MEXIKID

A GRAPHIC MEMOIR

BY

PEDRO MARTÍN

DIAL BOOKS FOR YOUNG READERS

DIAL BOOKS FOR YOUNG READERS

An imprint of Penguin Random House LLC, New York

First published in the United States of America by Dial Books for Young Readers,
an imprint of Penguin Random House LLC, 2023
Copyright © 2023 by Pedro Martín

Dial & colophon are registered trademarks of Penguin Random House LLC.
The Penguin colophon is a registered trademark of Penguin Books Limited.
Visit us online at penguinrandomhouse.com.

Library of Congress Cataloging-in-Publication Data is available.
Printed in the United States of America

ISBN 9780593462294 (pbk)
9 10

ISBN 9780593462287 (hc)
5 7 9 10 8 6

Design by Jennifer Kelly
Text set in Mexikid with permission from the author

FOR MY WIFE, GINA.
The love of my life, my best friend, and my North Star.
She makes me want to be better.

FOR PEDRO MARTÍN. APÁ.
The funniest, most loving dad in the world.
His almost-daily calls at "tequila o' clock" have
given me endless things to write about.

TO MERCEDES MARTÍN. AMÁ.
My inspiration.

CHAPTER 1
READY. SET. GO?!

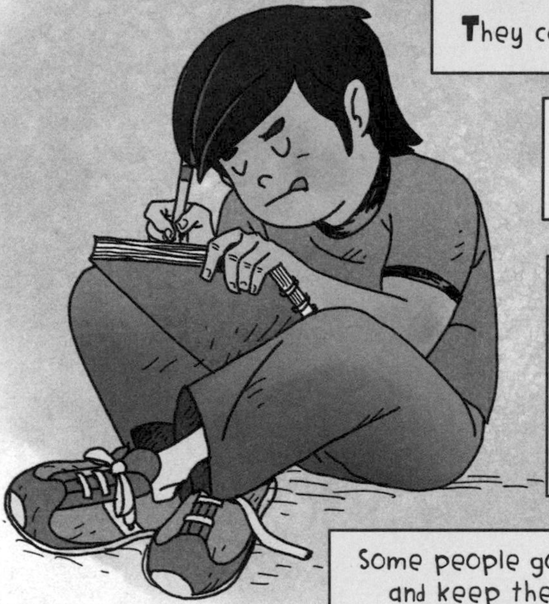

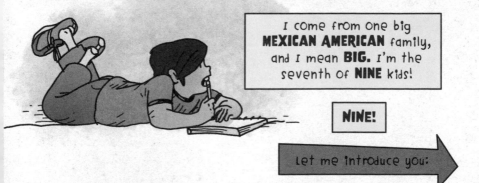

They call me **PETER...**

but my **REAL** name is **PEDRO.**

If your family's from **MEXICO,** like mine is, you usually have a couple of names you can go by.

Some people go full-on Mexican and keep their real names.

Some of us slip and slide between an **AMERICAN-STYLE NAME** and a Mexican one.

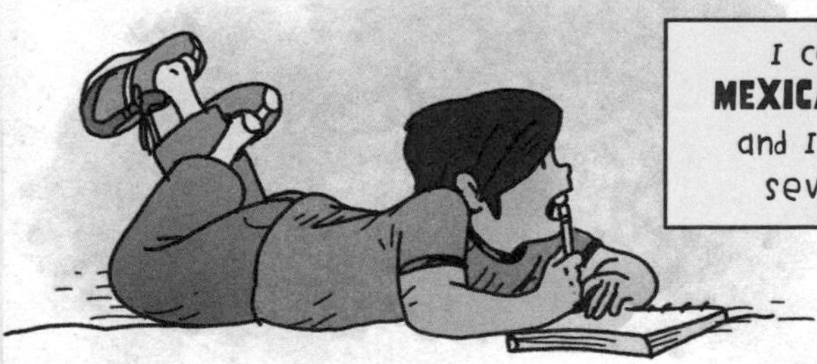

I come from one big **MEXICAN AMERICAN** family, and I mean **BIG.** I'm the seventh of **NINE** kids!

NINE!

Let me introduce you:

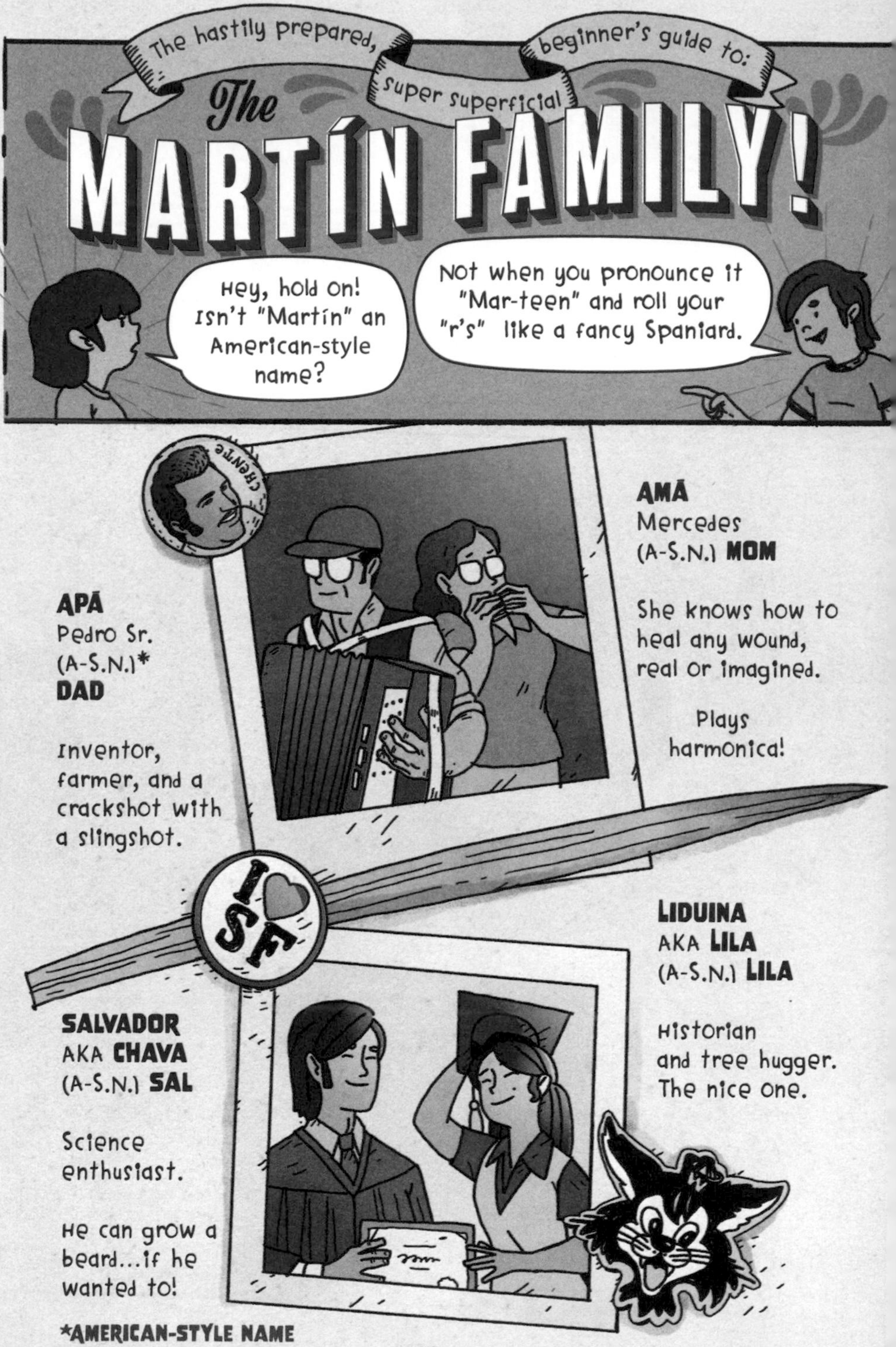
The hastily prepared, super superficial beginner's guide to:
The MARTÍN FAMILY!
Hey, hold on! Isn't "Martín" an American-style name?
Not when you pronounce it "Mar-teen" and roll your "r's" like a fancy Spaniard.
AMÁ
Mercedes
(A-S.N.) MOM
She knows how to heal any wound, real or imagined.
Plays harmonica!
APÁ
Pedro Sr.
(A-S.N.)*
DAD
Inventor, farmer, and a crackshot with a slingshot.
I SF
LIDUINA
AKA LILA
(A-S.N.) LILA
Historian and tree hugger. The nice one.
SALVADOR
AKA CHAVA
(A-S.N.) SAL
Science enthusiast.
He can grow a beard...if he wanted to!
*AMERICAN-STYLE NAME

LEÓN
(A-S.N.) **LEON**
(some of us get off easy on the name-switch thing.)

Half of the "Leon and Noe punching and pranking team."

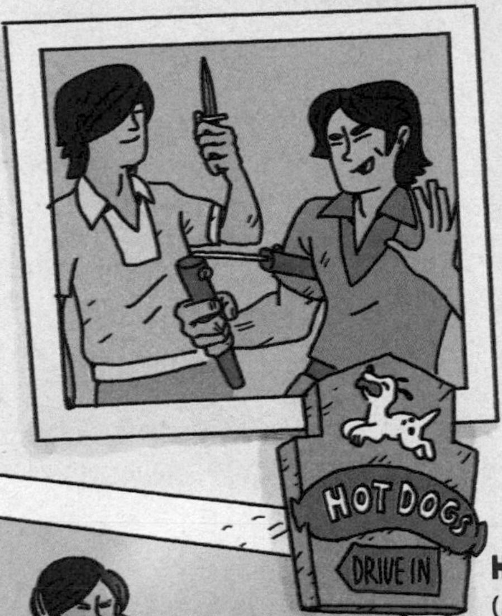
HOT DOGS
DRIVE IN

NOÉ
(A-S.N.): **NOE**
(pronounced "NO-ee")

He loves flowers!

Kidding.
He loves **PUNCHING.**

RUTH
(A-S.N.): **RUTH**
(In Spanish it sounds like "Root.")

Business-minded adventurer. Ghost whisperer.

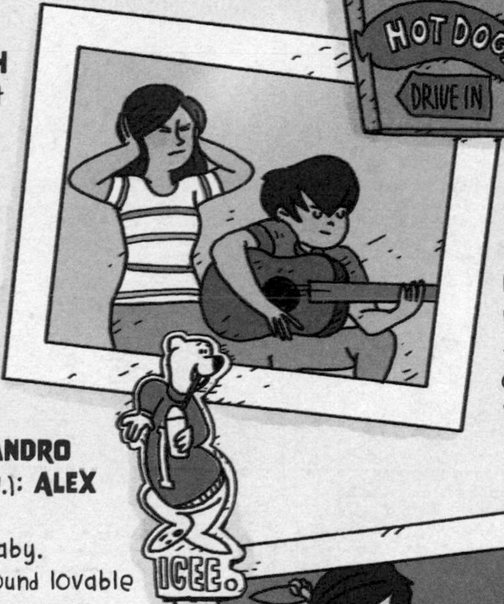
ICEE.

HUGO
(A-S.N.): **HUGO**
('Cuz in spanish it's "Oogo." It's a no-win scenario.)

Best guitar player in the family. Also the only guitar player in the family.

ALEJANDRO
(A-S.N.): **ALEX**

The baby.
All-around lovable smart-ass and poop-stirrer.

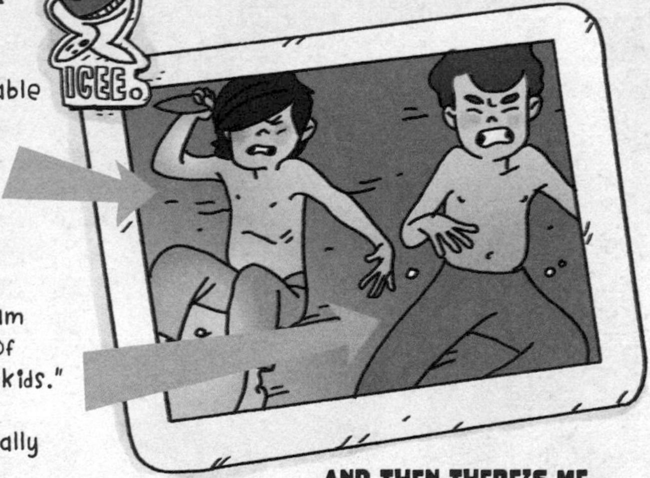

ADÁN
(A-S.N.): **ADAM**

Half of the "Adam and Alex team of Amá's favorite kids."

He's almost totally unflappable.

AND THEN THERE'S ME...

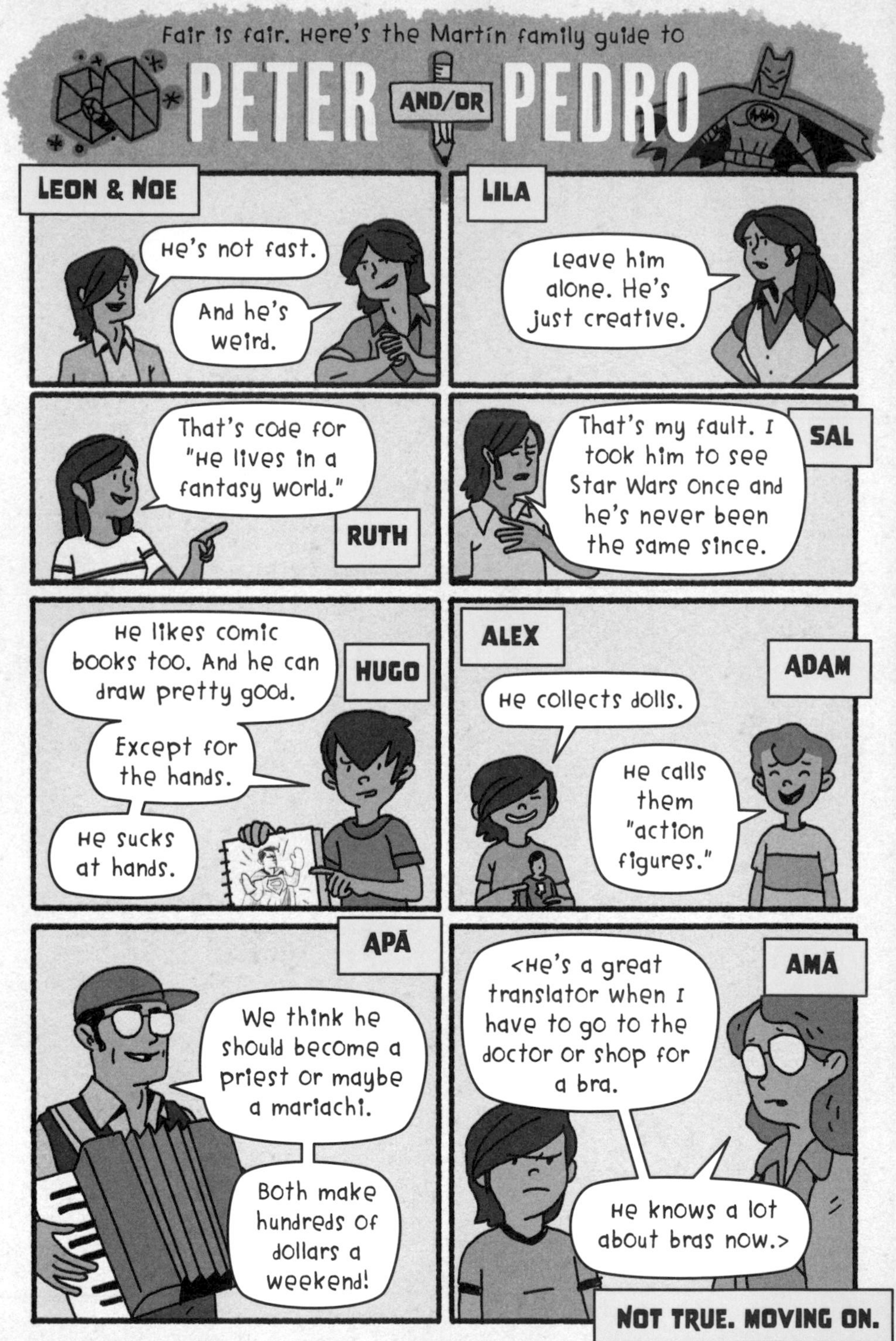

Fair is fair. Here's the Martín family guide to
PETER AND/OR PEDRO
LEON & NOE
He's not fast.
And he's weird.
LILA
Leave him alone. He's just creative.
That's code for "He lives in a fantasy world."
RUTH
That's my fault. I took him to see Star Wars once and he's never been the same since.
SAL
He likes comic books too. And he can draw pretty good.
Except for the hands.
He sucks at hands.
HUGO
ALEX
ADAM
He collects dolls.
He calls them "action figures."
APÁ
We think he should become a priest or maybe a mariachi.
Both make hundreds of dollars a weekend!
AMÁ
<He's a great translator when I have to go to the doctor or shop for a bra.
He knows a lot about bras now.>
NOT TRUE. MOVING ON.

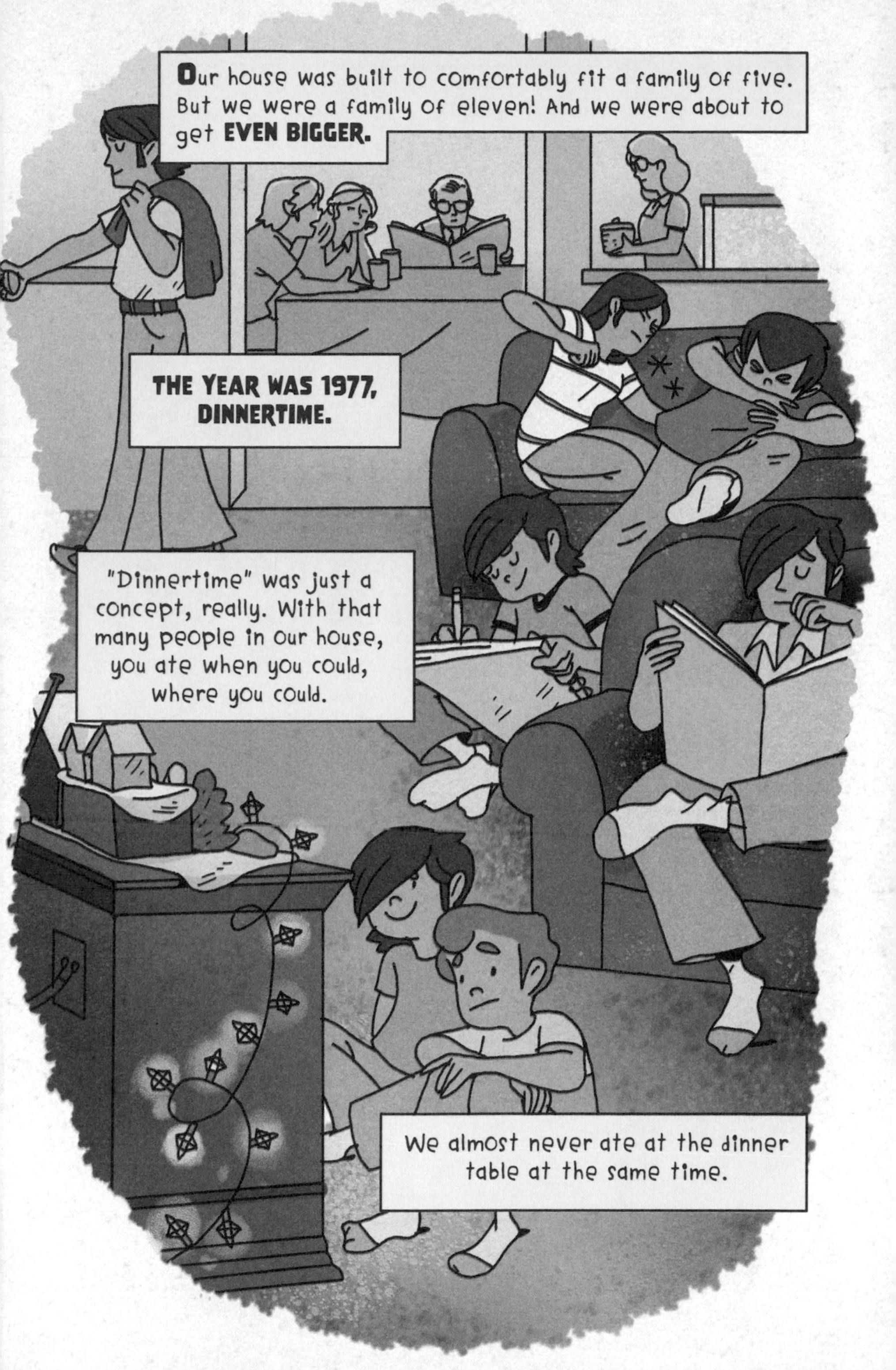
Our house was built to comfortably fit a family of five. But we were a family of eleven! And we were about to get EVEN BIGGER.
THE YEAR WAS 1977, DINNERTIME.
"Dinnertime" was just a concept, really. With that many people in our house, you ate when you could, where you could.
We almost never ate at the dinner table at the same time.

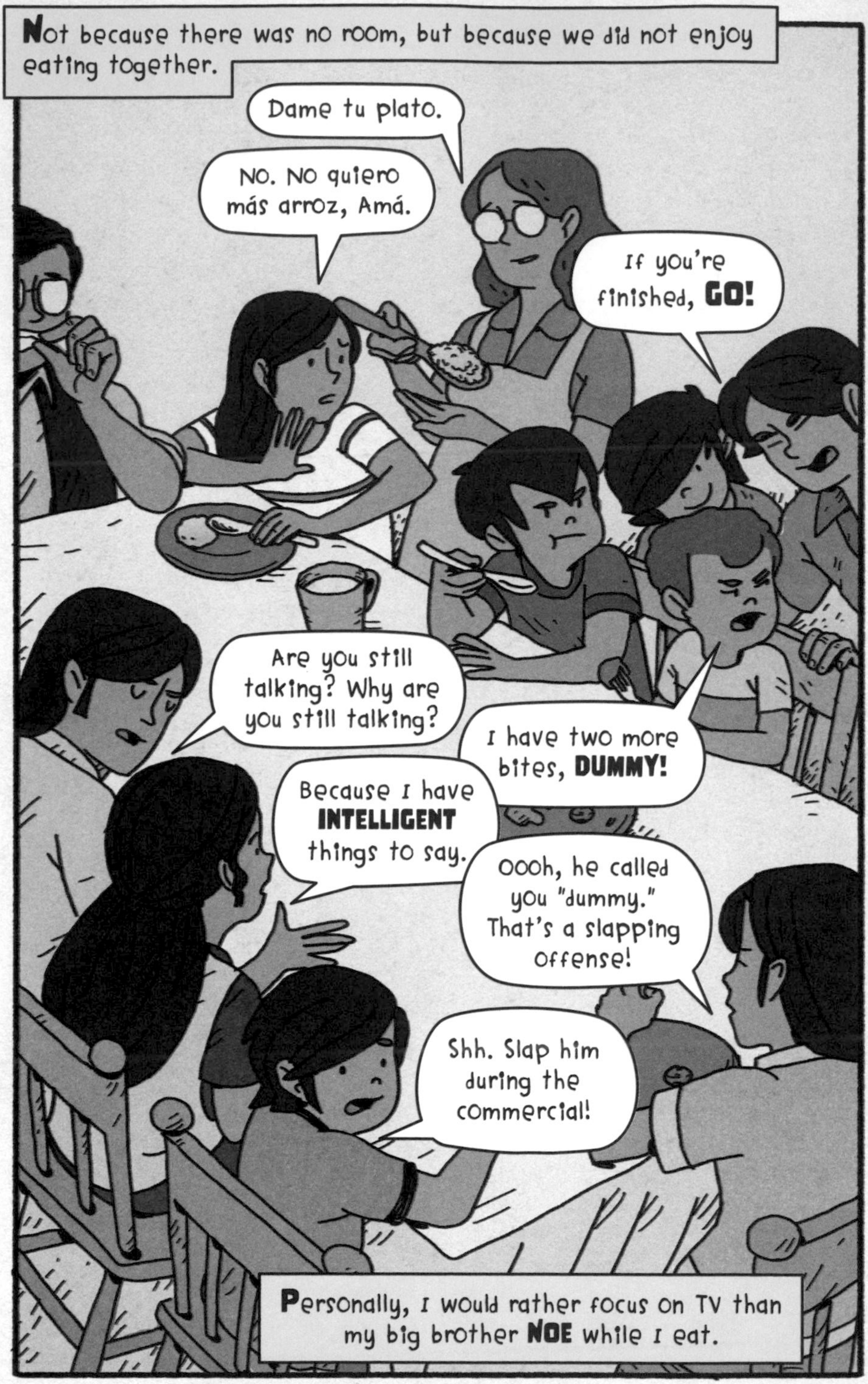
Not because there was no room, but because we did not enjoy eating together.
Dame tu plato.
NO. NO quiero más arroz, Amá.
If you're finished, GO!
Are you still talking? Why are you still talking?
I have two more bites, DUMMY!
Because I have INTELLIGENT things to say.
Oooh, he called you "dummy." That's a slapping offense!
Shh. Slap him during the commercial!
Personally, I would rather focus on TV than my big brother NOE while I eat.

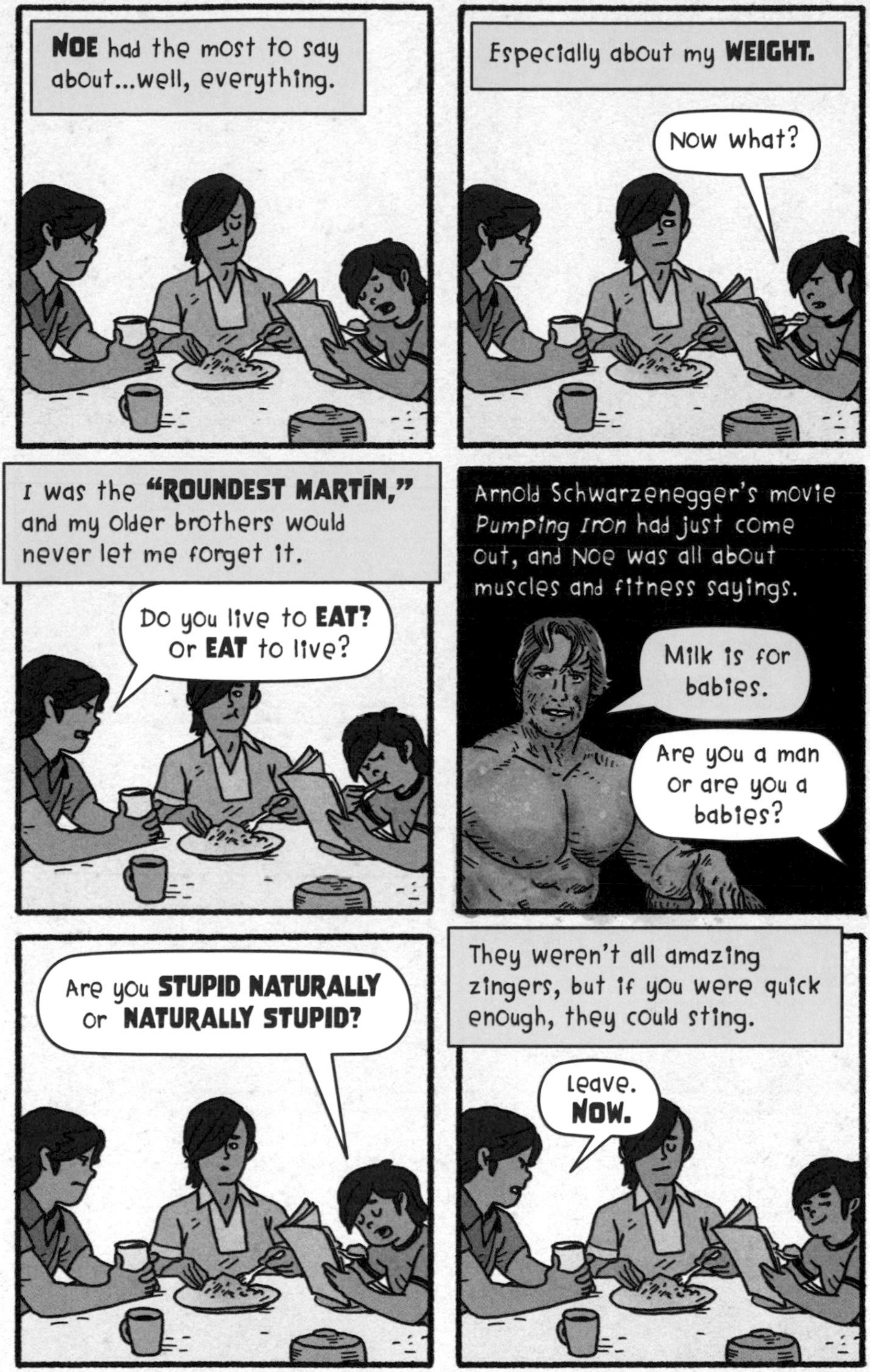
NOE had the most to say about...well, everything.
Especially about my **WEIGHT.**
Now what?
I was the **"ROUNDEST MARTÍN,"** and my older brothers would never let me forget it.
Do you live to **EAT?** Or **EAT** to live?
Arnold Schwarzenegger's movie *Pumping Iron* had just come out, and Noe was all about muscles and fitness sayings.
Milk is for babies.
Are you a man or are you a babies?
Are you **STUPID NATURALLY** or **NATURALLY STUPID?**
They weren't all amazing zingers, but if you were quick enough, they could sting.
Leave.
NOW.

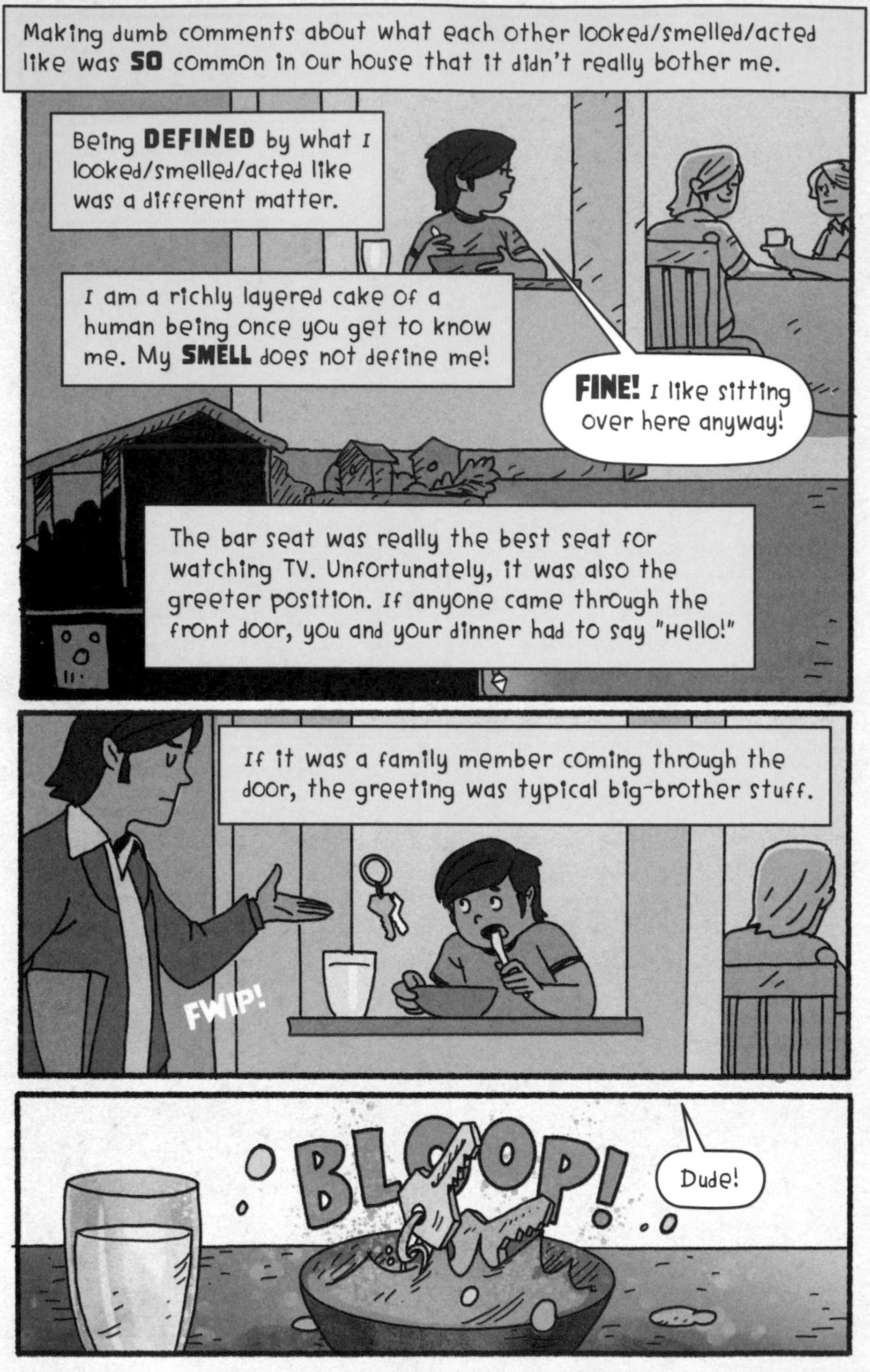

Making dumb comments about what each other looked/smelled/acted like was SO common in our house that it didn't really bother me.
Being DEFINED by what I looked/smelled/acted like was a different matter.
I am a richly layered cake of a human being once you get to know me. My SMELL does not define me!
FINE! I like sitting over here anyway!
The bar seat was really the best seat for watching TV. Unfortunately, it was also the greeter position. If anyone came through the front door, you and your dinner had to say "Hello!"
If it was a family member coming through the door, the greeting was typical big-brother stuff.
FWIP!
BLOOP!
Dude!

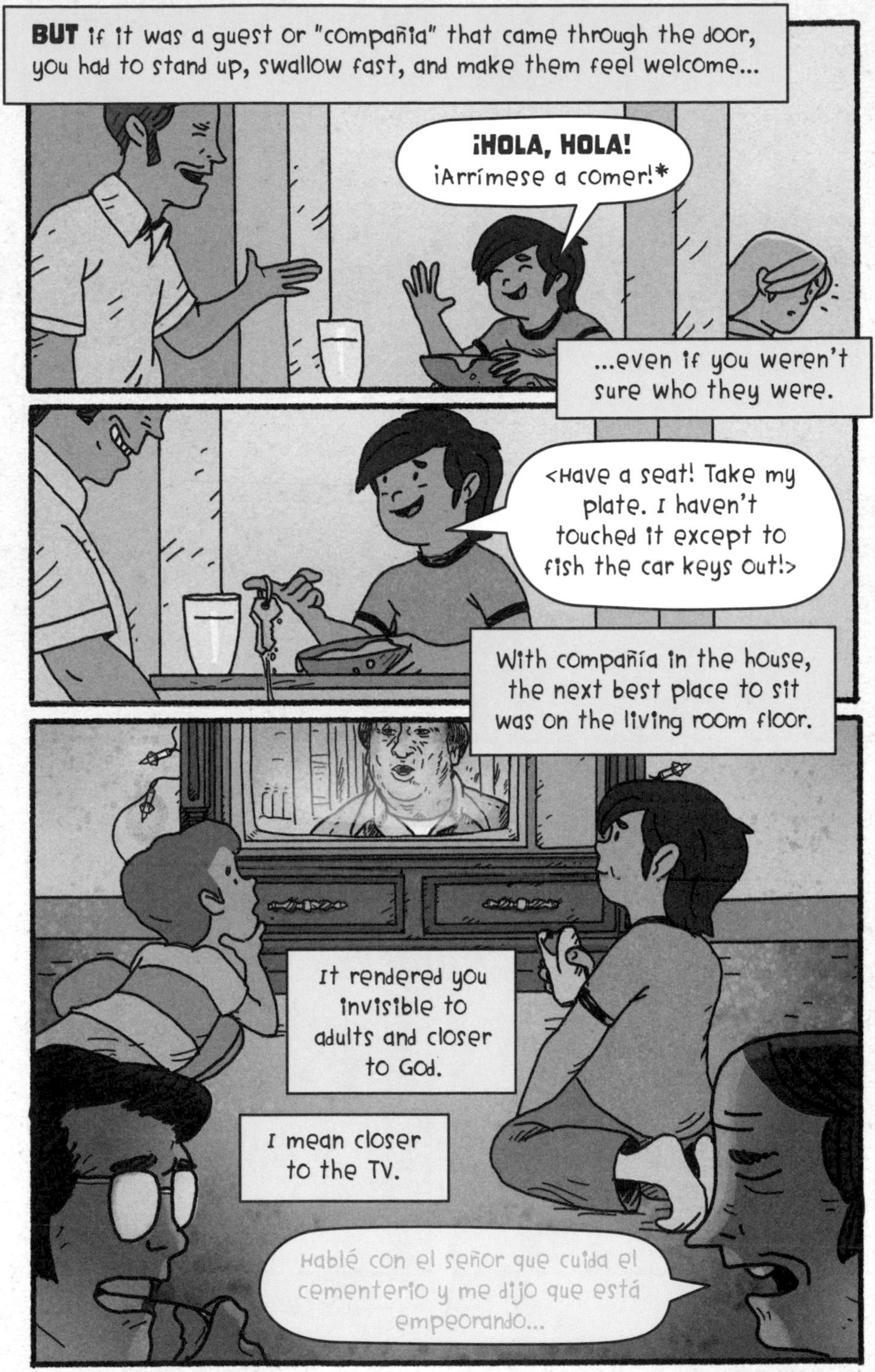

BUT if it was a guest or "compañía" that came through the door, you had to stand up, swallow fast, and make them feel welcome...
¡HOLA, HOLA! ¡Arrímese a comer!*
...even if you weren't sure who they were.
<Have a seat! Take my plate. I haven't touched it except to fish the car keys out!>
With compañía in the house, the next best place to sit was on the living room floor.
It rendered you invisible to adults and closer to God.
I mean closer to the TV.
Hablé con el señor que cuida el cementerio y me dijo que está empeorando...

*Hello, hello! Come and eat!

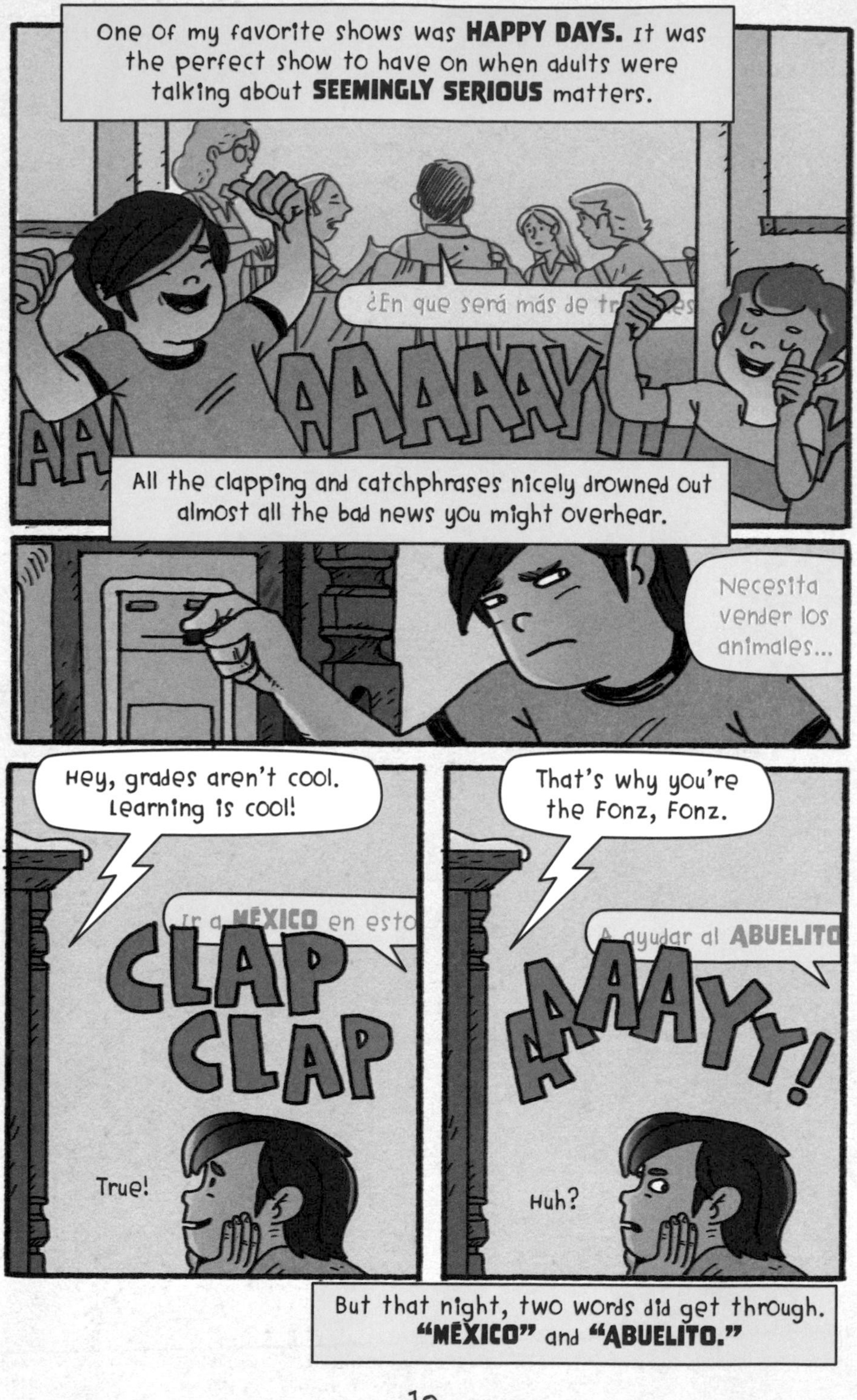
One of my favorite shows was **HAPPY DAYS.** It was the perfect show to have on when adults were talking about **SEEMINGLY SERIOUS** matters.
AAAAAY!
All the clapping and catchphrases nicely drowned out almost all the bad news you might overhear.
Necesita vender los animales...
Hey, grades aren't cool. Learning is cool!
CLAP CLAP
True!
That's why you're the Fonz, Fonz.
AAAAYY!
Huh?
But that night, two words did get through. **"MÉXICO"** and **"ABUELITO."**

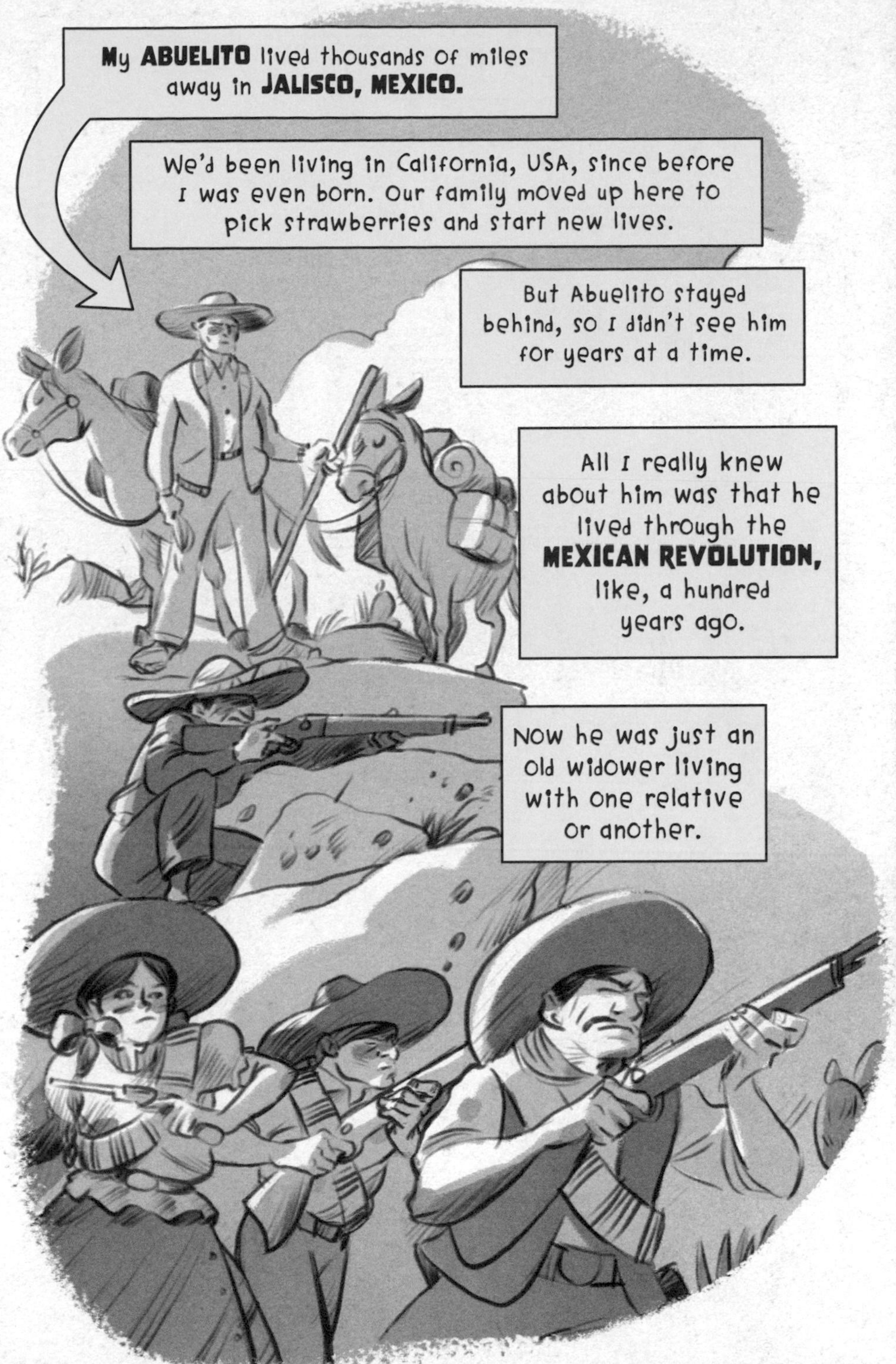
My **ABUELITO** lived thousands of miles away in **JALISCO, MEXICO.**
We'd been living in California, USA, since before I was even born. Our family moved up here to pick strawberries and start new lives.
But Abuelito stayed behind, so I didn't see him for years at a time.
All I really knew about him was that he lived through the **MEXICAN REVOLUTION,** like, a hundred years ago.
Now he was just an old widower living with one relative or another.

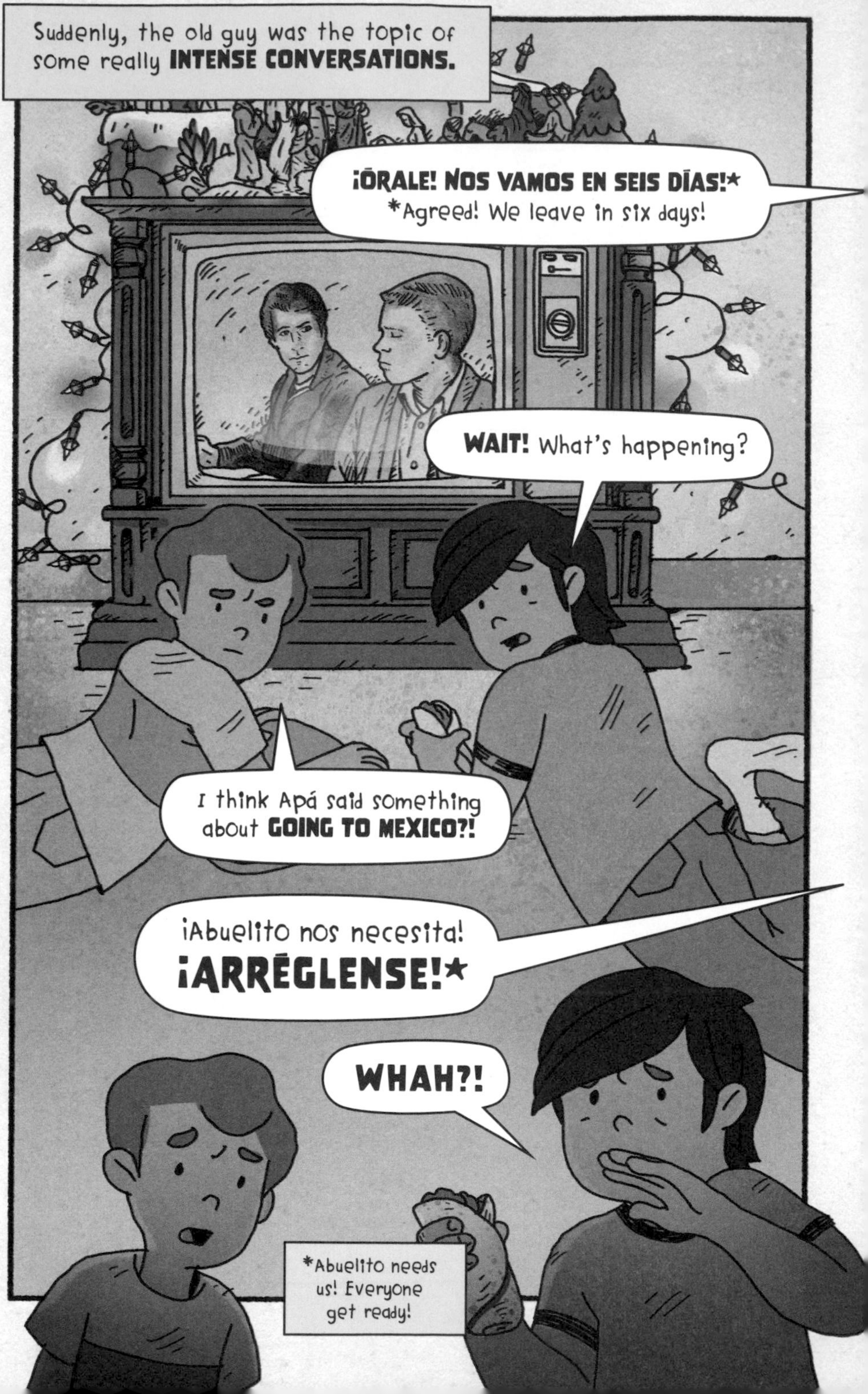

Suddenly, the old guy was the topic of some really **INTENSE CONVERSATIONS.**
¡ÓRALE! NOS VAMOS EN SEIS DÍAS!*
*Agreed! We leave in six days!
WAIT! What's happening?
I think Apá said something about **GOING TO MEXICO?!**
¡Abuelito nos necesita! **¡ARRÉGLENSE!***
WHAH?!
*Abuelito needs us! Everyone get ready!

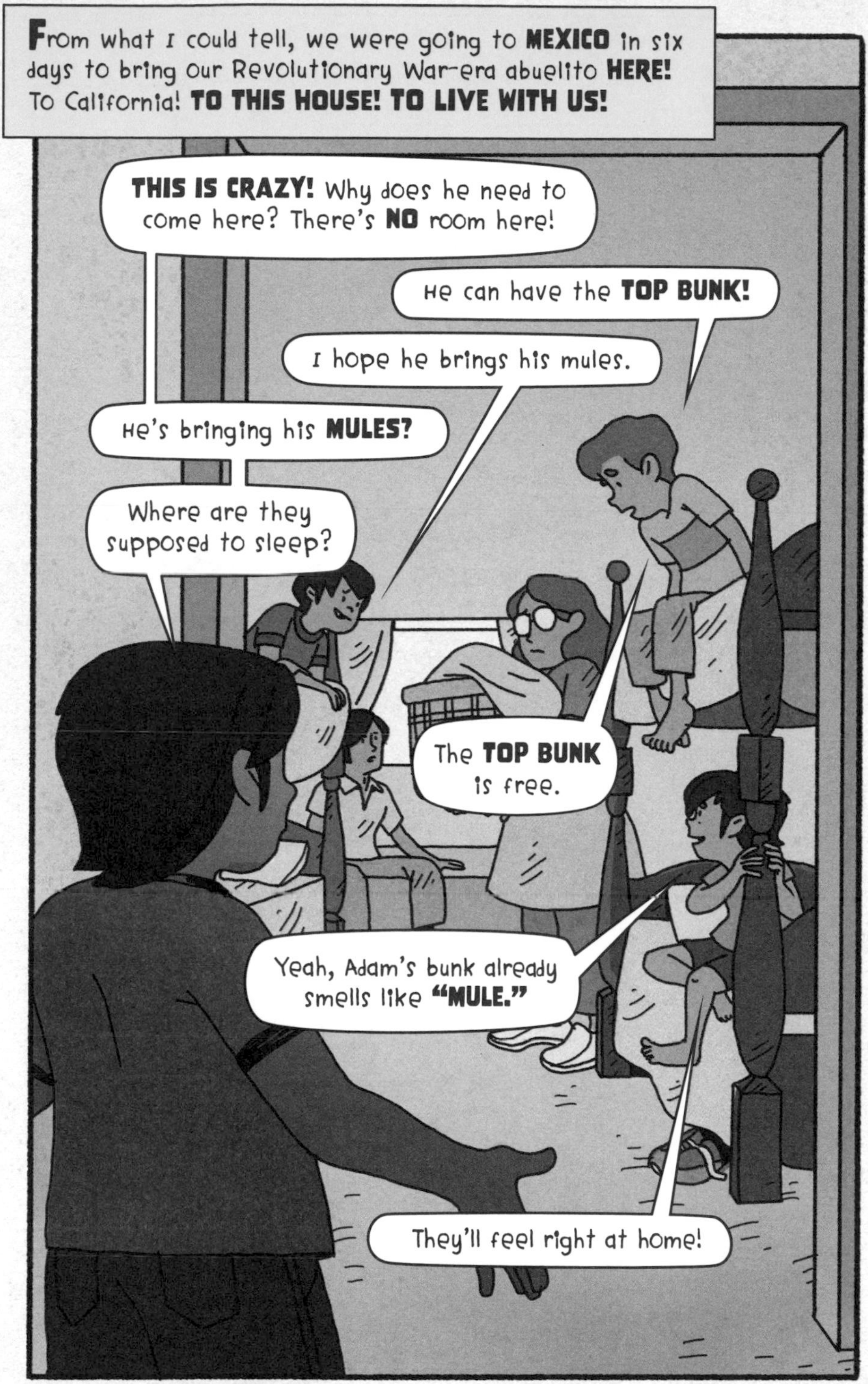
From what I could tell, we were going to MEXICO in six days to bring our Revolutionary War-era abuelito HERE! To California! TO THIS HOUSE! TO LIVE WITH US!
THIS IS CRAZY! Why does he need to come here? There's NO room here!
He can have the TOP BUNK!
I hope he brings his mules.
He's bringing his MULES?
Where are they supposed to sleep?
The TOP BUNK is free.
Yeah, Adam's bunk already smells like "MULE."
They'll feel right at home!

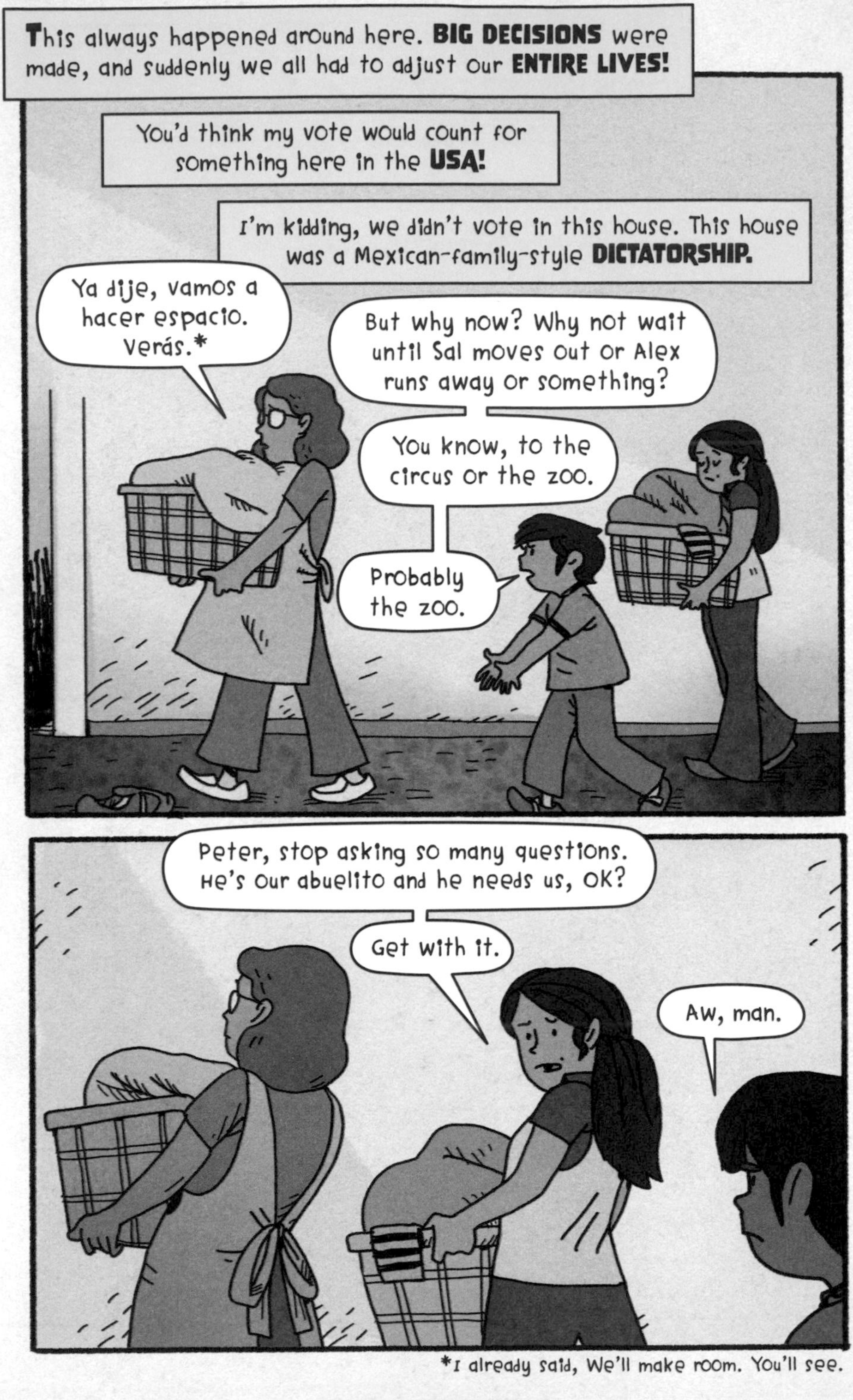
This always happened around here. BIG DECISIONS were made, and suddenly we all had to adjust our ENTIRE LIVES!
You'd think my vote would count for something here in the USA!
I'm kidding, we didn't vote in this house. This house was a Mexican-family-style DICTATORSHIP.
Ya dije, vamos a hacer espacio. Verás.*
But why now? Why not wait until Sal moves out or Alex runs away or something?
You know, to the circus or the zoo.
Probably the zoo.
Peter, stop asking so many questions. He's our abuelito and he needs us, OK?
Get with it.
Aw, man.

*I already said, We'll make room. You'll see.

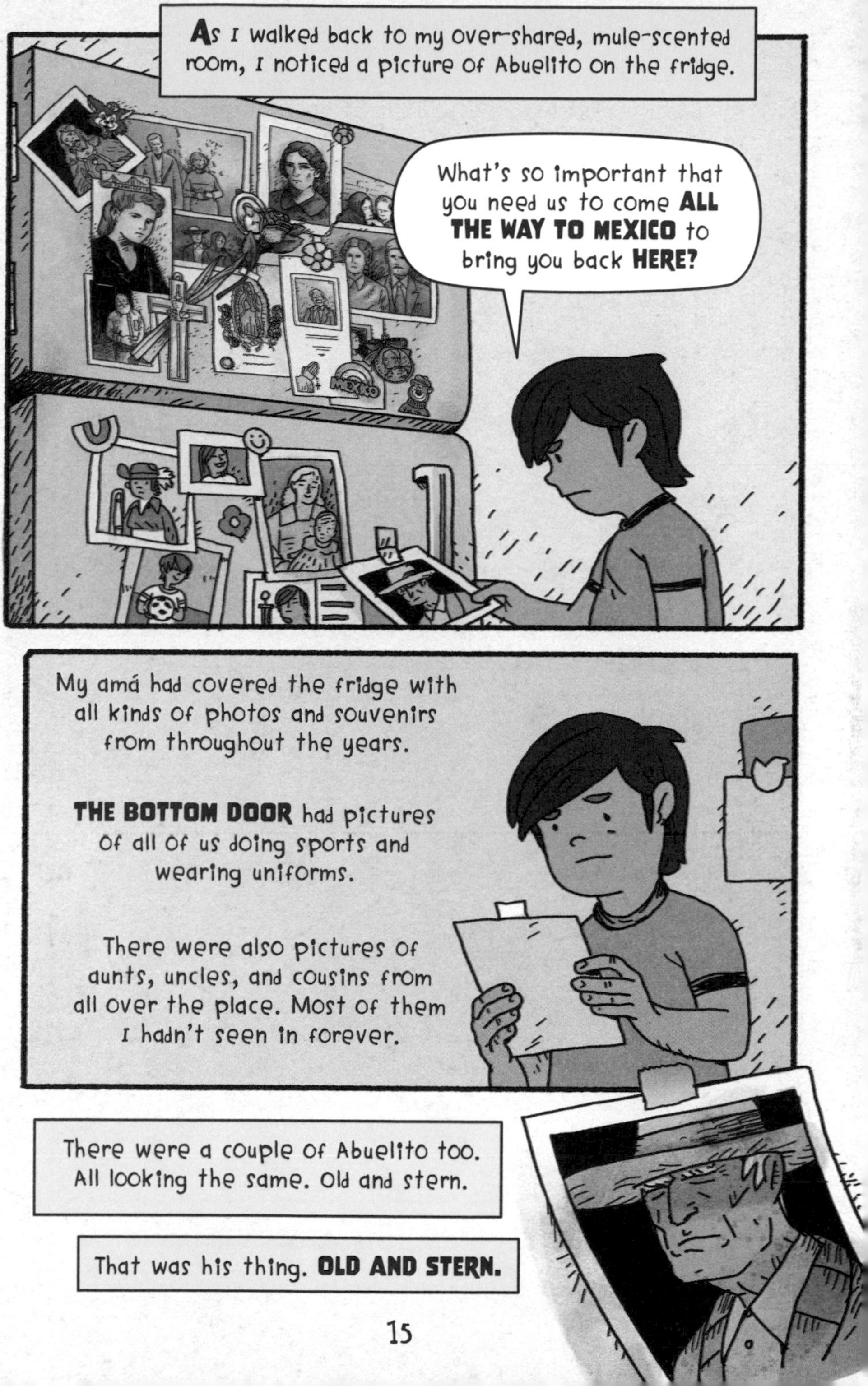
As I walked back to my over-shared, mule-scented room, I noticed a picture of Abuelito on the fridge.
What's so important that you need us to come ALL THE WAY TO MEXICO to bring you back HERE?
MEXICO
My amá had covered the fridge with all kinds of photos and souvenirs from throughout the years.
THE BOTTOM DOOR had pictures of all of us doing sports and wearing uniforms.
There were also pictures of aunts, uncles, and cousins from all over the place. Most of them I hadn't seen in forever.
There were a couple of Abuelito too. All looking the same. Old and stern.
That was his thing. OLD AND STERN.

I'd see my **ABUELITO** every few years or so, but I remembered the very **FIRST TIME** I met him. I was really little and he was **SUPER OLD,** even back then.

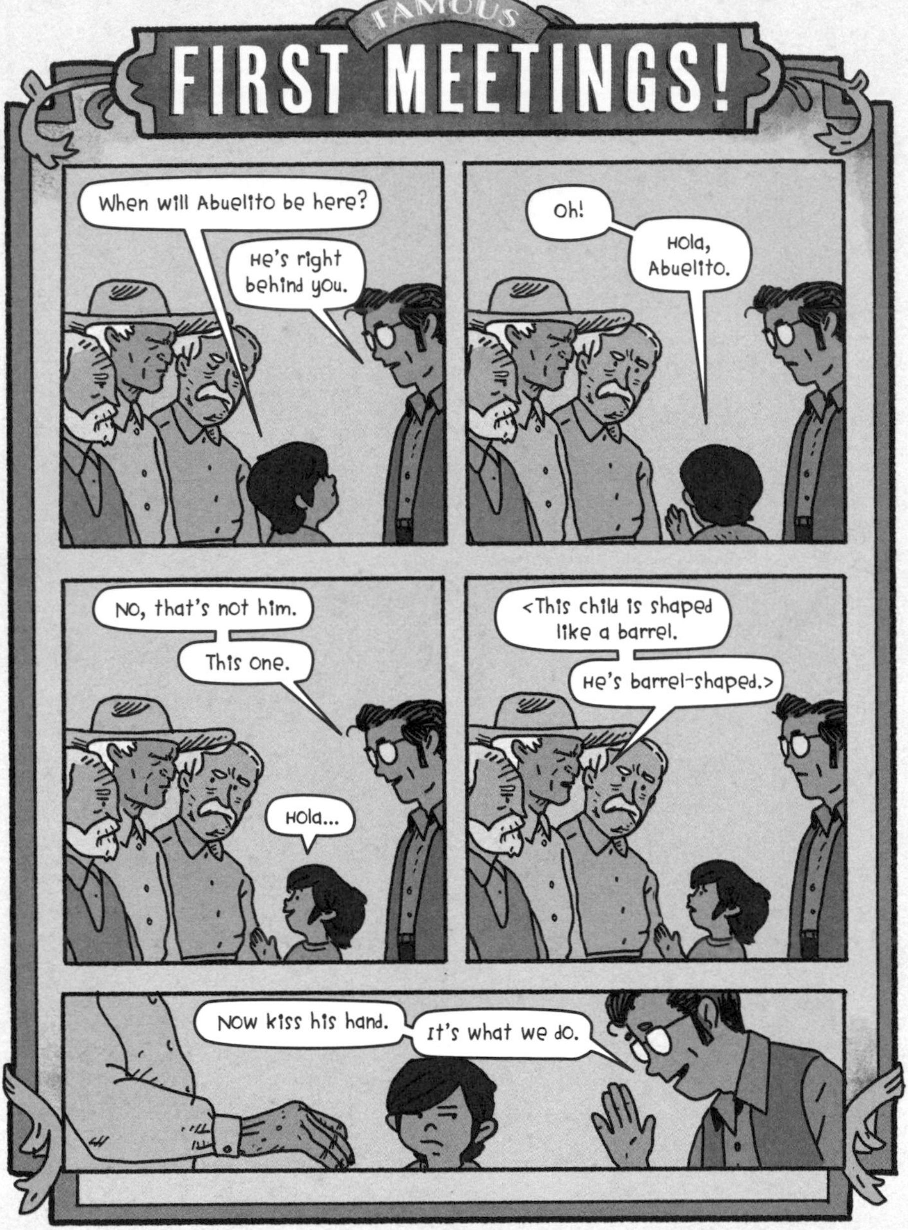
FAMOUS
FIRST MEETINGS!
When will Abuelito be here?
He's right behind you.
Oh!
Hola, Abuelito.
No, that's not him.
This one.
Hola...
<This child is shaped like a barrel.
He's barrel-shaped.>
Now kiss his hand.
It's what we do.

(In our family, you can either kiss an elder's hand or get pinched by an elder's hand. The choice is yours!)

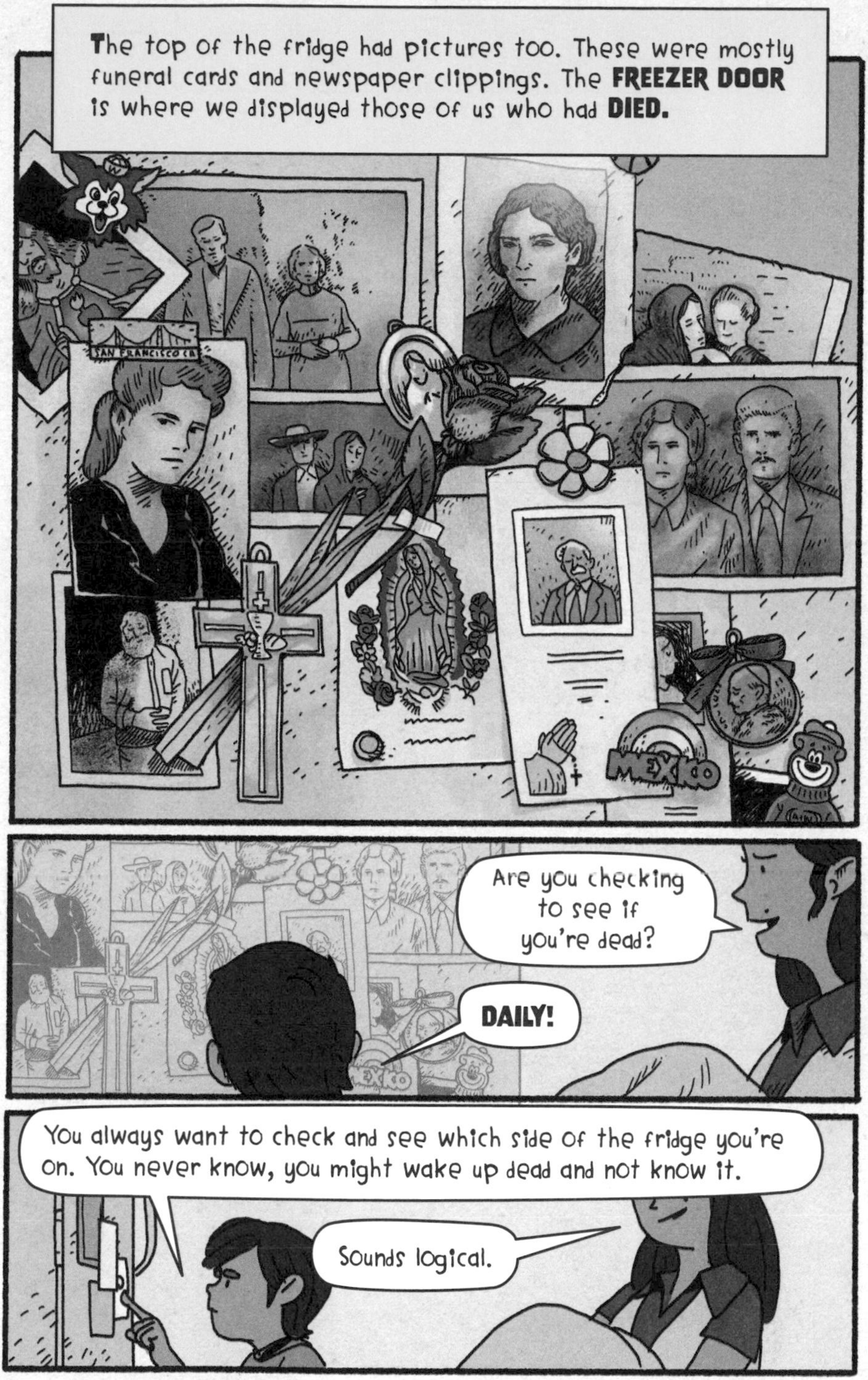
The top of the fridge had pictures too. These were mostly funeral cards and newspaper clippings. The **FREEZER DOOR** is where we displayed those of us who had **DIED.**
SAN FRANCISCO CA
MEXICO
Are you checking to see if you're dead?
DAILY!
You always want to check and see which side of the fridge you're on. You never know, you might wake up dead and not know it.
Sounds logical.

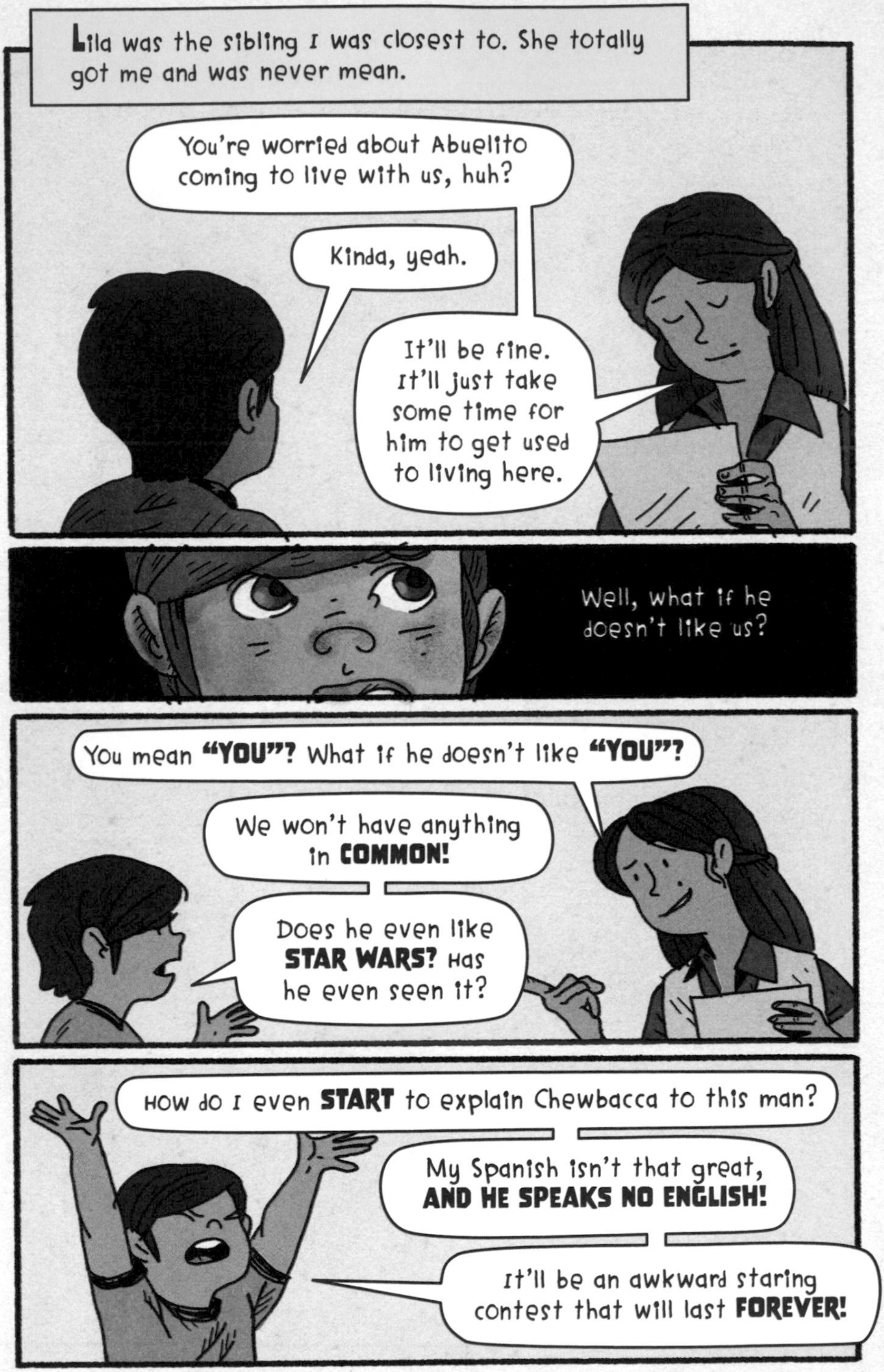
Lila was the sibling I was closest to. She totally got me and was never mean.
You're worried about Abuelito coming to live with us, huh?
Kinda, yeah.
It'll be fine. It'll just take some time for him to get used to living here.
Well, what if he doesn't like us?
You mean "YOU"? What if he doesn't like "YOU"?
We won't have anything in COMMON!
Does he even like STAR WARS? Has he even seen it?
How do I even START to explain Chewbacca to this man?
My Spanish isn't that great, AND HE SPEAKS NO ENGLISH!
It'll be an awkward staring contest that will last FOREVER!

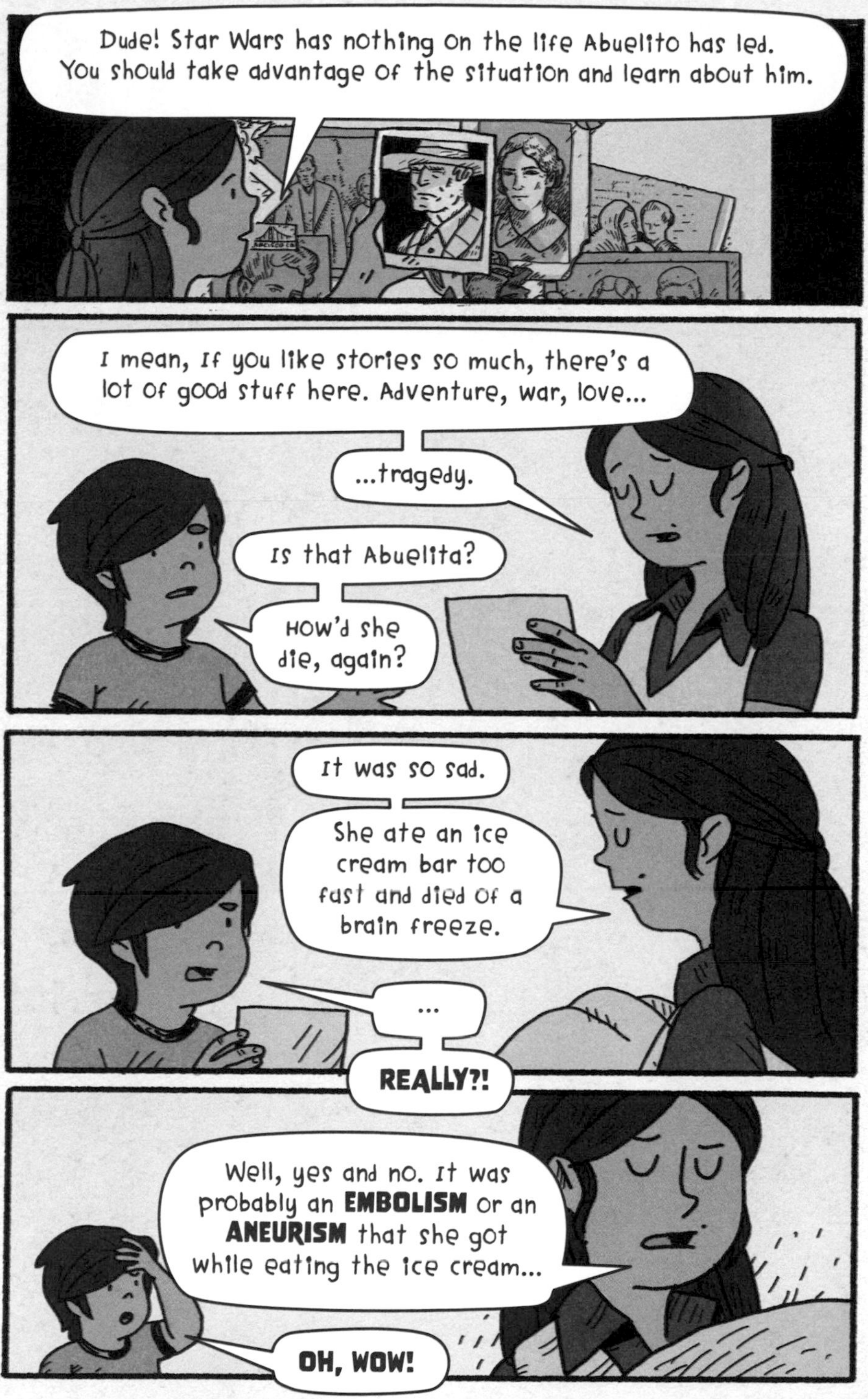
Dude! Star Wars has nothing on the life Abuelito has led. You should take advantage of the situation and learn about him.
I mean, if you like stories so much, there's a lot of good stuff here. Adventure, war, love...
...tragedy.
Is that Abuelita?
How'd she die, again?
It was so sad.
She ate an ice cream bar too fast and died of a brain freeze.
...
REALLY?!
Well, yes and no. It was probably an EMBOLISM or an ANEURISM that she got while eating the ice cream...
OH, WOW!

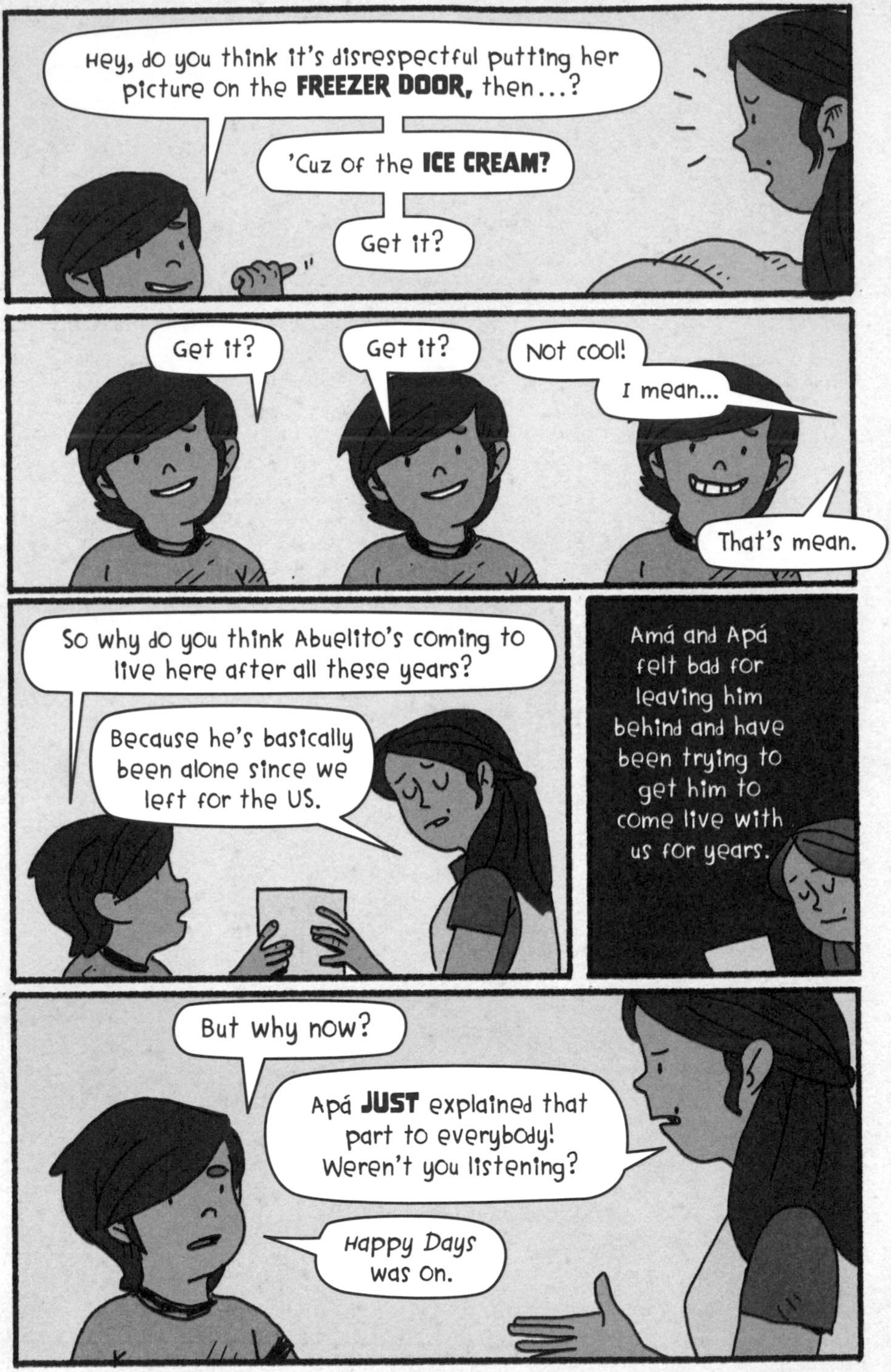
Hey, do you think it's disrespectful putting her picture on the FREEZER DOOR, then...?
'Cuz of the ICE CREAM?
Get it?
Get it?
Get it?
Not cool!
I mean...
That's mean.
So why do you think Abuelito's coming to live here after all these years?
Because he's basically been alone since we left for the US.
Amá and Apá felt bad for leaving him behind and have been trying to get him to come live with us for years.
But why now?
Apá JUST explained that part to everybody! Weren't you listening?
Happy Days was on.

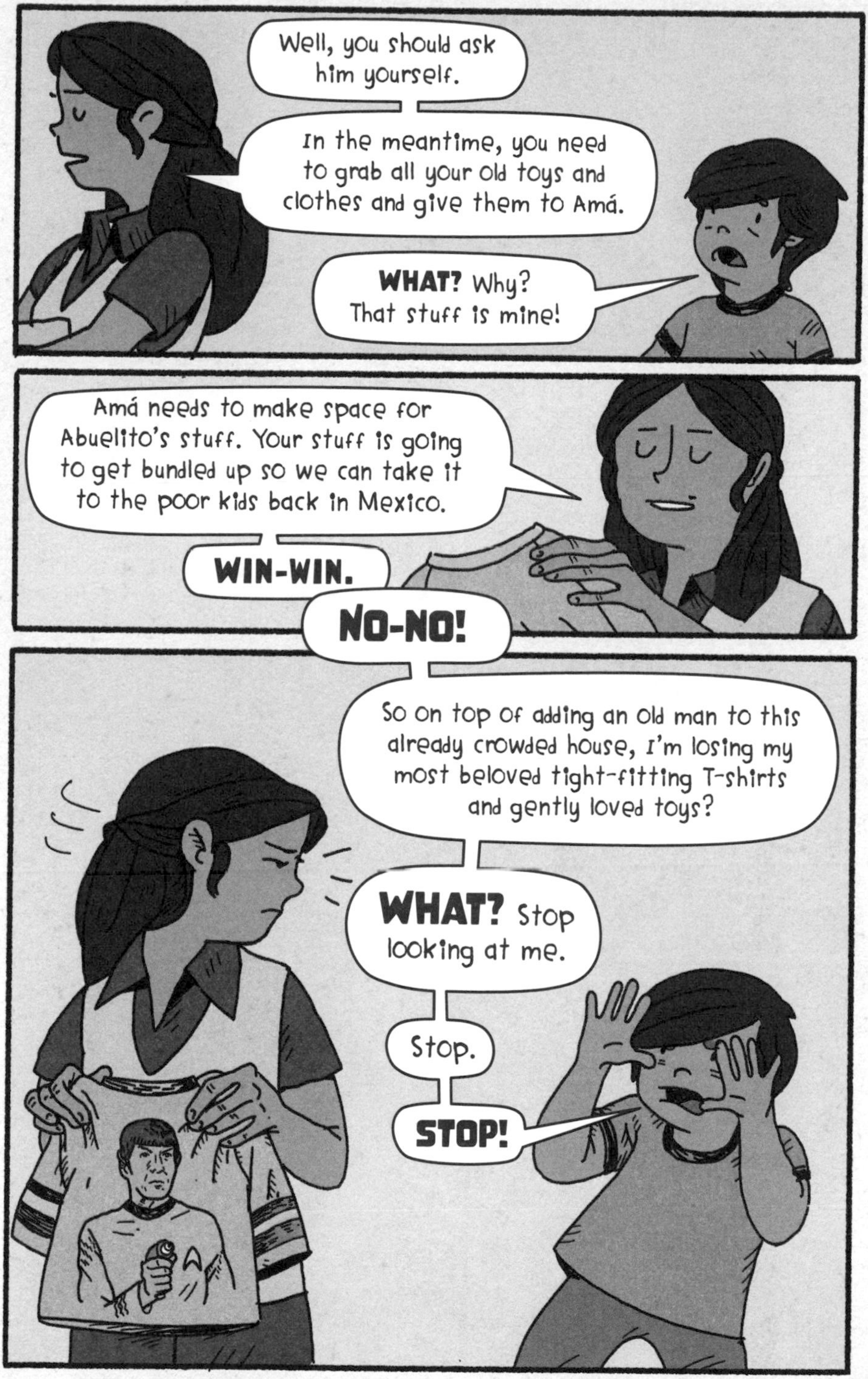
Well, you should ask him yourself.
In the meantime, you need to grab all your old toys and clothes and give them to Amá.
WHAT? Why? That stuff is mine!
Amá needs to make space for Abuelito's stuff. Your stuff is going to get bundled up so we can take it to the poor kids back in Mexico.
WIN-WIN.
NO-NO!
So on top of adding an old man to this already crowded house, I'm losing my most beloved tight-fitting T-shirts and gently loved toys?
WHAT? Stop looking at me.
Stop.
STOP!

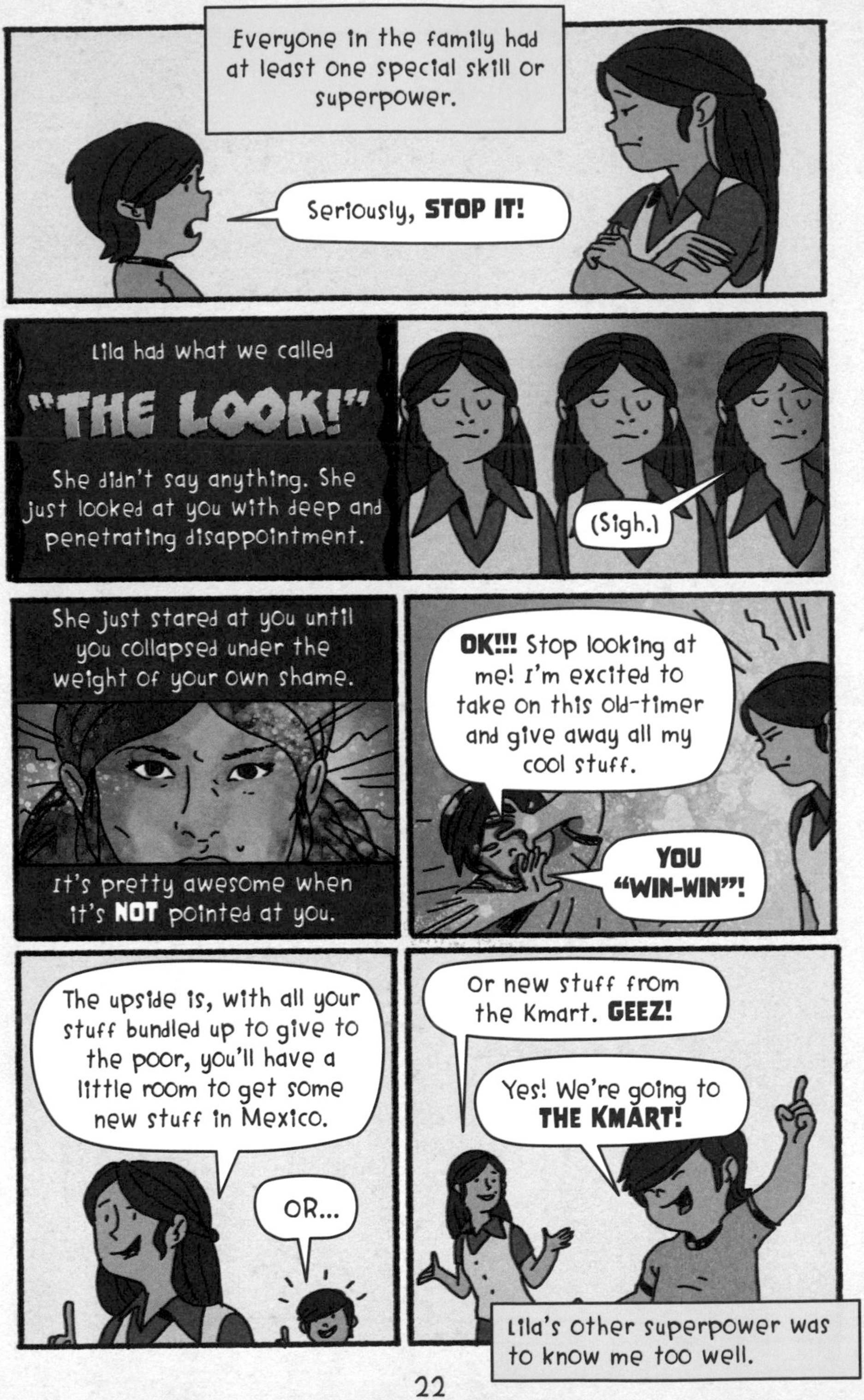
Everyone in the family had at least one special skill or superpower.
Seriously, **STOP IT!**
Lila had what we called
"THE LOOK!"
She didn't say anything. She just looked at you with deep and penetrating disappointment.
(Sigh.)
She just stared at you until you collapsed under the weight of your own shame.
It's pretty awesome when it's **NOT** pointed at you.
OK!!! Stop looking at me! I'm excited to take on this old-timer and give away all my cool stuff.
YOU "WIN-WIN"!
The upside is, with all your stuff bundled up to give to the poor, you'll have a little room to get some new stuff in Mexico.
OR...
Or new stuff from the Kmart. **GEEZ!**
Yes! We're going to **THE KMART!**
Lila's other superpower was to know me too well.

CHAPTER 2 SOLO LO ESENCIAL

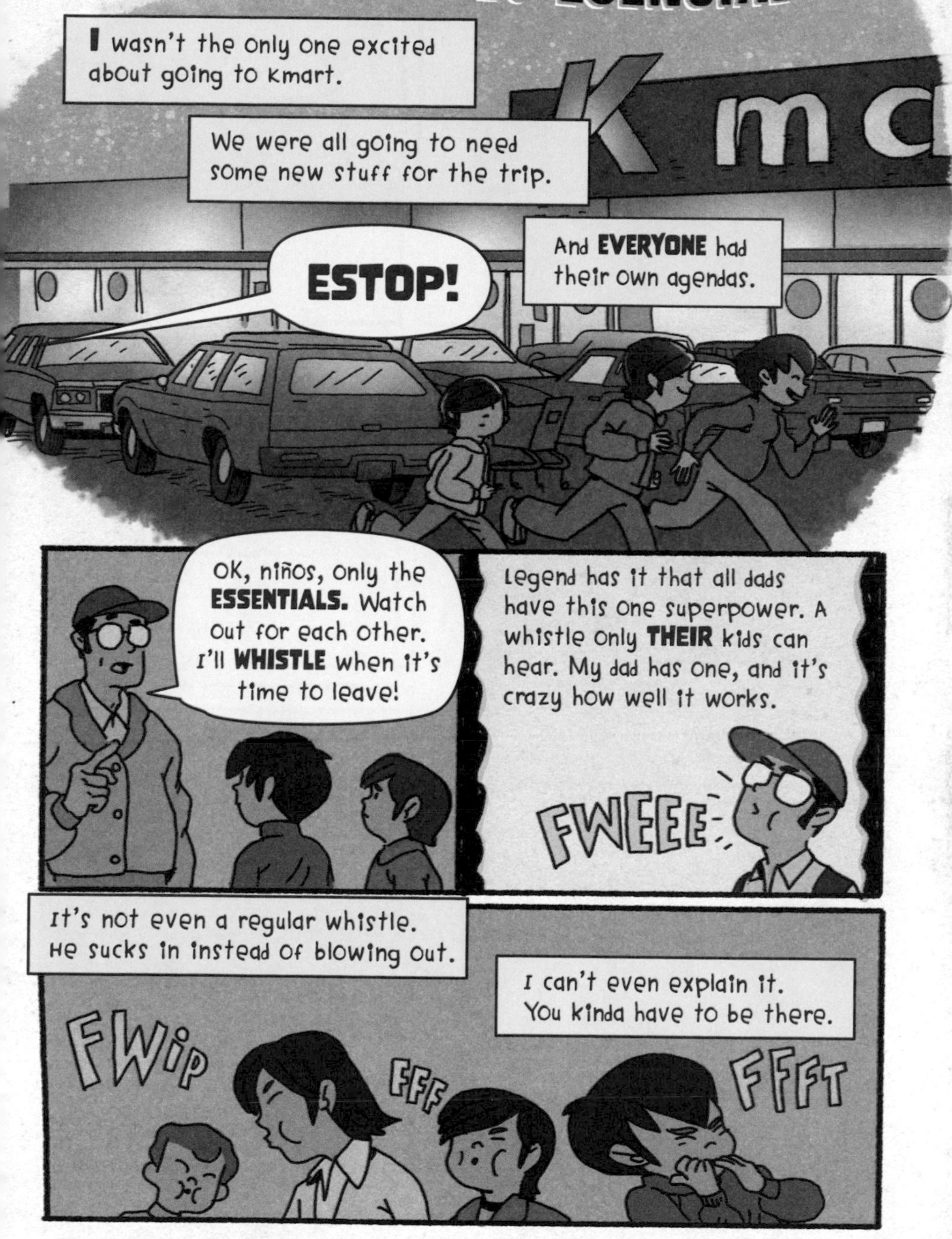
I wasn't the only one excited about going to Kmart.
We were all going to need some new stuff for the trip.
ESTOP!
And EVERYONE had their own agendas.
OK, niños, only the ESSENTIALS. Watch out for each other. I'll WHISTLE when it's time to leave!
Legend has it that all dads have this one superpower. A whistle only THEIR kids can hear. My dad has one, and it's crazy how well it works.
FWEEE
It's not even a regular whistle. He sucks in instead of blowing out.
I can't even explain it. You kinda have to be there.
FWip
FFF
FFFT

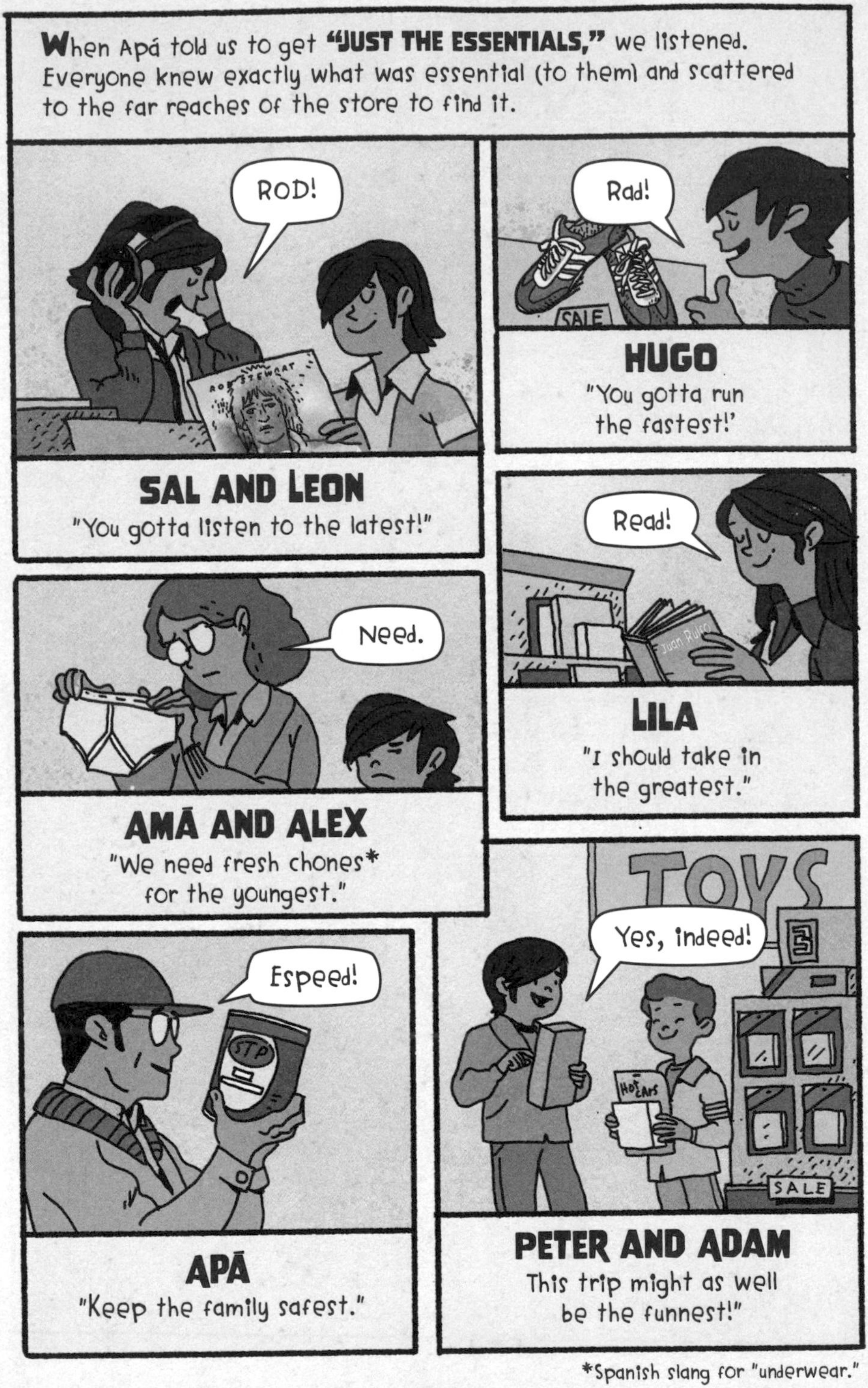
When Apá told us to get "JUST THE ESSENTIALS," we listened. Everyone knew exactly what was essential (to them) and scattered to the far reaches of the store to find it.
ROD!
ROD STEWART
SAL AND LEON
"You gotta listen to the latest!"
Rad!
SALE
HUGO
"You gotta run the fastest!'
Need.
AMÁ AND ALEX
"We need fresh chones* for the youngest."
Read!
Juan Rulfo
LILA
"I should take in the greatest."
Espeed!
STP
APÁ
"Keep the family safest."
TOYS
Yes, indeed!
HOT CARS
SALE
PETER AND ADAM
This trip might as well be the funnest!"

*Spanish slang for "underwear."

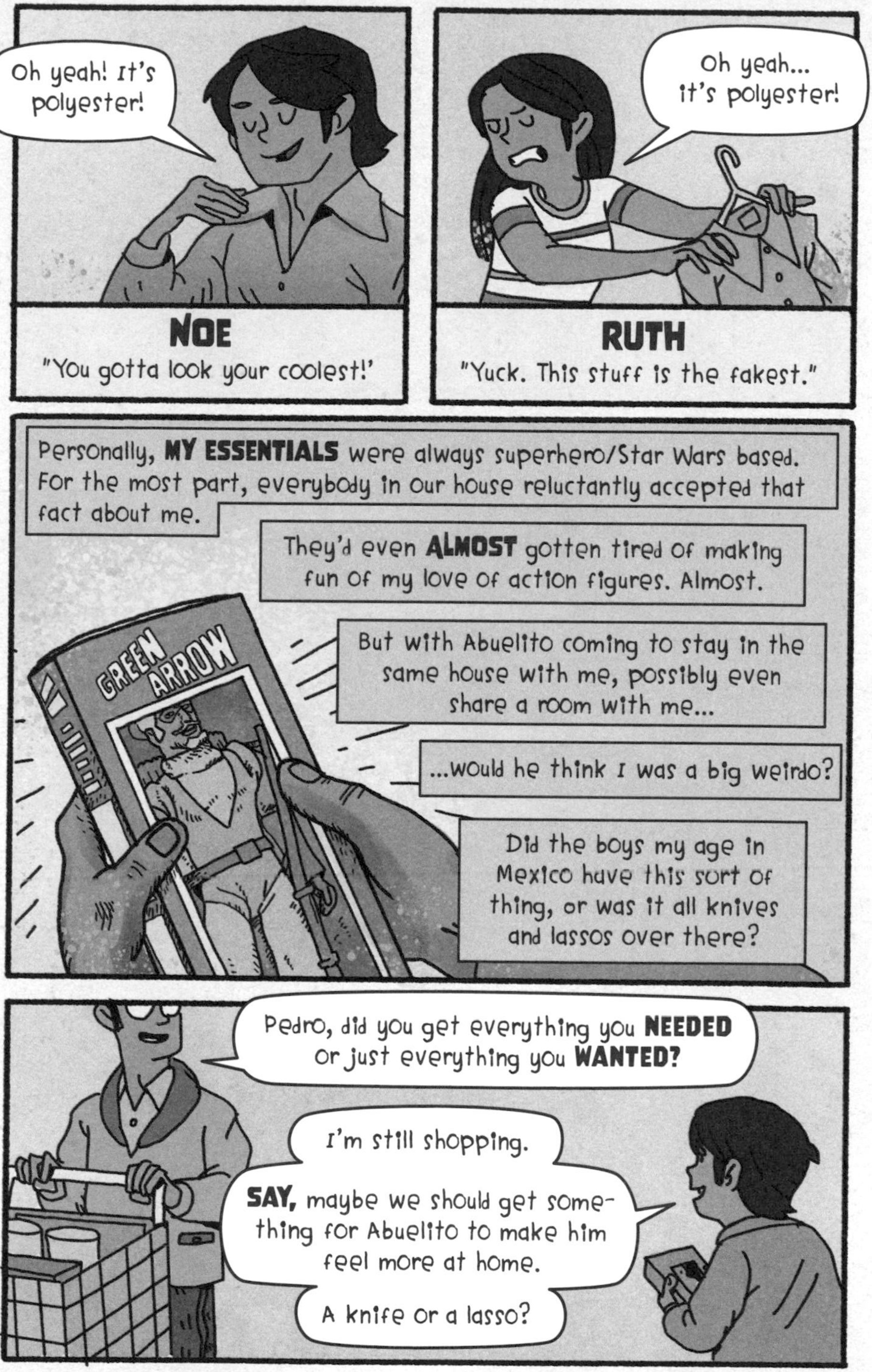

Oh yeah! It's polyester!
NOE
"You gotta look your coolest!'
Oh yeah... it's polyester!
RUTH
"Yuck. This stuff is the fakest."
Personally, MY ESSENTIALS were always superhero/Star Wars based. For the most part, everybody in our house reluctantly accepted that fact about me.
They'd even ALMOST gotten tired of making fun of my love of action figures. Almost.
GREEN ARROW
But with Abuelito coming to stay in the same house with me, possibly even share a room with me...
...would he think I was a big weirdo?
Did the boys my age in Mexico have this sort of thing, or was it all knives and lassos over there?
Pedro, did you get everything you NEEDED or just everything you WANTED?
I'm still shopping.
SAY, maybe we should get something for Abuelito to make him feel more at home.
A knife or a lasso?

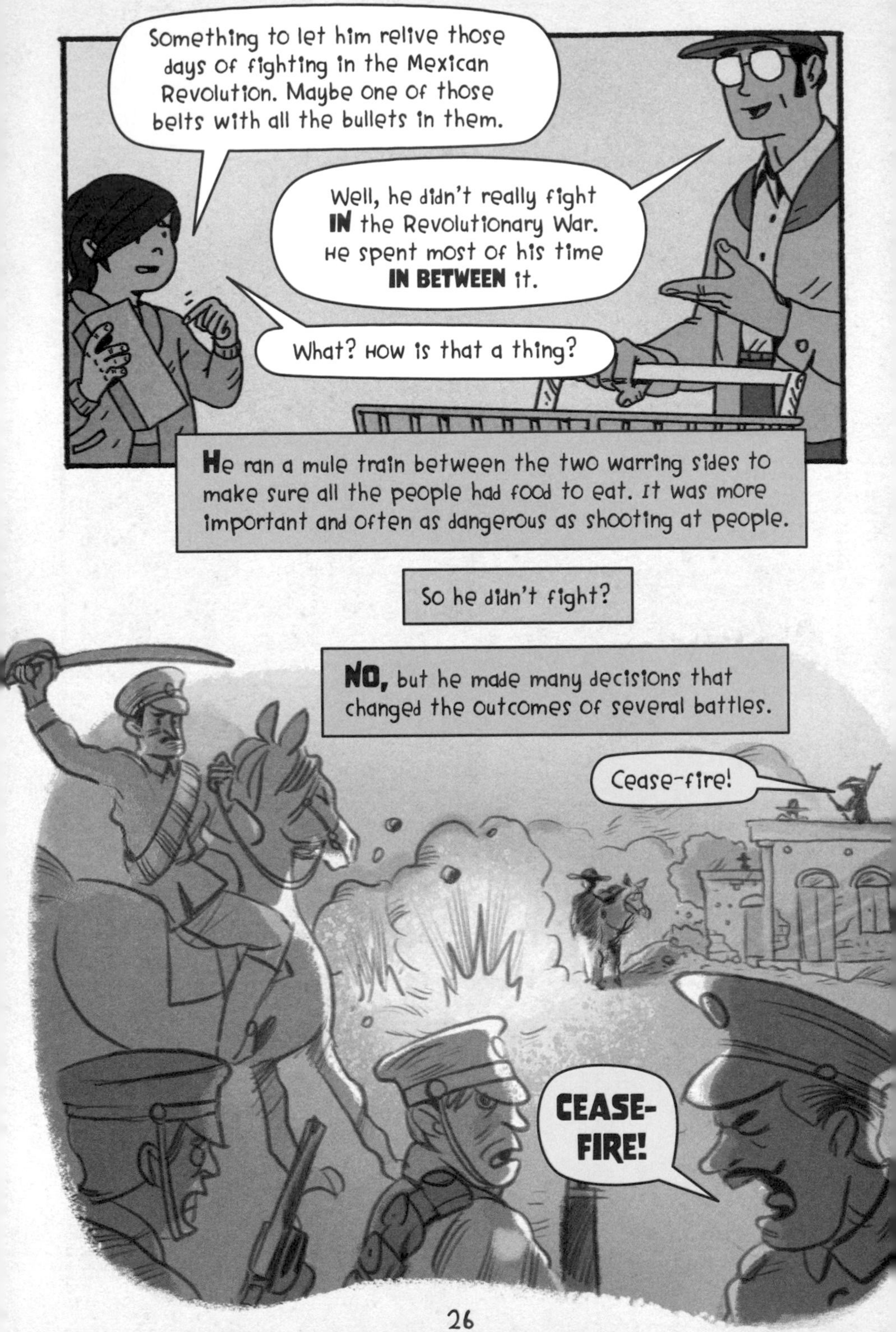
Something to let him relive those days of fighting in the Mexican Revolution. Maybe one of those belts with all the bullets in them.
Well, he didn't really fight IN the Revolutionary War. He spent most of his time IN BETWEEN it.
What? How is that a thing?
He ran a mule train between the two warring sides to make sure all the people had food to eat. It was more important and often as dangerous as shooting at people.
So he didn't fight?
NO, but he made many decisions that changed the outcomes of several battles.
Cease-fire!
CEASE-FIRE!

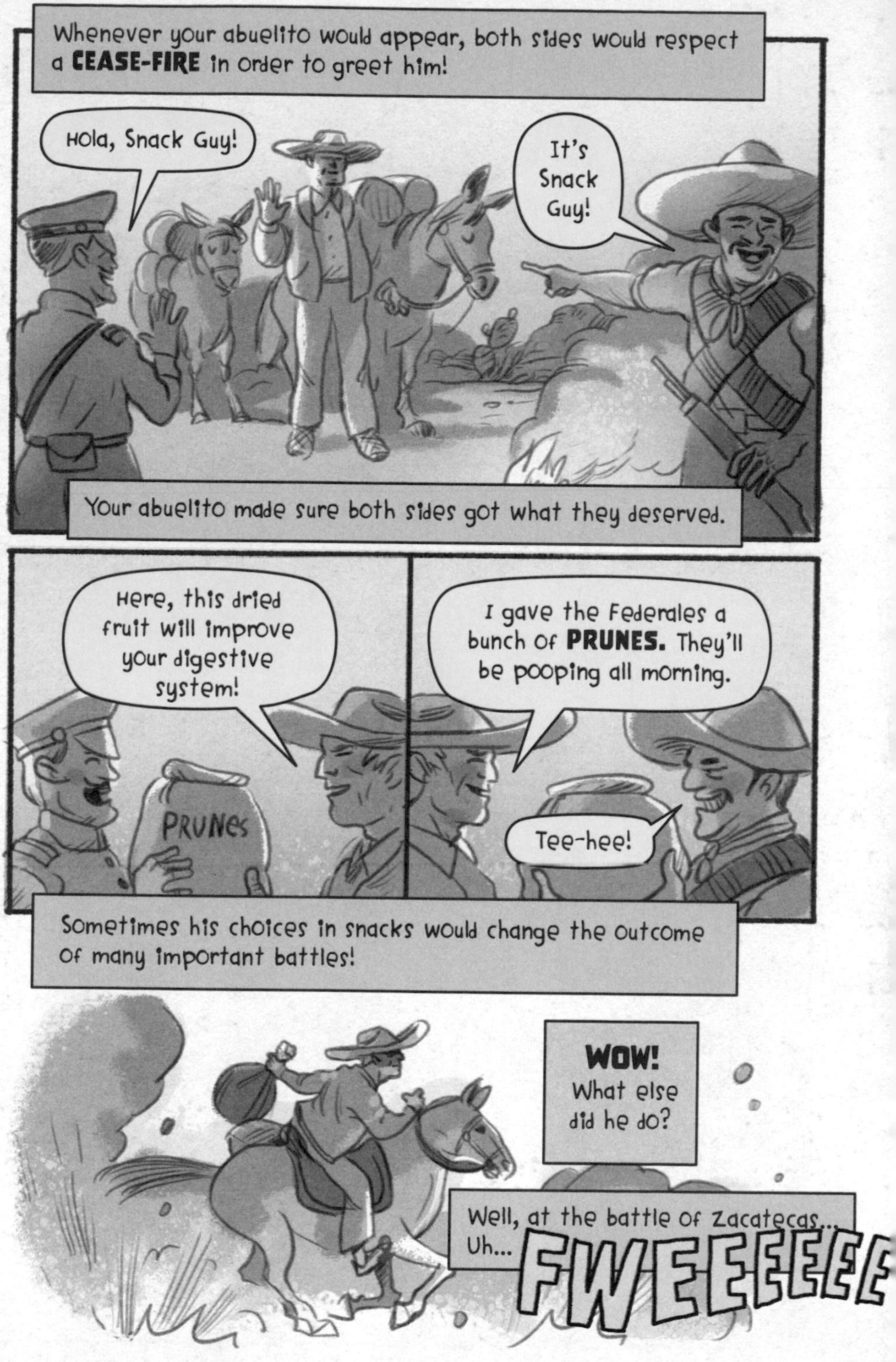
Whenever your abuelito would appear, both sides would respect a CEASE-FIRE in order to greet him!
Hola, Snack Guy!
It's Snack Guy!
Your abuelito made sure both sides got what they deserved.
Here, this dried fruit will improve your digestive system!
PRUNES
I gave the Federales a bunch of PRUNES. They'll be pooping all morning.
Tee-hee!
Sometimes his choices in snacks would change the outcome of many important battles!
WOW! What else did he do?
Well, at the battle of Zacatecas... Uh...
FWEEEEEE

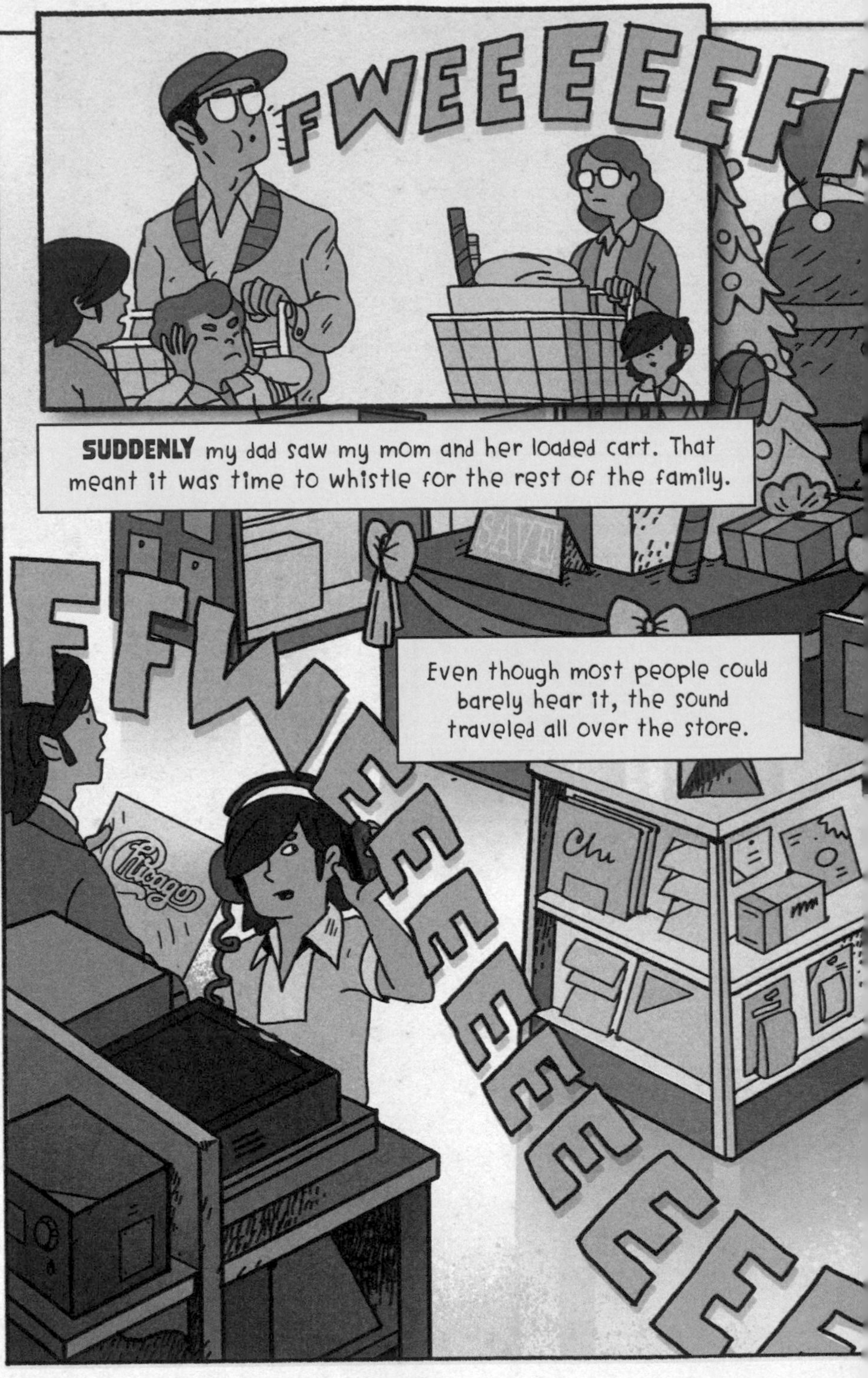
FWEEEEEFF
SUDDENLY my dad saw my mom and her loaded cart. That meant it was time to whistle for the rest of the family.
FFFWEEEEEEEEEEE
Even though most people could barely hear it, the sound traveled all over the store.
SAVE

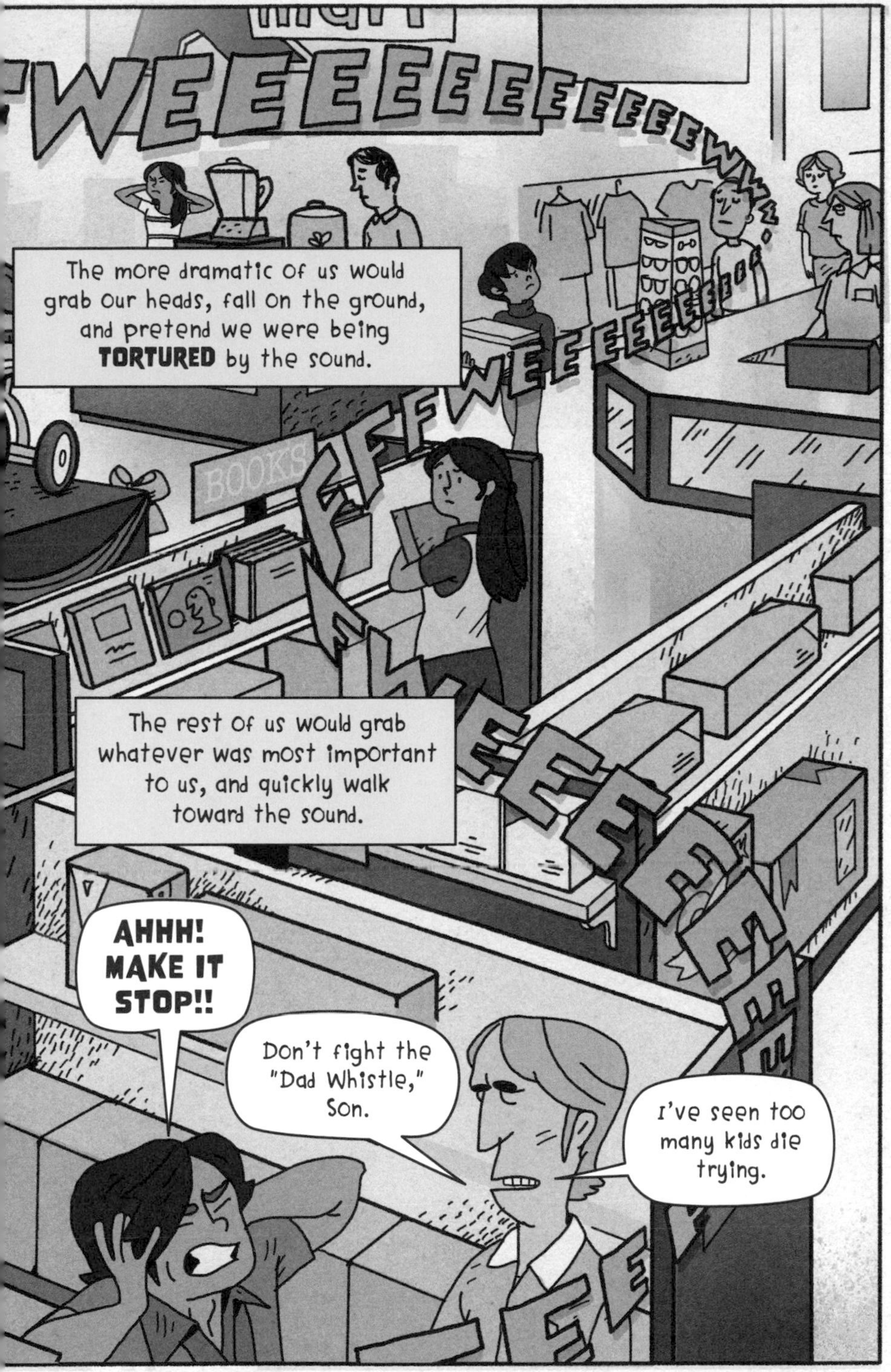
FWEEEEEEEEEEEEEWW
The more dramatic of us would grab our heads, fall on the ground, and pretend we were being **TORTURED** by the sound.
BOOKS
FFWEEEEEEEE
The rest of us would grab whatever was most important to us, and quickly walk toward the sound.
AHHH! MAKE IT STOP!!
Don't fight the "Dad Whistle," Son.
I've seen too many kids die trying.

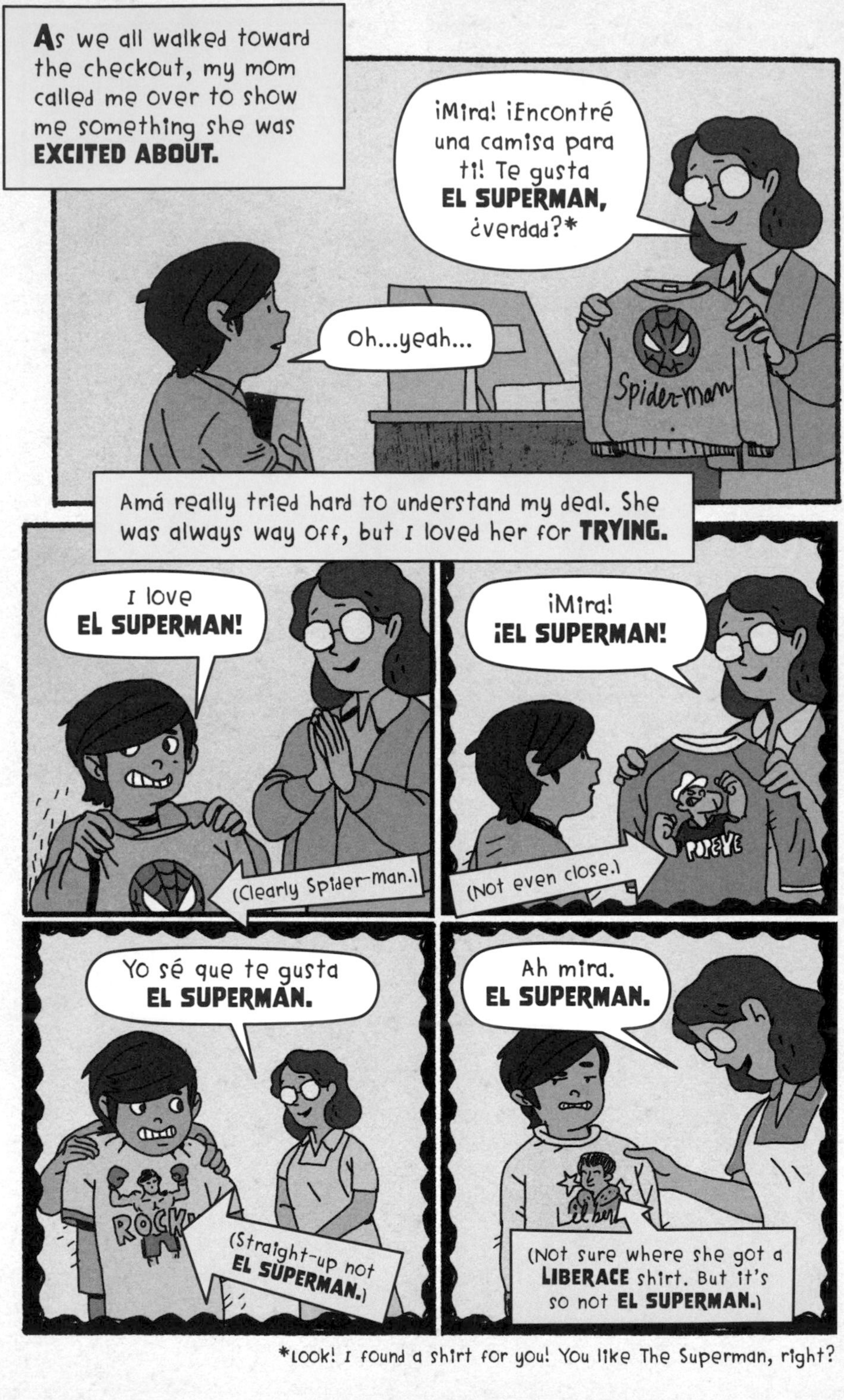
As we all walked toward the checkout, my mom called me over to show me something she was **EXCITED ABOUT.**
¡Mira! ¡Encontré una camisa para ti! Te gusta **EL SUPERMAN,** ¿verdad?*
Oh...yeah...
Spider-man
Amá really tried hard to understand my deal. She was always way off, but I loved her for **TRYING.**
I love **EL SUPERMAN!**
(Clearly Spider-man.)
¡Mira! **¡EL SUPERMAN!**
POPEYE
(Not even close.)
Yo sé que te gusta **EL SUPERMAN.**
ROCK
(Straight-up not **EL SUPERMAN.**)
Ah mira. **EL SUPERMAN.**
(Not sure where she got a **LIBERACE** shirt. But it's so not **EL SUPERMAN.**)

*Look! I found a shirt for you! You like The Superman, right?

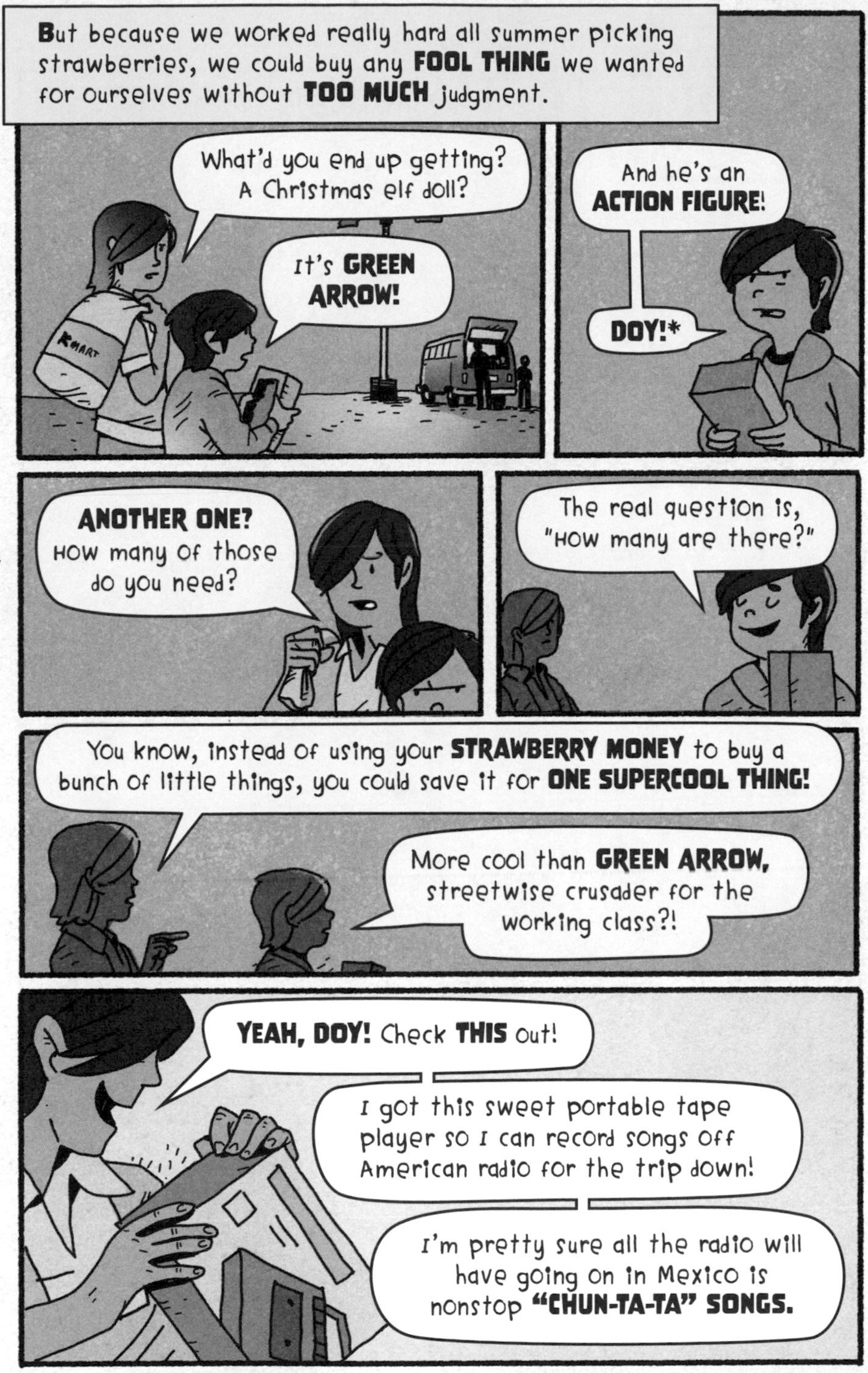
But because we worked really hard all summer picking strawberries, we could buy any FOOL THING we wanted for ourselves without TOO MUCH judgment.
What'd you end up getting? A Christmas elf doll?
It's GREEN ARROW!
And he's an ACTION FIGURE!
DOY!*
ANOTHER ONE? How many of those do you need?
The real question is, "How many are there?"
You know, instead of using your STRAWBERRY MONEY to buy a bunch of little things, you could save it for ONE SUPERCOOL THING!
More cool than GREEN ARROW, streetwise crusader for the working class?!
YEAH, DOY! Check THIS out!
I got this sweet portable tape player so I can record songs off American radio for the trip down!
I'm pretty sure all the radio will have going on in Mexico is nonstop "CHUN-TA-TA" SONGS.

*No kidding, Sherlock. AKA, "Durhay" or "Duh."

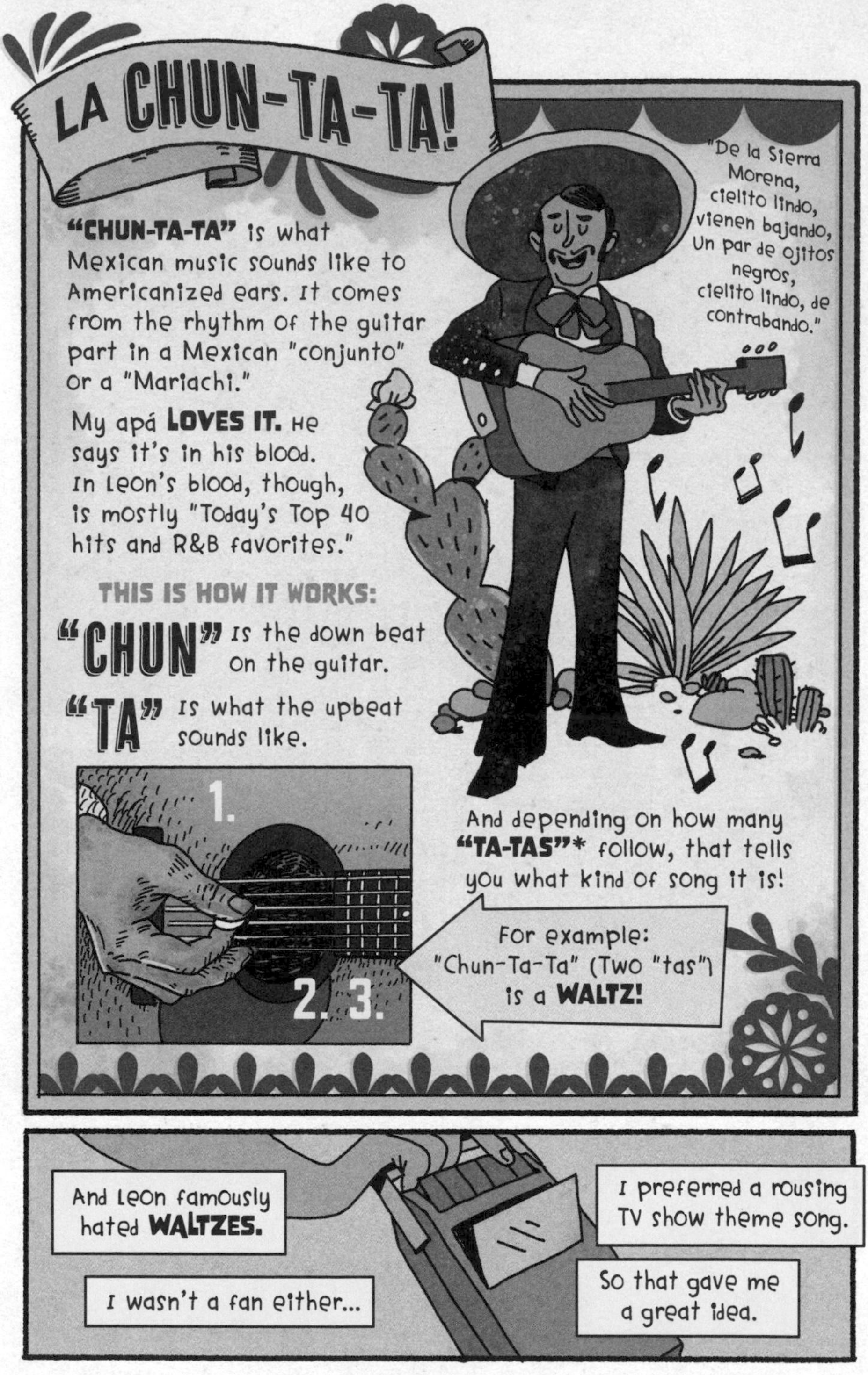
LA CHUN-TA-TA!
"CHUN-TA-TA" is what Mexican music sounds like to Americanized ears. It comes from the rhythm of the guitar part in a Mexican "conjunto" or a "Mariachi."
"De la Sierra Morena, cielito lindo, vienen bajando, Un par de ojitos negros, cielito lindo, de contrabando."
My apá LOVES IT. He says it's in his blood. In Leon's blood, though, is mostly "Today's Top 40 hits and R&B favorites."
THIS IS HOW IT WORKS:
"CHUN" is the down beat on the guitar.
"TA" is what the upbeat sounds like.
1.
2. 3.
And depending on how many "TA-TAS"* follow, that tells you what kind of song it is!
For example: "Chun-Ta-Ta" (Two "tas") is a WALTZ!
And Leon famously hated WALTZES.
I wasn't a fan either...
I preferred a rousing TV show theme song.
So that gave me a great idea.

* "Ta-tas." Tee-hee.

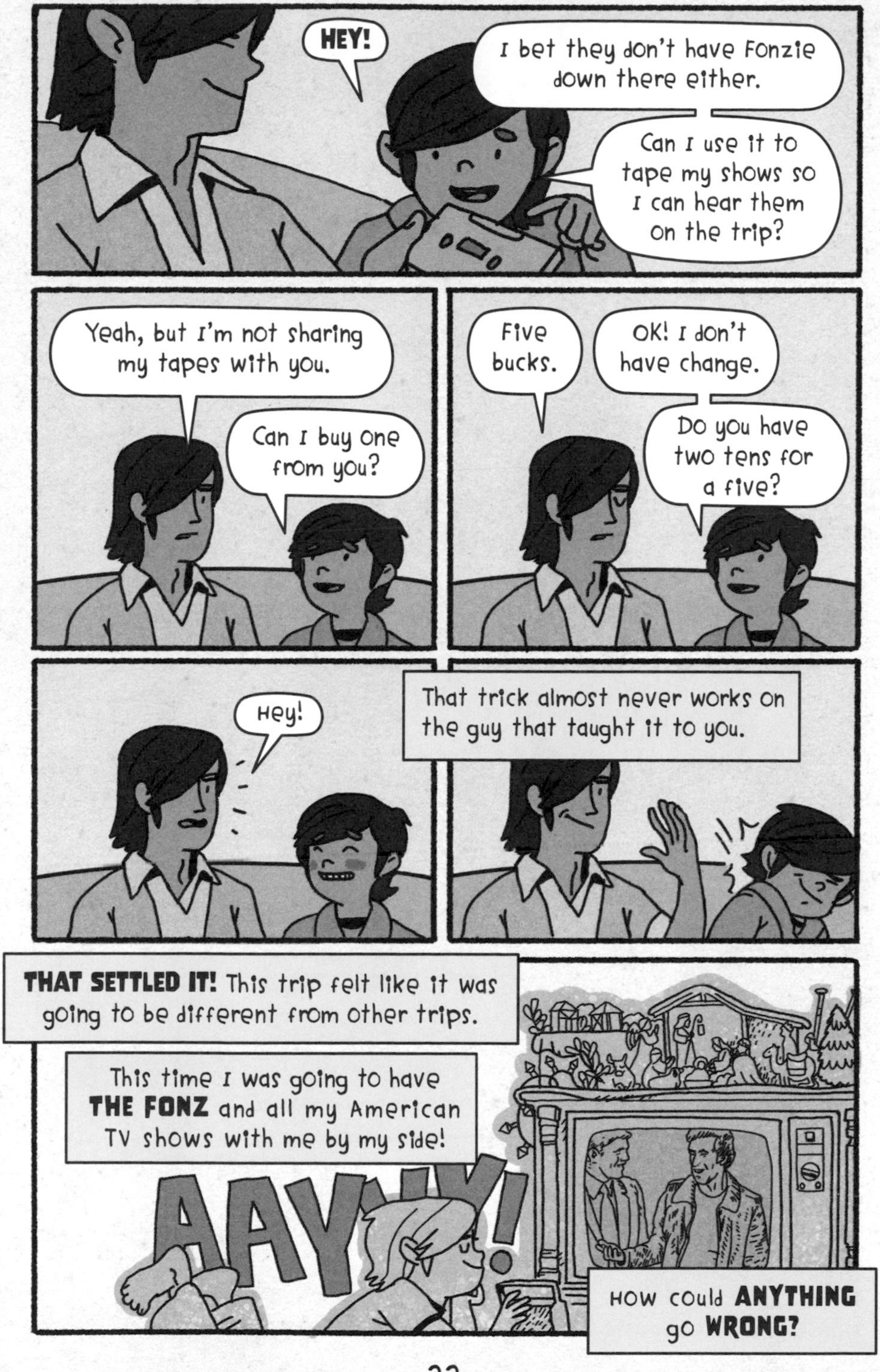
HEY!
I bet they don't have Fonzie down there either.
Can I use it to tape my shows so I can hear them on the trip?
Yeah, but I'm not sharing my tapes with you.
Can I buy one from you?
Five bucks.
OK! I don't have change.
Do you have two tens for a five?
Hey!
That trick almost never works on the guy that taught it to you.
THAT SETTLED IT! This trip felt like it was going to be different from other trips.
This time I was going to have THE FONZ and all my American TV shows with me by my side!
AAYY!
How could ANYTHING go WRONG?

CHAPTER 3 EL MOTORHOME

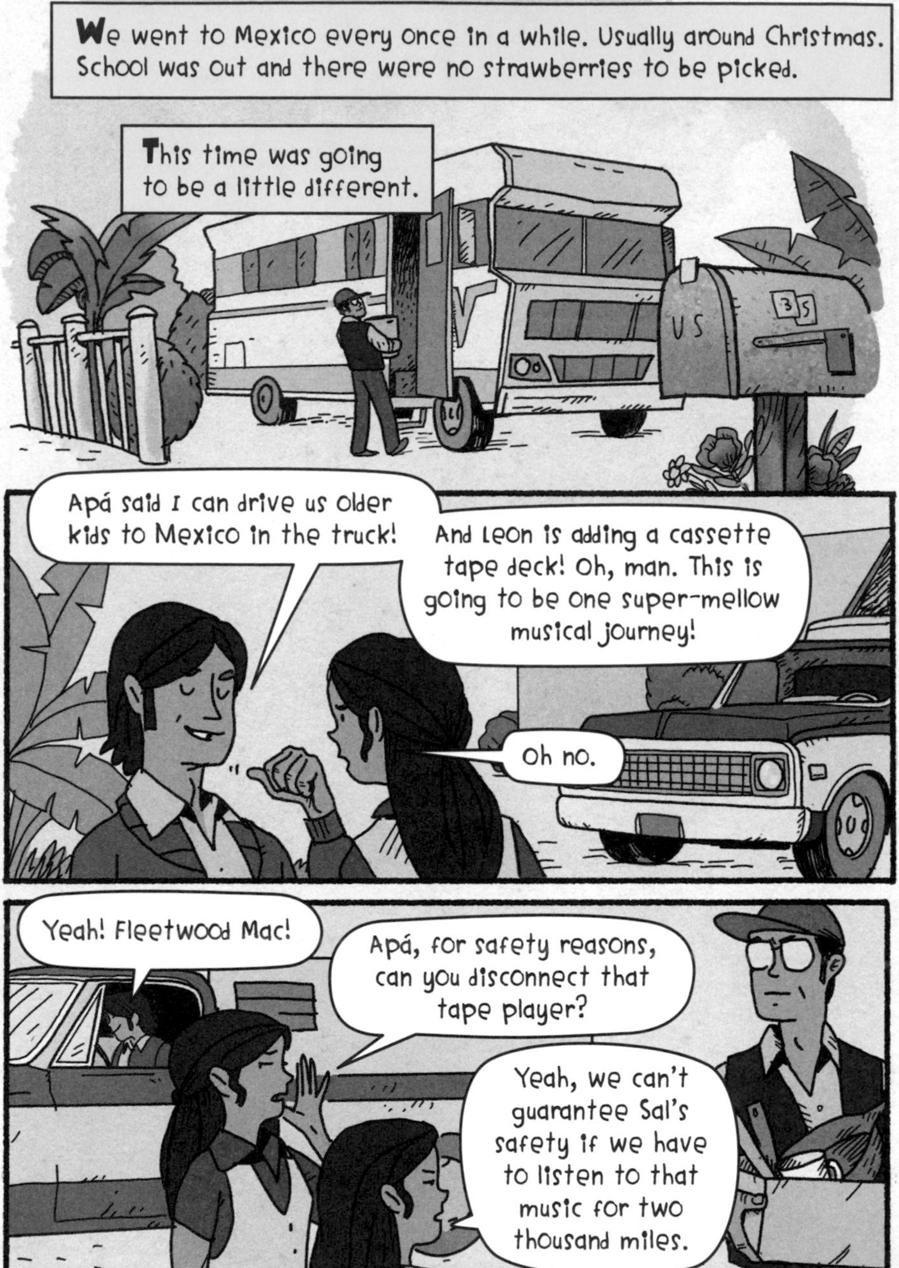
We went to Mexico every once in a while. Usually around Christmas. School was out and there were no strawberries to be picked.
This time was going to be a little different.
US
35
Apá said I can drive us older kids to Mexico in the truck!
And Leon is adding a cassette tape deck! Oh, man. This is going to be one super-mellow musical journey!
Oh no.
Yeah! Fleetwood Mac!
Apá, for safety reasons, can you disconnect that tape player?
Yeah, we can't guarantee Sal's safety if we have to listen to that music for two thousand miles.

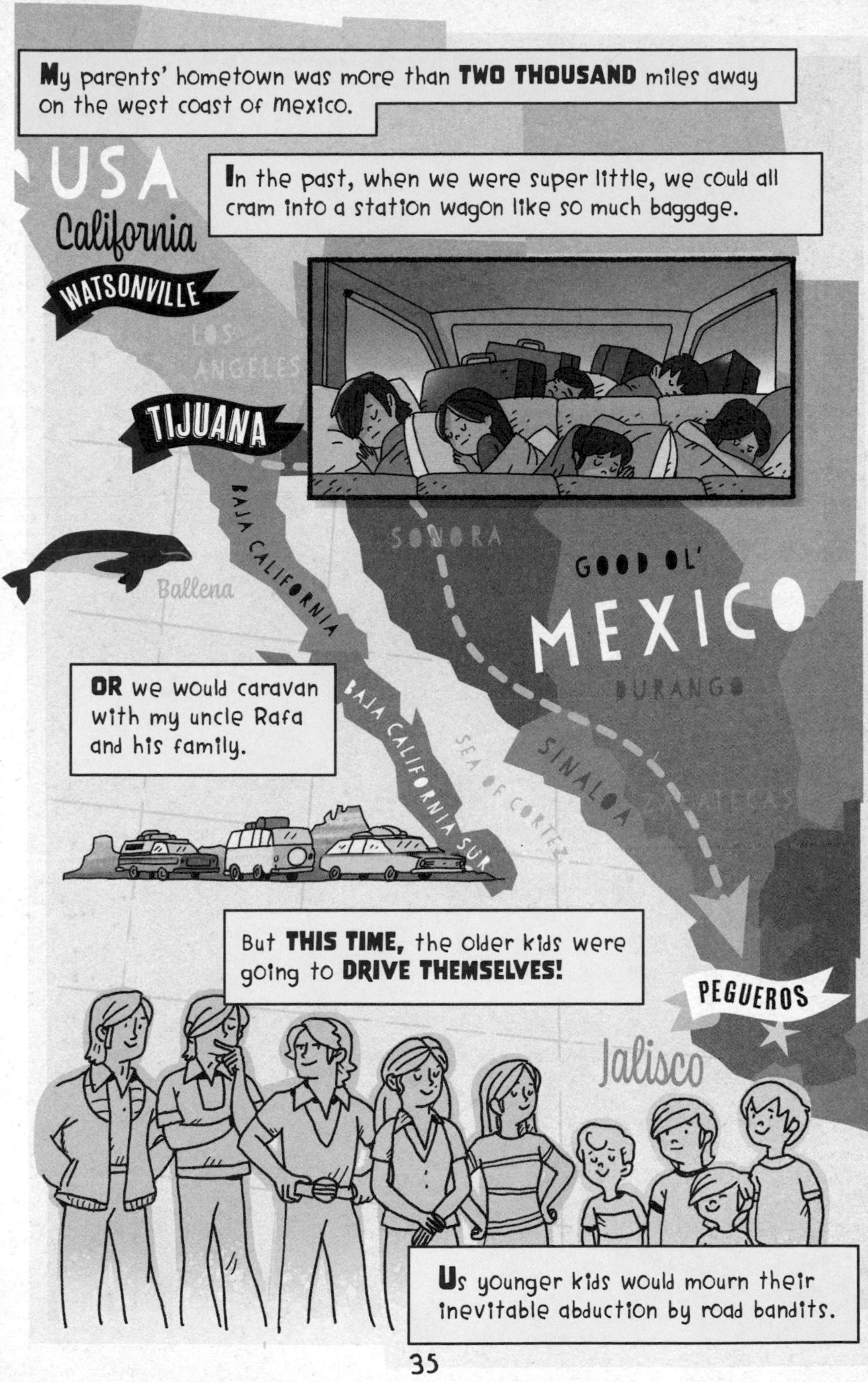
My parents' hometown was more than TWO THOUSAND miles away on the west coast of mexico.
USA
California
WATSONVILLE
In the past, when we were super little, we could all cram into a station wagon like so much baggage.
LOS ANGELES
TIJUANA
BAJA CALIFORNIA
SONORA
Ballena
GOOD OL'
MEXICO
DURANGO
OR we would caravan with my uncle Rafa and his family.
BAJA CALIFORNIA SUR
SEA OF CORTEZ
SINALOA
ZACATECAS
But THIS TIME, the older kids were going to DRIVE THEMSELVES!
PEGUEROS
Jalisco
Us younger kids would mourn their inevitable abduction by road bandits.

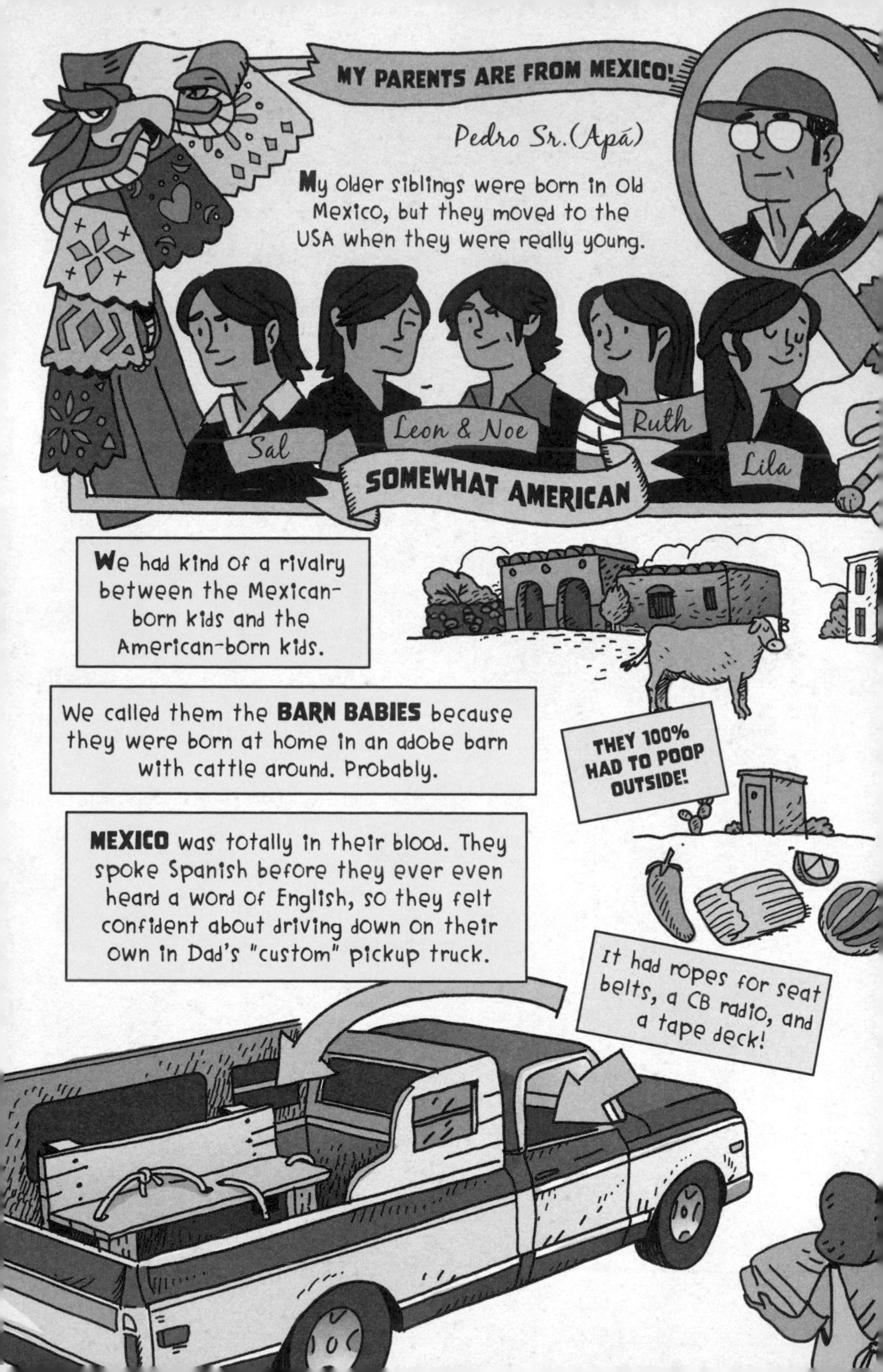

MY PARENTS ARE FROM MEXICO!
Pedro Sr. (Apá)
My older siblings were born in Old Mexico, but they moved to the USA when they were really young.
Sal
Leon & Noe
Ruth
Lila
SOMEWHAT AMERICAN
We had kind of a rivalry between the Mexican-born kids and the American-born kids.
We called them the BARN BABIES because they were born at home in an adobe barn with cattle around. Probably.
THEY 100% HAD TO POOP OUTSIDE!
MEXICO was totally in their blood. They spoke Spanish before they ever even heard a word of English, so they felt confident about driving down on their own in Dad's "custom" pickup truck.
It had ropes for seat belts, a CB radio, and a tape deck!

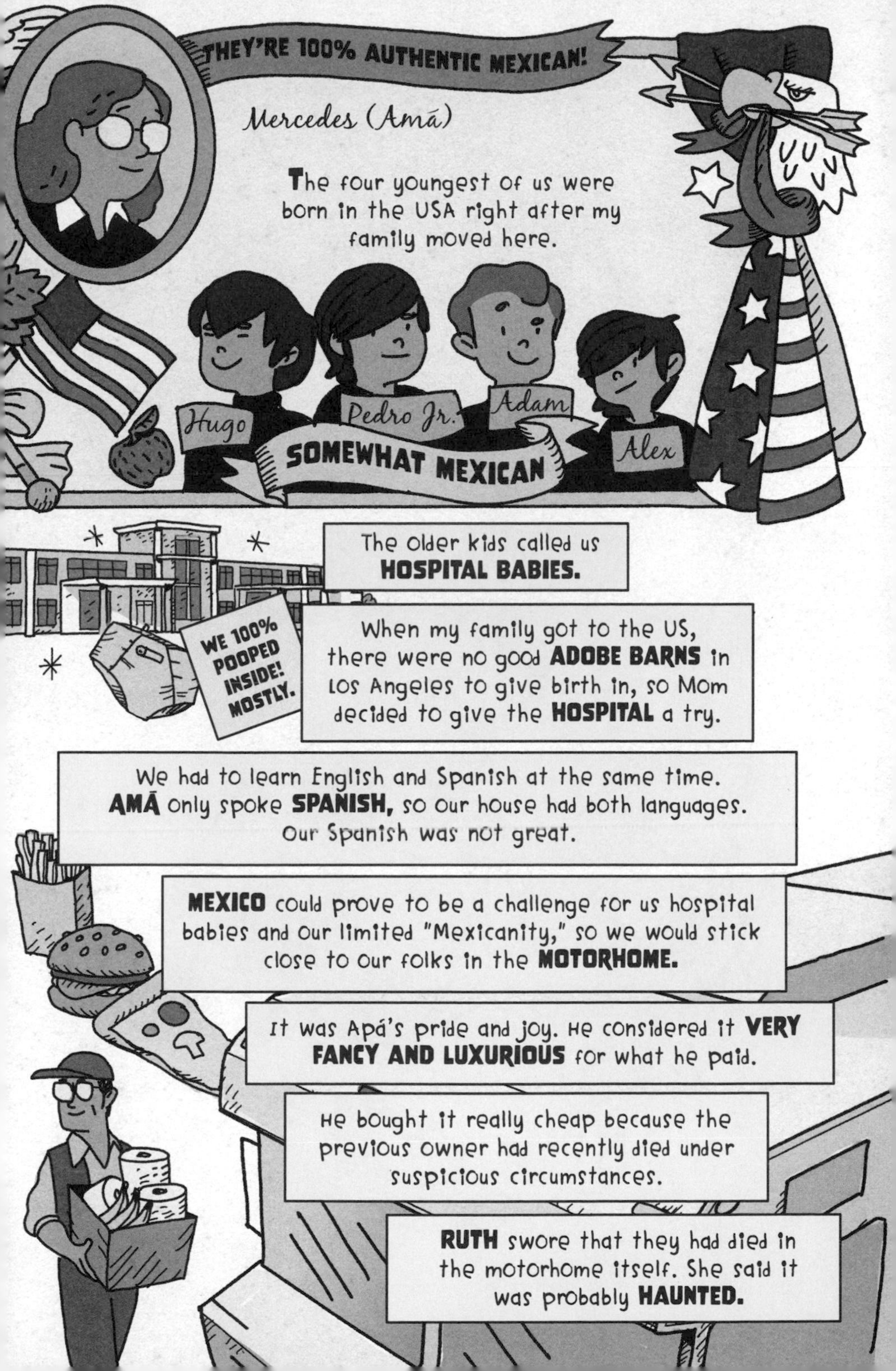

THEY'RE 100% AUTHENTIC MEXICAN!
Mercedes (Amá)
The four youngest of us were born in the USA right after my family moved here.
Hugo
Pedro Jr.
Adam
Alex
SOMEWHAT MEXICAN
The older kids called us HOSPITAL BABIES.
WE 100% POOPED INSIDE! MOSTLY.
When my family got to the US, there were no good ADOBE BARNS in Los Angeles to give birth in, so Mom decided to give the HOSPITAL a try.
We had to learn English and Spanish at the same time. AMÁ only spoke SPANISH, so our house had both languages. Our Spanish was not great.
MEXICO could prove to be a challenge for us hospital babies and our limited "Mexicanity," so we would stick close to our folks in the MOTORHOME.
It was Apá's pride and joy. He considered it VERY FANCY AND LUXURIOUS for what he paid.
He bought it really cheap because the previous owner had recently died under suspicious circumstances.
RUTH swore that they had died in the motorhome itself. She said it was probably HAUNTED.

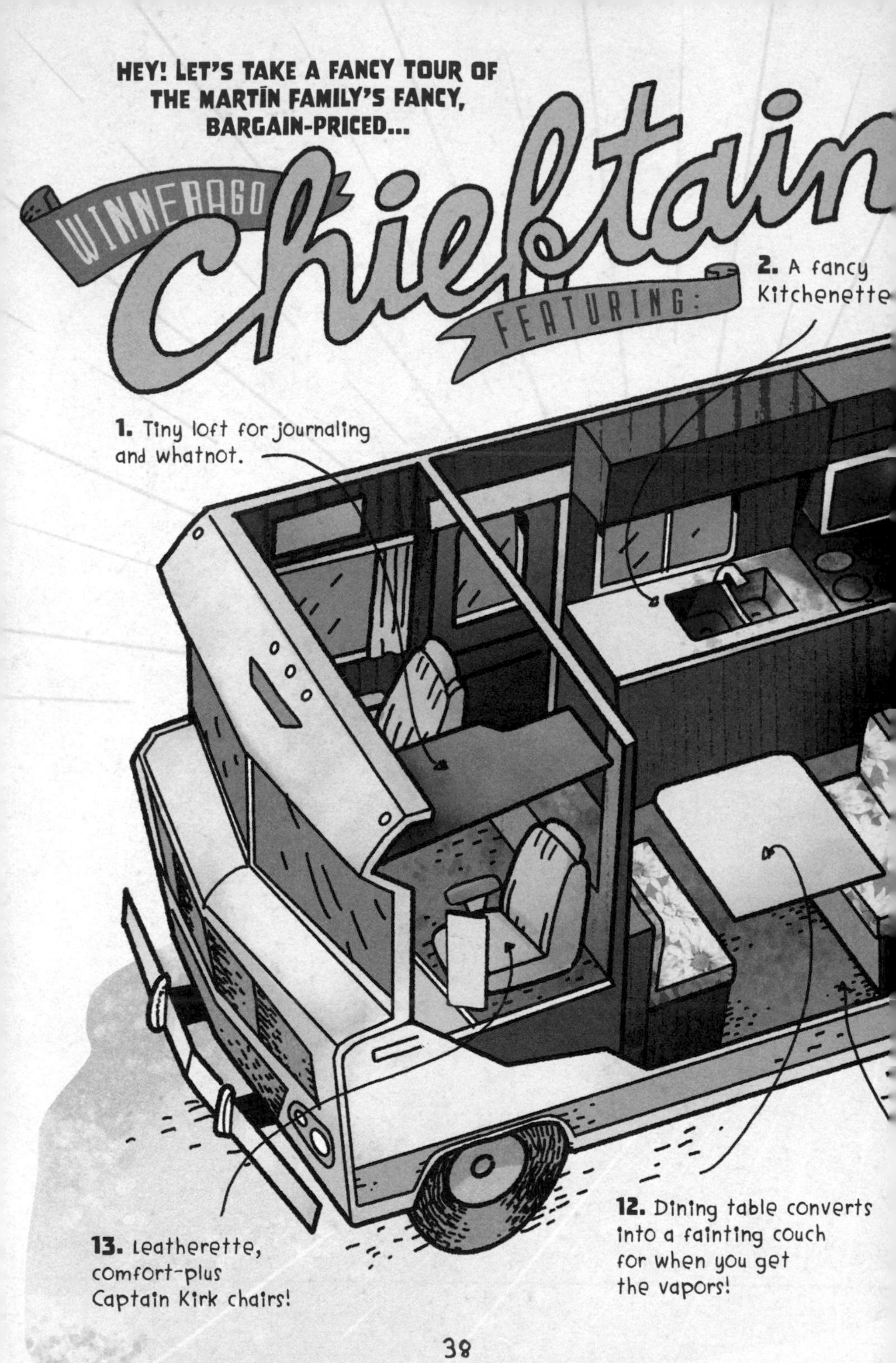
HEY! LET'S TAKE A FANCY TOUR OF THE MARTĪN FAMILY'S FANCY, BARGAIN-PRICED...
WINNEBAGO
Chieftain
FEATURING:
2. A fancy Kitchenette
1. Tiny loft for journaling and whatnot.
12. Dining table converts into a fainting couch for when you get the vapors!
13. Leatherette, comfort-plus Captain Kirk chairs!

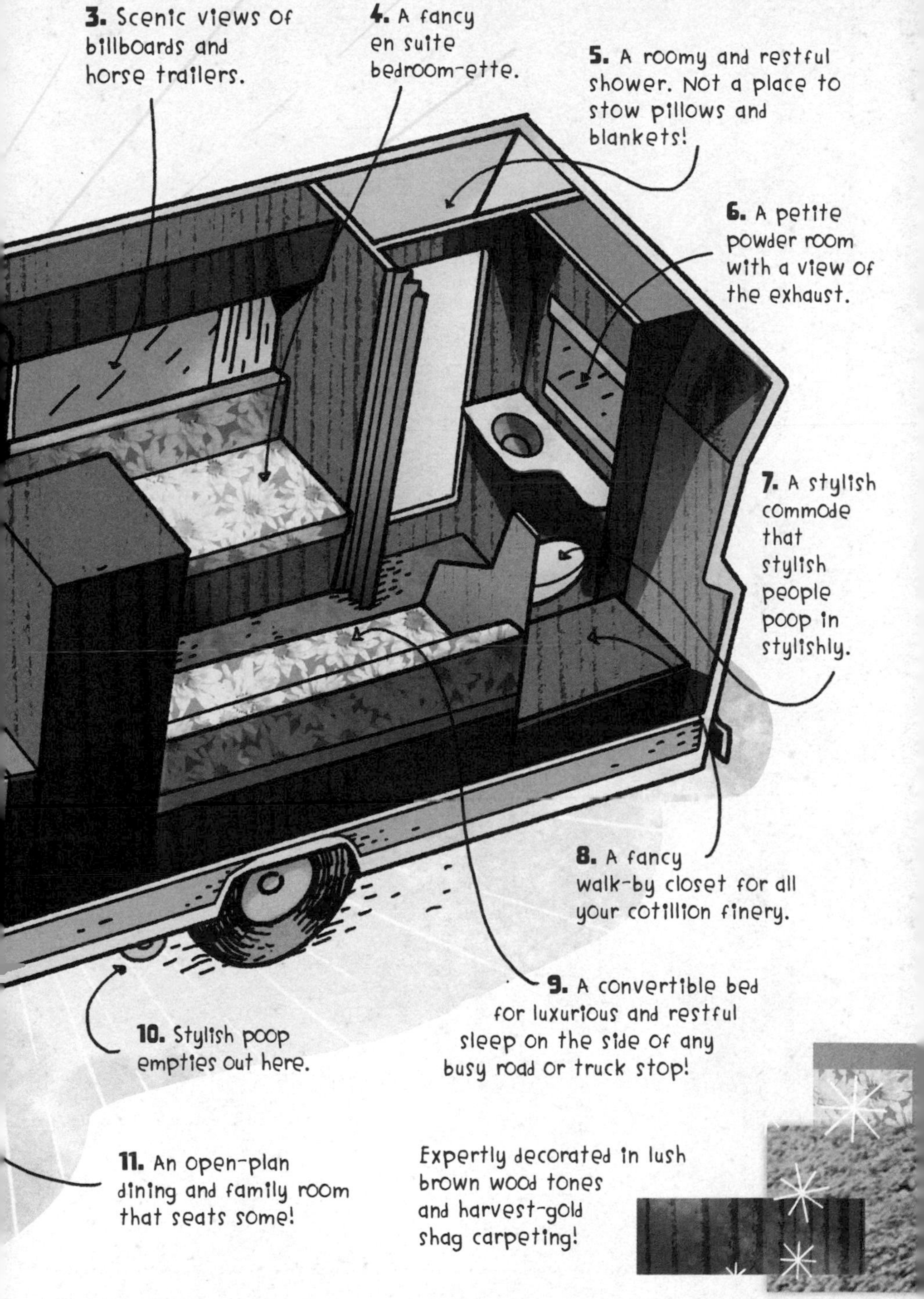

3. Scenic views of billboards and horse trailers.
4. A fancy en suite bedroom-ette.
5. A roomy and restful shower. Not a place to stow pillows and blankets!
6. A petite powder room with a view of the exhaust.
7. A stylish commode that stylish people poop in stylishly.
8. A fancy walk-by closet for all your cotillion finery.
9. A convertible bed for luxurious and restful sleep on the side of any busy road or truck stop!
10. Stylish poop empties out here.
11. An open-plan dining and family room that seats some!
Expertly decorated in lush brown wood tones and harvest-gold shag carpeting!

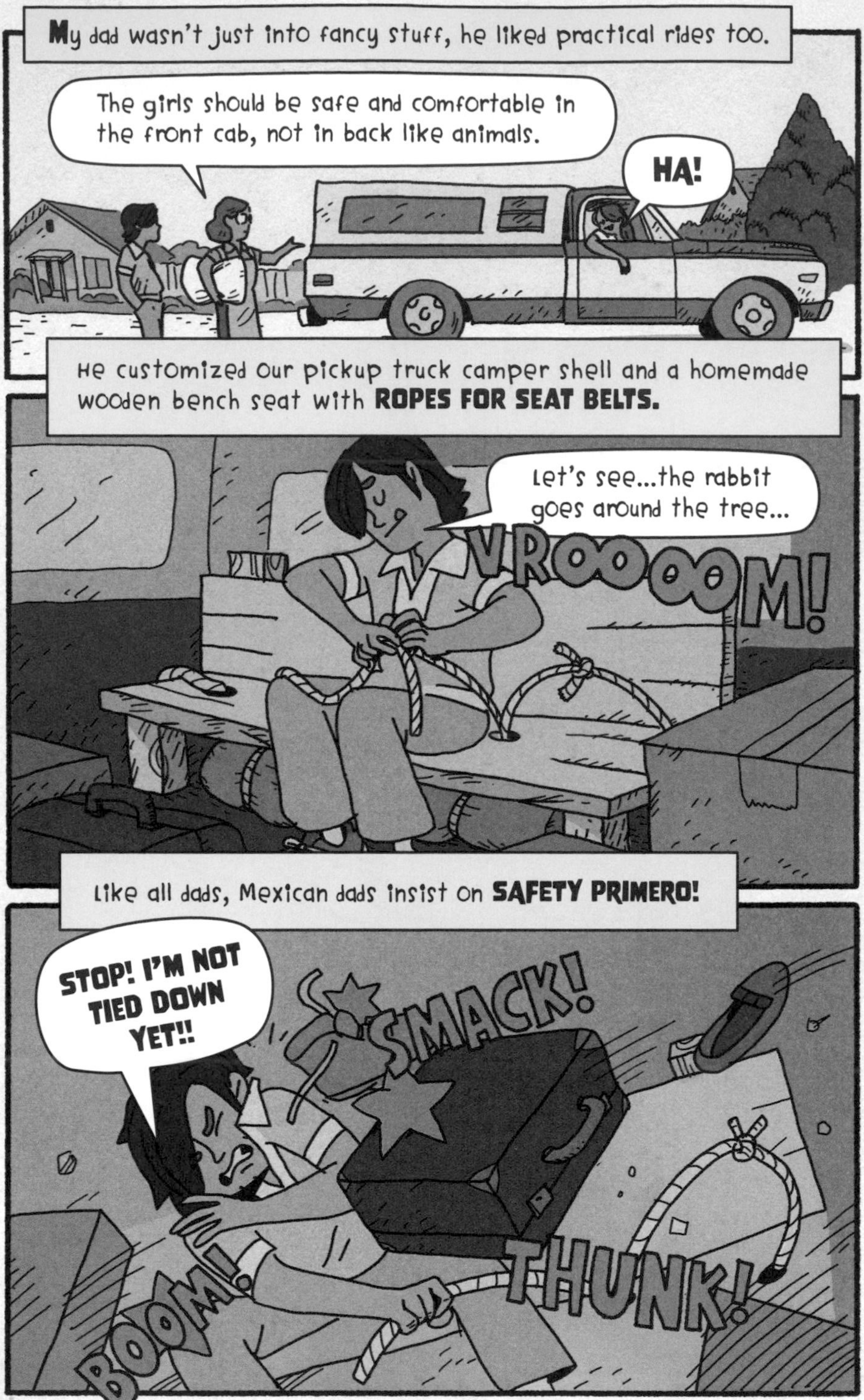
My dad wasn't just into fancy stuff, he liked practical rides too.
The girls should be safe and comfortable in the front cab, not in back like animals.
HA!
He customized our pickup truck camper shell and a homemade wooden bench seat with ROPES FOR SEAT BELTS.
Let's see...the rabbit goes around the tree...
VROOOOM!
Like all dads, Mexican dads insist on SAFETY PRIMERO!
STOP! I'M NOT TIED DOWN YET!!
SMACK!
THUNK!
BOOM!

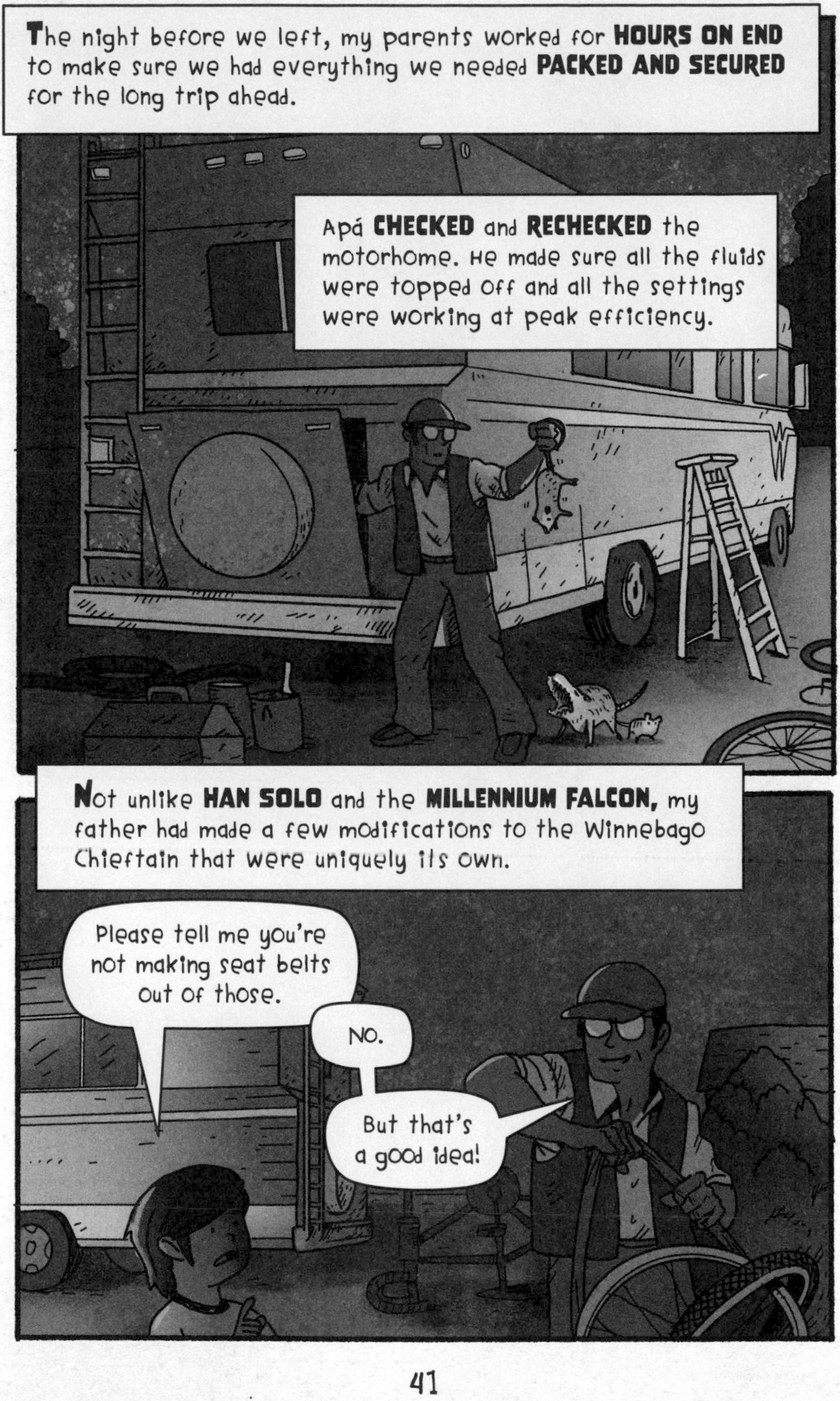
The night before we left, my parents worked for HOURS ON END to make sure we had everything we needed PACKED AND SECURED for the long trip ahead.
Apá CHECKED and RECHECKED the motorhome. He made sure all the fluids were topped off and all the settings were working at peak efficiency.
Not unlike HAN SOLO and the MILLENNIUM FALCON, my father had made a few modifications to the Winnebago Chieftain that were uniquely its own.
Please tell me you're not making seat belts out of those.
NO.
But that's a good idea!

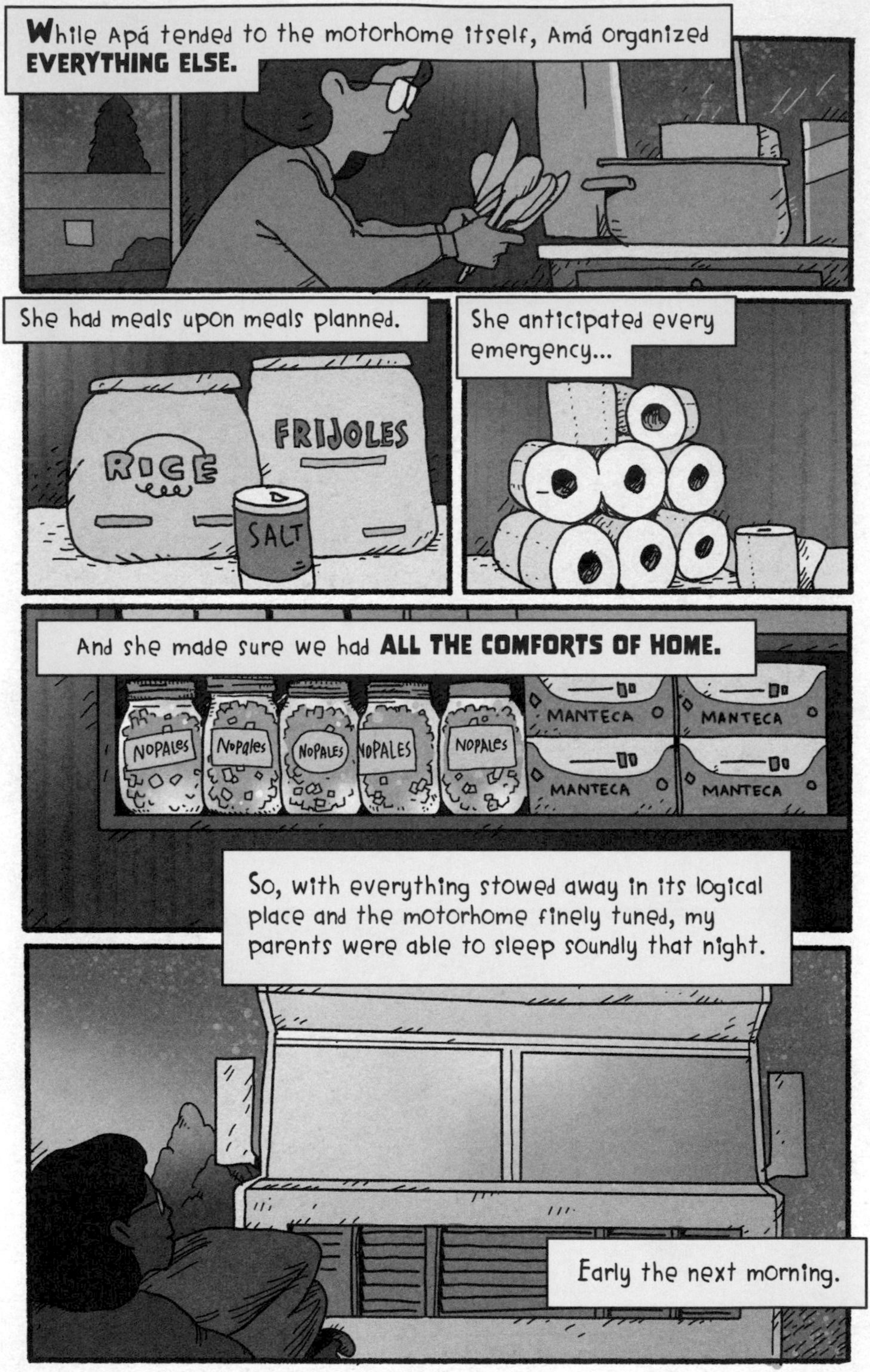

While Apá tended to the motorhome itself, Amá organized **EVERYTHING ELSE.**
She had meals upon meals planned.
RICE
FRIJOLES
SALT
She anticipated every emergency...
And she made sure we had **ALL THE COMFORTS OF HOME.**
NOPALES
NOPALES
NOPALES
NOPALES
NOPALES
MANTECA
MANTECA
MANTECA
MANTECA
So, with everything stowed away in its logical place and the motorhome finely tuned, my parents were able to sleep soundly that night.
Early the next morning.

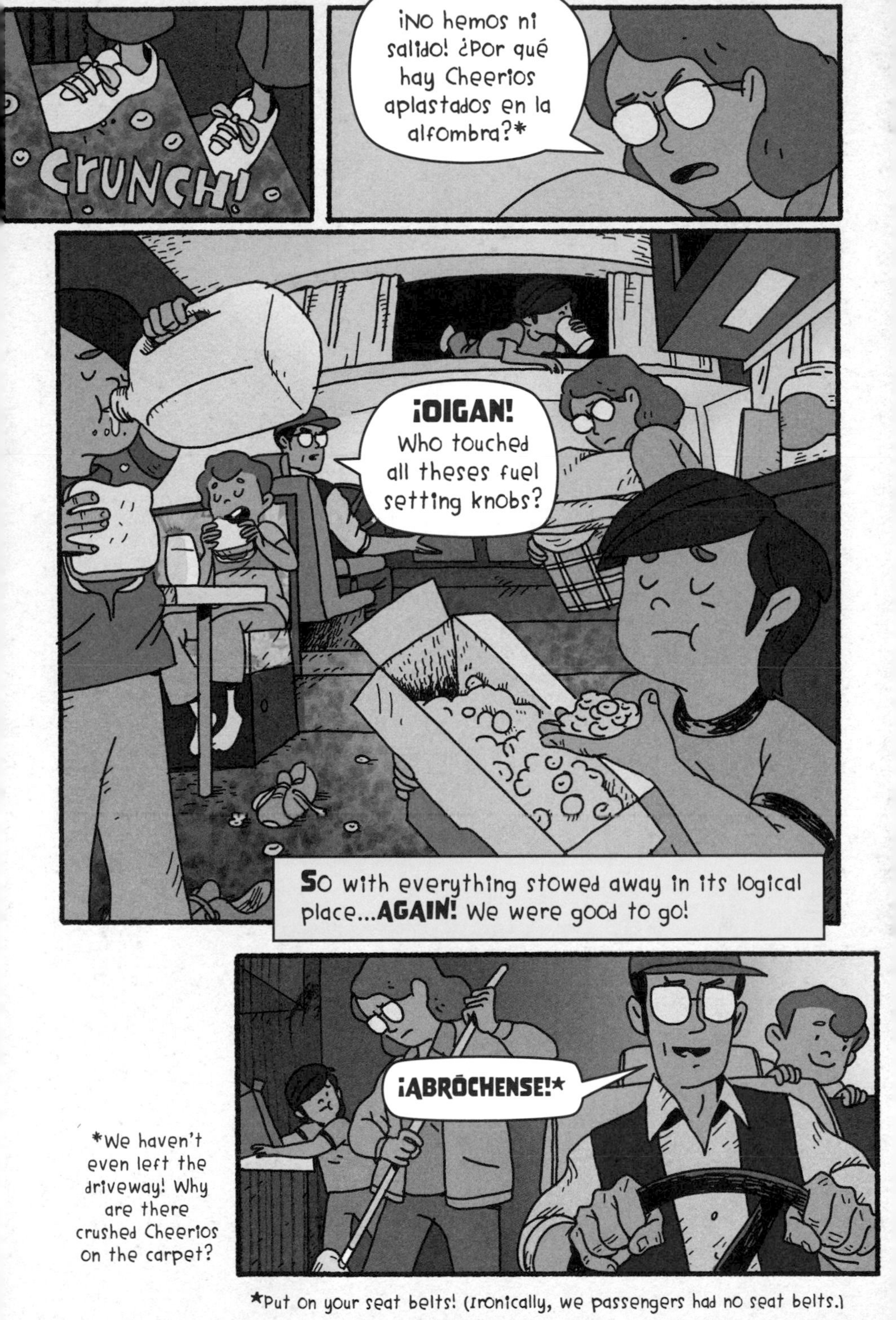
CRUNCH!
¡NO hemos ni salido! ¿Por qué hay Cheerios aplastados en la alfombra?*
¡OIGAN! Who touched all theses fuel setting knobs?
SO with everything stowed away in its logical place...AGAIN! We were good to go!
¡ABRÓCHENSE!*

*We haven't even left the driveway! Why are there crushed Cheerios on the carpet?

*Put on your seat belts! (Ironically, we passengers had no seat belts.)

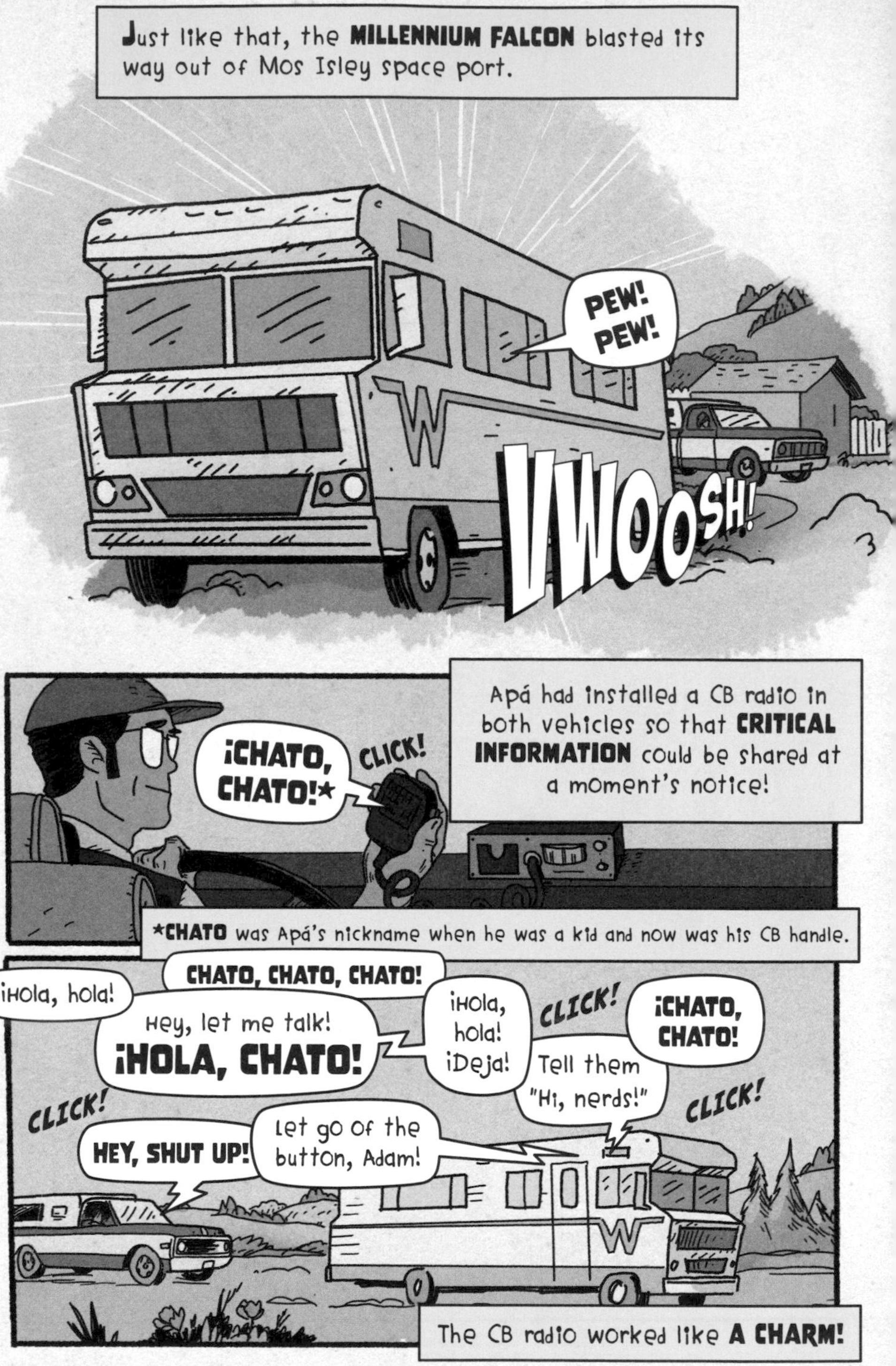
Just like that, the MILLENNIUM FALCON blasted its way out of Mos Isley space port.
PEW! PEW!
VWOOSH!
Apá had installed a CB radio in both vehicles so that CRITICAL INFORMATION could be shared at a moment's notice!
¡CHATO, CHATO!*
CLICK!
*CHATO was Apá's nickname when he was a kid and now was his CB handle.
CHATO, CHATO, CHATO!
¡Hola, hola!
Hey, let me talk! ¡HOLA, CHATO!
¡Hola, hola! ¡Deja!
CLICK!
¡CHATO, CHATO!
Tell them "Hi, nerds!"
CLICK!
CLICK!
HEY, SHUT UP!
Let go of the button, Adam!
The CB radio worked like A CHARM!

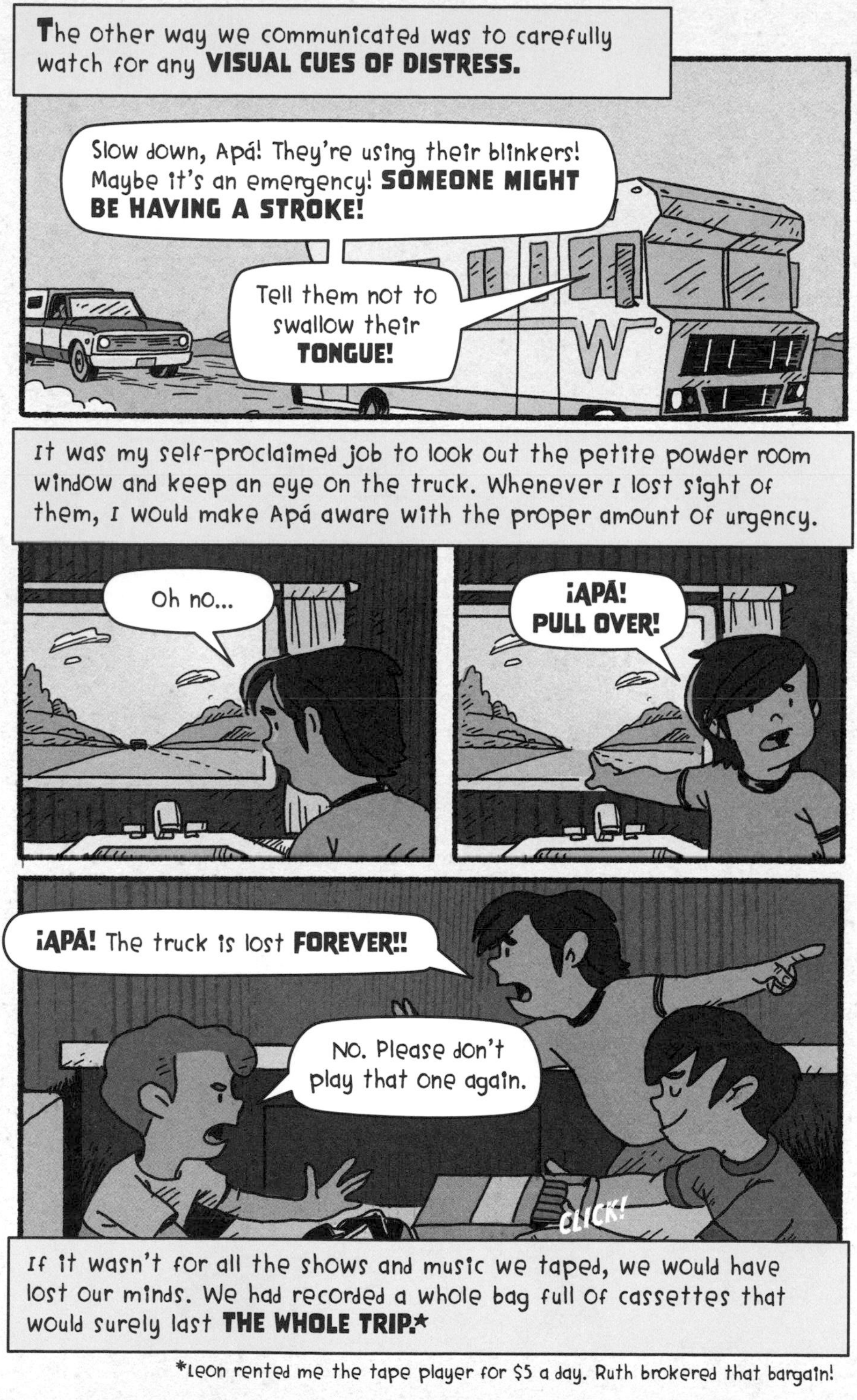
The other way we communicated was to carefully watch for any VISUAL CUES OF DISTRESS.
Slow down, Apá! They're using their blinkers! Maybe it's an emergency! SOMEONE MIGHT BE HAVING A STROKE!
Tell them not to swallow their TONGUE!
It was my self-proclaimed job to look out the petite powder room window and keep an eye on the truck. Whenever I lost sight of them, I would make Apá aware with the proper amount of urgency.
Oh no...
¡APÁ! PULL OVER!
¡APÁ! The truck is lost FOREVER!!
No. Please don't play that one again.
CLICK!
If it wasn't for all the shows and music we taped, we would have lost our minds. We had recorded a whole bag full of cassettes that would surely last THE WHOLE TRIP.*

*Leon rented me the tape player for $5 a day. Ruth brokered that bargain!

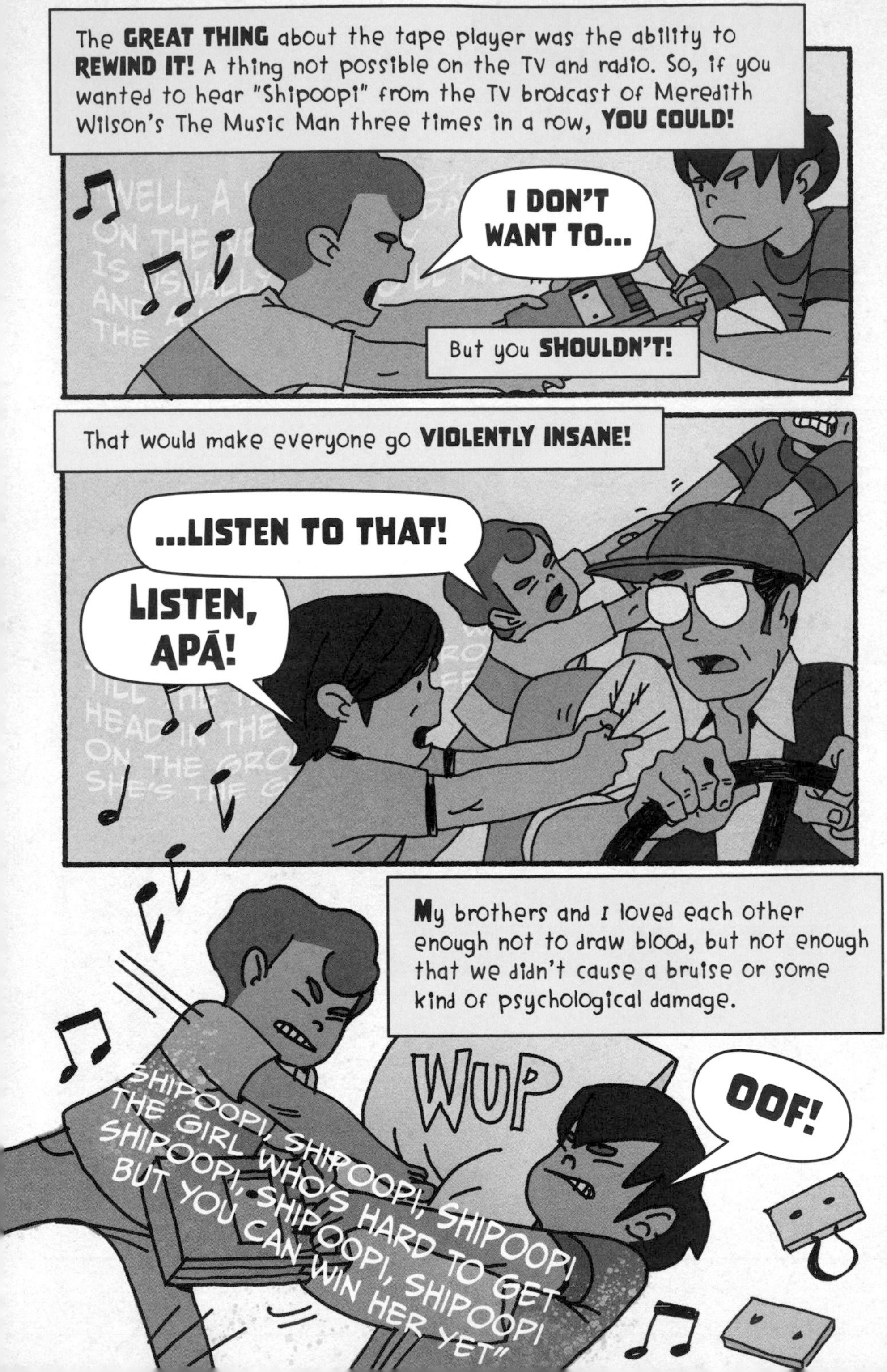
The GREAT THING about the tape player was the ability to REWIND IT! A thing not possible on the TV and radio. So, if you wanted to hear "Shipoopi" from the TV brodcast of Meredith Wilson's The Music Man three times in a row, YOU COULD!
I DON'T WANT TO...
But you SHOULDN'T!
That would make everyone go VIOLENTLY INSANE!
...LISTEN TO THAT!
LISTEN, APÁ!
My brothers and I loved each other enough not to draw blood, but not enough that we didn't cause a bruise or some kind of psychological damage.
WUP
OOF!
"SHIPOOPI, SHIPOOPI, SHIPOOPI
THE GIRL WHO'S HARD TO GET
SHIPOOPI, SHIPOOPI, SHIPOOPI
BUT YOU CAN WIN HER YET"

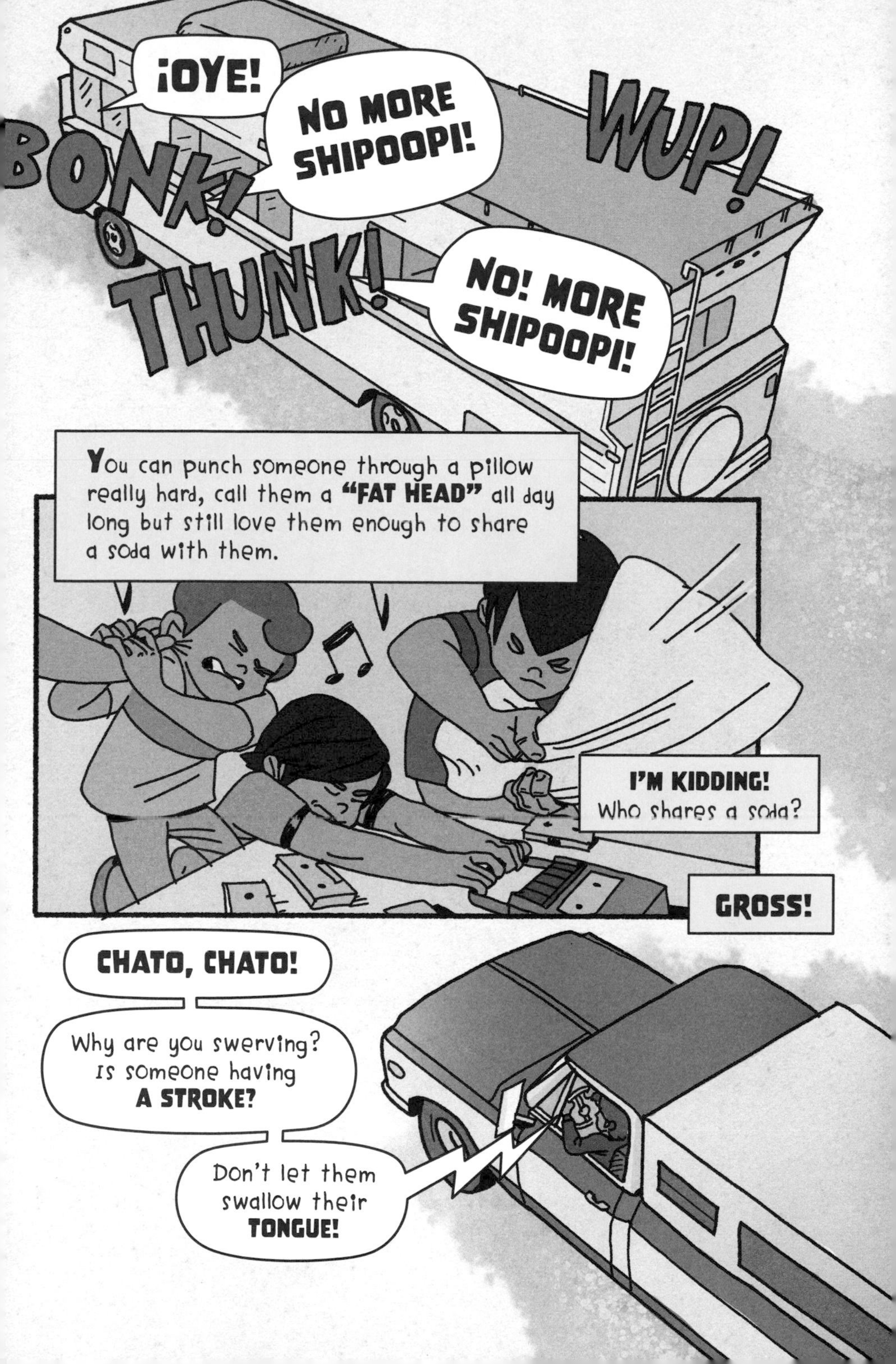
¡OYE!
NO MORE SHIPOOPI!
WUP!
BONK!
THUNK!
NO! MORE SHIPOOPI!
You can punch someone through a pillow really hard, call them a "FAT HEAD" all day long but still love them enough to share a soda with them.
I'M KIDDING! Who shares a soda?
GROSS!
CHATO, CHATO!
Why are you swerving? Is someone having A STROKE?
Don't let them swallow their TONGUE!

CHAPTER 4 THE NONSTOP ADVENTURE

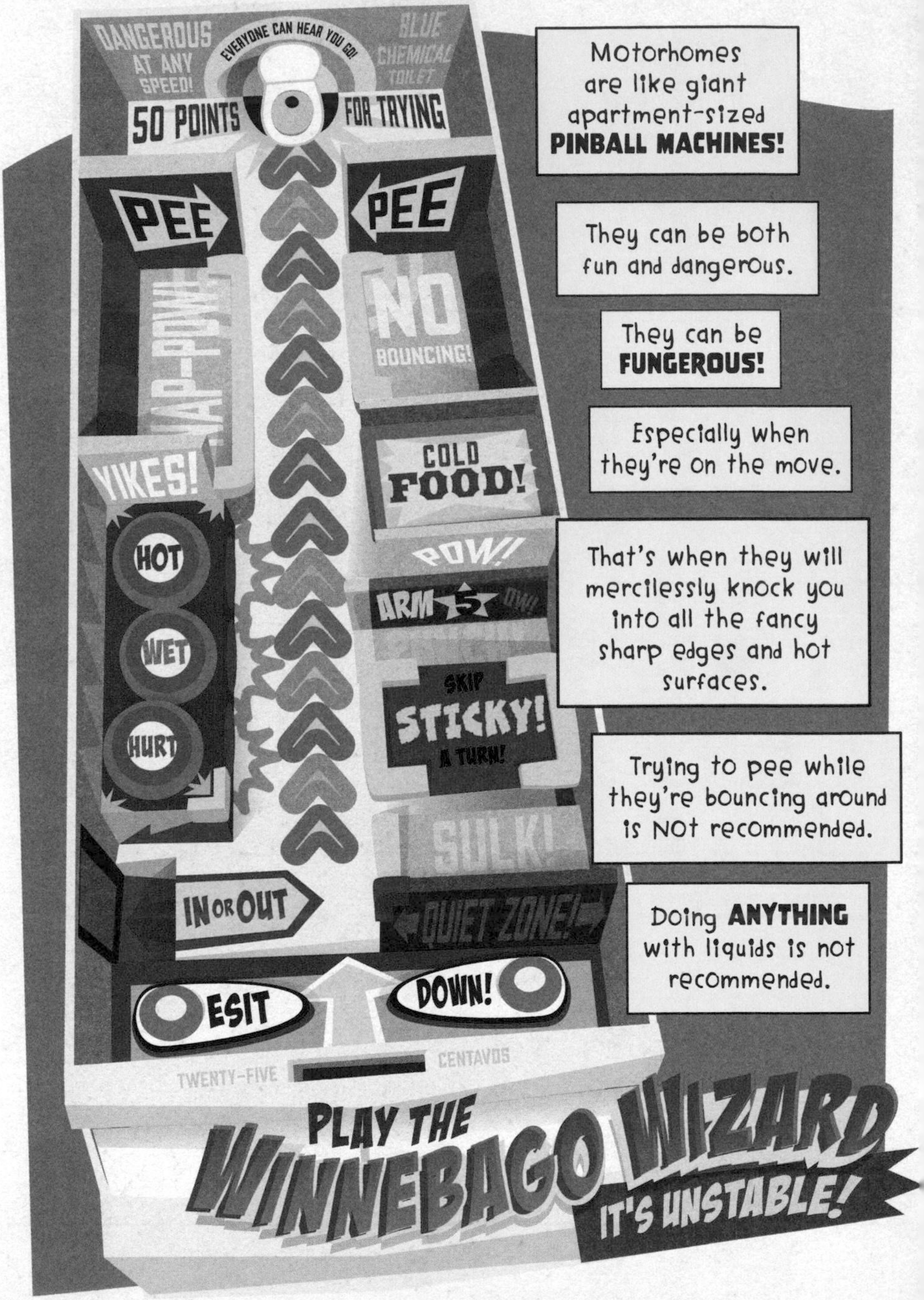
DANGEROUS AT ANY SPEED!
EVERYONE CAN HEAR YOU GO!
BLUE CHEMICAL TOILET
50 POINTS
FOR TRYING
PEE
PEE
YAP-POW!
NO BOUNCING!
YIKES!
COLD FOOD!
HOT
WET
HURT
POW!
ARM 5 OW!
SKIP STICKY! A TURN!
SULK!
IN OR OUT
QUIET ZONE!
ESIT
DOWN!
TWENTY-FIVE
CENTAVOS
PLAY THE WINNEBAGO WIZARD
IT'S UNSTABLE!

Motorhomes are like giant apartment-sized **PINBALL MACHINES!**

They can be both fun and dangerous.

They can be **FUNGEROUS!**

Especially when they're on the move.

That's when they will mercilessly knock you into all the fancy sharp edges and hot surfaces.

Trying to pee while they're bouncing around is NOT recommended.

Doing **ANYTHING** with liquids is not recommended.

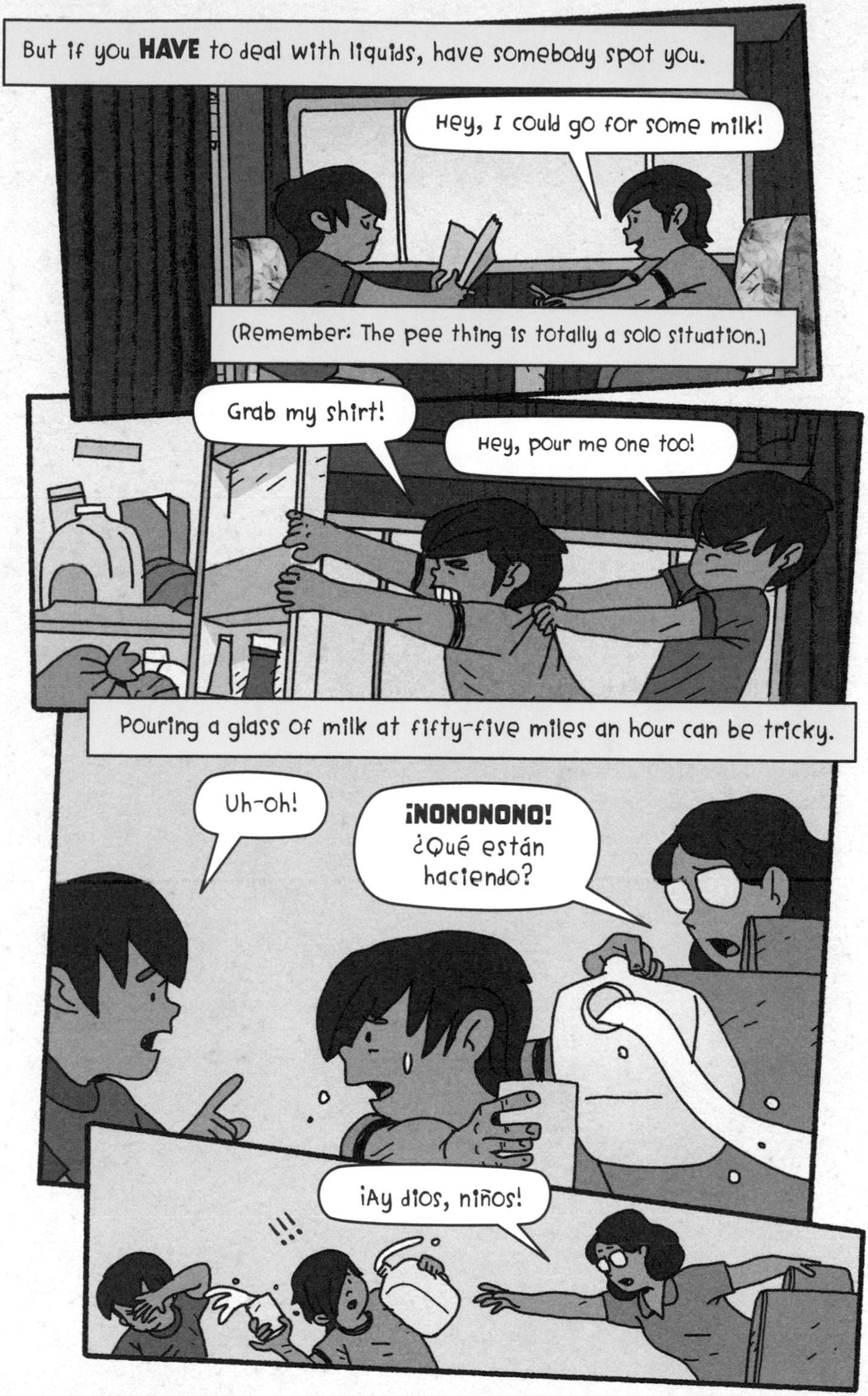

But if you **HAVE** to deal with liquids, have somebody spot you.
Hey, I could go for some milk!
(Remember: The pee thing is totally a solo situation.)
Grab my shirt!
Hey, pour me one too!
Pouring a glass of milk at fifty-five miles an hour can be tricky.
Uh-oh!
¡NONONONO! ¿Qué están haciendo?
!!!
¡Ay dios, niños!

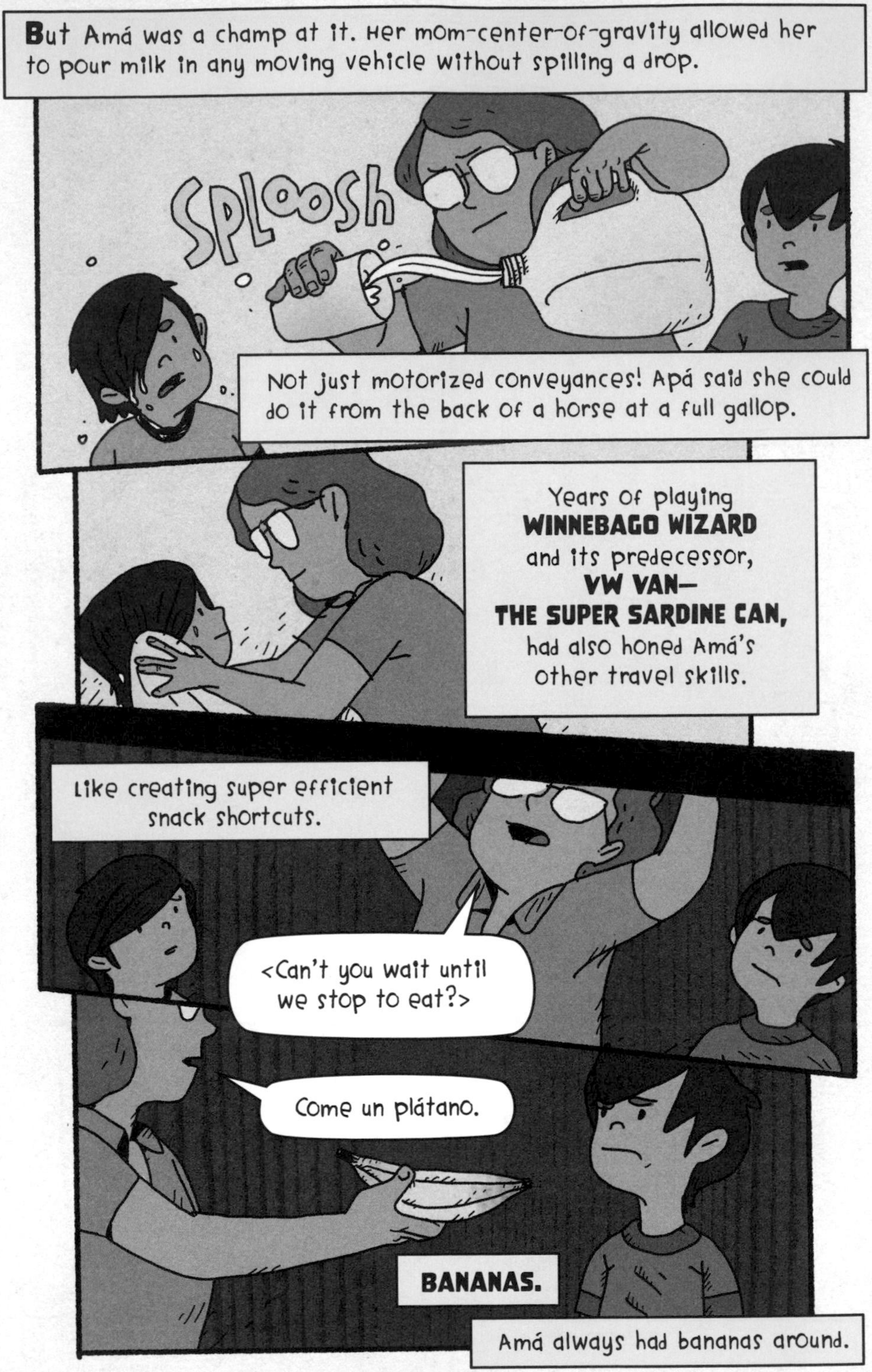
But Amá was a champ at it. Her mom-center-of-gravity allowed her to pour milk in any moving vehicle without spilling a drop.
SPLOOSH
Not just motorized conveyances! Apá said she could do it from the back of a horse at a full gallop.
Years of playing WINNEBAGO WIZARD and its predecessor, VW VAN— THE SUPER SARDINE CAN, had also honed Amá's other travel skills.
Like creating super efficient snack shortcuts.
<Can't you wait until we stop to eat?>
Come un plátano.
BANANAS.
Amá always had bananas around.

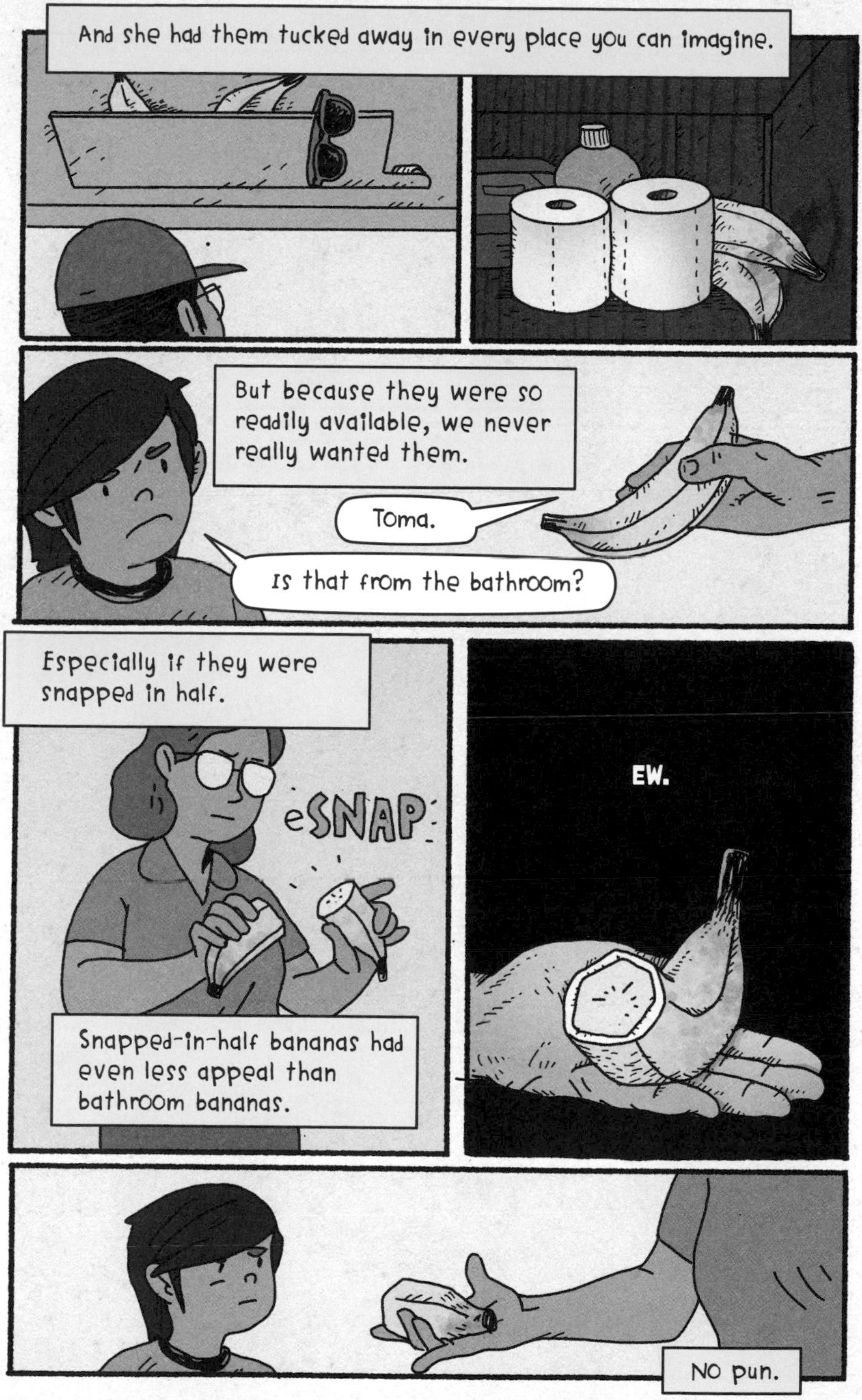

And she had them tucked away in every place you can imagine.
But because they were so readily available, we never really wanted them.
Toma.
Is that from the bathroom?
Especially if they were snapped in half.
eSNAP
Snapped-in-half bananas had even less appeal than bathroom bananas.
EW.
No pun.

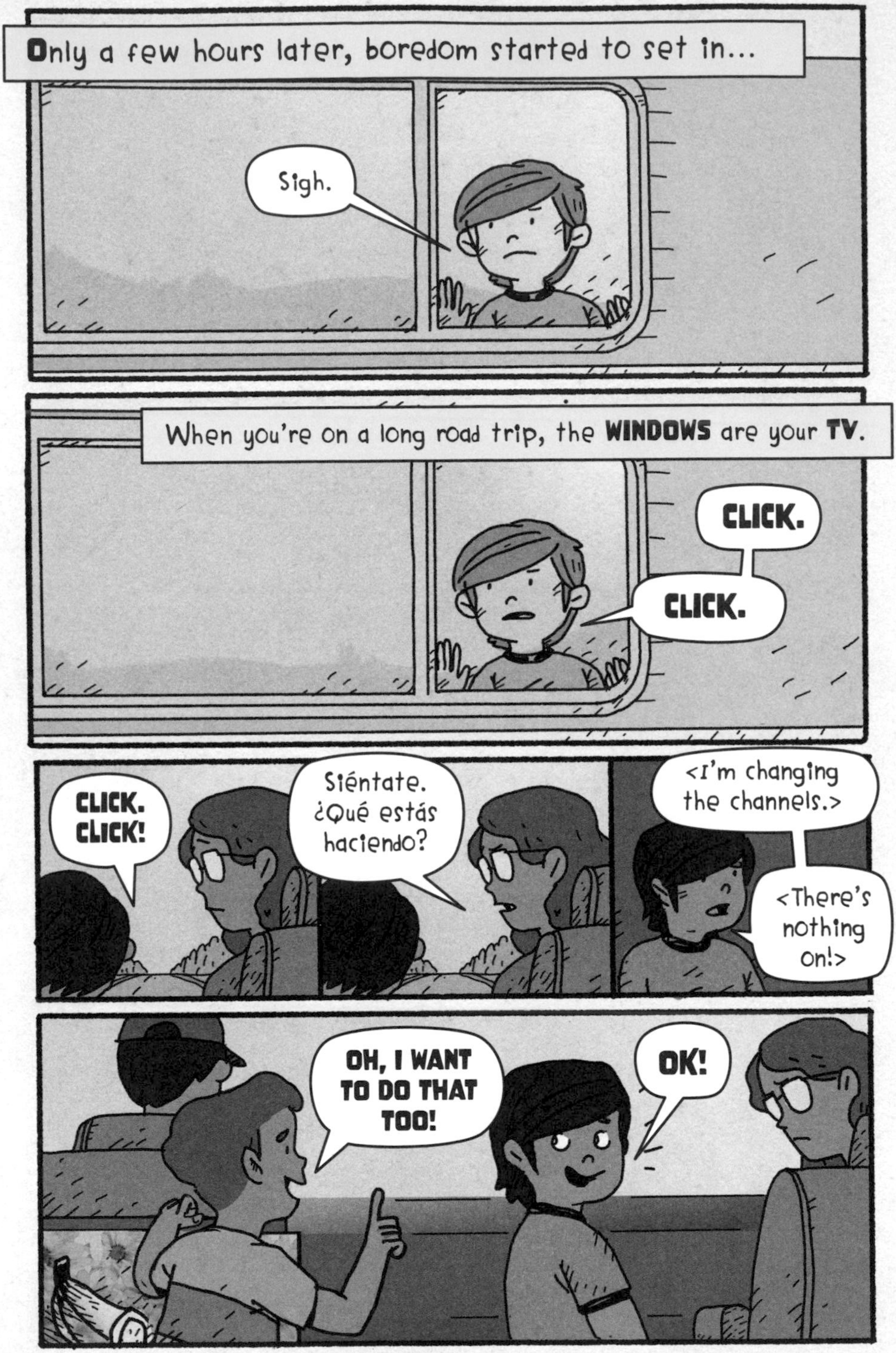
Only a few hours later, boredom started to set in...
Sigh.
When you're on a long road trip, the WINDOWS are your TV.
CLICK.
CLICK.
CLICK. CLICK!
Siéntate. ¿Qué estás haciendo?
<I'm changing the channels.>
<There's nothing on!>
OH, I WANT TO DO THAT TOO!
OK!

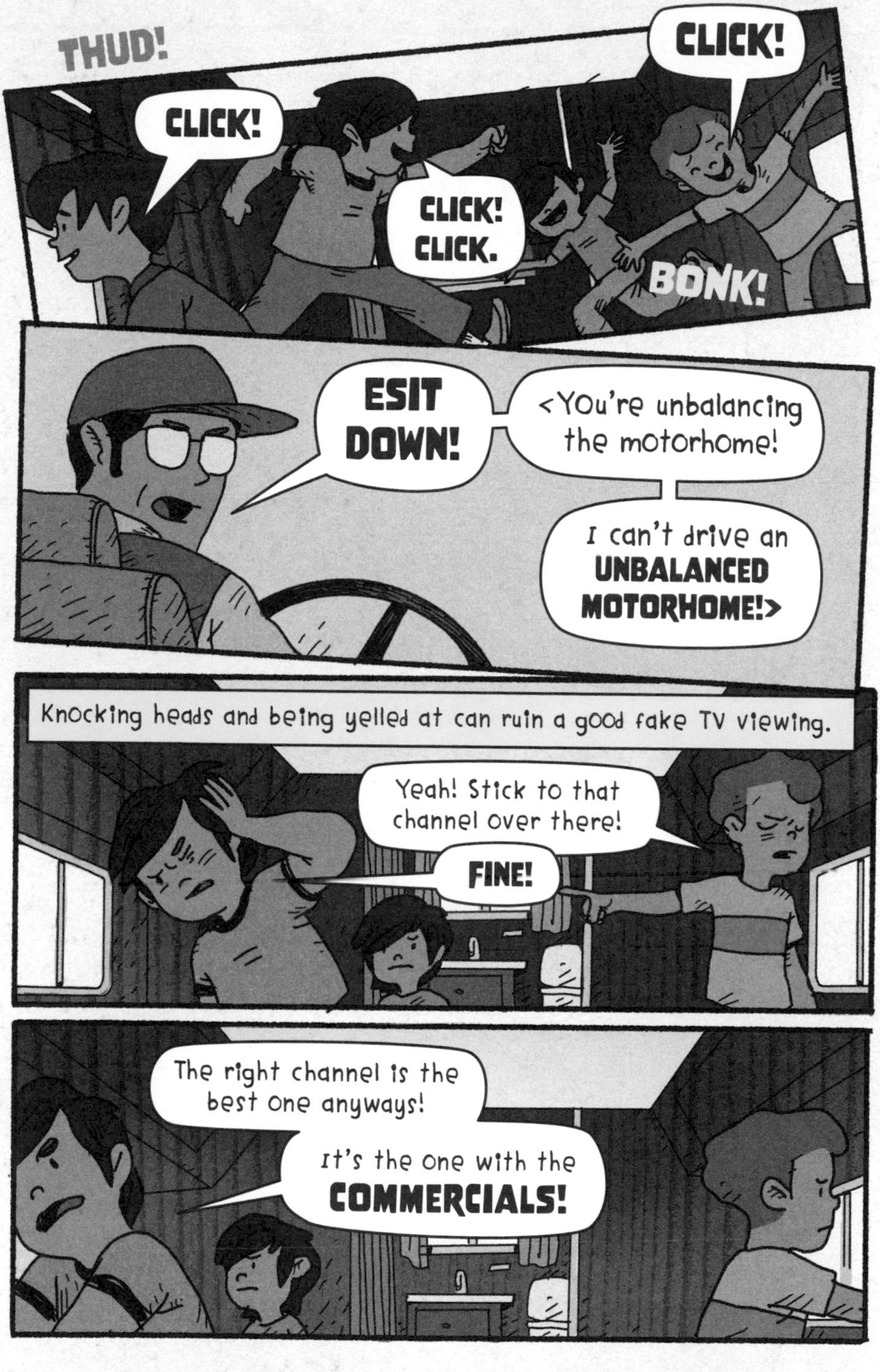
THUD!
CLICK!
CLICK! CLICK.
CLICK!
BONK!
ESIT DOWN!
<You're unbalancing the motorhome!
I can't drive an UNBALANCED MOTORHOME!>
Knocking heads and being yelled at can ruin a good fake TV viewing.
Yeah! Stick to that channel over there!
FINE!
The right channel is the best one anyways!
It's the one with the COMMERCIALS!

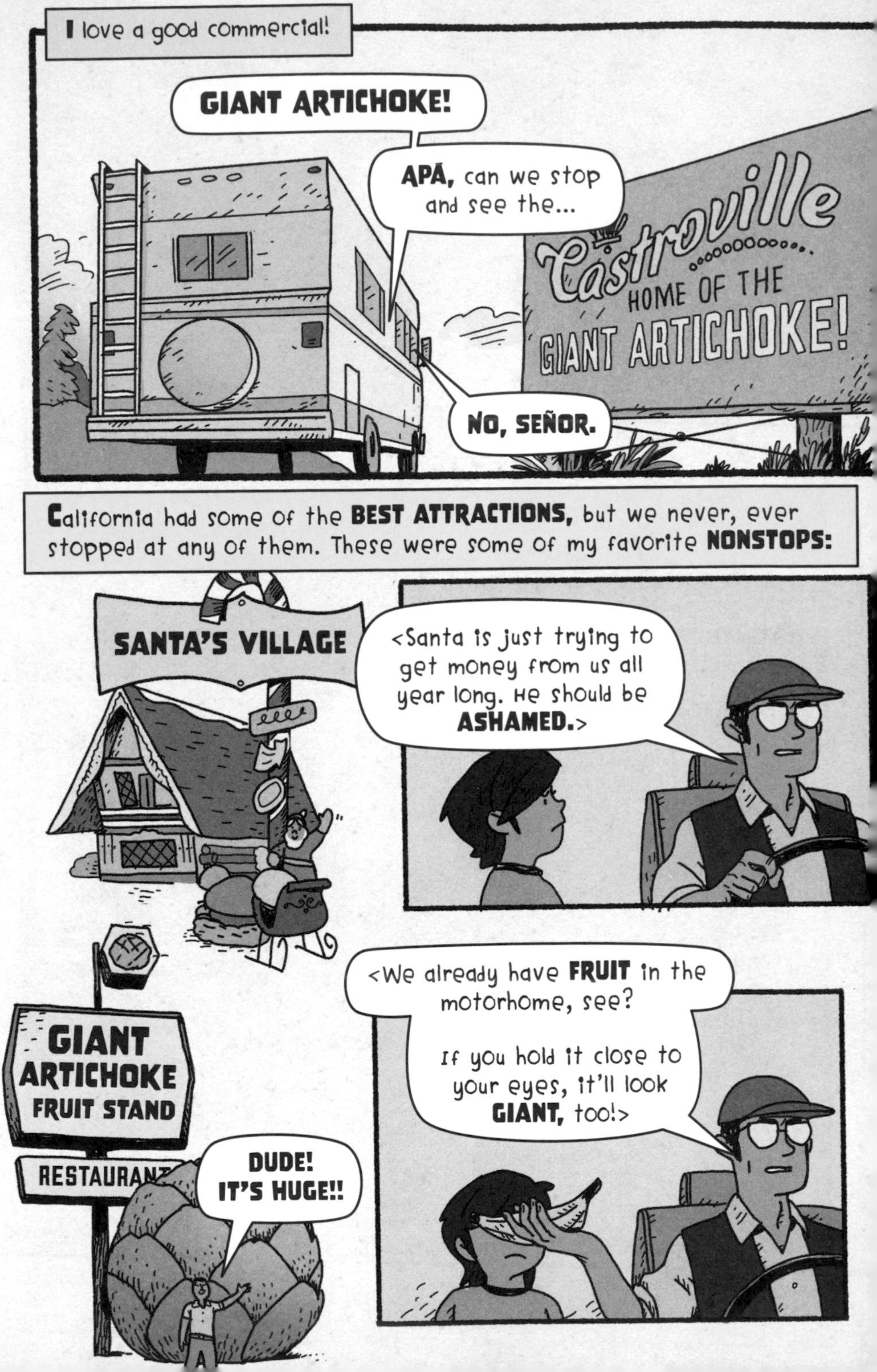
I love a good commercial!
GIANT ARTICHOKE!
APÁ, can we stop and see the...
Castroville HOME OF THE GIANT ARTICHOKE!
NO, SEÑOR.
California had some of the BEST ATTRACTIONS, but we never, ever stopped at any of them. These were some of my favorite NONSTOPS:
SANTA'S VILLAGE
<Santa is just trying to get money from us all year long. He should be ASHAMED.>
GIANT ARTICHOKE FRUIT STAND
RESTAURANT
DUDE! IT'S HUGE!!
<We already have FRUIT in the motorhome, see?
If you hold it close to your eyes, it'll look GIANT, too!>

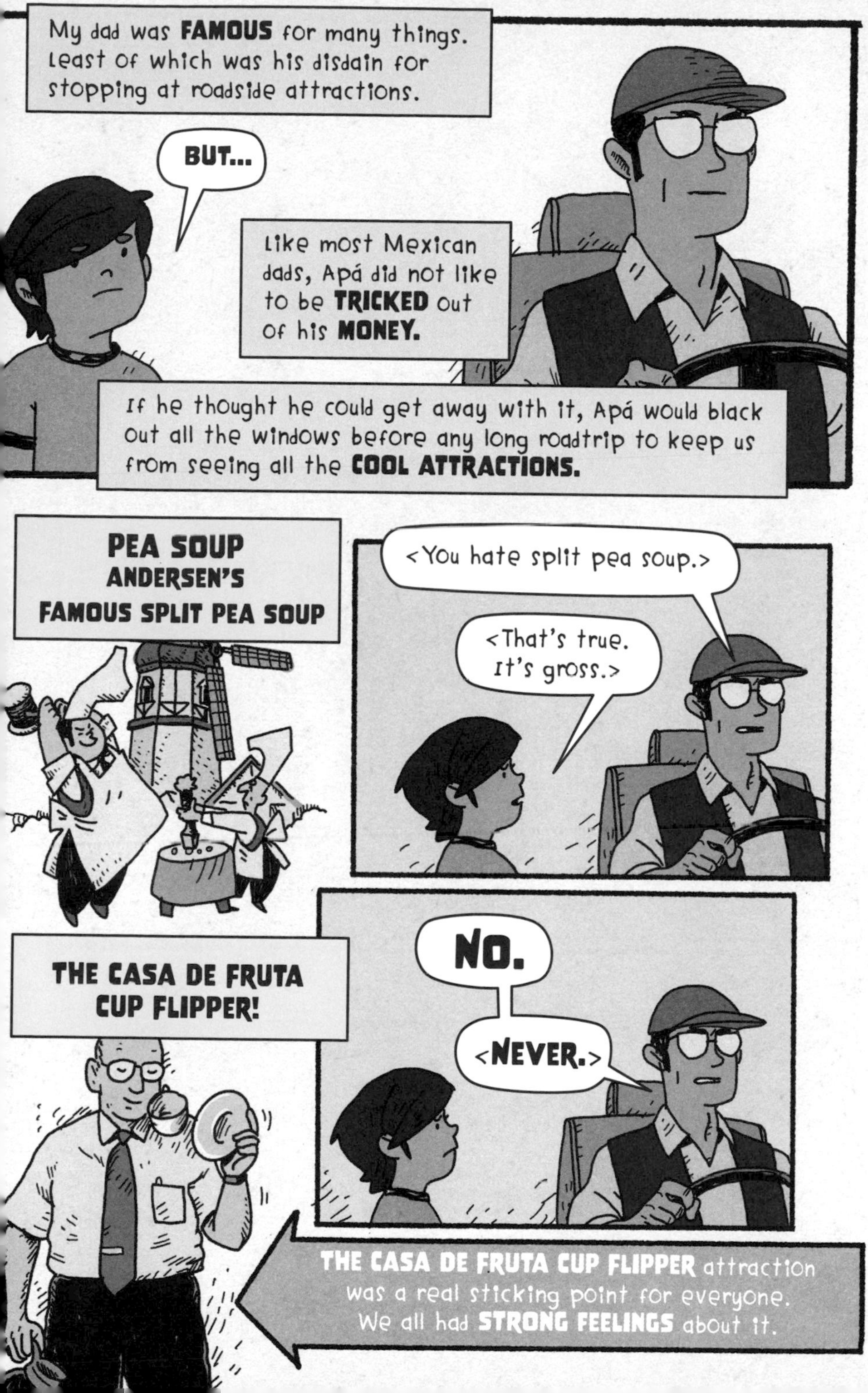
My dad was FAMOUS for many things. Least of which was his disdain for stopping at roadside attractions.
BUT...
Like most Mexican dads, Apá did not like to be TRICKED out of his MONEY.
If he thought he could get away with it, Apá would black out all the windows before any long roadtrip to keep us from seeing all the COOL ATTRACTIONS.
PEA SOUP ANDERSEN'S FAMOUS SPLIT PEA SOUP
<You hate split pea soup.>
<That's true. It's gross.>
THE CASA DE FRUTA CUP FLIPPER!
NO.
<NEVER.>
THE CASA DE FRUTA CUP FLIPPER attraction was a real sticking point for everyone. We all had STRONG FEELINGS about it.

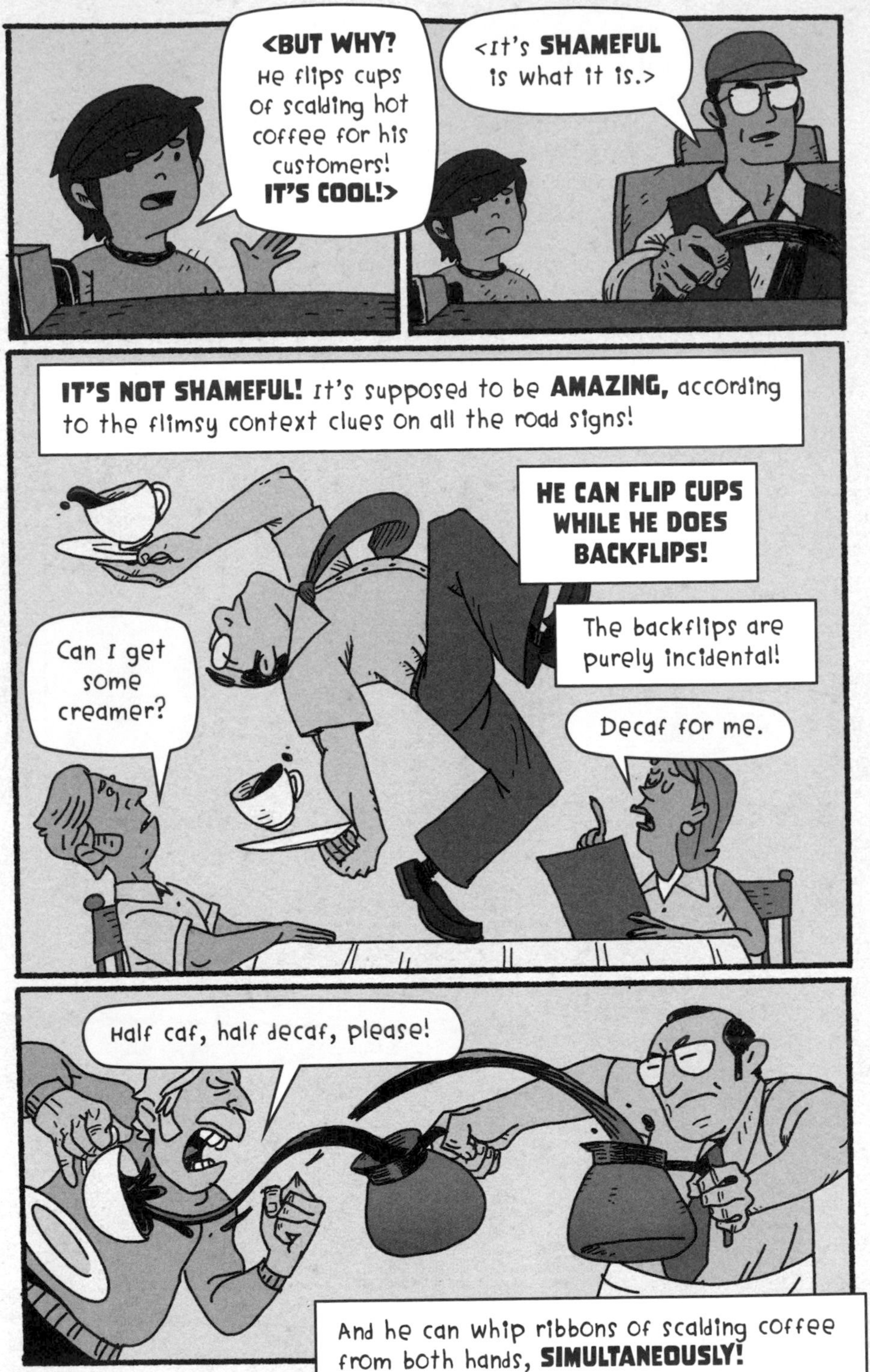
<**BUT WHY?** He flips cups of scalding hot coffee for his customers! **IT'S COOL!**>
<It's **SHAMEFUL** is what it is.>
IT'S NOT SHAMEFUL! It's supposed to be **AMAZING,** according to the flimsy context clues on all the road signs!
HE CAN FLIP CUPS WHILE HE DOES BACKFLIPS!
The backflips are purely incidental!
Can I get some creamer?
Decaf for me.
Half caf, half decaf, please!
And he can whip ribbons of scalding coffee from both hands, **SIMULTANEOUSLY!**

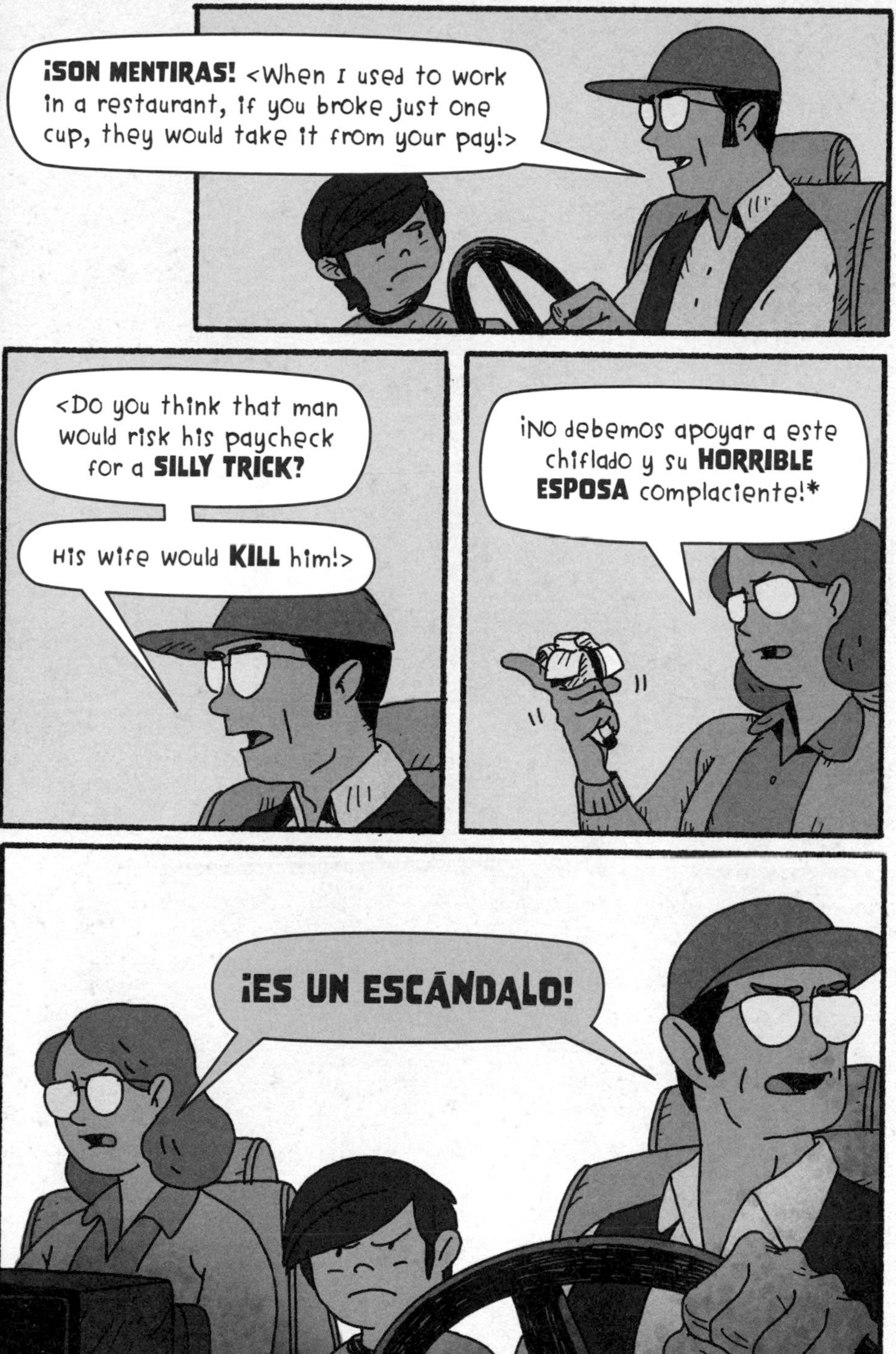
¡SON MENTIRAS! <When I used to work in a restaurant, if you broke just one cup, they would take it from your pay!>
<Do you think that man would risk his paycheck for a SILLY TRICK?
His wife would KILL him!>
¡No debemos apoyar a este chiflado y su HORRIBLE ESPOSA complaciente!*
¡ES UN ESCÁNDALO!

*We shouldn't support this screwball and his awful accommodating wife.

CHAPTER 5 LOS ANGELES

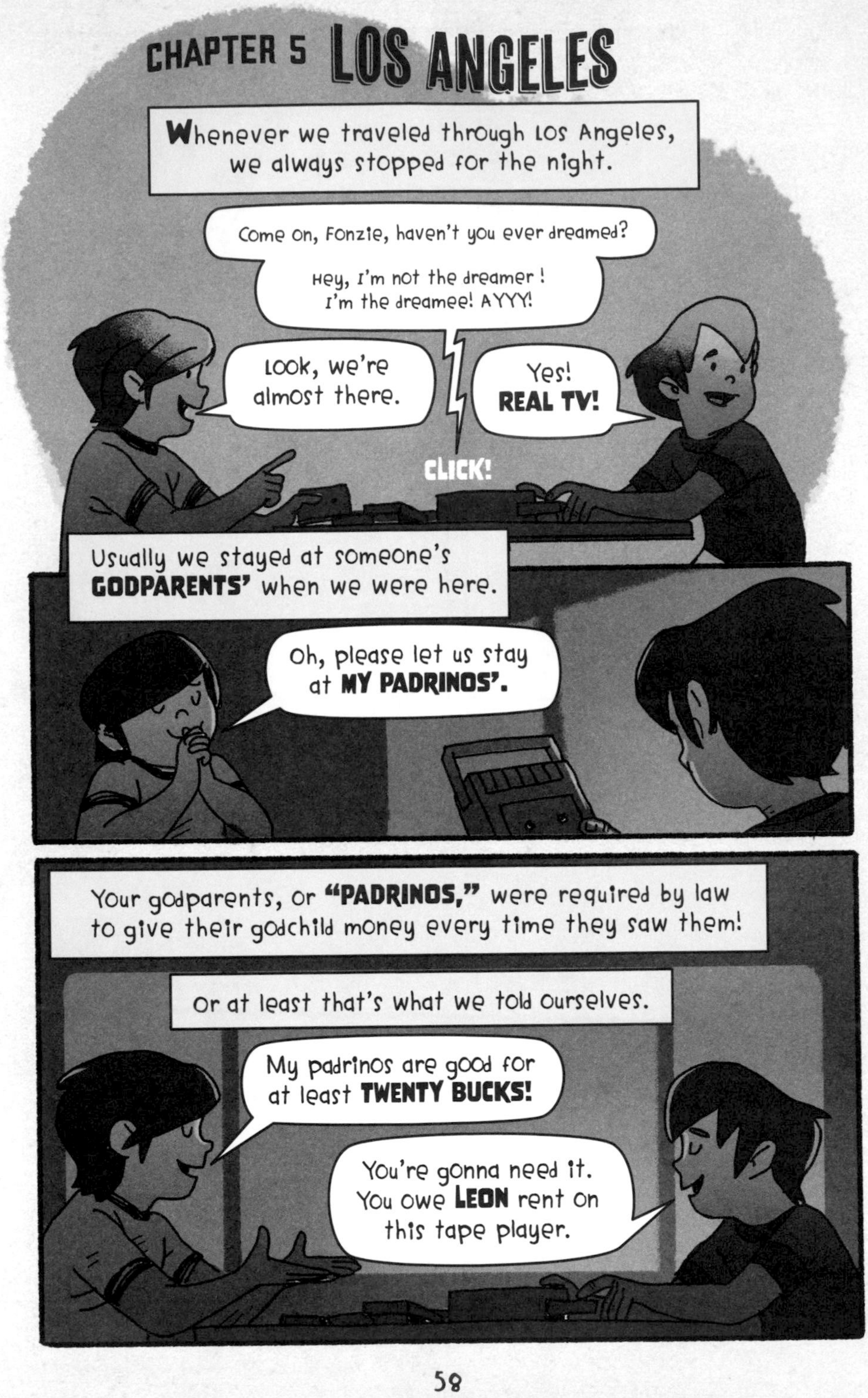
Whenever we traveled through Los Angeles, we always stopped for the night.
Come on, Fonzie, haven't you ever dreamed?
Hey, I'm not the dreamer ! I'm the dreamee! AYYY!
Look, we're almost there.
Yes! REAL TV!
CLICK!
Usually we stayed at someone's GODPARENTS' when we were here.
Oh, please let us stay at MY PADRINOS'.
Your godparents, or "PADRINOS," were required by law to give their godchild money every time they saw them!
Or at least that's what we told ourselves.
My padrinos are good for at least TWENTY BUCKS!
You're gonna need it. You owe LEON rent on this tape player.

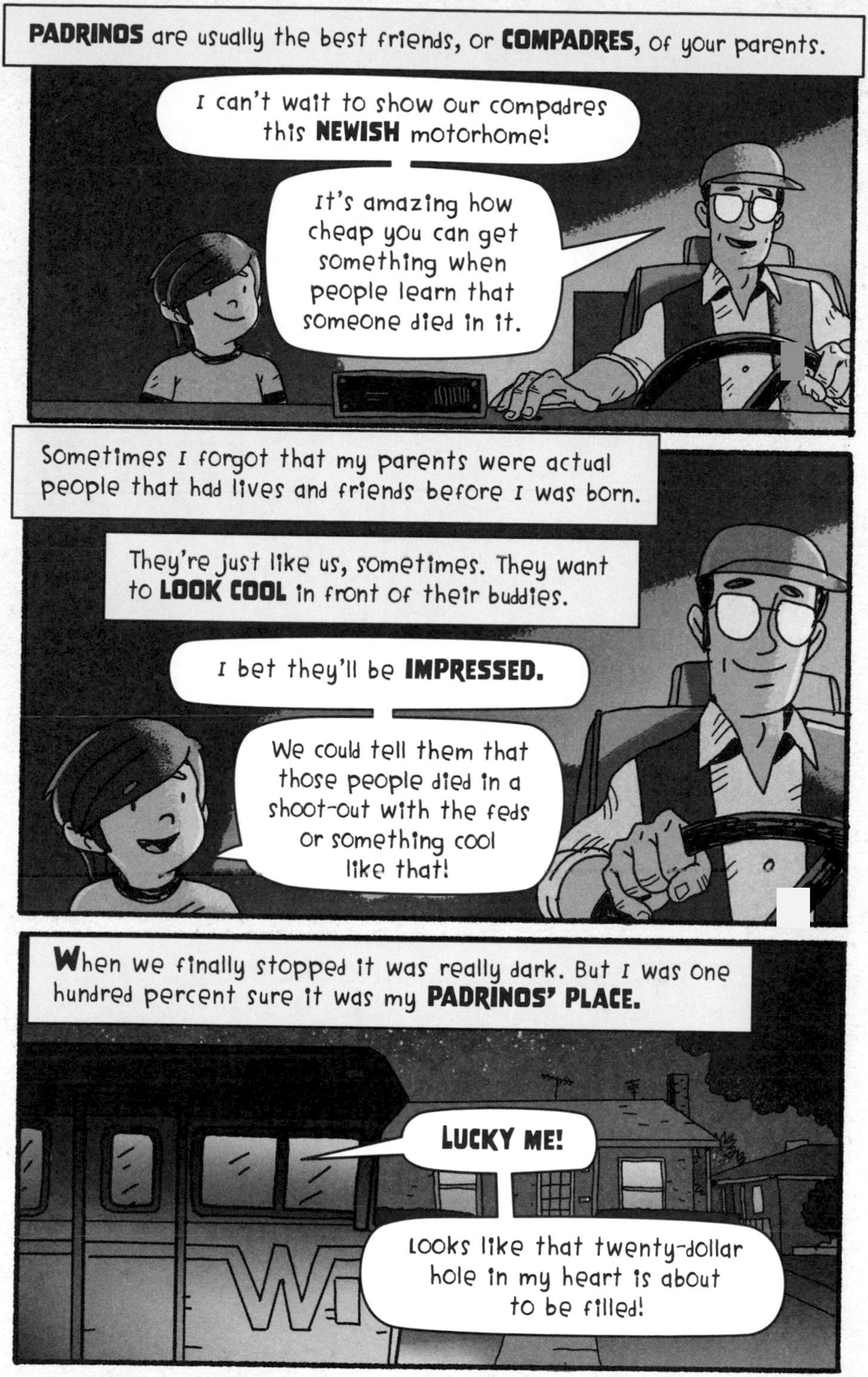
PADRINOS are usually the best friends, or COMPADRES, of your parents.
I can't wait to show our compadres this NEWISH motorhome!
It's amazing how cheap you can get something when people learn that someone died in it.
Sometimes I forgot that my parents were actual people that had lives and friends before I was born.
They're just like us, sometimes. They want to LOOK COOL in front of their buddies.
I bet they'll be IMPRESSED.
We could tell them that those people died in a shoot-out with the feds or something cool like that!
When we finally stopped it was really dark. But I was one hundred percent sure it was my PADRINOS' PLACE.
LUCKY ME!
Looks like that twenty-dollar hole in my heart is about to be filled!

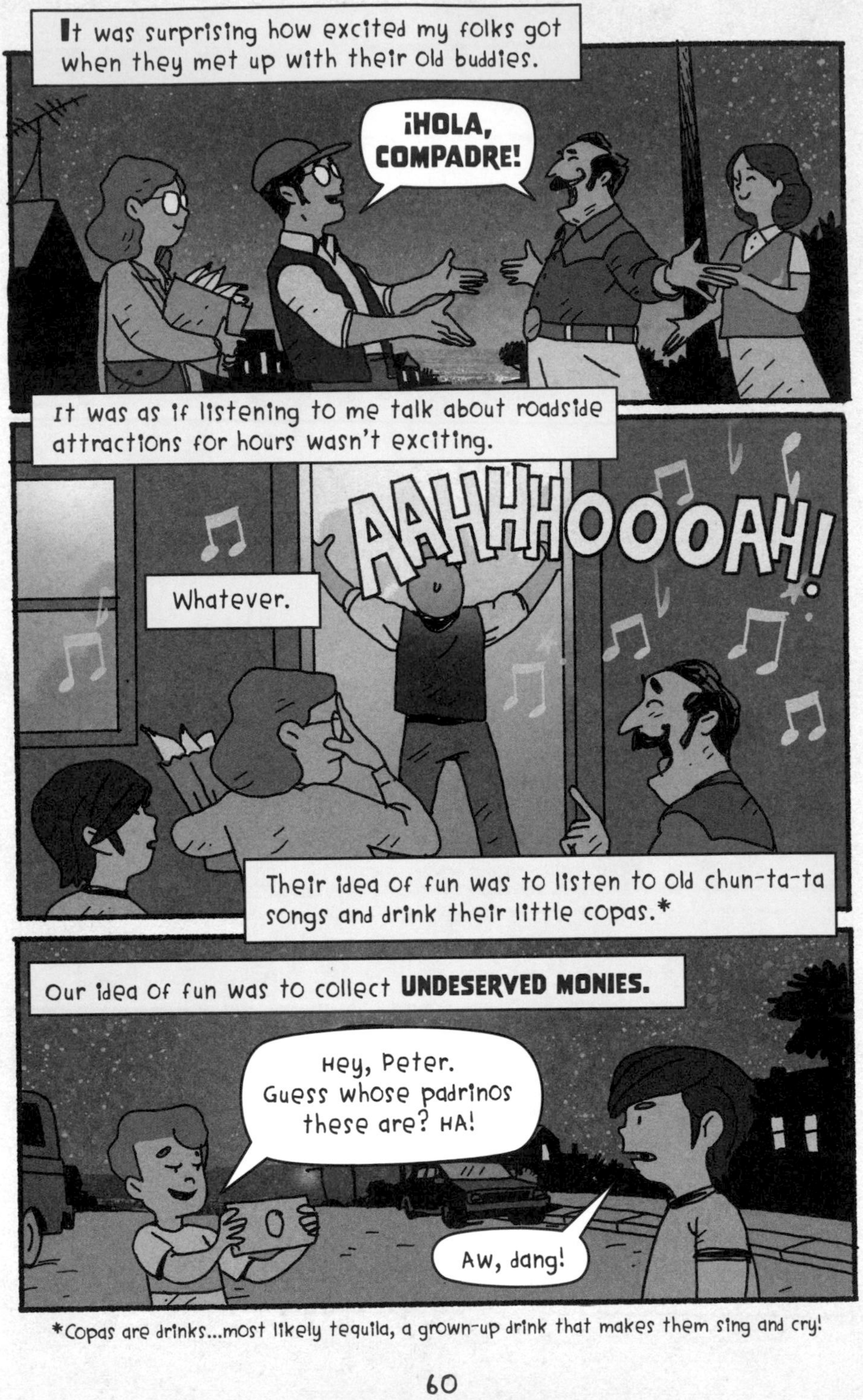
It was surprising how excited my folks got when they met up with their old buddies.
¡HOLA, COMPADRE!
It was as if listening to me talk about roadside attractions for hours wasn't exciting.
AAHHHOOOAH!
Whatever.
Their idea of fun was to listen to old chun-ta-ta songs and drink their little copas.*
Our idea of fun was to collect **UNDESERVED MONIES.**
Hey, Peter. Guess whose padrinos these are? HA!
Aw, dang!

*Copas are drinks...most likely tequila, a grown-up drink that makes them sing and cry!

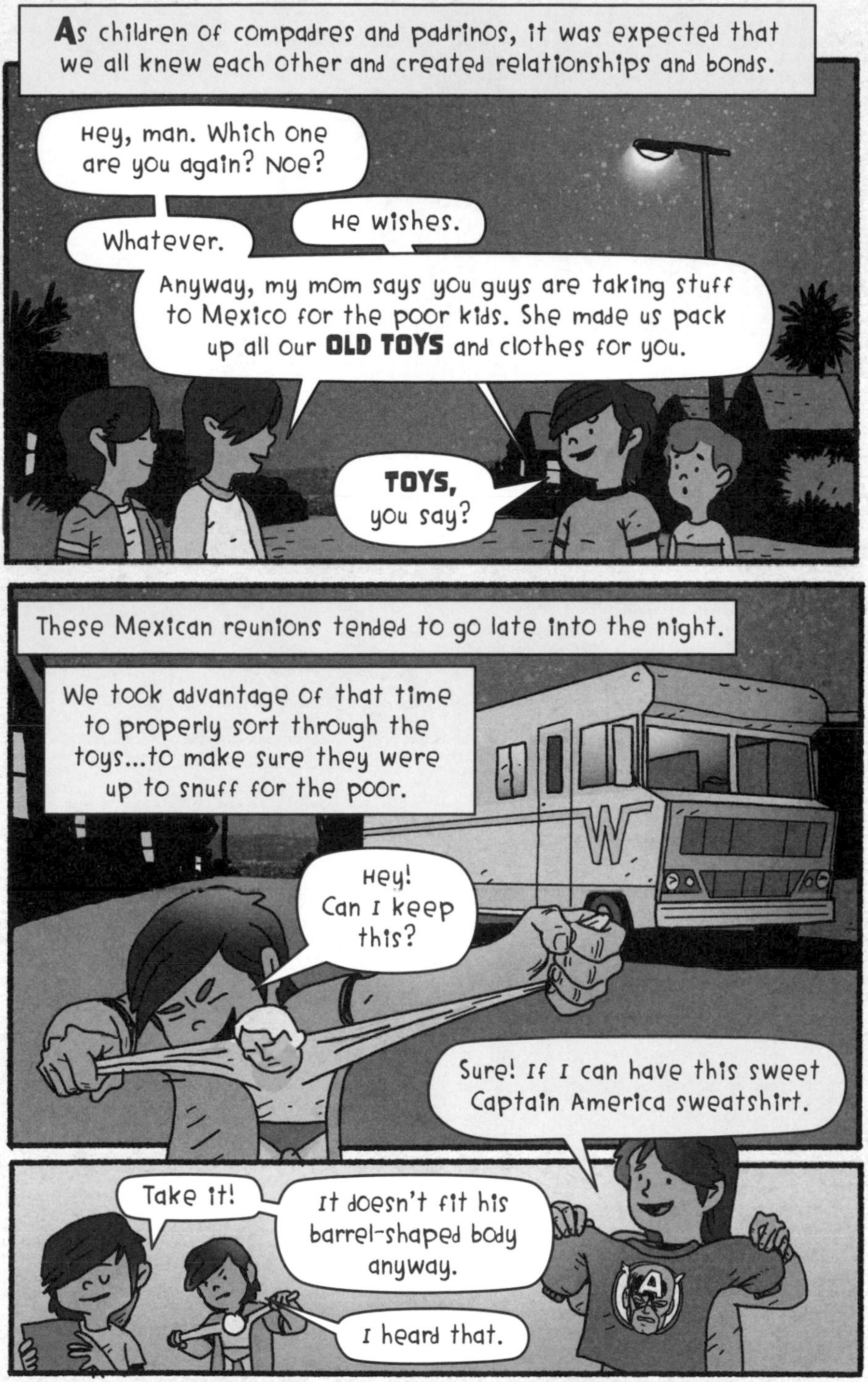
As children of compadres and padrinos, it was expected that we all knew each other and created relationships and bonds.
Hey, man. Which one are you again? Noe?
Whatever.
He wishes.
Anyway, my mom says you guys are taking stuff to Mexico for the poor kids. She made us pack up all our OLD TOYS and clothes for you.
TOYS, you say?
These Mexican reunions tended to go late into the night.
We took advantage of that time to properly sort through the toys...to make sure they were up to snuff for the poor.
Hey! Can I keep this?
Sure! If I can have this sweet Captain America sweatshirt.
Take it!
It doesn't fit his barrel-shaped body anyway.
I heard that.

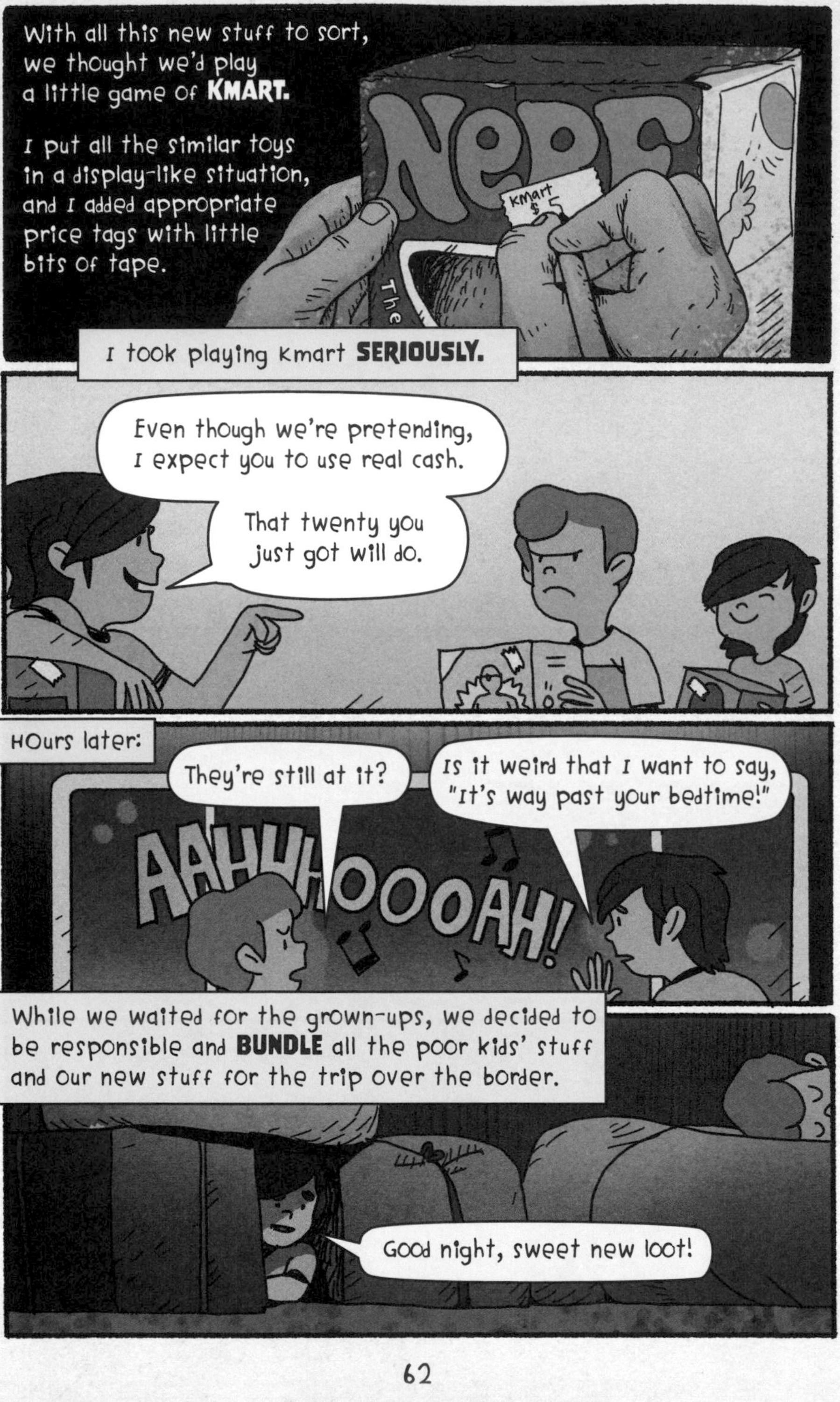
With all this new stuff to sort, we thought we'd play a little game of **KMART.**
I put all the similar toys in a display-like situation, and I added appropriate price tags with little bits of tape.
NERF
The
Kmart $
I took playing Kmart **SERIOUSLY.**
Even though we're pretending, I expect you to use real cash.
That twenty you just got will do.
Hours later:
They're still at it?
Is it weird that I want to say, "It's way past your bedtime!"
AAHUHOOOOAH!
While we waited for the grown-ups, we decided to be responsible and **BUNDLE** all the poor kids' stuff and our new stuff for the trip over the border.
Good night, sweet new loot!

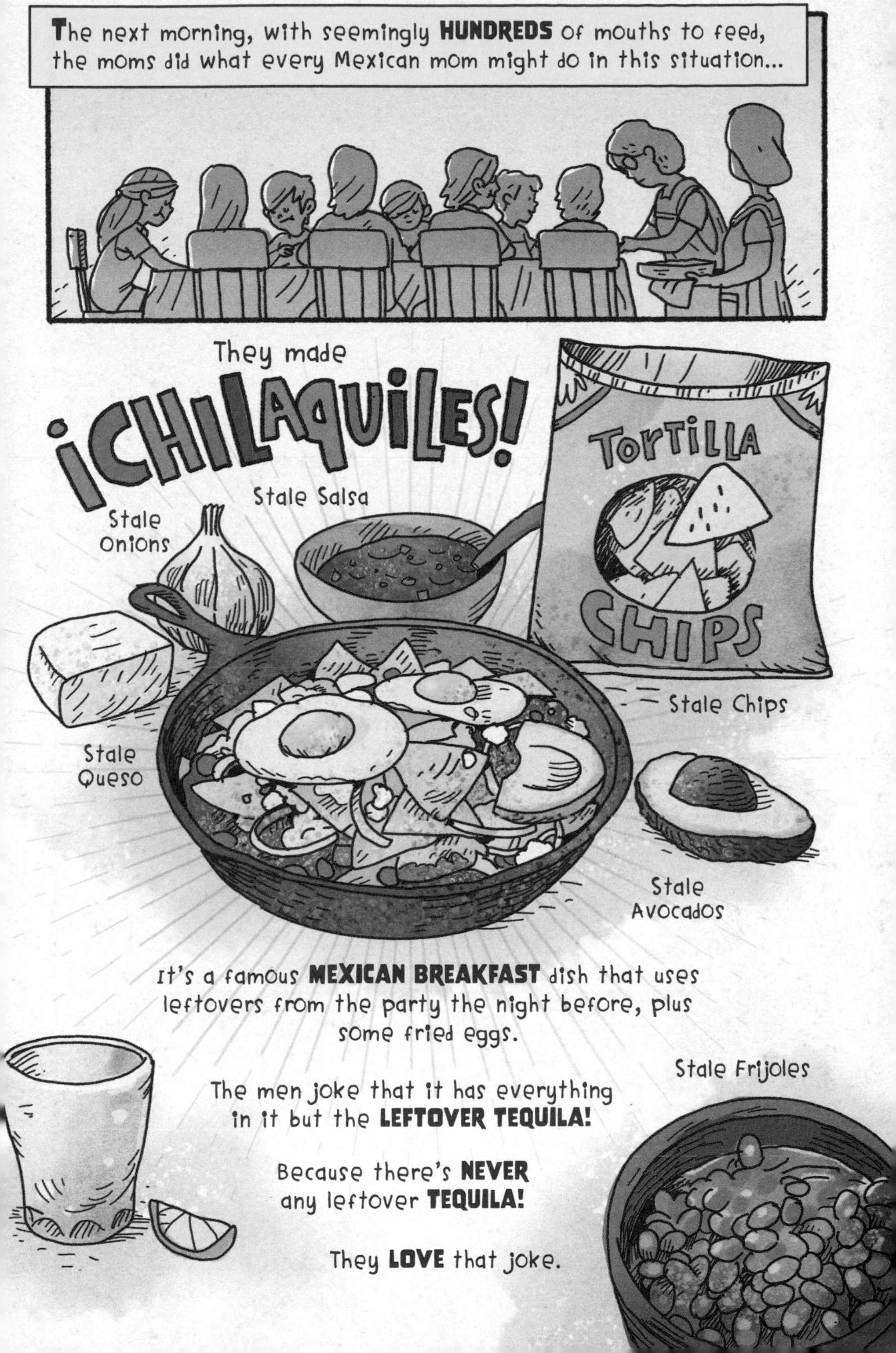
The next morning, with seemingly HUNDREDS of mouths to feed, the moms did what every Mexican mom might do in this situation...
They made
¡CHILAQUILES!
Stale Salsa
Stale Onions
TORTILLA CHIPS
Stale Chips
Stale Queso
Stale Avocados
It's a famous MEXICAN BREAKFAST dish that uses leftovers from the party the night before, plus some fried eggs.
Stale Frijoles
The men joke that it has everything in it but the LEFTOVER TEQUILA!
Because there's NEVER any leftover TEQUILA!
They LOVE that joke.

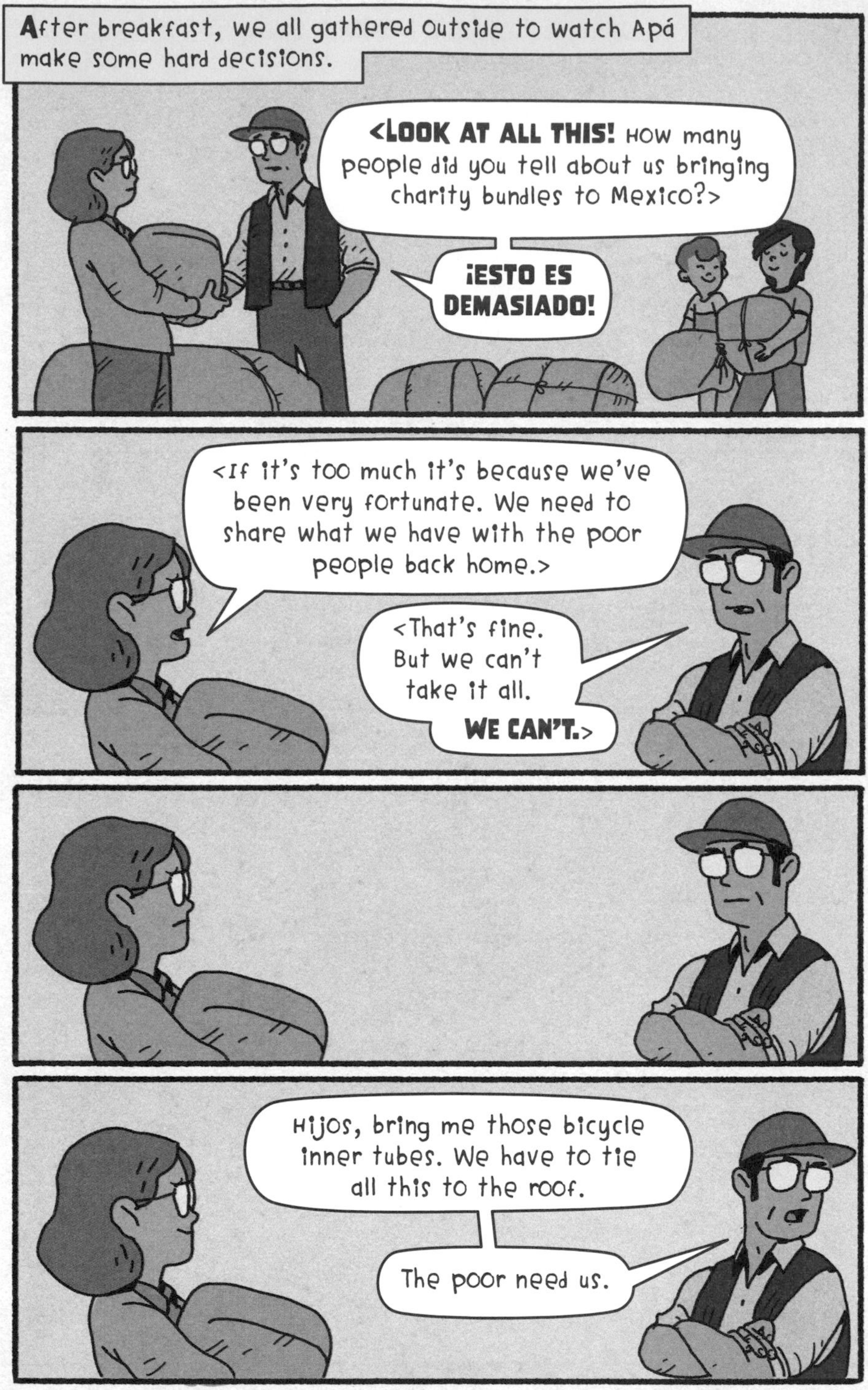
After breakfast, we all gathered outside to watch Apá make some hard decisions.
<LOOK AT ALL THIS! How many people did you tell about us bringing charity bundles to Mexico?>
¡ESTO ES DEMASIADO!
<If it's too much it's because we've been very fortunate. We need to share what we have with the poor people back home.>
<That's fine. But we can't take it all.
WE CAN'T.>
Hijos, bring me those bicycle inner tubes. We have to tie all this to the roof.
The poor need us.

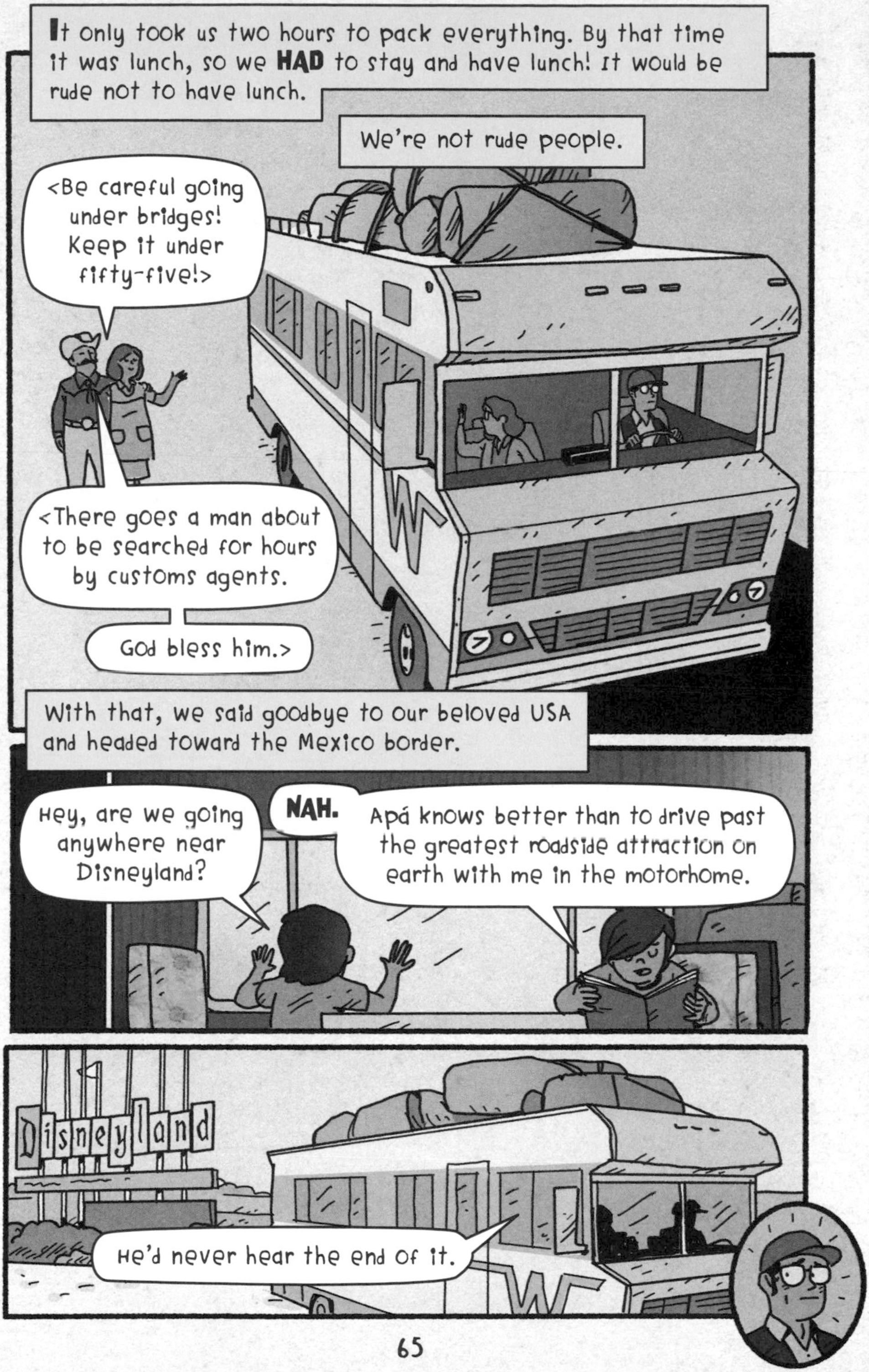
It only took us two hours to pack everything. By that time it was lunch, so we **HAD** to stay and have lunch! It would be rude not to have lunch.
We're not rude people.
<Be careful going under bridges! Keep it under fifty-five!>
<There goes a man about to be searched for hours by customs agents.
God bless him.>
With that, we said goodbye to our beloved USA and headed toward the Mexico border.
Hey, are we going anywhere near Disneyland?
NAH.
Apá knows better than to drive past the greatest roadside attraction on earth with me in the motorhome.
Disneyland
He'd never hear the end of it.

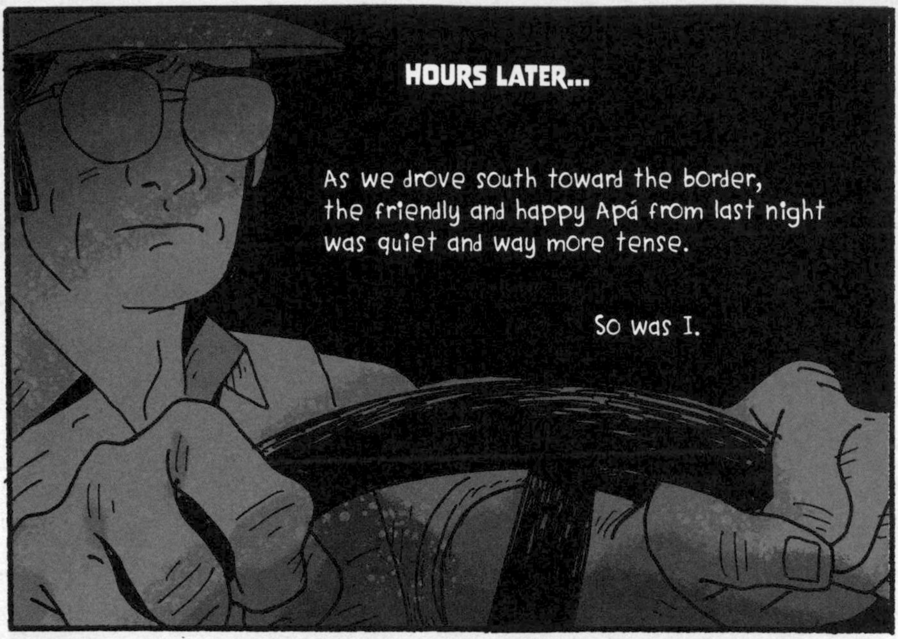
HOURS LATER...
As we drove south toward the border, the friendly and happy Apá from last night was quiet and way more tense.
So was I.

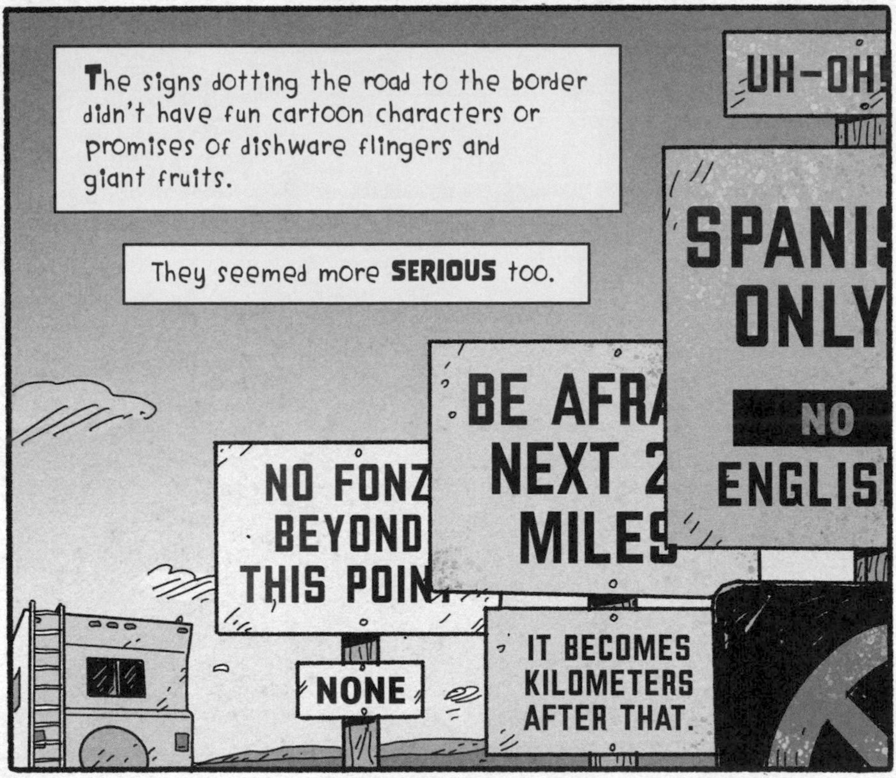
The signs dotting the road to the border didn't have fun cartoon characters or promises of dishware flingers and giant fruits.
They seemed more **SERIOUS** too.
UH-OH
SPANIS ONLY
NO ENGLIS
BE AFRA NEXT 2 MILES
NO FONZ BEYOND THIS POIN
NONE
IT BECOMES KILOMETERS AFTER THAT.

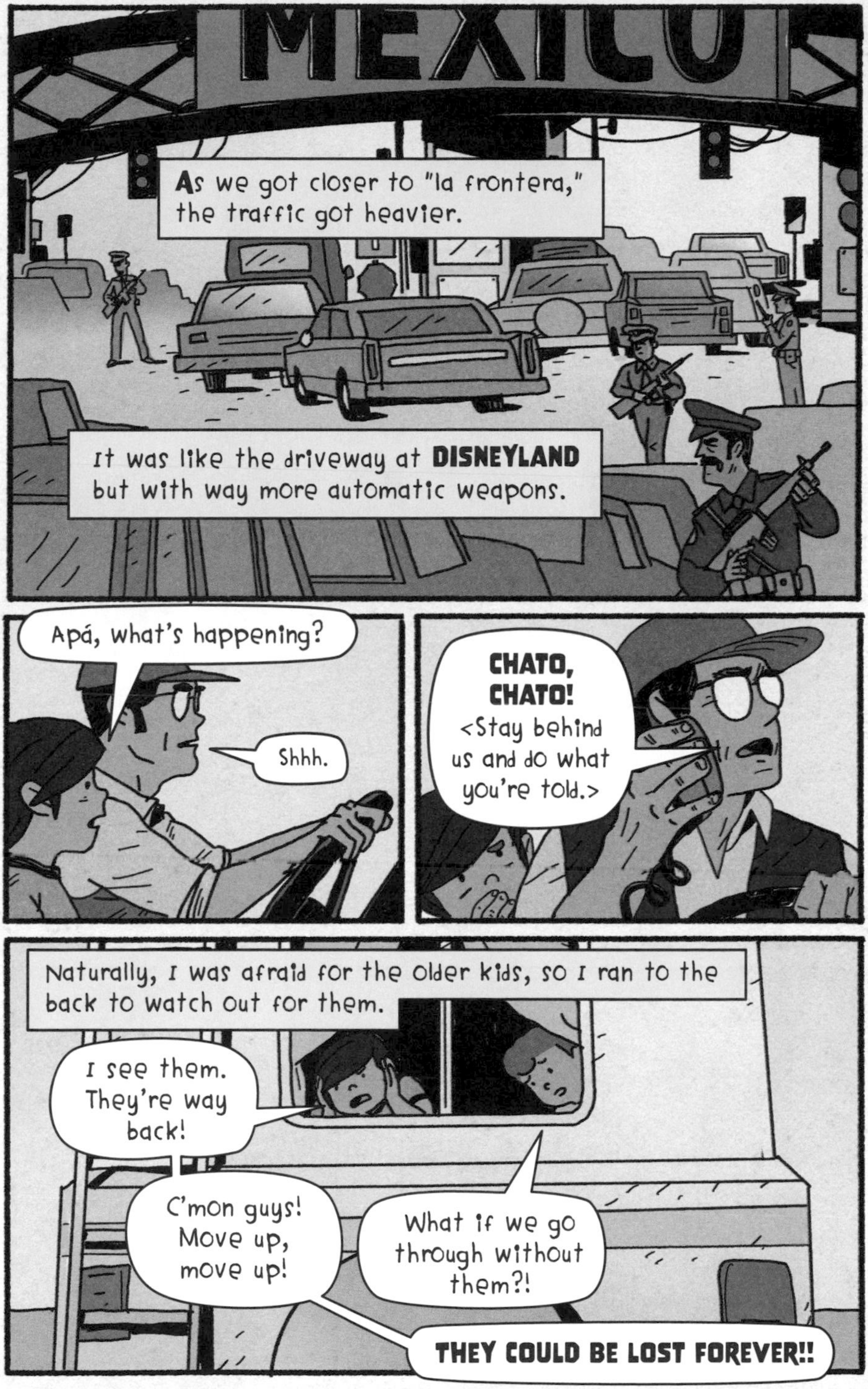
MEXICO
As we got closer to "la frontera," the traffic got heavier.
It was like the driveway at **DISNEYLAND** but with way more automatic weapons.
Apá, what's happening?
Shhh.
CHATO, CHATO!
<Stay behind us and do what you're told.>
Naturally, I was afraid for the older kids, so I ran to the back to watch out for them.
I see them. They're way back!
C'mon guys! Move up, move up!
What if we go through without them?!
THEY COULD BE LOST FOREVER!!

CHAPTER 6 ¡LA MORDIDA!

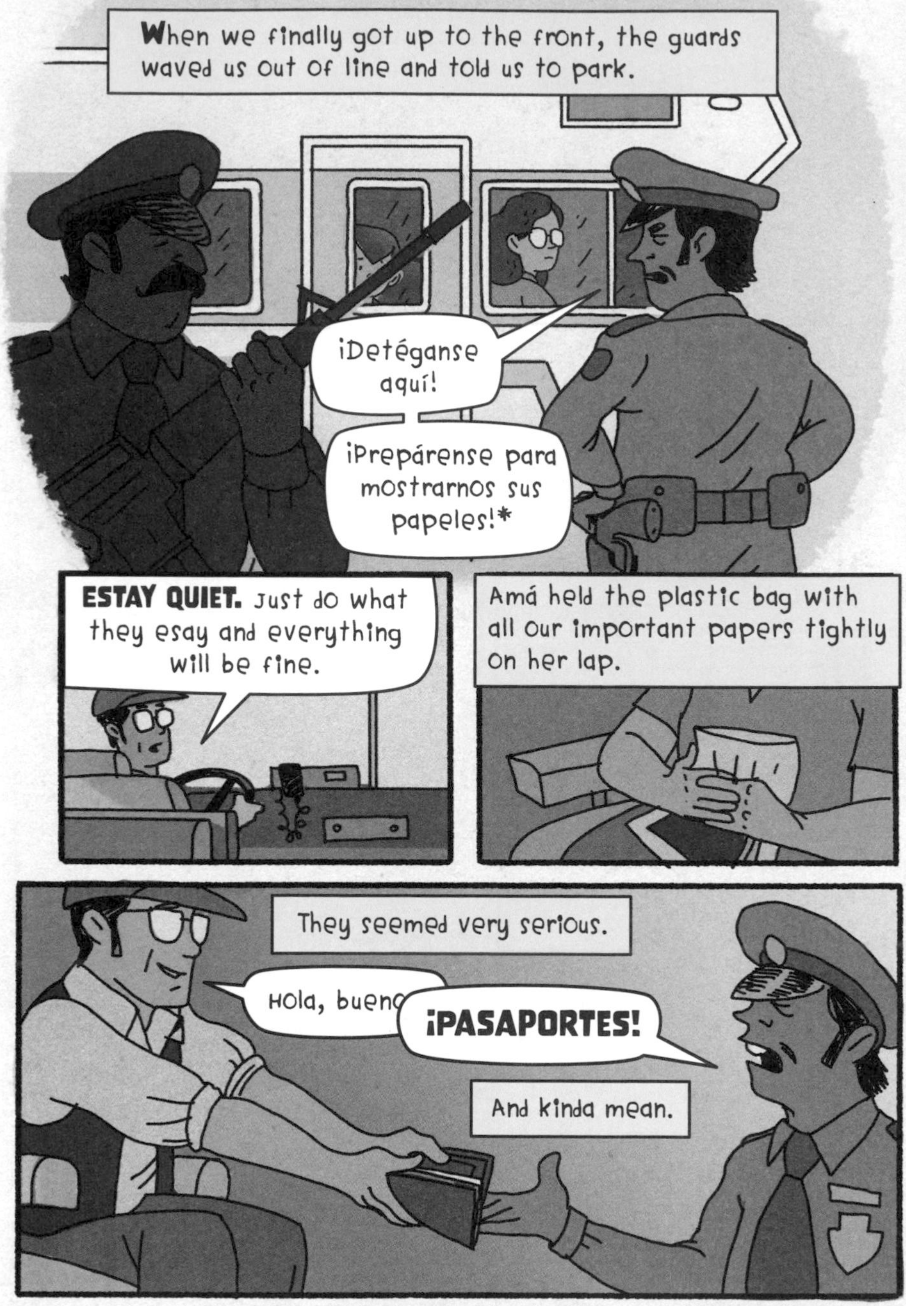

When we finally got up to the front, the guards waved us out of line and told us to park.
¡Detéganse aquí!
¡Prepárense para mostrarnos sus papeles!*
ESTAY QUIET. Just do what they esay and everything will be fine.
Amá held the plastic bag with all our important papers tightly on her lap.
They seemed very serious.
Hola, buen
¡PASAPORTES!
And kinda mean.

*Get ready to show us your papers!

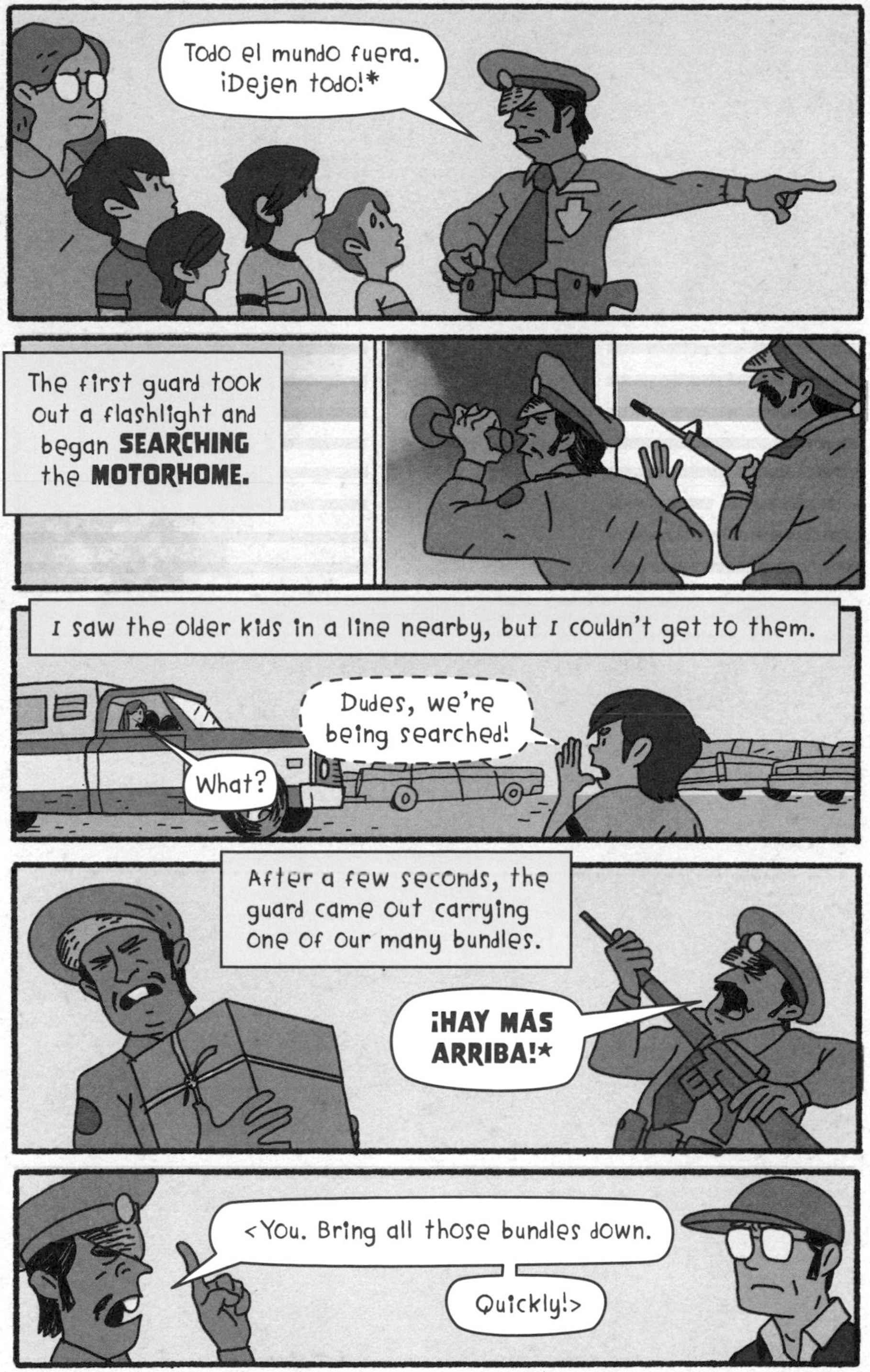
Todo el mundo fuera. ¡Dejen todo!*
The first guard took out a flashlight and began **SEARCHING** the **MOTORHOME.**
I saw the older kids in a line nearby, but I couldn't get to them.
Dudes, we're being searched!
What?
After a few seconds, the guard came out carrying one of our many bundles.
¡HAY MÁS ARRIBA!*
<You. Bring all those bundles down.
Quickly!>

*Everybody out. Drop everything!

*There's more on top!

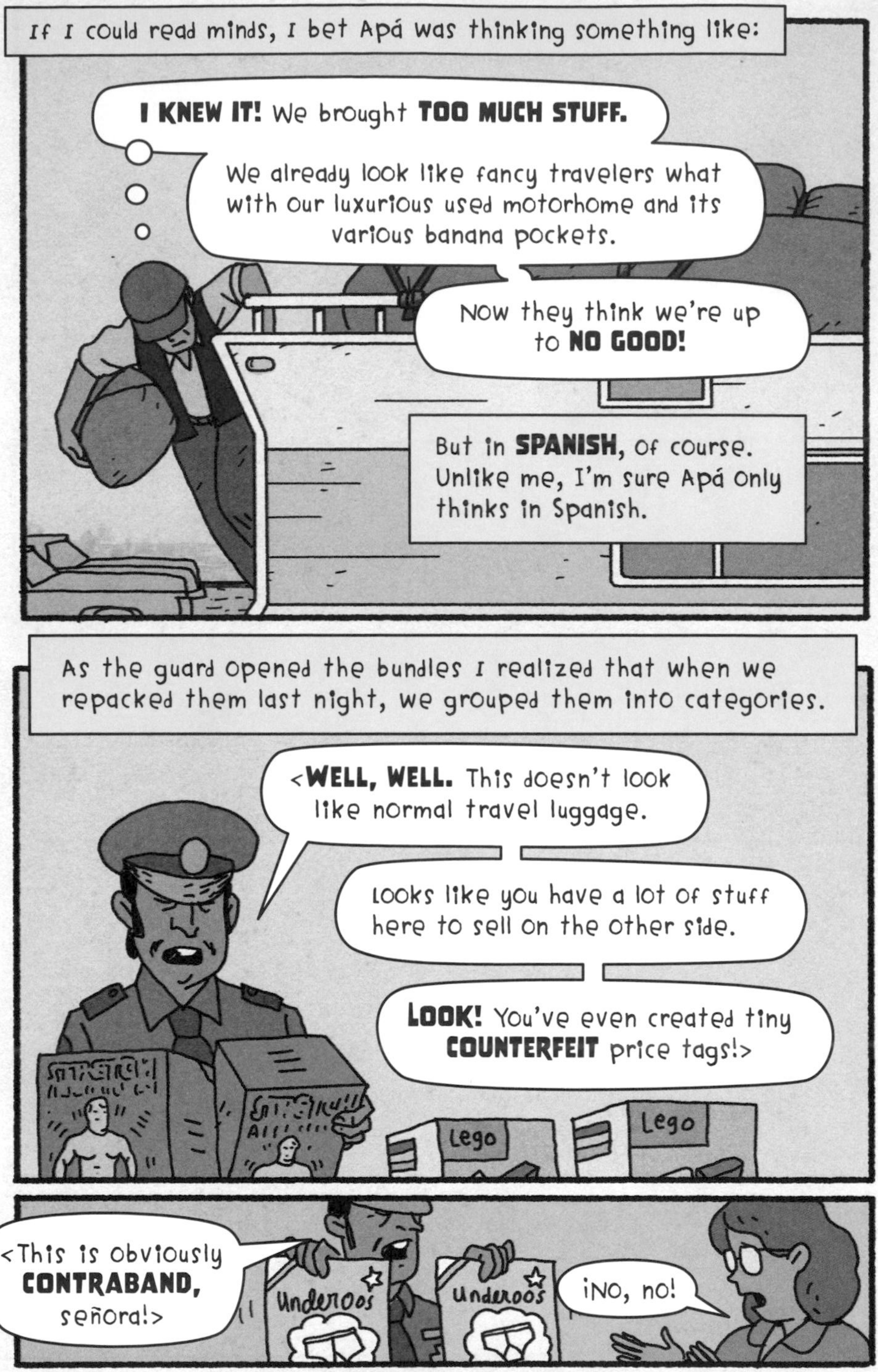
If I could read minds, I bet Apá was thinking something like:
I KNEW IT! We brought TOO MUCH STUFF.
We already look like fancy travelers what with our luxurious used motorhome and its various banana pockets.
Now they think we're up to NO GOOD!
But in SPANISH, of course. Unlike me, I'm sure Apá only thinks in Spanish.
As the guard opened the bundles I realized that when we repacked them last night, we grouped them into categories.
<WELL, WELL. This doesn't look like normal travel luggage.
Looks like you have a lot of stuff here to sell on the other side.
LOOK! You've even created tiny COUNTERFEIT price tags!>
Lego
Lego
<This is obviously CONTRABAND, señora!>
Underoos
Underoos
¡No, no!

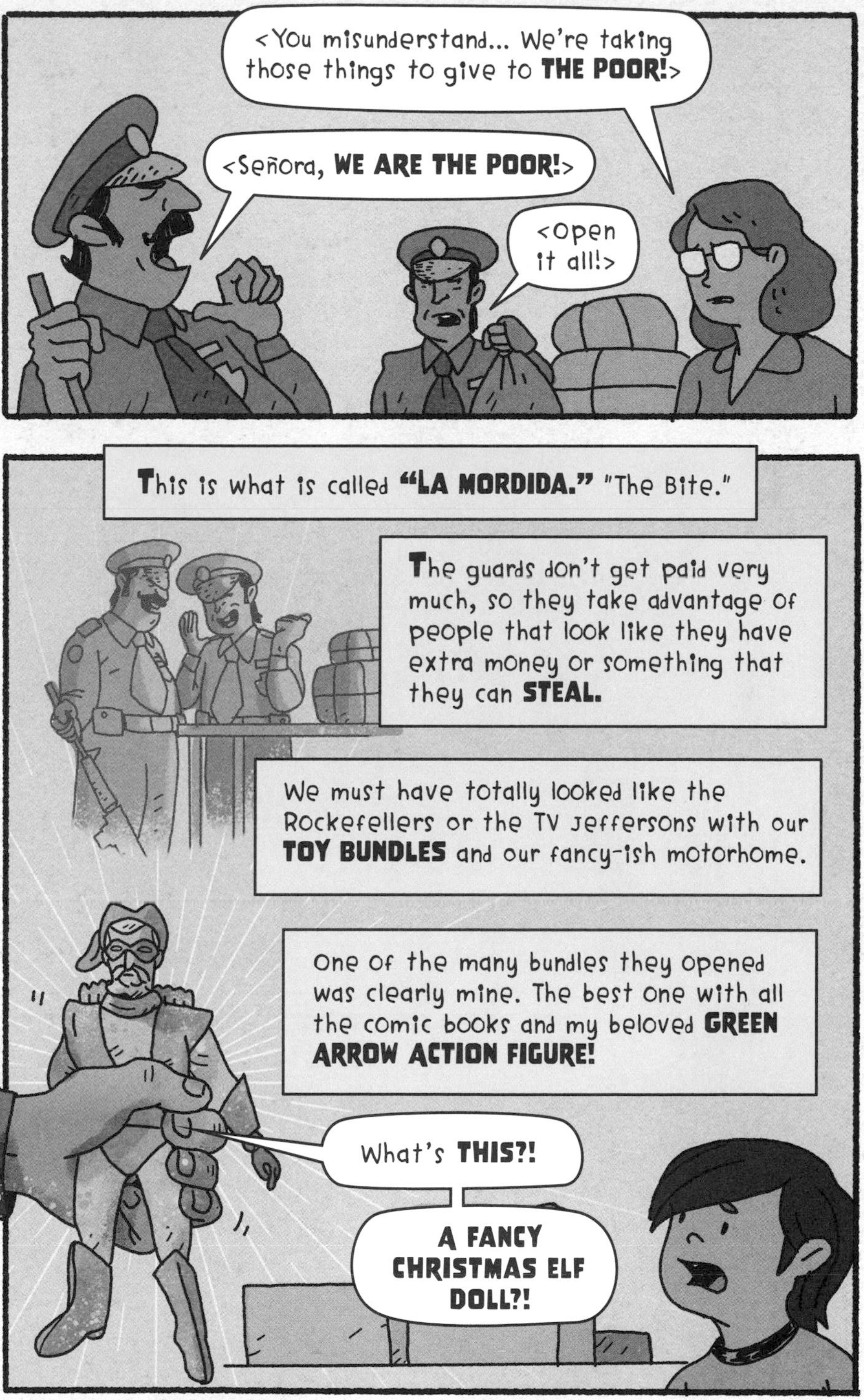
<You misunderstand... We're taking those things to give to **THE POOR!**>
<Señora, **WE ARE THE POOR!**>
<Open it all!>
This is what is called **"LA MORDIDA."** "The Bite."
The guards don't get paid very much, so they take advantage of people that look like they have extra money or something that they can **STEAL.**
We must have totally looked like the Rockefellers or the TV Jeffersons with our **TOY BUNDLES** and our fancy-ish motorhome.
One of the many bundles they opened was clearly mine. The best one with all the comic books and my beloved **GREEN ARROW ACTION FIGURE!**
What's **THIS?!**
A FANCY CHRISTMAS ELF DOLL?!

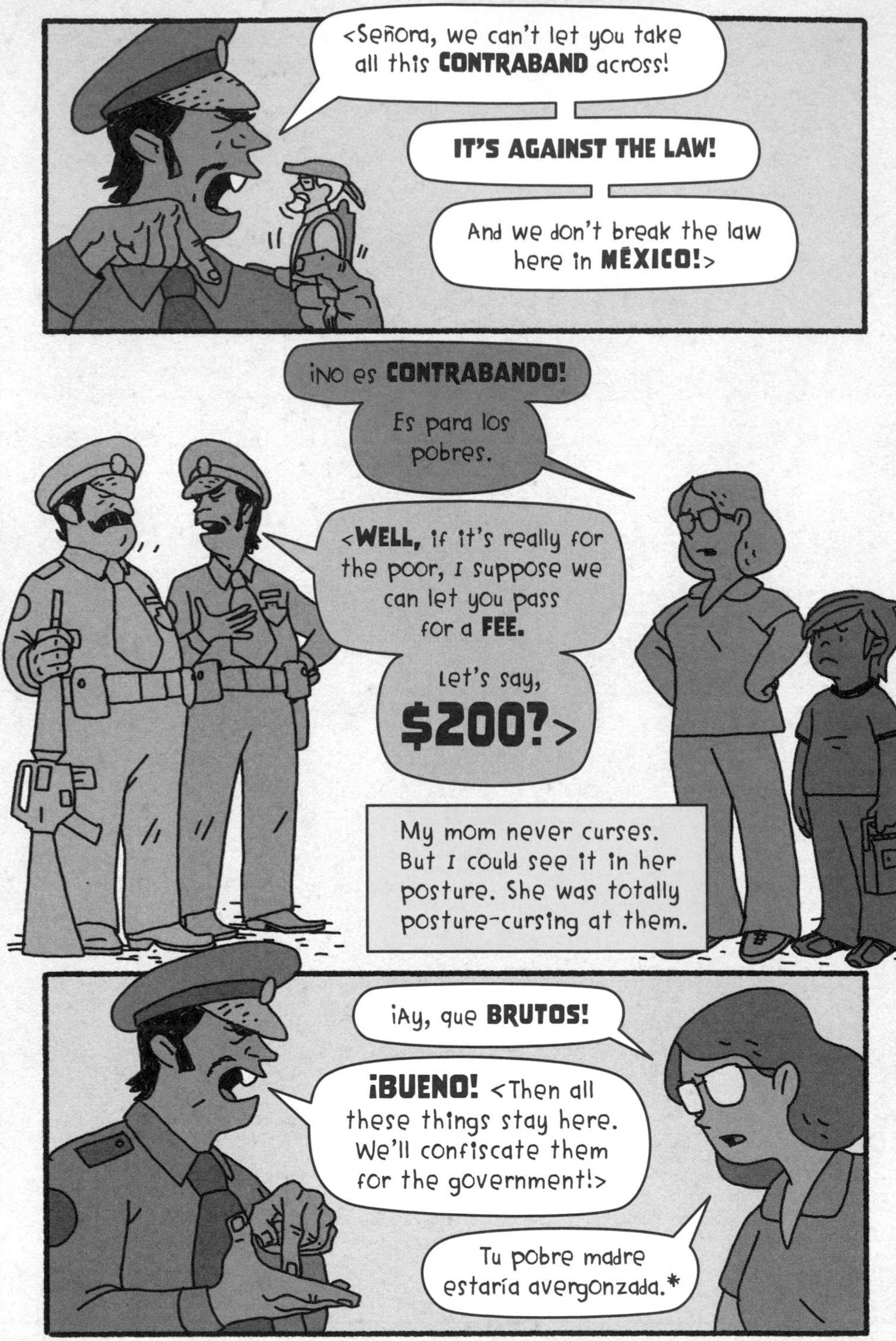
<Señora, we can't let you take all this CONTRABAND across!
IT'S AGAINST THE LAW!
And we don't break the law here in MÉXICO!>
¡No es CONTRABANDO!
Es para los pobres.
<WELL, if it's really for the poor, I suppose we can let you pass for a FEE.
Let's say, $200?>
My mom never curses. But I could see it in her posture. She was totally posture-cursing at them.
¡Ay, que BRUTOS!
¡BUENO! <Then all these things stay here. We'll confiscate them for the government!>
Tu pobre madre estaría avergonzada.*

*Your poor mother would be ashamed.

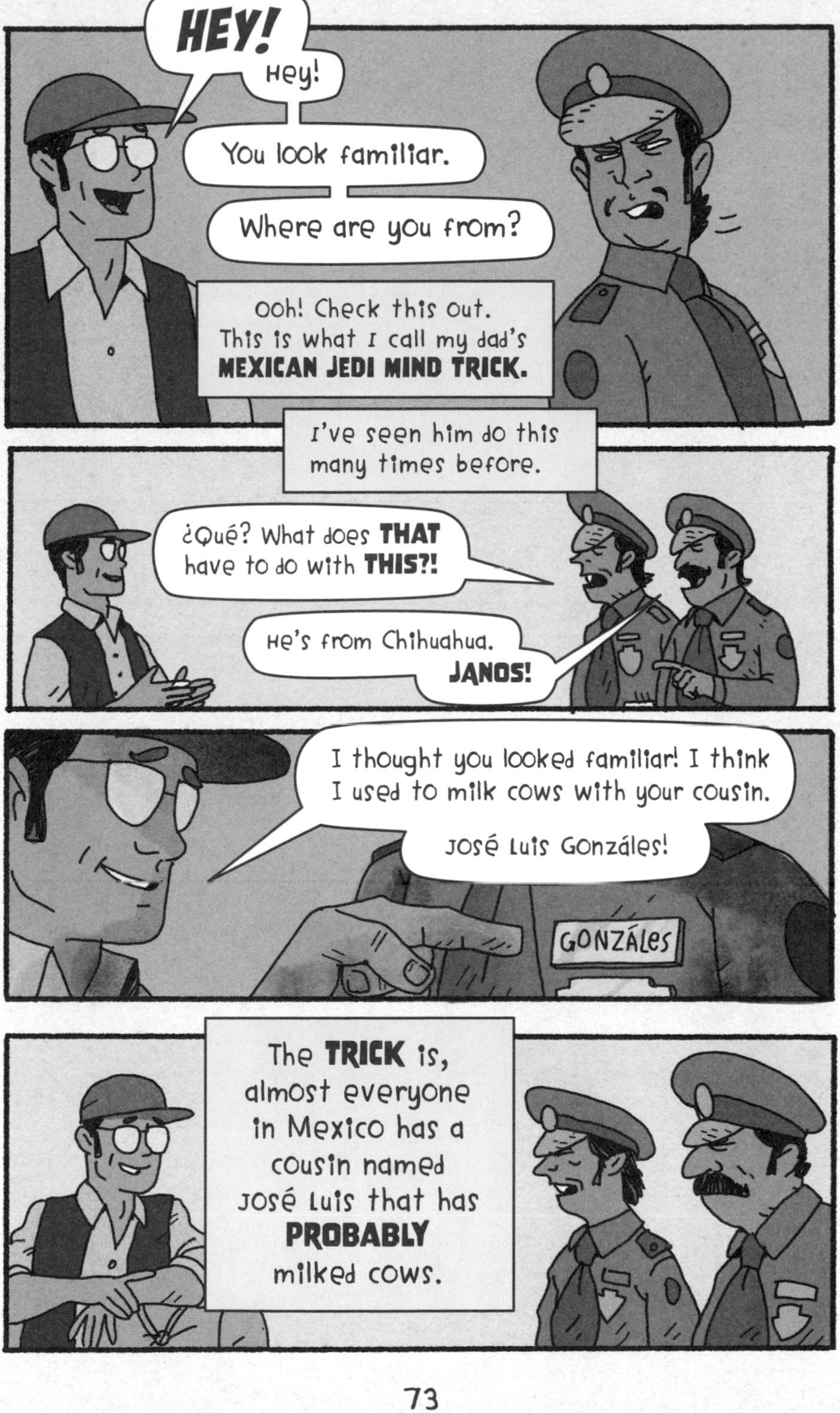
HEY!
Hey!
You look familiar.
Where are you from?
Ooh! Check this out. This is what I call my dad's **MEXICAN JEDI MIND TRICK.**
I've seen him do this many times before.
¿Qué? What does **THAT** have to do with **THIS?!**
He's from Chihuahua. **JANOS!**
I thought you looked familiar! I think I used to milk cows with your cousin.
José Luis Gonzáles!
GONZÁLES
The **TRICK** is, almost everyone in Mexico has a cousin named José Luis that has **PROBABLY** milked cows.

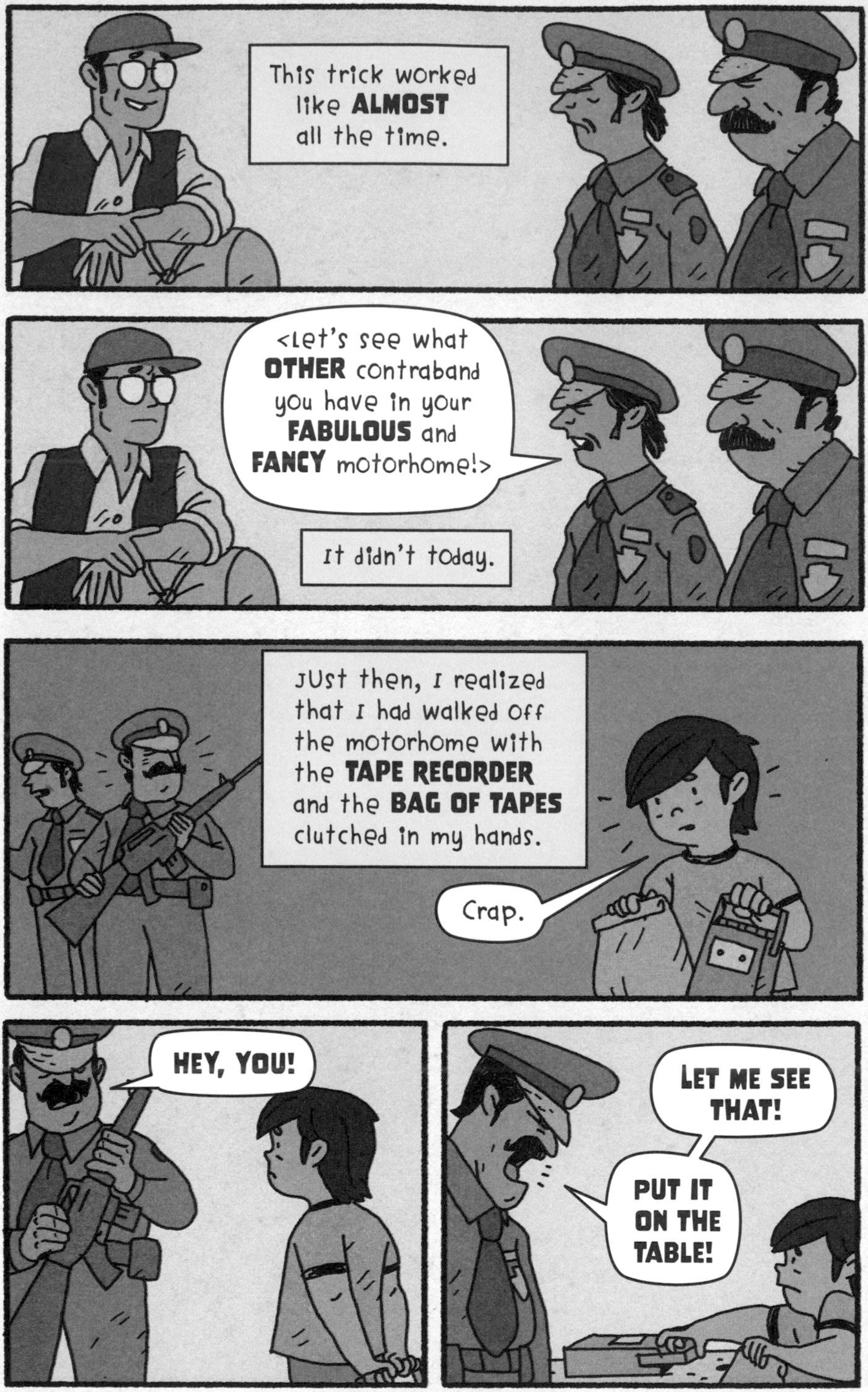
This trick worked like **ALMOST** all the time.
<Let's see what **OTHER** contraband you have in your **FABULOUS** and **FANCY** motorhome!>
It didn't today.
Just then, I realized that I had walked off the motorhome with the **TAPE RECORDER** and the **BAG OF TAPES** clutched in my hands.
Crap.
HEY, YOU!
LET ME SEE THAT!
PUT IT ON THE TABLE!

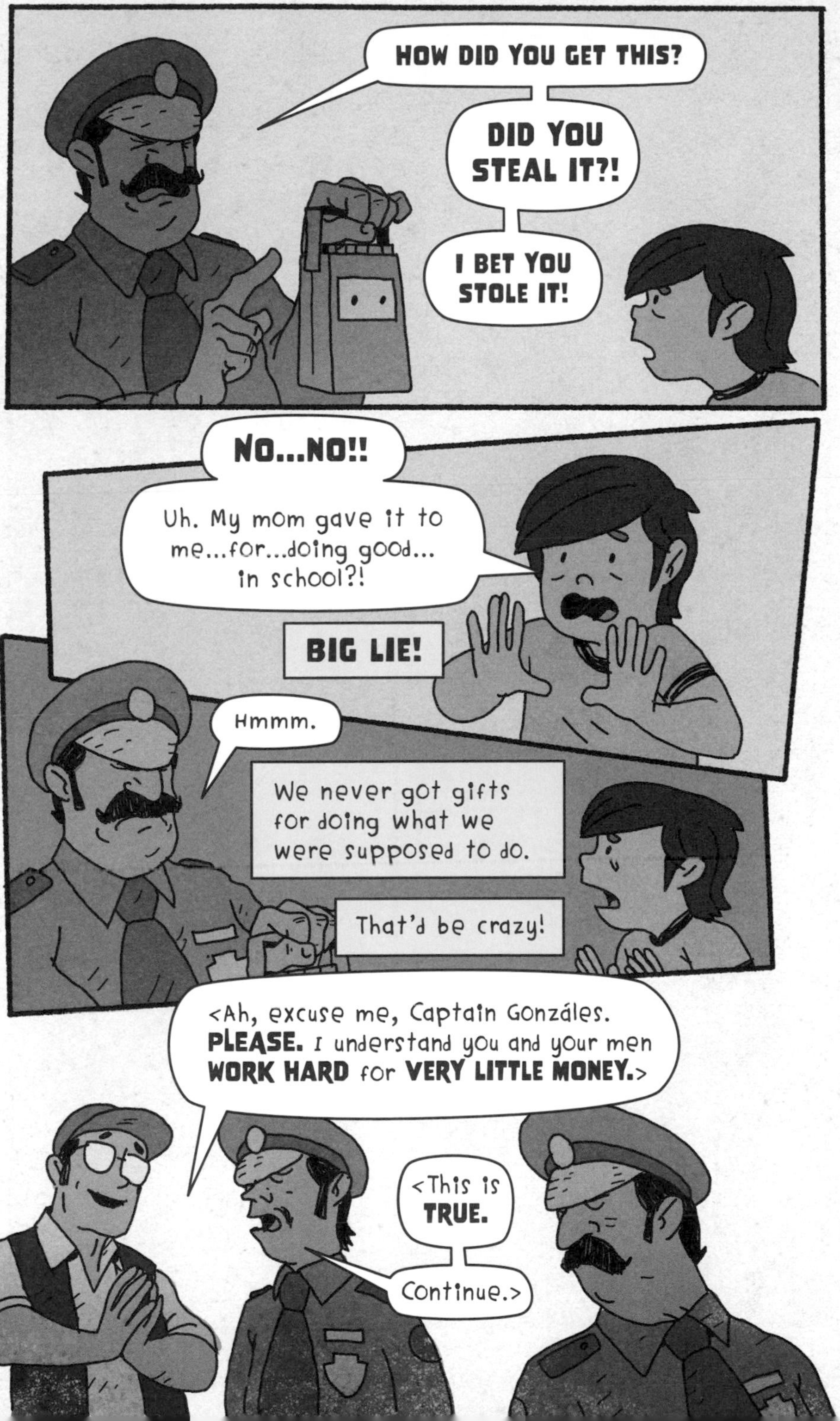
HOW DID YOU GET THIS?
DID YOU STEAL IT?!
I BET YOU STOLE IT!
NO...NO!!
Uh. My mom gave it to me...for...doing good... in school?!
BIG LIE!
Hmmm.
We never got gifts for doing what we were supposed to do.
That'd be crazy!
<Ah, excuse me, Captain Gonzáles. **PLEASE.** I understand you and your men **WORK HARD** for **VERY LITTLE MONEY.**>
<This is **TRUE.**
Continue.>

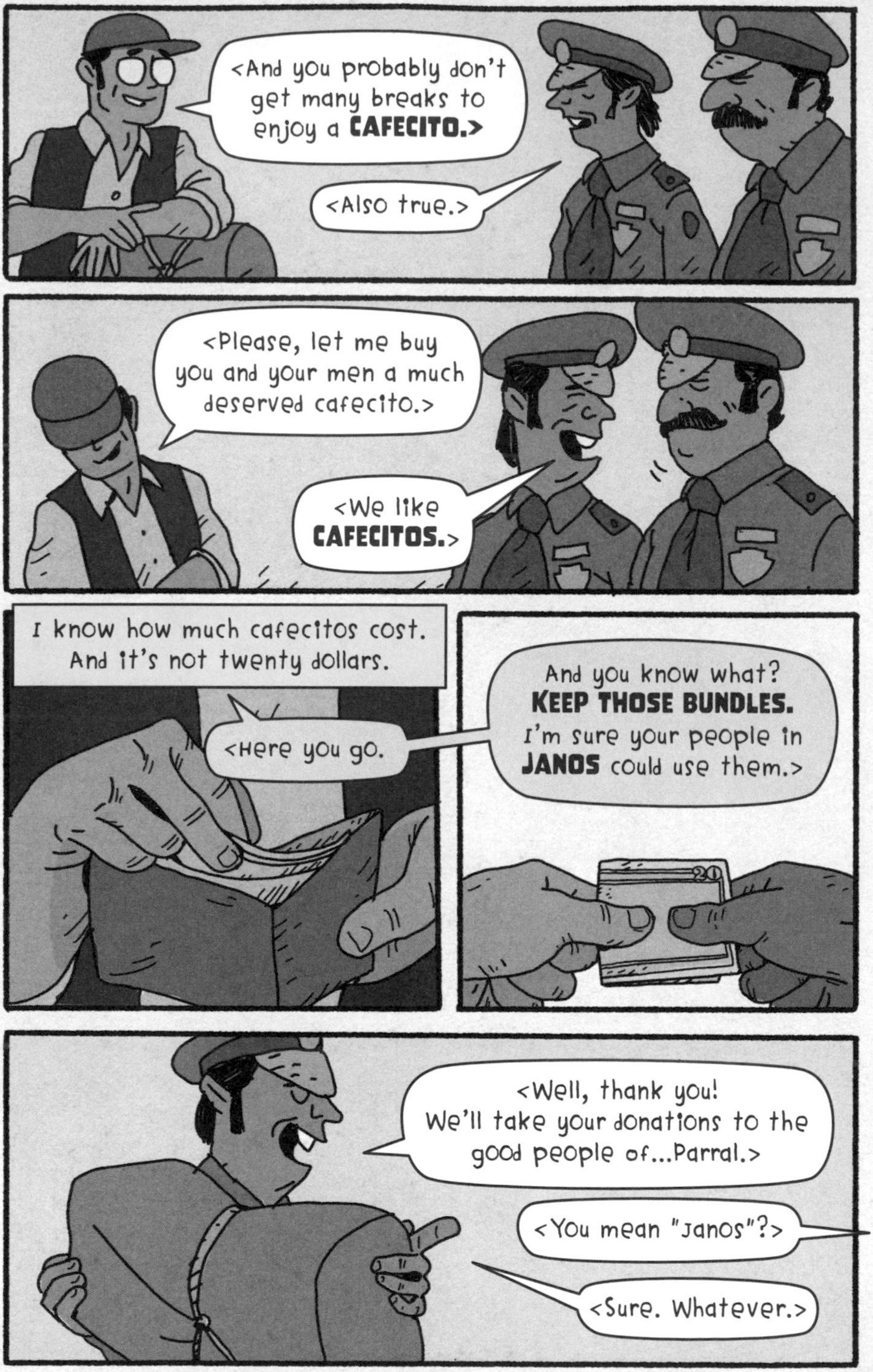
<And you probably don't get many breaks to enjoy a **CAFECITO.**>
<Also true.>
<Please, let me buy you and your men a much deserved cafecito.>
<We like **CAFECITOS.**>
I know how much cafecitos cost. And it's not twenty dollars.
<Here you go.
And you know what? **KEEP THOSE BUNDLES.** I'm sure your people in **JANOS** could use them.>
20
<Well, thank you! We'll take your donations to the good people of...Parral.>
<You mean "Janos"?>
<Sure. Whatever.>

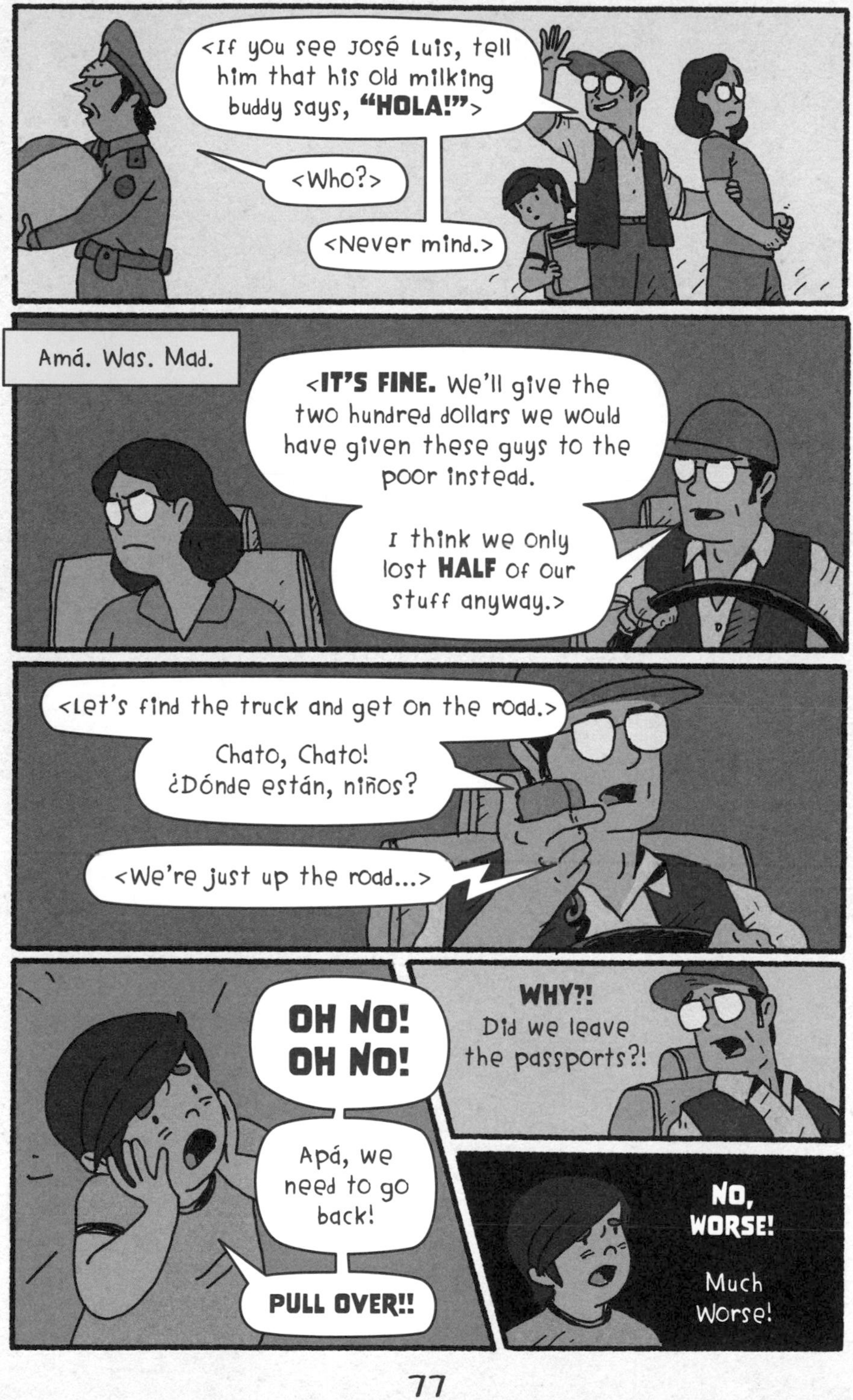
<If you see José Luis, tell him that his old milking buddy says, **"HOLA!"**>
<Who?>
<Never mind.>
Amá. Was. Mad.
<**IT'S FINE.** We'll give the two hundred dollars we would have given these guys to the poor instead.
I think we only lost **HALF** of our stuff anyway.>
<Let's find the truck and get on the road.>
Chato, Chato! ¿Dónde están, niños?
<We're just up the road...>
OH NO! OH NO!
Apá, we need to go back!
PULL OVER!!
WHY?! Did we leave the passports?!
NO, WORSE!
Much Worse!

CHAPTER 7 THE OTHER SIDE

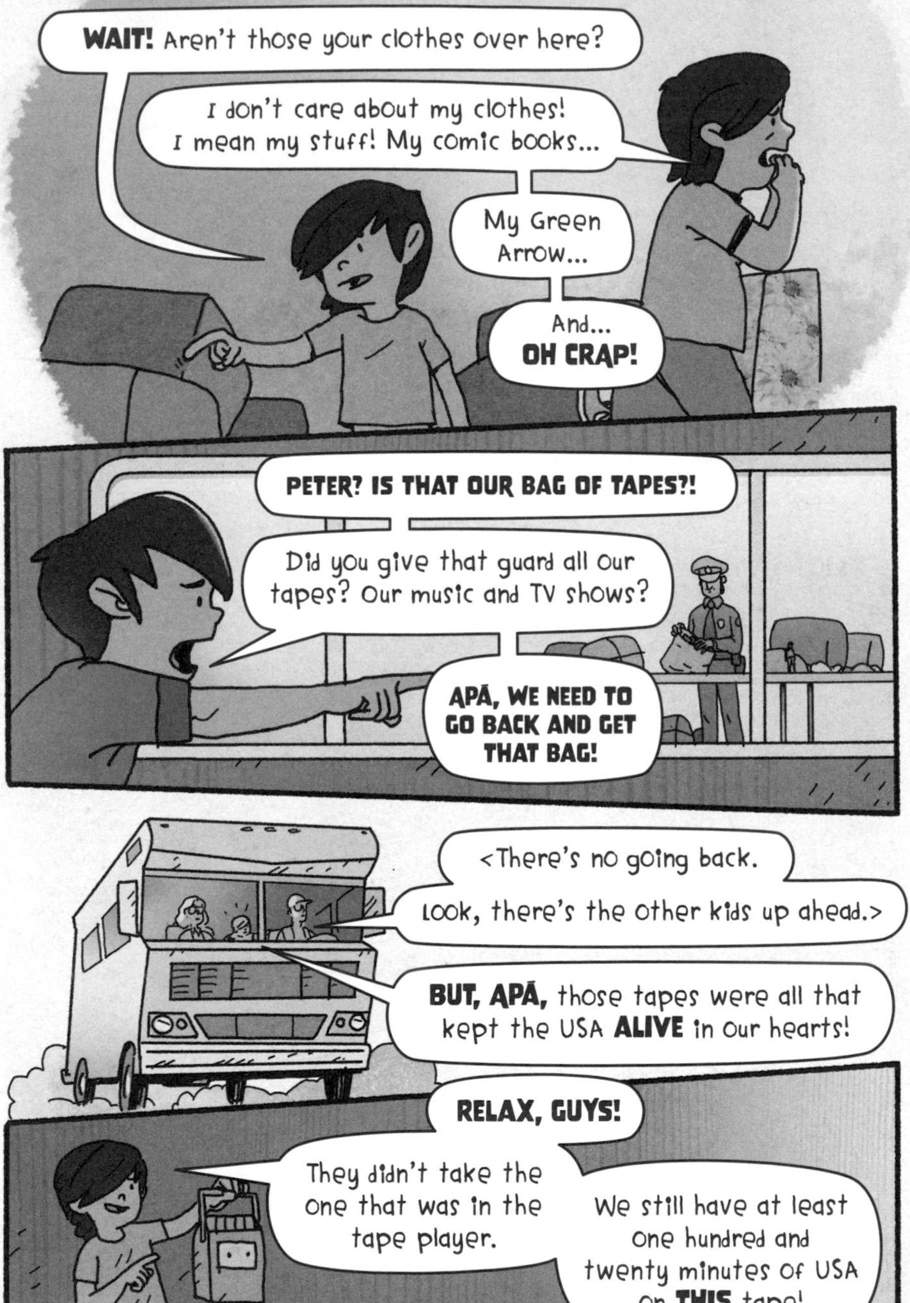

WAIT! Aren't those your clothes over here?
I don't care about my clothes! I mean my stuff! My comic books...
My Green Arrow...
And... OH CRAP!
PETER? IS THAT OUR BAG OF TAPES?!
Did you give that guard all our tapes? Our music and TV shows?
APĀ, WE NEED TO GO BACK AND GET THAT BAG!
<There's no going back.
Look, there's the other kids up ahead.>
BUT, APĀ, those tapes were all that kept the USA ALIVE in our hearts!
RELAX, GUYS!
They didn't take the one that was in the tape player.
We still have at least one hundred and twenty minutes of USA on THIS tape!

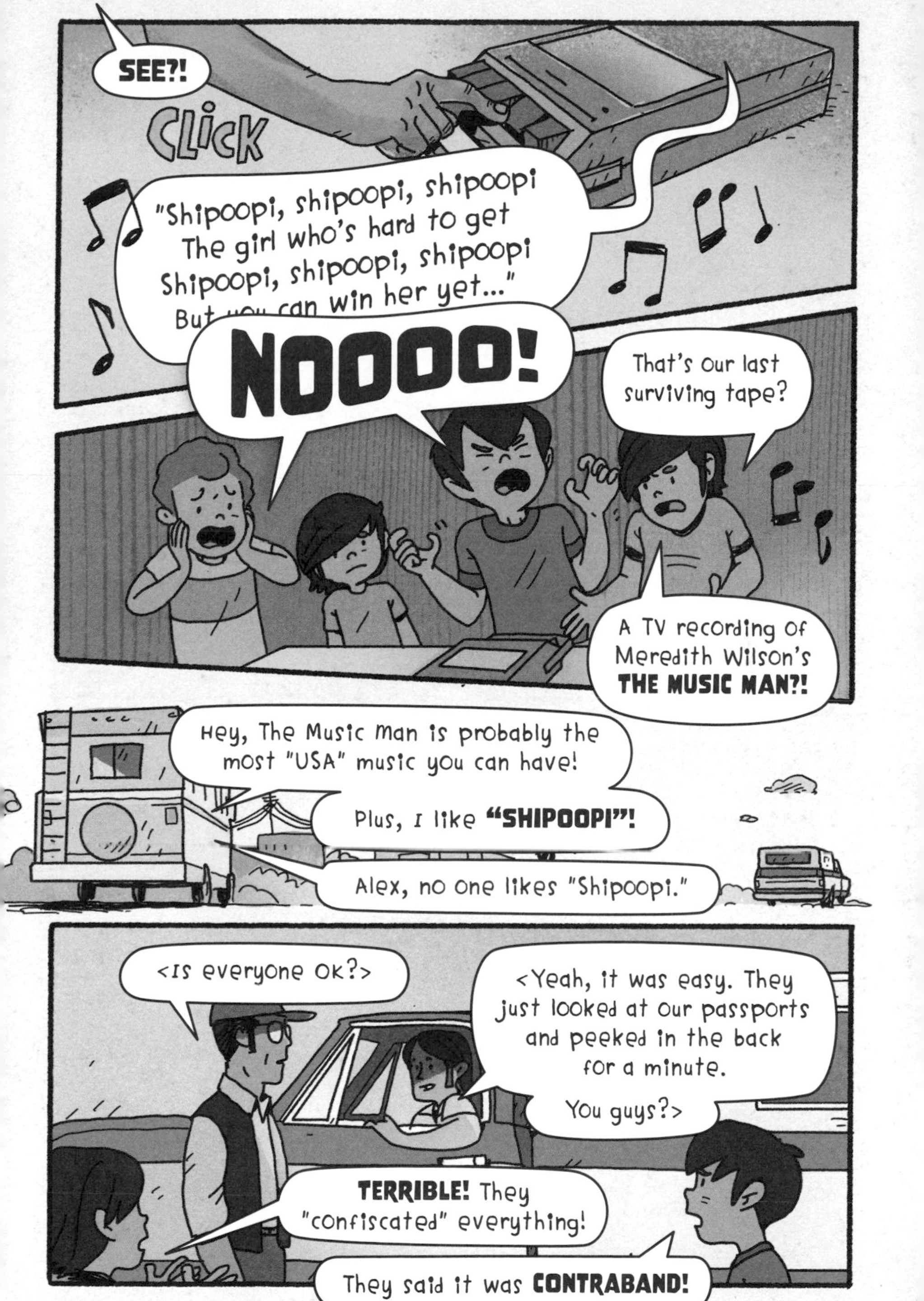

SEE?!
CLICK
"Shipoopi, shipoopi, shipoopi The girl who's hard to get Shipoopi, shipoopi, shipoopi Bu can win her yet..."
NOOOO!
That's our last surviving tape?
A TV recording of Meredith Wilson's **THE MUSIC MAN?!**
Hey, The Music Man is probably the most "USA" music you can have!
Plus, I like **"SHIPOOPI"!**
Alex, no one likes "Shipoopi."
<Is everyone OK?>
<Yeah, it was easy. They just looked at our passports and peeked in the back for a minute.
You guys?>
TERRIBLE! They "confiscated" everything!
They said it was **CONTRABAND!**

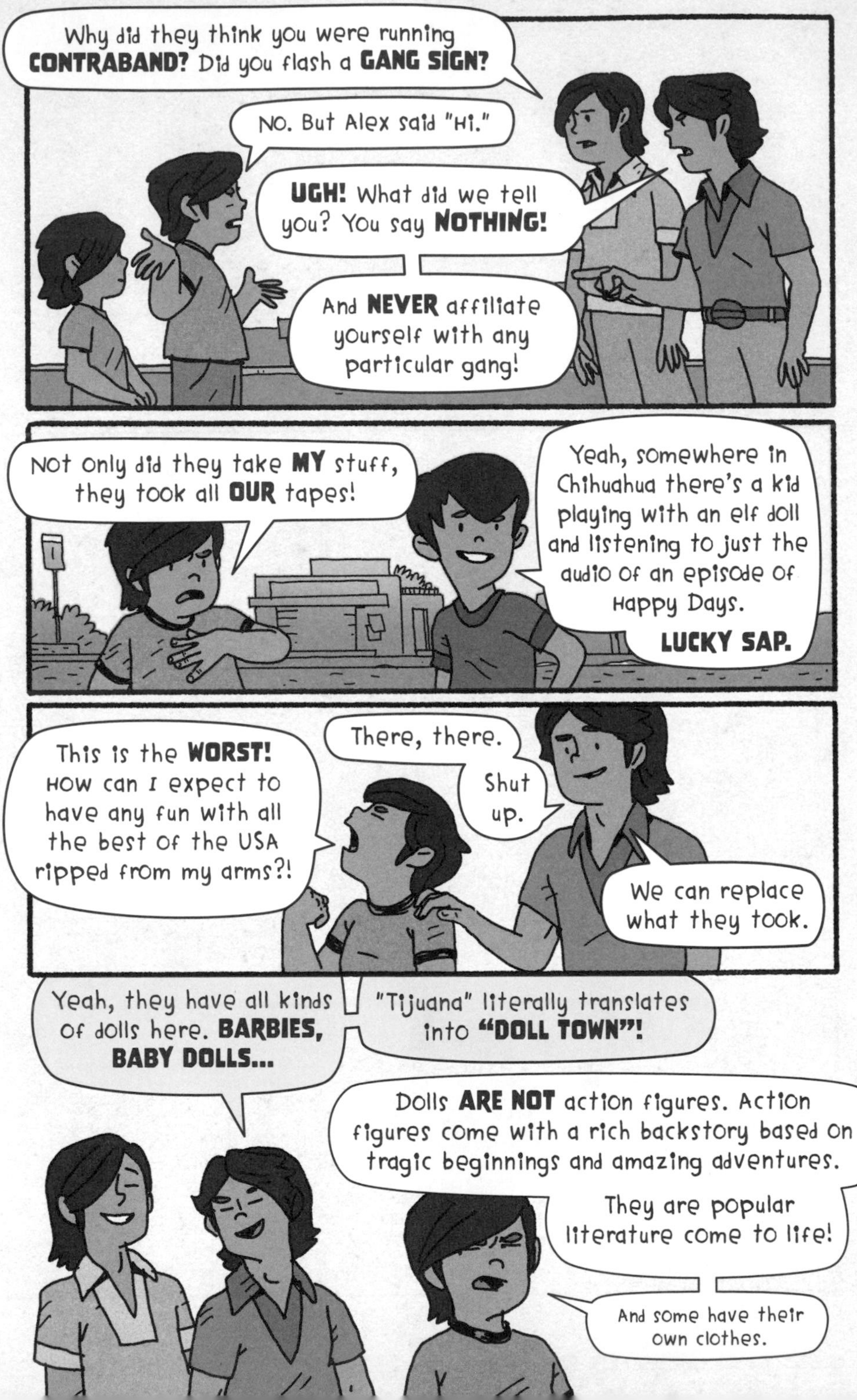
Why did they think you were running CONTRABAND? Did you flash a GANG SIGN?
NO. But Alex said "Hi."
UGH! What did we tell you? You say NOTHING!
And NEVER affiliate yourself with any particular gang!
Not only did they take MY stuff, they took all OUR tapes!
Yeah, somewhere in Chihuahua there's a kid playing with an elf doll and listening to just the audio of an episode of Happy Days.
LUCKY SAP.
This is the WORST! How can I expect to have any fun with all the best of the USA ripped from my arms?!
There, there.
Shut up.
We can replace what they took.
Yeah, they have all kinds of dolls here. BARBIES, BABY DOLLS...
"Tijuana" literally translates into "DOLL TOWN"!
Dolls ARE NOT action figures. Action figures come with a rich backstory based on tragic beginnings and amazing adventures.
They are popular literature come to life!
And some have their own clothes.

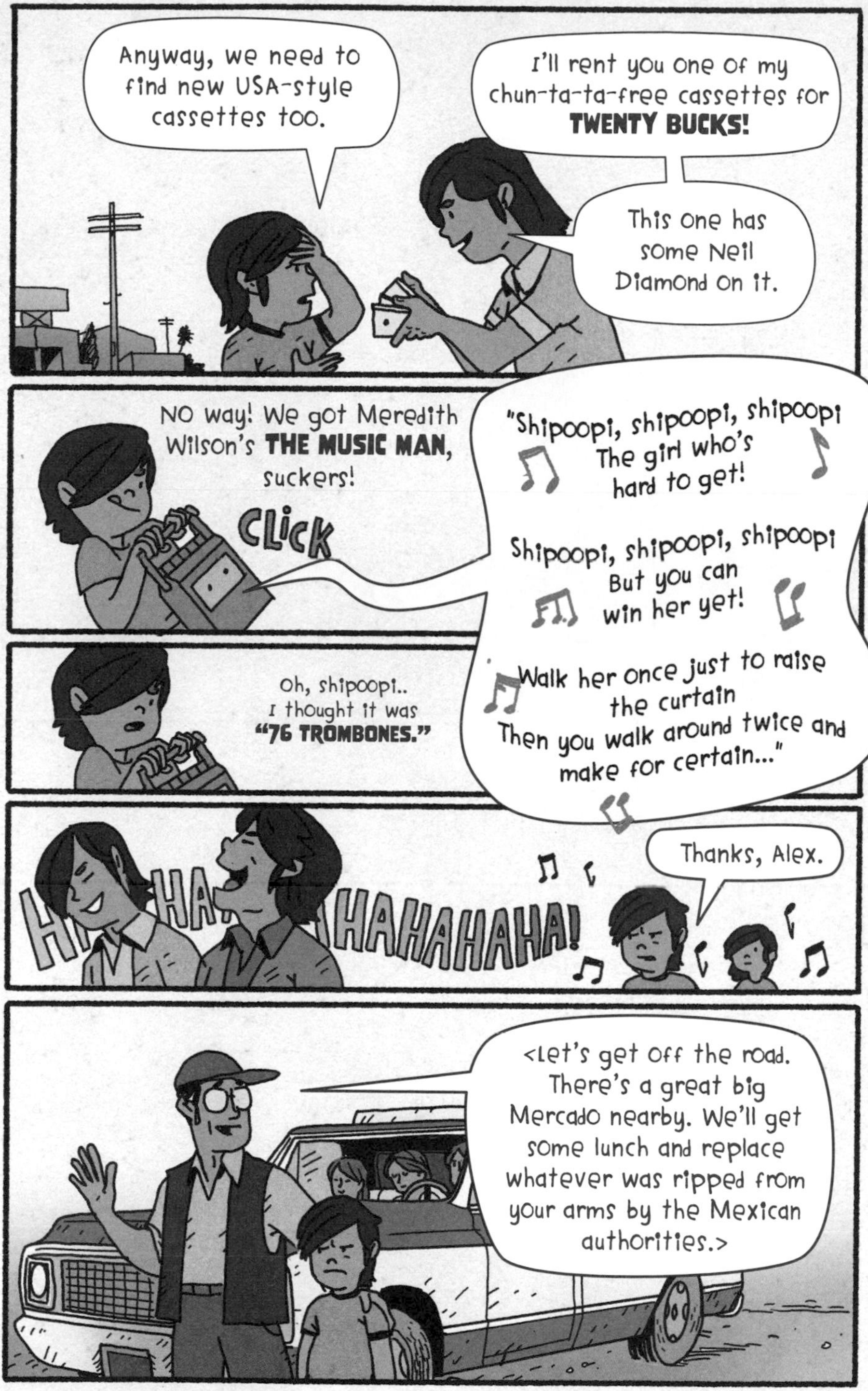

Anyway, we need to find new USA-style cassettes too.
I'll rent you one of my chun-ta-ta-free cassettes for **TWENTY BUCKS!**
This one has some Neil Diamond on it.
NO way! We got Meredith Wilson's **THE MUSIC MAN**, suckers!
CLICK
"Shipoopi, shipoopi, shipoopi The girl who's hard to get! Shipoopi, shipoopi, shipoopi But you can win her yet! Walk her once just to raise the curtain Then you walk around twice and make for certain..."
Oh, shipoopi.. I thought it was **"76 TROMBONES."**
HAHAHAHAHA!
Thanks, Alex.
<Let's get off the road. There's a great big Mercado nearby. We'll get some lunch and replace whatever was ripped from your arms by the Mexican authorities.>

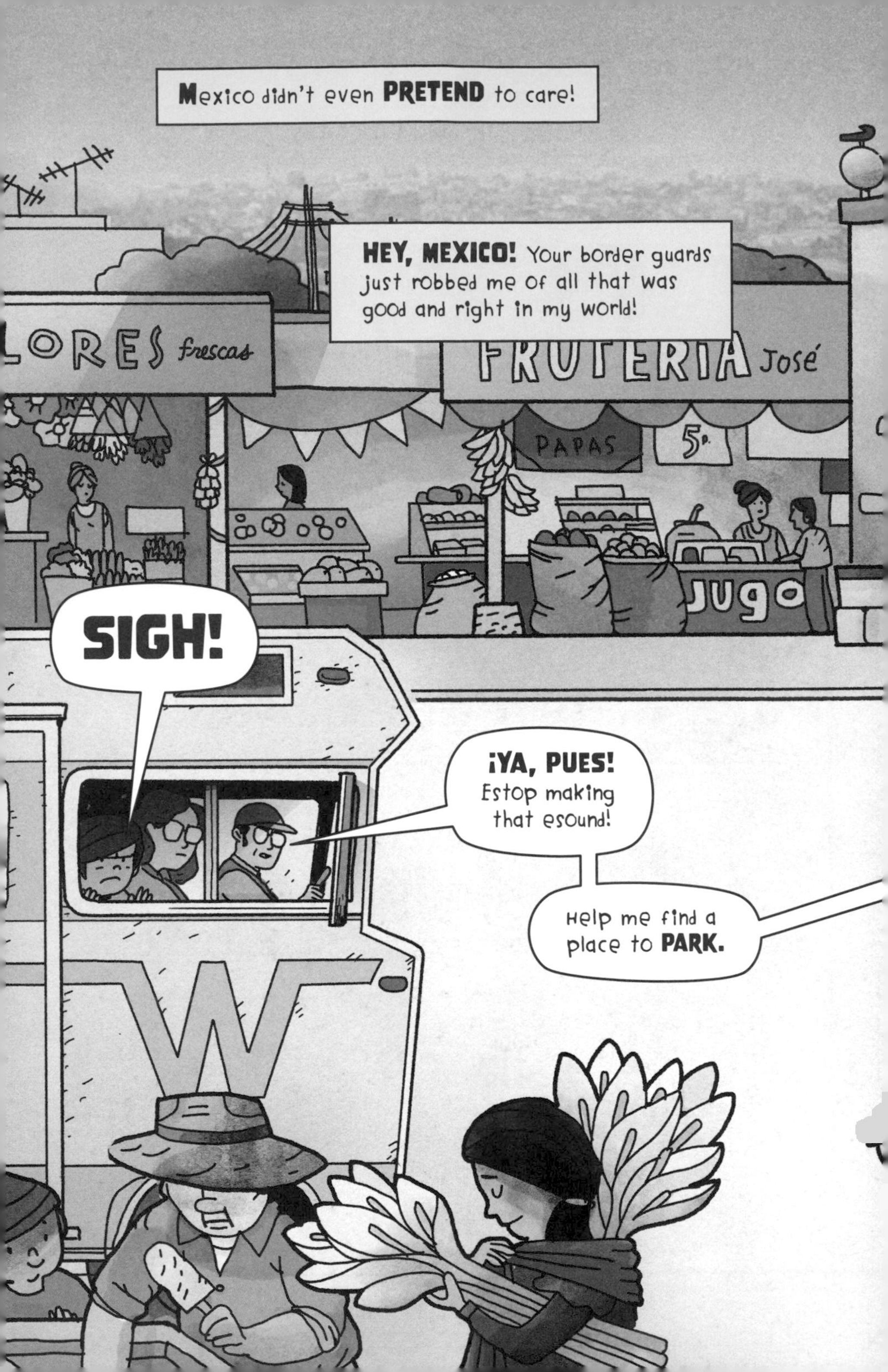
Mexico didn't even PRETEND to care!
HEY, MEXICO! Your border guards just robbed me of all that was good and right in my world!
LORES frescas
FRUTERIA José
PAPAS
5p.
JUGO
SIGH!
¡YA, PUES! Estop making that esound!
Help me find a place to PARK.

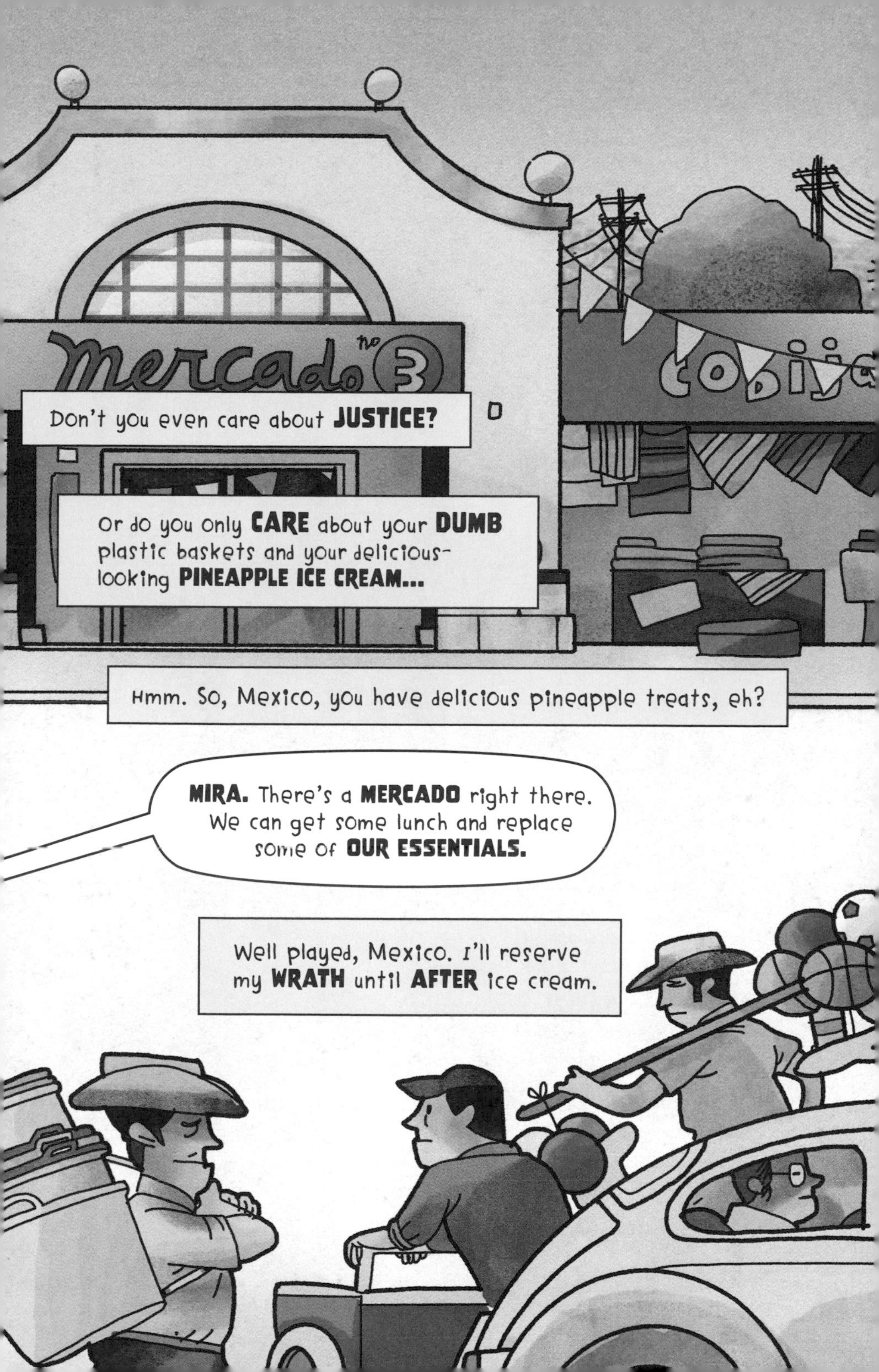
Mercado No 3
Don't you even care about JUSTICE?
Or do you only CARE about your DUMB plastic baskets and your delicious-looking PINEAPPLE ICE CREAM...
Hmm. So, Mexico, you have delicious pineapple treats, eh?
MIRA. There's a MERCADO right there. We can get some lunch and replace some of OUR ESSENTIALS.
Well played, Mexico. I'll reserve my WRATH until AFTER ice cream.

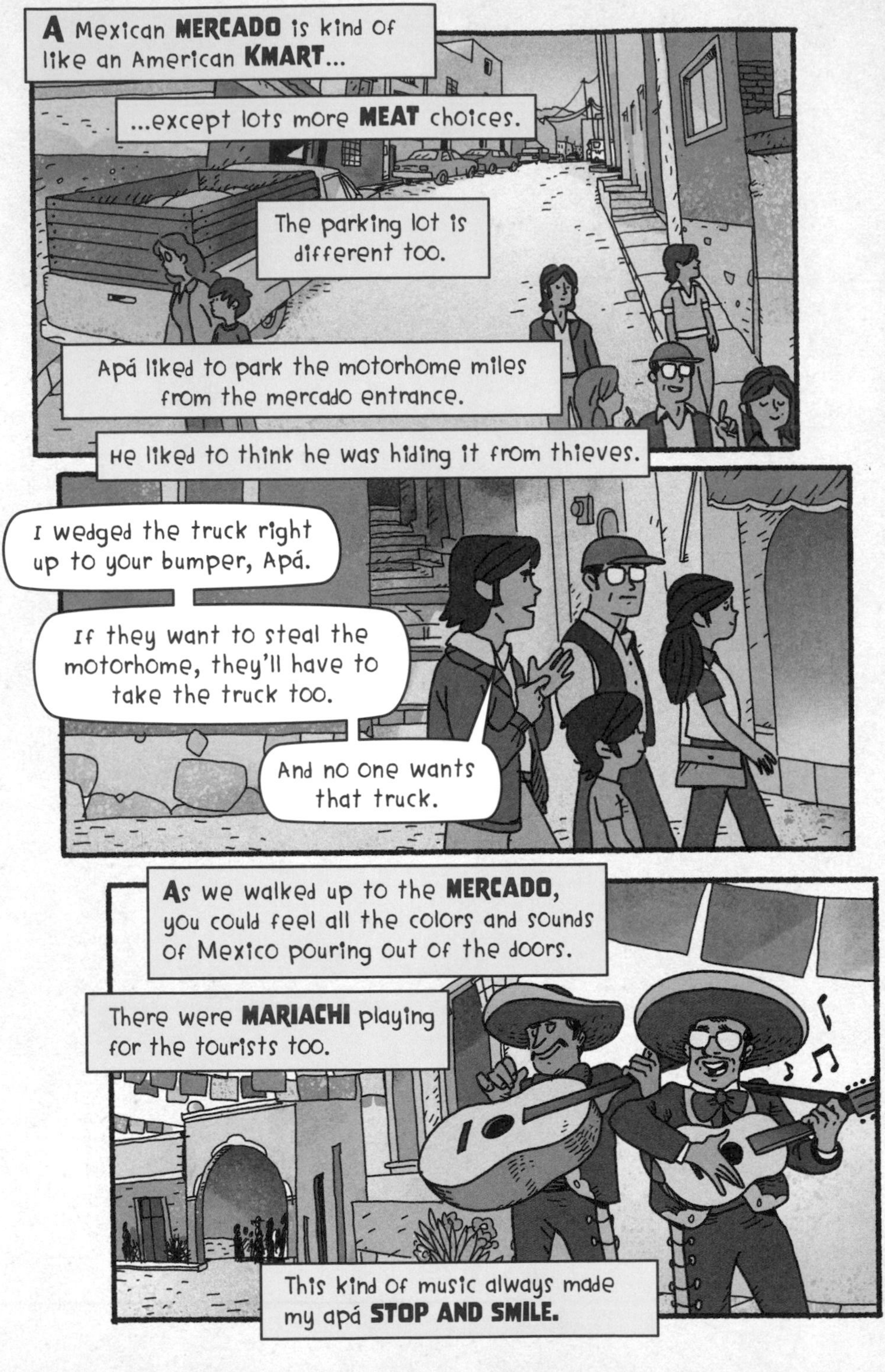
A Mexican **MERCADO** is kind of like an American **KMART**...
...except lots more **MEAT** choices.
The parking lot is different too.
Apá liked to park the motorhome miles from the mercado entrance.
He liked to think he was hiding it from thieves.
I wedged the truck right up to your bumper, Apá.
If they want to steal the motorhome, they'll have to take the truck too.
And no one wants that truck.
As we walked up to the **MERCADO**, you could feel all the colors and sounds of Mexico pouring out of the doors.
There were **MARIACHI** playing for the tourists too.
This kind of music always made my apá **STOP AND SMILE.**

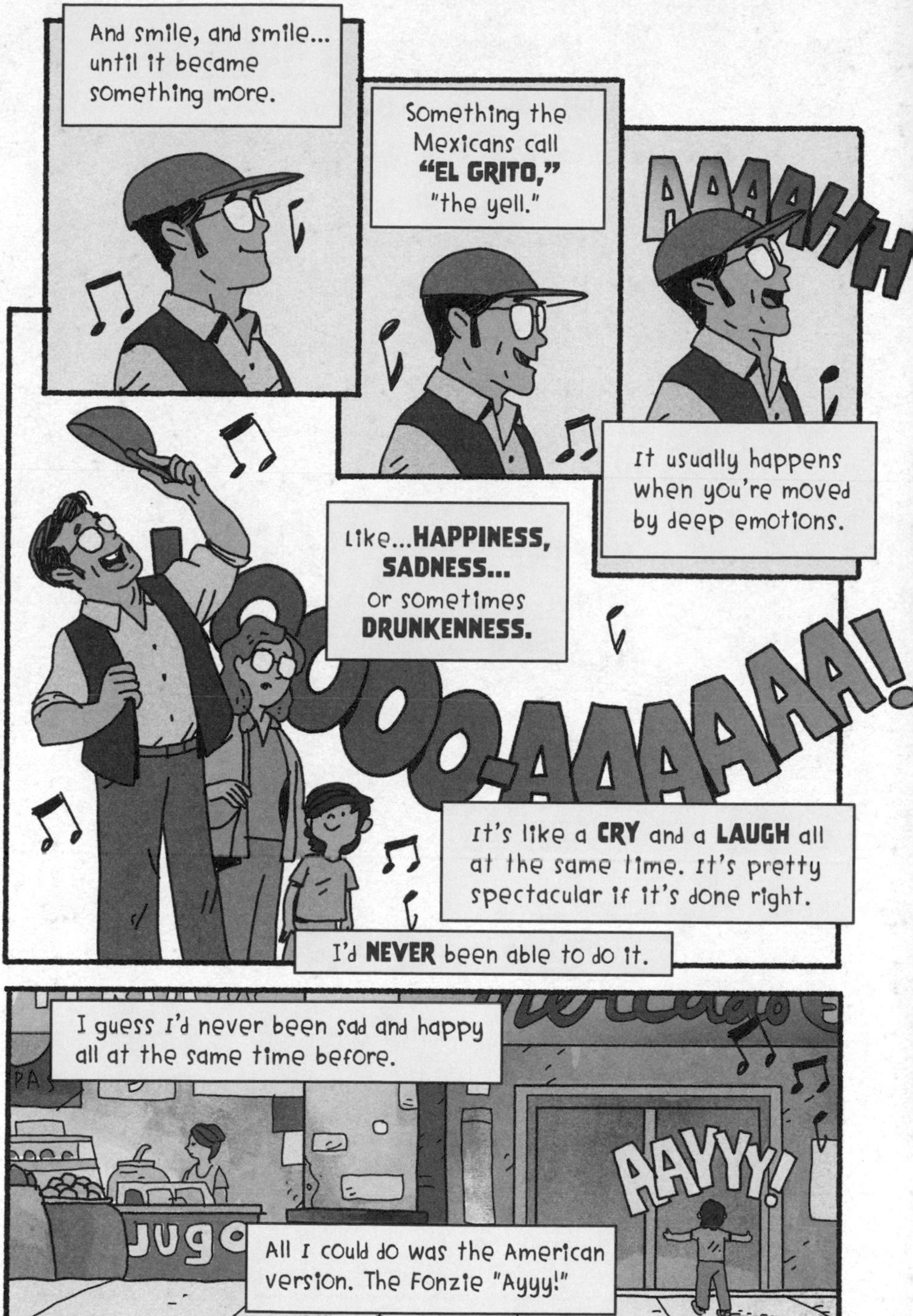
And smile, and smile... until it became something more.
Something the Mexicans call **"EL GRITO,"** "the yell."
AAAAHHH
It usually happens when you're moved by deep emotions.
Like...**HAPPINESS, SADNESS...** or sometimes **DRUNKENNESS.**
OOOOO-AAAAAAA!
It's like a **CRY** and a **LAUGH** all at the same time. It's pretty spectacular if it's done right.
I'd **NEVER** been able to do it.
I guess I'd never been sad and happy all at the same time before.
JUGO
AAYYY!
All I could do was the American version. The Fonzie "Ayyy!"

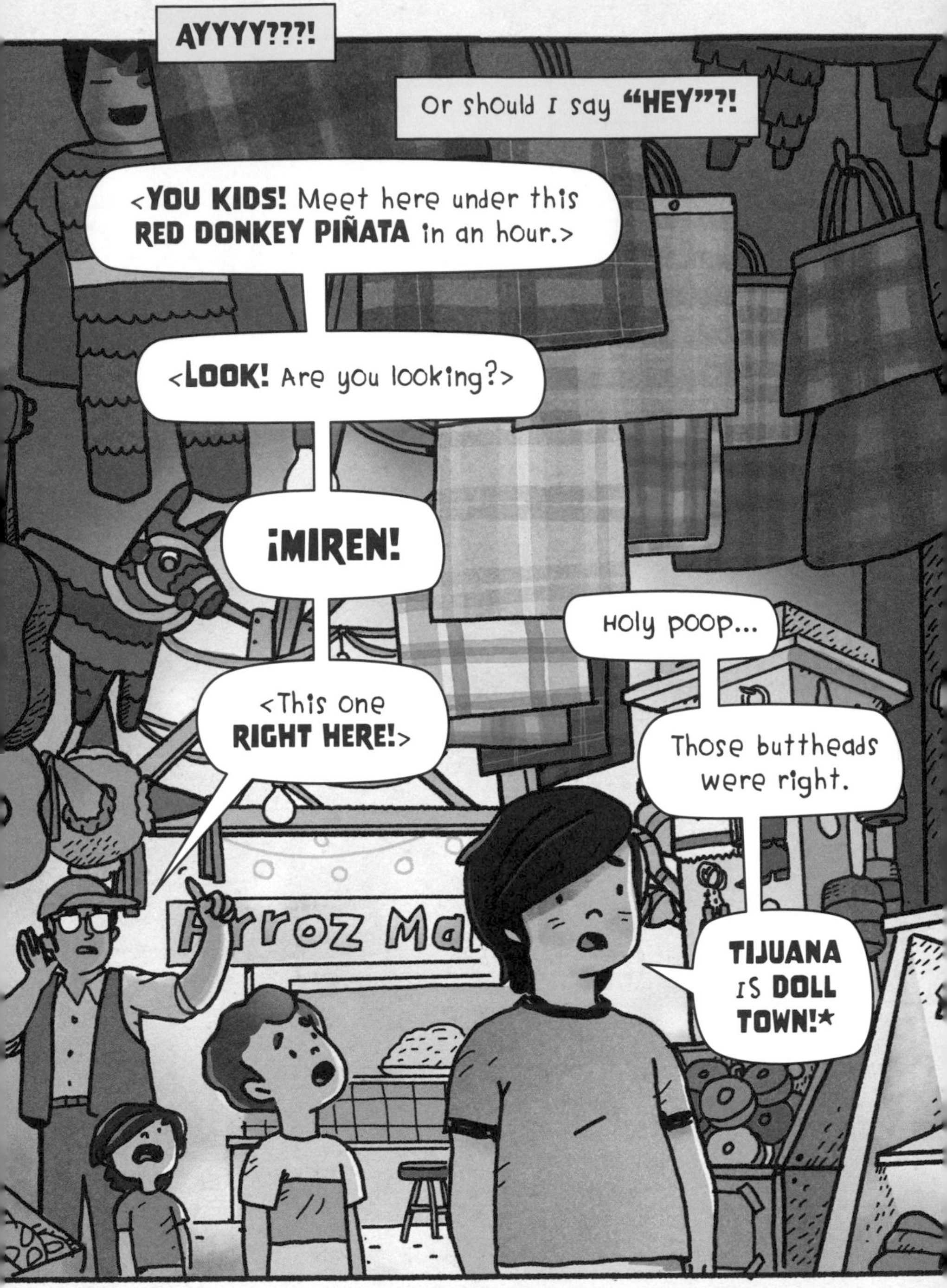
AYYYY???!
Or should I say "HEY"?!
<YOU KIDS! Meet here under this RED DONKEY PIÑATA in an hour.>
<LOOK! Are you looking?>
¡MIREN!
<This one RIGHT HERE!>
Arroz Ma
Holy poop...
Those buttheads were right.
TIJUANA IS DOLL TOWN!*

*Shut up, you know I meant "Action figures"!

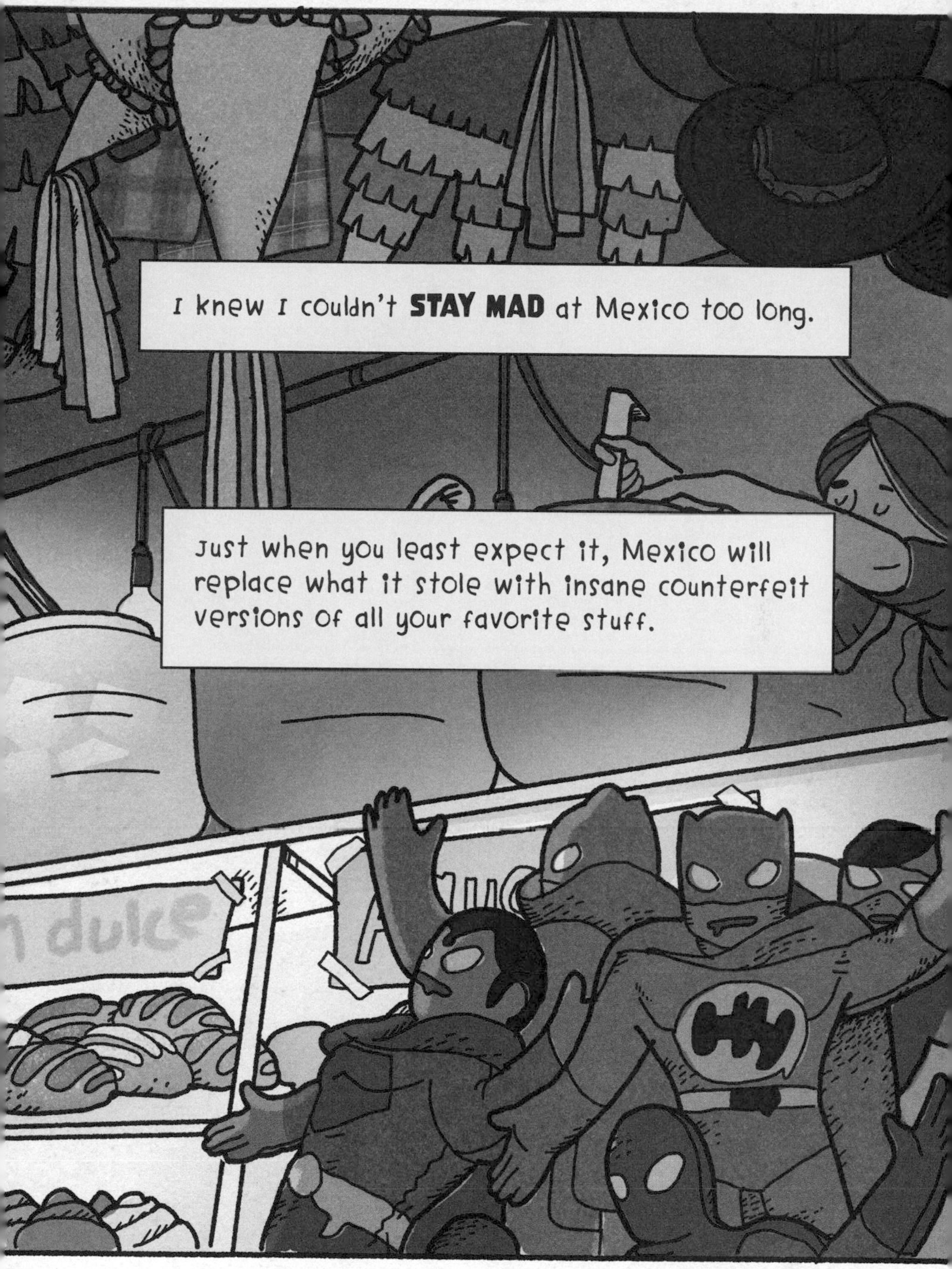

I knew I couldn't **STAY MAD** at Mexico too long.
Just when you least expect it, Mexico will replace what it stole with insane counterfeit versions of all your favorite stuff.
dulce

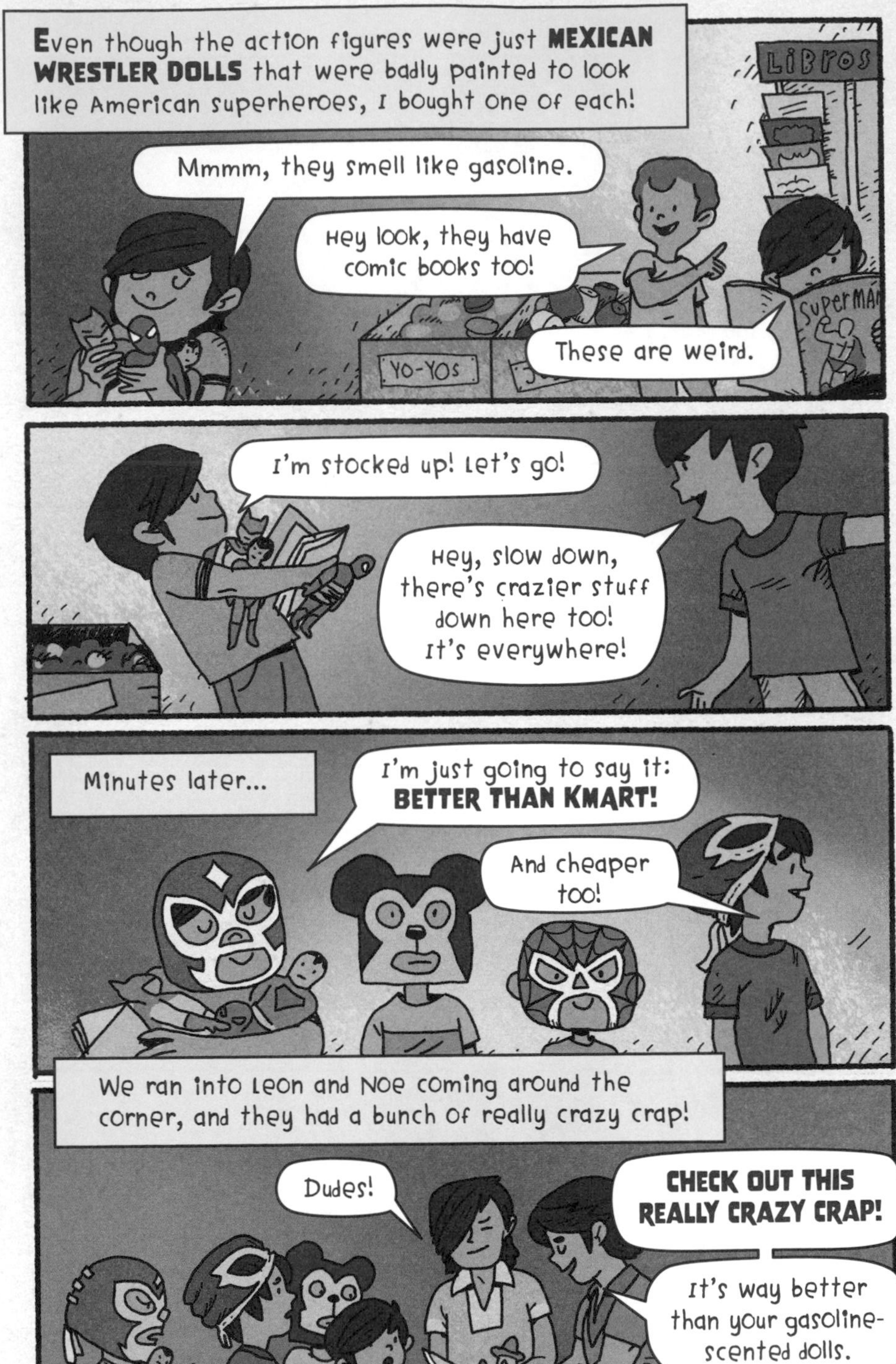

Even though the action figures were just **MEXICAN WRESTLER DOLLS** that were badly painted to look like American superheroes, I bought one of each!
LIBROS
Mmmm, they smell like gasoline.
Hey look, they have comic books too!
YO-YOS
SUPERMAN
These are weird.
I'm stocked up! Let's go!
Hey, slow down, there's crazier stuff down here too! It's everywhere!
Minutes later...
I'm just going to say it: **BETTER THAN KMART!**
And cheaper too!
We ran into Leon and Noe coming around the corner, and they had a bunch of really crazy crap!
Dudes!
CHECK OUT THIS REALLY CRAZY CRAP!
It's way better than your gasoline-scented dolls.

A MEXICAN BOY'S GUIDE TO:

UNREGULATED TOYS

Made FOR CHILDREN OF MEXICO BY CHILDREN

MEXICAN INGENUITY + NO OVERSIGHT = FUN!

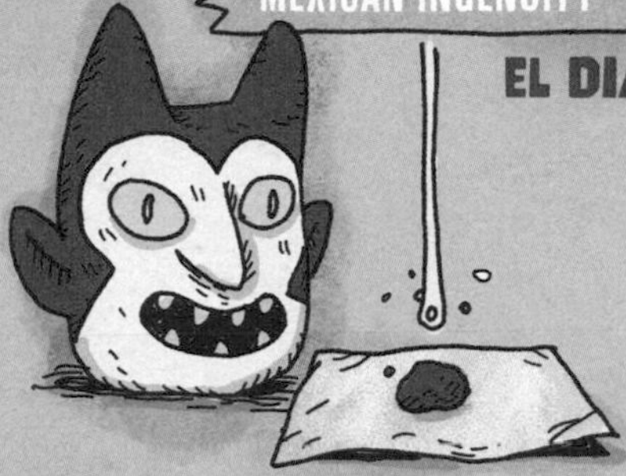

EL DIABLO'S HEAD

Generates incredible heat when you spit on a piece of tinfoil and scrape off bits of the horn into it. My oldest brother, Sal (science is his thing), says that it's quicklime (calcium oxide).

"TOY" BULLWHIP

An actual whip made for tourists and child-like teens who enjoy **TORTURING** their younger siblings (oddly specific).

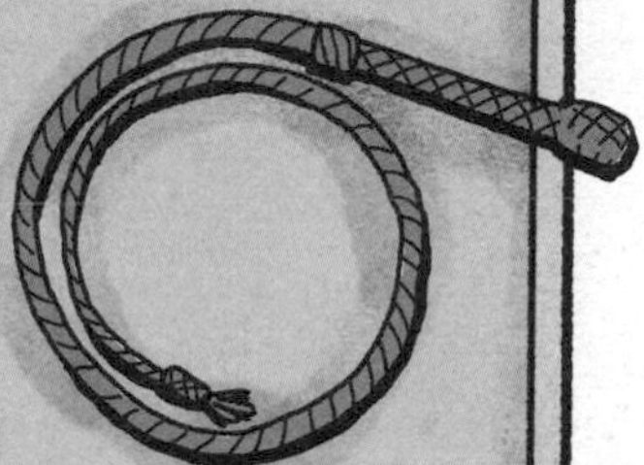

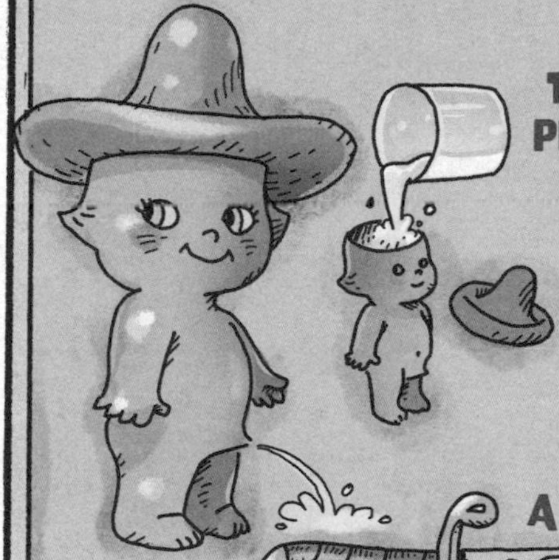

THE LITTLE PEEPEE MAN

A hollow kewpie Doll wearing a pink sombrero that looks like a baby bottle nipple. When you fill it with water and then squeeze the hat, a stream of **"PEE"** comes out of his little peepee (for fun)!

A MINI MACHETE

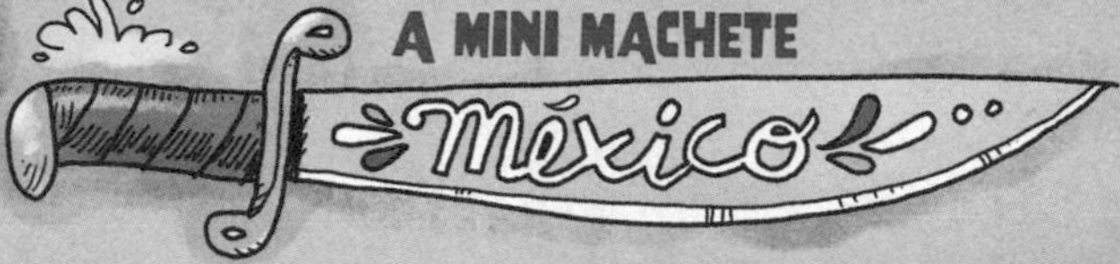
México

It's actually sharp and has the word **"MÉXICO"** painted on it so you know that the guy killing you is **FROM MEXICO** (or just a classy tourist like my brothers)!

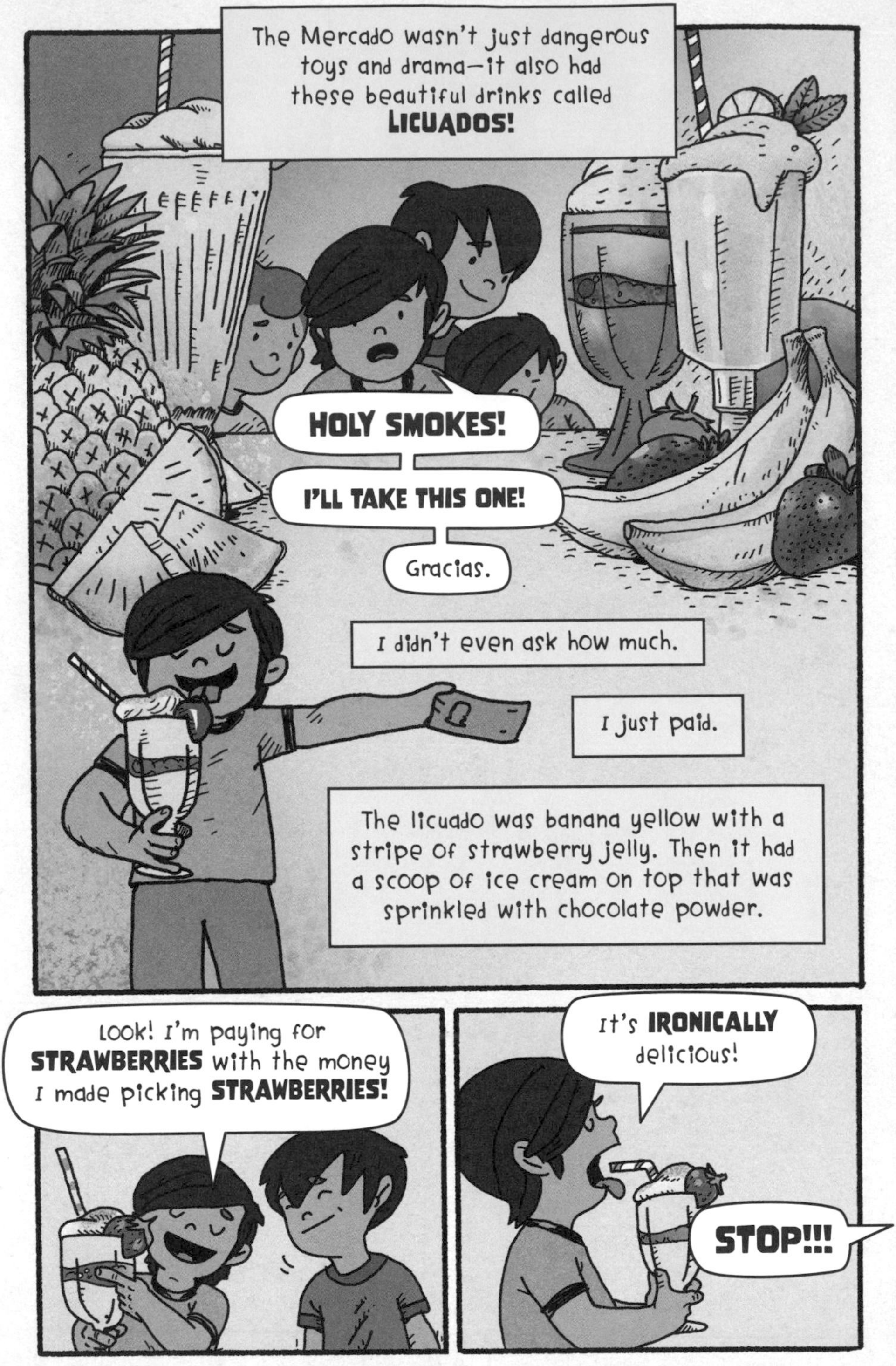
The Mercado wasn't just dangerous toys and drama—it also had these beautiful drinks called **LICUADOS!**
HOLY SMOKES!
I'LL TAKE THIS ONE!
Gracias.
I didn't even ask how much.
I just paid.
The licuado was banana yellow with a stripe of strawberry jelly. Then it had a scoop of ice cream on top that was sprinkled with chocolate powder.
Look! I'm paying for **STRAWBERRIES** with the money I made picking **STRAWBERRIES!**
It's **IRONICALLY** delicious!
STOP!!!

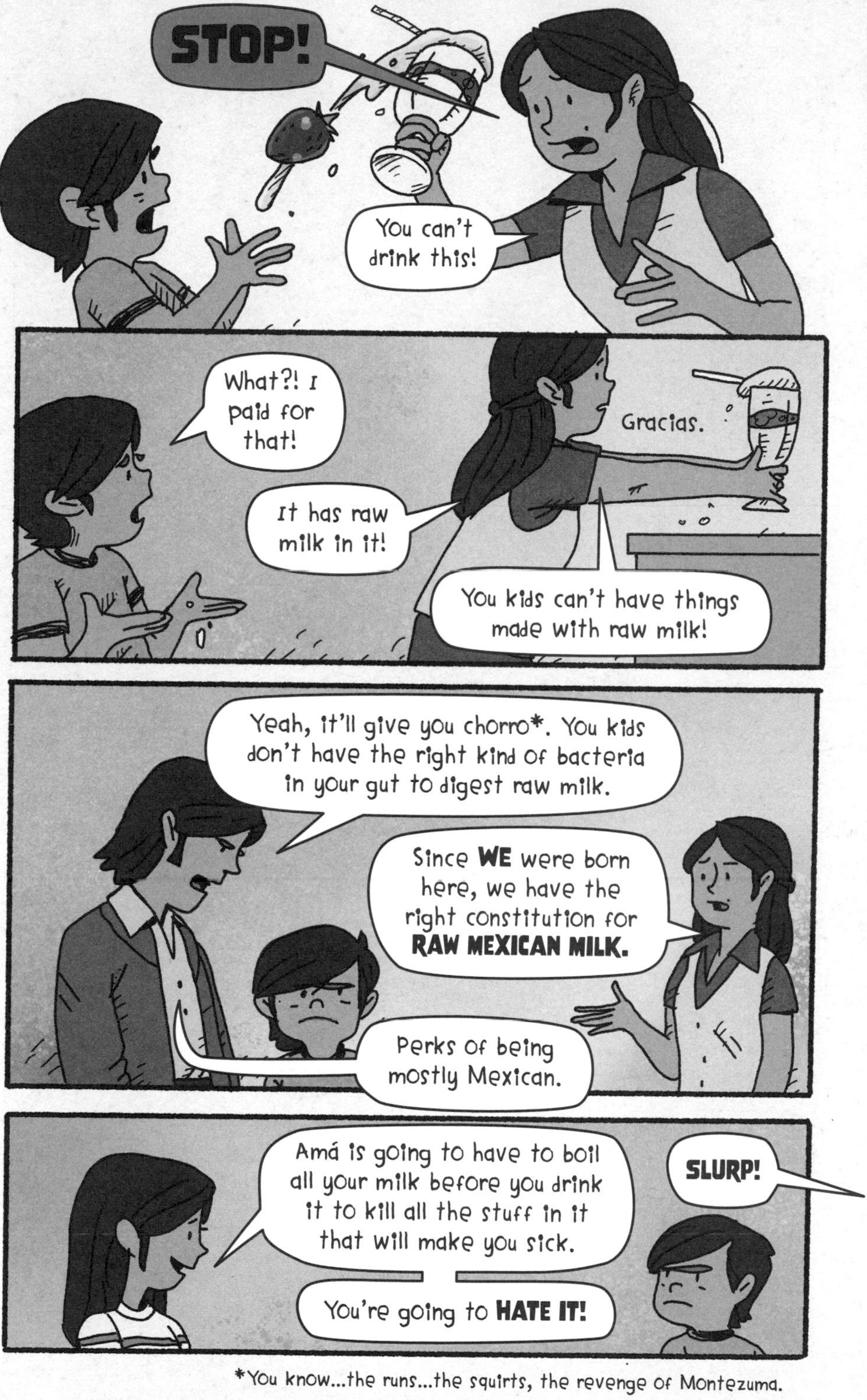
STOP!
You can't drink this!
What?! I paid for that!
It has raw milk in it!
Gracias.
You kids can't have things made with raw milk!
Yeah, it'll give you chorro*. You kids don't have the right kind of bacteria in your gut to digest raw milk.
Since WE were born here, we have the right constitution for RAW MEXICAN MILK.
Perks of being mostly Mexican.
Amá is going to have to boil all your milk before you drink it to kill all the stuff in it that will make you sick.
You're going to HATE IT!
SLURP!

*You know...the runs...the squirts, the revenge of Montezuma.

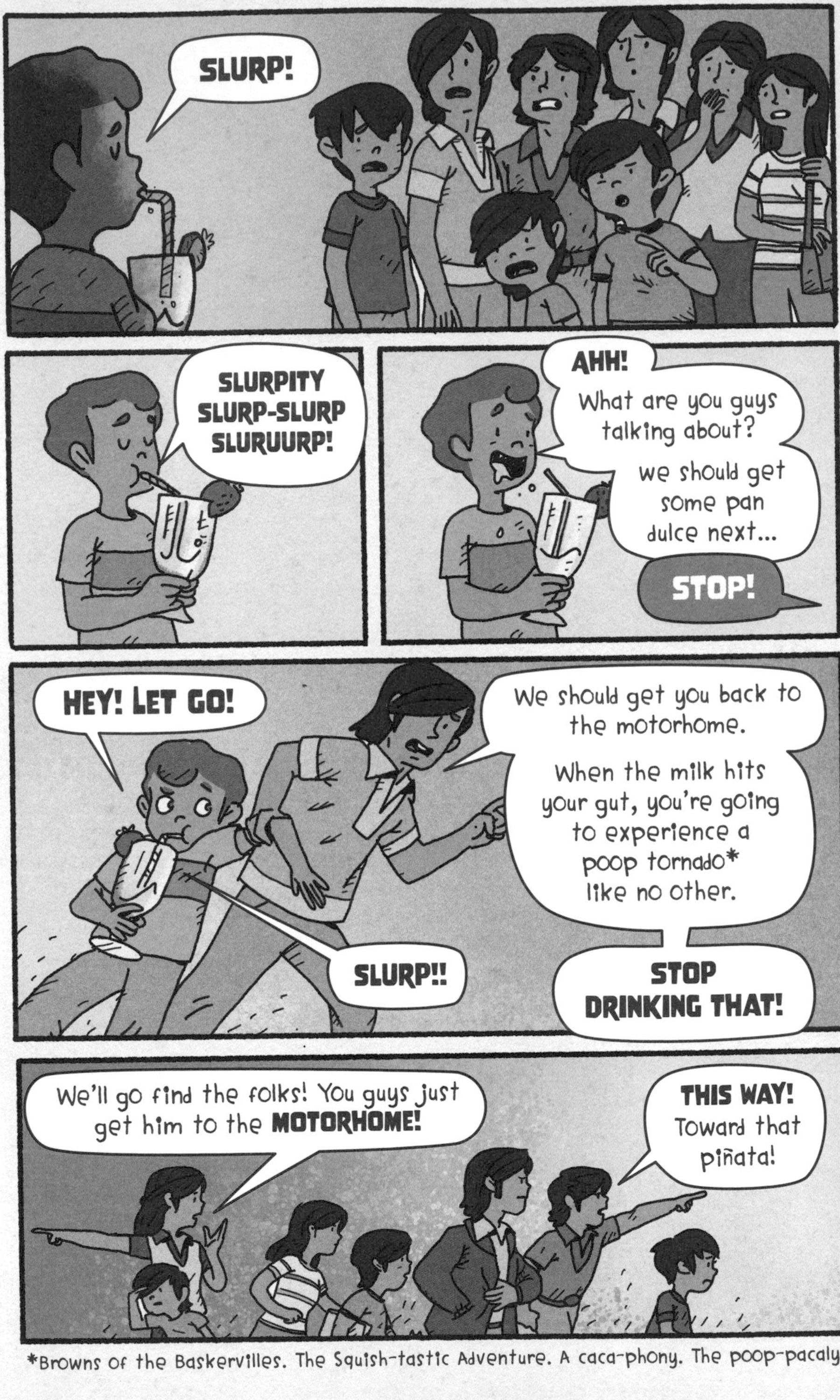
SLURP!
SLURPITY SLURP-SLURP SLURUURP!
AHH!
What are you guys talking about?
we should get some pan dulce next...
STOP!
HEY! LET GO!
We should get you back to the motorhome.
When the milk hits your gut, you're going to experience a poop tornado* like no other.
SLURP!!
STOP DRINKING THAT!
We'll go find the folks! You guys just get him to the **MOTORHOME!**
THIS WAY! Toward that piñata!

*Browns of the Baskervilles. The Squish-tastic Adventure. A caca-phony. The poop-pacalypse. The terrible trots. The Doom Poop-trol. The tourist two-step. The Avocado Avalanche. Liquid assets. Misty, watercolor memories.

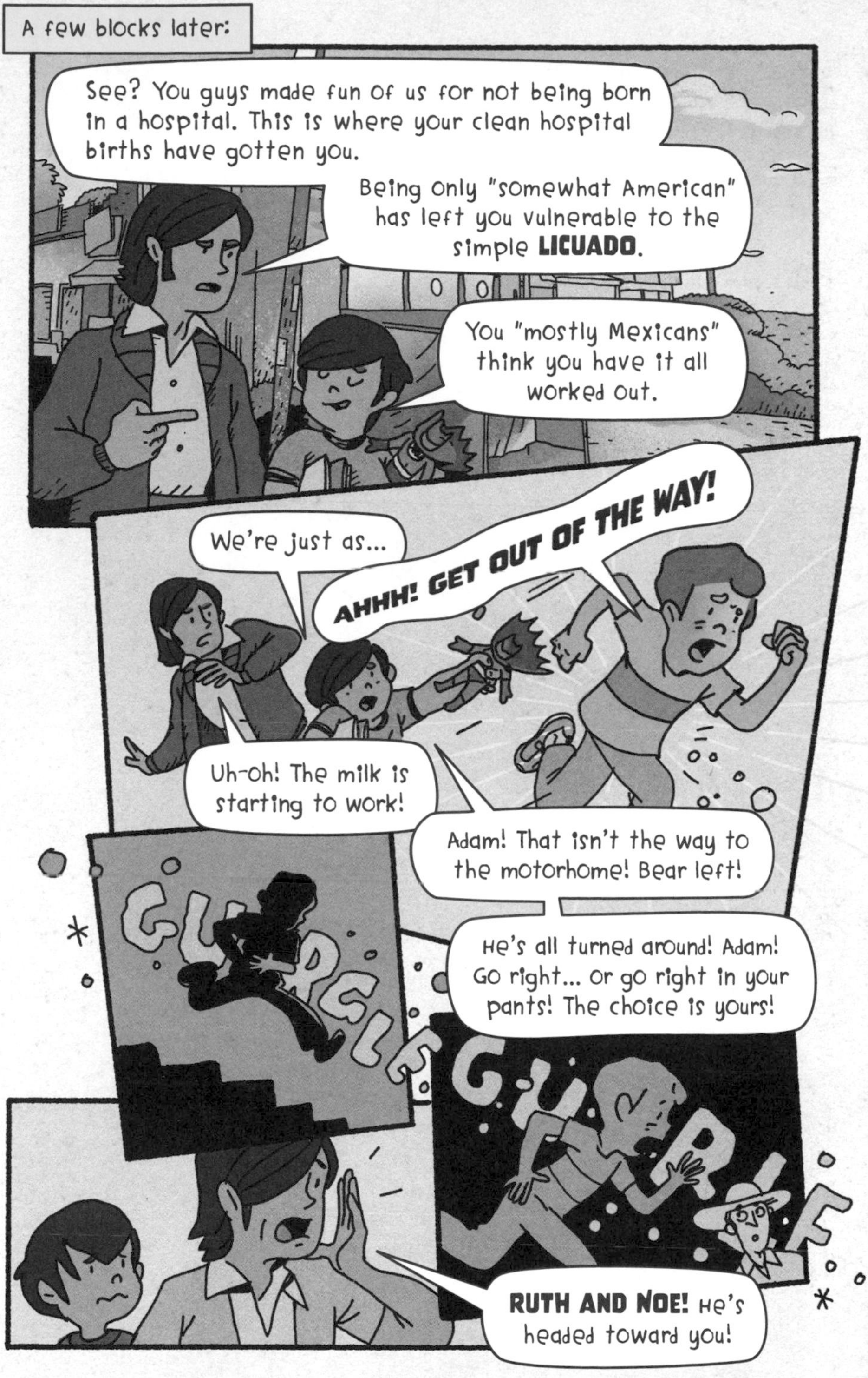
A few blocks later:
See? You guys made fun of us for not being born in a hospital. This is where your clean hospital births have gotten you.
Being only "somewhat American" has left you vulnerable to the simple LICUADO.
You "mostly Mexicans" think you have it all worked out.
We're just as...
AHHH! GET OUT OF THE WAY!
Uh-oh! The milk is starting to work!
Adam! That isn't the way to the motorhome! Bear left!
He's all turned around! Adam! Go right... or go right in your pants! The choice is yours!
GURGLE
GURGLE
RUTH AND NOE! He's headed toward you!

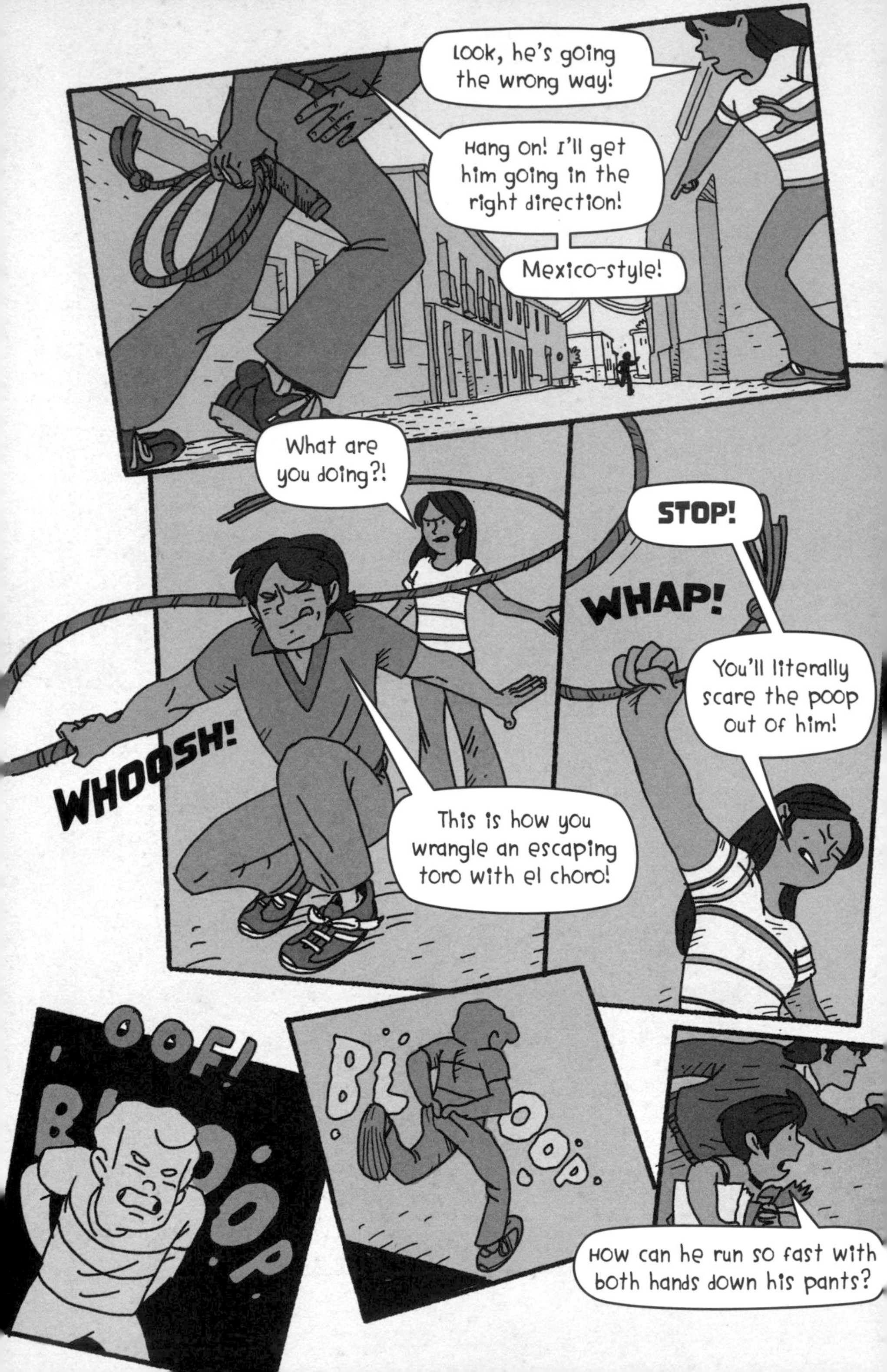
Look, he's going the wrong way!
Hang on! I'll get him going in the right direction!
Mexico-style!
What are you doing?!
WHOOSH!
This is how you wrangle an escaping toro with el choro!
STOP!
WHAP!
You'll literally scare the poop out of him!
OOF!
BLOOP.
How can he run so fast with both hands down his pants?

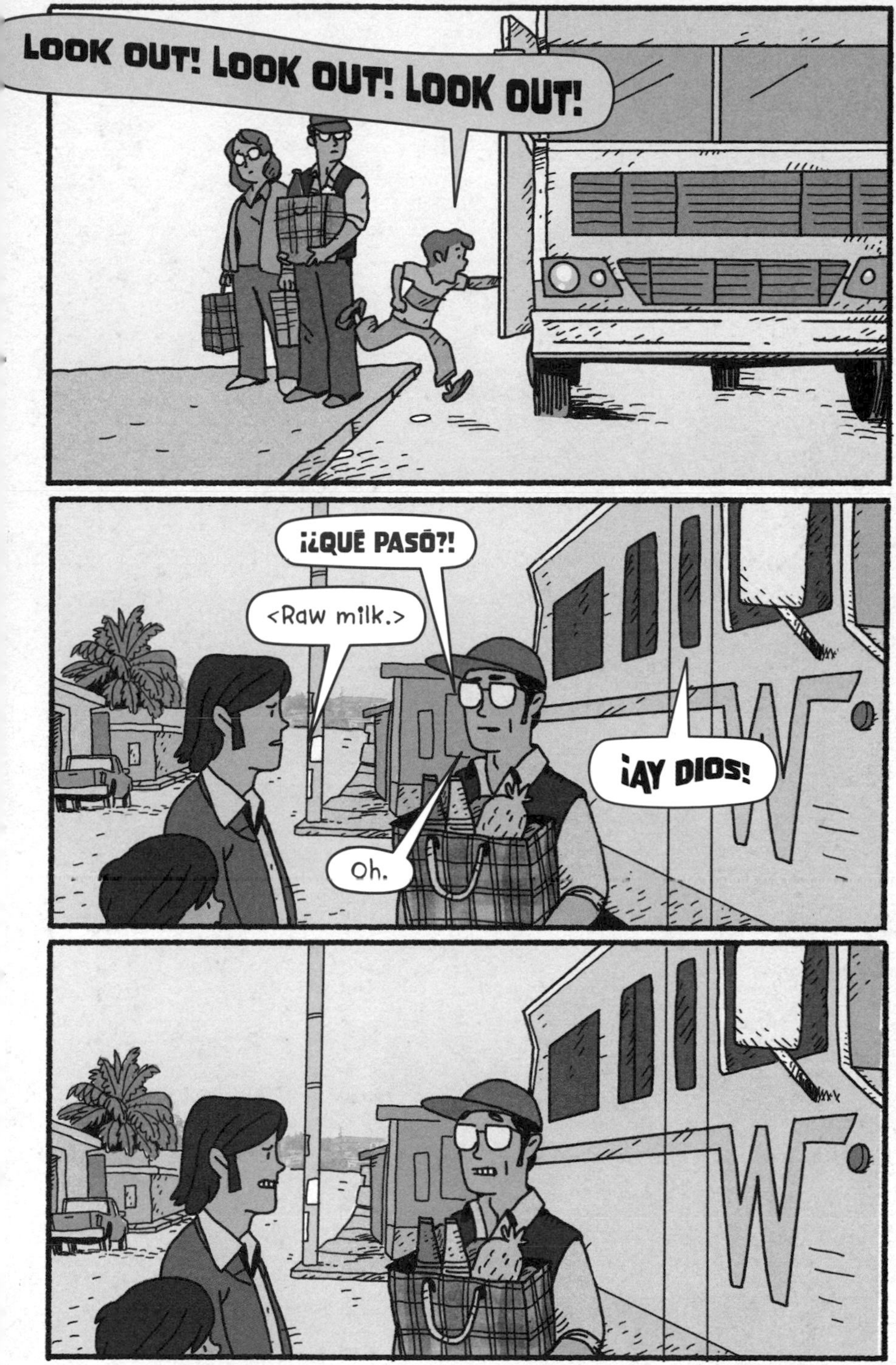
LOOK OUT! LOOK OUT! LOOK OUT!
¡¿QUÉ PASÓ?!
<Raw milk.>
¡AY DIOS!
Oh.

CHAPTER 8
PLAN DE BARRANCAS

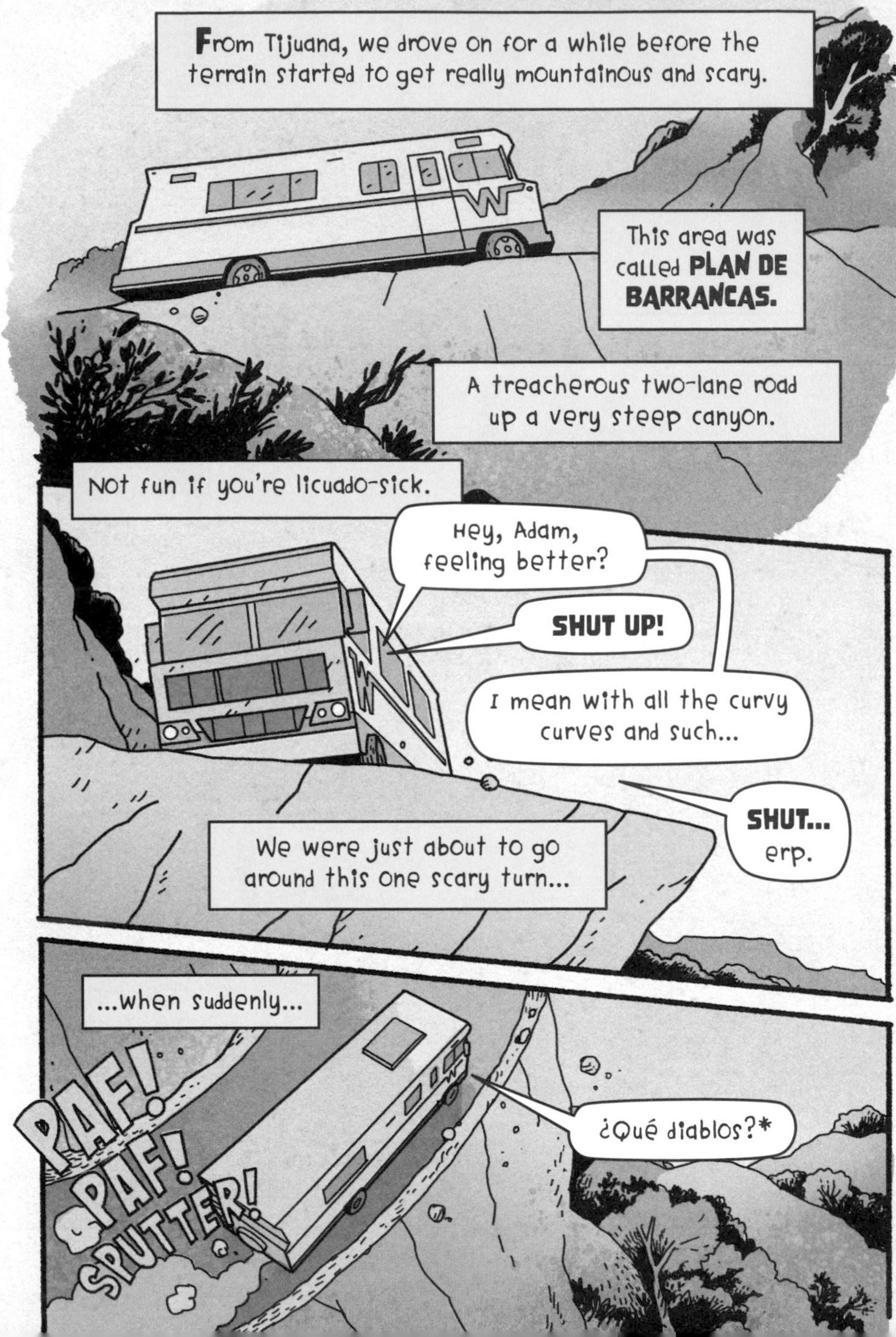
From Tijuana, we drove on for a while before the terrain started to get really mountainous and scary.
This area was called PLAN DE BARRANCAS.
A treacherous two-lane road up a very steep canyon.
Not fun if you're licuado-sick.
Hey, Adam, feeling better?
SHUT UP!
I mean with all the curvy curves and such...
SHUT... erp.
We were just about to go around this one scary turn...
...when suddenly...
PAF! PAF! SPUTTER!
¿Qué diablos?*

*What the devil?

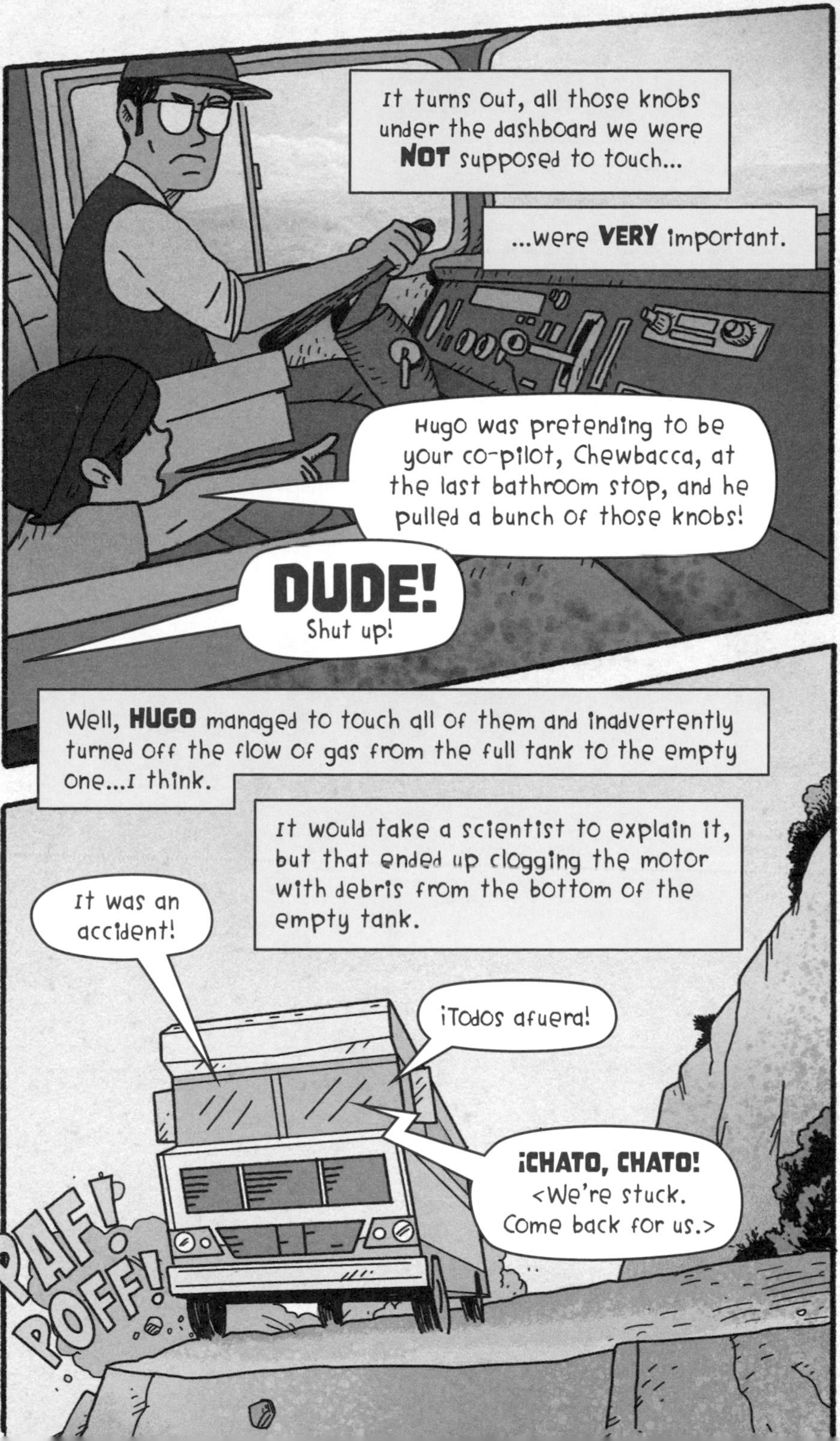

It turns out, all those knobs under the dashboard we were **NOT** supposed to touch...
...were **VERY** important.
Hugo was pretending to be your co-pilot, Chewbacca, at the last bathroom stop, and he pulled a bunch of those knobs!
DUDE! Shut up!
Well, **HUGO** managed to touch all of them and inadvertently turned off the flow of gas from the full tank to the empty one...I think.
It would take a scientist to explain it, but that ended up clogging the motor with debris from the bottom of the empty tank.
It was an accident!
¡Todos afuera!
¡CHATO, CHATO! <We're stuck. Come back for us.>
PAF! POFF!

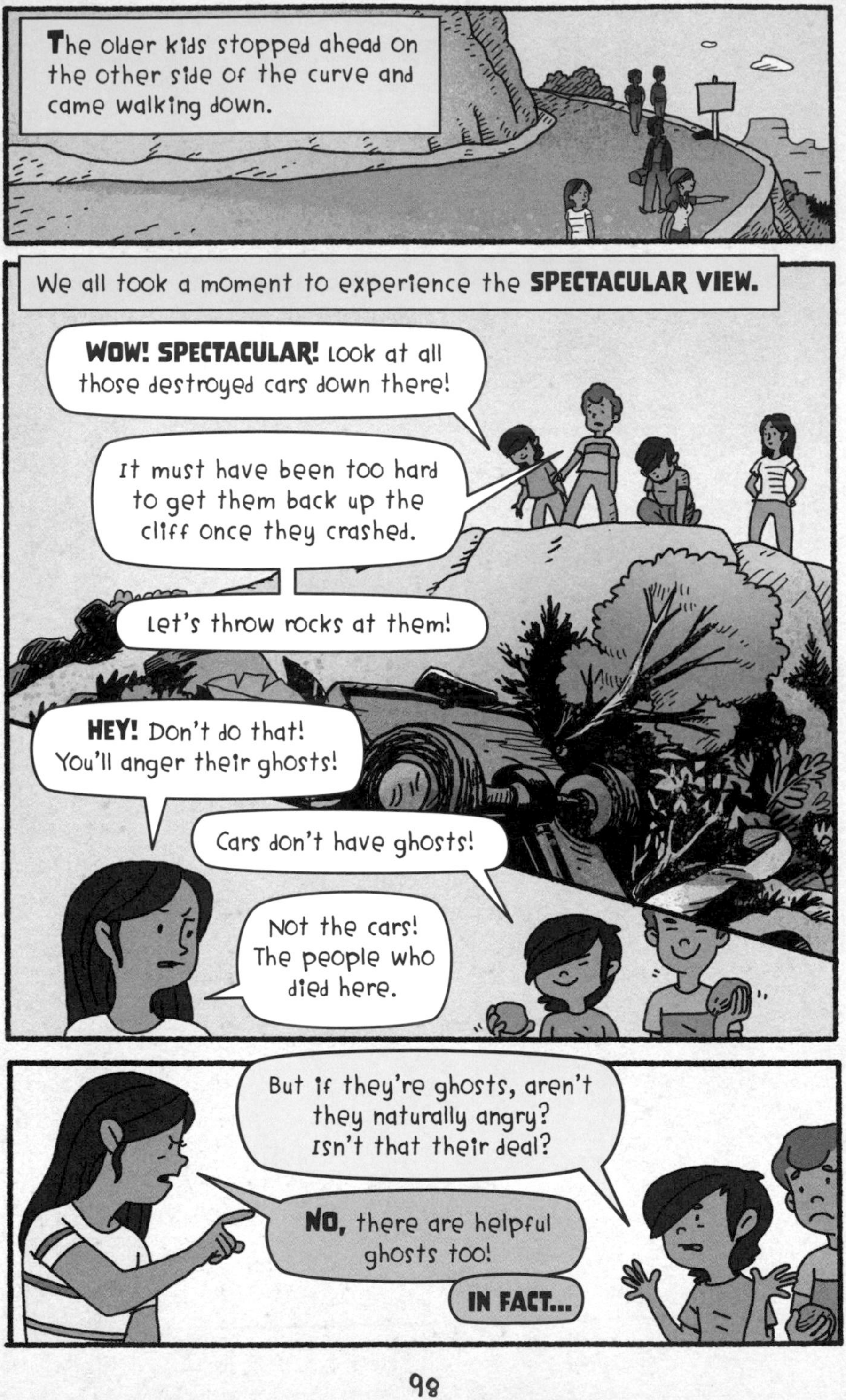

The older kids stopped ahead on the other side of the curve and came walking down.
We all took a moment to experience the SPECTACULAR VIEW.
WOW! SPECTACULAR! Look at all those destroyed cars down there!
It must have been too hard to get them back up the cliff once they crashed.
Let's throw rocks at them!
HEY! Don't do that! You'll anger their ghosts!
Cars don't have ghosts!
Not the cars! The people who died here.
But if they're ghosts, aren't they naturally angry? Isn't that their deal?
NO, there are helpful ghosts too!
IN FACT...

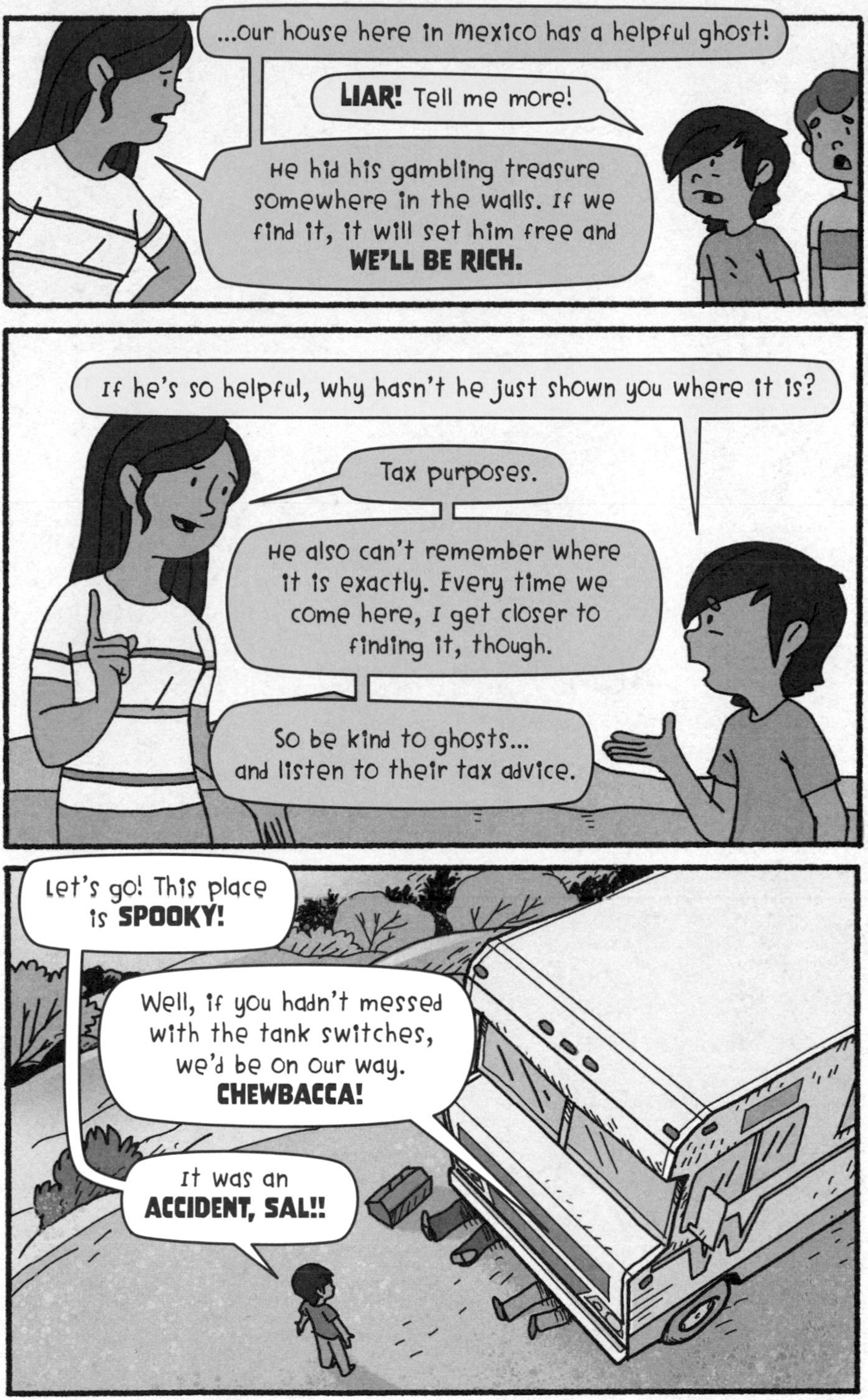
...our house here in mexico has a helpful ghost!
LIAR! Tell me more!
He hid his gambling treasure somewhere in the walls. If we find it, it will set him free and WE'LL BE RICH.
If he's so helpful, why hasn't he just shown you where it is?
Tax purposes.
He also can't remember where it is exactly. Every time we come here, I get closer to finding it, though.
So be kind to ghosts... and listen to their tax advice.
Let's go! This place is SPOOKY!
Well, if you hadn't messed with the tank switches, we'd be on our way. CHEWBACCA!
It was an ACCIDENT, SAL!!

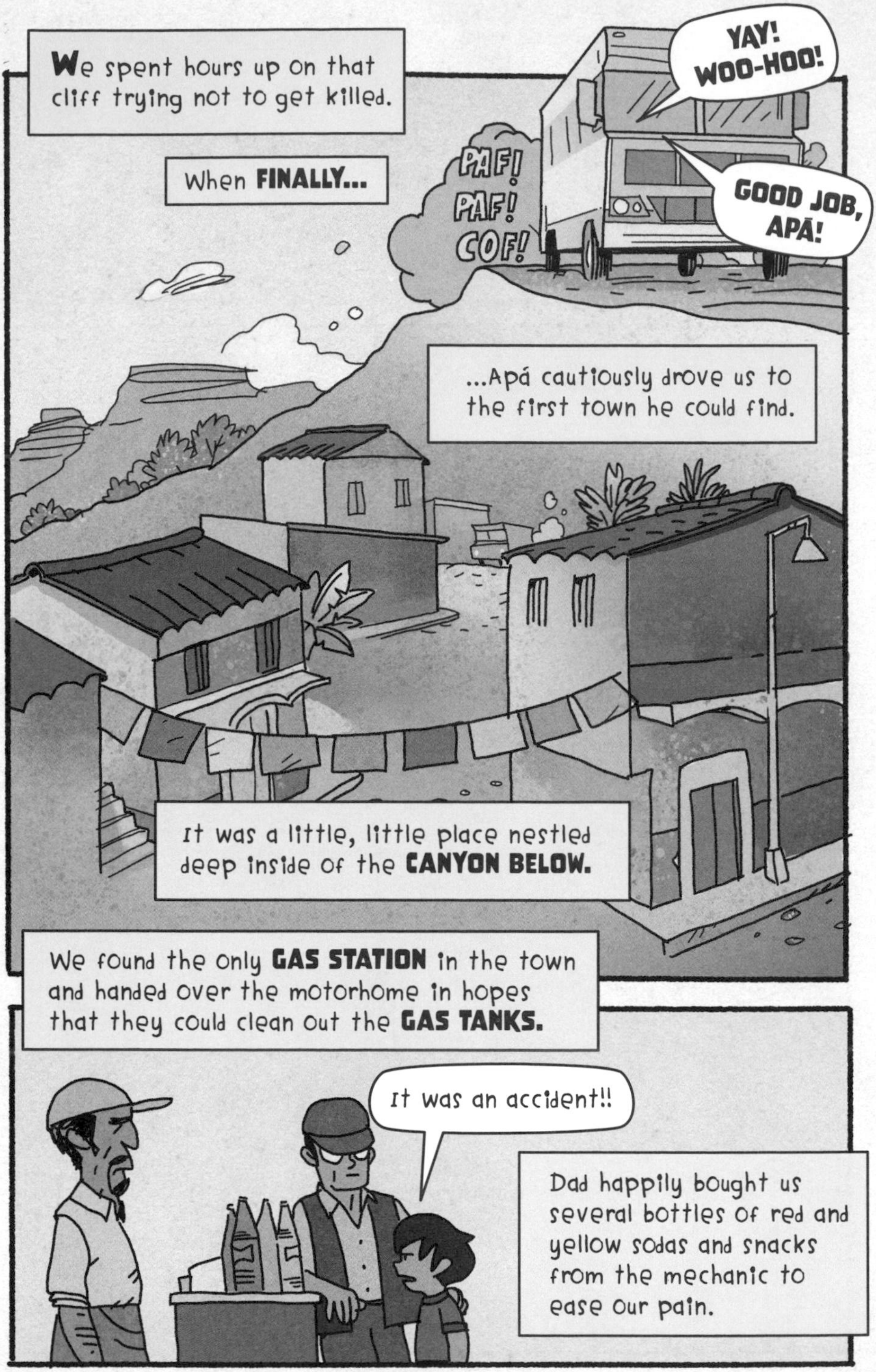

We spent hours up on that cliff trying not to get killed.
YAY! WOO-HOO!
When FINALLY...
PAF! PAF! COF!
GOOD JOB, APÁ!
...Apá cautiously drove us to the first town he could find.
It was a little, little place nestled deep inside of the CANYON BELOW.
We found the only GAS STATION in the town and handed over the motorhome in hopes that they could clean out the GAS TANKS.
It was an accident!!
Dad happily bought us several bottles of red and yellow sodas and snacks from the mechanic to ease our pain.

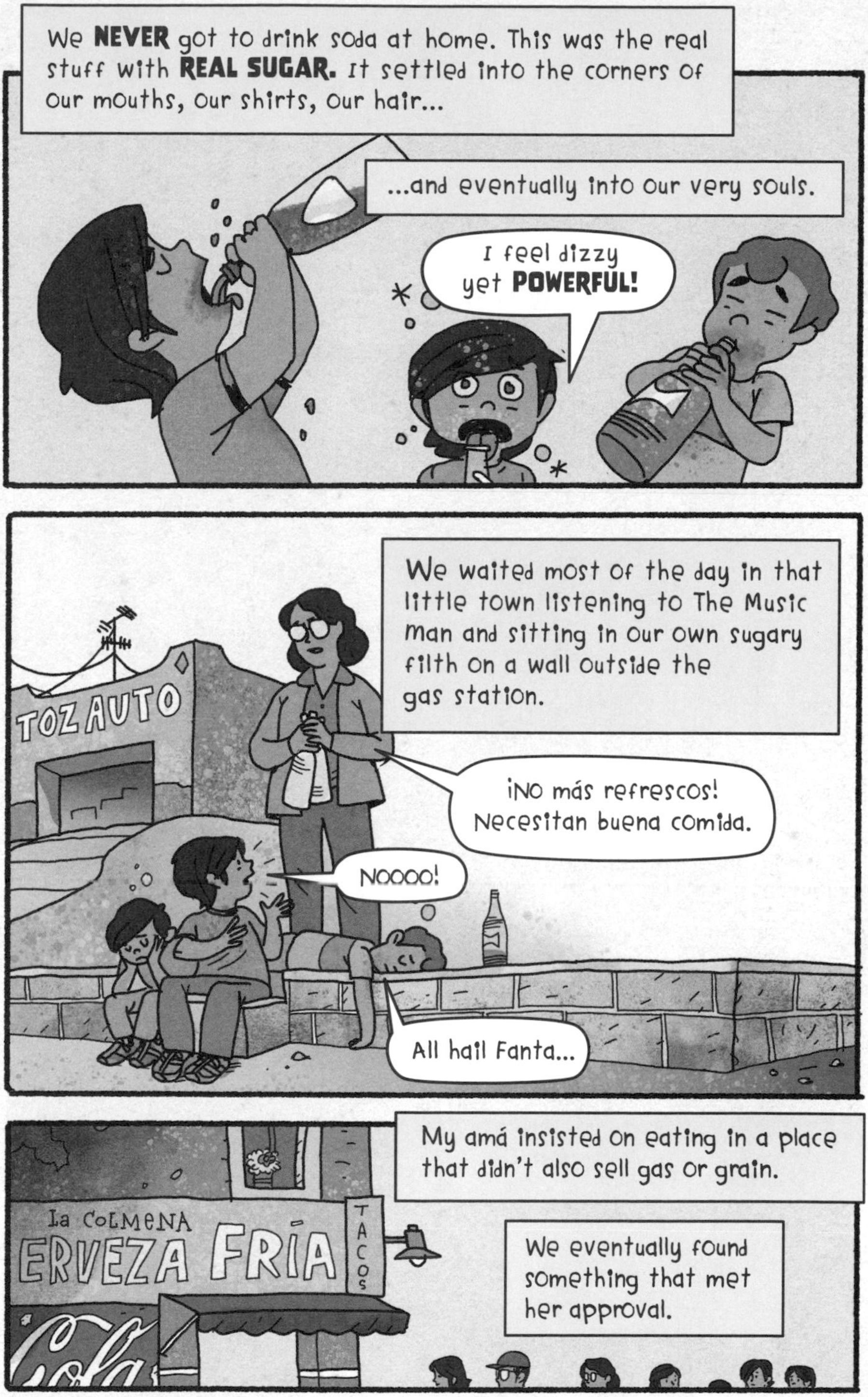
We **NEVER** got to drink soda at home. This was the real stuff with **REAL SUGAR.** It settled into the corners of our mouths, our shirts, our hair...
...and eventually into our very souls.
I feel dizzy yet **POWERFUL!**
We waited most of the day in that little town listening to The Music man and sitting in our own sugary filth on a wall outside the gas station.
TOZ AUTO
¡No más refrescos! Necesitan buena comida.
NOOOO!
All hail Fanta...
My amá insisted on eating in a place that didn't also sell gas or grain.
We eventually found something that met her approval.
La COLMENA
ERVEZA FRIA
TACOS
Cola

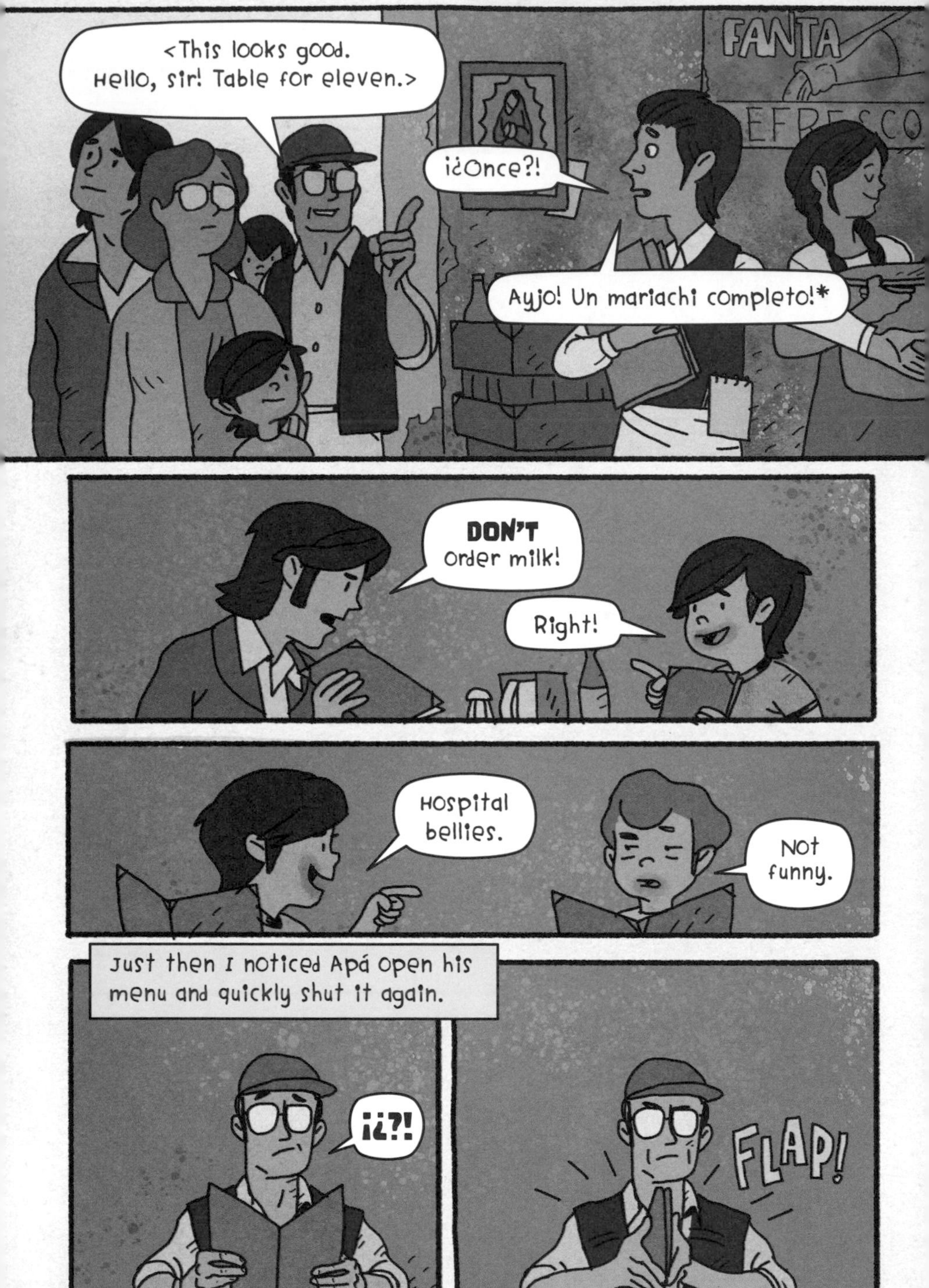
<This looks good. Hello, sir! Table for eleven.>
¡¿Once?!
Ayjo! Un mariachi completo!*
FANTA
DON'T order milk!
Right!
Hospital bellies.
Not funny.
Just then I noticed Apá open his menu and quickly shut it again.
¡¿?!
FLAP!

*Eleven? That's practically a complete mariachi band!

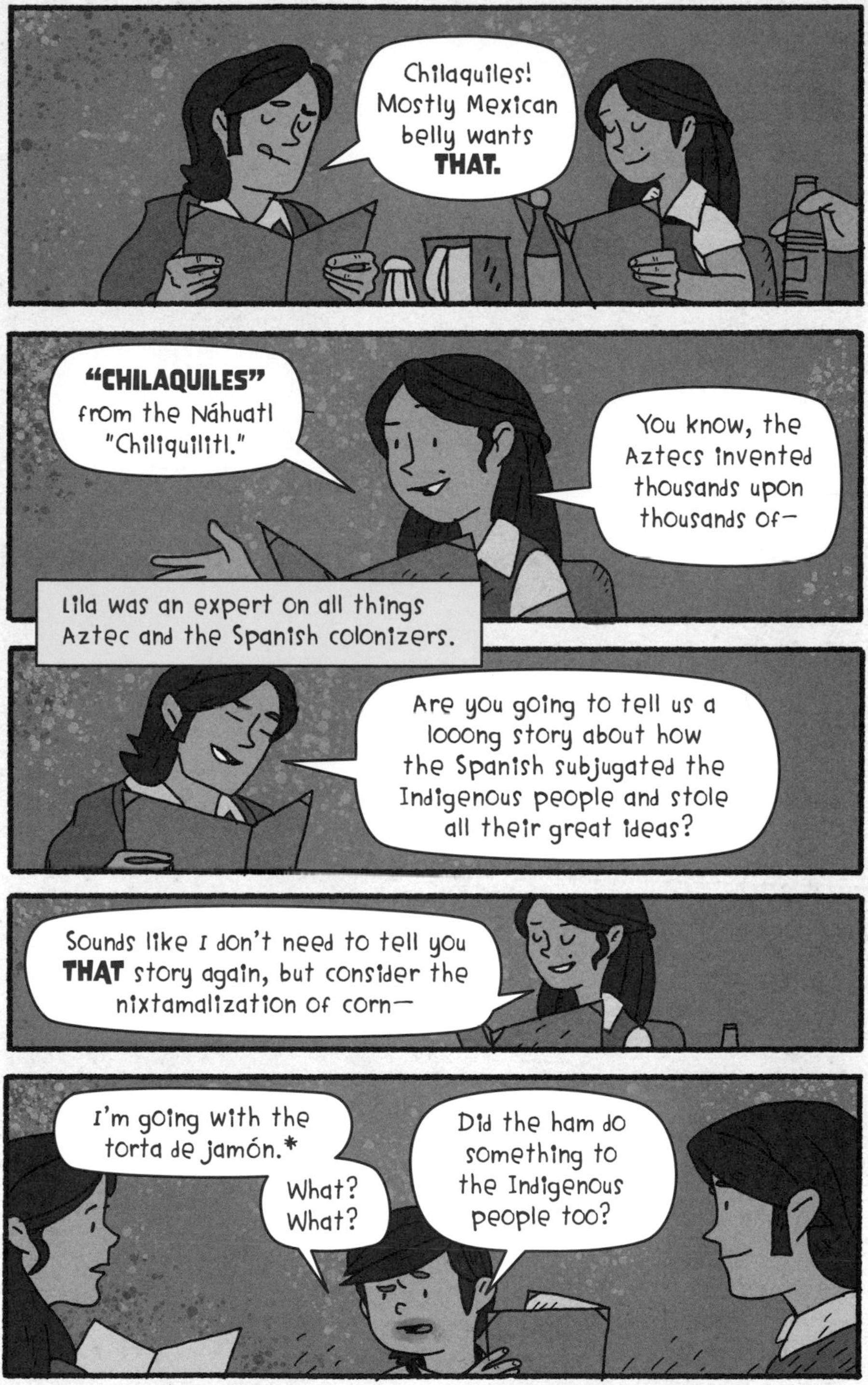
Chilaquiles! Mostly Mexican belly wants **THAT.**
"CHILAQUILES" from the Náhuatl "Chiliquilitl."
You know, the Aztecs invented thousands upon thousands of—
Lila was an expert on all things Aztec and the Spanish colonizers.
Are you going to tell us a looong story about how the Spanish subjugated the Indigenous people and stole all their great ideas?
Sounds like I don't need to tell you **THAT** story again, but consider the nixtamalization of corn—
I'm going with the torta de jamón.*
What? What?
Did the ham do something to the Indigenous people too?

*Ham sandwich.

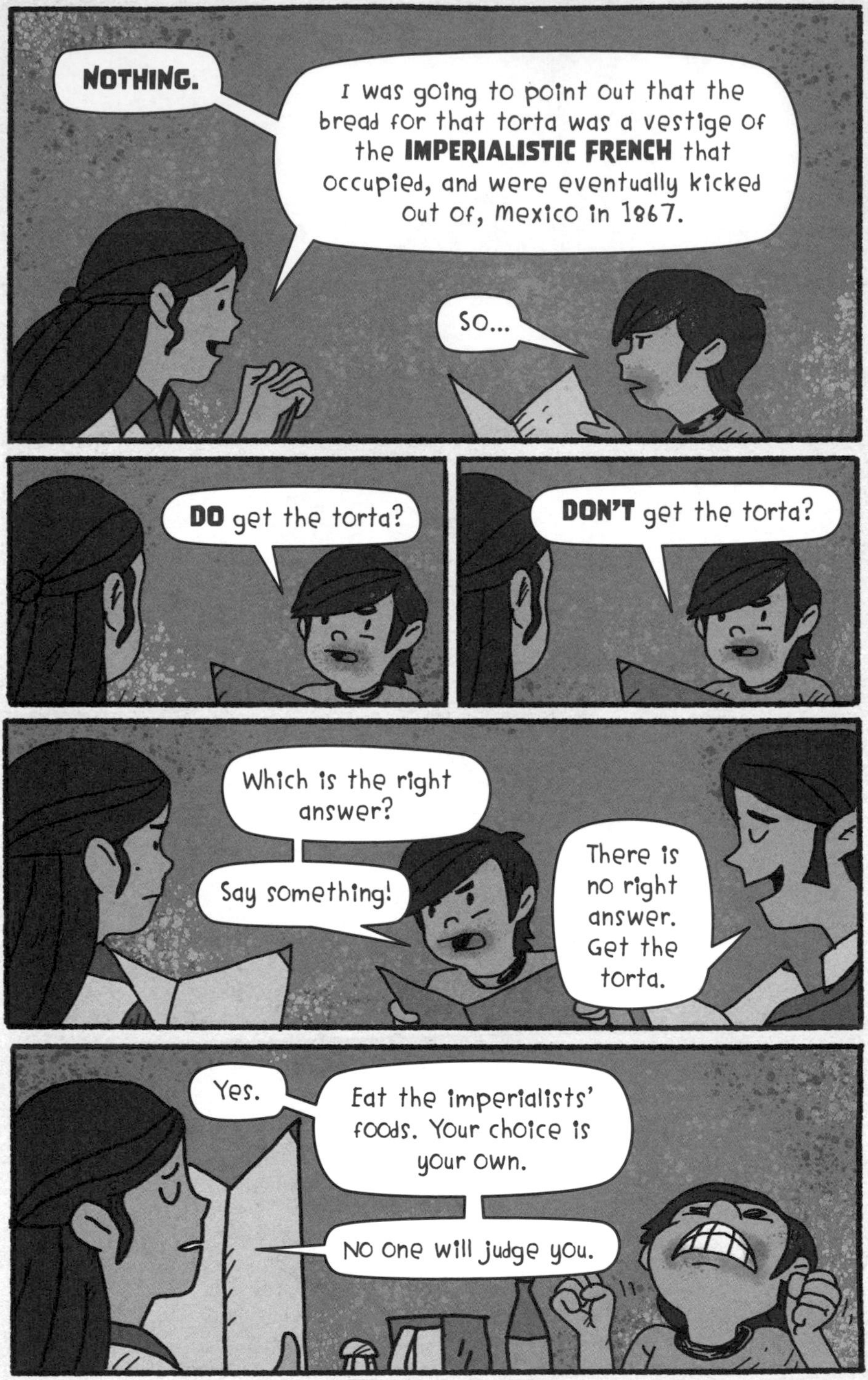
NOTHING.
I was going to point out that the bread for that torta was a vestige of the IMPERIALISTIC FRENCH that occupied, and were eventually kicked out of, mexico in 1867.
So...
DO get the torta?
DON'T get the torta?
Which is the right answer?
Say something!
There is no right answer. Get the torta.
Yes.
Eat the imperialists' foods. Your choice is your own.
No one will judge you.

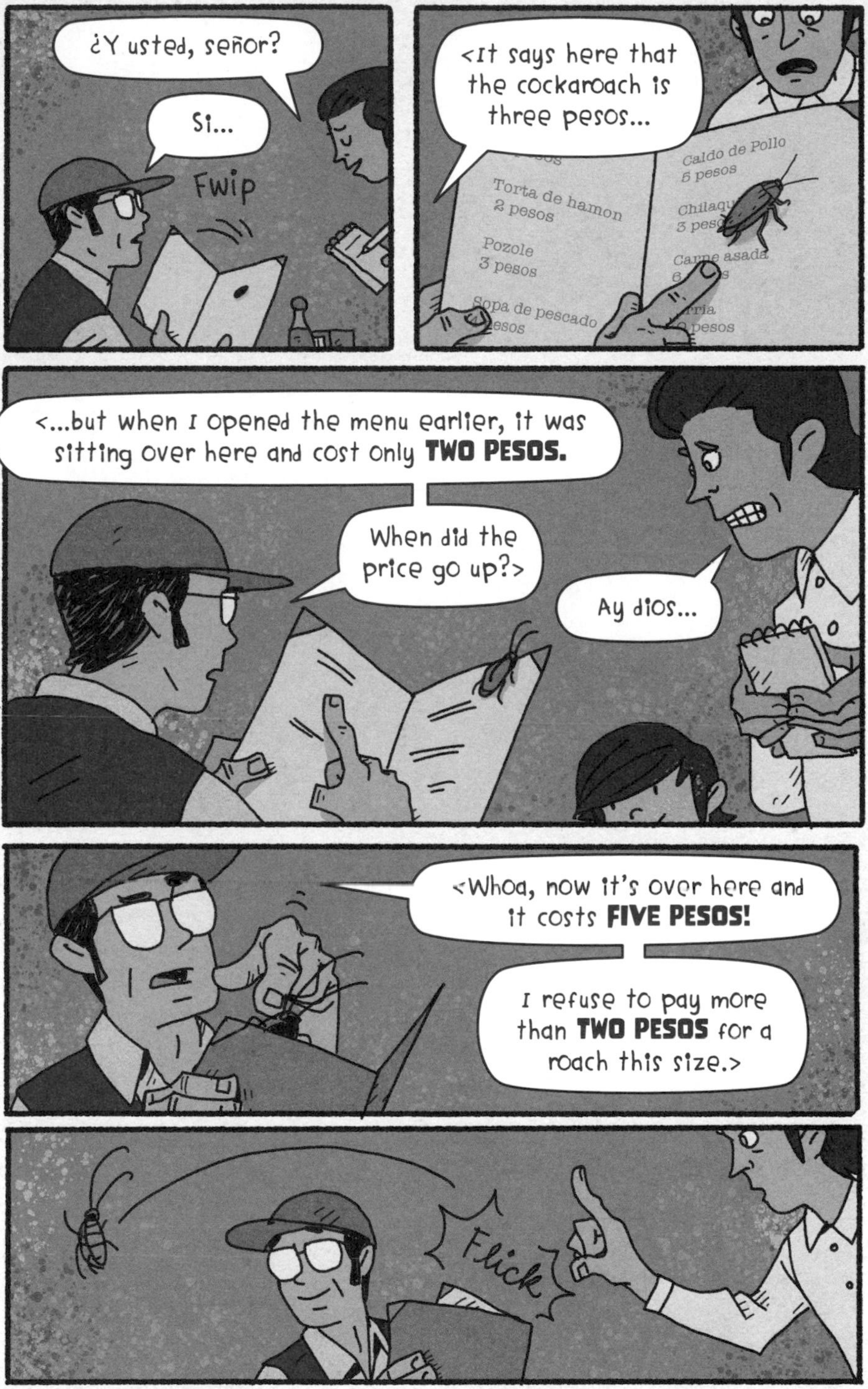
¿Y usted, señor?
Si...
Fwip
<It says here that the cockaroach is three pesos...
Torta de hamon
2 pesos
Pozole
3 pesos
Caldo de Pollo
5 pesos
Sopa de pescado
<...but when I opened the menu earlier, it was sitting over here and cost only **TWO PESOS.**
When did the price go up?>
Ay dios...
<Whoa, now it's over here and it costs **FIVE PESOS!**
I refuse to pay more than **TWO PESOS** for a roach this size.>
Flick

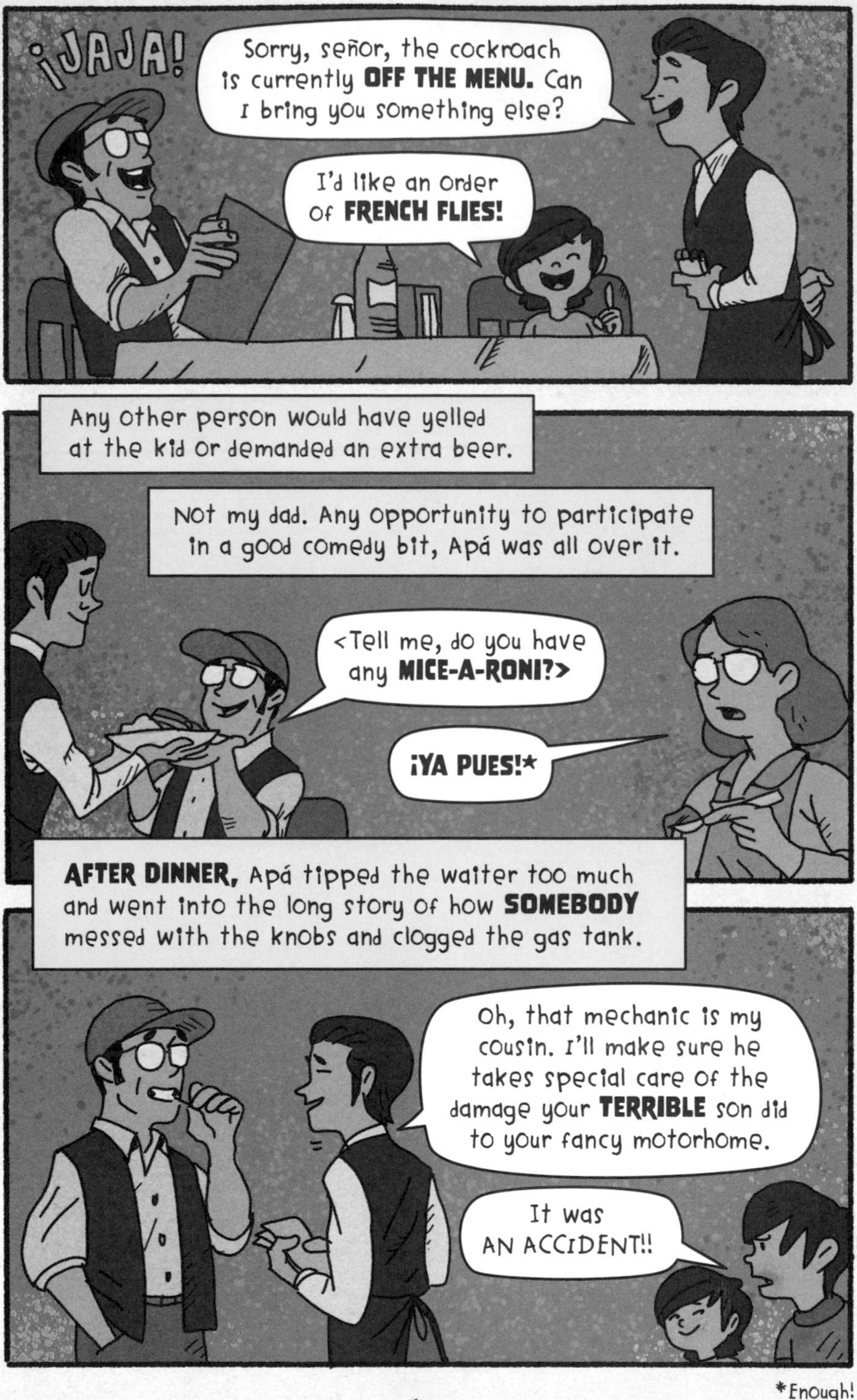
¡JAJA!
Sorry, señor, the cockroach is currently OFF THE MENU. Can I bring you something else?
I'd like an order of FRENCH FLIES!
Any other person would have yelled at the kid or demanded an extra beer.
Not my dad. Any opportunity to participate in a good comedy bit, Apá was all over it.
<Tell me, do you have any MICE-A-RONI?>
¡YA PUES!*
AFTER DINNER, Apá tipped the waiter too much and went into the long story of how SOMEBODY messed with the knobs and clogged the gas tank.
Oh, that mechanic is my cousin. I'll make sure he takes special care of the damage your TERRIBLE son did to your fancy motorhome.
It was AN ACCIDENT!!

*Enough!

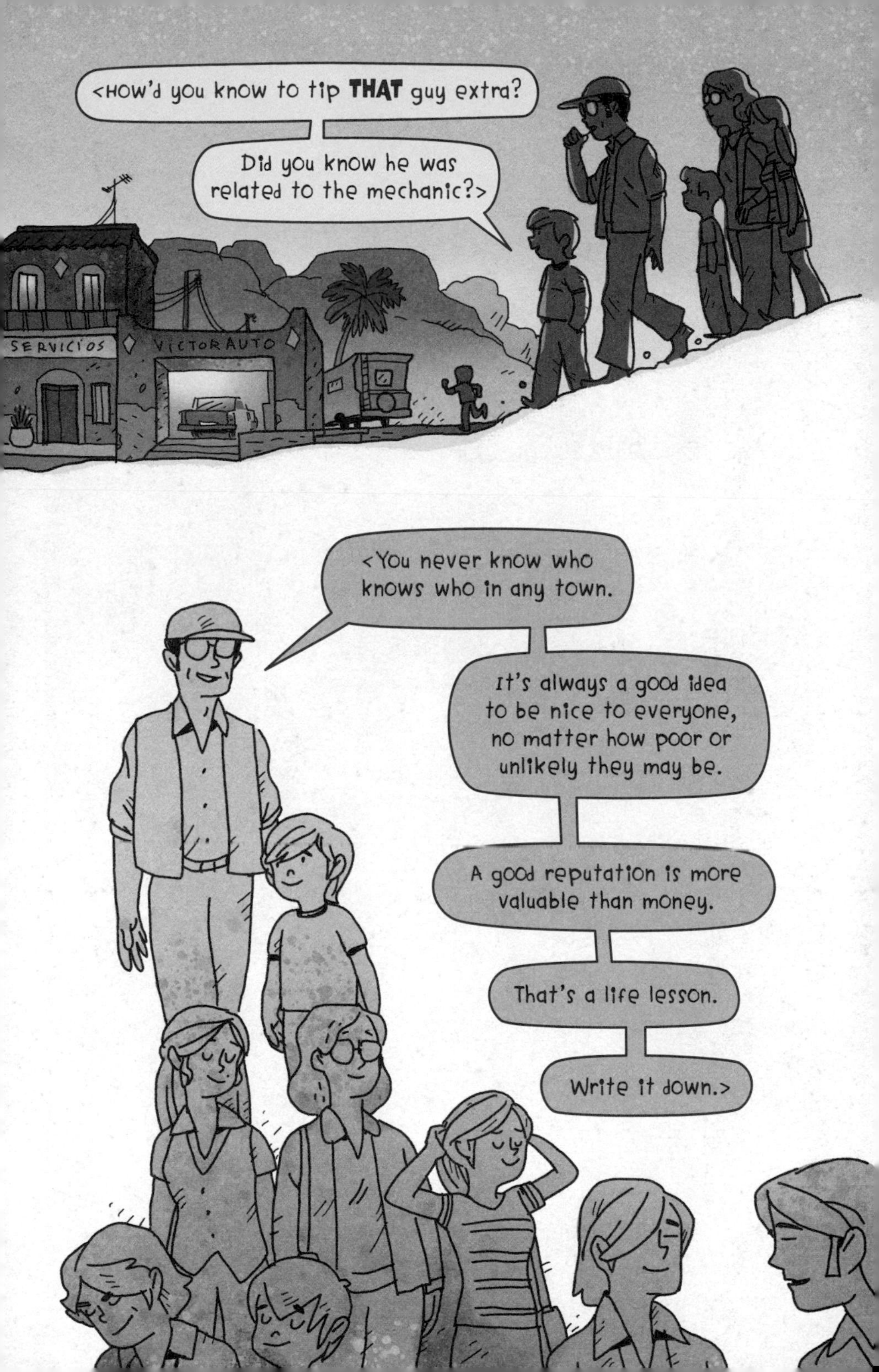
<HOW'd you know to tip **THAT** guy extra?
Did you know he was related to the mechanic?>
SERVICIOS
VICTOR AUTO
<You never know who knows who in any town.
It's always a good idea to be nice to everyone, no matter how poor or unlikely they may be.
A good reputation is more valuable than money.
That's a life lesson.
Write it down.>

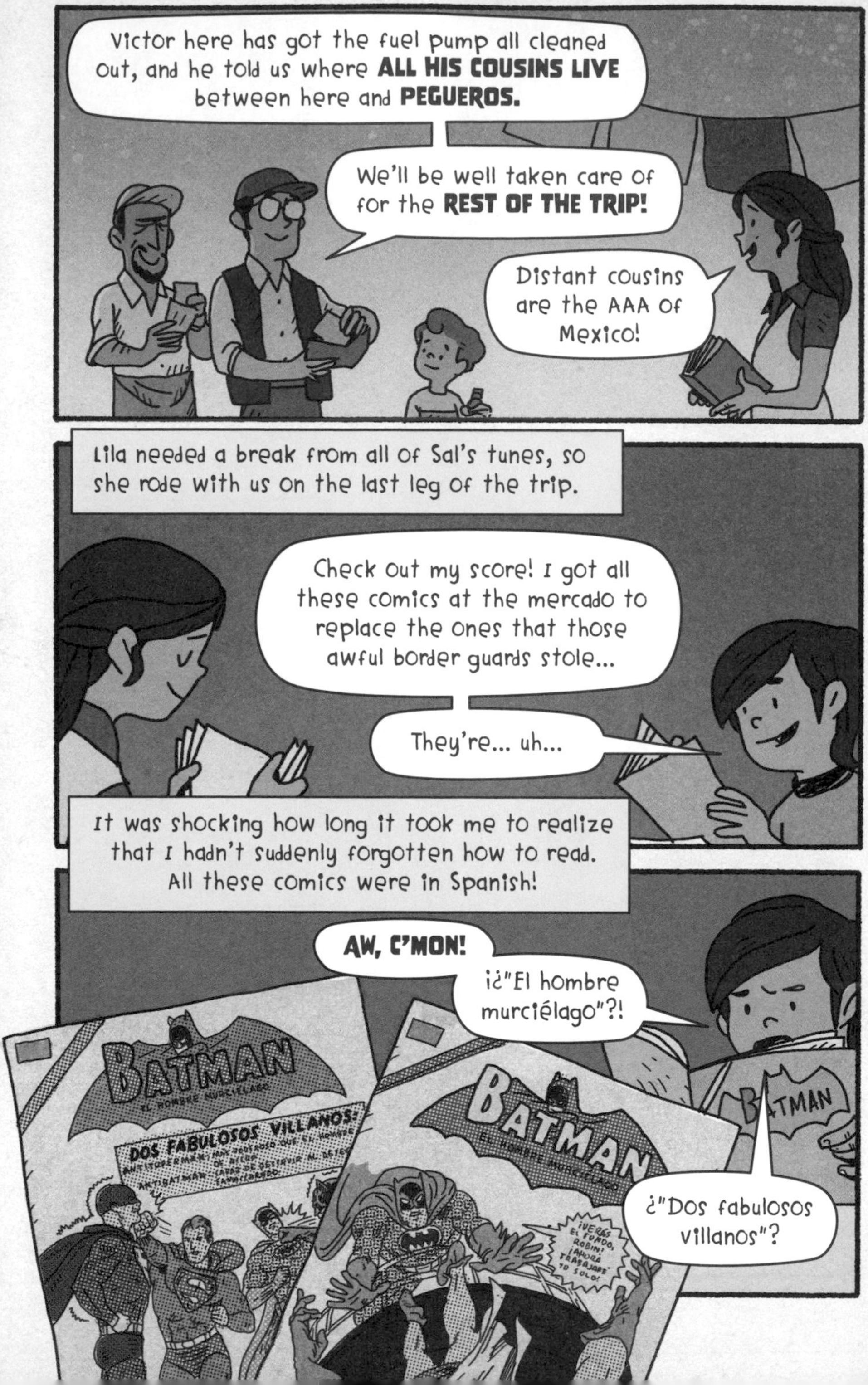
Victor here has got the fuel pump all cleaned out, and he told us where ALL HIS COUSINS LIVE between here and PEGUEROS.
We'll be well taken care of for the REST OF THE TRIP!
Distant cousins are the AAA of Mexico!
Lila needed a break from all of Sal's tunes, so she rode with us on the last leg of the trip.
Check out my score! I got all these comics at the mercado to replace the ones that those awful border guards stole...
They're... uh...
It was shocking how long it took me to realize that I hadn't suddenly forgotten how to read. All these comics were in Spanish!
AW, C'MON!
¡¿"El hombre murciélago"?!
BATMAN
DOS FABULOSOS VILLANOS:
BATMAN
¿"Dos fabulosos villanos"?

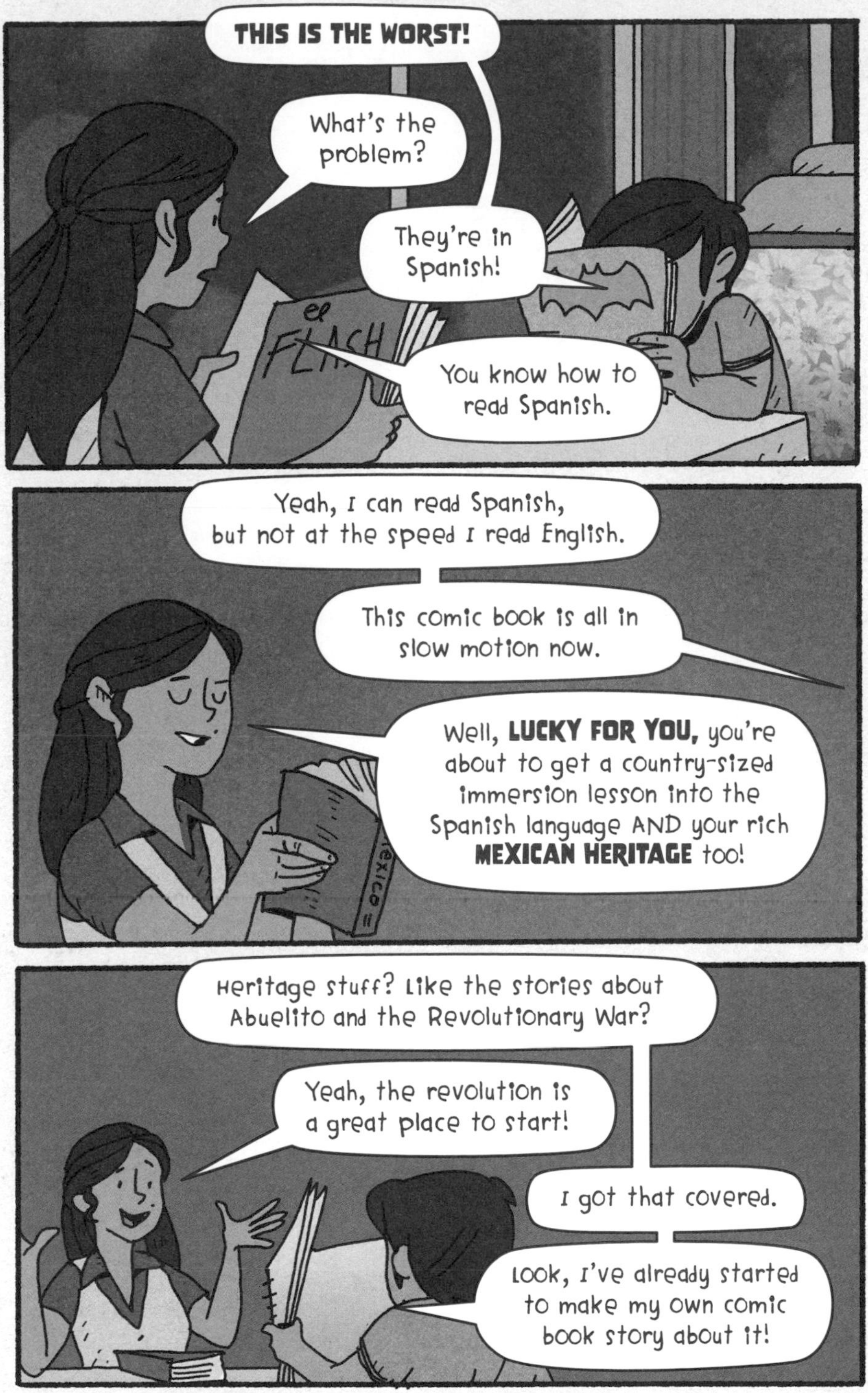
THIS IS THE WORST!
What's the problem?
They're in Spanish!
el FLASH
You know how to read Spanish.
Yeah, I can read Spanish, but not at the speed I read English.
This comic book is all in slow motion now.
Well, LUCKY FOR YOU, you're about to get a country-sized immersion lesson into the Spanish language AND your rich MEXICAN HERITAGE too!
Heritage stuff? Like the stories about Abuelito and the Revolutionary War?
Yeah, the revolution is a great place to start!
I got that covered.
Look, I've already started to make my own comic book story about it!

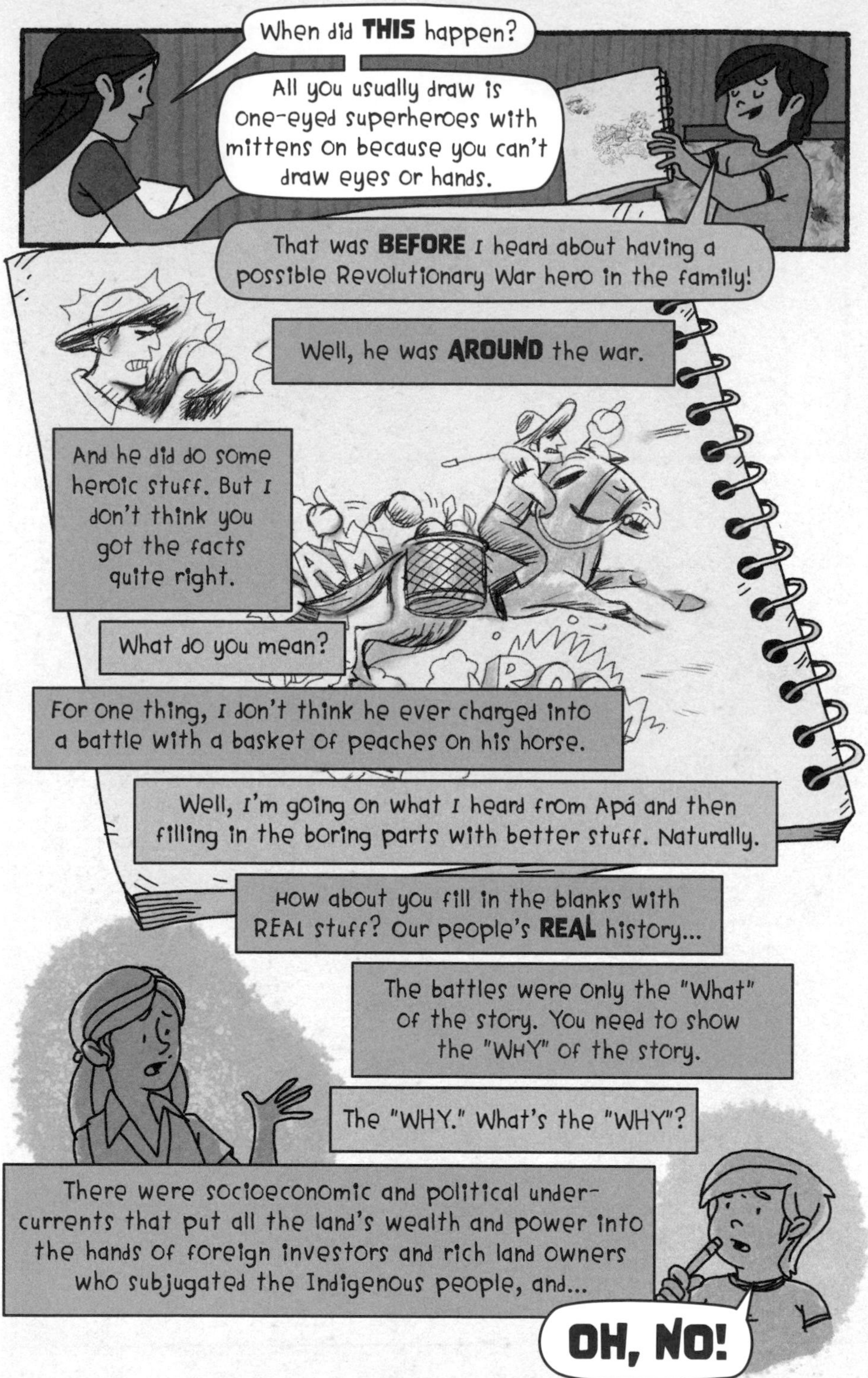
When did THIS happen?
All you usually draw is one-eyed superheroes with mittens on because you can't draw eyes or hands.
That was BEFORE I heard about having a possible Revolutionary War hero in the family!
Well, he was AROUND the war.
And he did do some heroic stuff. But I don't think you got the facts quite right.
What do you mean?
For one thing, I don't think he ever charged into a battle with a basket of peaches on his horse.
Well, I'm going on what I heard from Apá and then filling in the boring parts with better stuff. Naturally.
How about you fill in the blanks with REAL stuff? Our people's REAL history...
The battles were only the "What" of the story. You need to show the "WHY" of the story.
The "WHY." What's the "WHY"?
There were socioeconomic and political undercurrents that put all the land's wealth and power into the hands of foreign investors and rich land owners who subjugated the Indigenous people, and...
OH, NO!

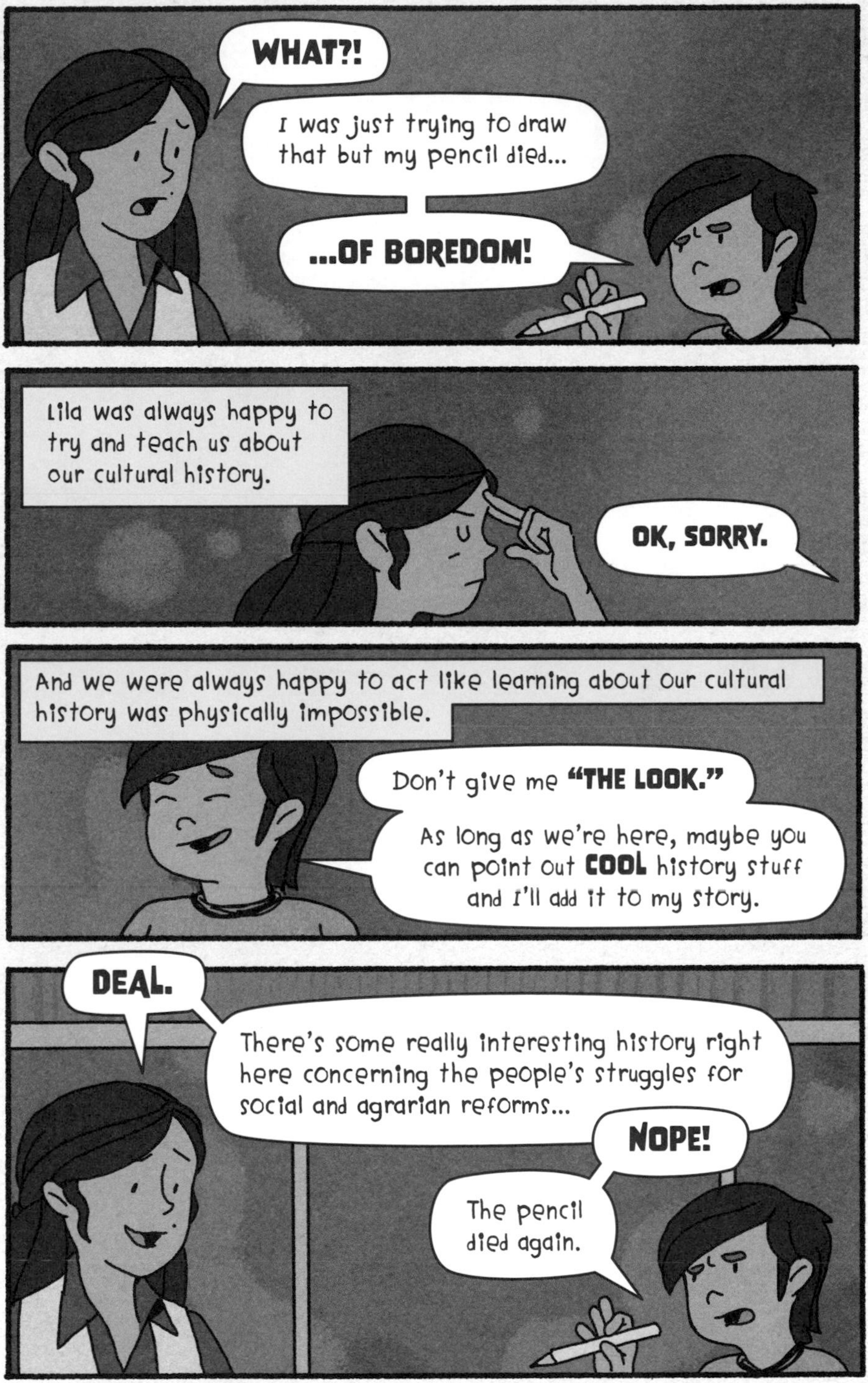
WHAT?!
I was just trying to draw that but my pencil died...
...OF BOREDOM!
Lila was always happy to try and teach us about our cultural history.
OK, SORRY.
And we were always happy to act like learning about our cultural history was physically impossible.
Don't give me "THE LOOK."
As long as we're here, maybe you can point out COOL history stuff and I'll add it to my story.
DEAL.
There's some really interesting history right here concerning the people's struggles for social and agrarian reforms...
NOPE!
The pencil died again.

CHAPTER 9
A HISTORICAL HAIRCUT

After hundreds of long miles and so many sugary sodas, we finally arrived at my parents' hometown, **PEGUEROS.**

It was tiny in comparison to the nearby town of Tepatitlán, but its church was as grand as you'd find in any big city.

Our house was right on the main street across from the big church.

My parents used to run a hotel and restaurant out of that house back when they were first married.

They had an ice cream shop in there too!

But now it was just a house they rented out when we weren't there.

Sadly, the ice cream shop was long gone.

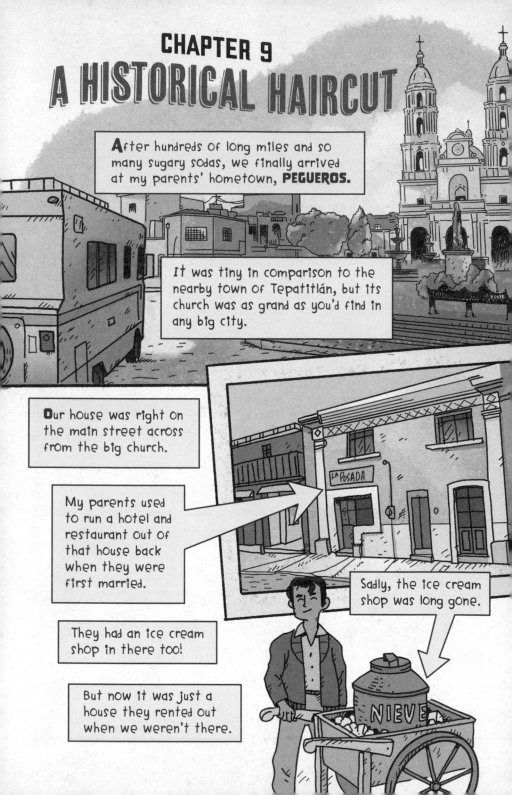

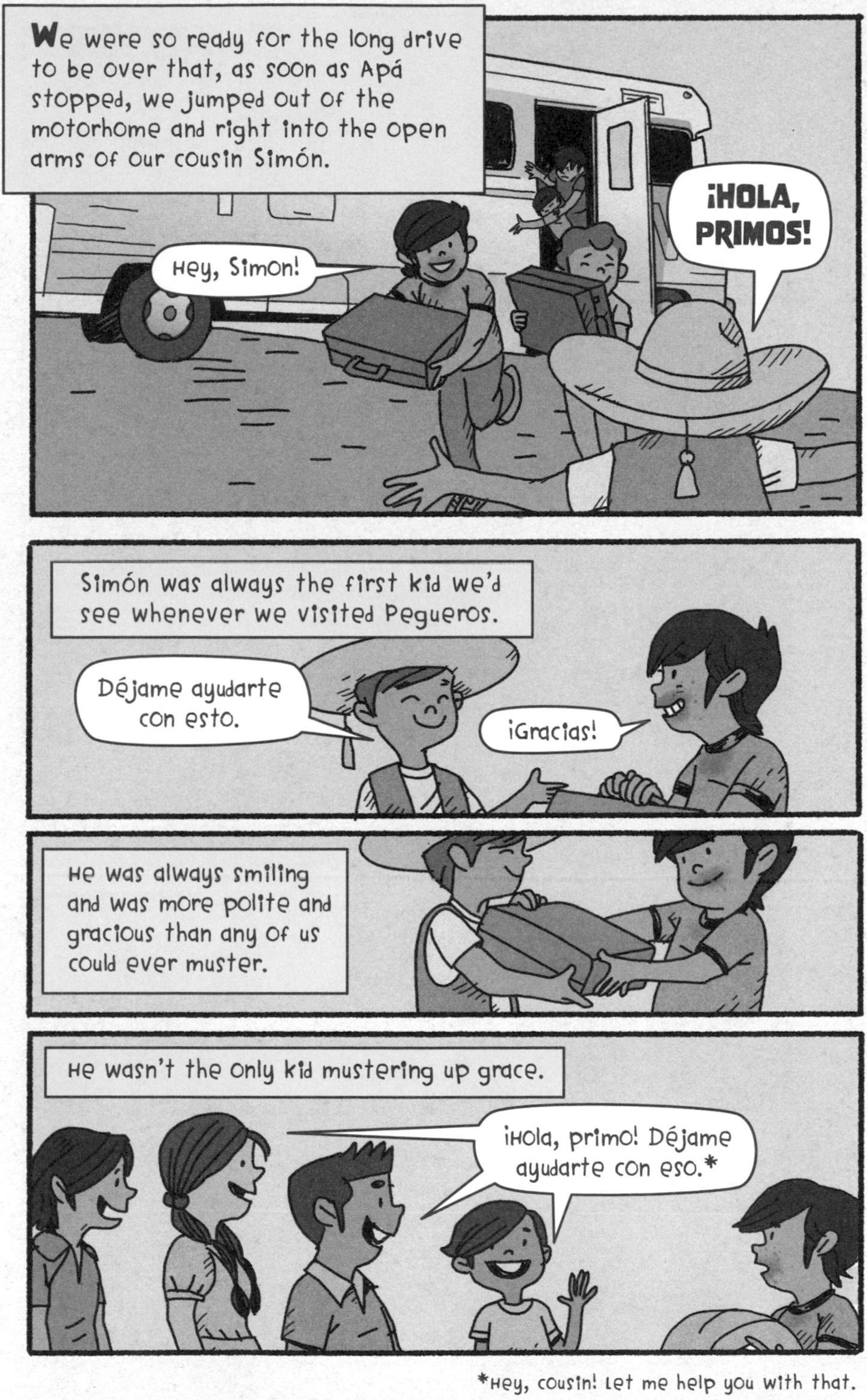
We were so ready for the long drive to be over that, as soon as Apá stopped, we jumped out of the motorhome and right into the open arms of our cousin Simón.
Hey, Simon!
¡HOLA, PRIMOS!
Simón was always the first kid we'd see whenever we visited Pegueros.
Déjame ayudarte con esto.
¡Gracias!
He was always smiling and was more polite and gracious than any of us could ever muster.
He wasn't the only kid mustering up grace.
¡Hola, primo! Déjame ayudarte con eso.*

*Hey, cousin! Let me help you with that.

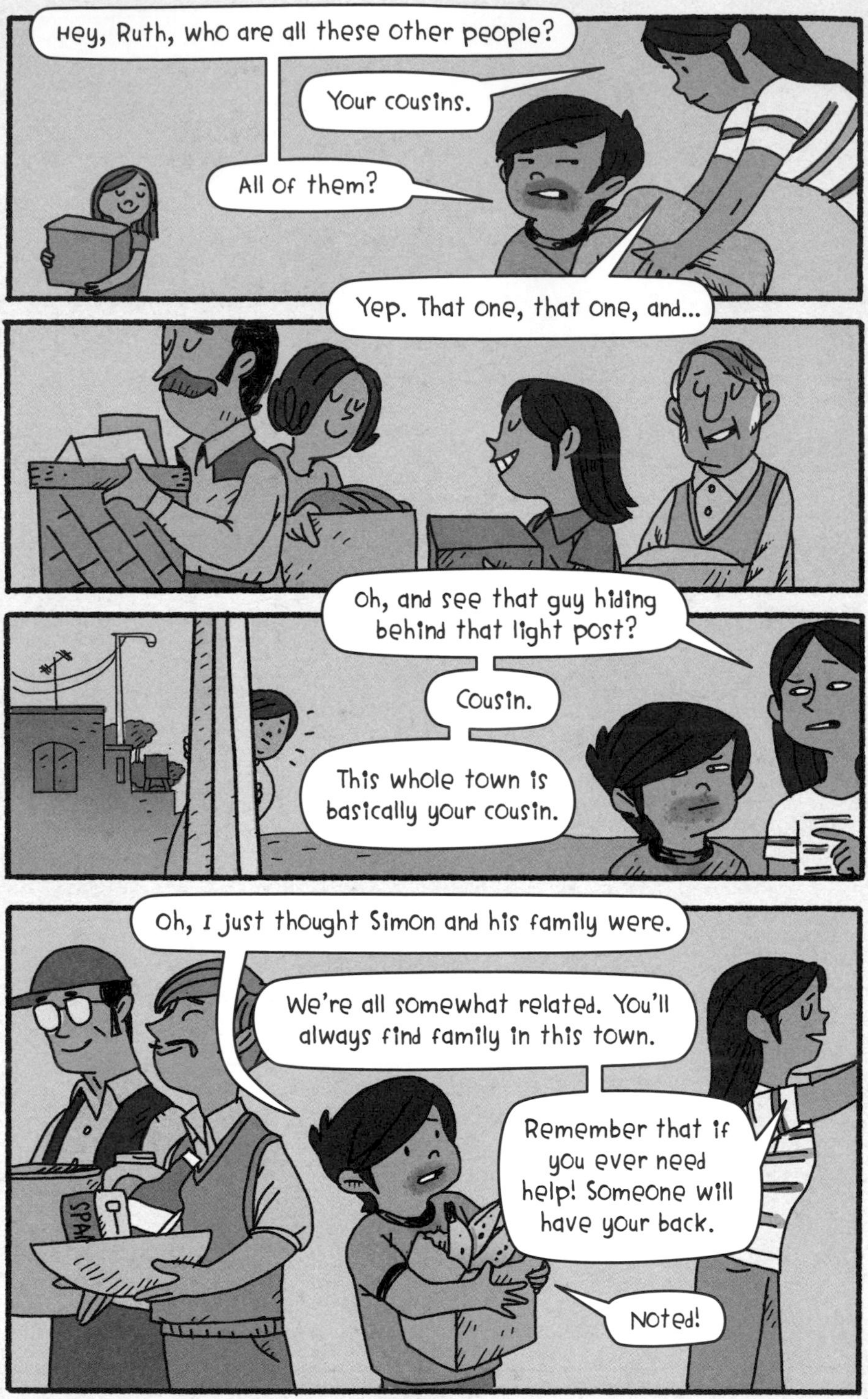
Hey, Ruth, who are all these other people?
Your cousins.
All of them?
Yep. That one, that one, and...
Oh, and see that guy hiding behind that light post?
Cousin.
This whole town is basically your cousin.
Oh, I just thought Simon and his family were.
We're all somewhat related. You'll always find family in this town.
Remember that if you ever need help! Someone will have your back.
Noted!

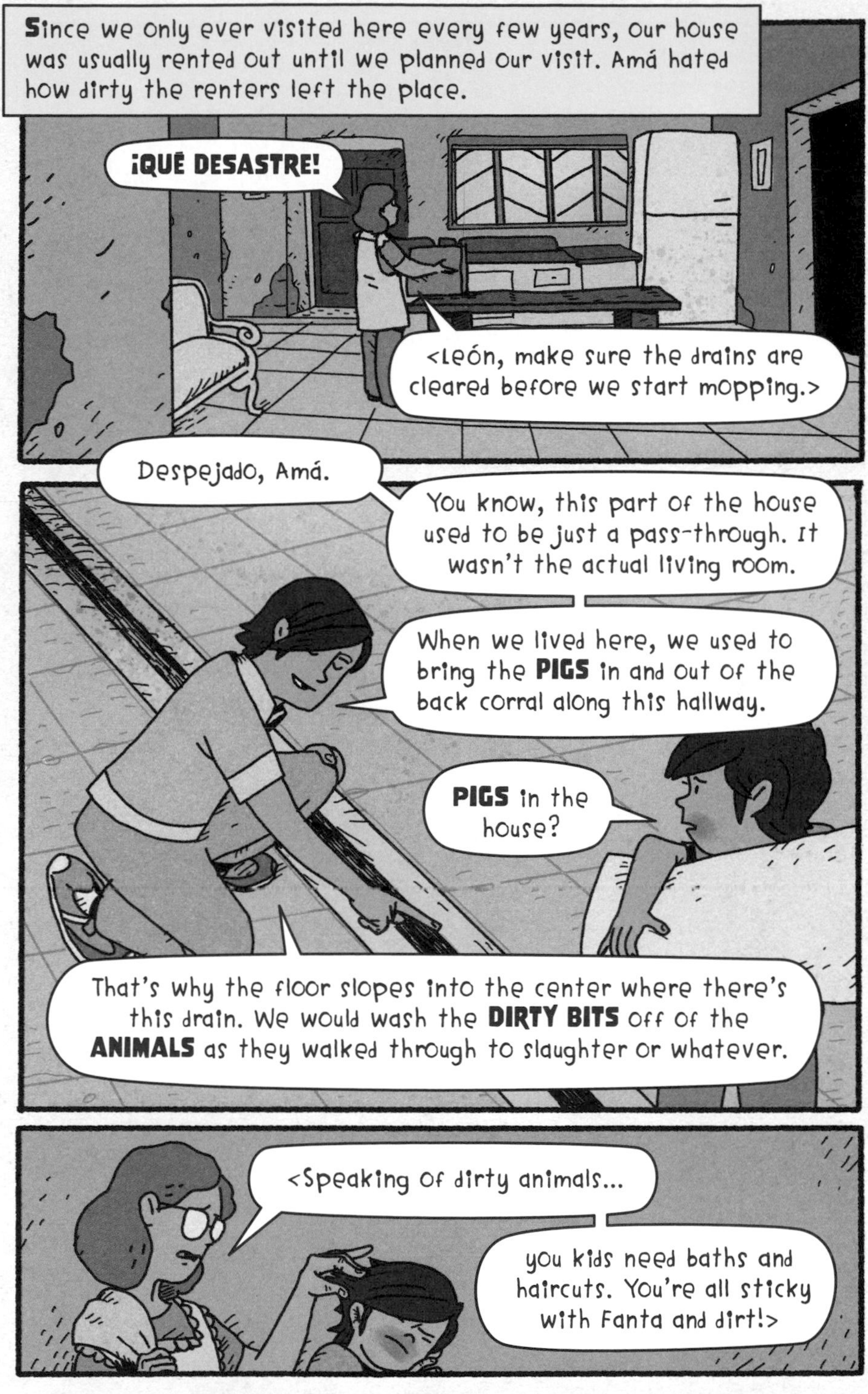
Since we only ever visited here every few years, our house was usually rented out until we planned our visit. Amá hated how dirty the renters left the place.
¡QUÉ DESASTRE!
<León, make sure the drains are cleared before we start mopping.>
Despejado, Amá.
You know, this part of the house used to be just a pass-through. It wasn't the actual living room.
When we lived here, we used to bring the PIGS in and out of the back corral along this hallway.
PIGS in the house?
That's why the floor slopes into the center where there's this drain. We would wash the DIRTY BITS off of the ANIMALS as they walked through to slaughter or whatever.
<Speaking of dirty animals...
you kids need baths and haircuts. You're all sticky with Fanta and dirt!>

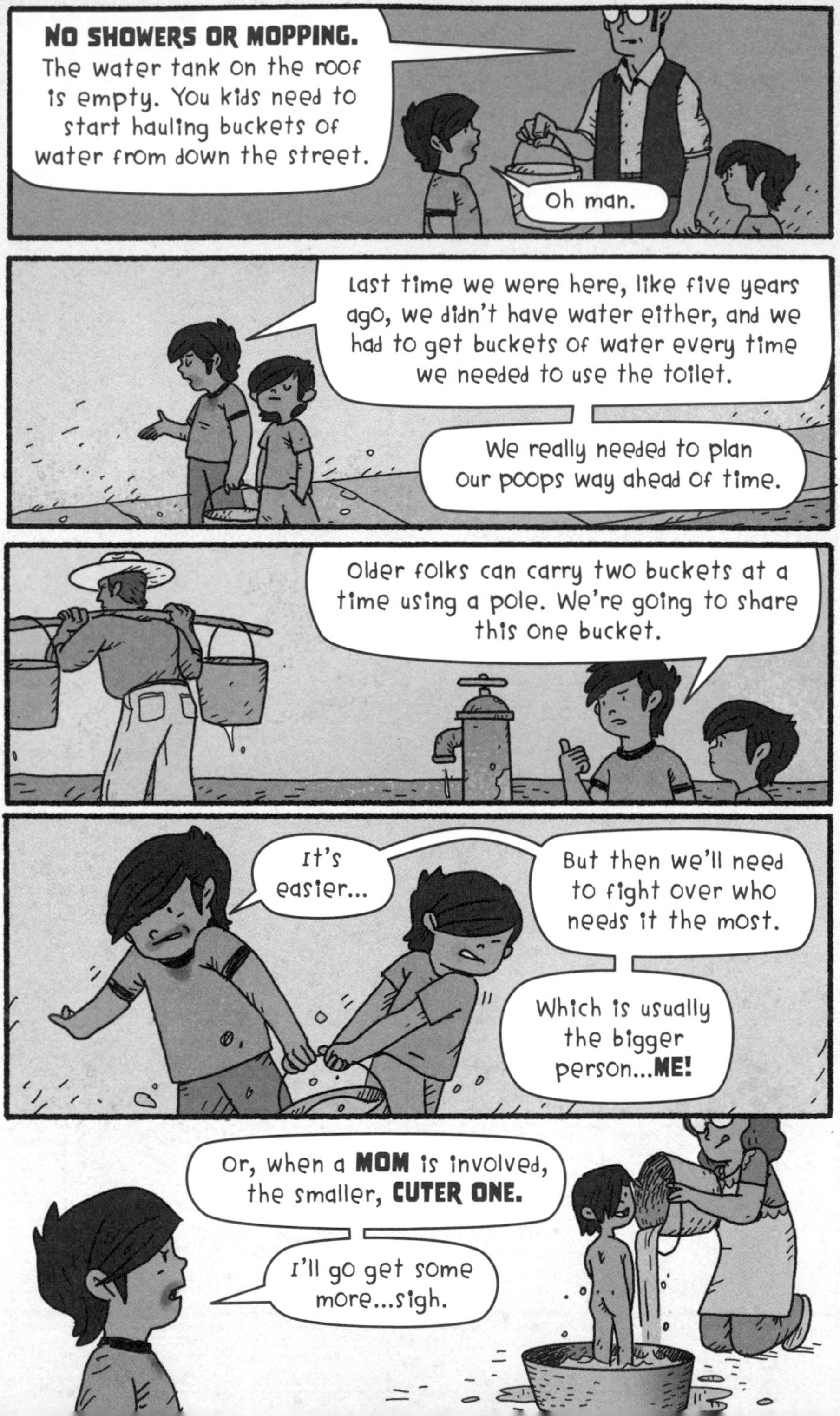

NO SHOWERS OR MOPPING. The water tank on the roof is empty. You kids need to start hauling buckets of water from down the street.
Oh man.
Last time we were here, like five years ago, we didn't have water either, and we had to get buckets of water every time we needed to use the toilet.
We really needed to plan our poops way ahead of time.
Older folks can carry two buckets at a time using a pole. We're going to share this one bucket.
It's easier...
But then we'll need to fight over who needs it the most.
Which is usually the bigger person...**ME!**
Or, when a **MOM** is involved, the smaller, **CUTER ONE.**
I'll go get some more...sigh.

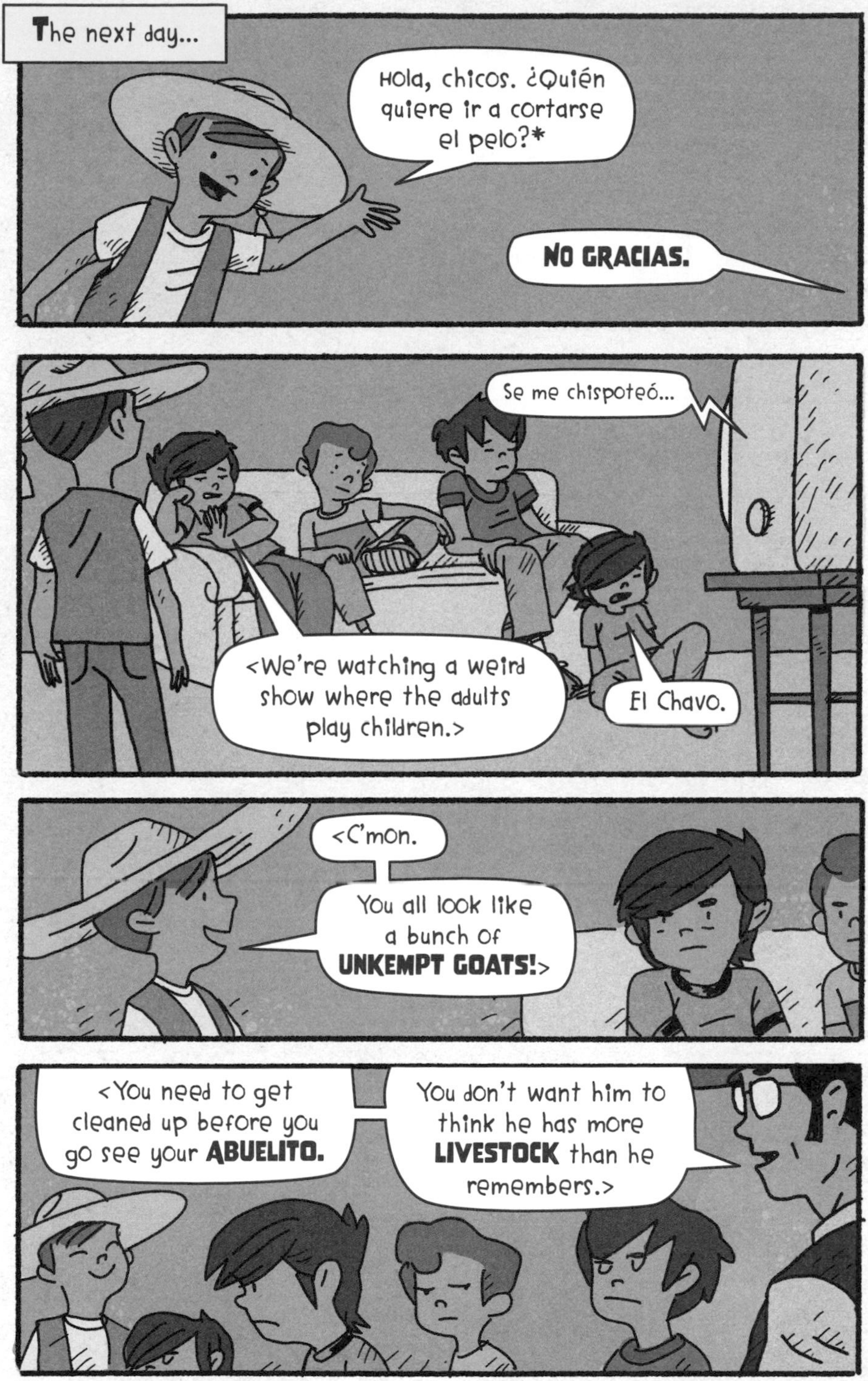
The next day...
Hola, chicos. ¿Quién quiere ir a cortarse el pelo?*
NO GRACIAS.
Se me chispoteó...
<We're watching a weird show where the adults play children.>
El Chavo.
<C'mon.
You all look like a bunch of UNKEMPT GOATS!>
<You need to get cleaned up before you go see your ABUELITO.
You don't want him to think he has more LIVESTOCK than he remembers.>

*Hi, guys. Who wants to go get a haircut?

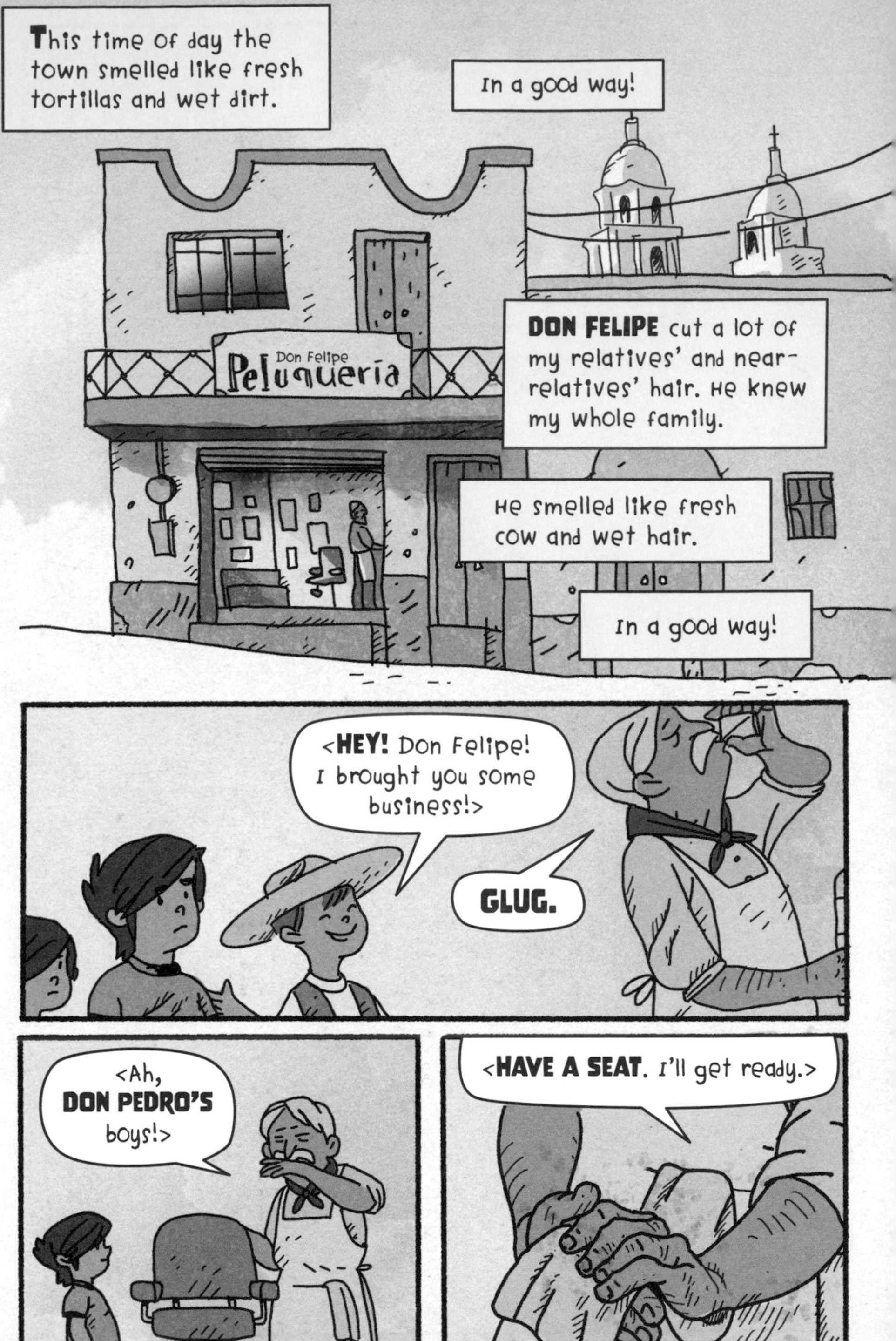
This time of day the town smelled like fresh tortillas and wet dirt.
In a good way!
Don Felipe Peluquería
DON FELIPE cut a lot of my relatives' and near-relatives' hair. He knew my whole family.
He smelled like fresh cow and wet hair.
In a good way!
<HEY! Don Felipe! I brought you some business!>
GLUG.
<Ah, DON PEDRO'S boys!>
<HAVE A SEAT. I'll get ready.>

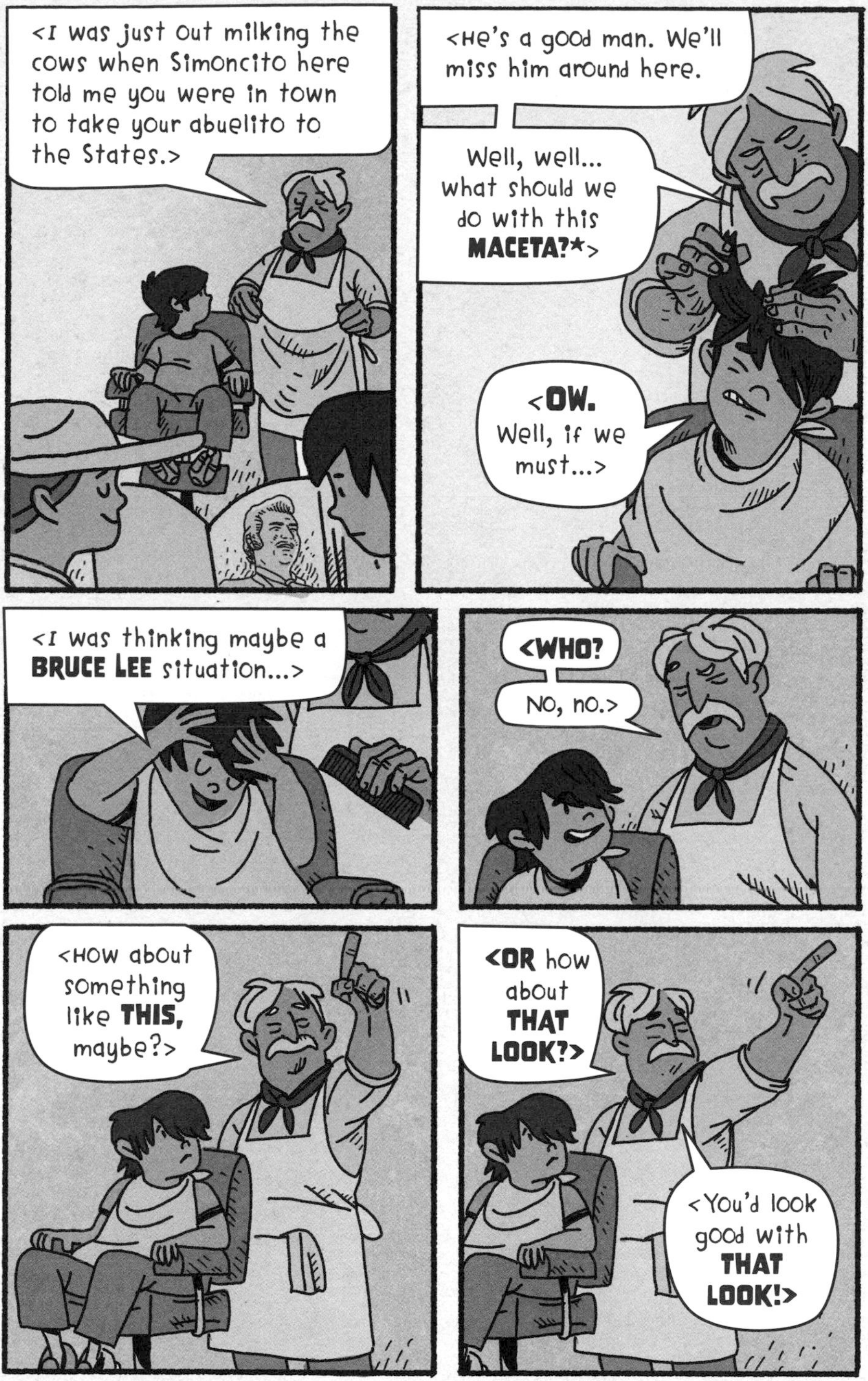
<I was just out milking the cows when Simoncito here told me you were in town to take your abuelito to the States.>
<He's a good man. We'll miss him around here.
Well, well... what should we do with this **MACETA?***>
<**OW.** Well, if we must...>
<I was thinking maybe a **BRUCE LEE** situation...>
<**WHO?**
No, no.>
<How about something like **THIS,** maybe?>
<**OR** how about **THAT LOOK?**>
<You'd look good with **THAT LOOK!**>

*A nice way to say "big head."

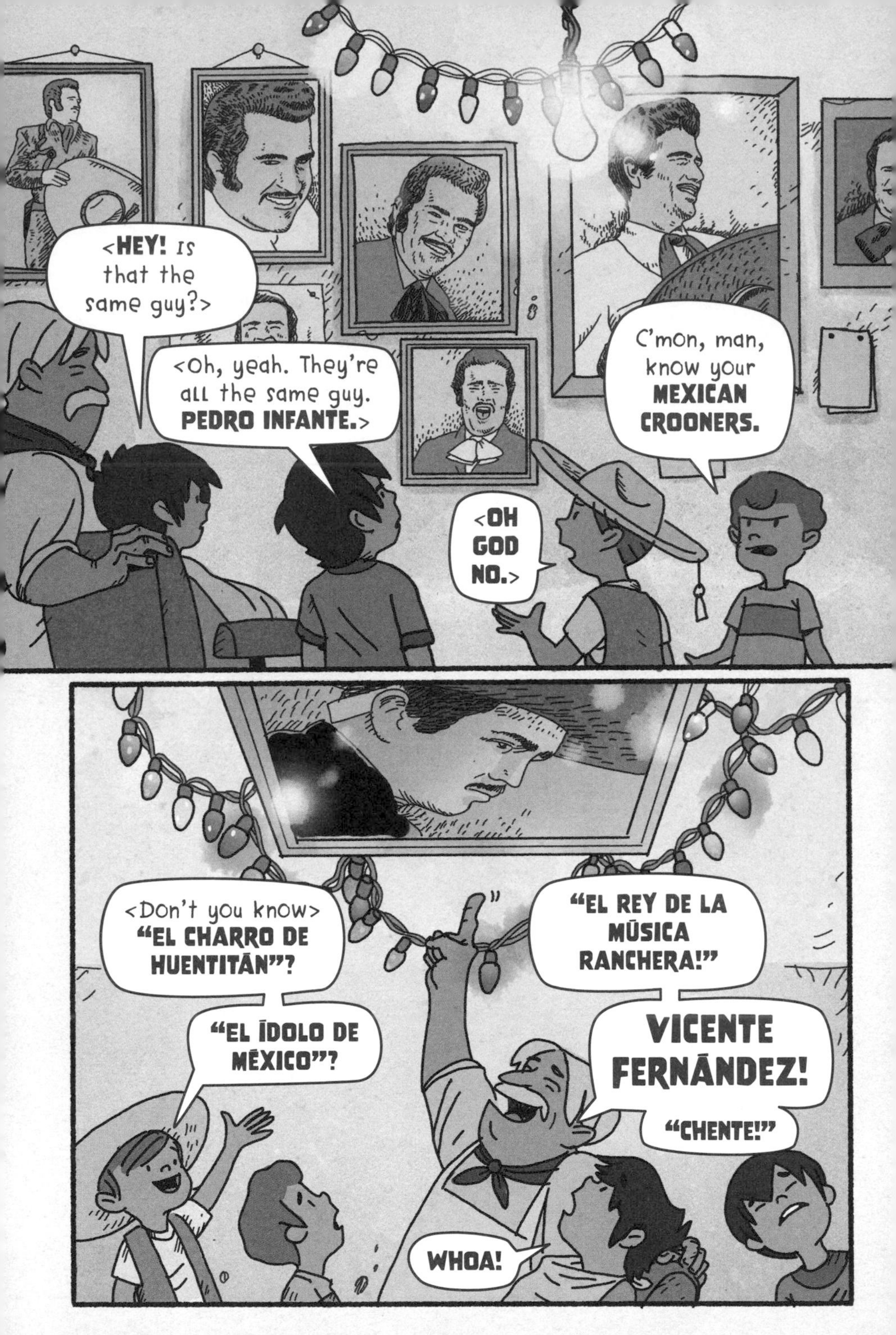
<HEY! is that the same guy?>
<Oh, yeah. They're all the same guy. PEDRO INFANTE.>
C'mon, man, know your MEXICAN CROONERS.
<OH GOD NO.>
<Don't you know> "EL CHARRO DE HUENTITÁN"?
"EL REY DE LA MÚSICA RANCHERA!"
"EL ÍDOLO DE MÉXICO"?
VICENTE FERNÁNDEZ!
"CHENTE!"
WHOA!

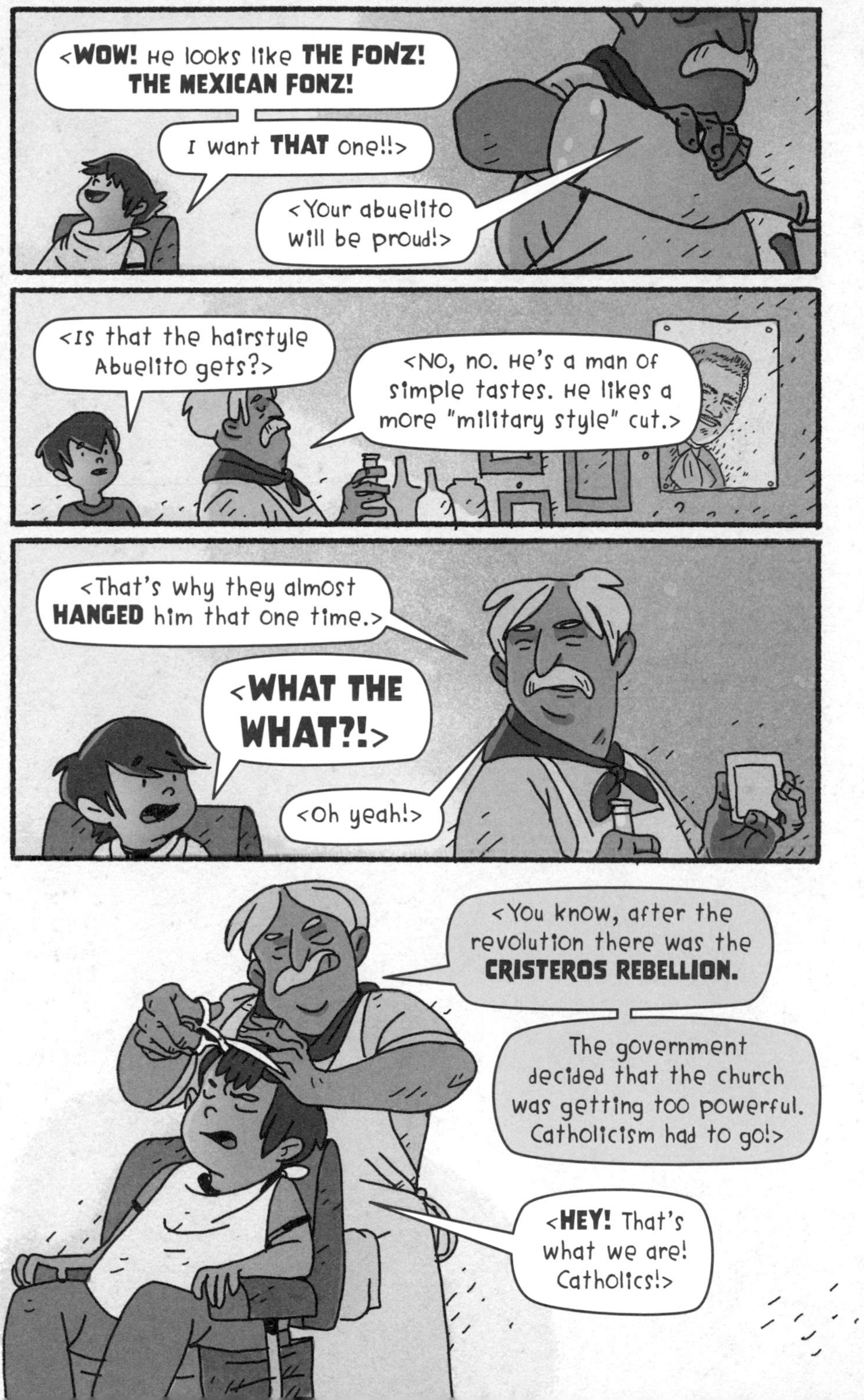
<WOW! He looks like THE FONZ! THE MEXICAN FONZ!
I want THAT one!!>
<Your abuelito will be proud!>
<Is that the hairstyle Abuelito gets?>
<No, no. He's a man of simple tastes. He likes a more "military style" cut.>
<That's why they almost HANGED him that one time.>
<WHAT THE WHAT?!>
<Oh yeah!>
<You know, after the revolution there was the CRISTEROS REBELLION.
The government decided that the church was getting too powerful. Catholicism had to go!>
<HEY! That's what we are! Catholics!>

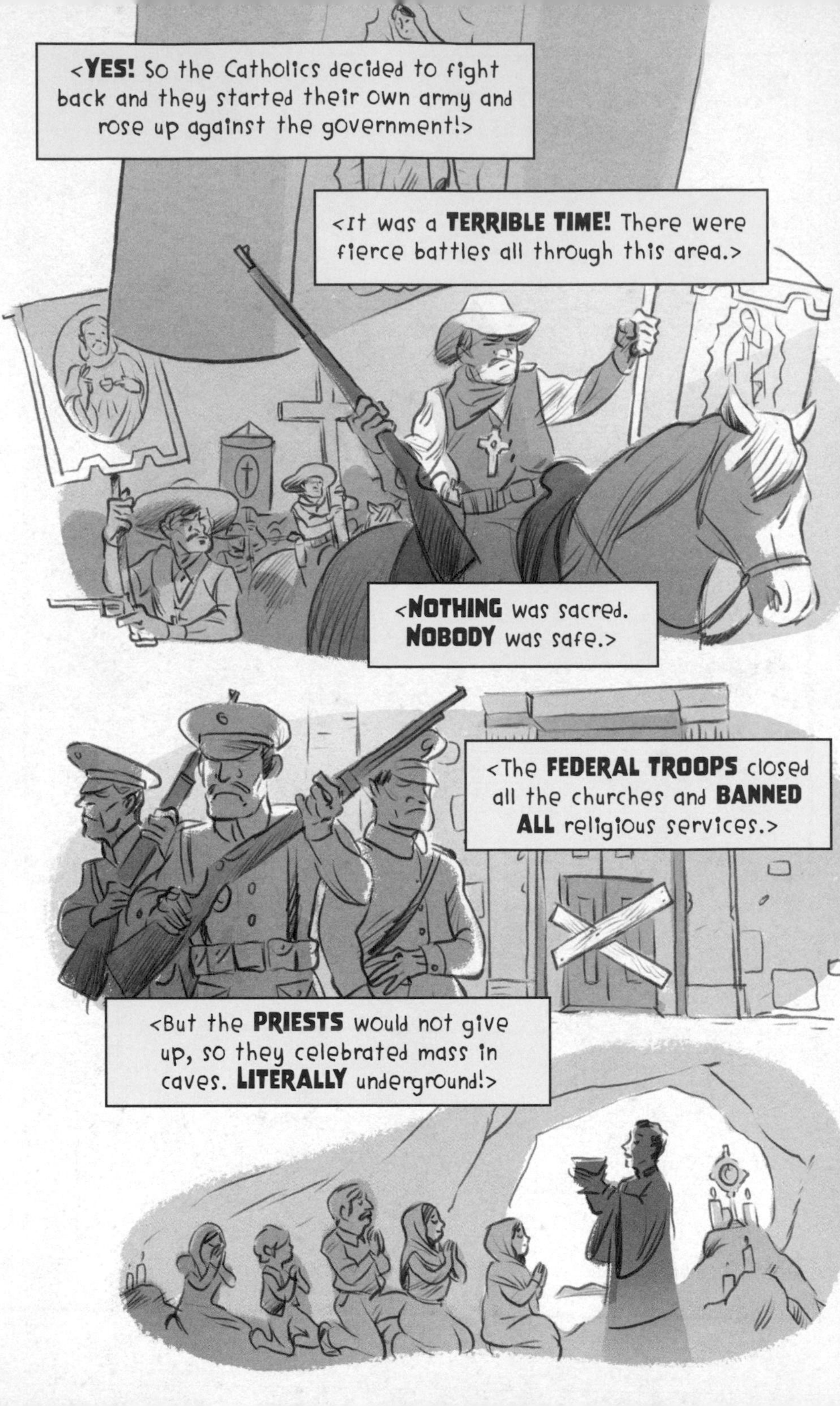
<YES! So the Catholics decided to fight back and they started their own army and rose up against the government!>
<It was a TERRIBLE TIME! There were fierce battles all through this area.>
<NOTHING was sacred. NOBODY was safe.>
<The FEDERAL TROOPS closed all the churches and BANNED ALL religious services.>
<But the PRIESTS would not give up, so they celebrated mass in caves. LITERALLY underground!>

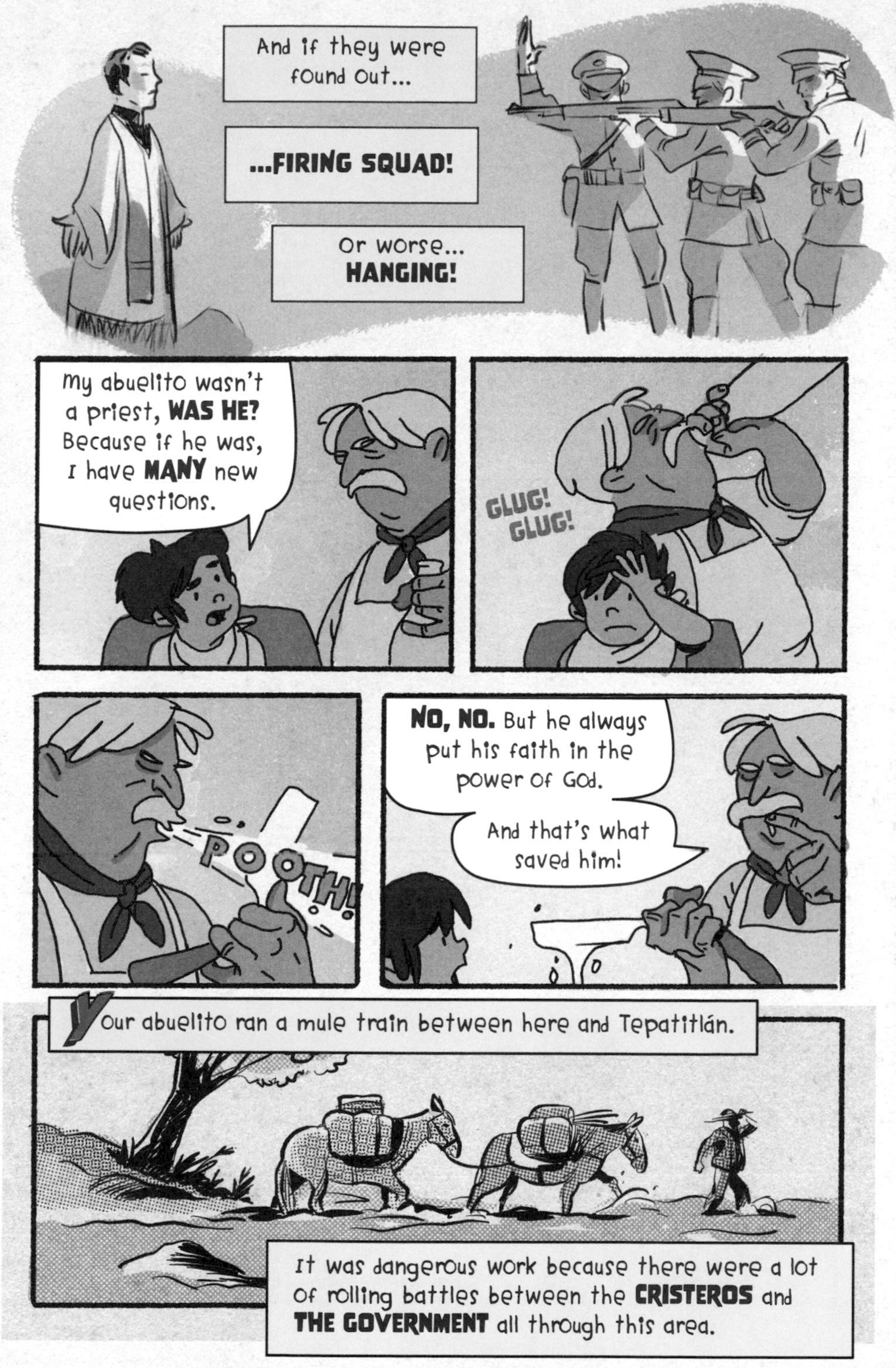
And if they were found out...
...FIRING SQUAD!
Or worse... HANGING!
My abuelito wasn't a priest, WAS HE? Because if he was, I have MANY new questions.
GLUG! GLUG!
POOTH!
NO, NO. But he always put his faith in the power of God.
And that's what saved him!
Your abuelito ran a mule train between here and Tepatitlán.
It was dangerous work because there were a lot of rolling battles between the CRISTEROS and THE GOVERNMENT all through this area.

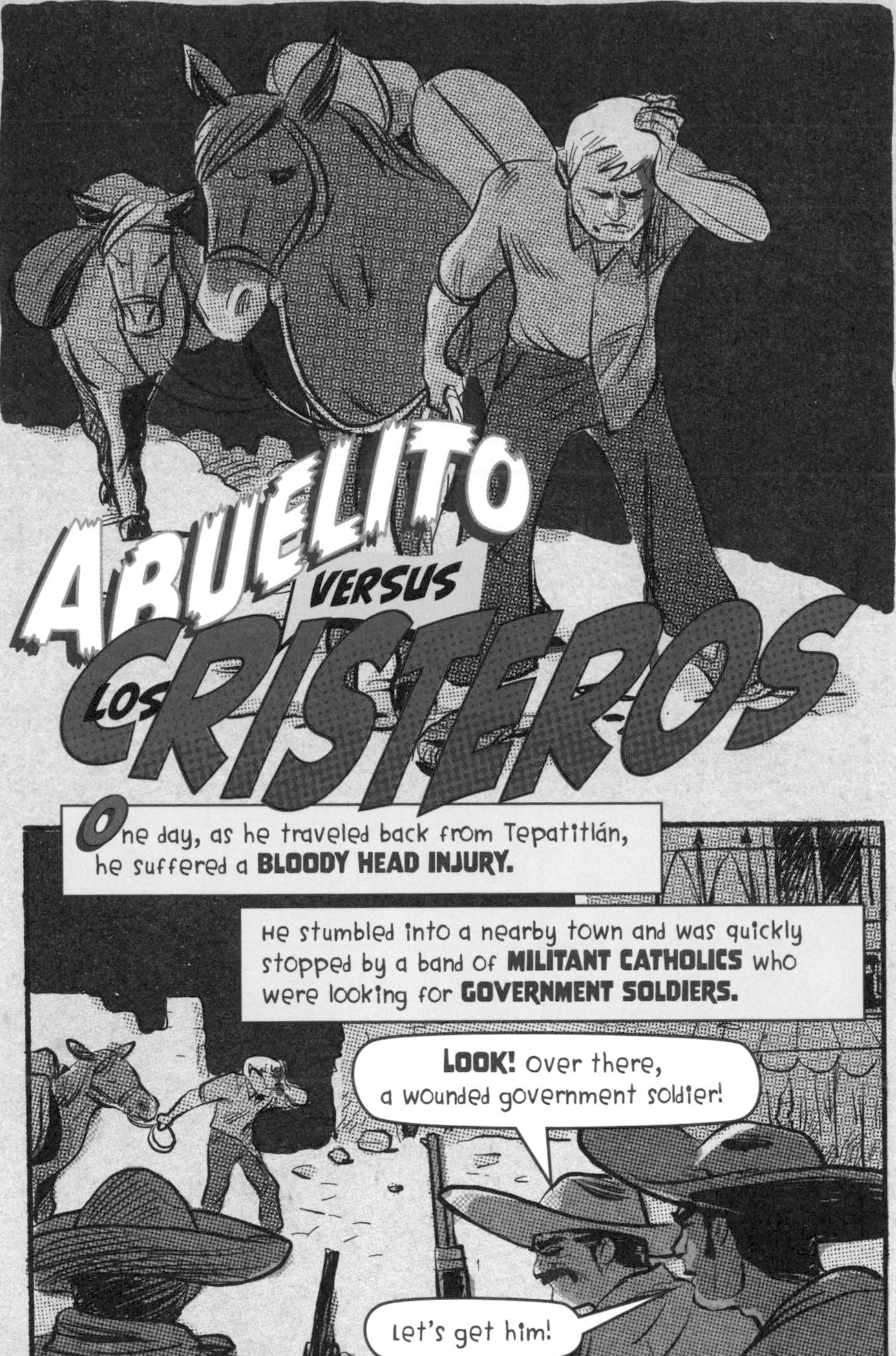
ABUELITO VERSUS LOS CRISTEROS
One day, as he traveled back from Tepatitlán, he suffered a BLOODY HEAD INJURY.
He stumbled into a nearby town and was quickly stopped by a band of MILITANT CATHOLICS who were looking for GOVERNMENT SOLDIERS.
LOOK! Over there, a wounded government soldier!
Let's get him!

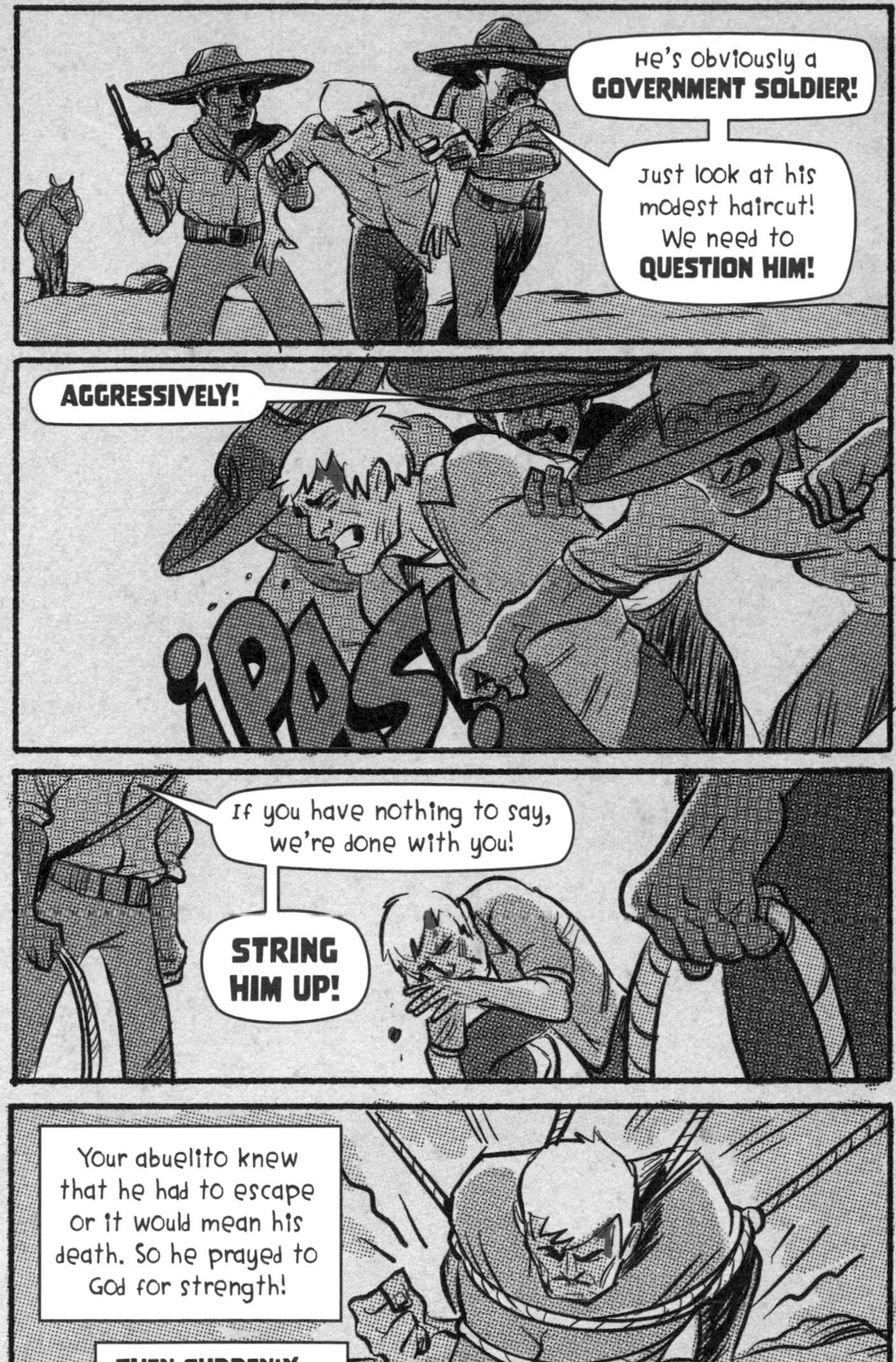
He's obviously a GOVERNMENT SOLDIER!
Just look at his modest haircut! We need to QUESTION HIM!
AGGRESSIVELY!
¡POS!
If you have nothing to say, we're done with you!
STRING HIM UP!
Your abuelito knew that he had to escape or it would mean his death. So he prayed to God for strength!
THEN SUDDENLY...

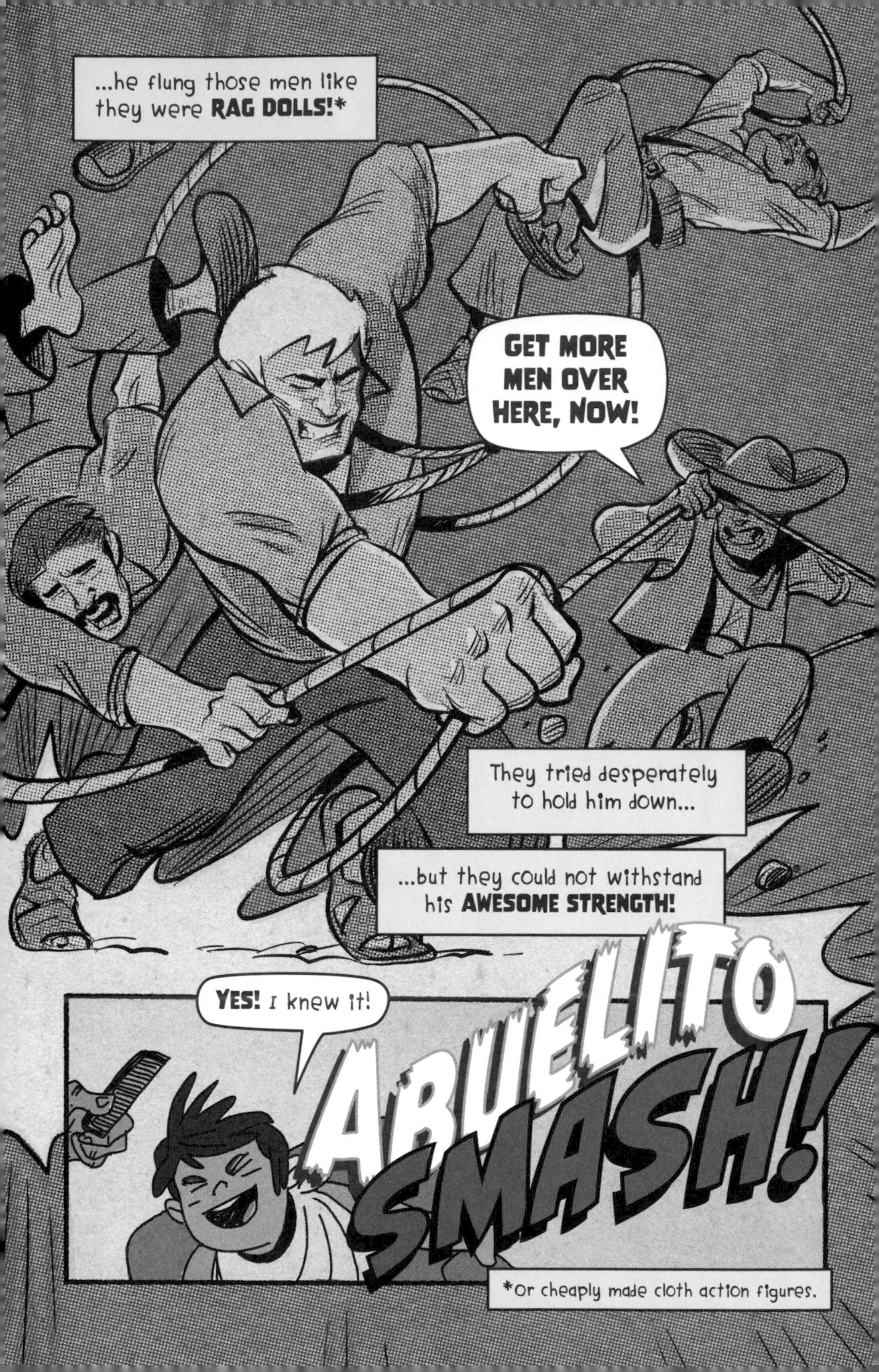
...he flung those men like they were RAG DOLLS!*
GET MORE MEN OVER HERE, NOW!
They tried desperately to hold him down...
...but they could not withstand his AWESOME STRENGTH!
YES! I knew it!
ABUELITO SMASH!
*Or cheaply made cloth action figures.

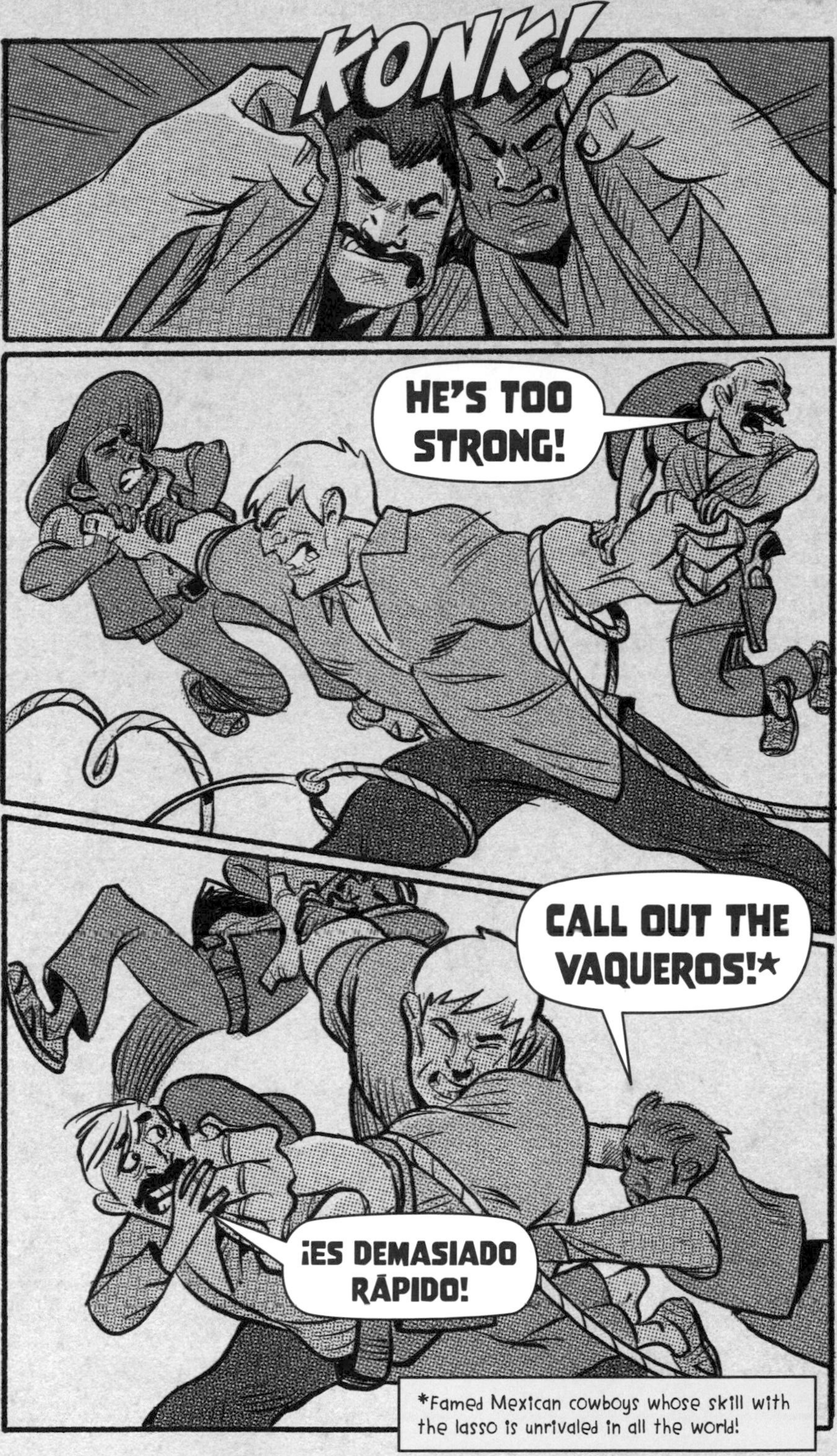
KONK!
HE'S TOO STRONG!
CALL OUT THE VAQUEROS!*
¡ES DEMASIADO RÁPIDO!
*Famed Mexican cowboys whose skill with the lasso is unrivaled in all the world!

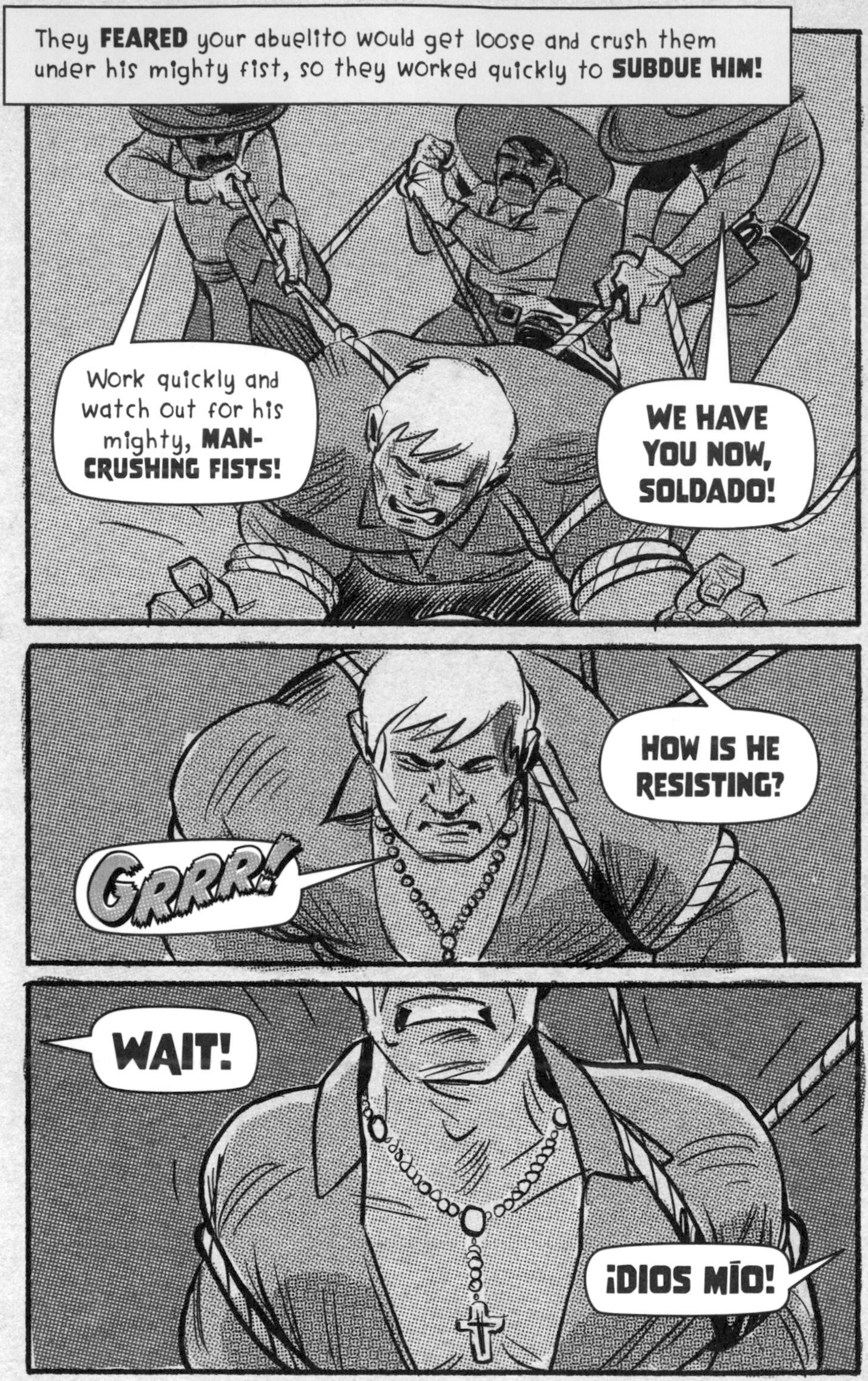

They FEARED your abuelito would get loose and crush them under his mighty fist, so they worked quickly to SUBDUE HIM!
Work quickly and watch out for his mighty, MAN-CRUSHING FISTS!
WE HAVE YOU NOW, SOLDADO!
HOW IS HE RESISTING?
GRRR!
WAIT!
¡DIOS MÍO!

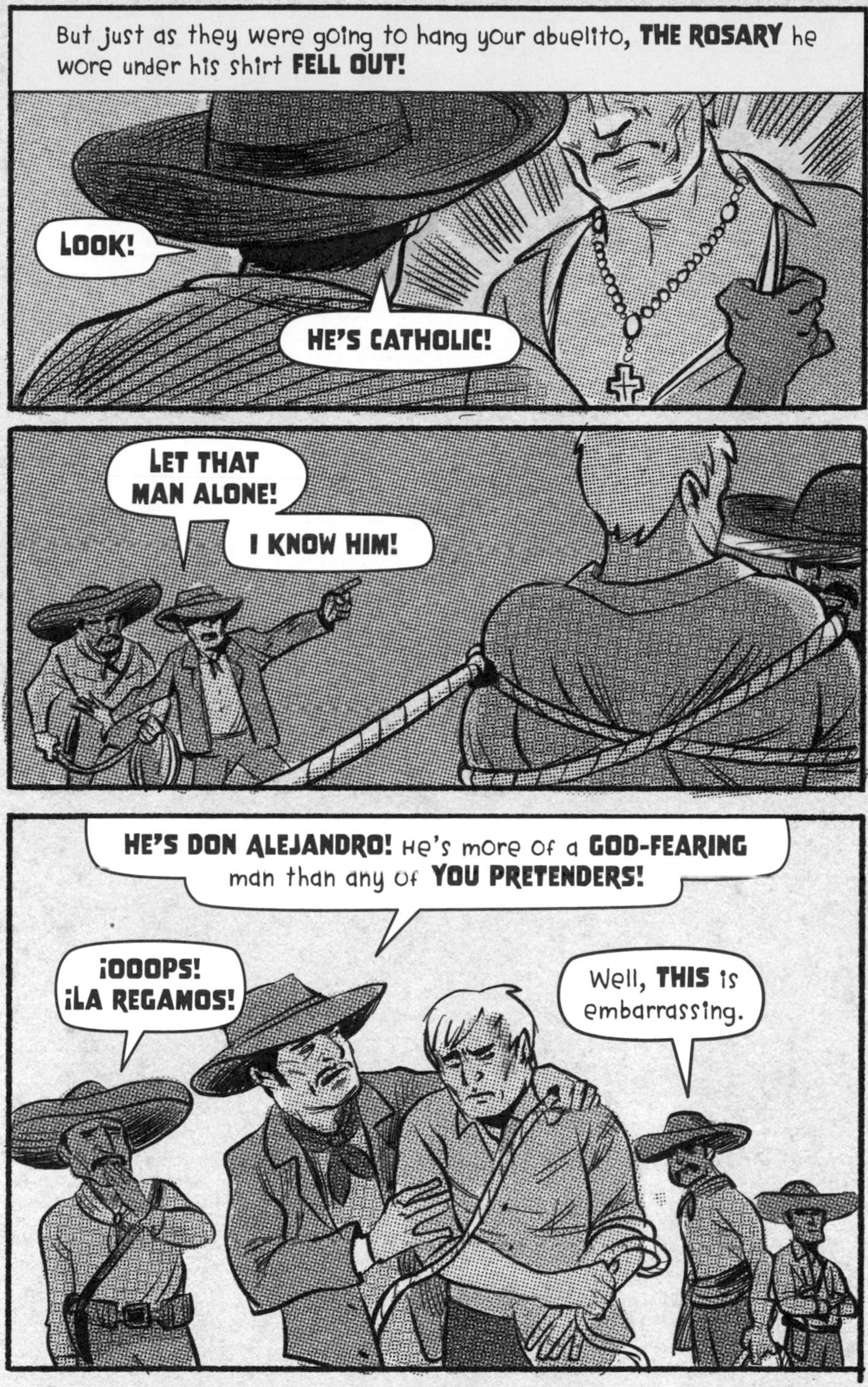
But just as they were going to hang your abuelito, THE ROSARY he wore under his shirt FELL OUT!
LOOK!
HE'S CATHOLIC!
LET THAT MAN ALONE!
I KNOW HIM!
HE'S DON ALEJANDRO! He's more of a GOD-FEARING man than any of YOU PRETENDERS!
¡OOOPS! ¡LA REGAMOS!
Well, THIS is embarrassing.

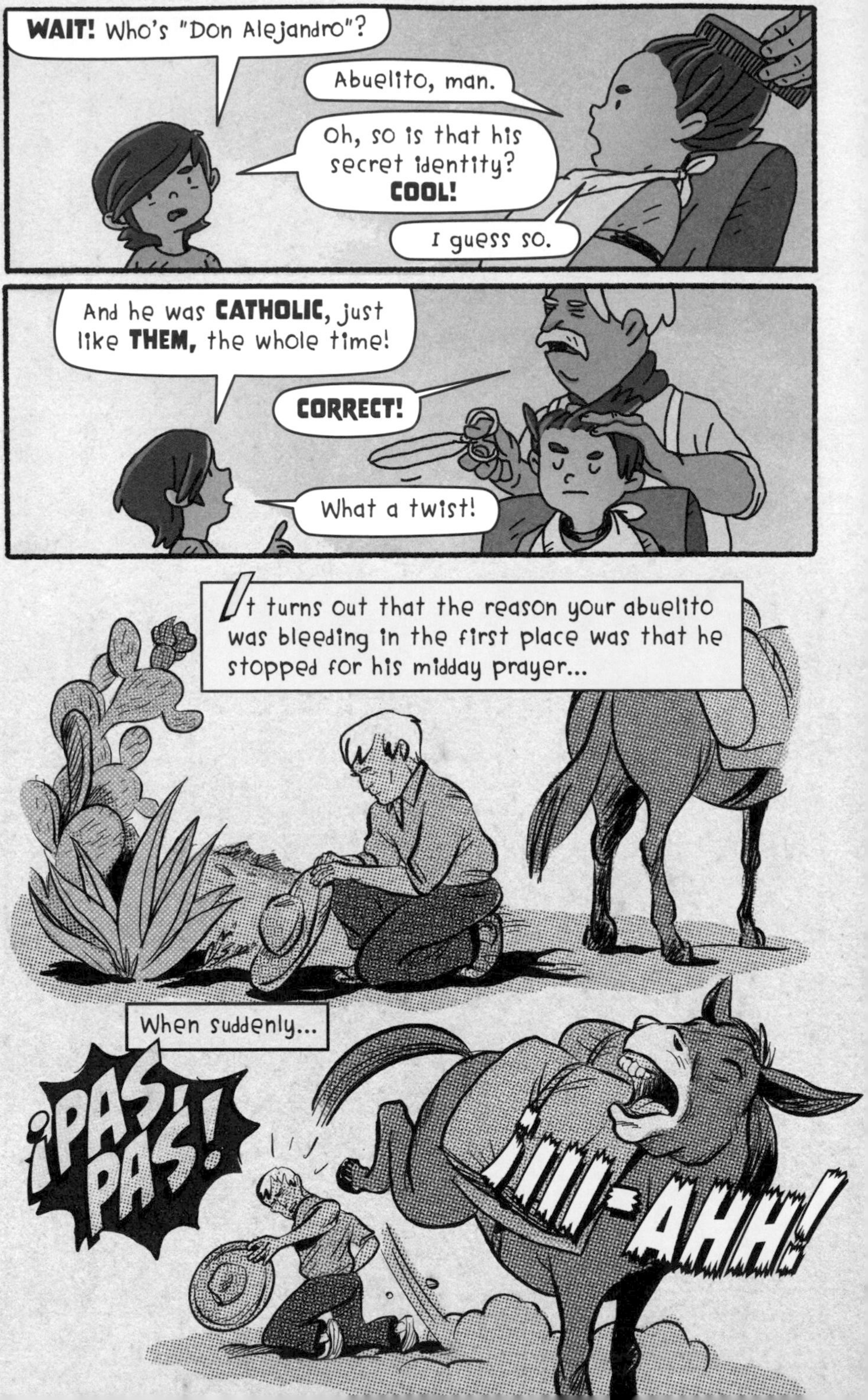
WAIT! Who's "Don Alejandro"?
Abuelito, man.
Oh, so is that his secret identity? COOL!
I guess so.
And he was CATHOLIC, just like THEM, the whole time!
CORRECT!
What a twist!
It turns out that the reason your abuelito was bleeding in the first place was that he stopped for his midday prayer...
When suddenly...
¡PAS, PAS!
IIII-AHH!

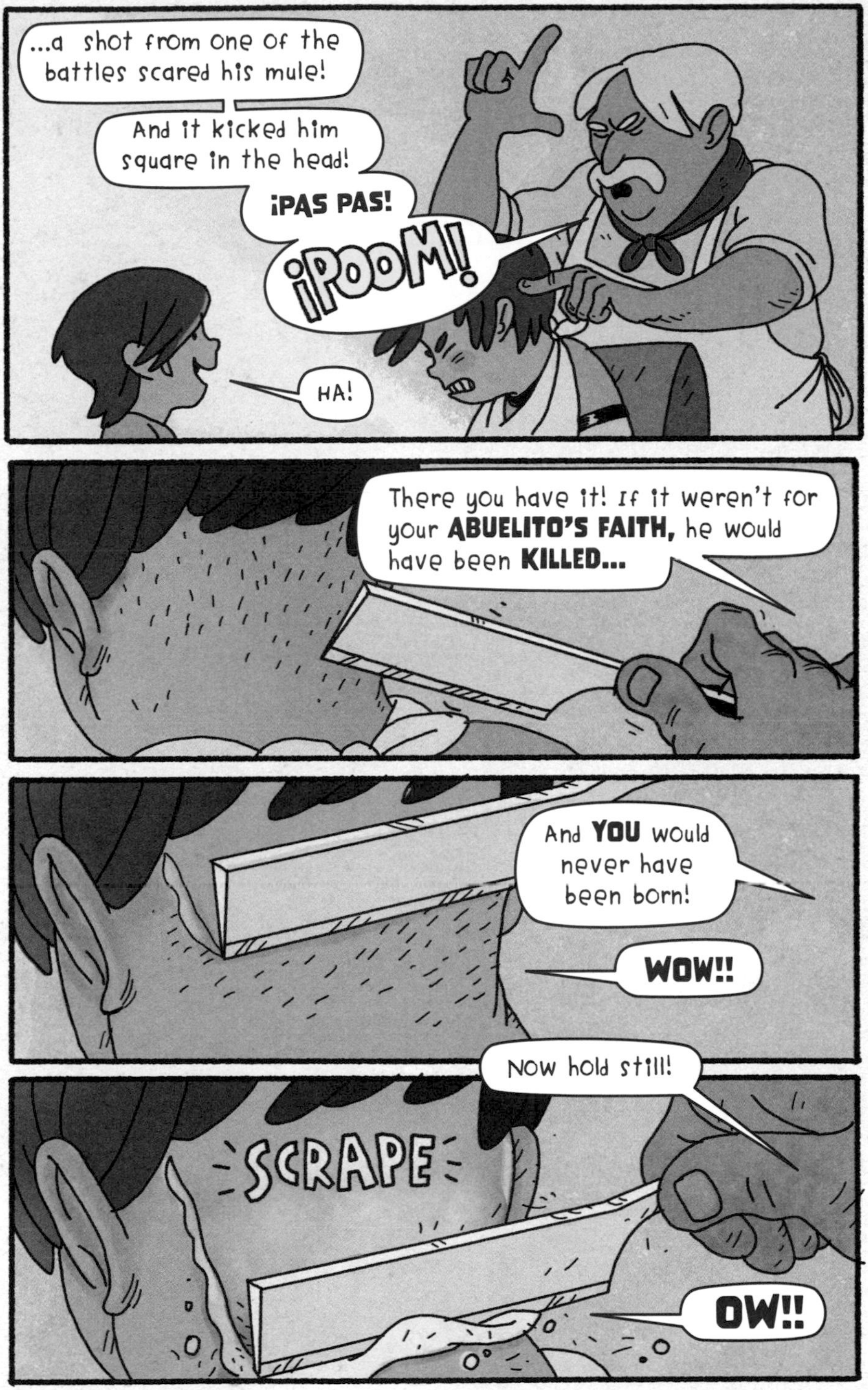

...a shot from one of the battles scared his mule!
And it kicked him square in the head!
¡PAS PAS!
¡POOM!
HA!
There you have it! If it weren't for your **ABUELITO'S FAITH,** he would have been **KILLED...**
And **YOU** would never have been born!
WOW!!
Now hold still!
SCRAPE
OW!!

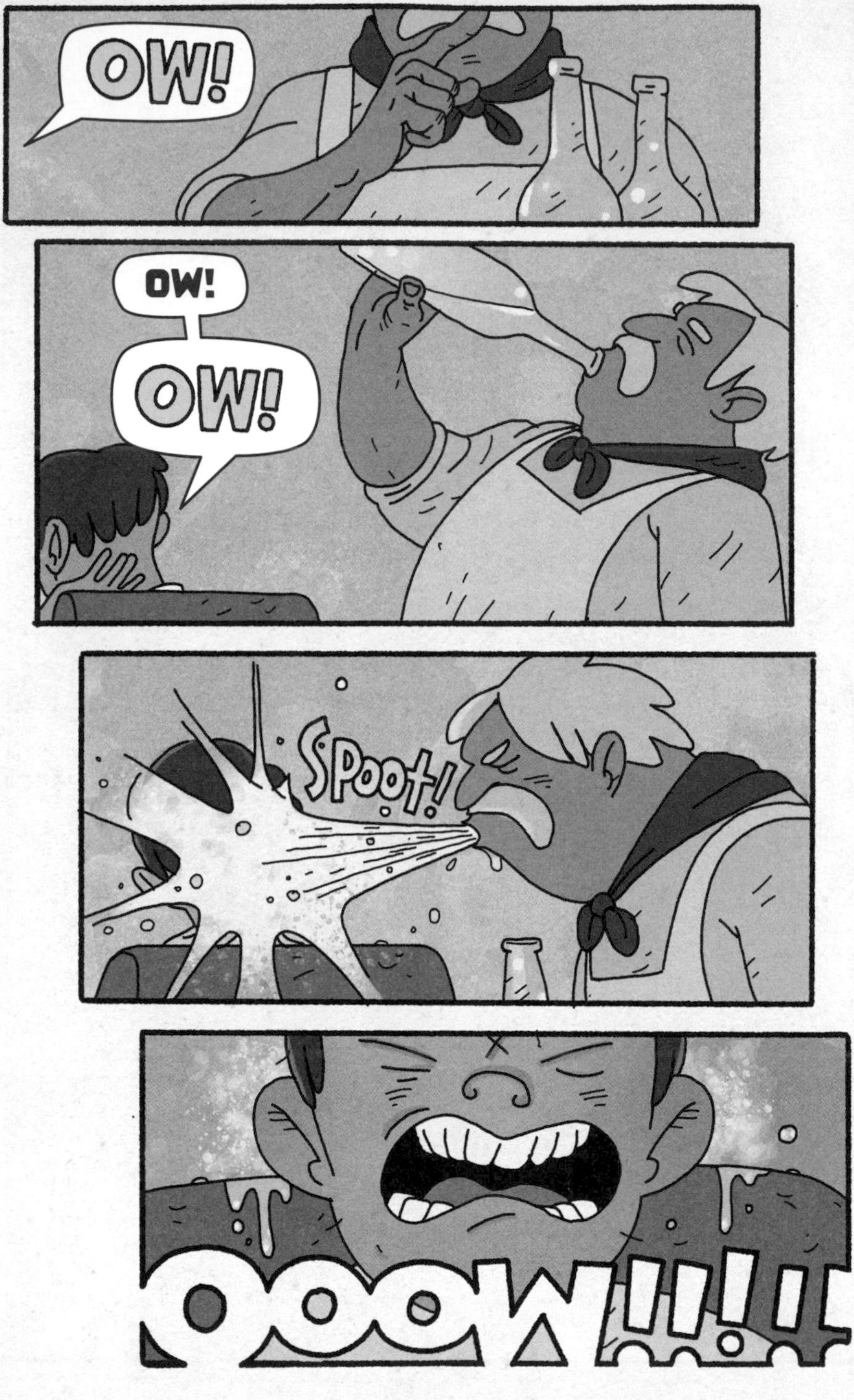
OW!
OW!
OW!
SPOOT!
OOOW!!!!

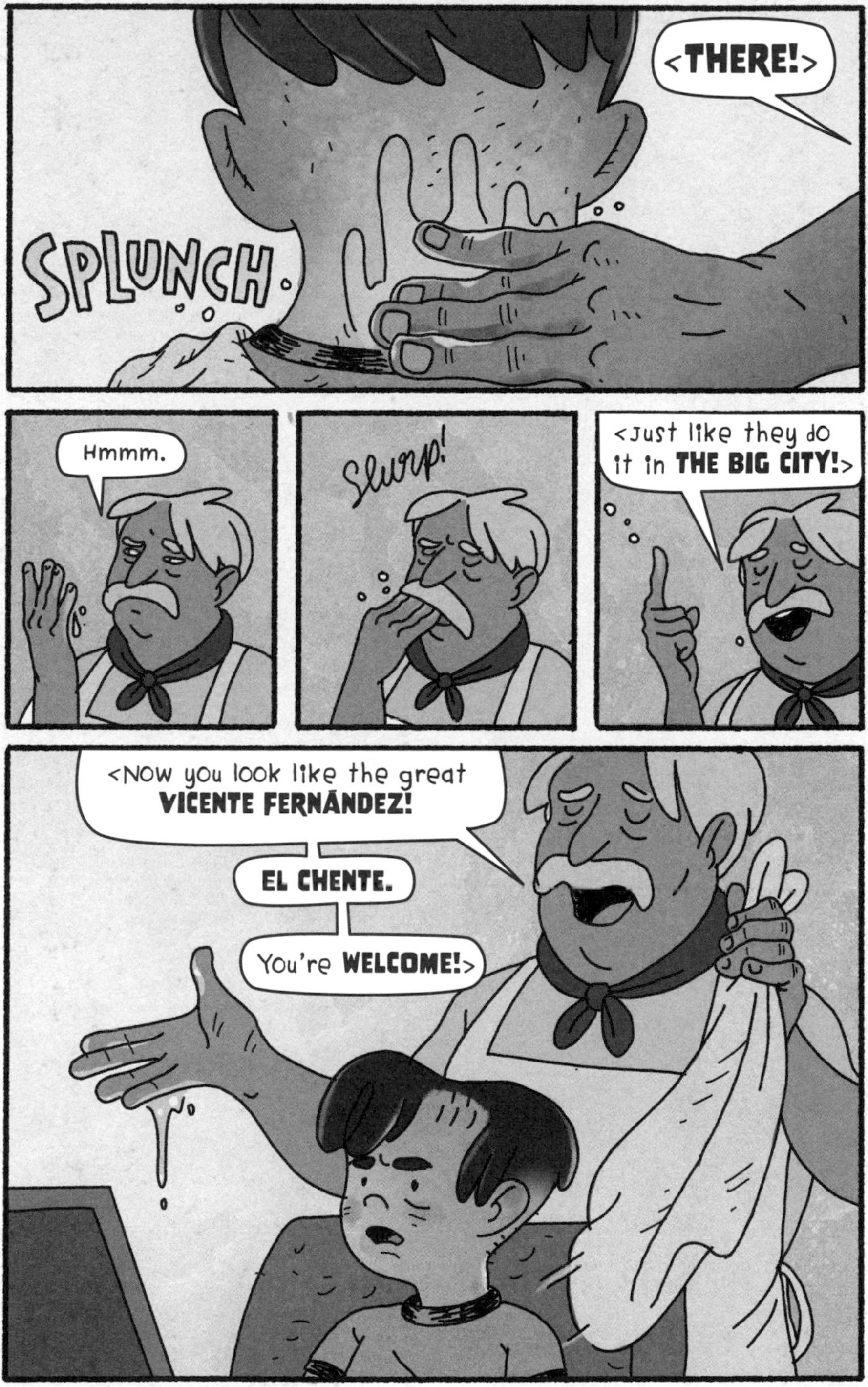

<THERE!>
SPLUNCH
Hmmm.
Slurp!
<Just like they do it in **THE BIG CITY!**>
<Now you look like the great **VICENTE FERNÁNDEZ!**
EL CHENTE.
You're **WELCOME!**>

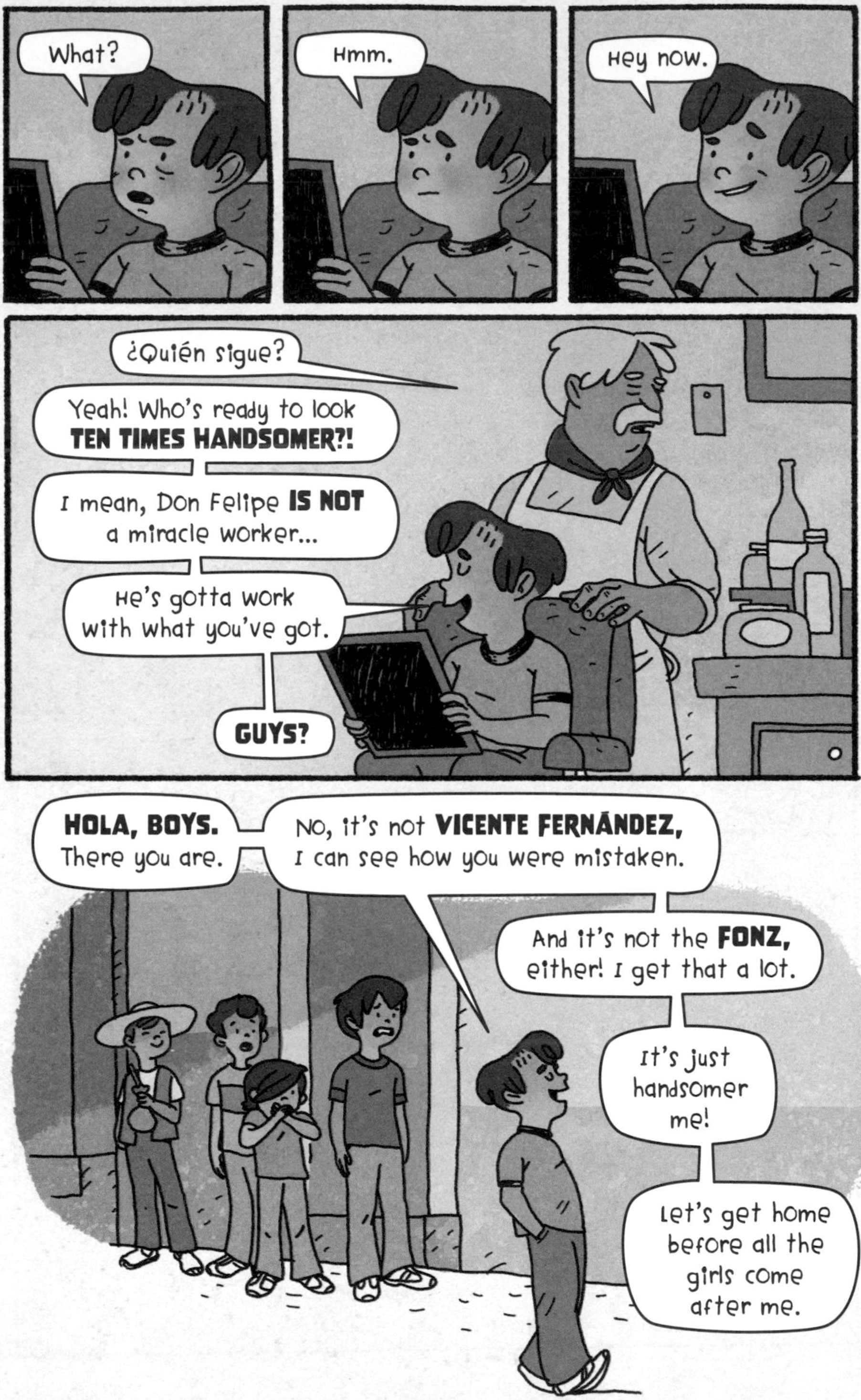
What?
Hmm.
Hey now.
¿Quién sigue?
Yeah! Who's ready to look TEN TIMES HANDSOMER?!
I mean, Don Felipe IS NOT a miracle worker...
He's gotta work with what you've got.
GUYS?
HOLA, BOYS. There you are.
No, it's not VICENTE FERNÁNDEZ, I can see how you were mistaken.
And it's not the FONZ, either! I get that a lot.
It's just handsomer me!
Let's get home before all the girls come after me.

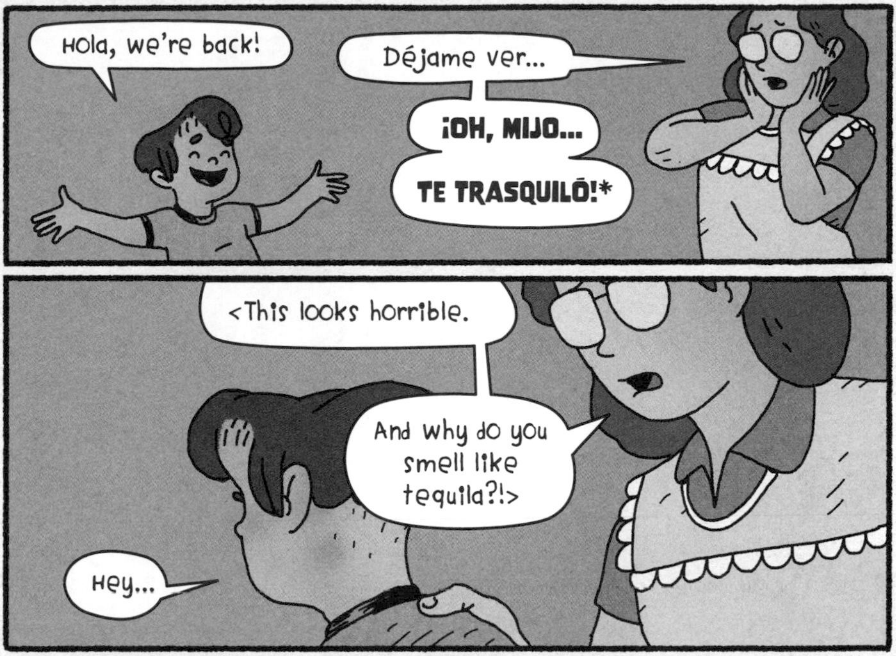
Hola, we're back!
Déjame ver...
¡OH, MIJO...
TE TRASQUILÓ!*
<This looks horrible.
And why do you smell like tequila?!>
Hey...

*Let me look. Oh, son, he really butchered you!

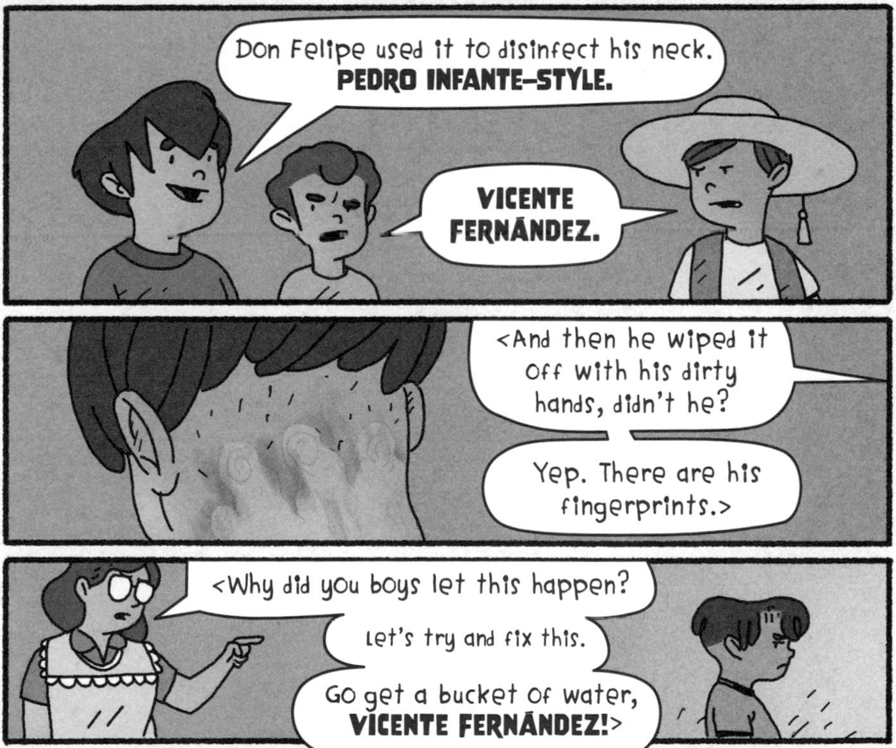
Don Felipe used it to disinfect his neck. PEDRO INFANTE–STYLE.
VICENTE FERNÁNDEZ.
<And then he wiped it off with his dirty hands, didn't he?
Yep. There are his fingerprints.>
<Why did you boys let this happen?
Let's try and fix this.
Go get a bucket of water, VICENTE FERNÁNDEZ!>

CHAPTER 10 THE MEXICAN JEDI

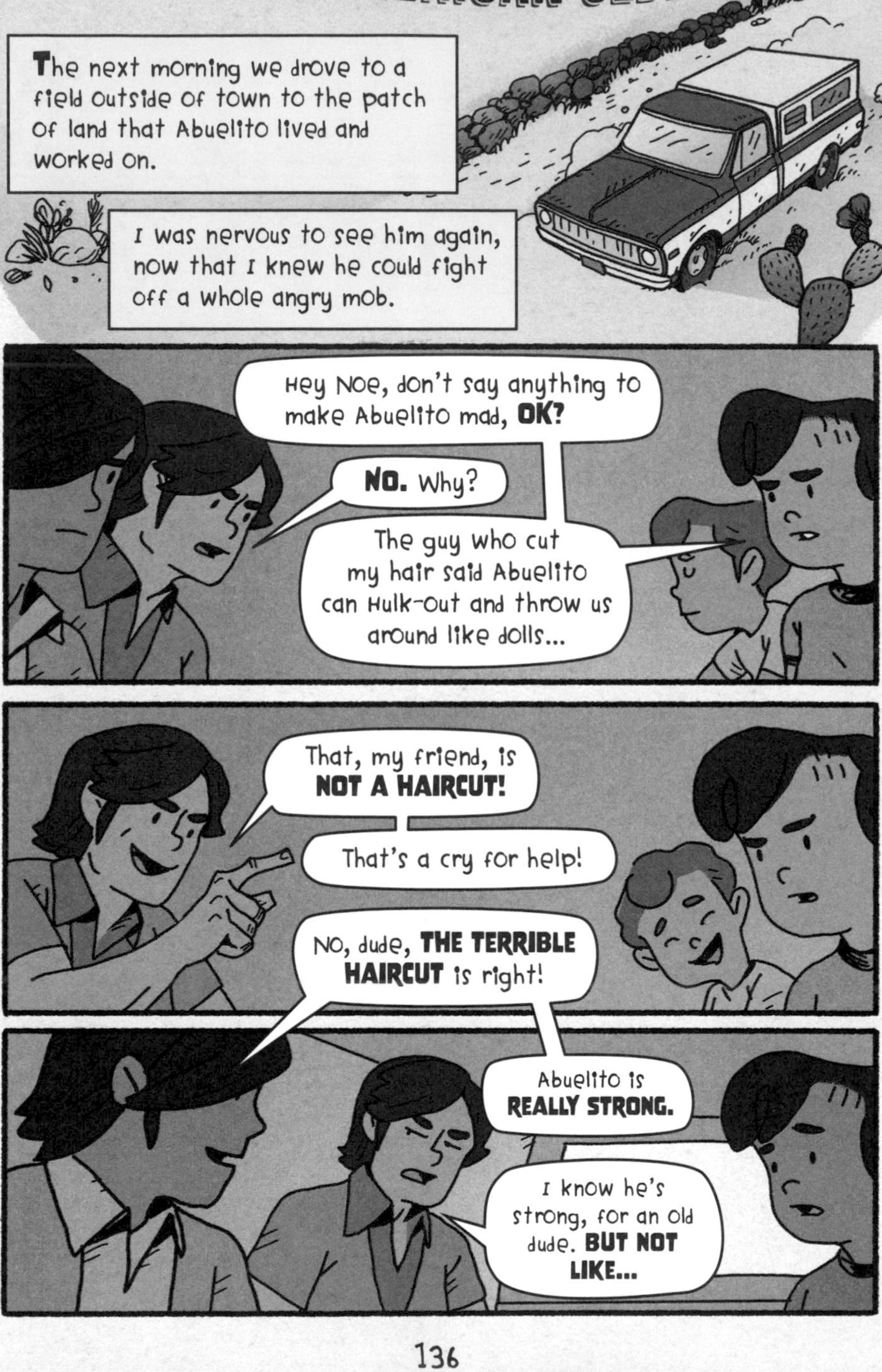
The next morning we drove to a field outside of town to the patch of land that Abuelito lived and worked on.
I was nervous to see him again, now that I knew he could fight off a whole angry mob.
Hey Noe, don't say anything to make Abuelito mad, OK?
NO. Why?
The guy who cut my hair said Abuelito can Hulk-out and throw us around like dolls...
That, my friend, is NOT A HAIRCUT!
That's a cry for help!
No, dude, THE TERRIBLE HAIRCUT is right!
Abuelito is REALLY STRONG.
I know he's strong, for an old dude. BUT NOT LIKE...

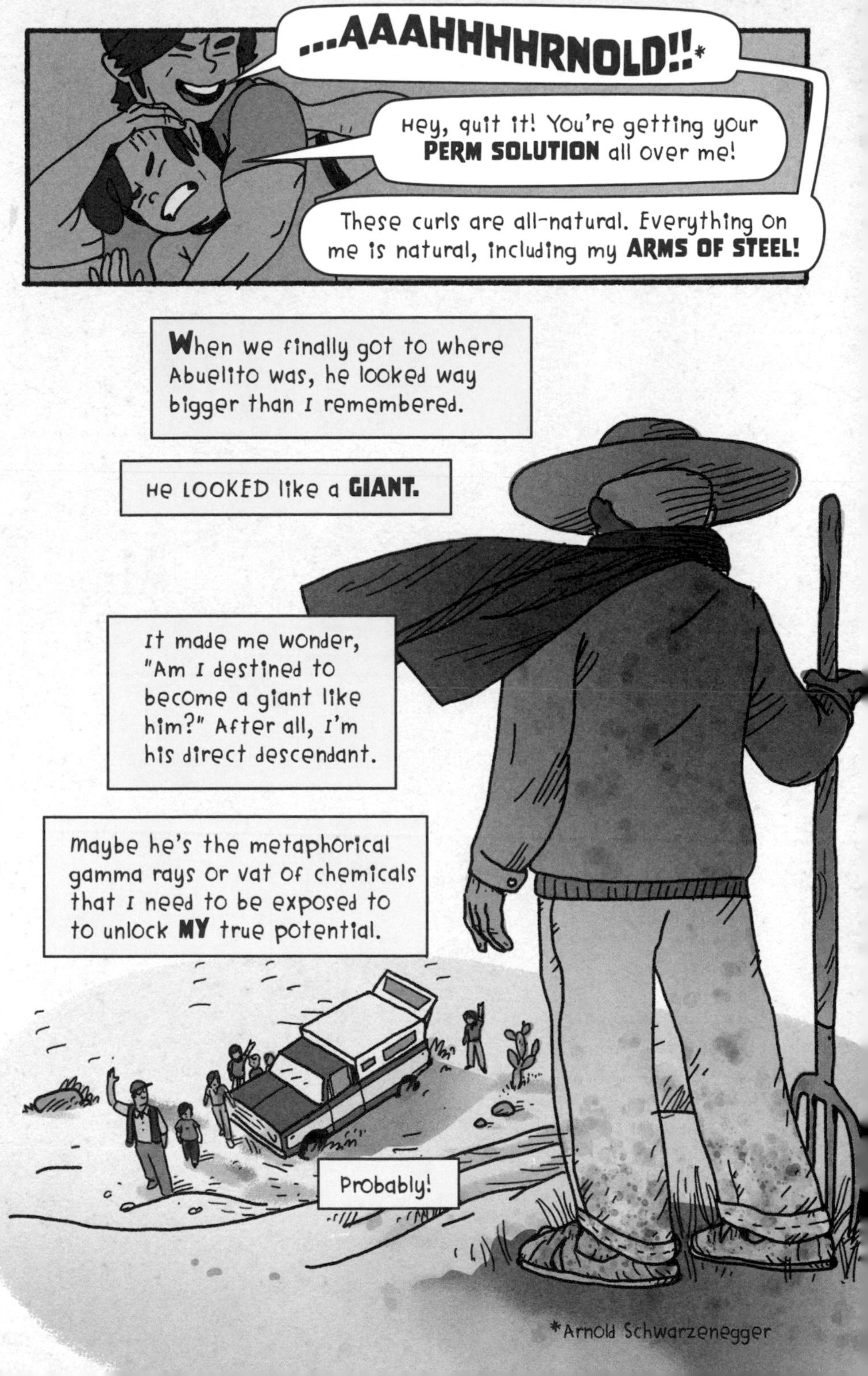

...AAAHHHHRNOLD!!*
Hey, quit it! You're getting your PERM SOLUTION all over me!
These curls are all-natural. Everything on me is natural, including my ARMS OF STEEL!
When we finally got to where Abuelito was, he looked way bigger than I remembered.
He LOOKED like a GIANT.
It made me wonder, "Am I destined to become a giant like him?" After all, I'm his direct descendant.
Maybe he's the metaphorical gamma rays or vat of chemicals that I need to be exposed to to unlock MY true potential.
Probably!
*Arnold Schwarzenegger

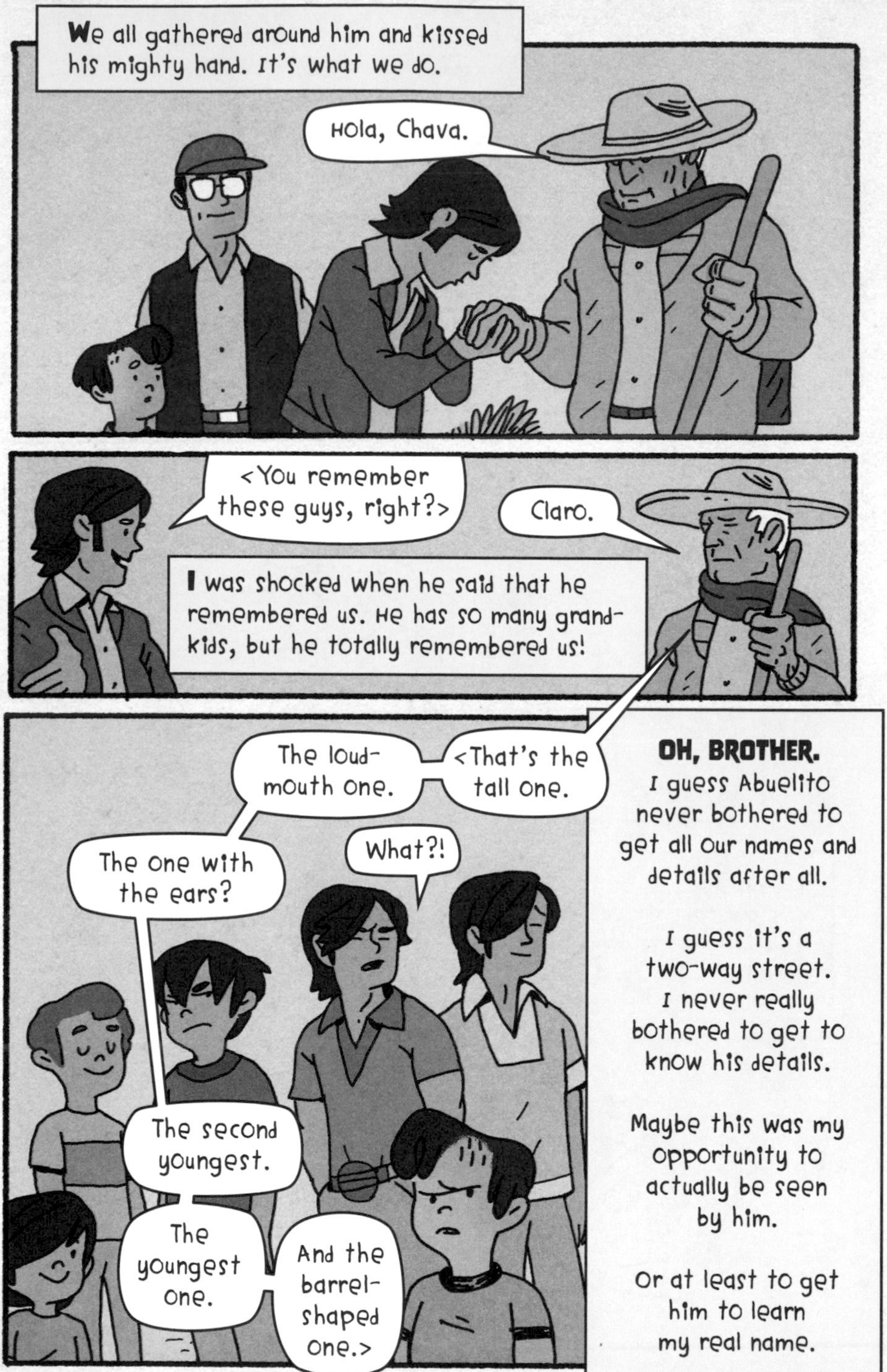

We all gathered around him and kissed his mighty hand. It's what we do.
Hola, Chava.
<You remember these guys, right?>
Claro.
I was shocked when he said that he remembered us. He has so many grand-kids, but he totally remembered us!
<That's the tall one.
The loud-mouth one.
The one with the ears?
What?!
The second youngest.
The youngest one.
And the barrel-shaped one.>
OH, BROTHER.
I guess Abuelito never bothered to get all our names and details after all.
I guess it's a two-way street. I never really bothered to get to know his details.
Maybe this was my opportunity to actually be seen by him.
Or at least to get him to learn my real name.

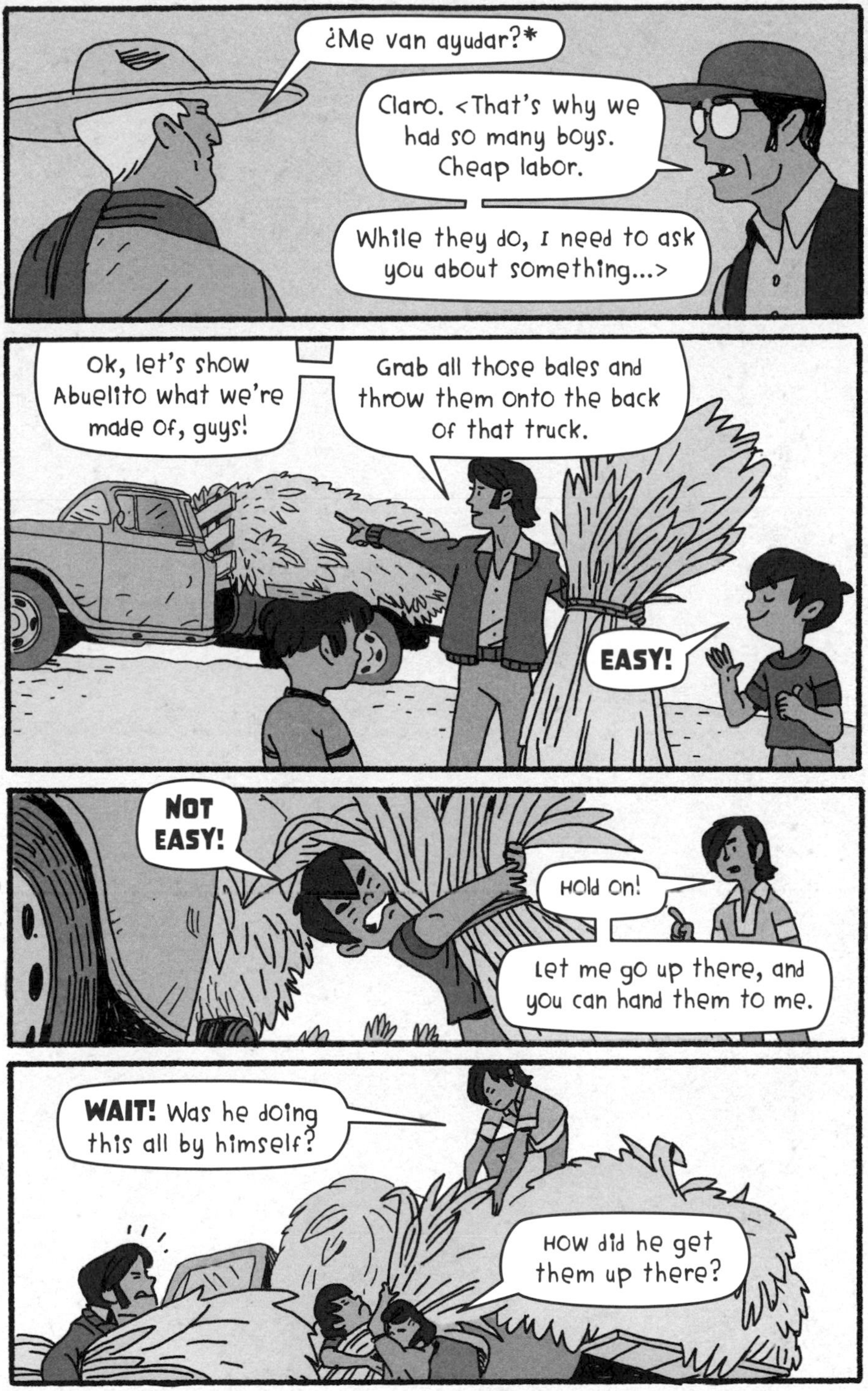
¿Me van ayudar?*
Claro. <That's why we had so many boys. Cheap labor.
While they do, I need to ask you about something...>
Ok, let's show Abuelito what we're made of, guys!
Grab all those bales and throw them onto the back of that truck.
EASY!
NOT EASY!
Hold on!
Let me go up there, and you can hand them to me.
WAIT! Was he doing this all by himself?
How did he get them up there?

*Are they going to help me?

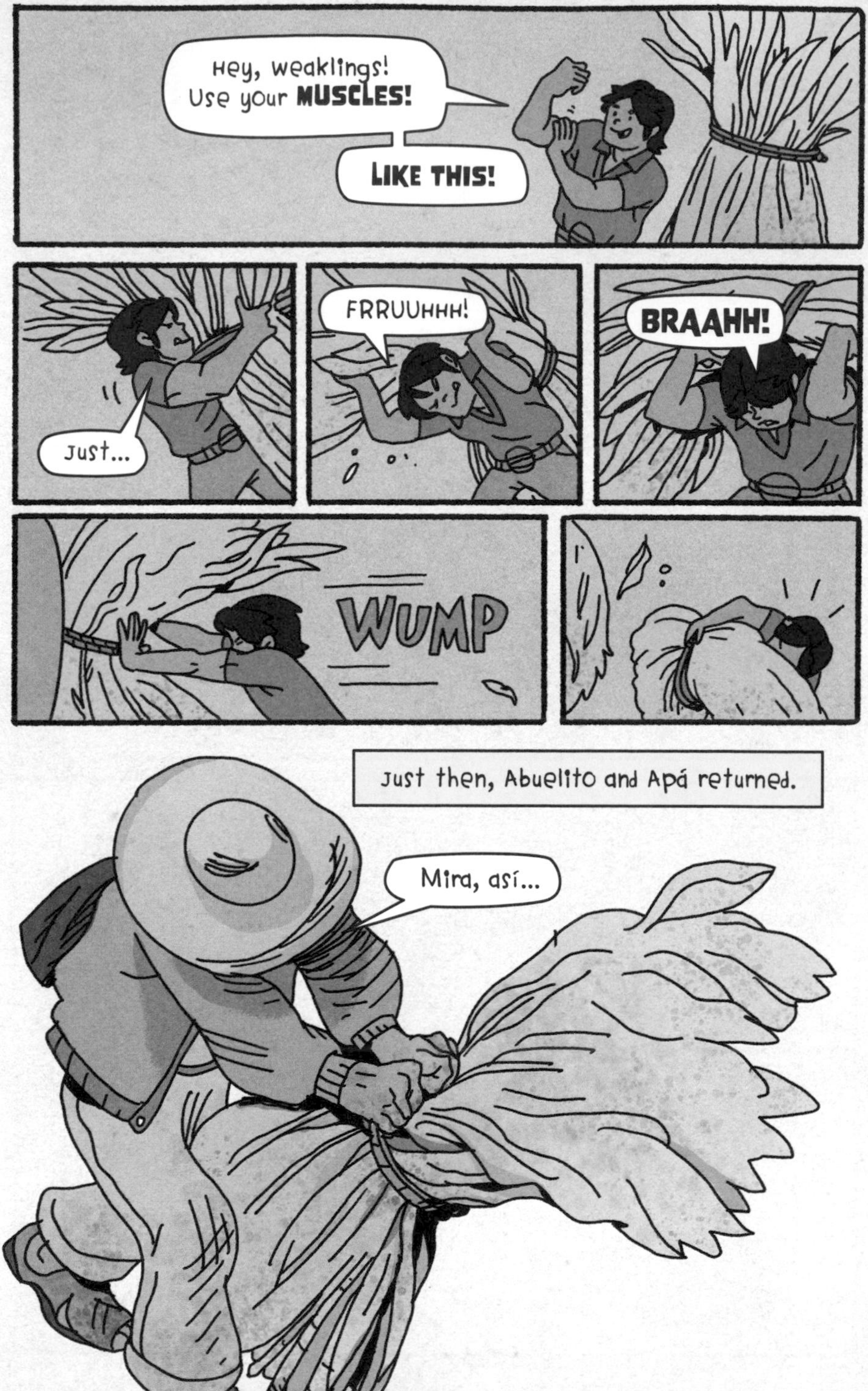
Hey, weaklings! Use your MUSCLES!
LIKE THIS!
Just...
FRRUUHHH!
BRAAHH!
WUMP
Just then, Abuelito and Apá returned.
Mira, así...

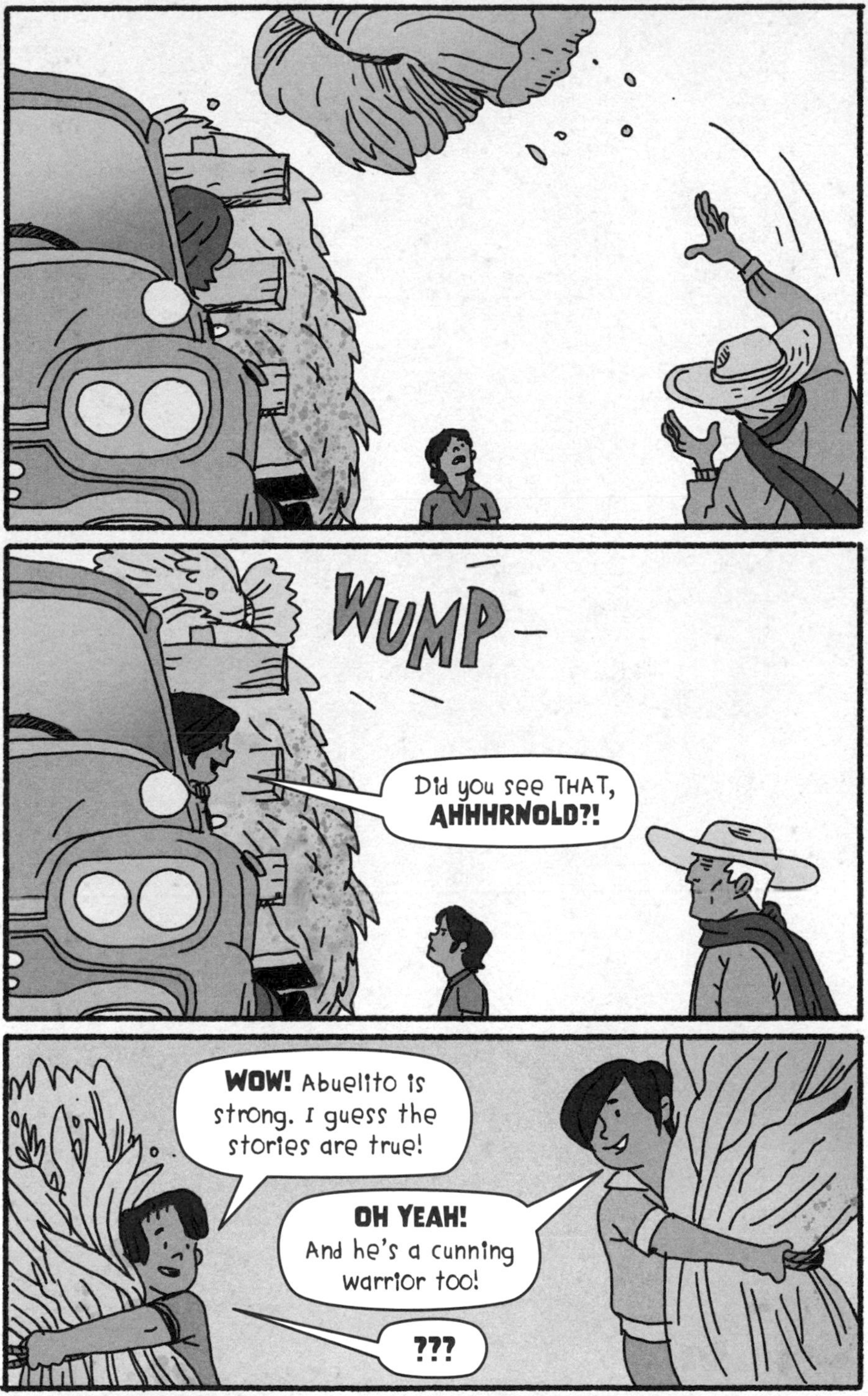
WUMP
Did you see THAT, AHHHRNOLD?!
WOW! Abuelito is strong. I guess the stories are true!
OH YEAH! And he's a cunning warrior too!
???

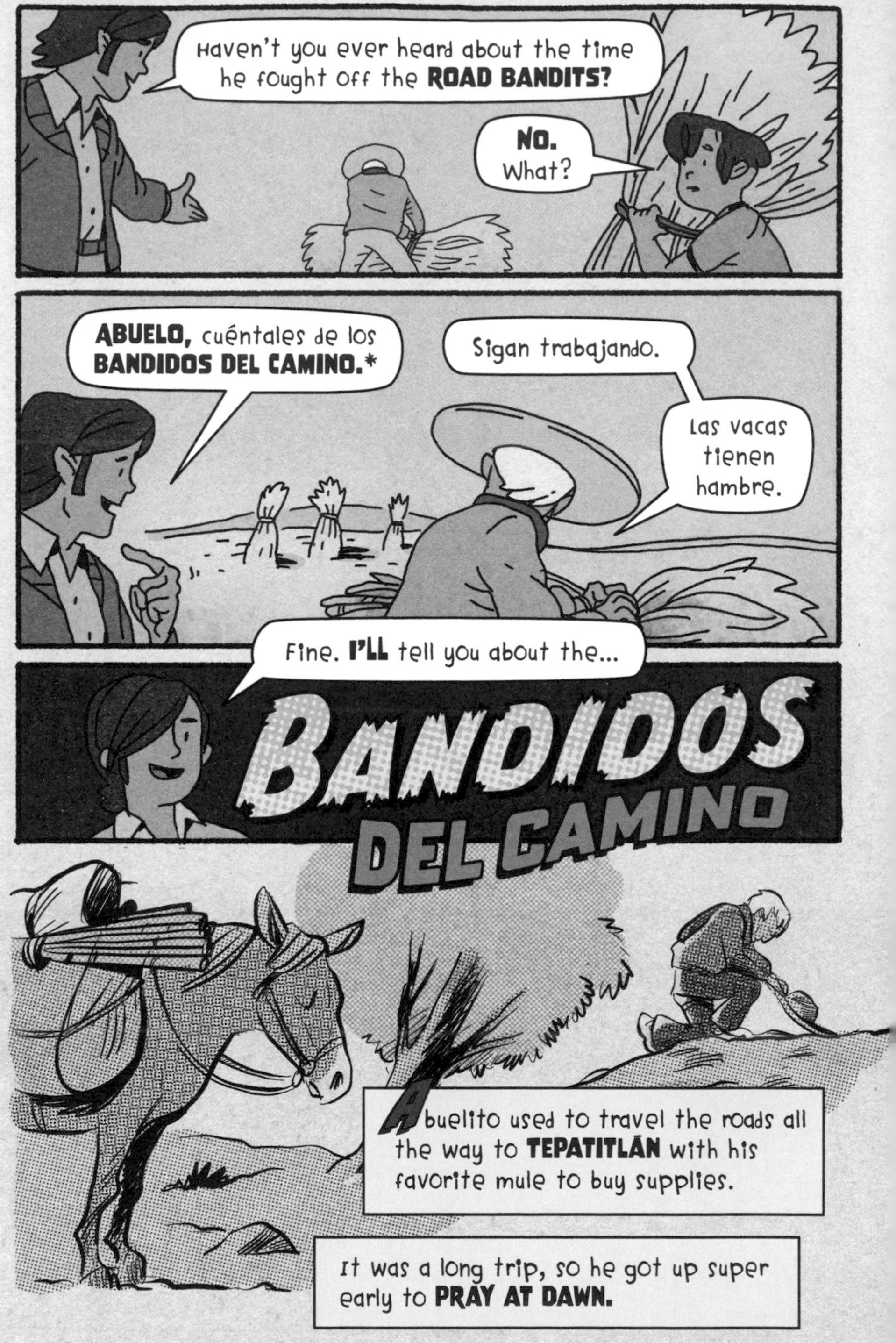
Haven't you ever heard about the time he fought off the ROAD BANDITS?
NO.
What?
ABUELO, cuéntales de los BANDIDOS DEL CAMINO.*
Sigan trabajando.
Las vacas tienen hambre.
Fine. I'LL tell you about the...
BANDIDOS DEL CAMINO
Abuelito used to travel the roads all the way to TEPATITLÁN with his favorite mule to buy supplies.
It was a long trip, so he got up super early to PRAY AT DAWN.

*Grandpa, tell them about the ROAD BANDITS!

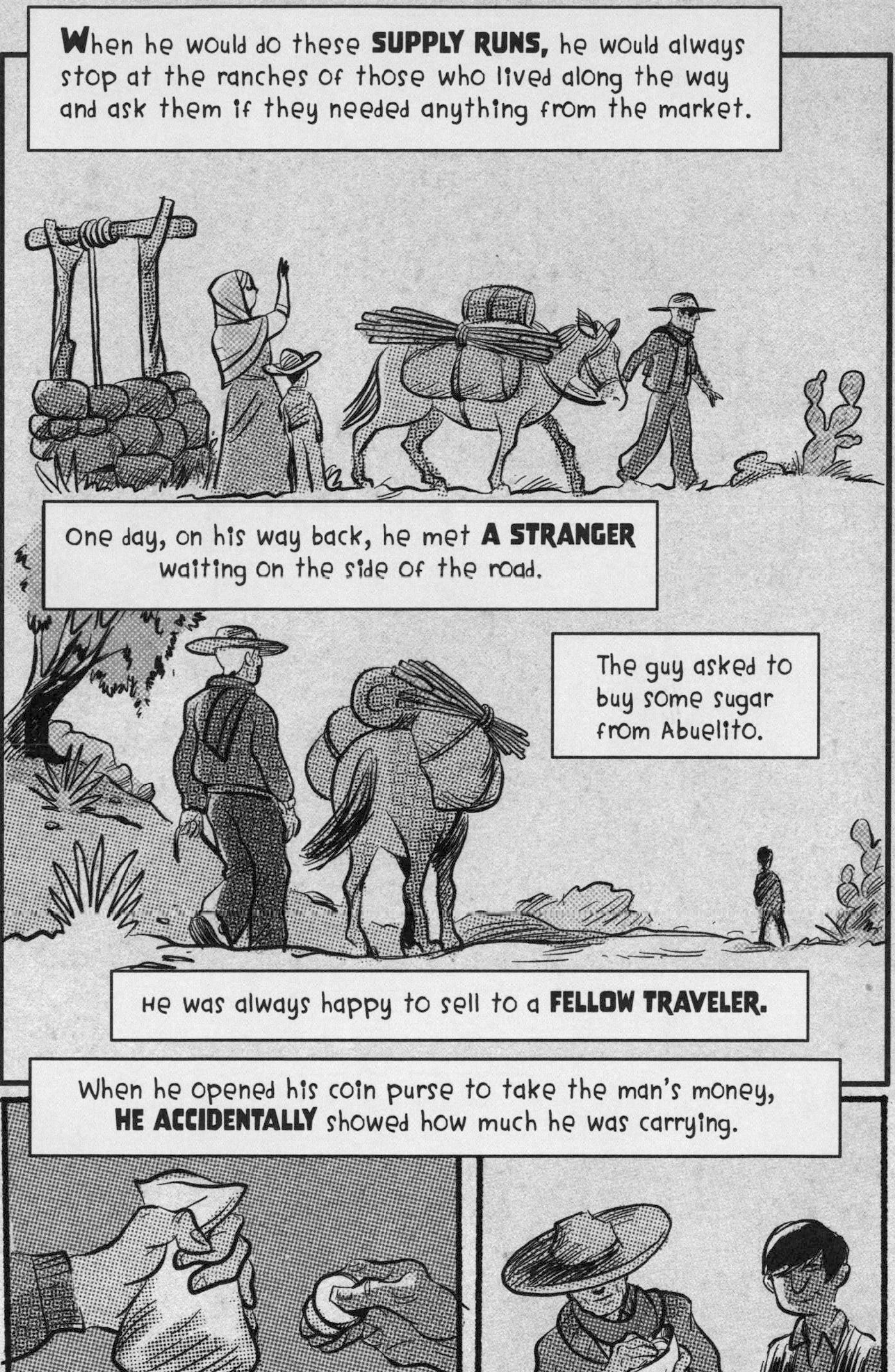
When he would do these SUPPLY RUNS, he would always stop at the ranches of those who lived along the way and ask them if they needed anything from the market.
One day, on his way back, he met A STRANGER waiting on the side of the road.
The guy asked to buy some sugar from Abuelito.
He was always happy to sell to a FELLOW TRAVELER.
When he opened his coin purse to take the man's money, HE ACCIDENTALLY showed how much he was carrying.

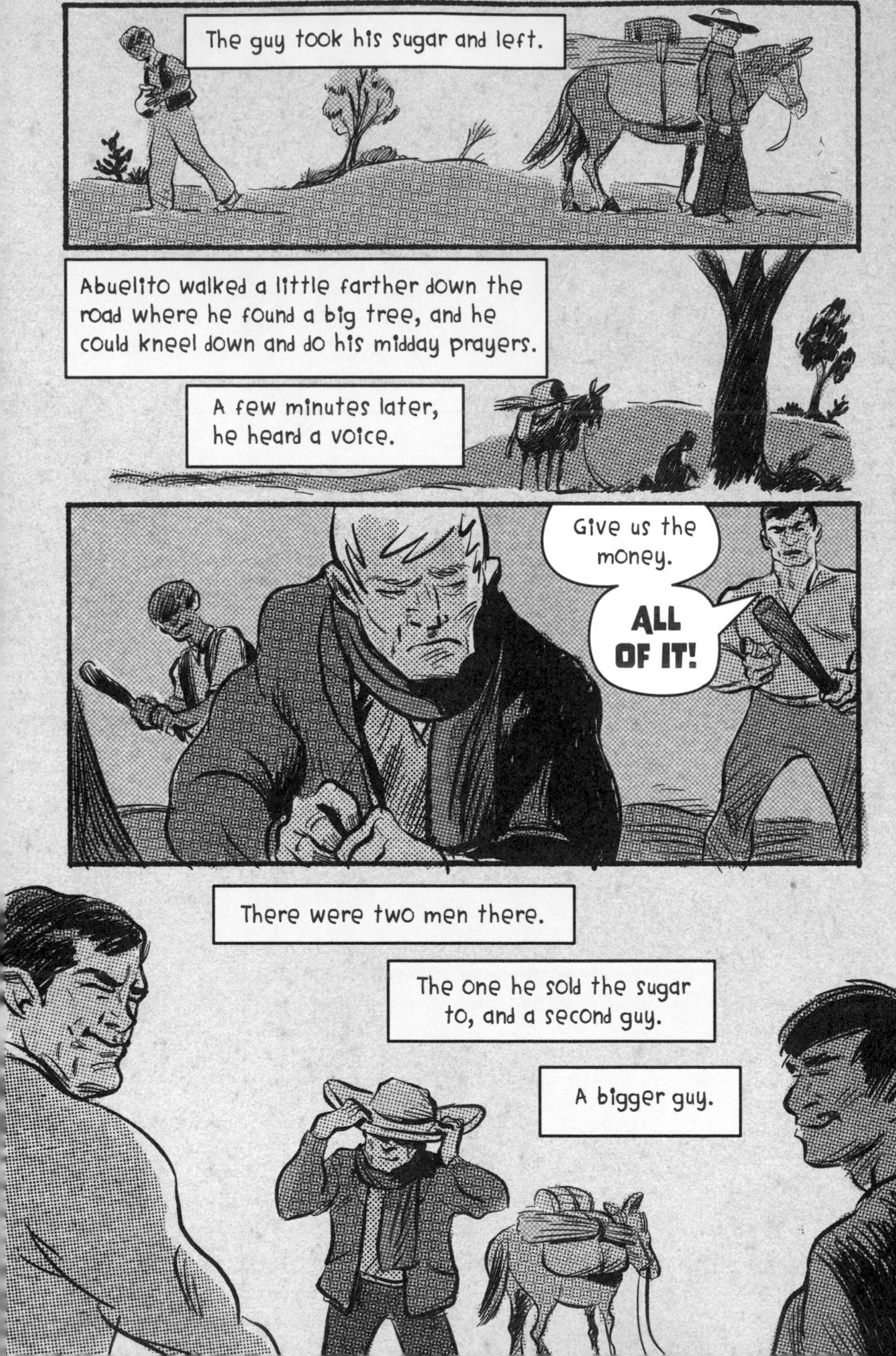
The guy took his sugar and left.
Abuelito walked a little farther down the road where he found a big tree, and he could kneel down and do his midday prayers.
A few minutes later, he heard a voice.
Give us the money.
ALL OF IT!
There were two men there.
The one he sold the sugar to, and a second guy.
A bigger guy.

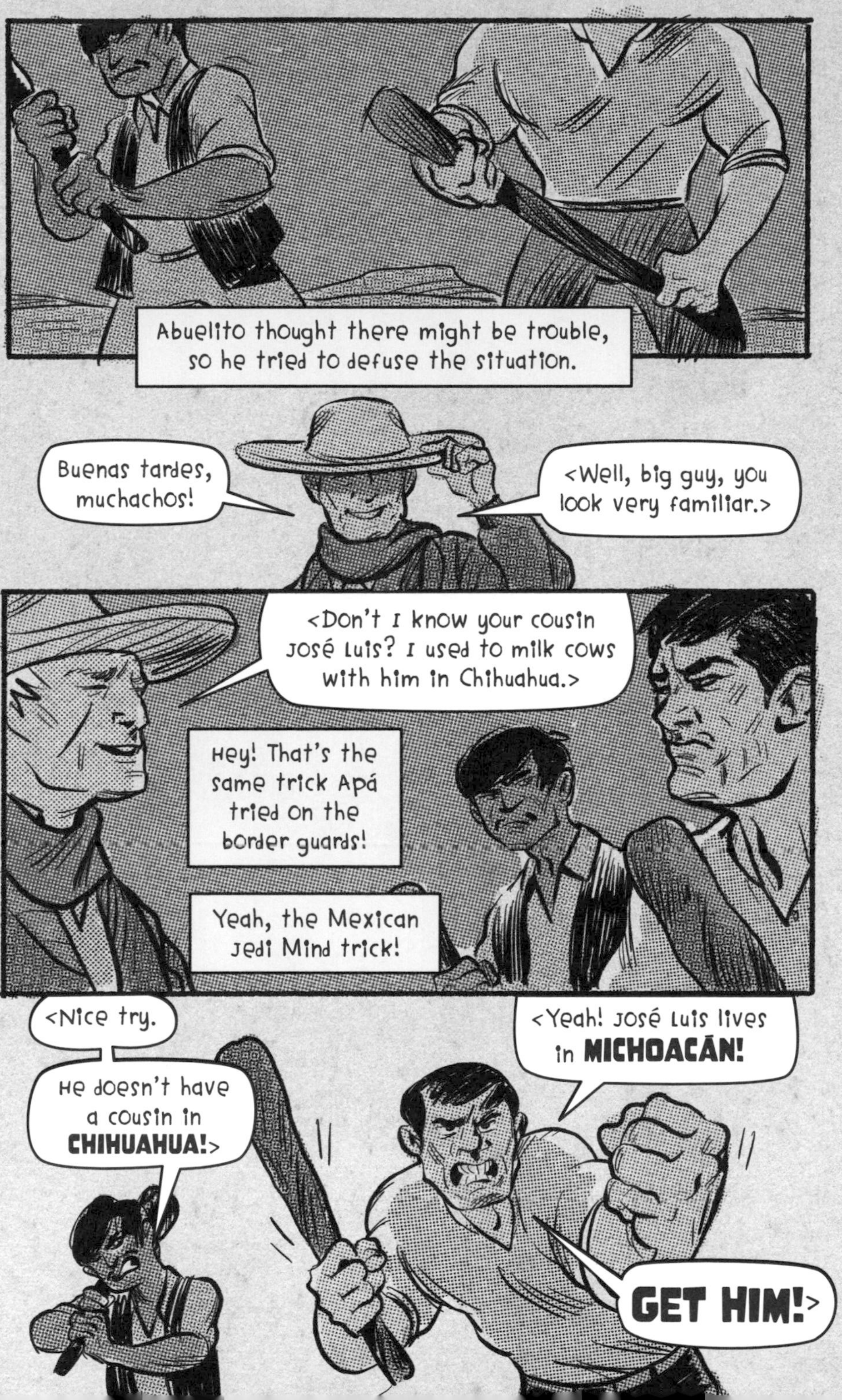
Abuelito thought there might be trouble, so he tried to defuse the situation.
Buenas tardes, muchachos!
<Well, big guy, you look very familiar.>
<Don't I know your cousin José Luis? I used to milk cows with him in Chihuahua.>
Hey! That's the same trick Apá tried on the border guards!
Yeah, the Mexican Jedi Mind trick!
<Nice try.
He doesn't have a cousin in CHIHUAHUA!>
<Yeah! José Luis lives in MICHOACÁN!
GET HIM!>

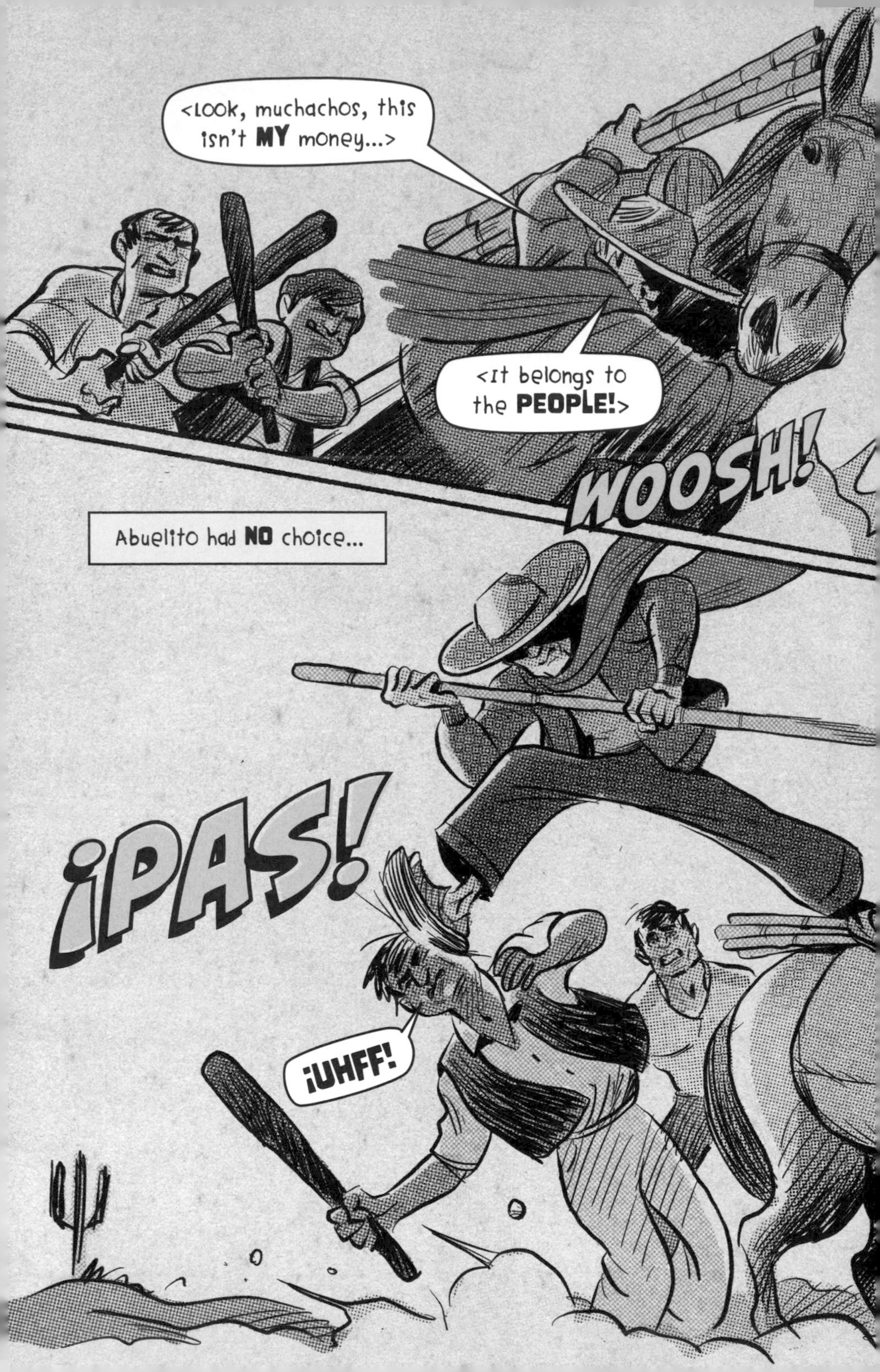
<Look, muchachos, this isn't **MY** money...>
<It belongs to the **PEOPLE!**>
WOOSH!
Abuelito had **NO** choice...
¡PAS!
¡UHFF!

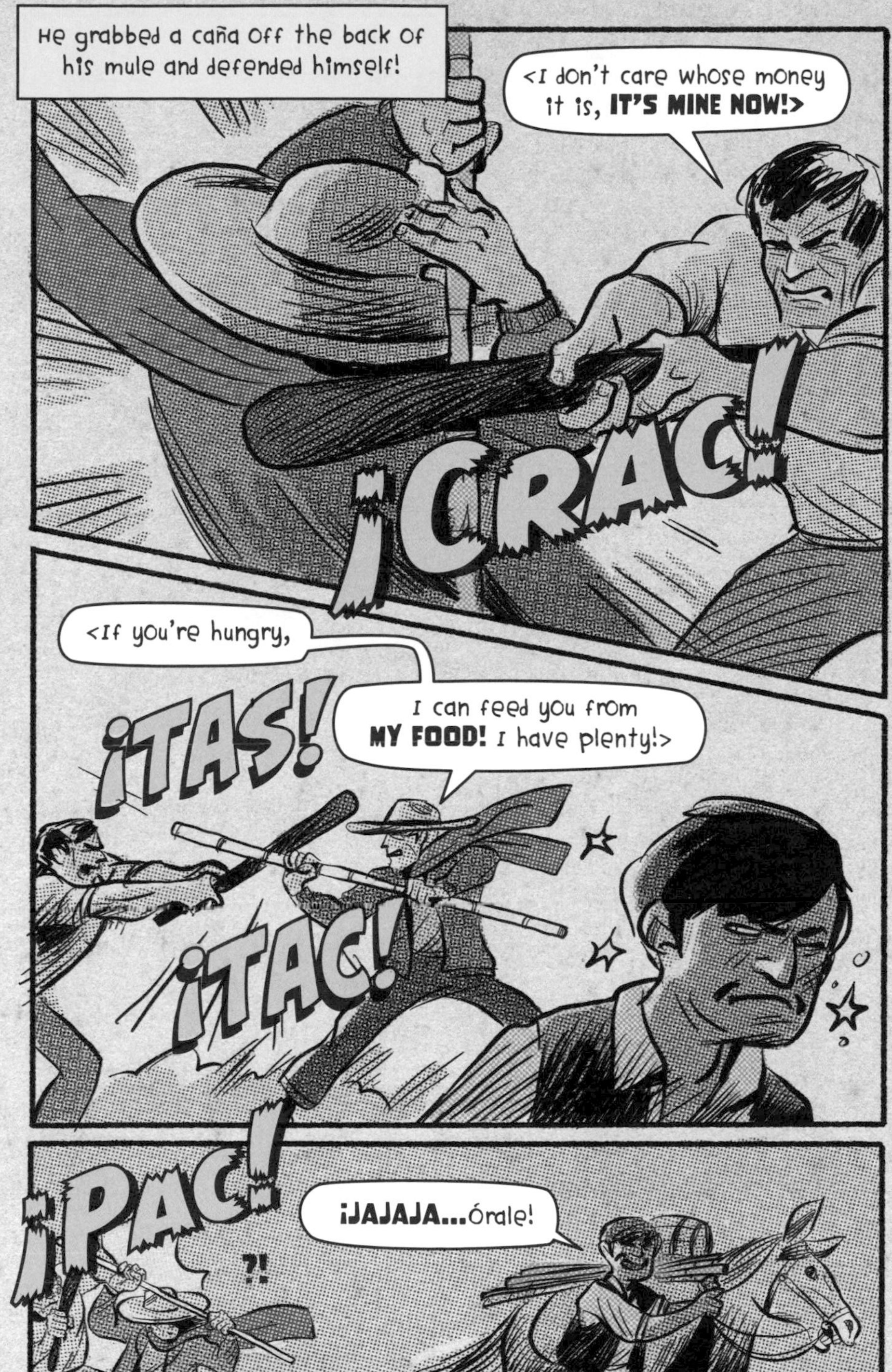
He grabbed a caña off the back of his mule and defended himself!
<I don't care whose money it is, IT'S MINE NOW!>
¡CRAC!
<If you're hungry,
I can feed you from MY FOOD! I have plenty!>
¡TAS!
¡TAC!
¡PAC!
?!
¡JAJAJA...órale!

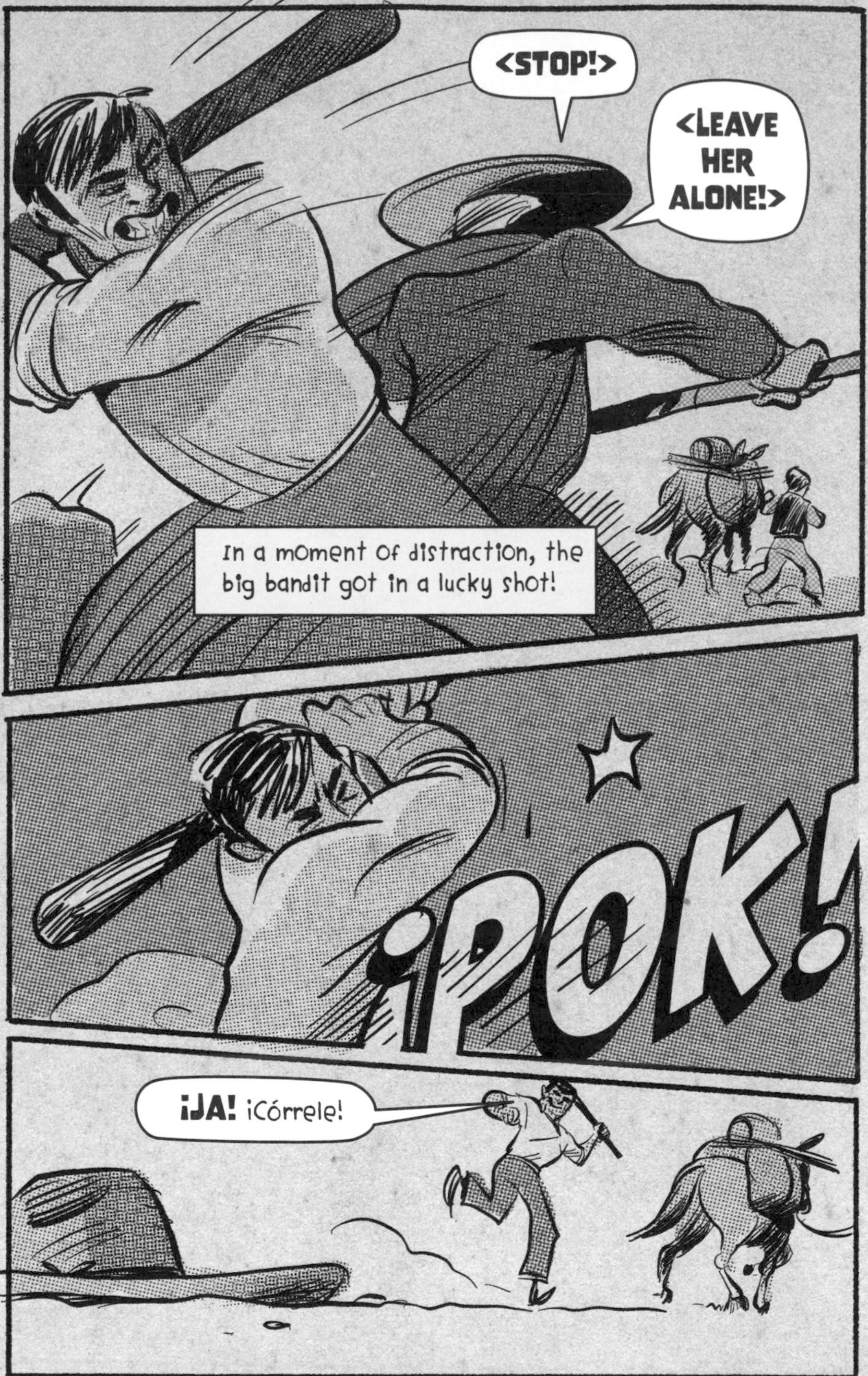
<STOP!>
<LEAVE HER ALONE!>
In a moment of distraction, the big bandit got in a lucky shot!
¡POK!
¡JA! ¡Córrele!

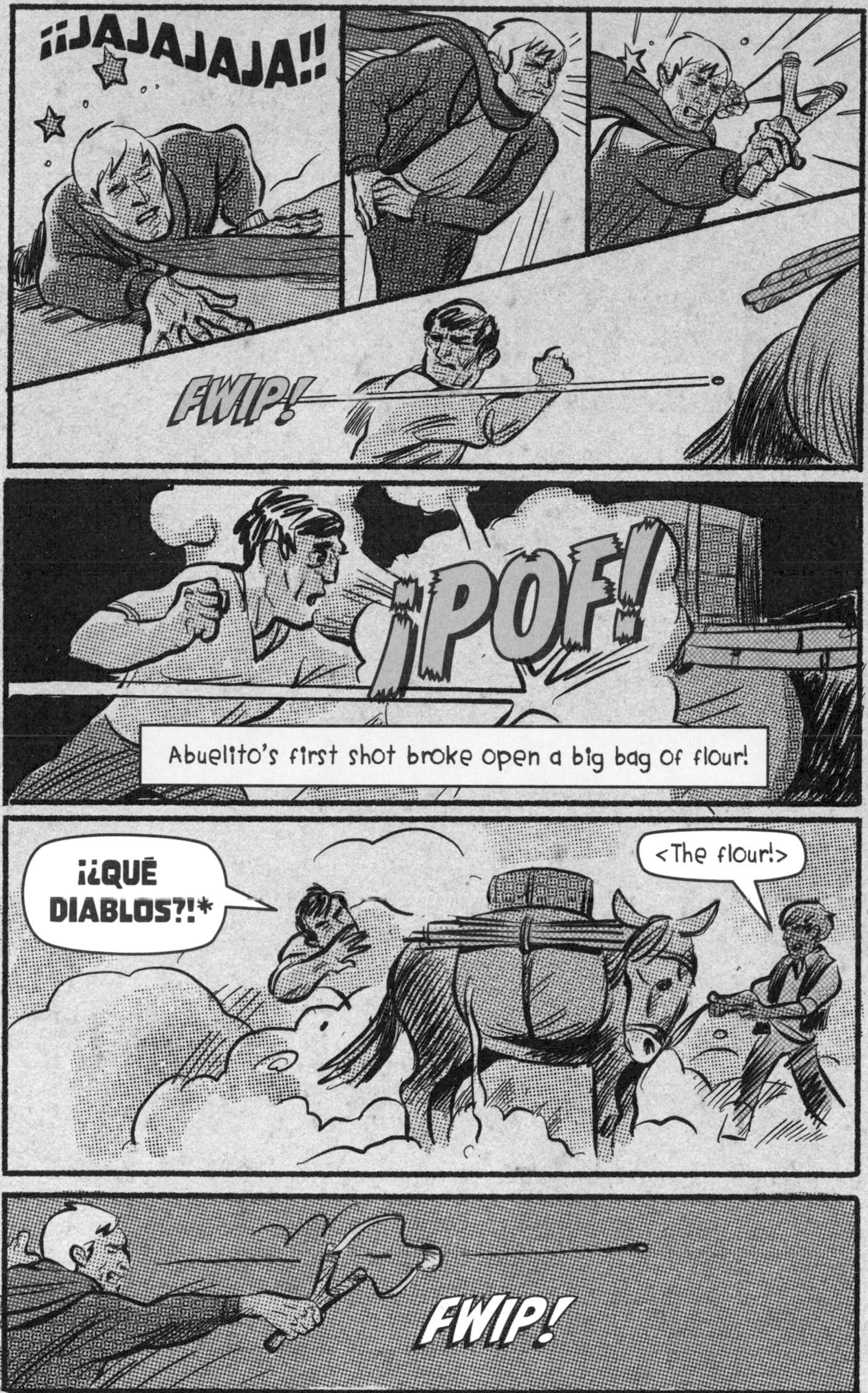
¡¡JAJAJAJA!!
FWIP!
¡POF!
Abuelito's first shot broke open a big bag of flour!
¡¿QUÉ DIABLOS?!*
<The flour!>
FWIP!

*What the devil?!

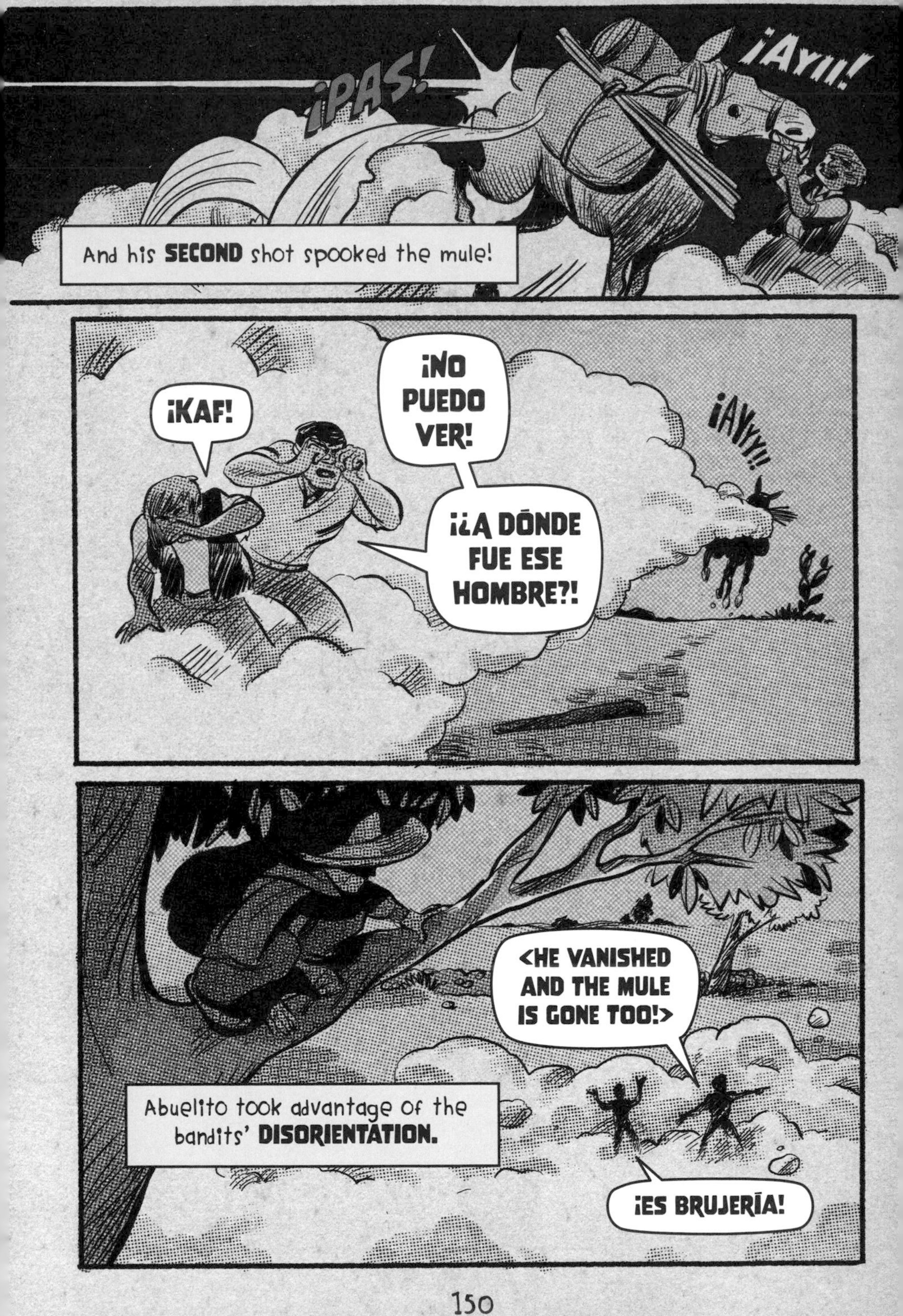
¡PAS!
¡AYII!
And his **SECOND** shot spooked the mule!
¡KAF!
¡NO PUEDO VER!
¡¿A DÓNDE FUE ESE HOMBRE?!
¡AYYY!!
Abuelito took advantage of the bandits' **DISORIENTATION.**
<HE VANISHED AND THE MULE IS GONE TOO!>
¡ES BRUJERÍA!

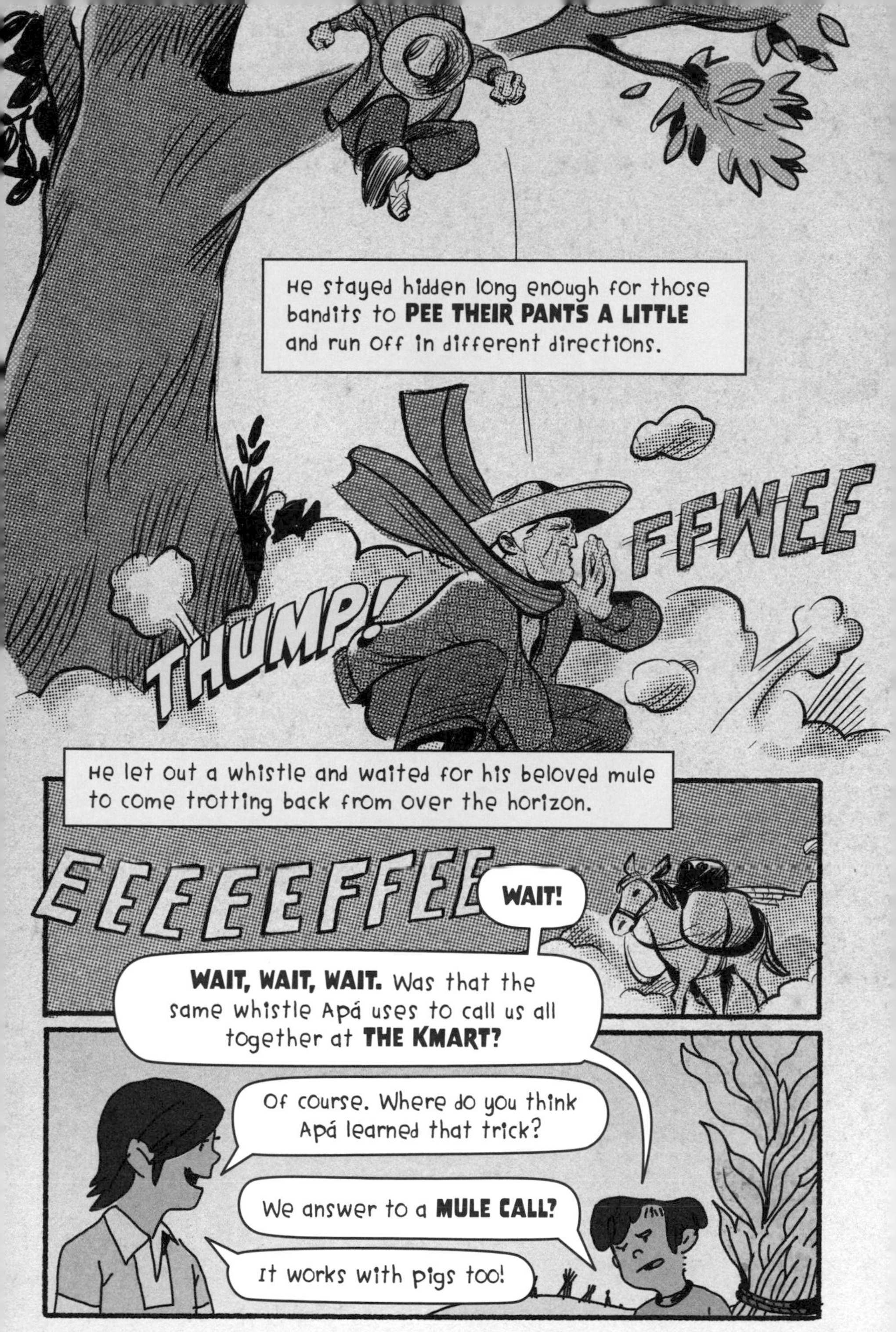
He stayed hidden long enough for those bandits to PEE THEIR PANTS A LITTLE and run off in different directions.
THUMP!
FFWEE
He let out a whistle and waited for his beloved mule to come trotting back from over the horizon.
EEEEEFFEE
WAIT!
WAIT, WAIT, WAIT. Was that the same whistle Apá uses to call us all together at THE KMART?
Of course. Where do you think Apá learned that trick?
We answer to a MULE CALL?
It works with pigs too!

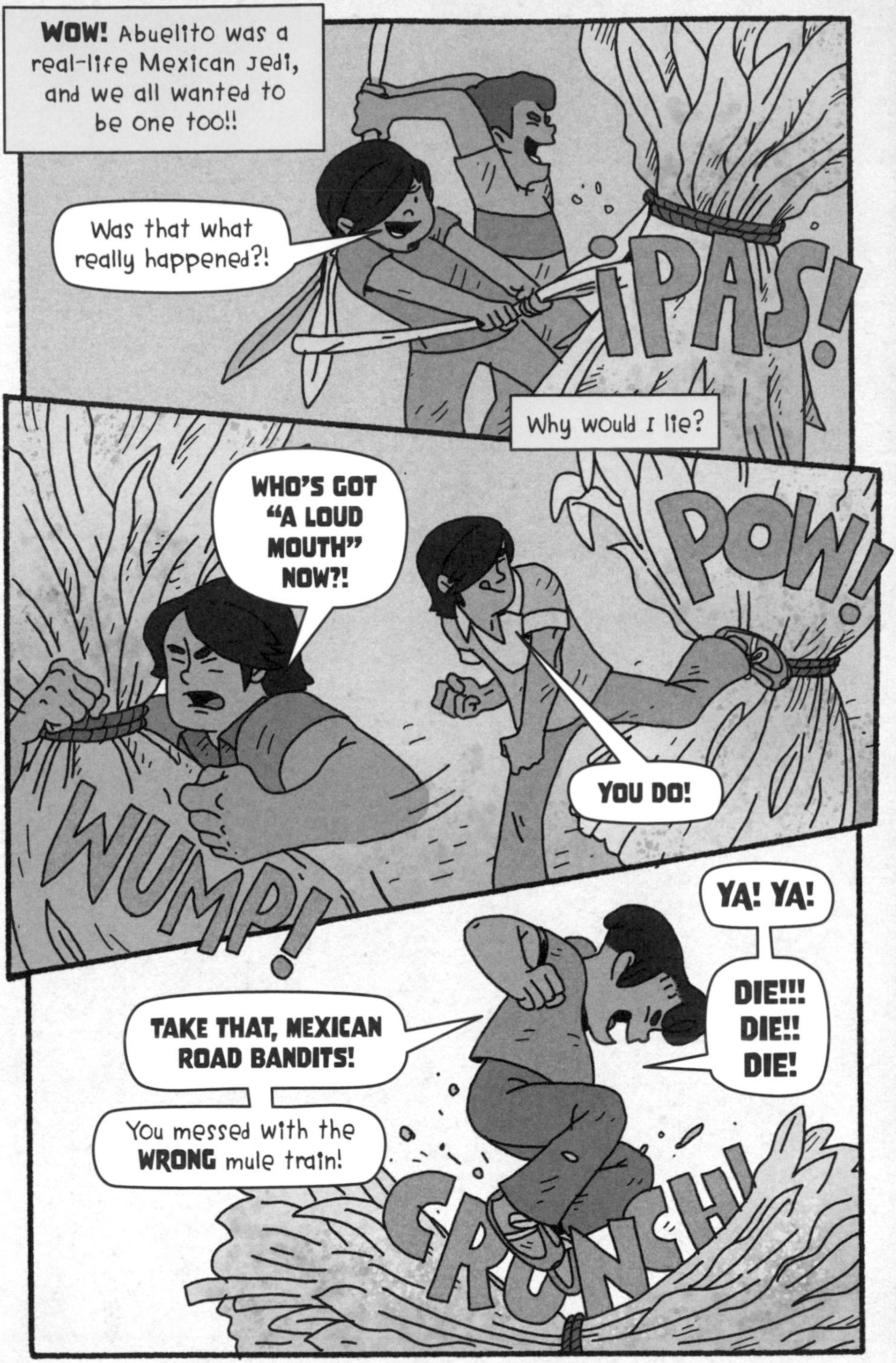
WOW! Abuelito was a real-life Mexican Jedi, and we all wanted to be one too!!
Was that what really happened?!
¡PAS!
Why would I lie?
WHO'S GOT "A LOUD MOUTH" NOW?!
POW!
YOU DO!
WUMP!
YA! YA!
DIE!!! DIE!! DIE!
TAKE THAT, MEXICAN ROAD BANDITS!
You messed with the WRONG mule train!
CRUNCH!

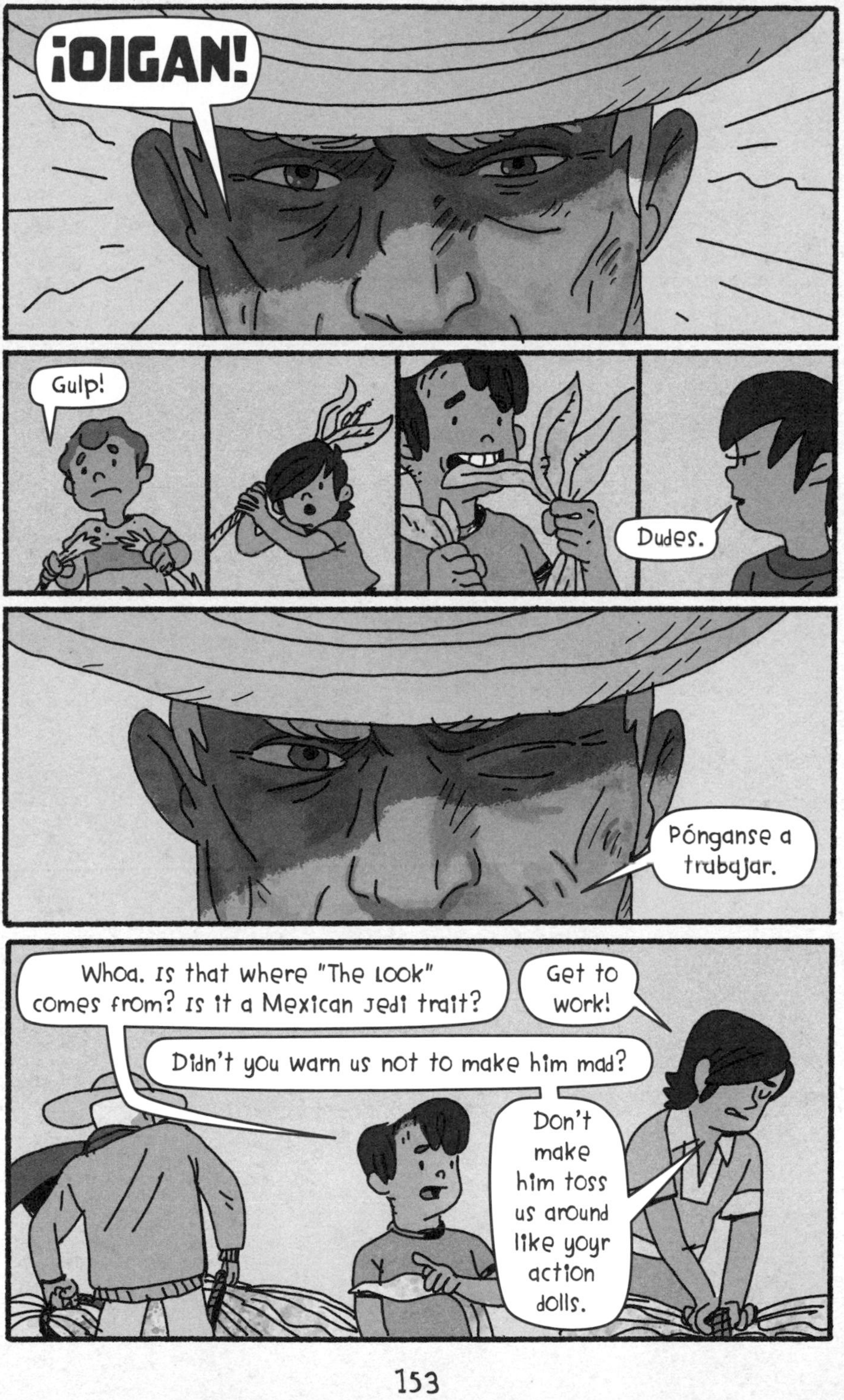
¡OIGAN!
Gulp!
Dudes.
Póngnse a trabajar.
Whoa. Is that where "The Look" comes from? Is it a Mexican Jedi trait?
Get to work!
Didn't you warn us not to make him mad?
Don't make him toss us around like yoyr action dolls.

CHAPTER 11
LOVE IN THE TIME OF FLIES

Our time in Pegueros wasn't all just work and road fighting. It was also a place to find love and besos (kisses).

The best way was the traditional "Serenata," or "Serenade." It's an activity that helps lovers find each other and enjoy music and candy!

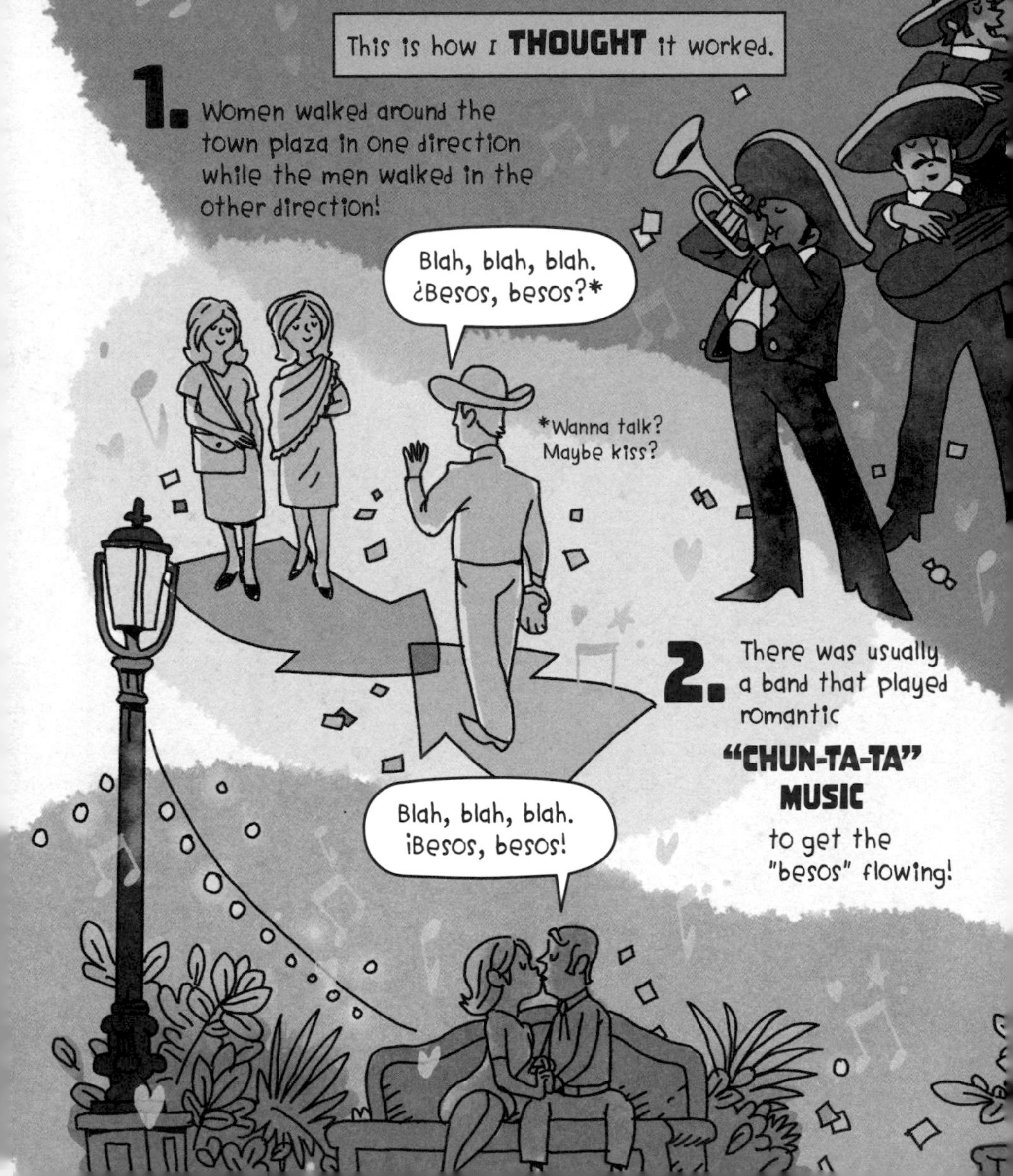
This is how I **THOUGHT** it worked.
1. Women walked around the town plaza in one direction while the men walked in the other direction!
Blah, blah, blah. ¿Besos, besos?*
*Wanna talk? Maybe kiss?
2. There was usually a band that played romantic
"CHUN-TA-TA" MUSIC
to get the "besos" flowing!
Blah, blah, blah. ¡Besos, besos!

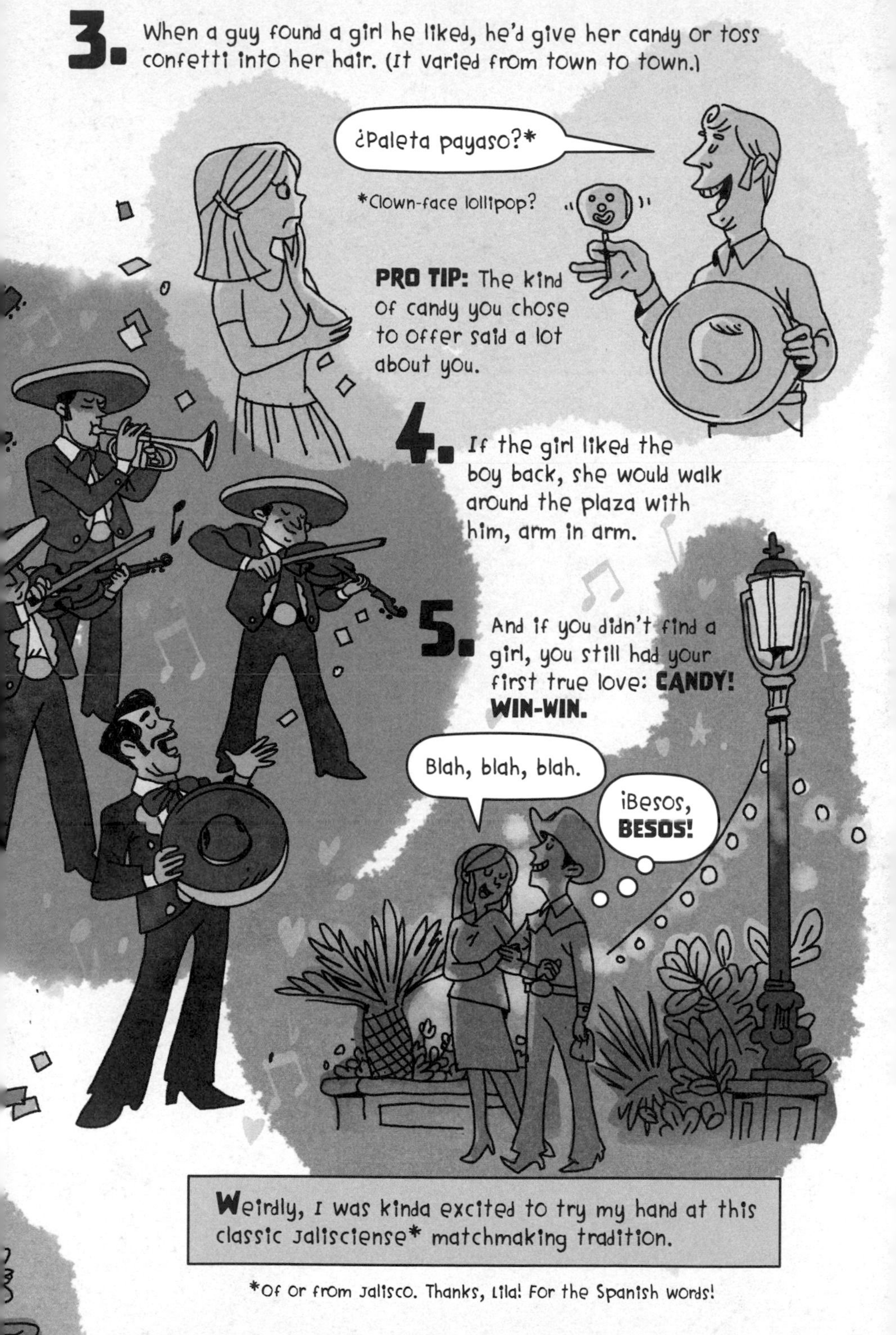
3. When a guy found a girl he liked, he'd give her candy or toss confetti into her hair. (It varied from town to town.)
¿Paleta payaso?*
*Clown-face lollipop?
PRO TIP: The kind of candy you chose to offer said a lot about you.
4. If the girl liked the boy back, she would walk around the plaza with him, arm in arm.
5. And if you didn't find a girl, you still had your first true love: CANDY! WIN-WIN.
Blah, blah, blah.
¡Besos, BESOS!
Weirdly, I was kinda excited to try my hand at this classic Jalisciense* matchmaking tradition.
*Of or from Jalisco. Thanks, Lila! For the Spanish words!

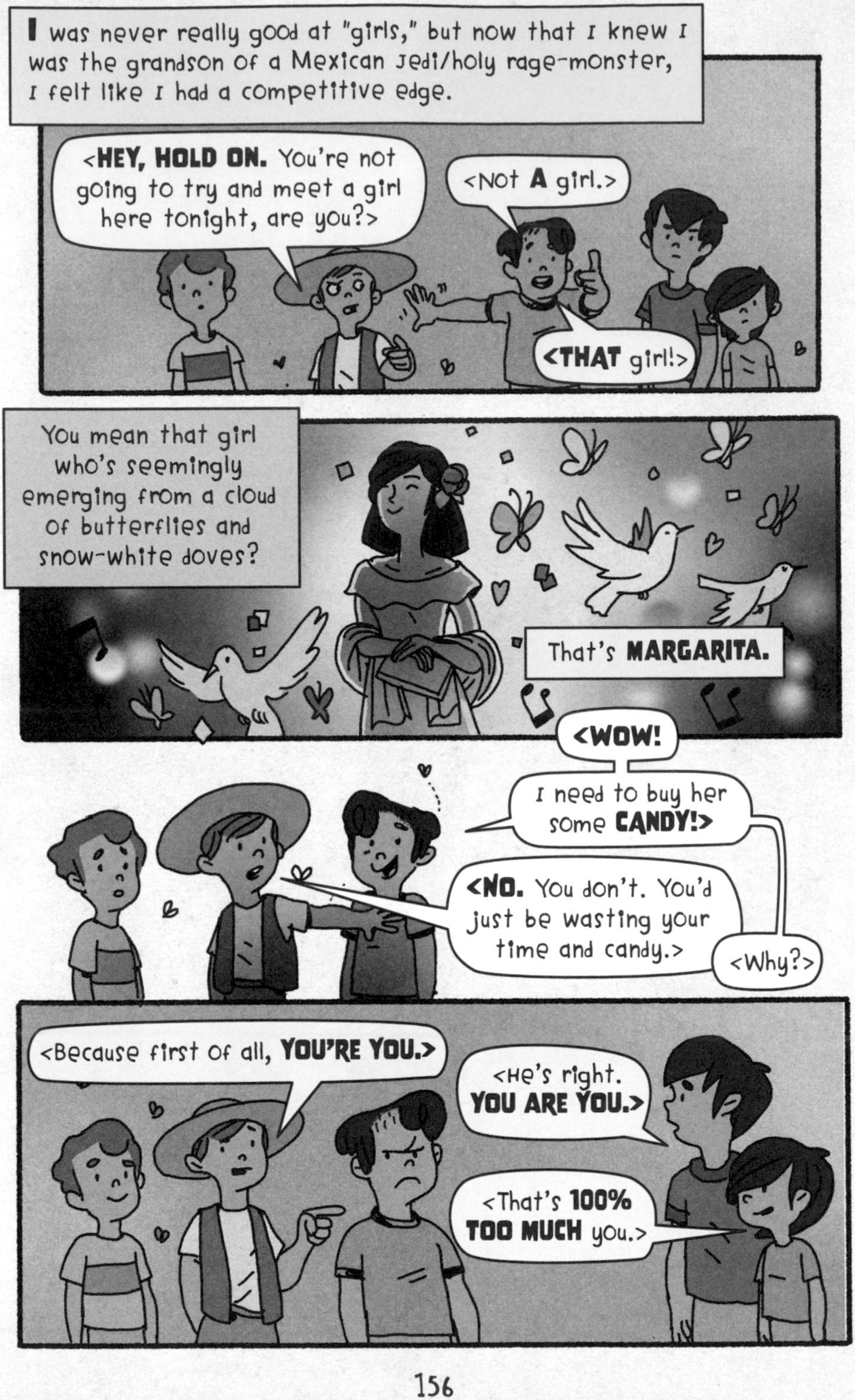
I was never really good at "girls," but now that I knew I was the grandson of a Mexican Jedi/holy rage-monster, I felt like I had a competitive edge.
<HEY, HOLD ON. You're not going to try and meet a girl here tonight, are you?>
<Not A girl.>
<THAT girl!>
You mean that girl who's seemingly emerging from a cloud of butterflies and snow-white doves?
That's MARGARITA.
<WOW!
I need to buy her some CANDY!>
<NO. You don't. You'd just be wasting your time and candy.>
<Why?>
<Because first of all, YOU'RE YOU.>
<He's right. YOU ARE YOU.>
<That's 100% TOO MUCH you.>

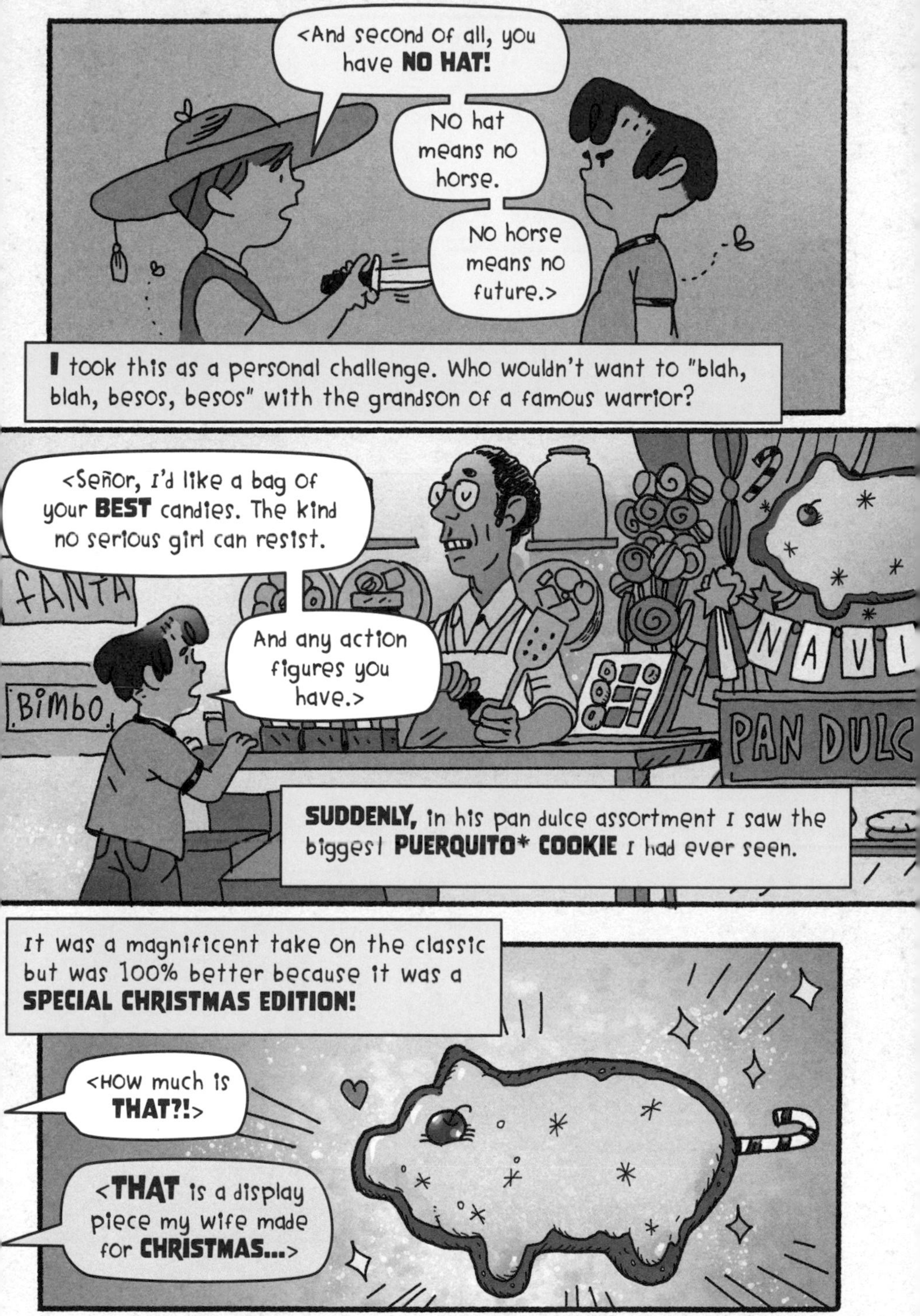
<And second of all, you have **NO HAT!**
No hat means no horse.
No horse means no future.>
I took this as a personal challenge. Who wouldn't want to "blah, blah, besos, besos" with the grandson of a famous warrior?
<Señor, I'd like a bag of your **BEST** candies. The kind no serious girl can resist.
And any action figures you have.>
FANTA
BIMBO
NAVI
PAN DULC
SUDDENLY, in his pan dulce assortment I saw the biggest **PUERQUITO* COOKIE** I had ever seen.
It was a magnificent take on the classic but was 100% better because it was a **SPECIAL CHRISTMAS EDITION!**
<HOW much is **THAT?!**>
<**THAT** is a display piece my wife made for **CHRISTMAS...**>

*A gingerbread cookie shaped like a pudgy piggy.

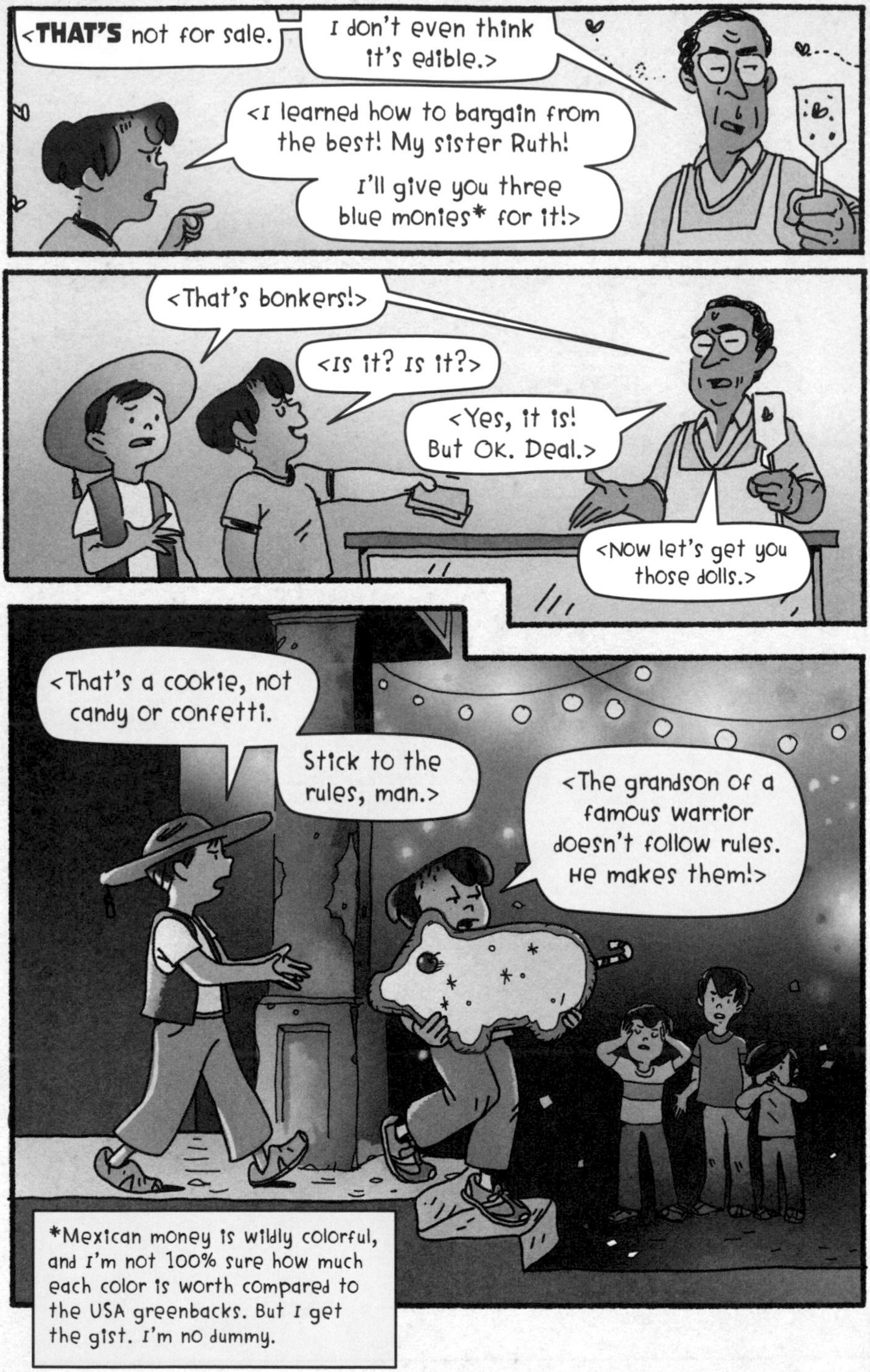
<**THAT'S** not for sale.
I don't even think it's edible.>
<I learned how to bargain from the best! My sister Ruth!
I'll give you three blue monies* for it!>
<That's bonkers!>
<Is it? Is it?>
<Yes, it is! But OK. Deal.>
<Now let's get you those dolls.>
<That's a cookie, not candy or confetti.
Stick to the rules, man.>
<The grandson of a famous warrior doesn't follow rules. He makes them!>
*Mexican money is wildly colorful, and I'm not 100% sure how much each color is worth compared to the USA greenbacks. But I get the gist. I'm no dummy.

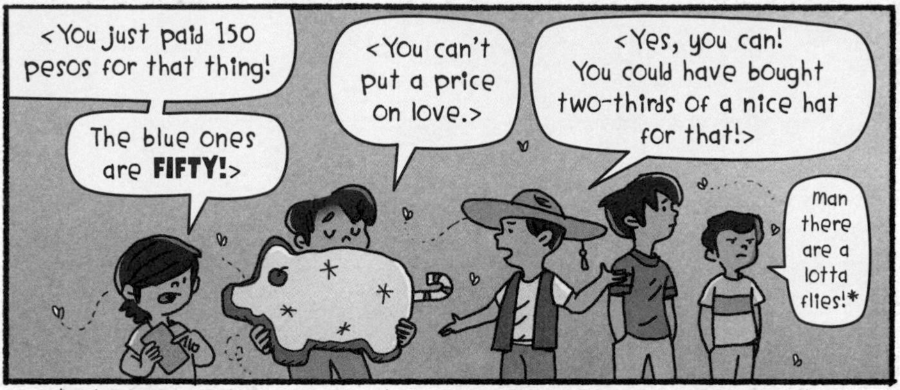
<You just paid 150 pesos for that thing!
The blue ones are **FIFTY!**>
<You can't put a price on love.>
<Yes, you can! You could have bought two-thirds of a nice hat for that!>
man there are a lotta flies!*

*It had been a bad year for flies. There were a lot of people keeping pigs in their backyards and the muck had no place to go. So they hung out on your food.

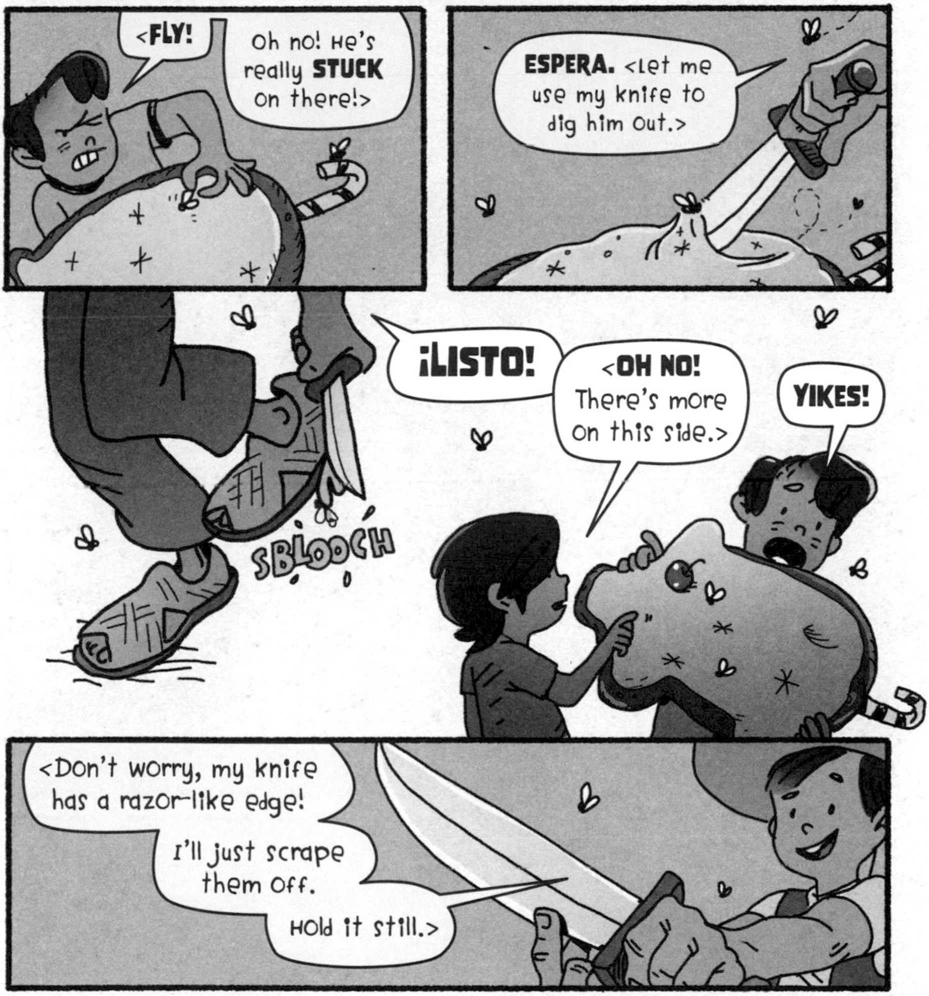
<**FLY!**
Oh no! He's really **STUCK** on there!>
ESPERA. <Let me use my knife to dig him out.>
¡LISTO!
SBLOOCH
<**OH NO!** There's more on this side.>
YIKES!
<Don't worry, my knife has a razor-like edge!
I'll just scrape them off.
Hold it still.>

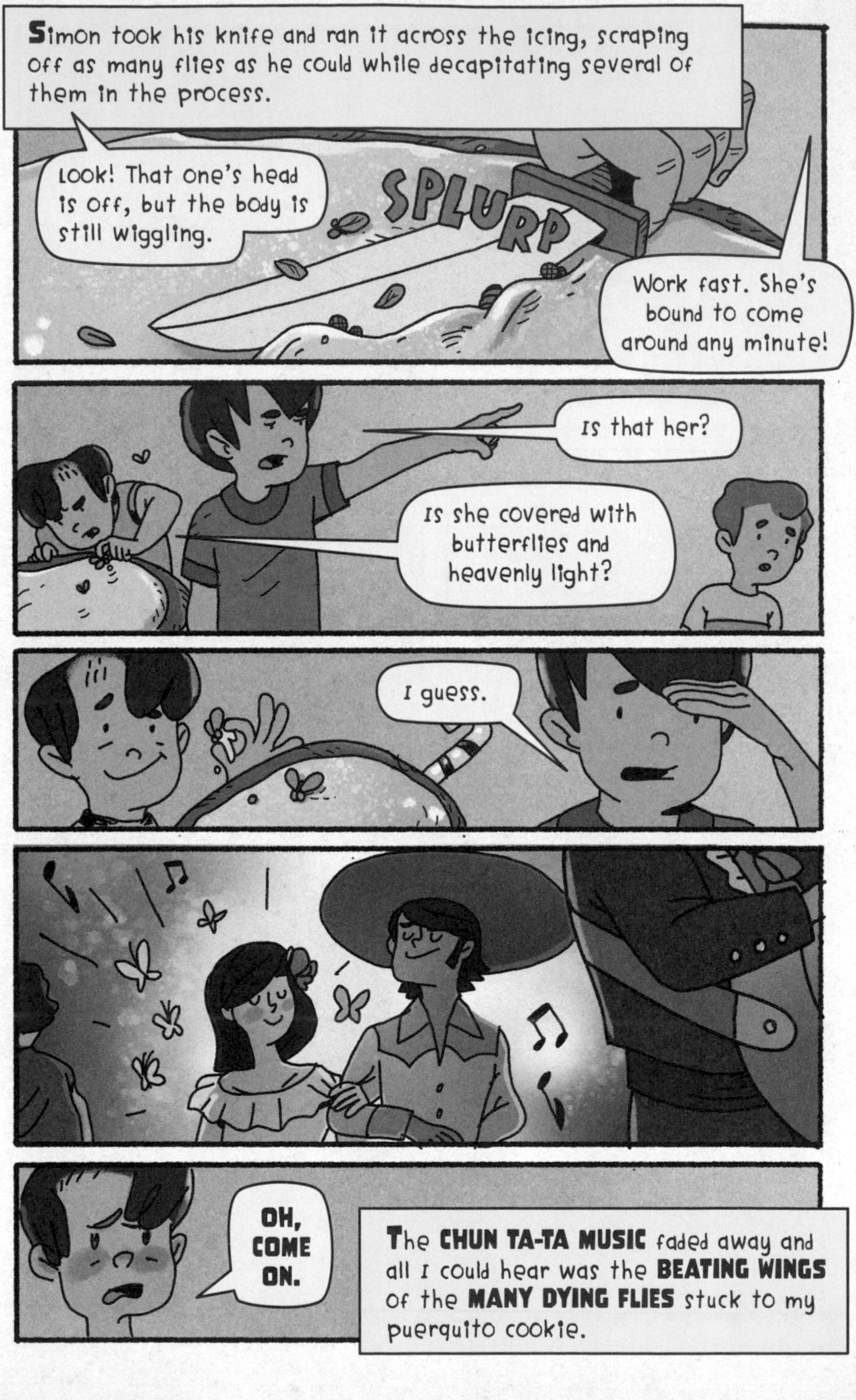
Simon took his knife and ran it across the icing, scraping off as many flies as he could while decapitating several of them in the process.
Look! That one's head is off, but the body is still wiggling.
SPLURP
Work fast. She's bound to come around any minute!
Is that her?
Is she covered with butterflies and heavenly light?
I guess.
OH, COME ON.
The CHUN TA-TA MUSIC faded away and all I could hear was the BEATING WINGS of the MANY DYING FLIES stuck to my puerquito cookie.

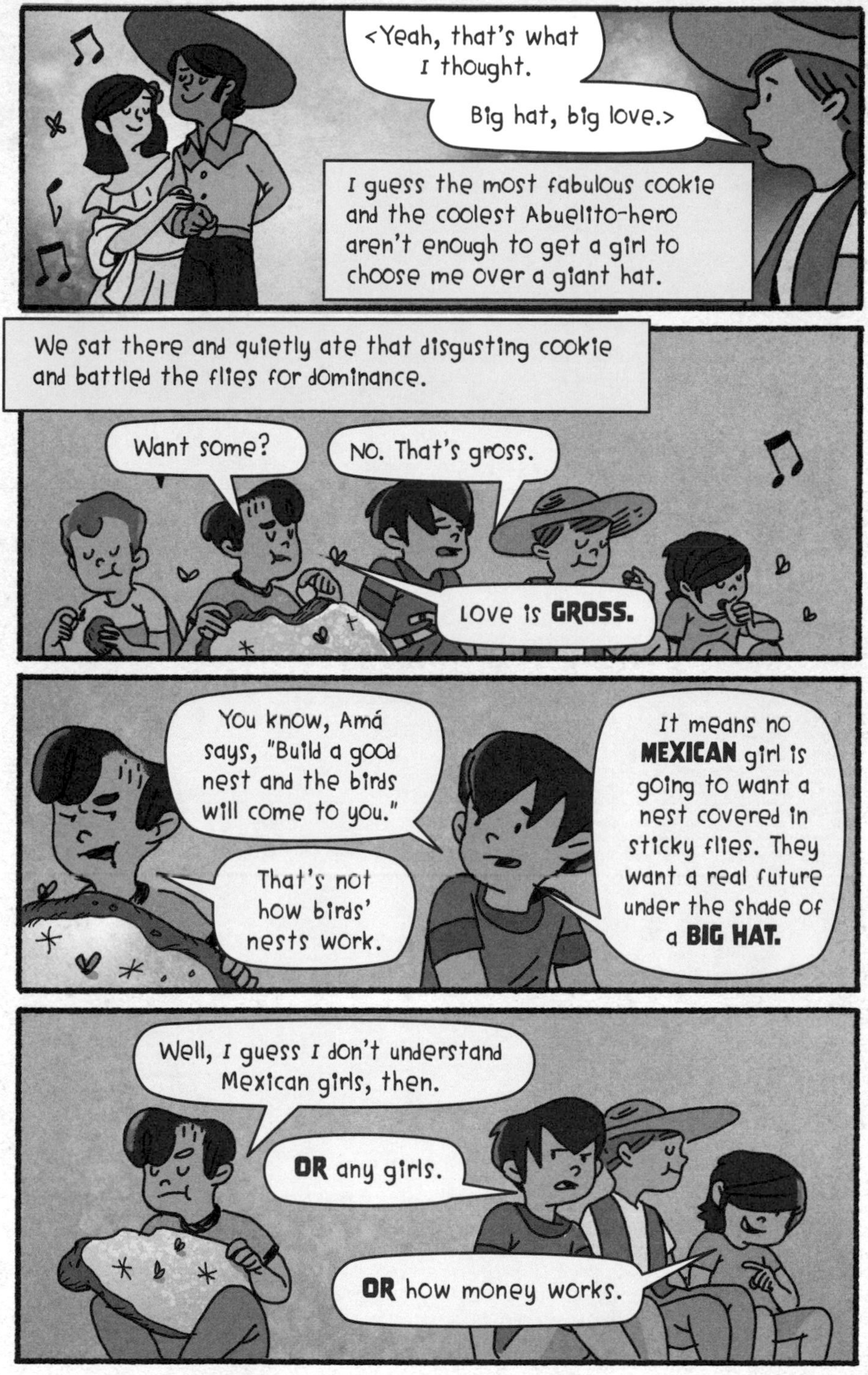
<Yeah, that's what I thought.
Big hat, big love.>
I guess the most fabulous cookie and the coolest Abuelito-hero aren't enough to get a girl to choose me over a giant hat.
We sat there and quietly ate that disgusting cookie and battled the flies for dominance.
Want some?
No. That's gross.
Love is **GROSS.**
You know, Amá says, "Build a good nest and the birds will come to you."
That's not how birds' nests work.
It means no **MEXICAN** girl is going to want a nest covered in sticky flies. They want a real future under the shade of a **BIG HAT.**
Well, I guess I don't understand Mexican girls, then.
OR any girls.
OR how money works.

CHAPTER 12 CROSSING ALONE

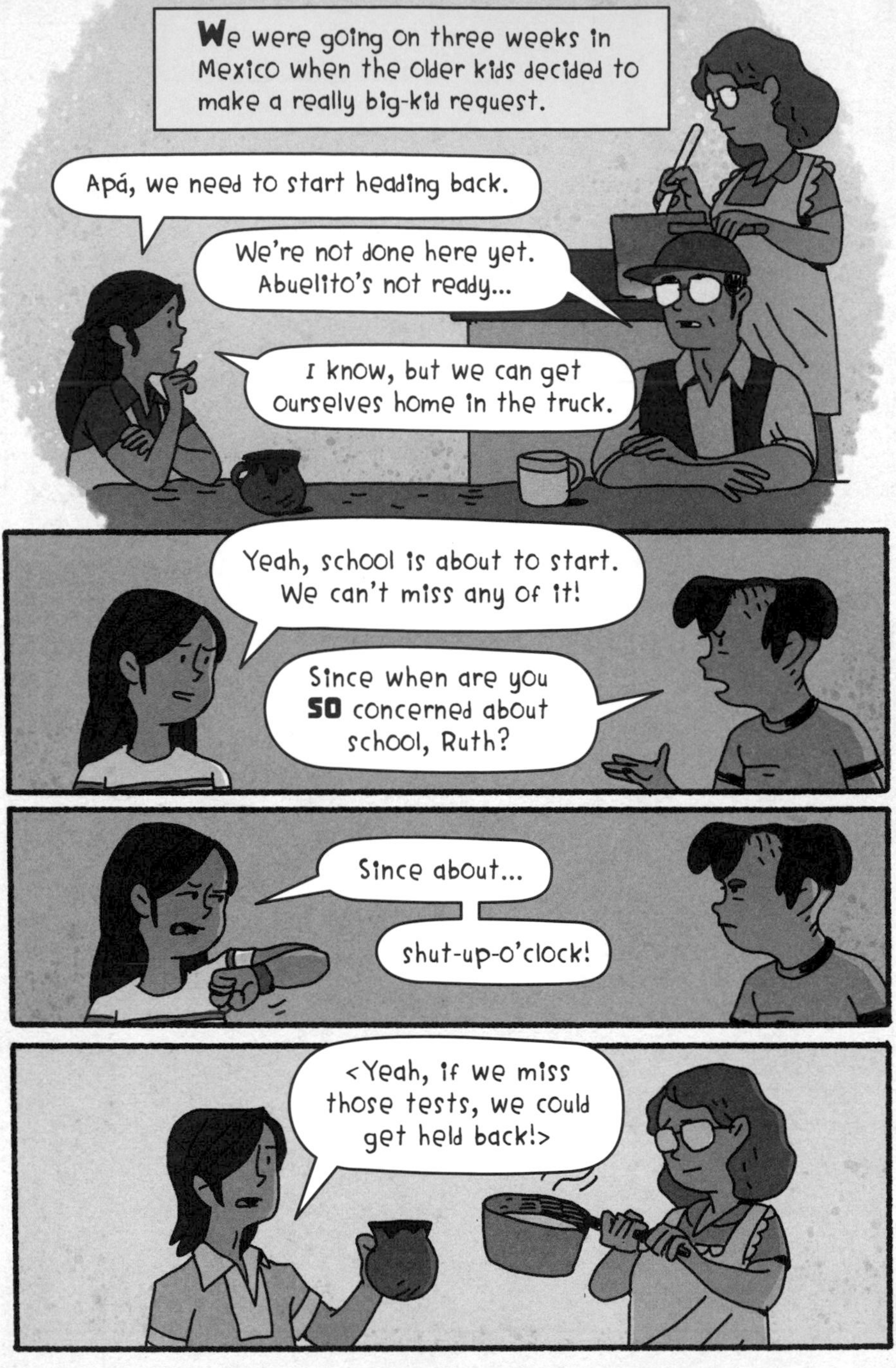

We were going on three weeks in Mexico when the older kids decided to make a really big-kid request.
Apá, we need to start heading back.
We're not done here yet. Abuelito's not ready...
I know, but we can get ourselves home in the truck.
Yeah, school is about to start. We can't miss any of it!
Since when are you **SO** concerned about school, Ruth?
Since about...
shut-up-o'clock!
<Yeah, if we miss those tests, we could get held back!>

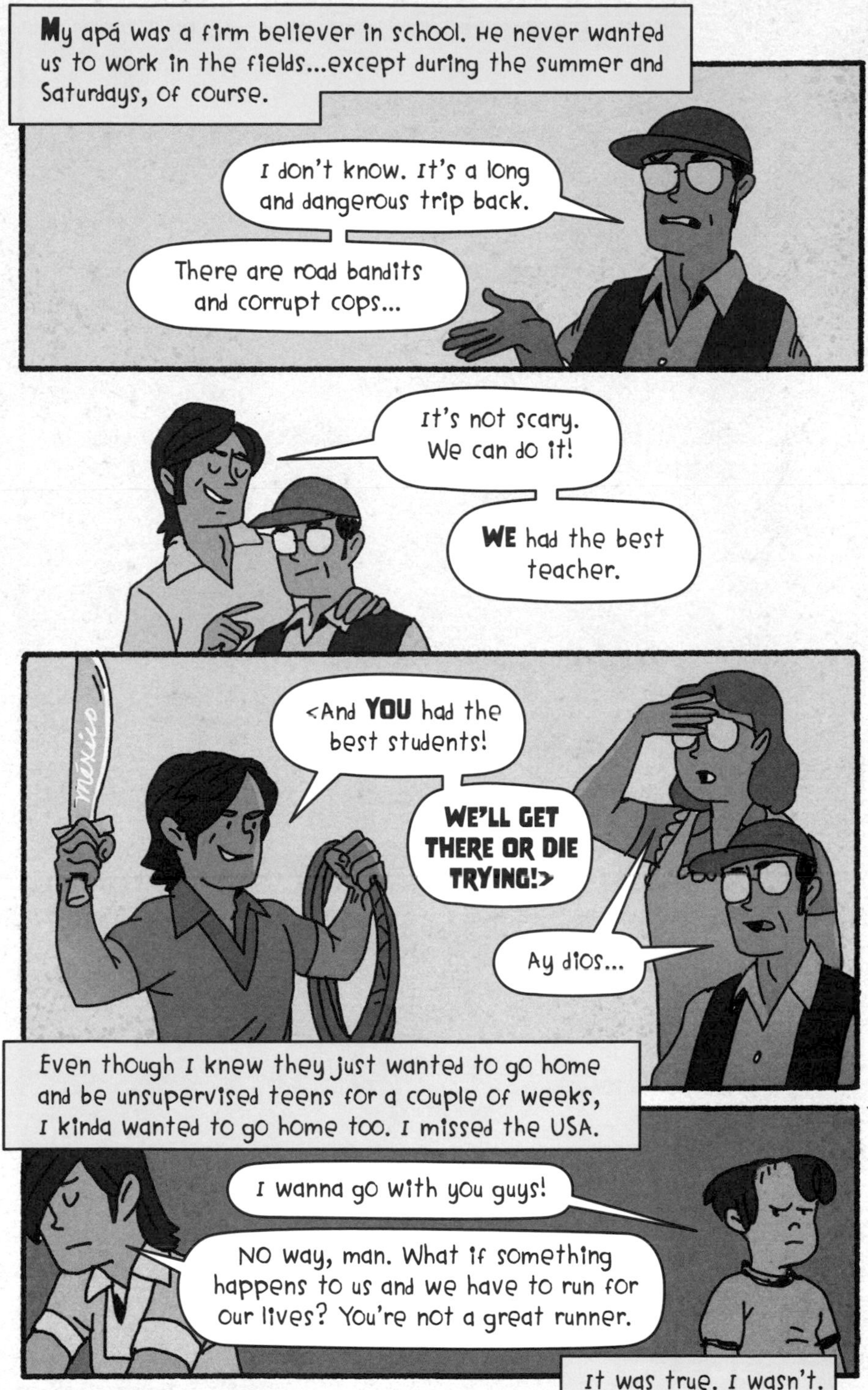
My apá was a firm believer in school. He never wanted us to work in the fields...except during the summer and Saturdays, of course.
I don't know. It's a long and dangerous trip back.
There are road bandits and corrupt cops...
It's not scary. We can do it!
WE had the best teacher.
<And **YOU** had the best students!
WE'LL GET THERE OR DIE TRYING!>
Ay dios...
Even though I knew they just wanted to go home and be unsupervised teens for a couple of weeks, I kinda wanted to go home too. I missed the USA.
I wanna go with you guys!
No way, man. What if something happens to us and we have to run for our lives? You're not a great runner.
It was true. I wasn't.

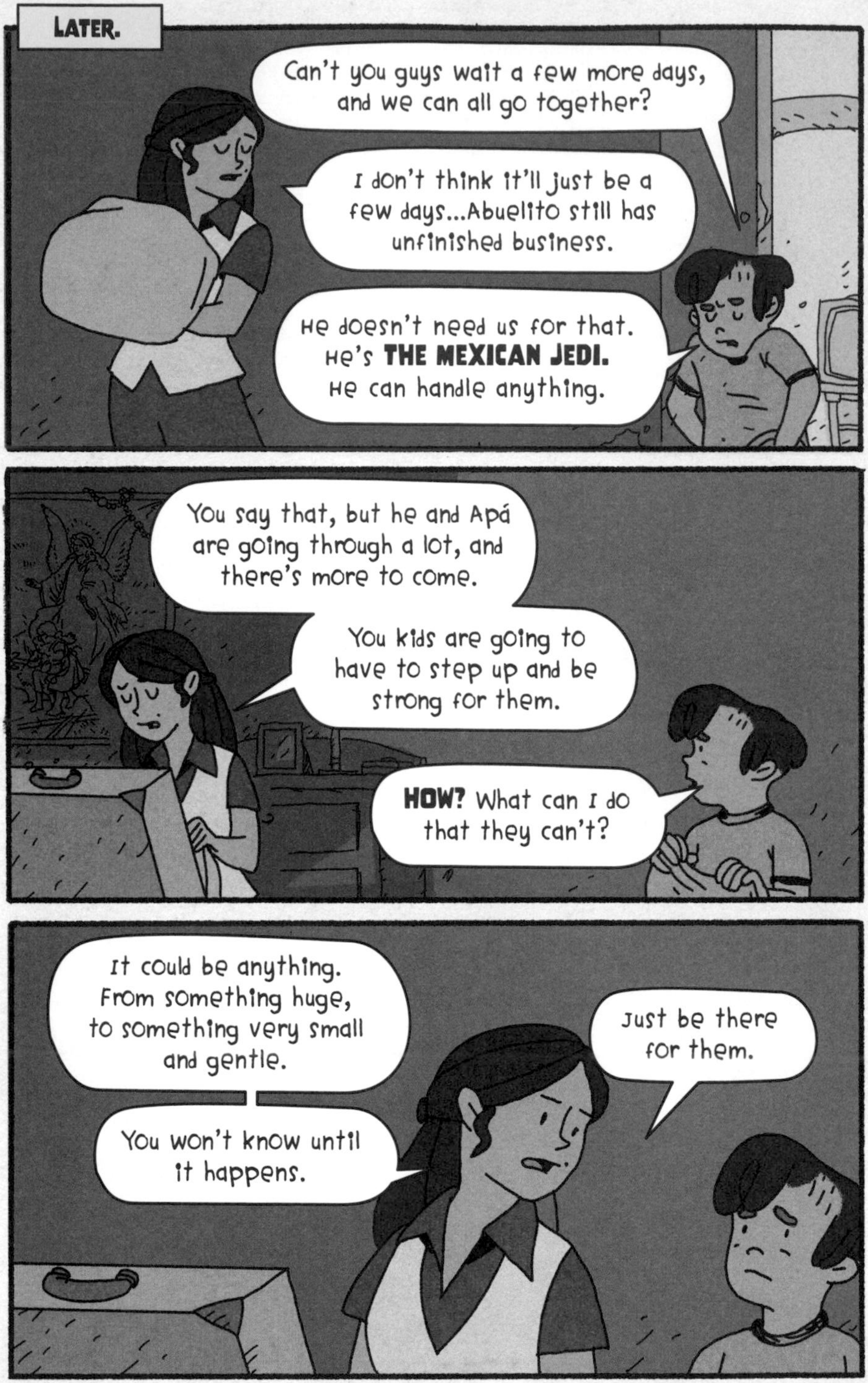
LATER.
Can't you guys wait a few more days, and we can all go together?
I don't think it'll just be a few days...Abuelito still has unfinished business.
He doesn't need us for that. He's **THE MEXICAN JEDI.** He can handle anything.
You say that, but he and Apá are going through a lot, and there's more to come.
You kids are going to have to step up and be strong for them.
HOW? What can I do that they can't?
It could be anything. From something huge, to something very small and gentle.
You won't know until it happens.
Just be there for them.

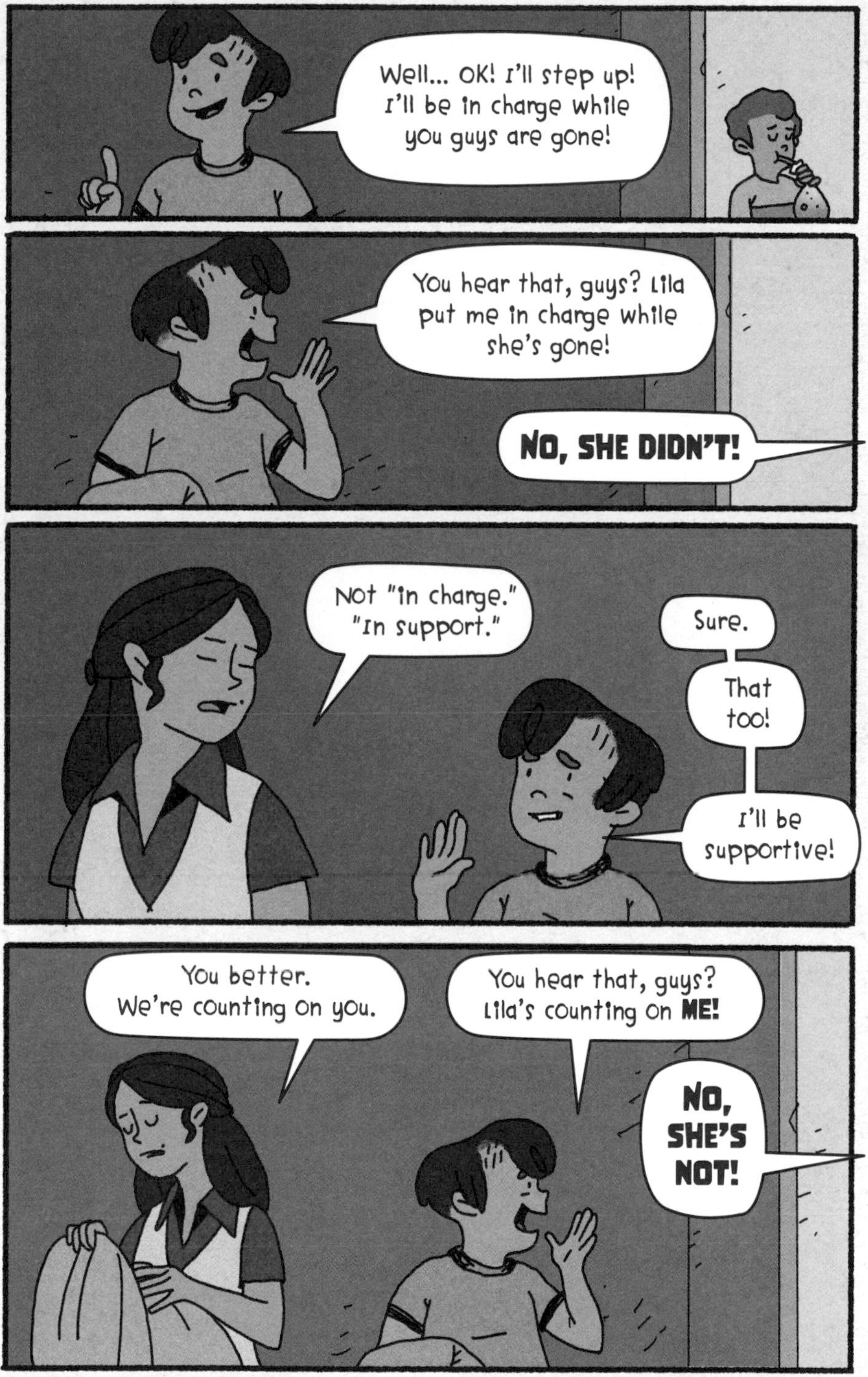
Well... OK! I'll step up! I'll be in charge while you guys are gone!
You hear that, guys? Lila put me in charge while she's gone!
NO, SHE DIDN'T!
Not "in charge." "In support."
Sure.
That too!
I'll be supportive!
You better. We're counting on you.
You hear that, guys? Lila's counting on **ME!**
NO, SHE'S NOT!

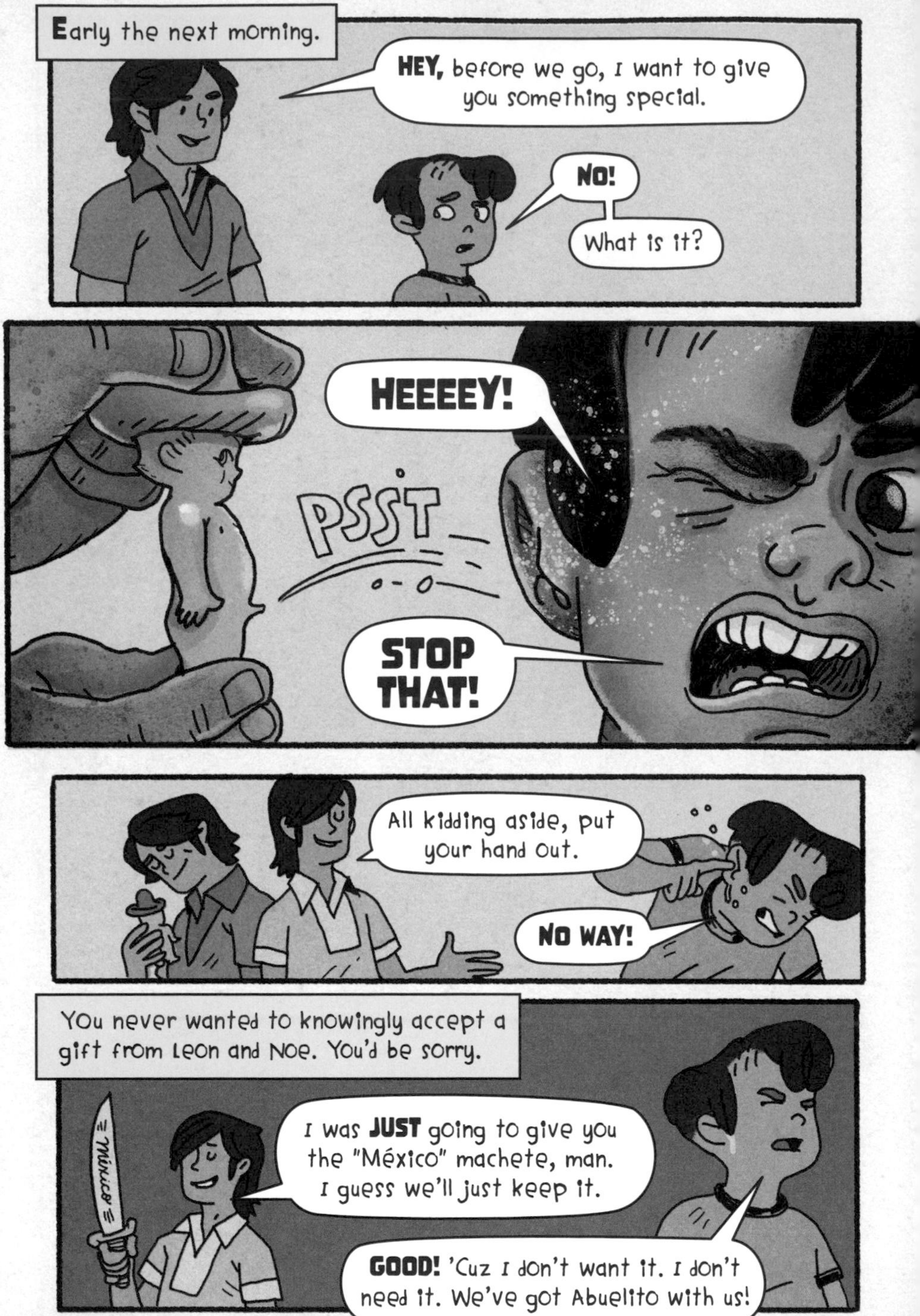

Early the next morning.
HEY, before we go, I want to give you something special.
NO!
What is it?
HEEEEY!
PSST
STOP THAT!
All kidding aside, put your hand out.
NO WAY!
You never wanted to knowingly accept a gift from Leon and Noe. You'd be sorry.
I was JUST going to give you the "México" machete, man. I guess we'll just keep it.
GOOD! 'Cuz I don't want it. I don't need it. We've got Abuelito with us!

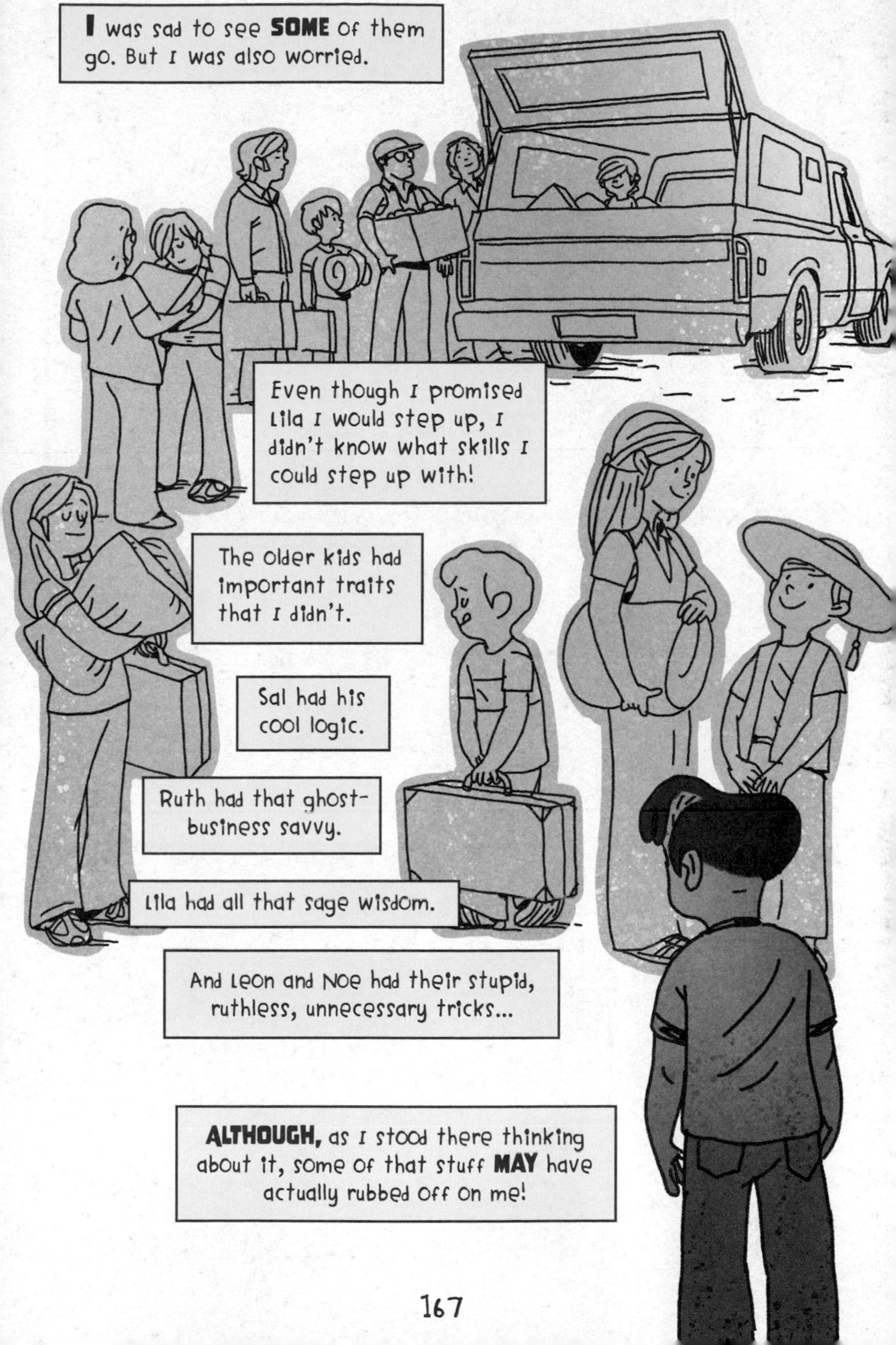
I was sad to see SOME of them go. But I was also worried.
Even though I promised Lila I would step up, I didn't know what skills I could step up with!
The older kids had important traits that I didn't.
Sal had his cool logic.
Ruth had that ghost-business savvy.
Lila had all that sage wisdom.
And Leon and Noe had their stupid, ruthless, unnecessary tricks...
ALTHOUGH, as I stood there thinking about it, some of that stuff MAY have actually rubbed off on me!

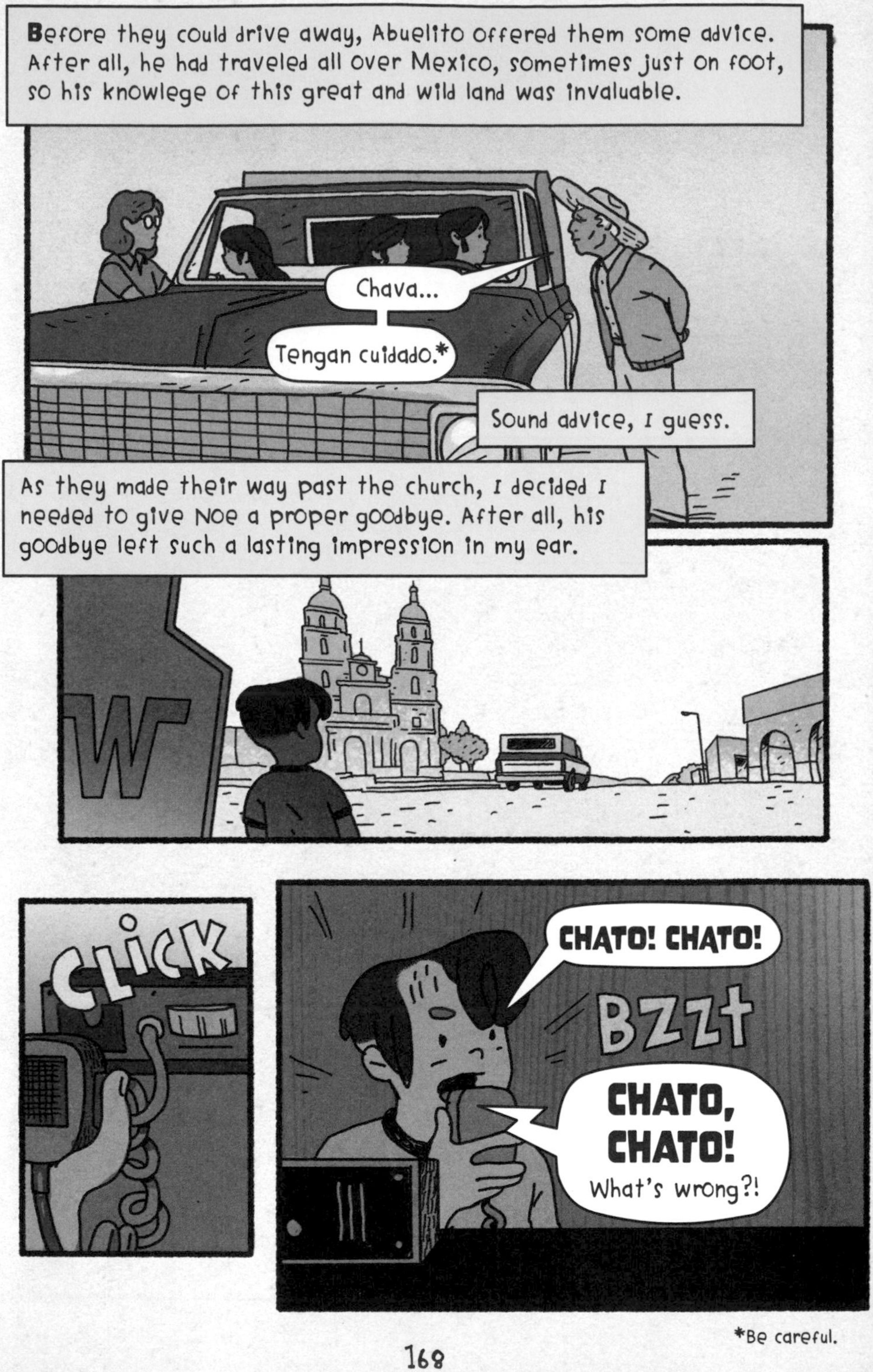
Before they could drive away, Abuelito offered them some advice. After all, he had traveled all over Mexico, sometimes just on foot, so his knowlege of this great and wild land was invaluable.
Chava...
Tengan cuidado.*
Sound advice, I guess.
As they made their way past the church, I decided I needed to give Noe a proper goodbye. After all, his goodbye left such a lasting impression in my ear.
W
CLICK
CHATO! CHATO!
BZZT
CHATO, CHATO! What's wrong?!

*Be careful.

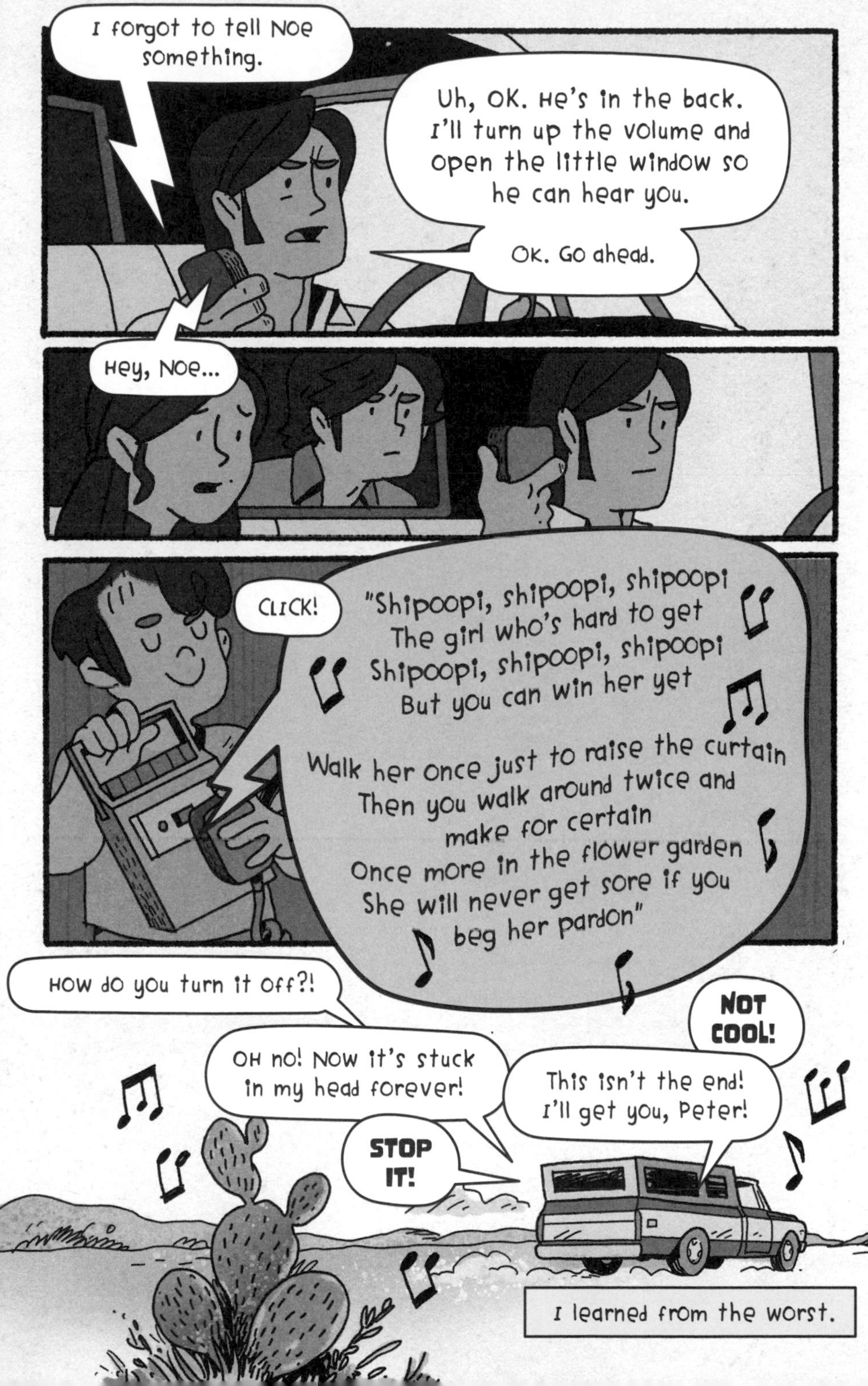

I forgot to tell Noe something.
Uh, OK. He's in the back. I'll turn up the volume and open the little window so he can hear you.
OK. Go ahead.
Hey, Noe...
CLICK!
"Shipoopi, shipoopi, shipoopi
The girl who's hard to get
Shipoopi, shipoopi, shipoopi
But you can win her yet
Walk her once just to raise the curtain
Then you walk around twice and make for certain
Once more in the flower garden
She will never get sore if you beg her pardon"
How do you turn it off?!
Oh no! Now it's stuck in my head forever!
STOP IT!
NOT COOL!
This isn't the end! I'll get you, Peter!
I learned from the worst.

CHAPTER 13 TEPATITLÁN

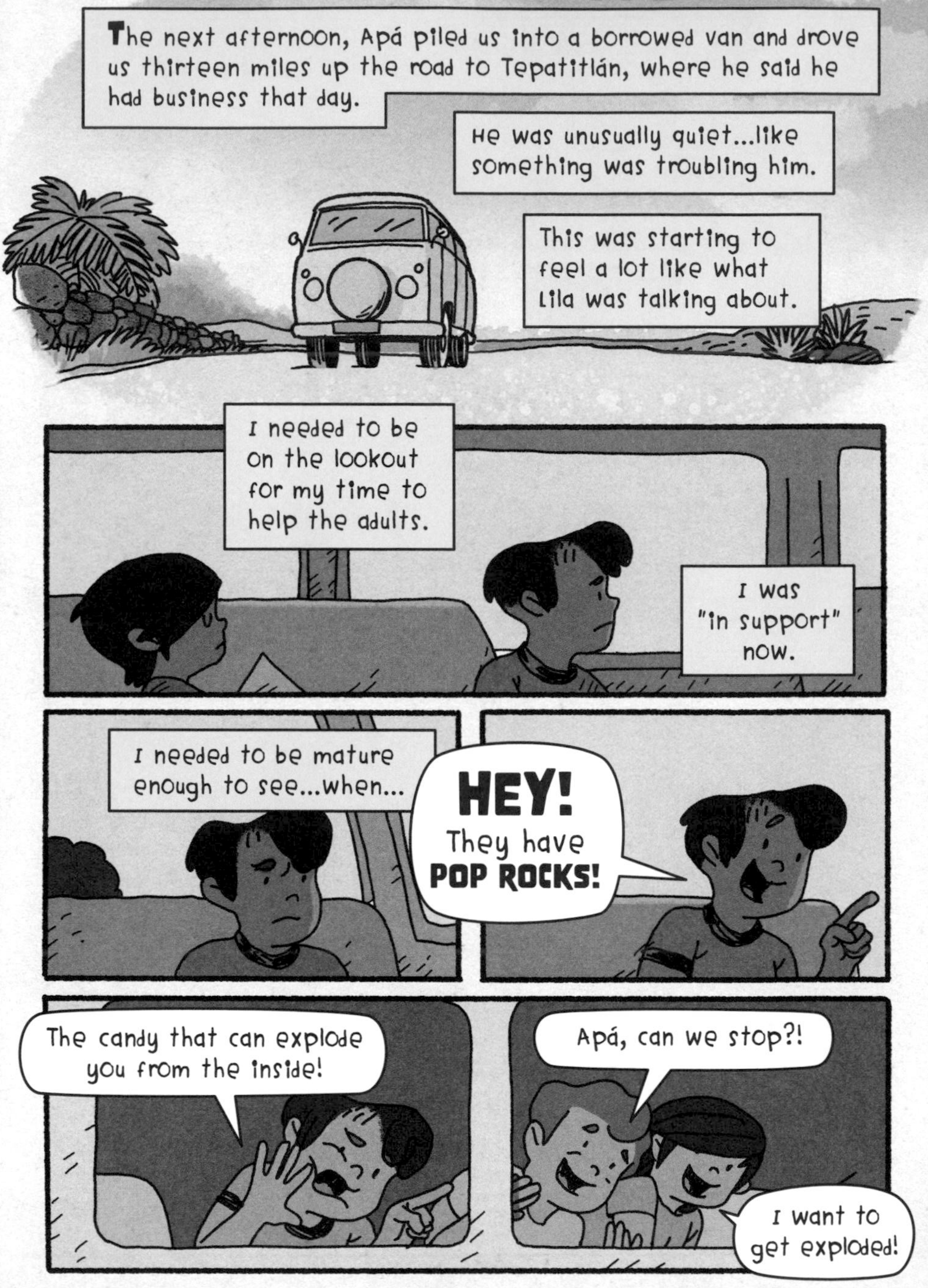

The next afternoon, Apá piled us into a borrowed van and drove us thirteen miles up the road to Tepatitlán, where he said he had business that day.
He was unusually quiet...like something was troubling him.
This was starting to feel a lot like what Lila was talking about.
I needed to be on the lookout for my time to help the adults.
I was "in support" now.
I needed to be mature enough to see...when...
HEY! They have POP ROCKS!
The candy that can explode you from the inside!
Apá, can we stop?!
I want to get exploded!

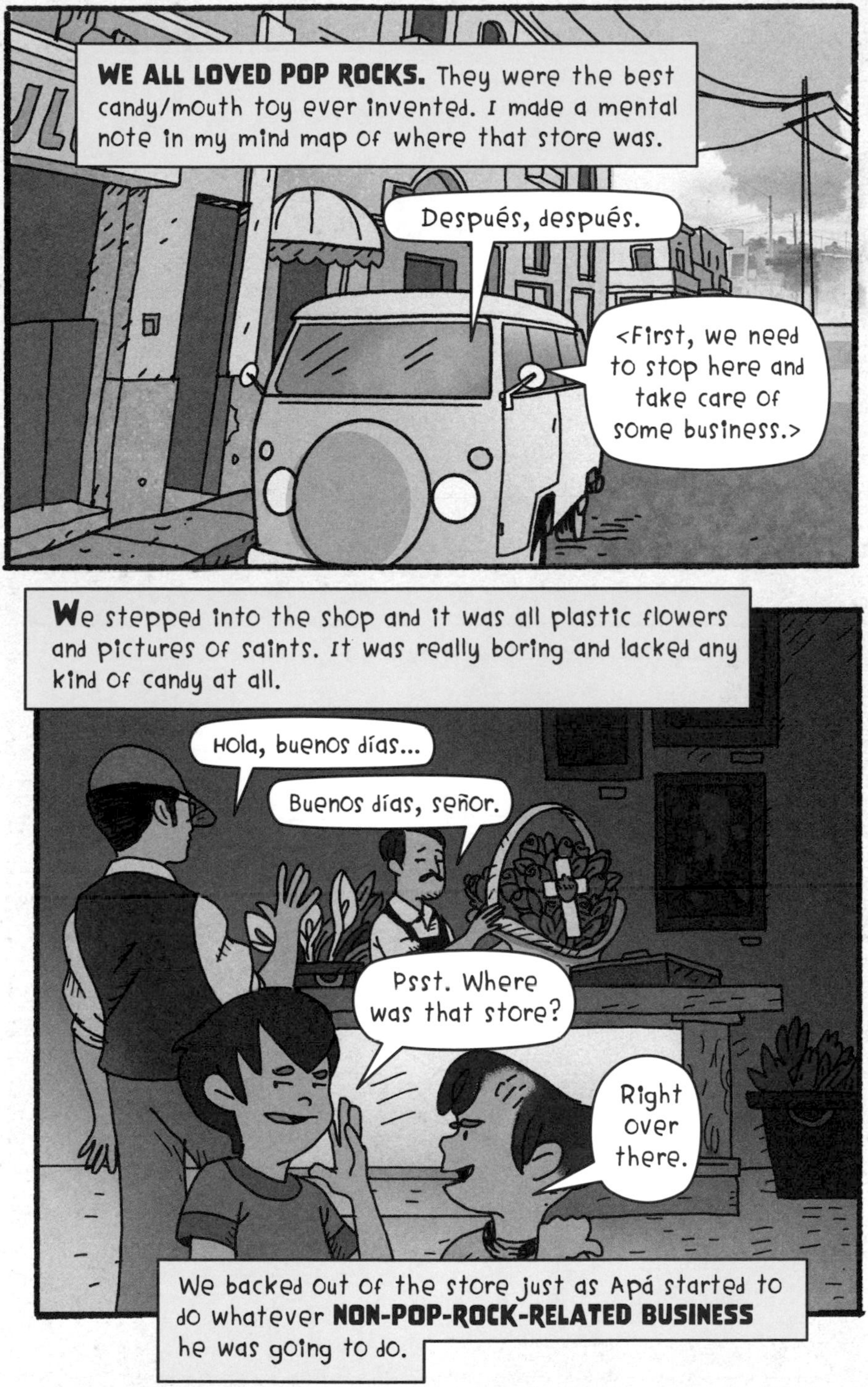
WE ALL LOVED POP ROCKS. They were the best candy/mouth toy ever invented. I made a mental note in my mind map of where that store was.
Después, después.
<First, we need to stop here and take care of some business.>
We stepped into the shop and it was all plastic flowers and pictures of saints. It was really boring and lacked any kind of candy at all.
Hola, buenos días...
Buenos días, señor.
Psst. Where was that store?
Right over there.
We backed out of the store just as Apá started to do whatever NON-POP-ROCK-RELATED BUSINESS he was going to do.

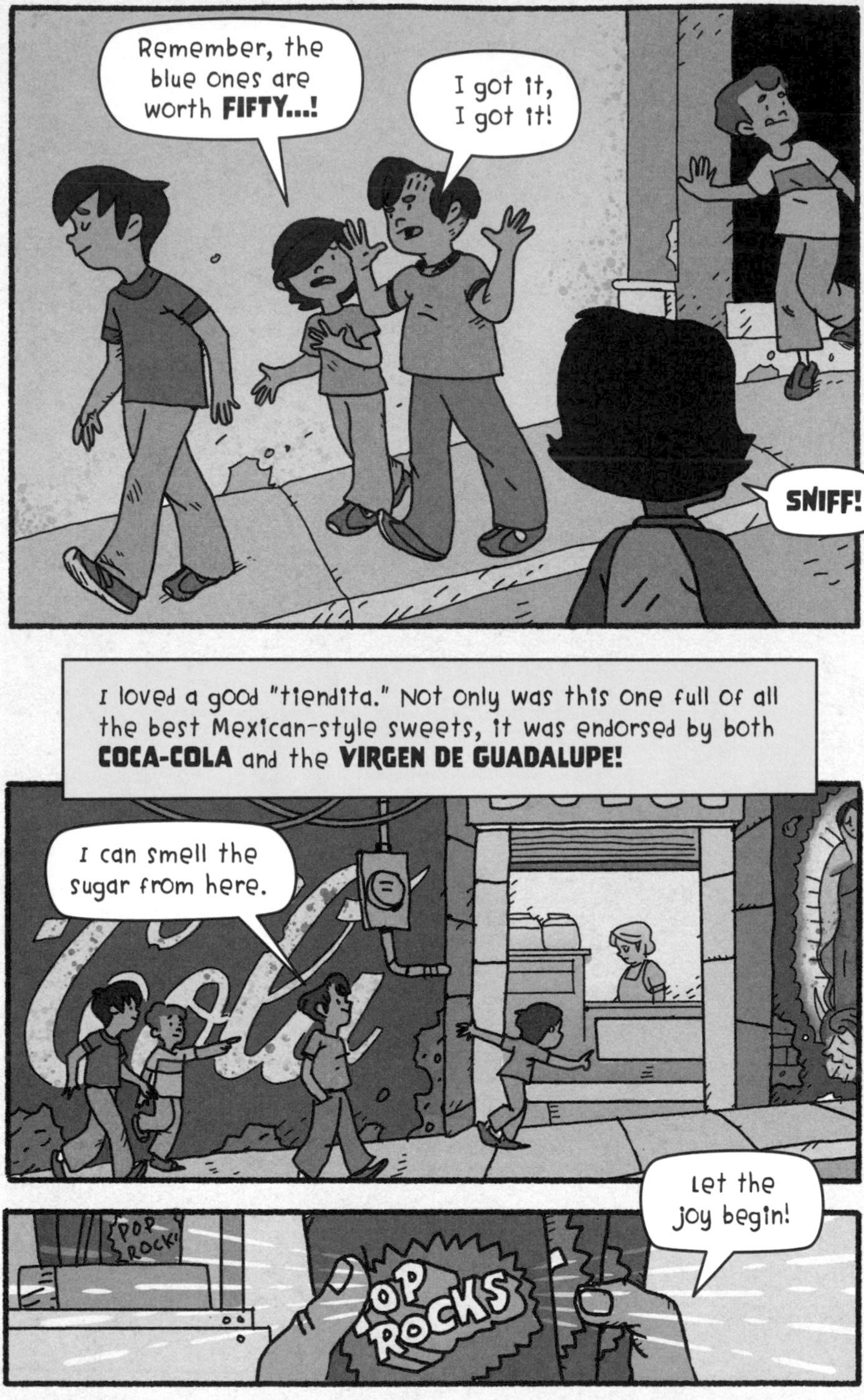
Remember, the blue ones are worth **FIFTY...!**
I got it, I got it!
SNIFF!
I loved a good "tiendita." Not only was this one full of all the best Mexican-style sweets, it was endorsed by both **COCA-COLA** and the **VIRGEN DE GUADALUPE!**
I can smell the sugar from here.
Let the joy begin!

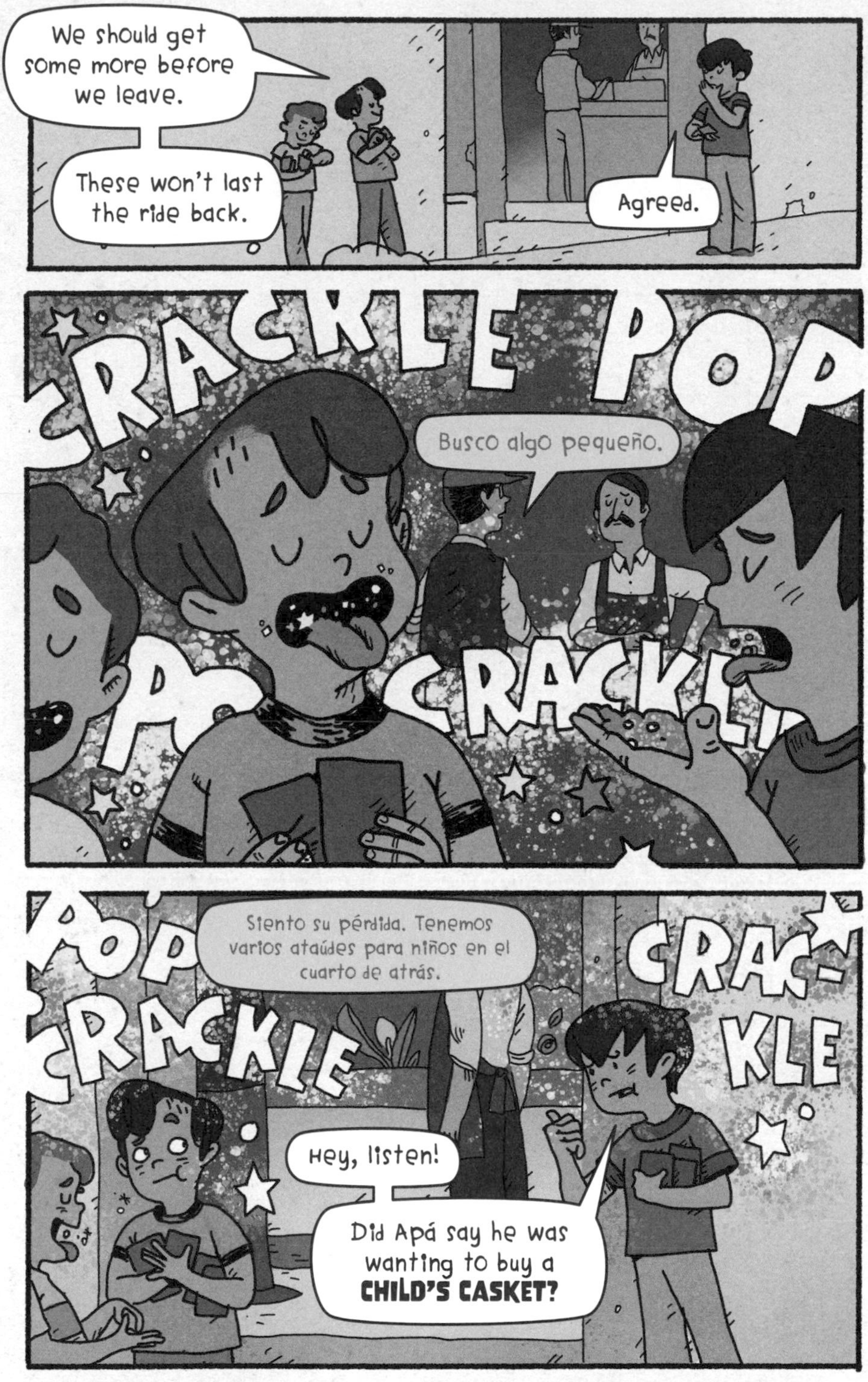
We should get some more before we leave.
These won't last the ride back.
Agreed.
CRACKLE POP
Busco algo pequeño.
POP
CRACKLE
POP
Siento su pérdida. Tenemos varios ataúdes para niños en el cuarto de atrás.
CRAC-KLE
CRACKLE
Hey, listen!
Did Apá say he was wanting to buy a **CHILD'S CASKET?**

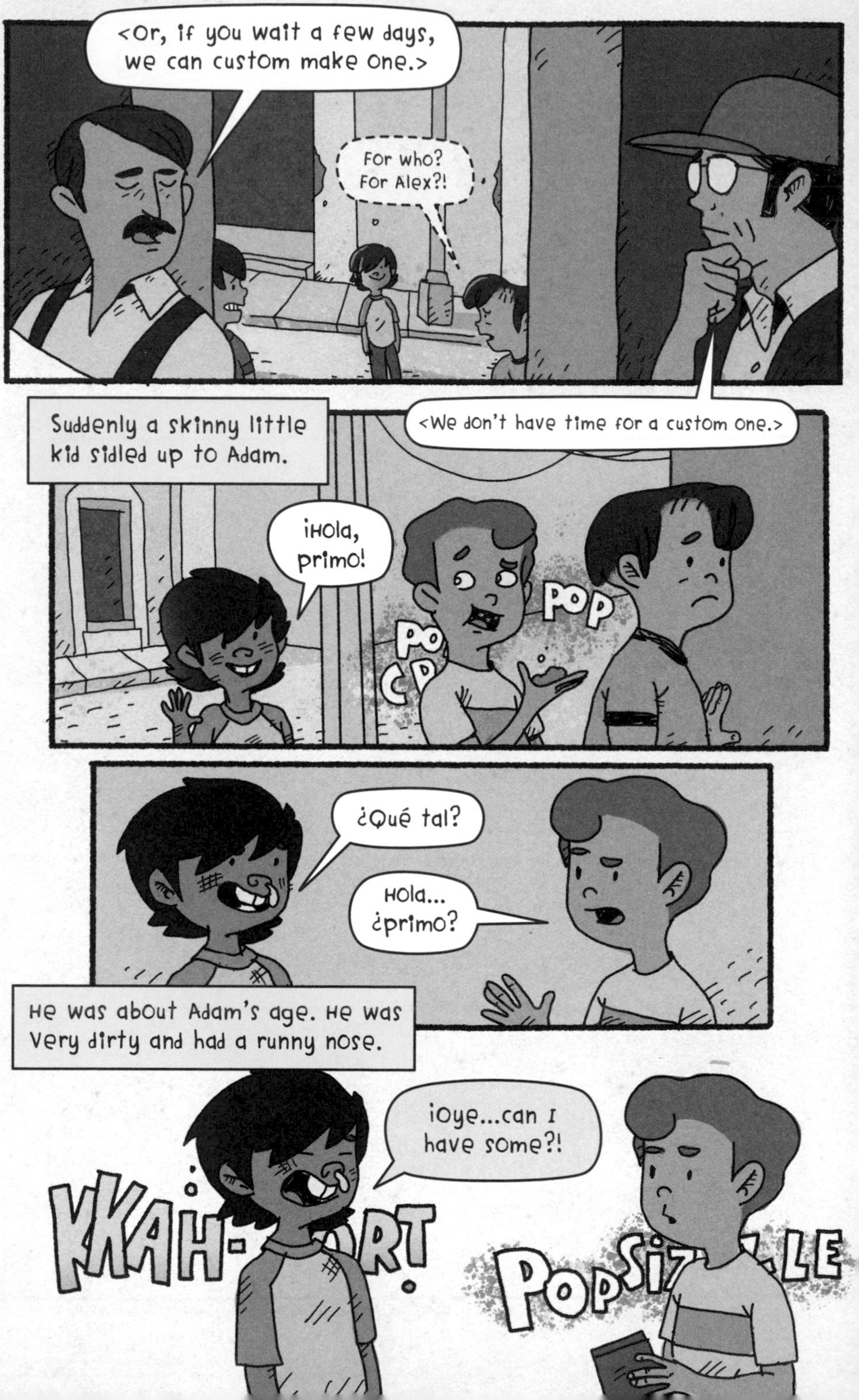
<Or, if you wait a few days, we can custom make one.>
For who? For Alex?!
<We don't have time for a custom one.>
Suddenly a skinny little kid sidled up to Adam.
¡Hola, primo!
POP
¿Qué tal?
Hola... ¿primo?
He was about Adam's age. He was very dirty and had a runny nose.
¡Oye...can I have some?!

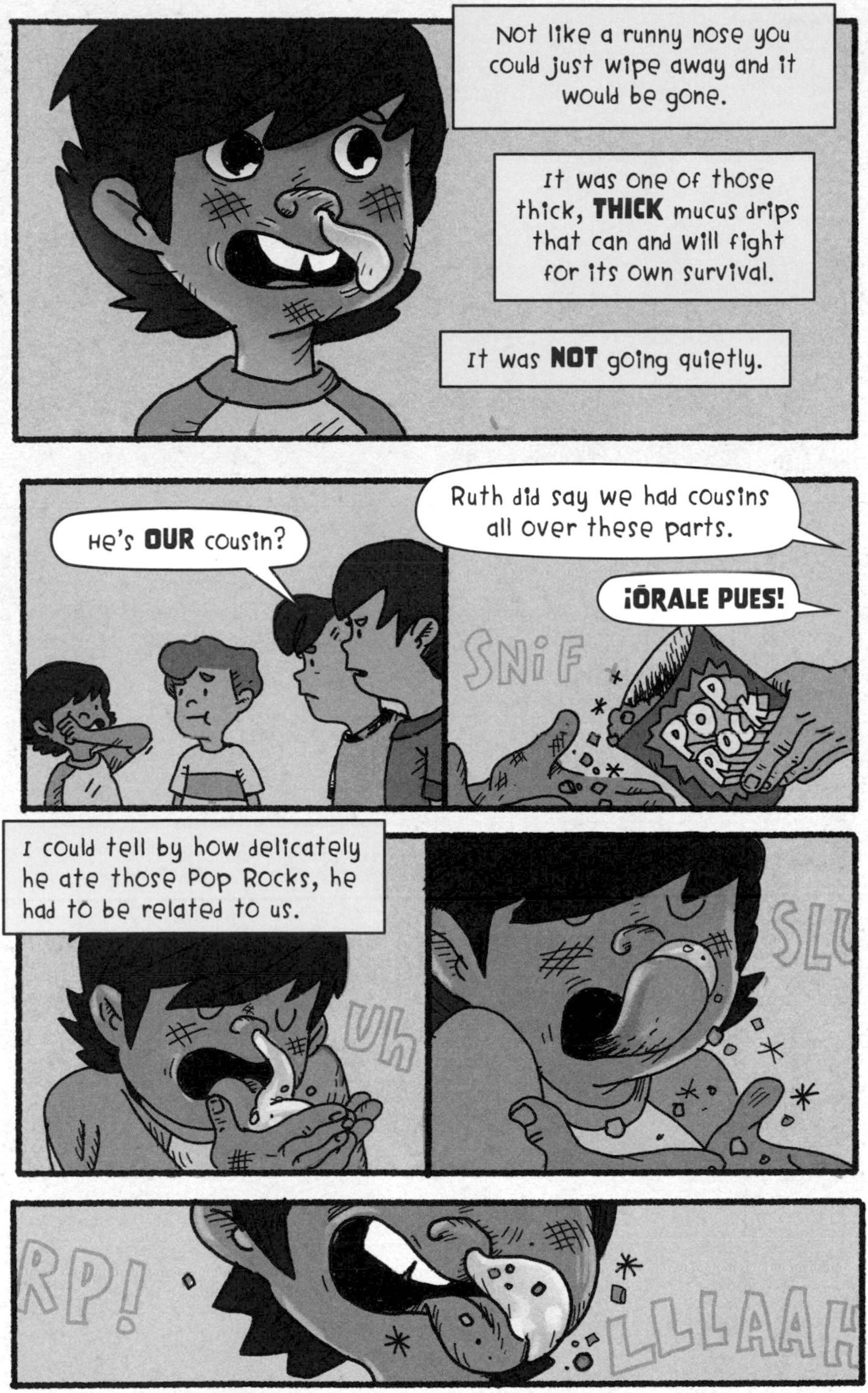
Not like a runny nose you could just wipe away and it would be gone.
It was one of those thick, THICK mucus drips that can and will fight for its own survival.
It was NOT going quietly.
He's OUR cousin?
Ruth did say we had cousins all over these parts.
SNIF
¡ÓRALE PUES!
POP ROCK
I could tell by how delicately he ate those Pop Rocks, he had to be related to us.
Uh
SLU
RP!
LLLAAH

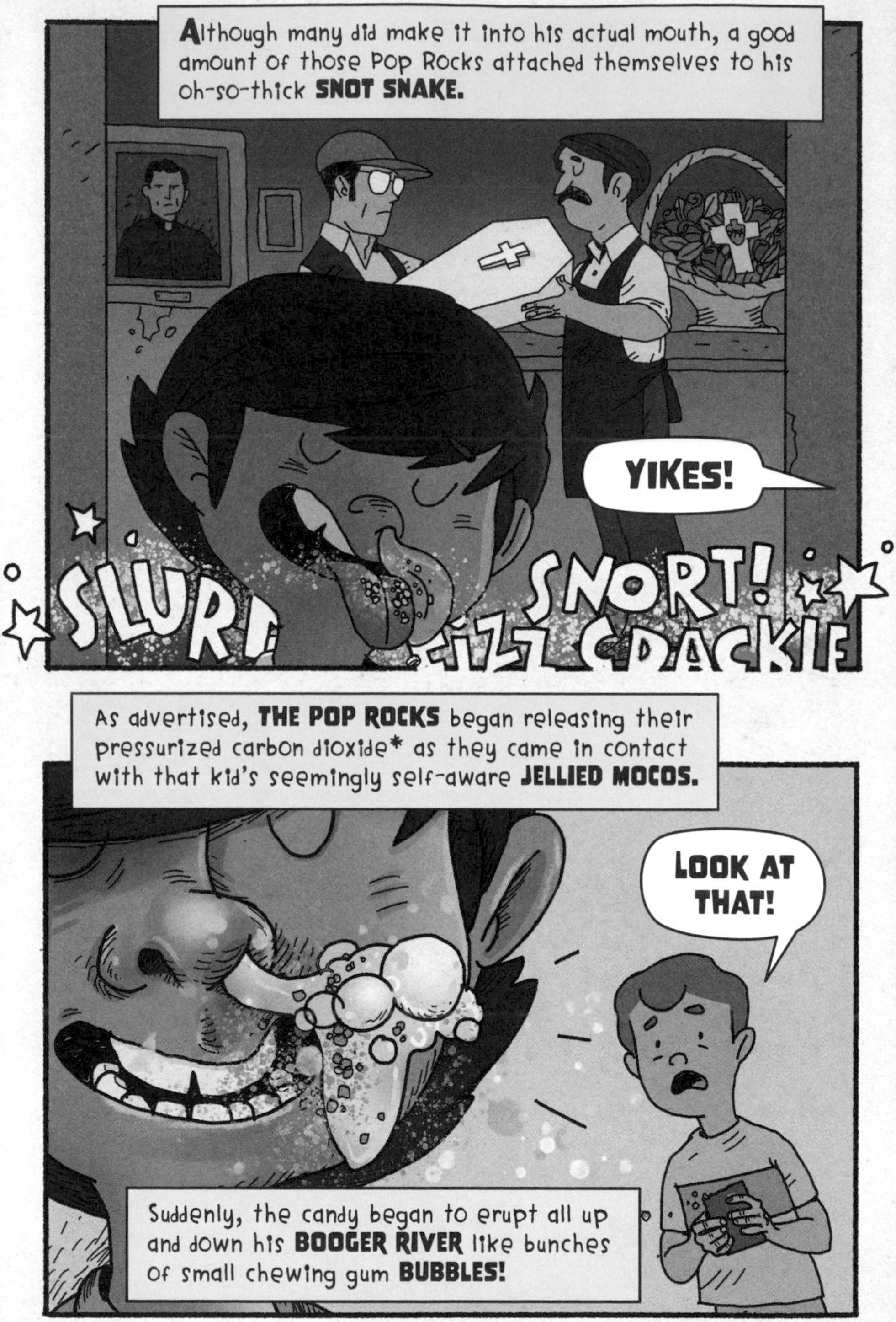
Although many did make it into his actual mouth, a good amount of those Pop Rocks attached themselves to his oh-so-thick **SNOT SNAKE.**
YIKES!
SNORT!
As advertised, **THE POP ROCKS** began releasing their pressurized carbon dioxide* as they came in contact with that kid's seemingly self-aware **JELLIED MOCOS.**
LOOK AT THAT!
Suddenly, the candy began to erupt all up and down his **BOOGER RIVER** like bunches of small chewing gum **BUBBLES!**

*My brother Sal told us that it's a chemical reaction, not a tool of the devil like I thought.

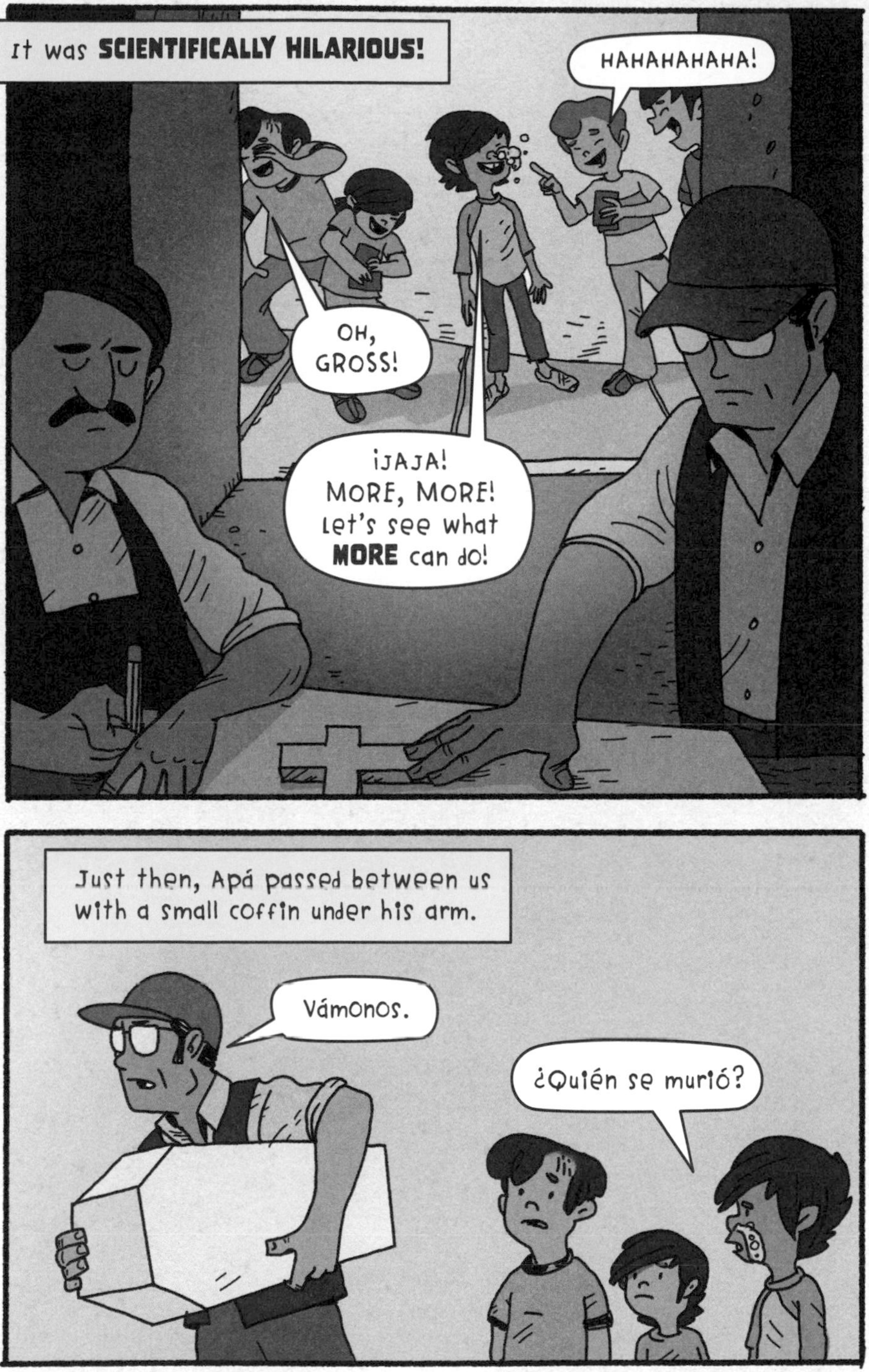
It was SCIENTIFICALLY HILARIOUS!
HAHAHAHAHA!
OH, GROSS!
¡JAJA! MORE, MORE! Let's see what MORE can do!
Just then, Apá passed between us with a small coffin under his arm.
Vámonos.
¿Quién se murió?

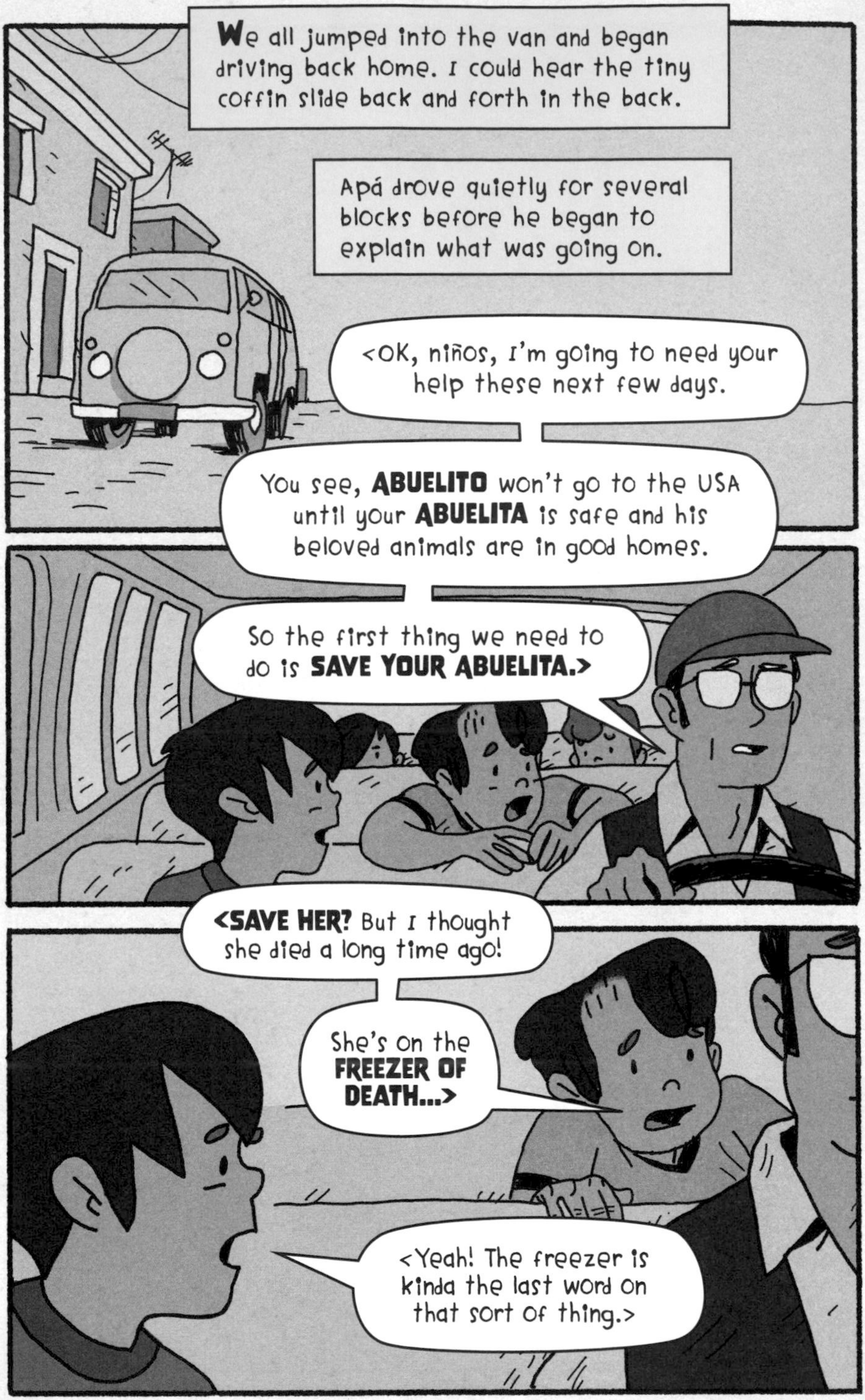
We all jumped into the van and began driving back home. I could hear the tiny coffin slide back and forth in the back.
Apá drove quietly for several blocks before he began to explain what was going on.
<OK, niños, I'm going to need your help these next few days.
You see, ABUELITO won't go to the USA until your ABUELITA is safe and his beloved animals are in good homes.
So the first thing we need to do is SAVE YOUR ABUELITA.>
<SAVE HER? But I thought she died a long time ago!
She's on the FREEZER OF DEATH...>
<Yeah! The freezer is kinda the last word on that sort of thing.>

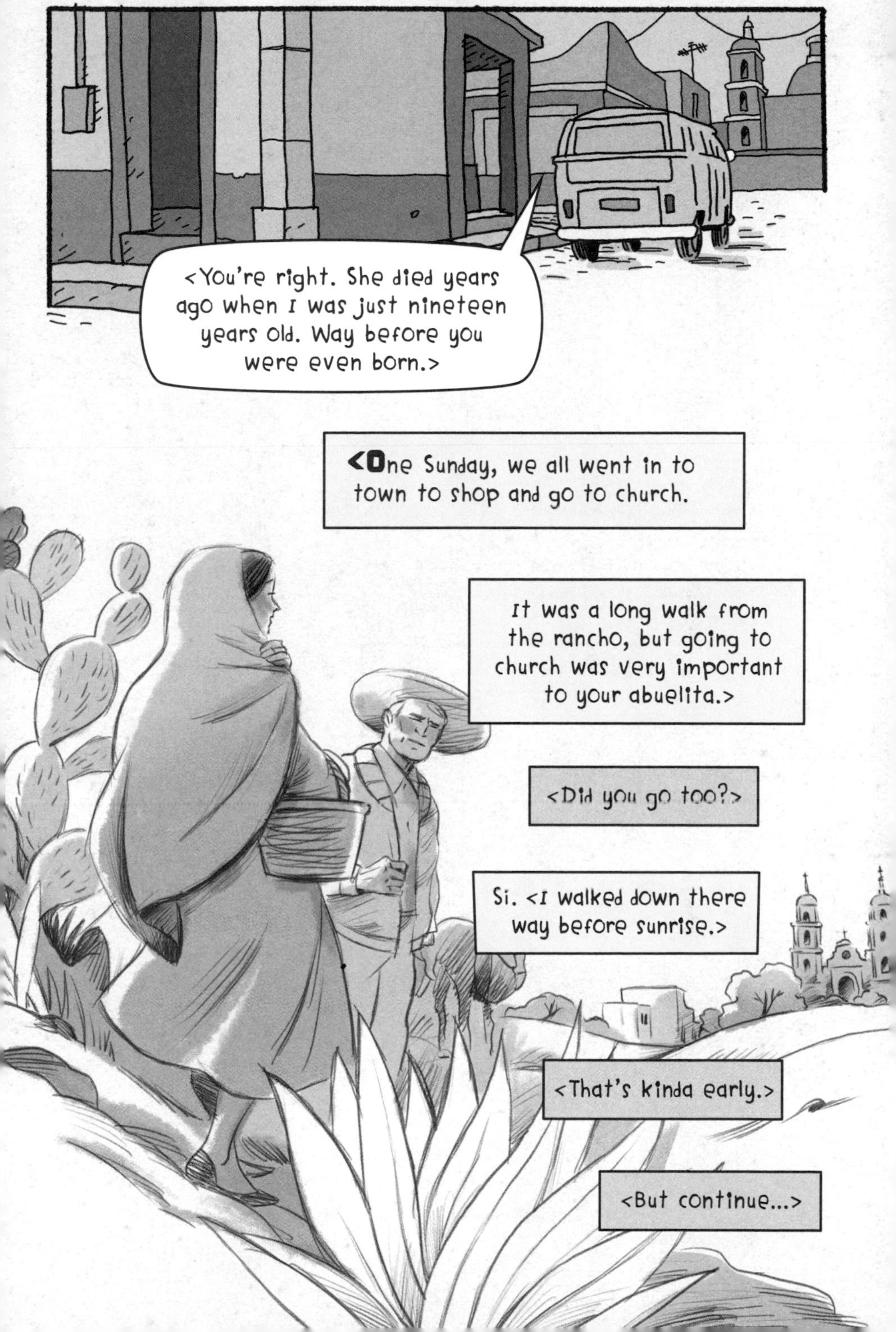
<You're right. She died years ago when I was just nineteen years old. Way before you were even born.>
<One Sunday, we all went in to town to shop and go to church.
It was a long walk from the rancho, but going to church was very important to your abuelita.>
<Did you go too?>
Si. <I walked down there way before sunrise.>
<That's kinda early.>
<But continue...>

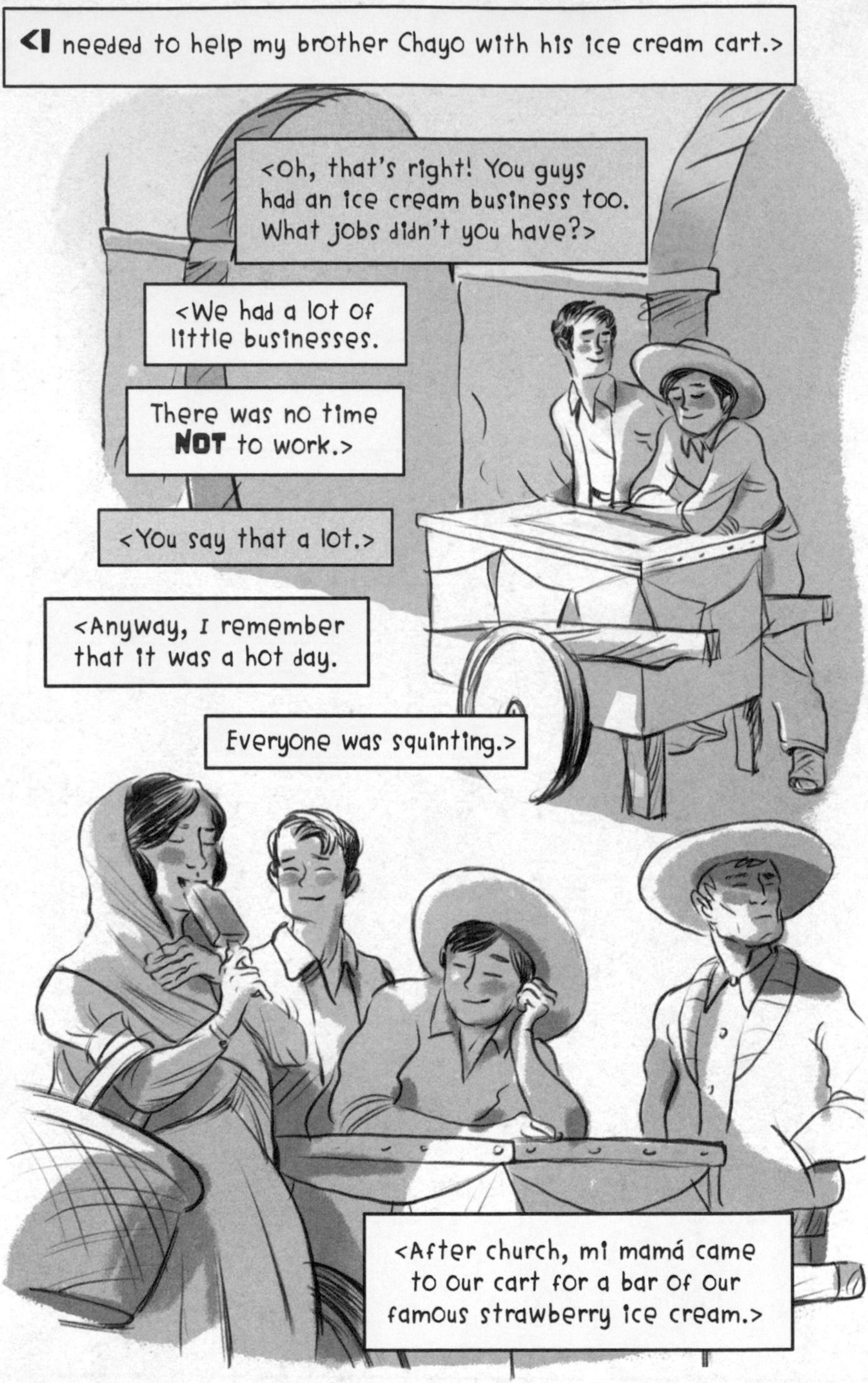
<I needed to help my brother Chayo with his ice cream cart.>
<Oh, that's right! You guys had an ice cream business too. What jobs didn't you have?>
<We had a lot of little businesses.
There was no time **NOT** to work.>
<You say that a lot.>
<Anyway, I remember that it was a hot day.
Everyone was squinting.>
<After church, mi mamá came to our cart for a bar of our famous strawberry ice cream.>

<It was her favorite.>

<She may have been partial, but she thought our ice cream was the best in town.

Suddenly, she got **THAT** headache.

You know, the one you get when you eat ice cream too fast?

Only **WORSE.>**

<A few days later, she passed away.>

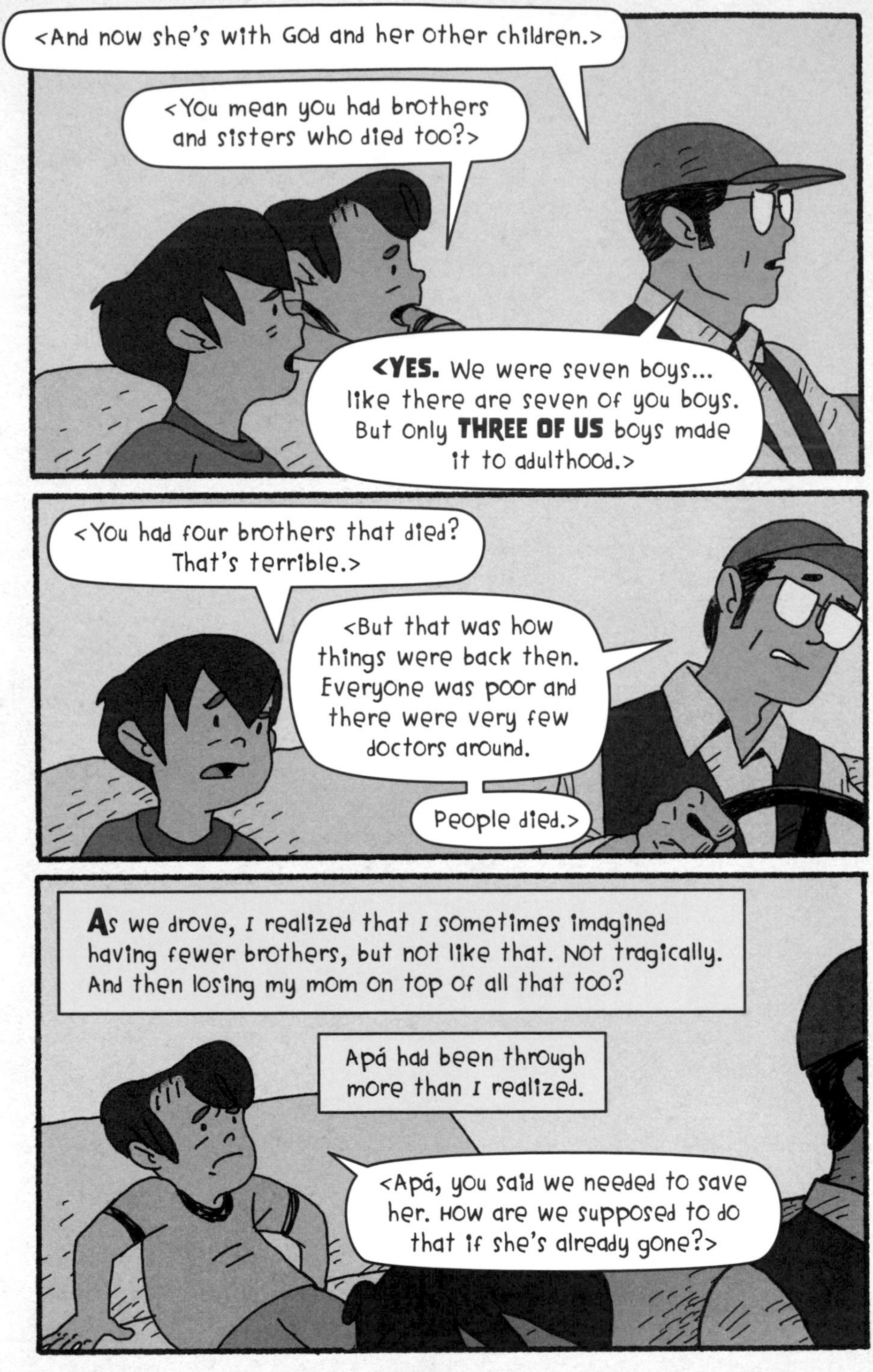
<And now she's with God and her other children.>
<You mean you had brothers and sisters who died too?>
<**YES.** We were seven boys... like there are seven of you boys. But only **THREE OF US** boys made it to adulthood.>
<You had four brothers that died? That's terrible.>
<But that was how things were back then. Everyone was poor and there were very few doctors around.
People died.>
As we drove, I realized that I sometimes imagined having fewer brothers, but not like that. Not tragically. And then losing my mom on top of all that too?
Apá had been through more than I realized.
<Apá, you said we needed to save her. How are we supposed to do that if she's already gone?>

CHAPTER 14
THE UNDERGROUND FLOW

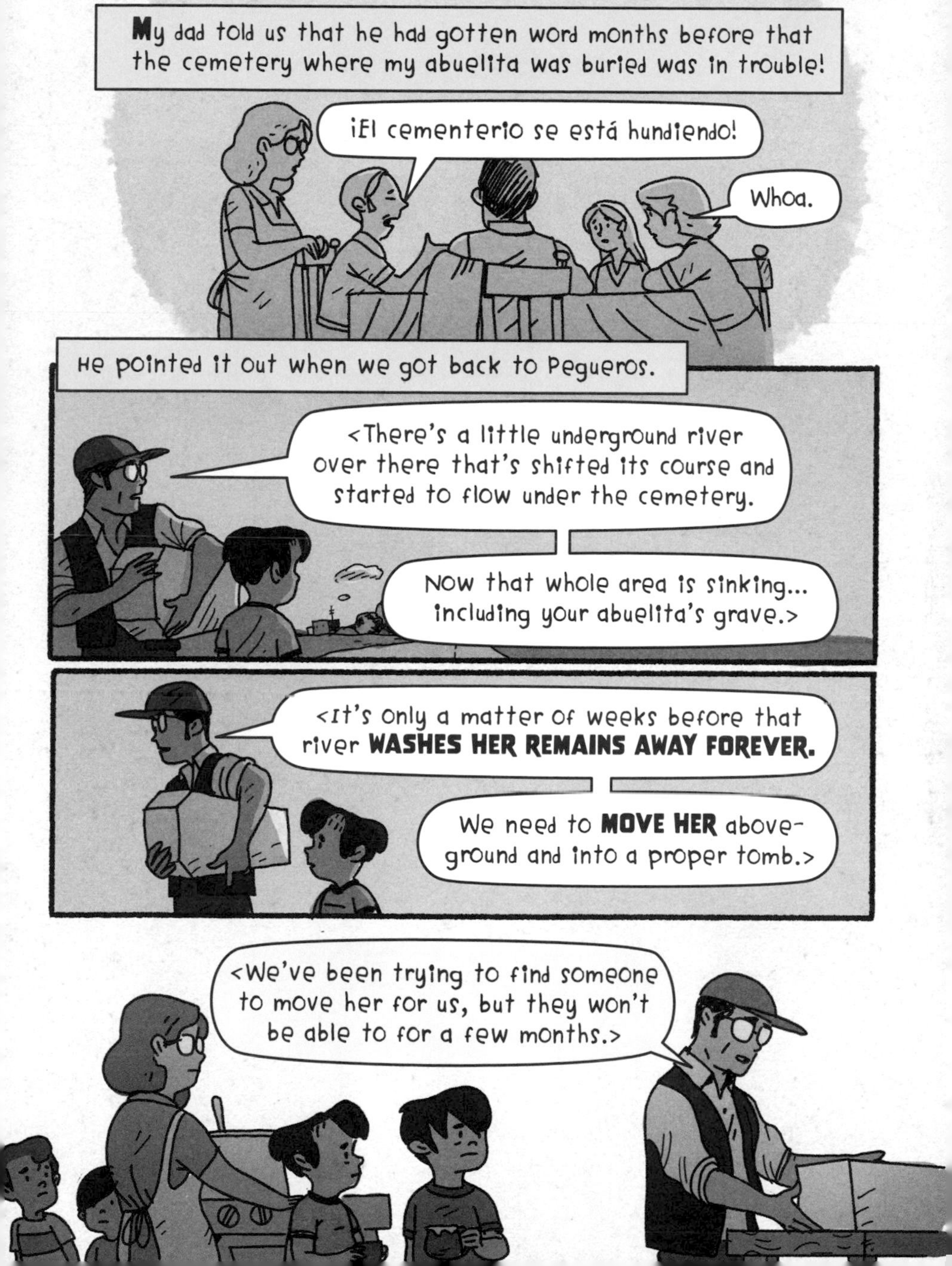
My dad told us that he had gotten word months before that the cemetery where my abuelita was buried was in trouble!
¡El cementerio se está hundiendo!
Whoa.
He pointed it out when we got back to Pegueros.
<There's a little underground river over there that's shifted its course and started to flow under the cemetery.
Now that whole area is sinking... including your abuelita's grave.>
<It's only a matter of weeks before that river **WASHES HER REMAINS AWAY FOREVER.**
We need to **MOVE HER** above-ground and into a proper tomb.>
<We've been trying to find someone to move her for us, but they won't be able to for a few months.>

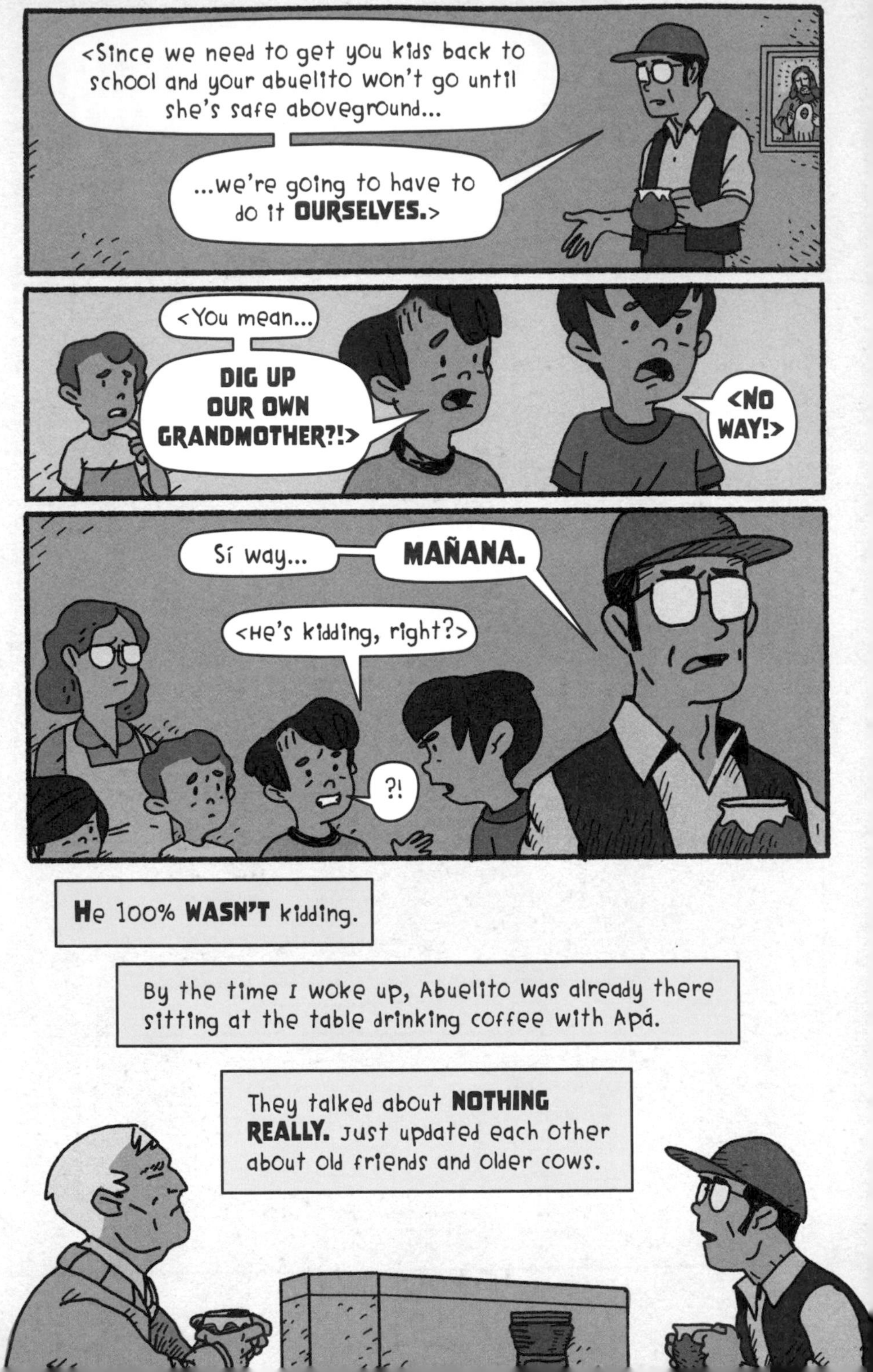
<Since we need to get you kids back to school and your abuelito won't go until she's safe aboveground...
...we're going to have to do it **OURSELVES.**>
<You mean...
DIG UP OUR OWN GRANDMOTHER?!>
<NO WAY!>
Sí way...
MAÑANA.
<He's kidding, right?>
?!
He 100% **WASN'T** kidding.
By the time I woke up, Abuelito was already there sitting at the table drinking coffee with Apá.
They talked about **NOTHING REALLY.** Just updated each other about old friends and older cows.

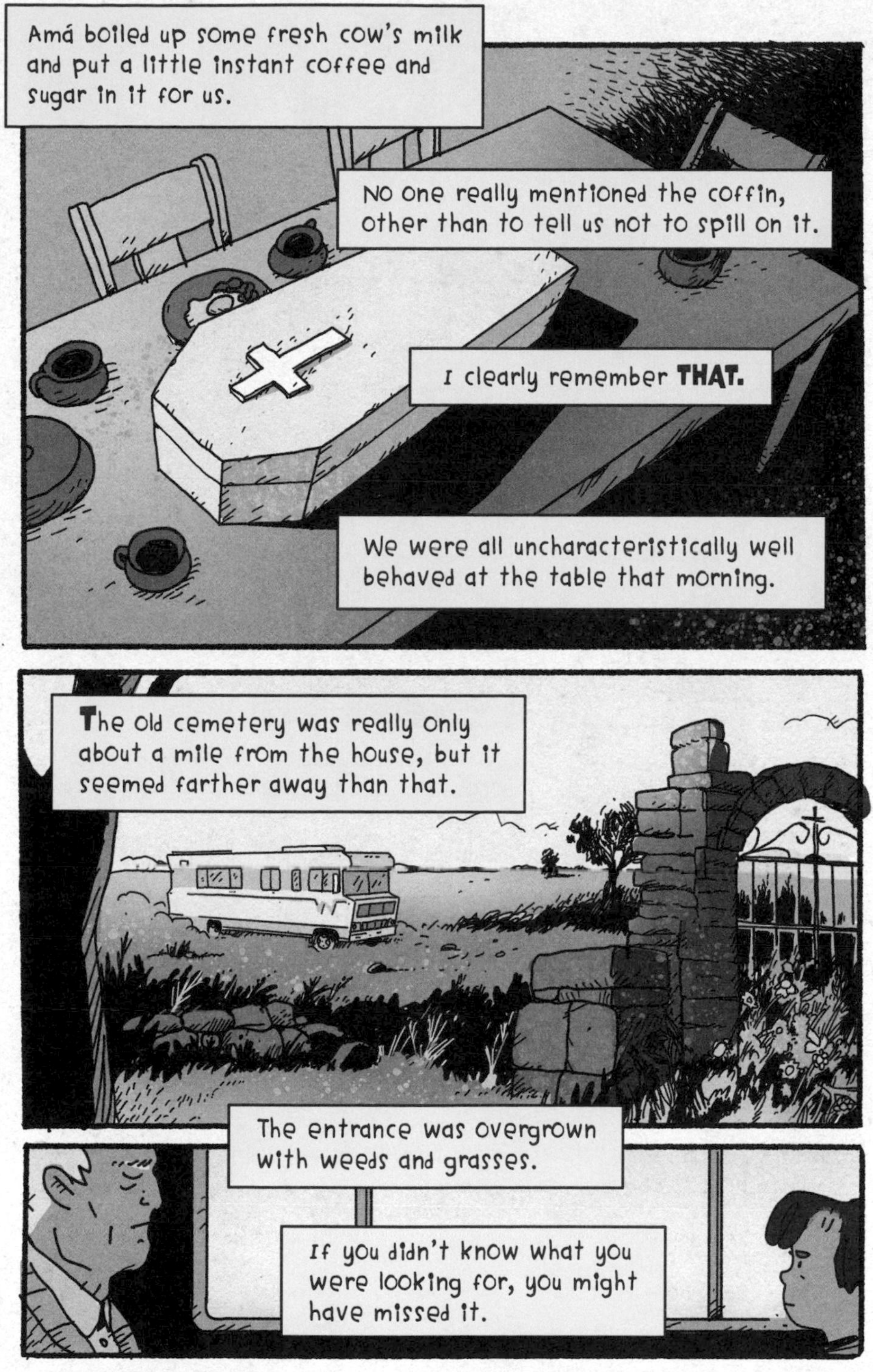
Amá boiled up some fresh cow's milk and put a little instant coffee and sugar in it for us.
No one really mentioned the coffin, other than to tell us not to spill on it.
I clearly remember **THAT.**
We were all uncharacteristically well behaved at the table that morning.
The old cemetery was really only about a mile from the house, but it seemed farther away than that.
The entrance was overgrown with weeds and grasses.
If you didn't know what you were looking for, you might have missed it.

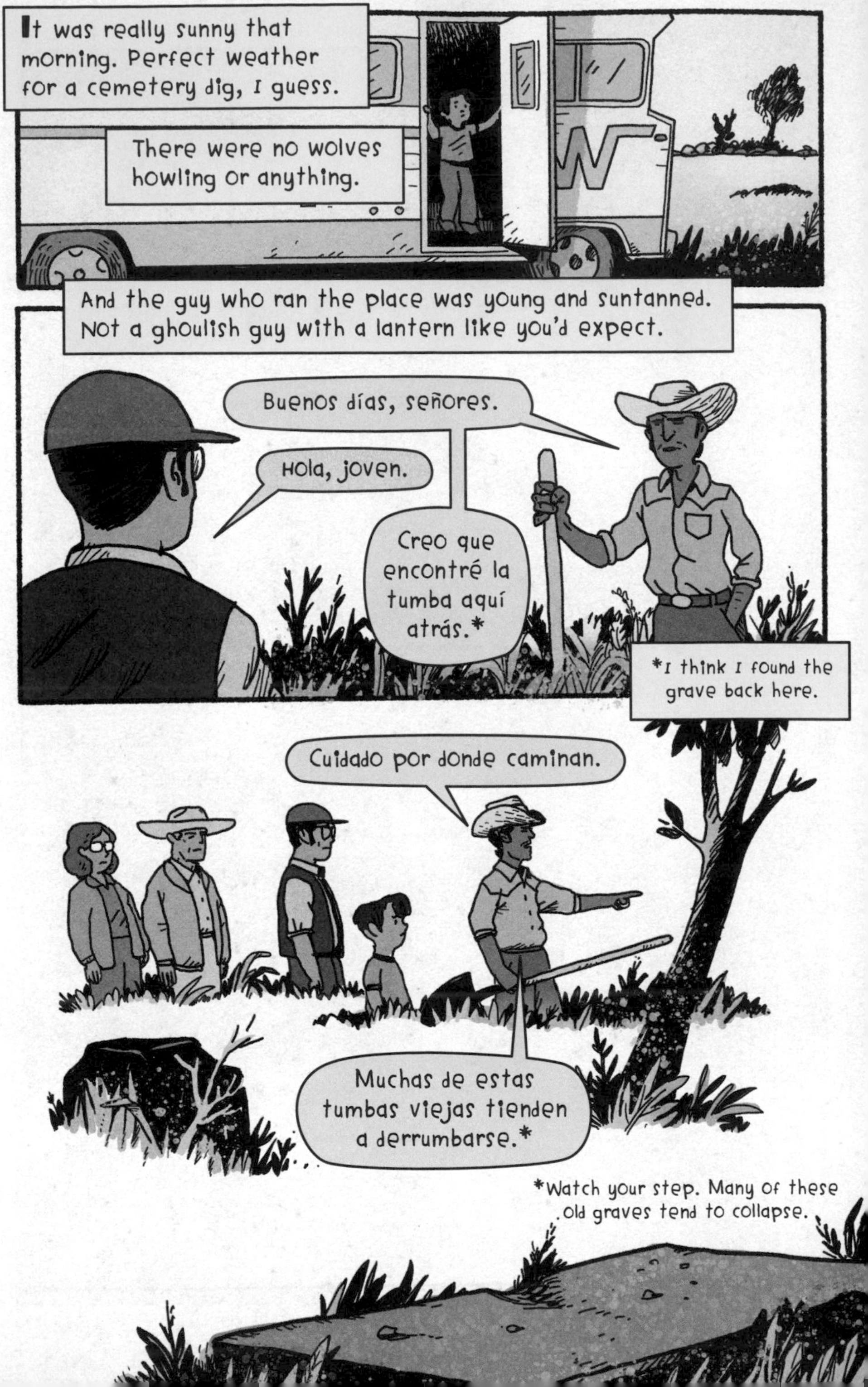
It was really sunny that morning. Perfect weather for a cemetery dig, I guess.
There were no wolves howling or anything.
And the guy who ran the place was young and suntanned. Not a ghoulish guy with a lantern like you'd expect.
Buenos días, señores.
Hola, joven.
Creo que encontré la tumba aquí atrás.*
*I think I found the grave back here.
Cuidado por donde caminan.
Muchas de estas tumbas viejas tienden a derrumbarse.*
*Watch your step. Many of these old graves tend to collapse.

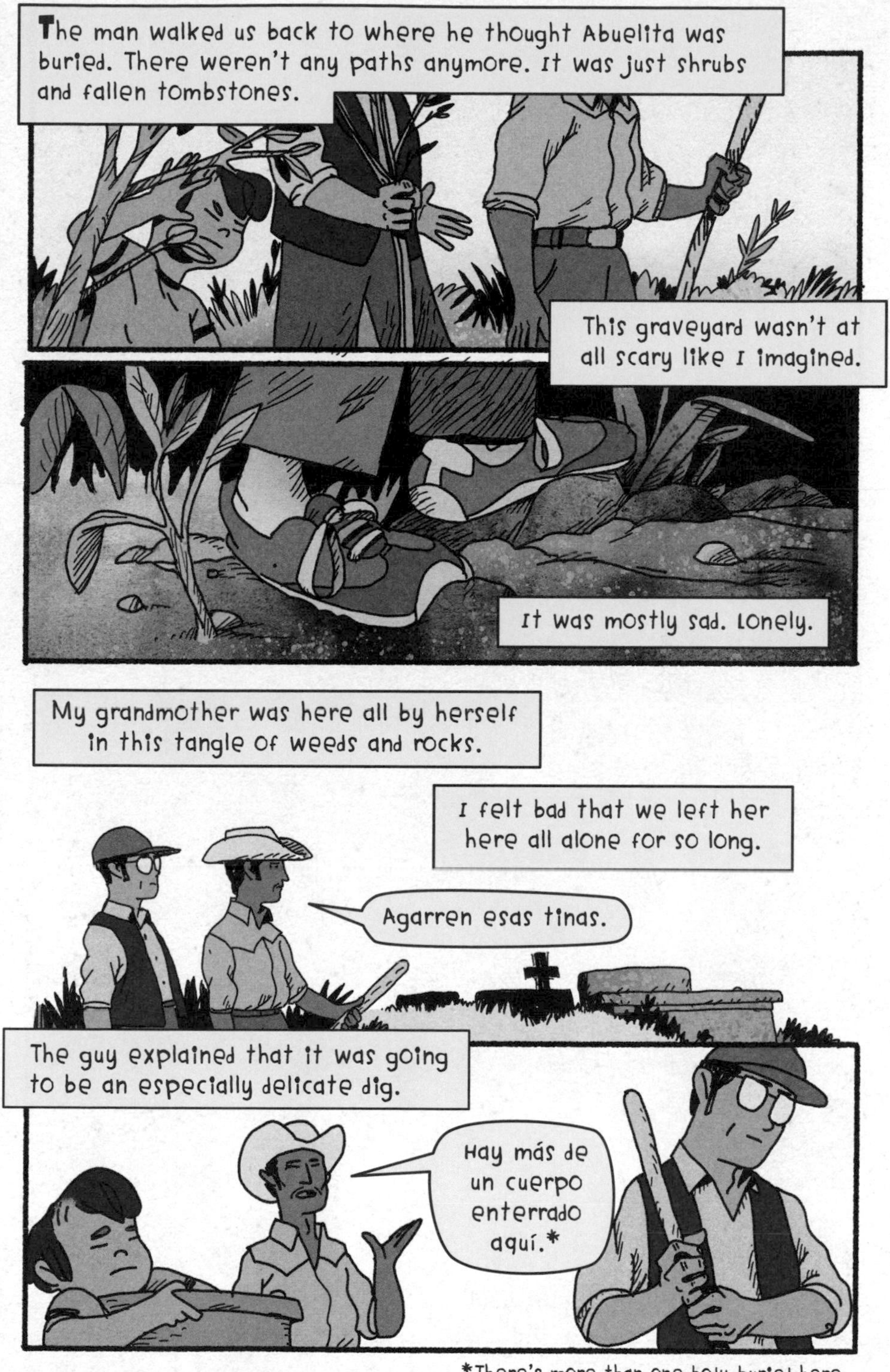
The man walked us back to where he thought Abuelita was buried. There weren't any paths anymore. It was just shrubs and fallen tombstones.
This graveyard wasn't at all scary like I imagined.
It was mostly sad. Lonely.
My grandmother was here all by herself in this tangle of weeds and rocks.
I felt bad that we left her here all alone for so long.
Agarren esas tinas.
The guy explained that it was going to be an especially delicate dig.
Hay más de un cuerpo enterrado aquí.*
*There's more than one body buried here.

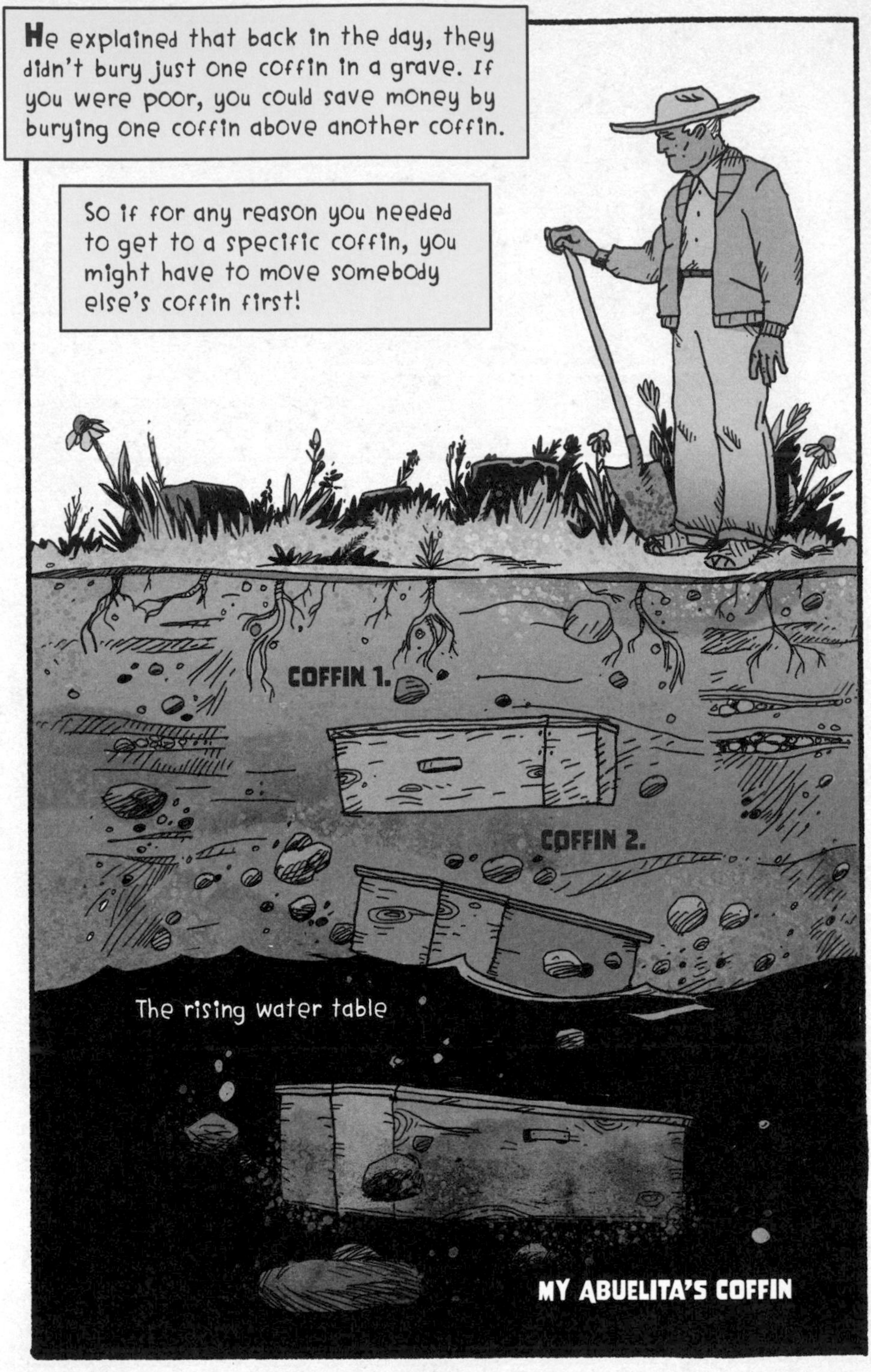
He explained that back in the day, they didn't bury just one coffin in a grave. If you were poor, you could save money by burying one coffin above another coffin.
So if for any reason you needed to get to a specific coffin, you might have to move somebody else's coffin first!
COFFIN 1.
COFFIN 2.
The rising water table
MY ABUELITA'S COFFIN

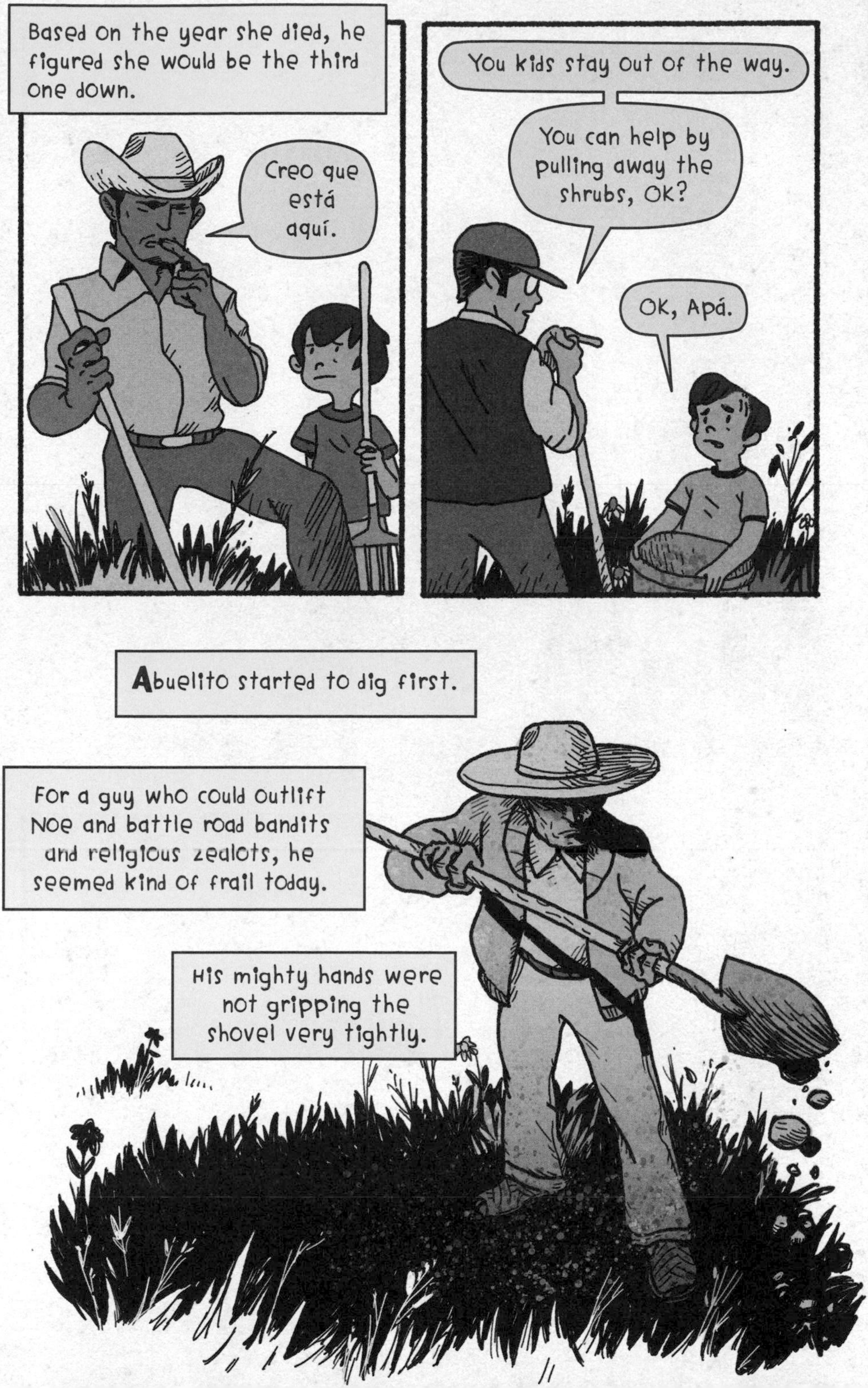

Based on the year she died, he figured she would be the third one down.
Creo que está aquí.
You kids stay out of the way.
You can help by pulling away the shrubs, OK?
OK, Apá.
Abuelito started to dig first.
For a guy who could outlift Noe and battle road bandits and religious zealots, he seemed kind of frail today.
His mighty hands were not gripping the shovel very tightly.

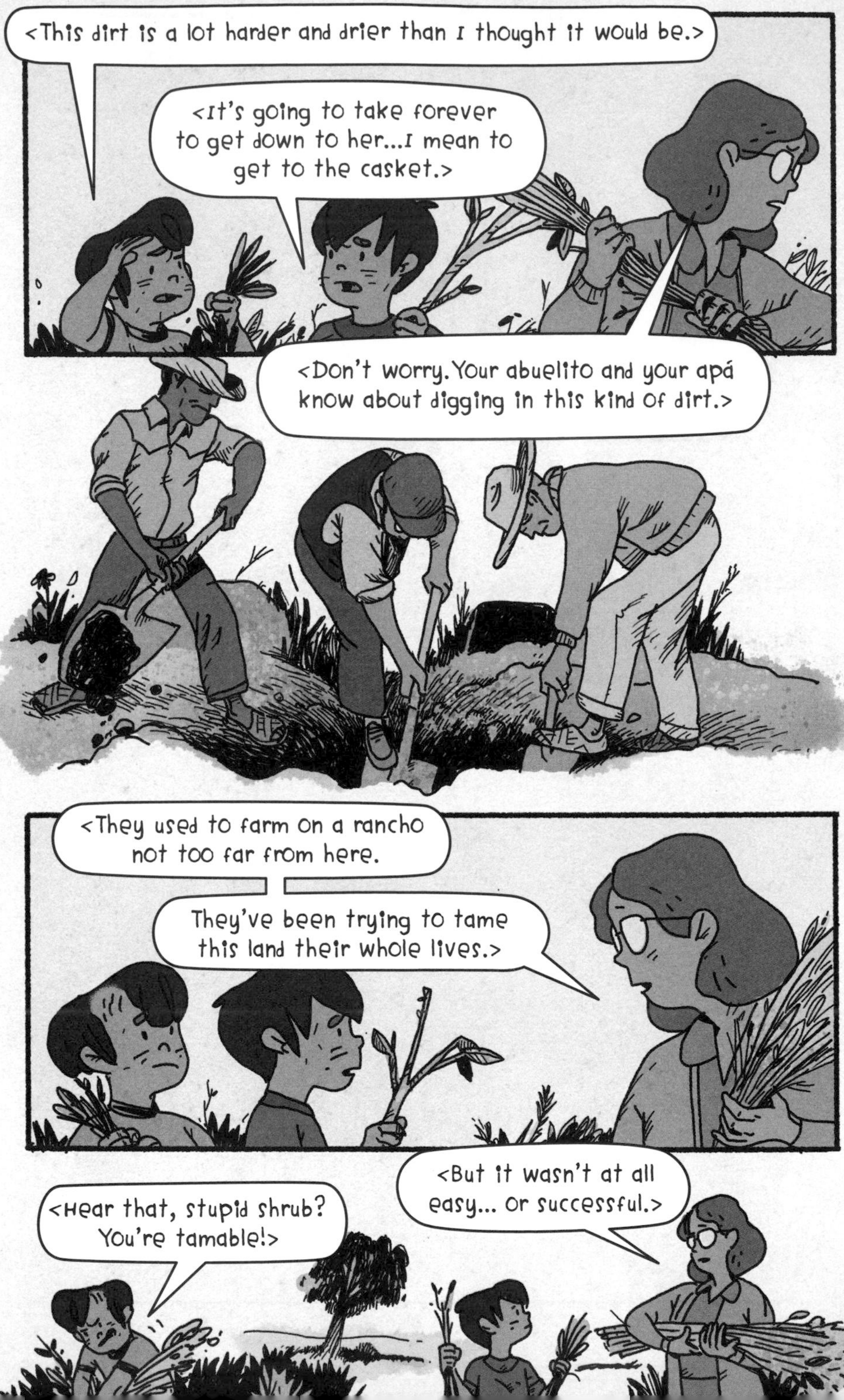
<This dirt is a lot harder and drier than I thought it would be.>
<It's going to take forever to get down to her...I mean to get to the casket.>
<Don't worry. Your abuelito and your apá know about digging in this kind of dirt.>
<They used to farm on a rancho not too far from here.
They've been trying to tame this land their whole lives.>
<Hear that, stupid shrub? You're tamable!>
<But it wasn't at all easy... or successful.>

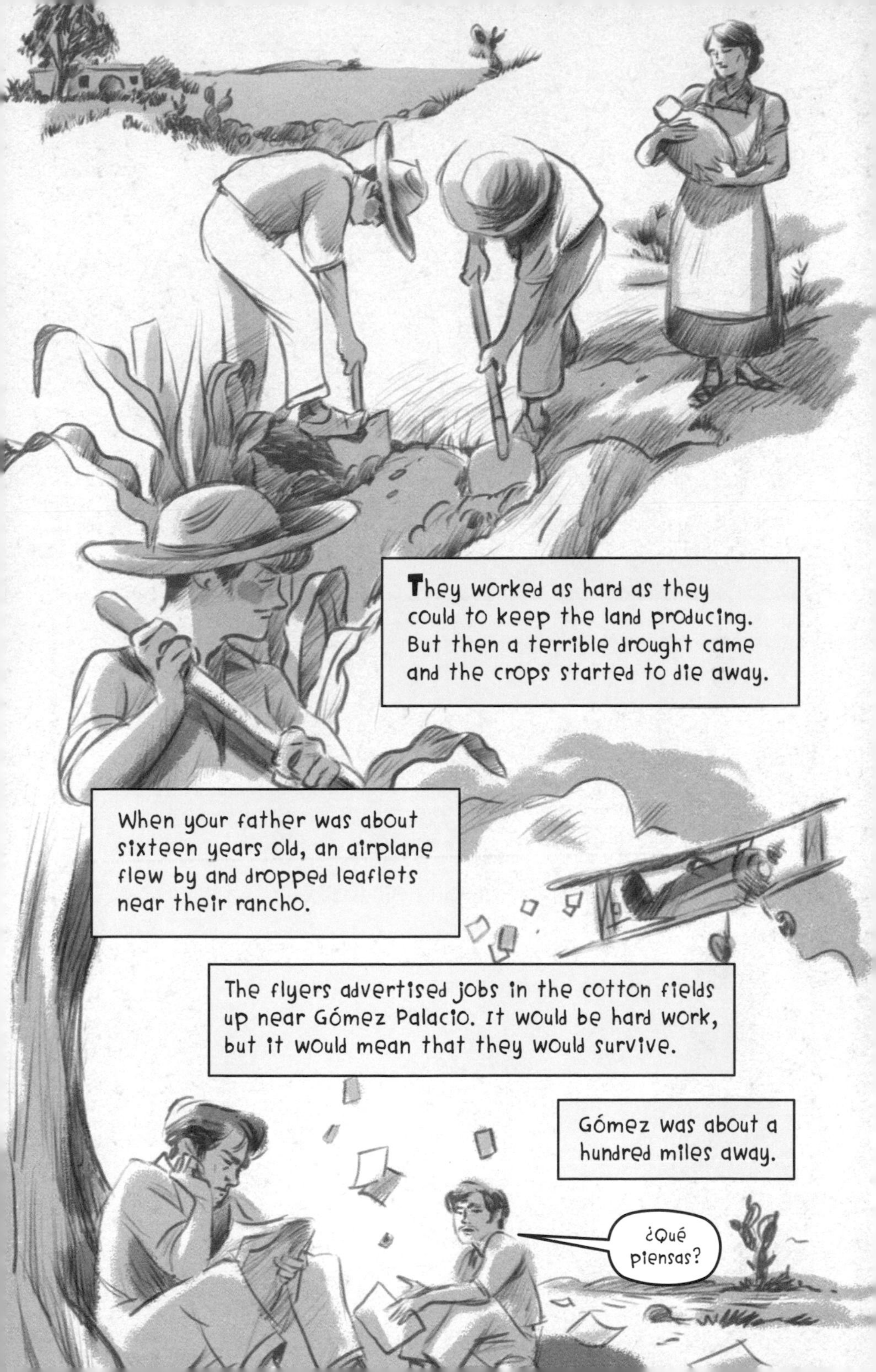
They worked as hard as they could to keep the land producing. But then a terrible drought came and the crops started to die away.
When your father was about sixteen years old, an airplane flew by and dropped leaflets near their rancho.
The flyers advertised jobs in the cotton fields up near Gómez Palacio. It would be hard work, but it would mean that they would survive.
Gómez was about a hundred miles away.
¿Qué piensas?

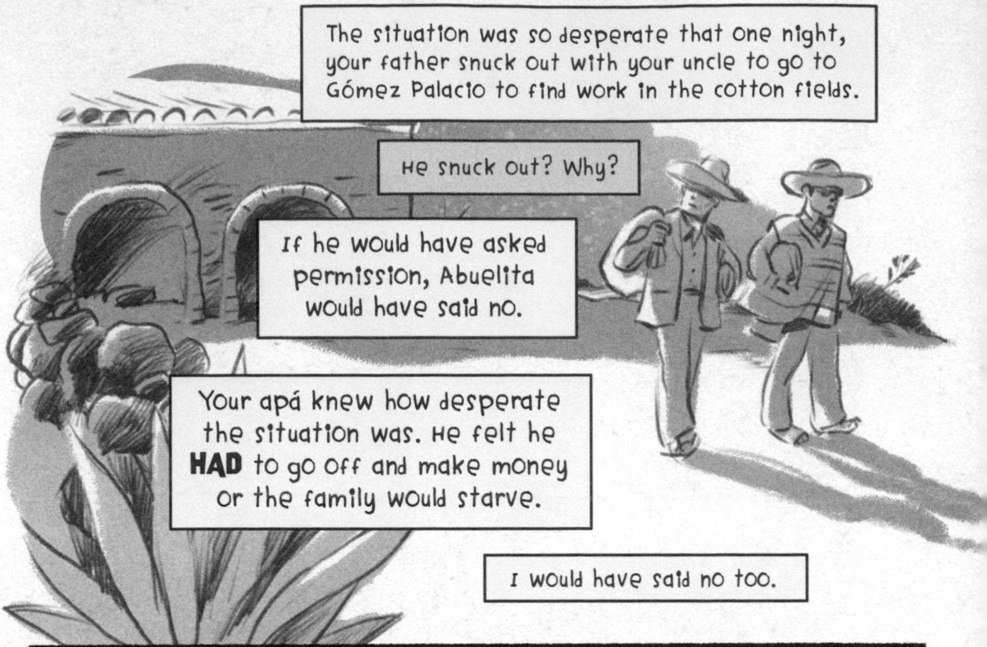
The situation was so desperate that one night, your father snuck out with your uncle to go to Gómez Palacio to find work in the cotton fields.
He snuck out? Why?
If he would have asked permission, Abuelita would have said no.
Your apá knew how desperate the situation was. He felt he HAD to go off and make money or the family would starve.
I would have said no too.

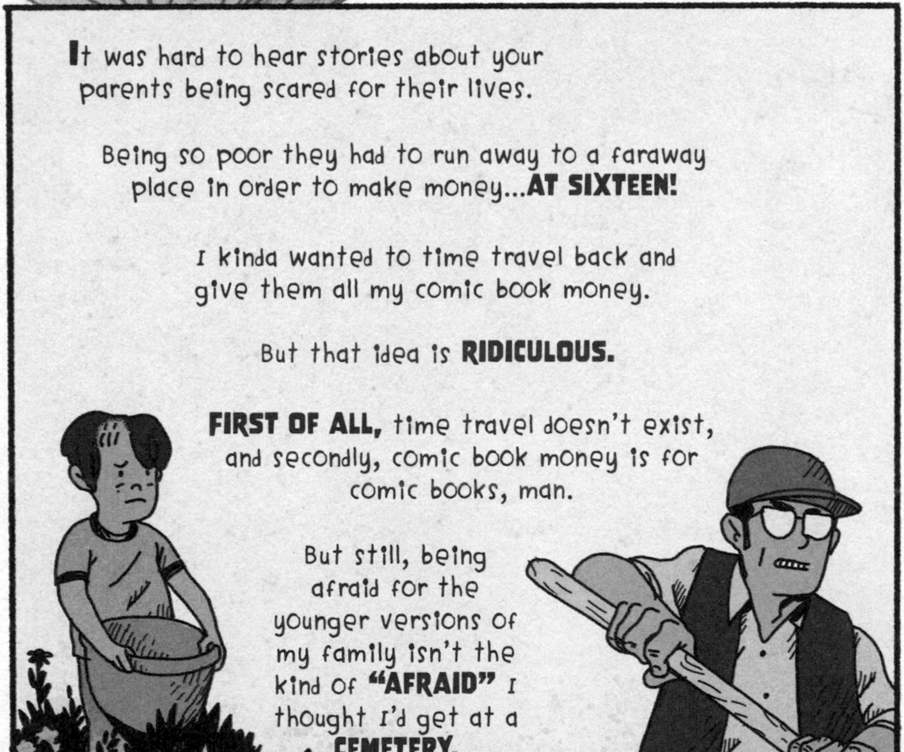
It was hard to hear stories about your parents being scared for their lives.
Being so poor they had to run away to a faraway place in order to make money...AT SIXTEEN!
I kinda wanted to time travel back and give them all my comic book money.
But that idea is RIDICULOUS.
FIRST OF ALL, time travel doesn't exist, and secondly, comic book money is for comic books, man.
But still, being afraid for the younger versions of my family isn't the kind of "AFRAID" I thought I'd get at a CEMETERY.

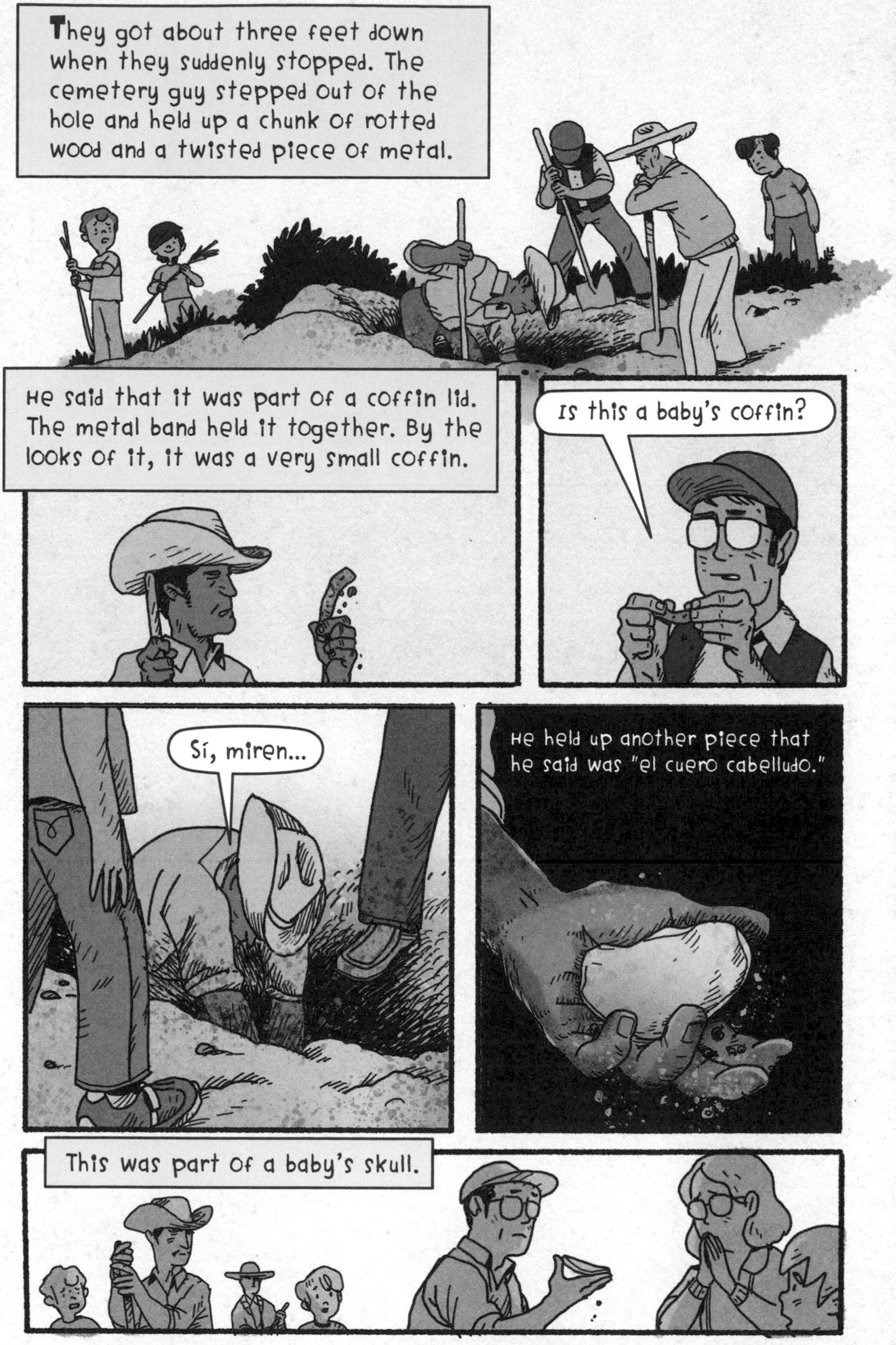
They got about three feet down when they suddenly stopped. The cemetery guy stepped out of the hole and held up a chunk of rotted wood and a twisted piece of metal.
He said that it was part of a coffin lid. The metal band held it together. By the looks of it, it was a very small coffin.
Is this a baby's coffin?
Sí, miren...
He held up another piece that he said was "el cuero cabelludo."
This was part of a baby's skull.

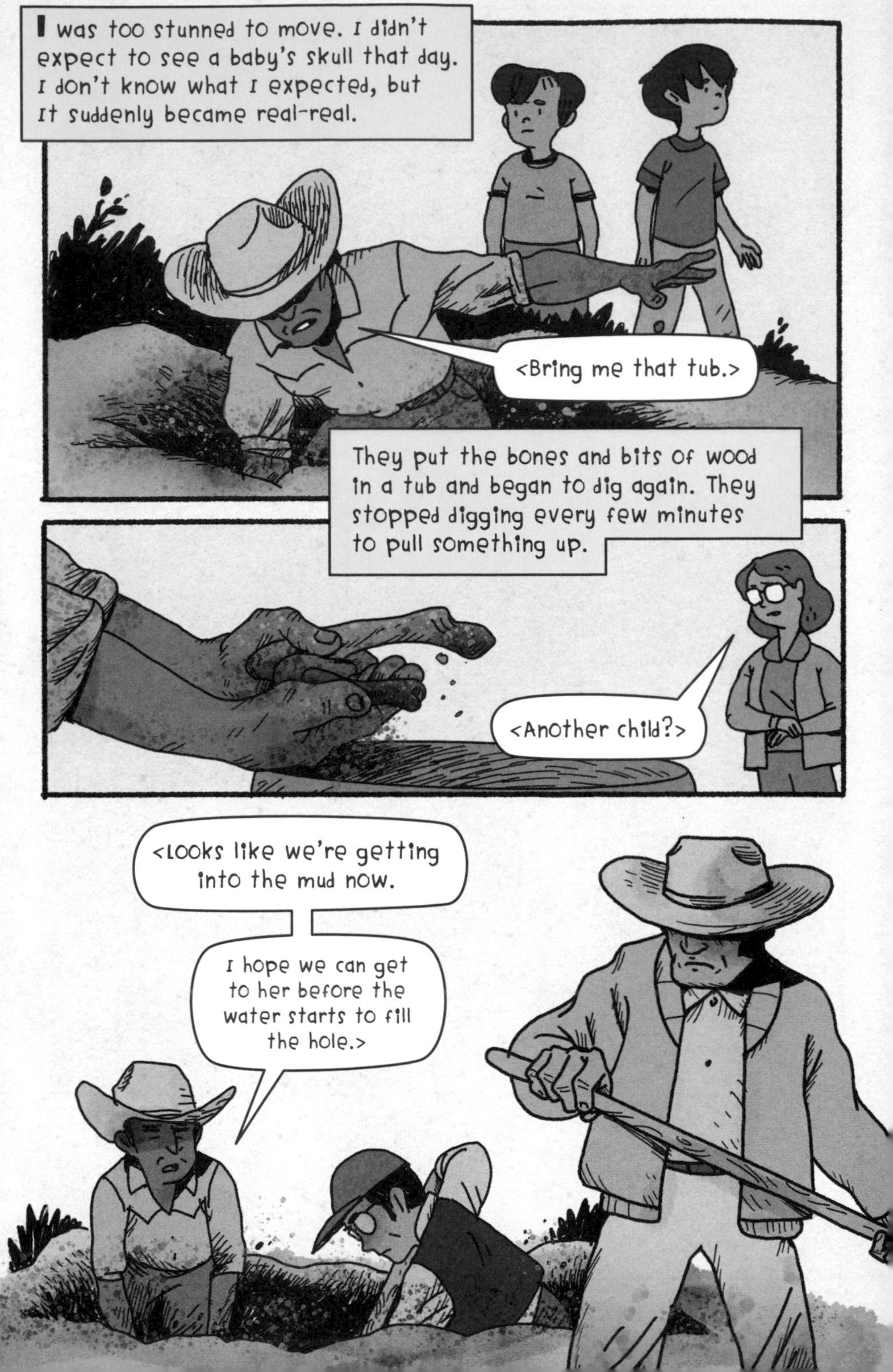
I was too stunned to move. I didn't expect to see a baby's skull that day. I don't know what I expected, but it suddenly became real-real.
<Bring me that tub.>
They put the bones and bits of wood in a tub and began to dig again. They stopped digging every few minutes to pull something up.
<Another child?>
<Looks like we're getting into the mud now.
I hope we can get to her before the water starts to fill the hole.>

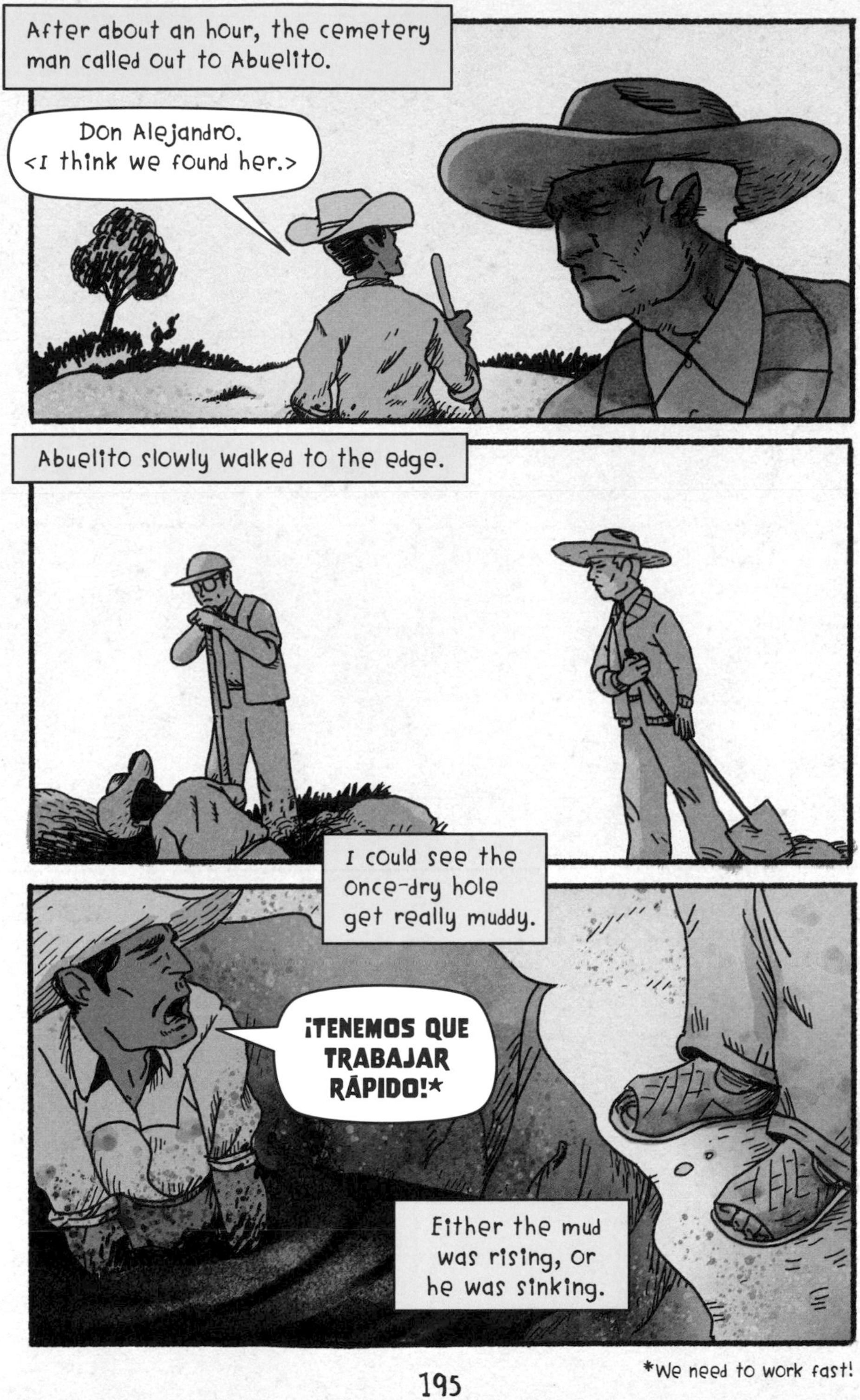
After about an hour, the cemetery man called out to Abuelito.
Don Alejandro. <I think we found her.>
Abuelito slowly walked to the edge.
I could see the once-dry hole get really muddy.
¡TENEMOS QUE TRABAJAR RÁPIDO!*
Either the mud was rising, or he was sinking.
*We need to work fast!

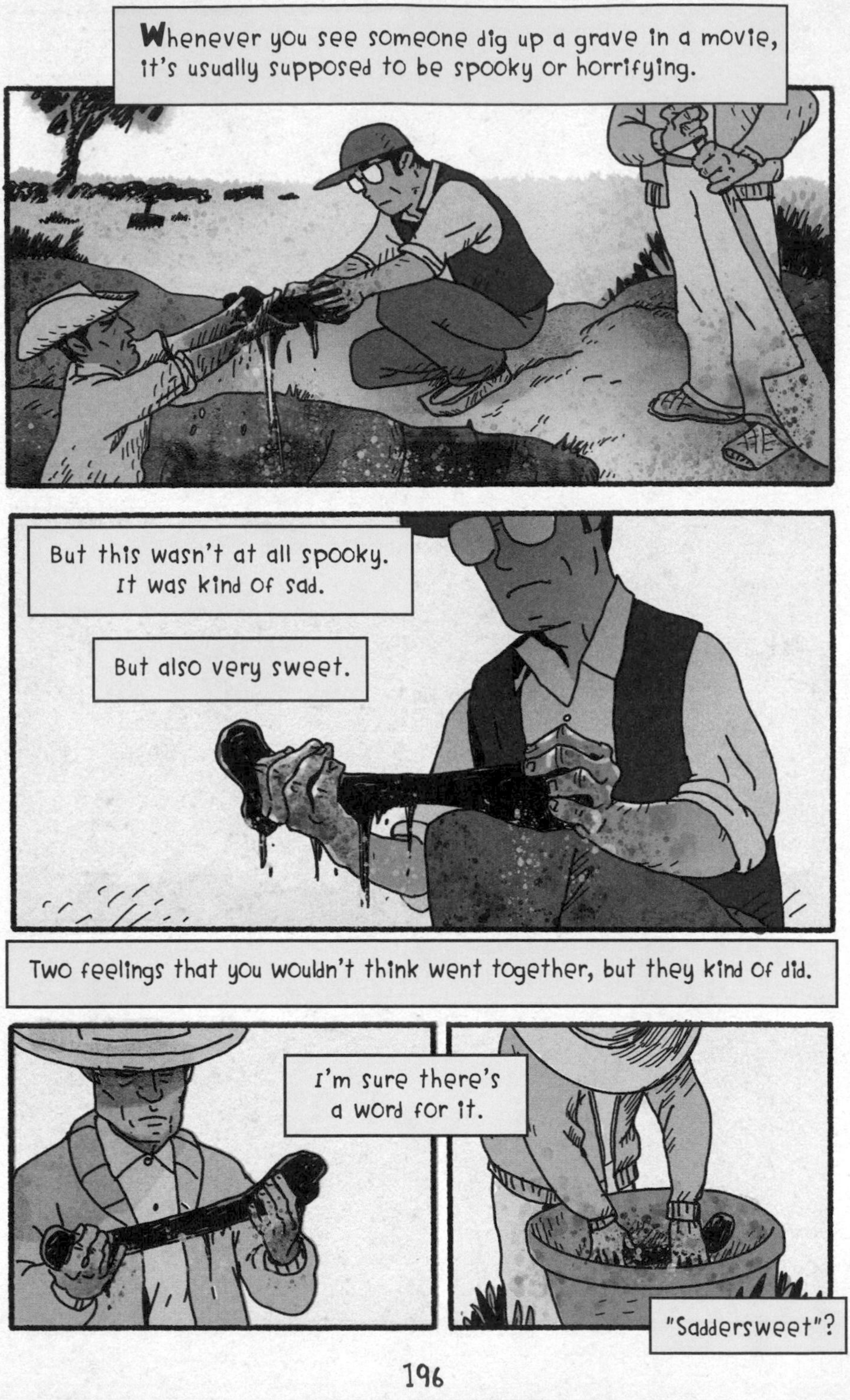
Whenever you see someone dig up a grave in a movie, it's usually supposed to be spooky or horrifying.
But this wasn't at all spooky. It was kind of sad.
But also very sweet.
Two feelings that you wouldn't think went together, but they kind of did.
I'm sure there's a word for it.
"Saddersweet"?

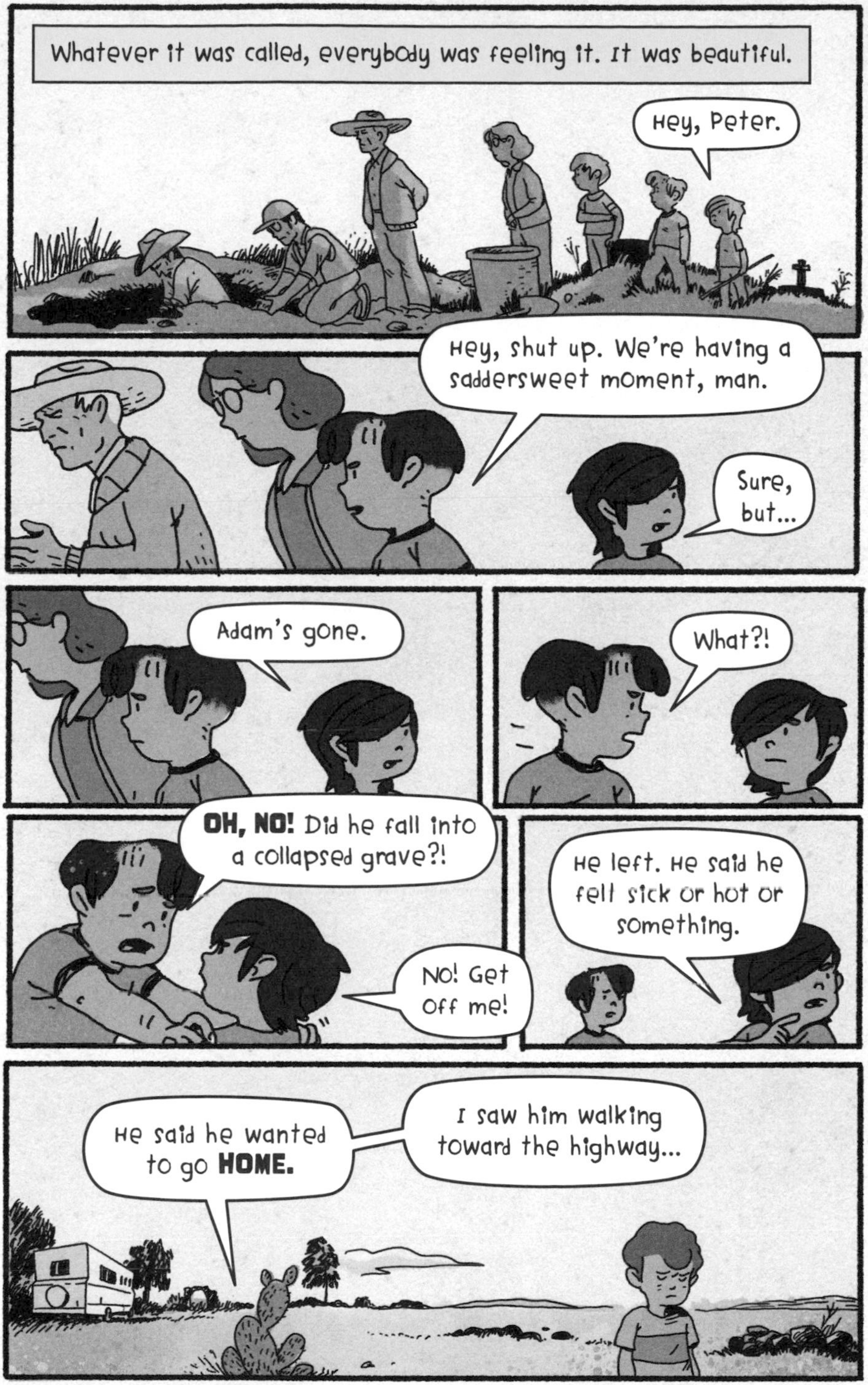
Whatever it was called, everybody was feeling it. It was beautiful.
Hey, Peter.
Hey, shut up. We're having a saddersweet moment, man.
Sure, but...
Adam's gone.
What?!
OH, NO! Did he fall into a collapsed grave?!
No! Get off me!
He left. He said he felt sick or hot or something.
He said he wanted to go HOME.
I saw him walking toward the highway...

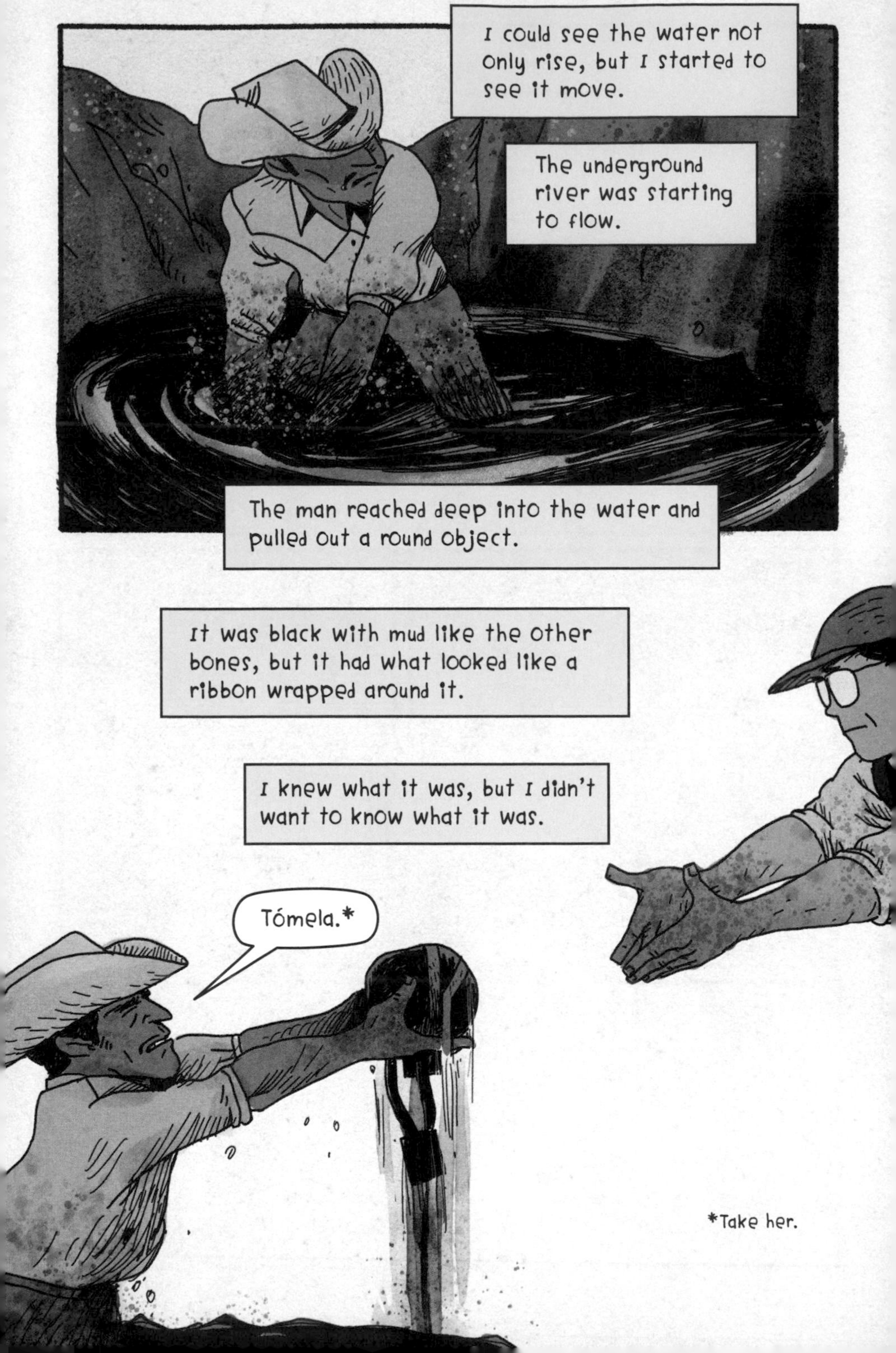
I could see the water not only rise, but I started to see it move.
The underground river was starting to flow.
The man reached deep into the water and pulled out a round object.
It was black with mud like the other bones, but it had what looked like a ribbon wrapped around it.
I knew what it was, but I didn't want to know what it was.
Tómela.*
*Take her.

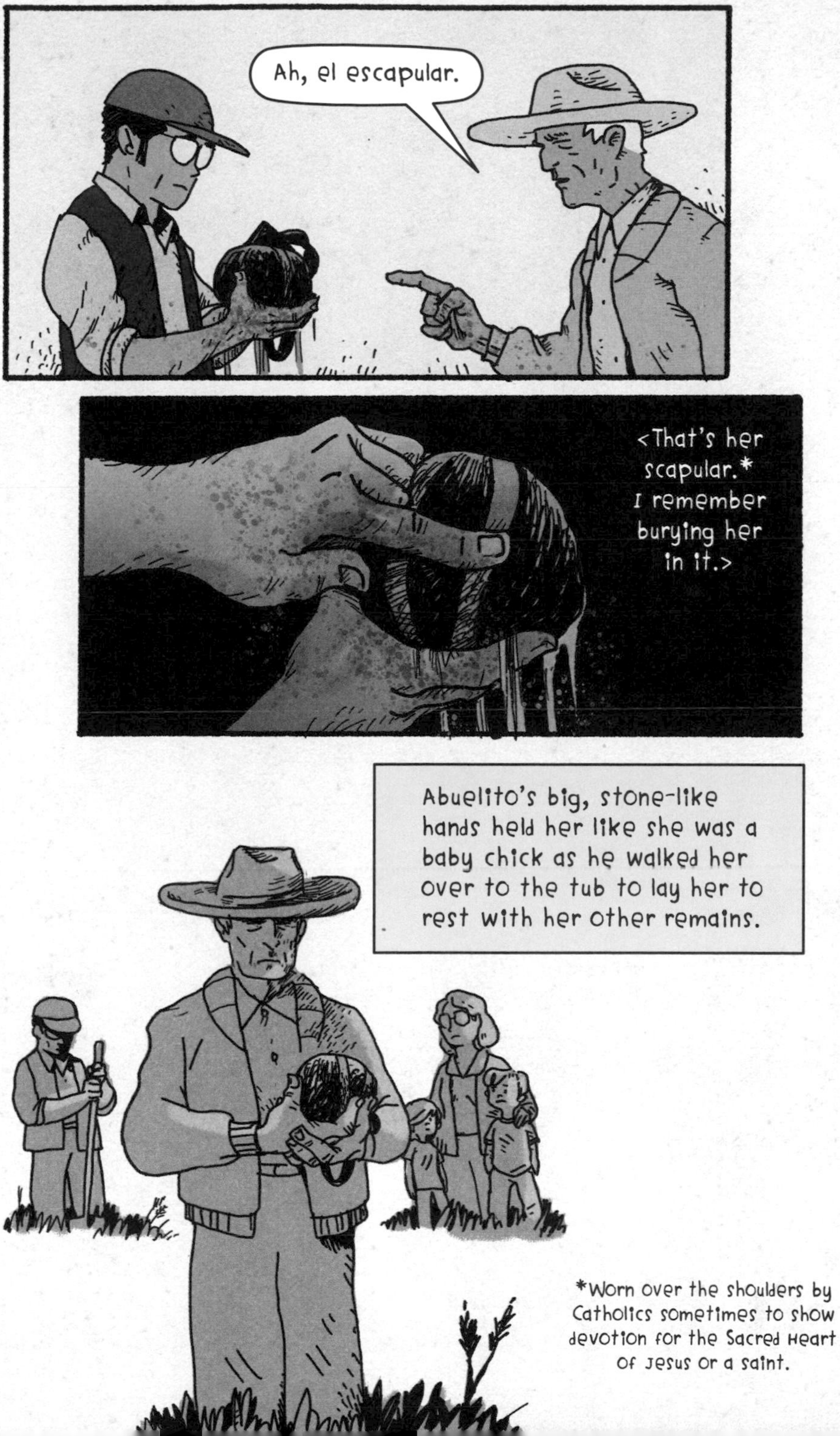
Ah, el escapular.
<That's her scapular.* I remember burying her in it.>
Abuelito's big, stone-like hands held her like she was a baby chick as he walked her over to the tub to lay her to rest with her other remains.
*Worn over the shoulders by Catholics sometimes to show devotion for the Sacred Heart of Jesus or a saint.

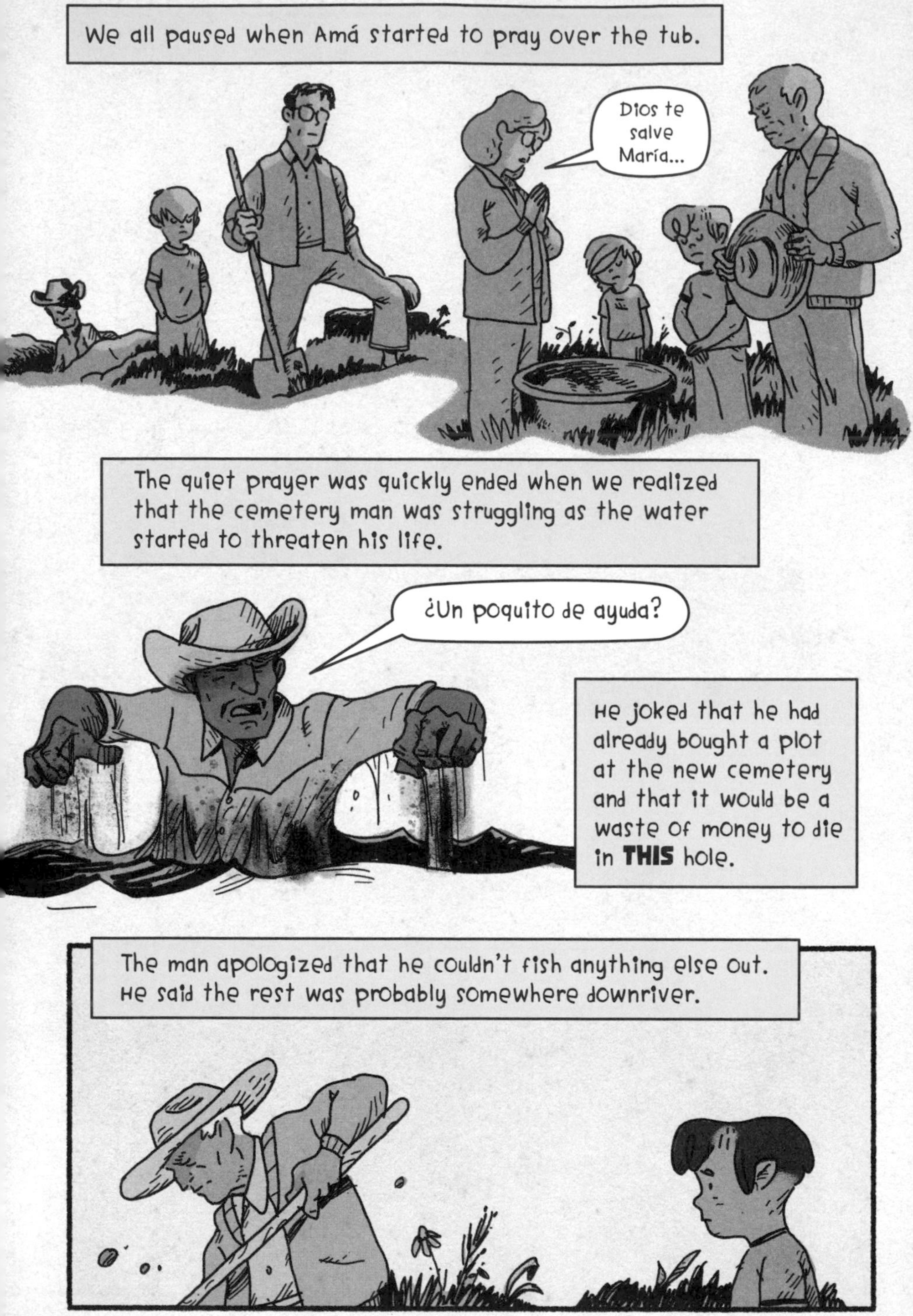
We all paused when Amá started to pray over the tub.
Dios te salve María...
The quiet prayer was quickly ended when we realized that the cemetery man was struggling as the water started to threaten his life.
¿Un poquito de ayuda?
He joked that he had already bought a plot at the new cemetery and that it would be a waste of money to die in THIS hole.
The man apologized that he couldn't fish anything else out. He said the rest was probably somewhere downriver.

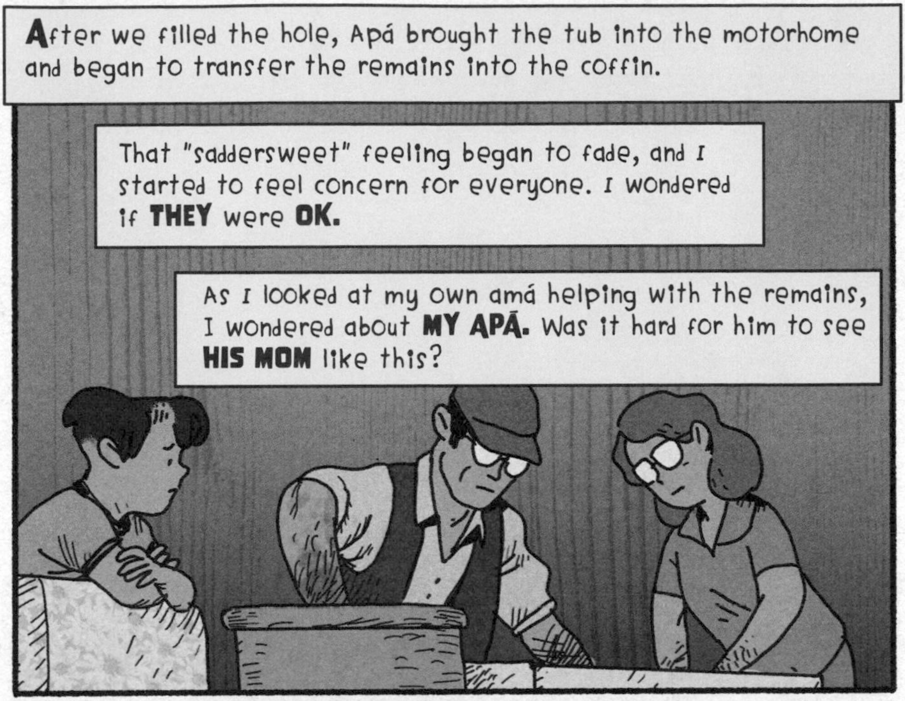
After we filled the hole, Apá brought the tub into the motorhome and began to transfer the remains into the coffin.
That "saddersweet" feeling began to fade, and I started to feel concern for everyone. I wondered if **THEY** were **OK.**
As I looked at my own amá helping with the remains, I wondered about **MY APÁ.** Was it hard for him to see **HIS MOM** like this?

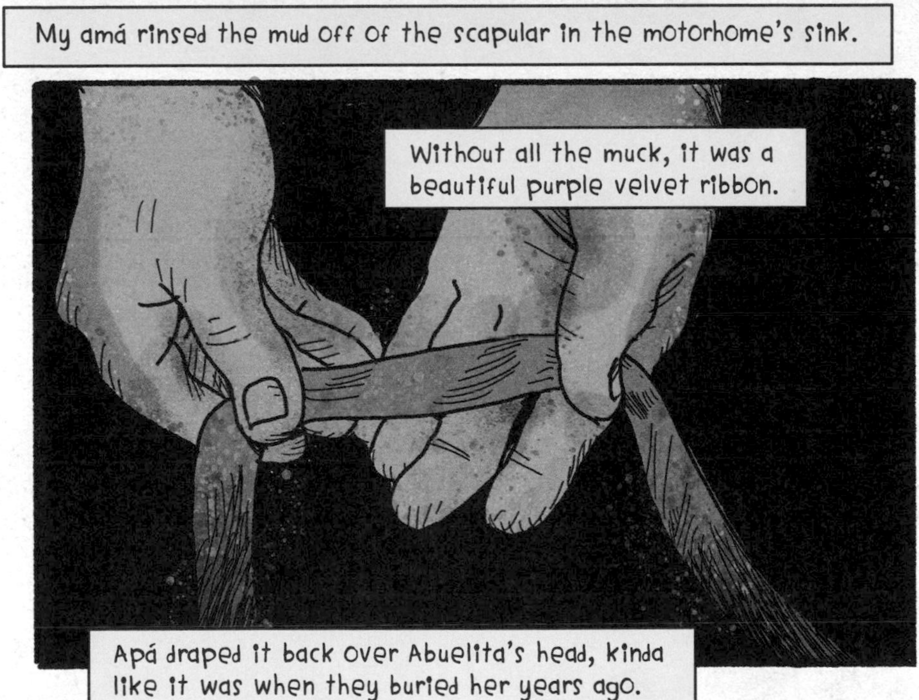
My amá rinsed the mud off of the scapular in the motorhome's sink.
Without all the muck, it was a beautiful purple velvet ribbon.
Apá draped it back over Abuelita's head, kinda like it was when they buried her years ago.

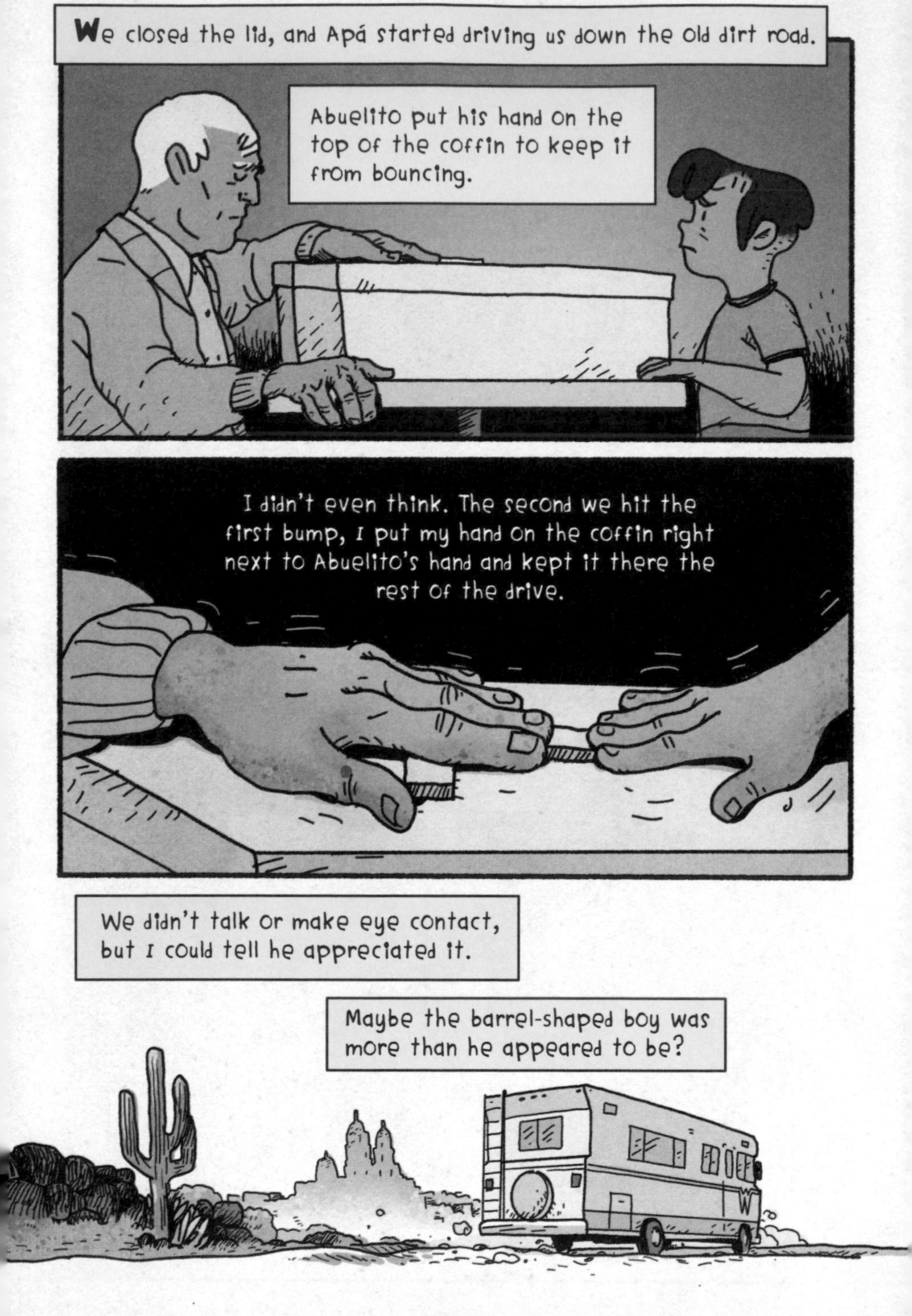
We closed the lid, and Apá started driving us down the old dirt road.
Abuelito put his hand on the top of the coffin to keep it from bouncing.
I didn't even think. The second we hit the first bump, I put my hand on the coffin right next to Abuelito's hand and kept it there the rest of the drive.
We didn't talk or make eye contact, but I could tell he appreciated it.
Maybe the barrel-shaped boy was more than he appeared to be?

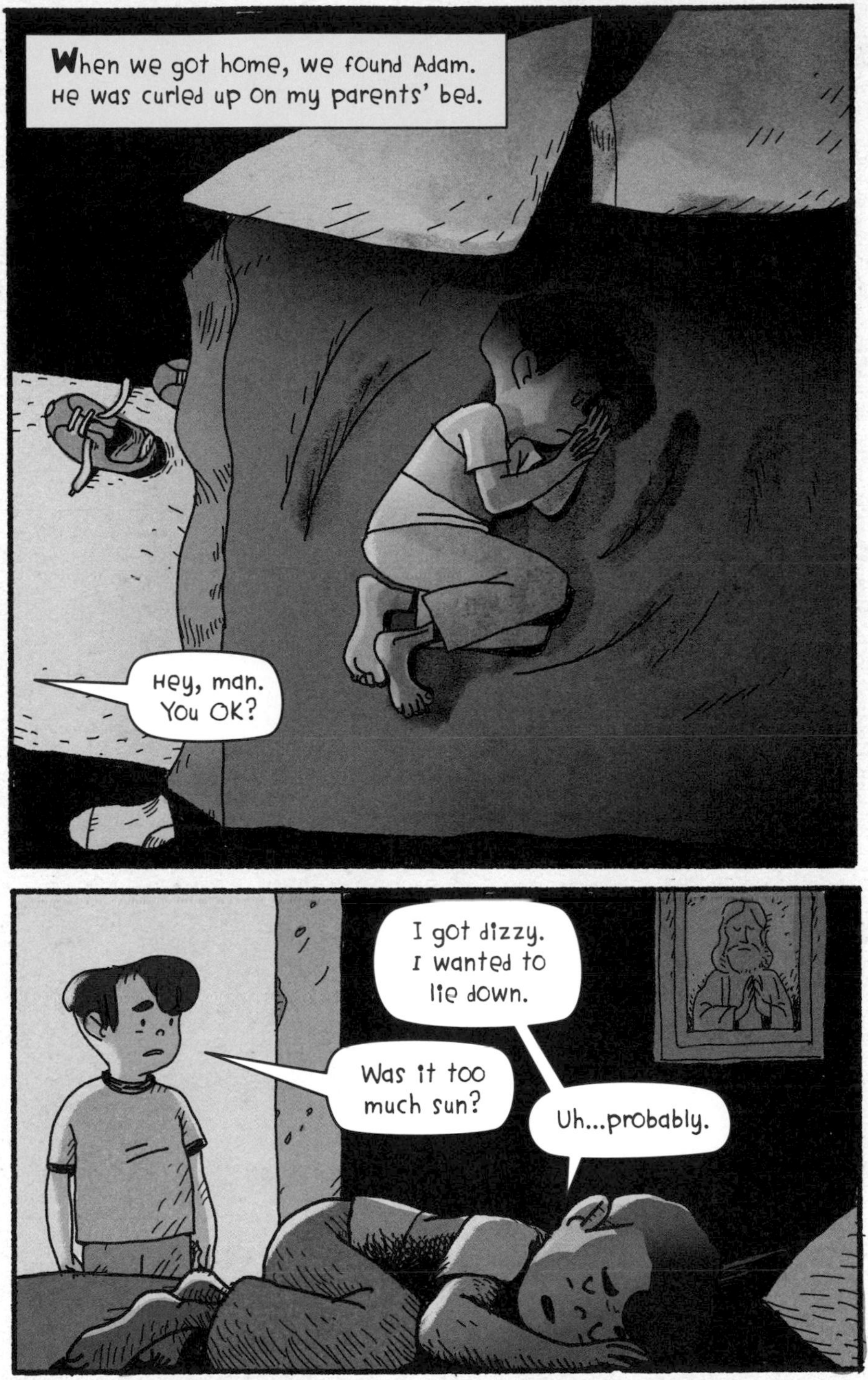
When we got home, we found Adam.
He was curled up on my parents' bed.
Hey, man.
You OK?
I got dizzy.
I wanted to
lie down.
Was it too
much sun?
Uh...probably.

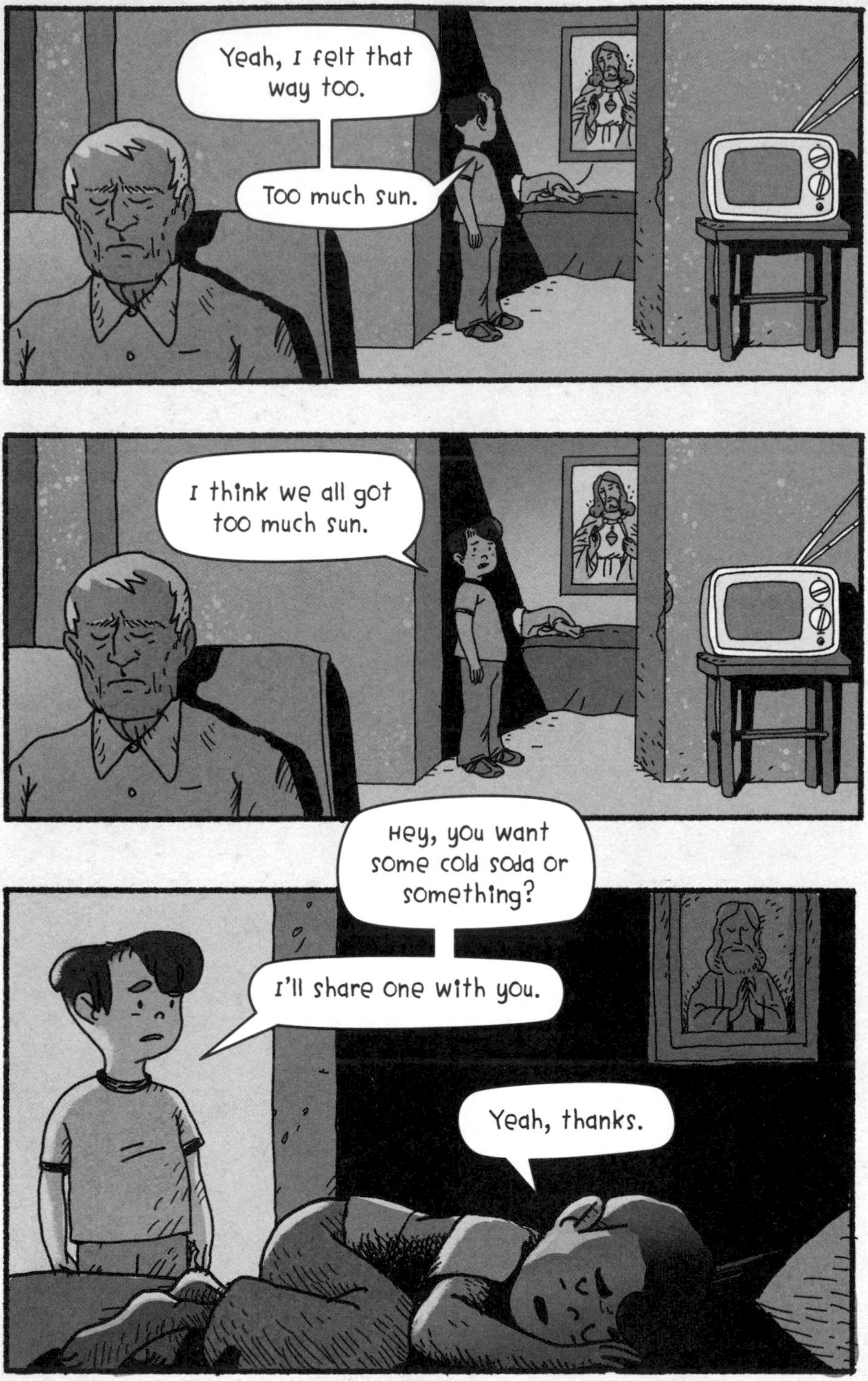
Yeah, I felt that way too.
Too much sun.
I think we all got too much sun.
Hey, you want some cold soda or something?
I'll share one with you.
Yeah, thanks.

CHAPTER 15
LA PRIETA LINDA

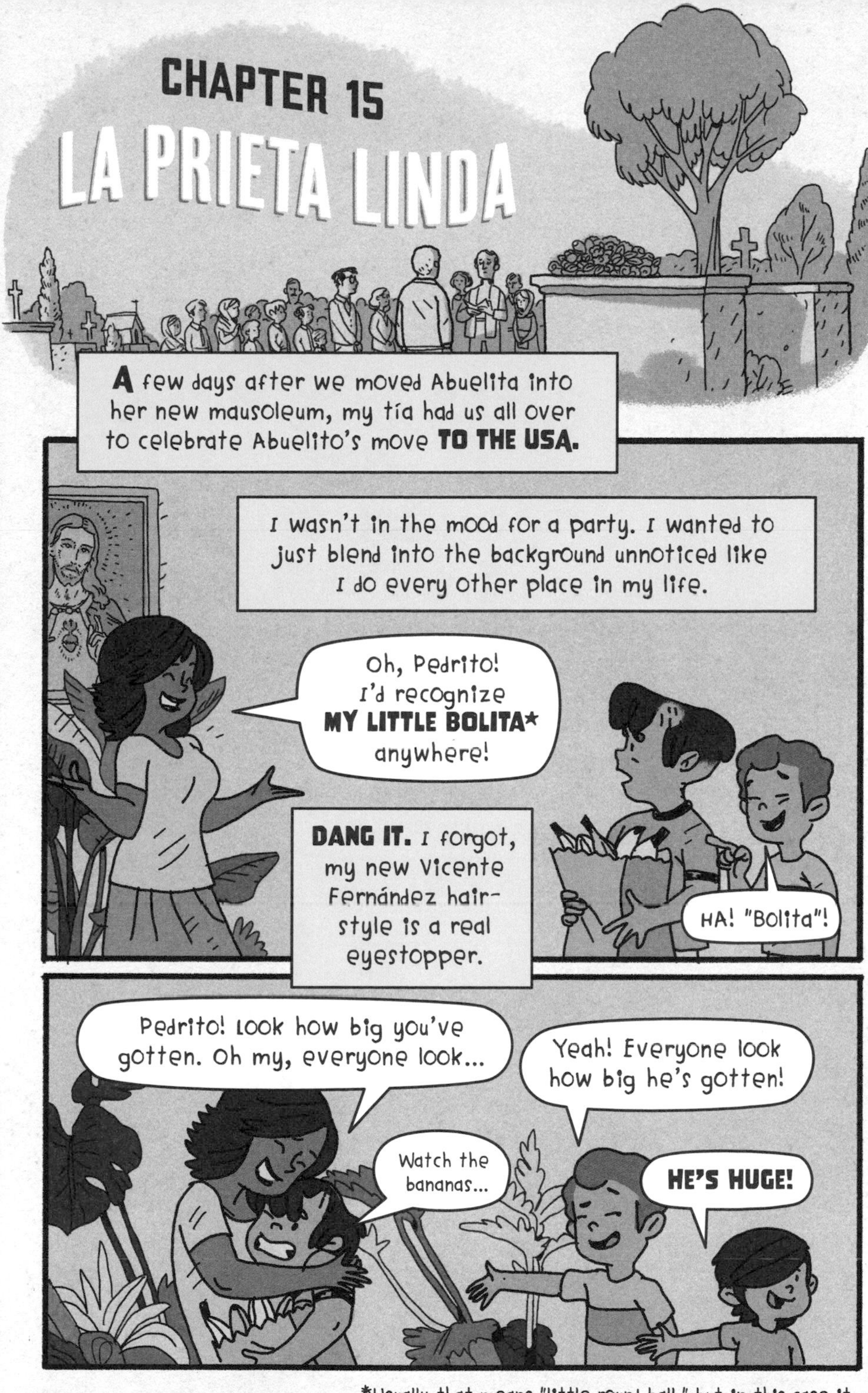

A few days after we moved Abuelita into her new mausoleum, my tía had us all over to celebrate Abuelito's move **TO THE USA.**
I wasn't in the mood for a party. I wanted to just blend into the background unnoticed like I do every other place in my life.
Oh, Pedrito! I'd recognize **MY LITTLE BOLITA*** anywhere!
DANG IT. I forgot, my new Vicente Fernández hair-style is a real eyestopper.
HA! "Bolita"!
Pedrito! Look how big you've gotten. Oh my, everyone look...
Yeah! Everyone look how big he's gotten!
Watch the bananas...
HE'S HUGE!

*Usually that means "little round ball," but in this case it might be one of Vicente Fernández's nicknames. Probably.

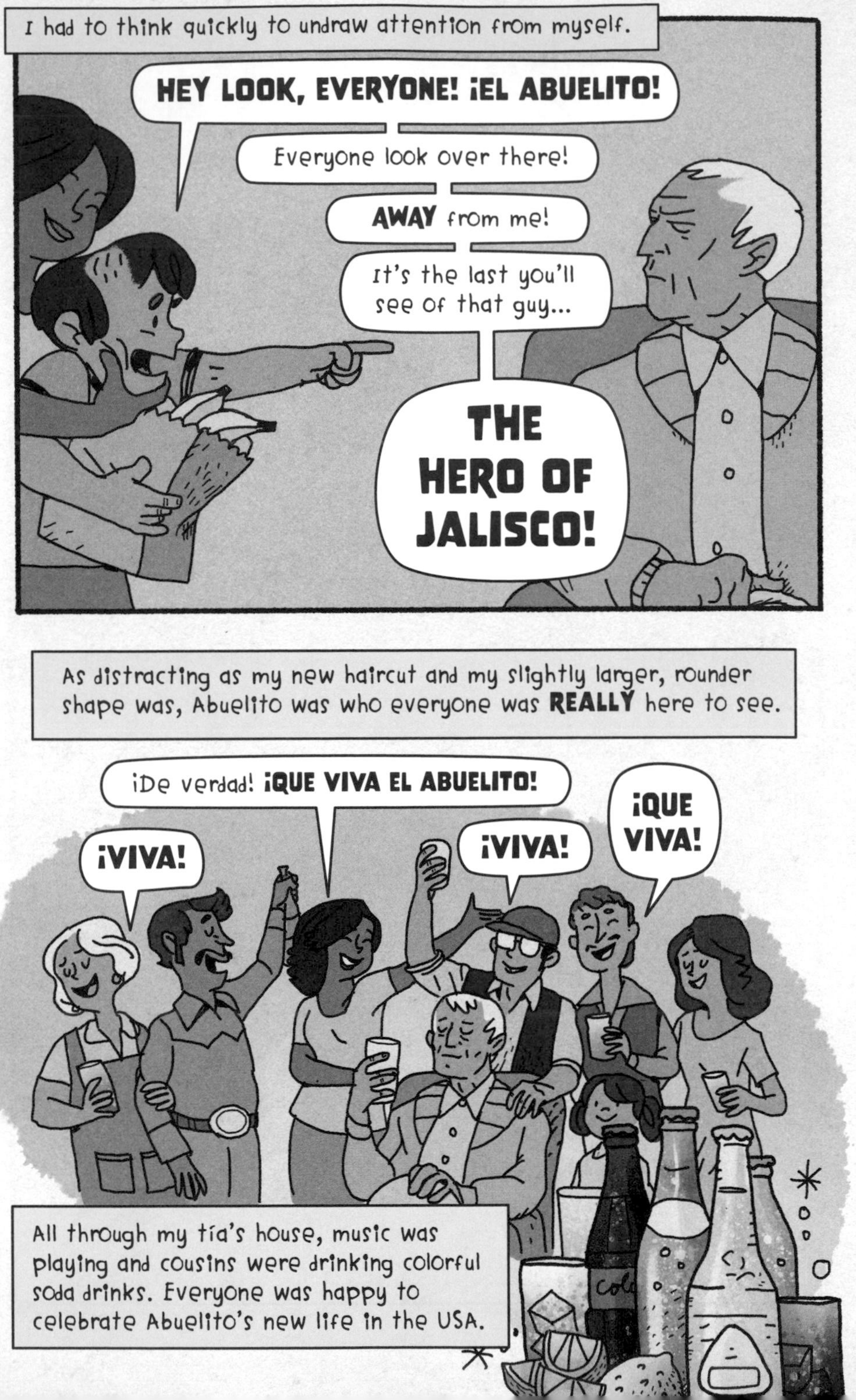
I had to think quickly to undraw attention from myself.
HEY LOOK, EVERYONE! ¡EL ABUELITO!
Everyone look over there!
AWAY from me!
It's the last you'll see of that guy...
THE HERO OF JALISCO!
As distracting as my new haircut and my slightly larger, rounder shape was, Abuelito was who everyone was REALLY here to see.
¡VIVA!
¡De verdad! ¡QUE VIVA EL ABUELITO!
¡VIVA!
¡QUE VIVA!
All through my tía's house, music was playing and cousins were drinking colorful soda drinks. Everyone was happy to celebrate Abuelito's new life in the USA.

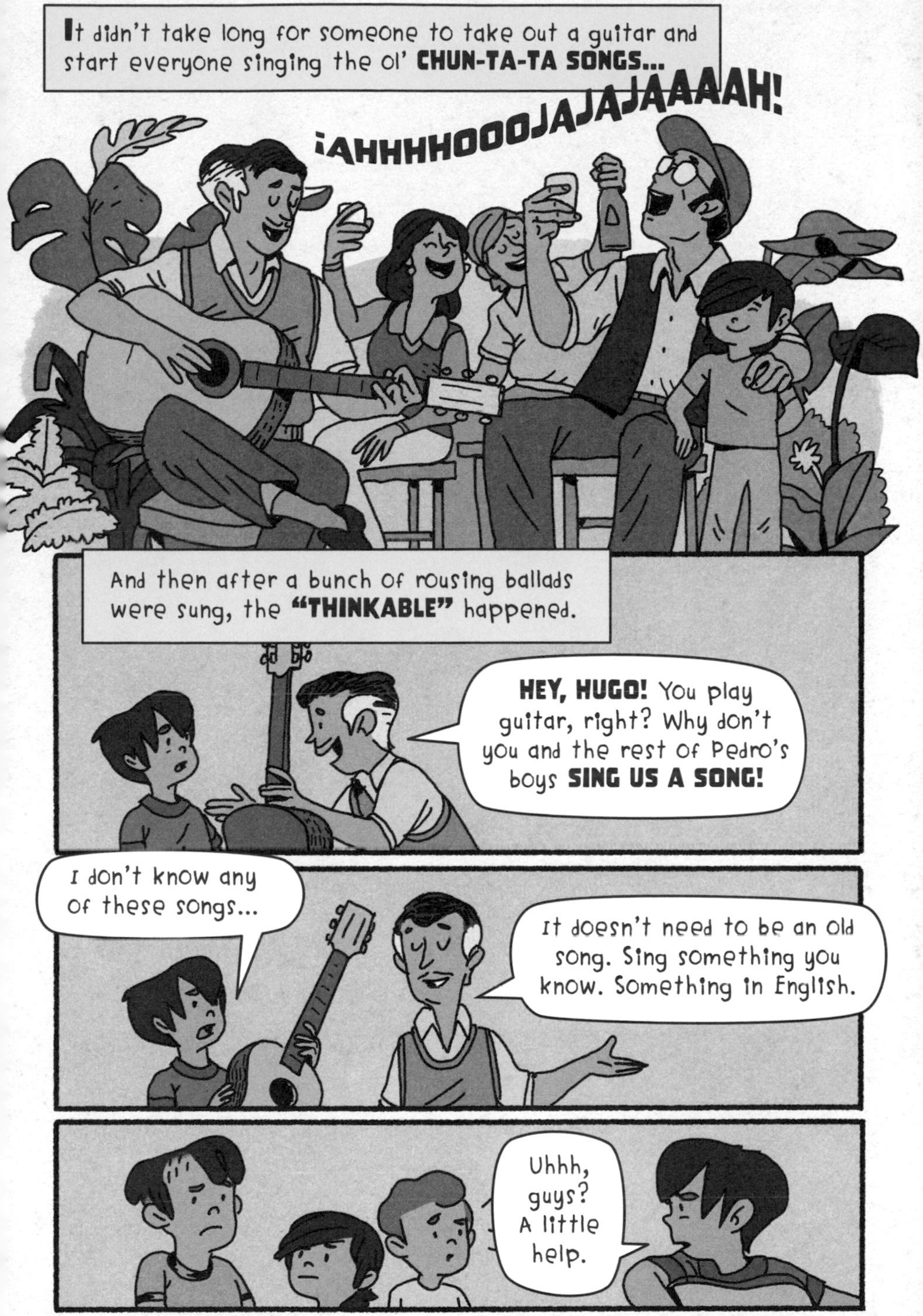
It didn't take long for someone to take out a guitar and start everyone singing the ol' CHUN-TA-TA SONGS...
¡AHHHHOOOJAJAJAAAAH!
And then after a bunch of rousing ballads were sung, the "THINKABLE" happened.
HEY, HUGO! You play guitar, right? Why don't you and the rest of Pedro's boys SING US A SONG!
I don't know any of these songs...
It doesn't need to be an old song. Sing something you know. Something in English.
Uhhh, guys? A little help.

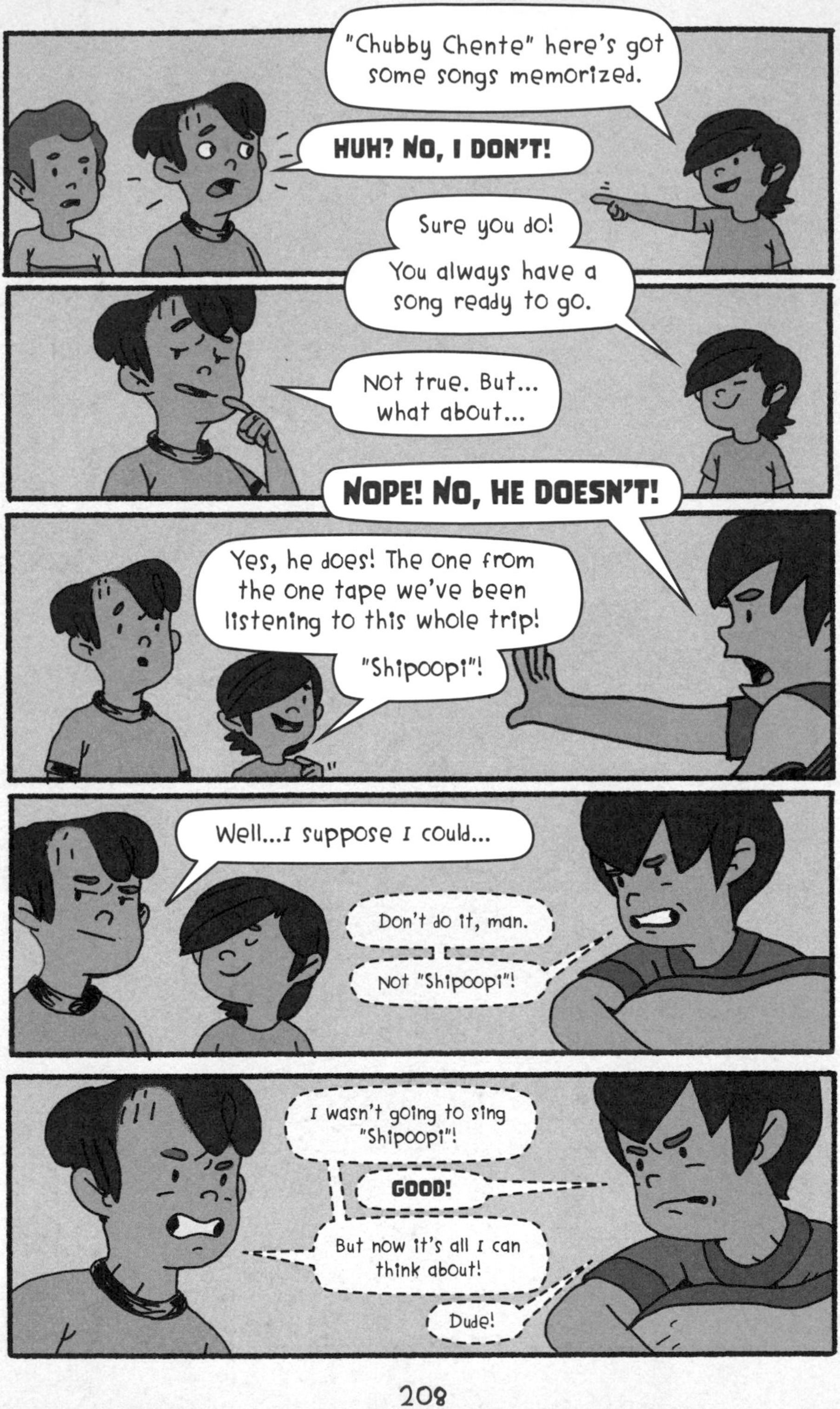
"Chubby Chente" here's got some songs memorized.
HUH? NO, I DON'T!
Sure you do!
You always have a song ready to go.
Not true. But... what about...
NOPE! NO, HE DOESN'T!
Yes, he does! The one from the one tape we've been listening to this whole trip!
"Shipoopi"!
Well...I suppose I could...
Don't do it, man.
Not "Shipoopi"!
I wasn't going to sing "Shipoopi"!
GOOD!
But now it's all I can think about!
Dude!

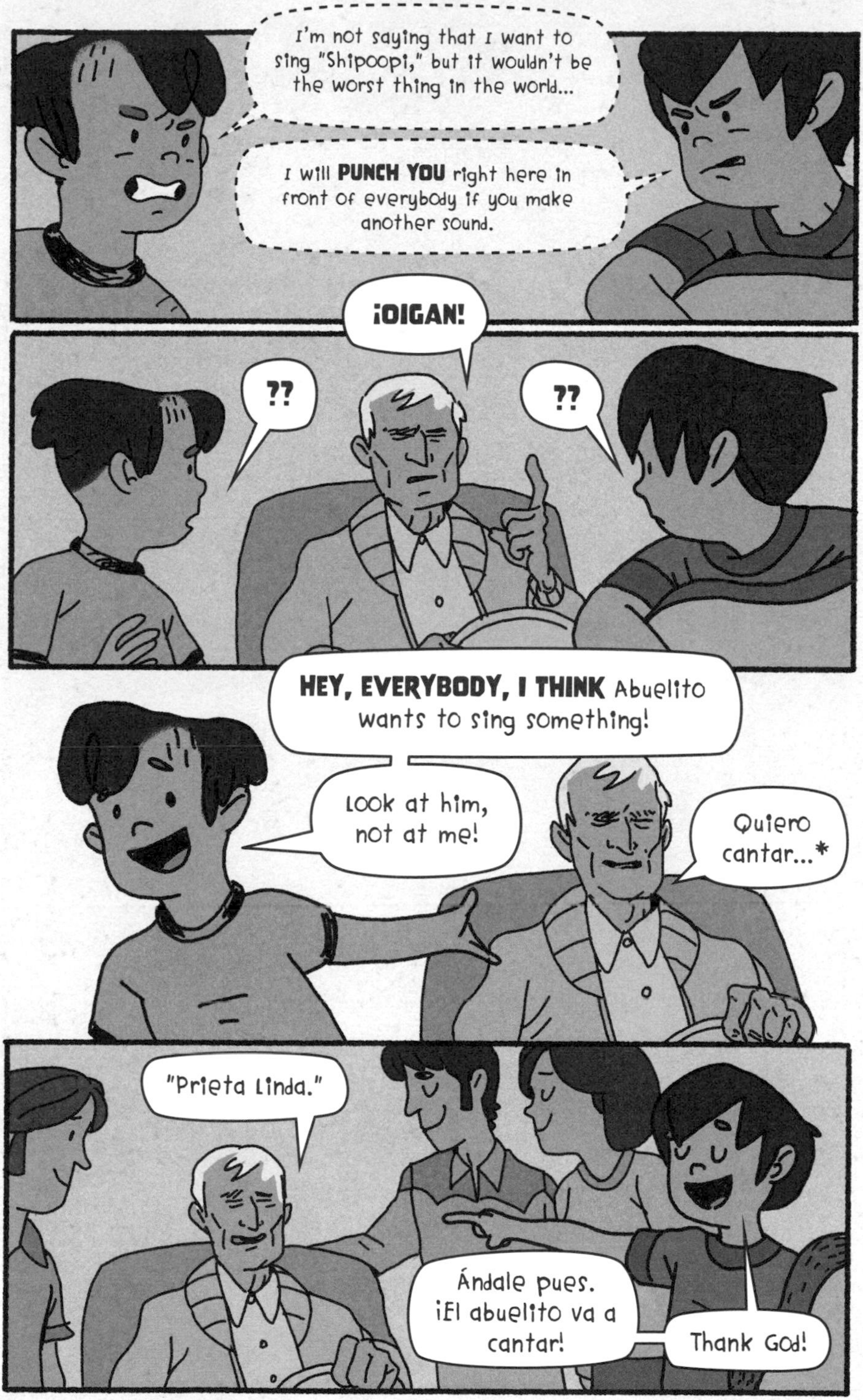

I'm not saying that I want to sing "Shipoopi," but it wouldn't be the worst thing in the world...
I will **PUNCH YOU** right here in front of everybody if you make another sound.
¡OIGAN!
??
??
HEY, EVERYBODY, I THINK Abuelito wants to sing something!
Look at him, not at me!
Quiero cantar...*
"Prieta Linda."
Ándale pues. ¡El abuelito va a cantar!
Thank God!

*I want to sing...

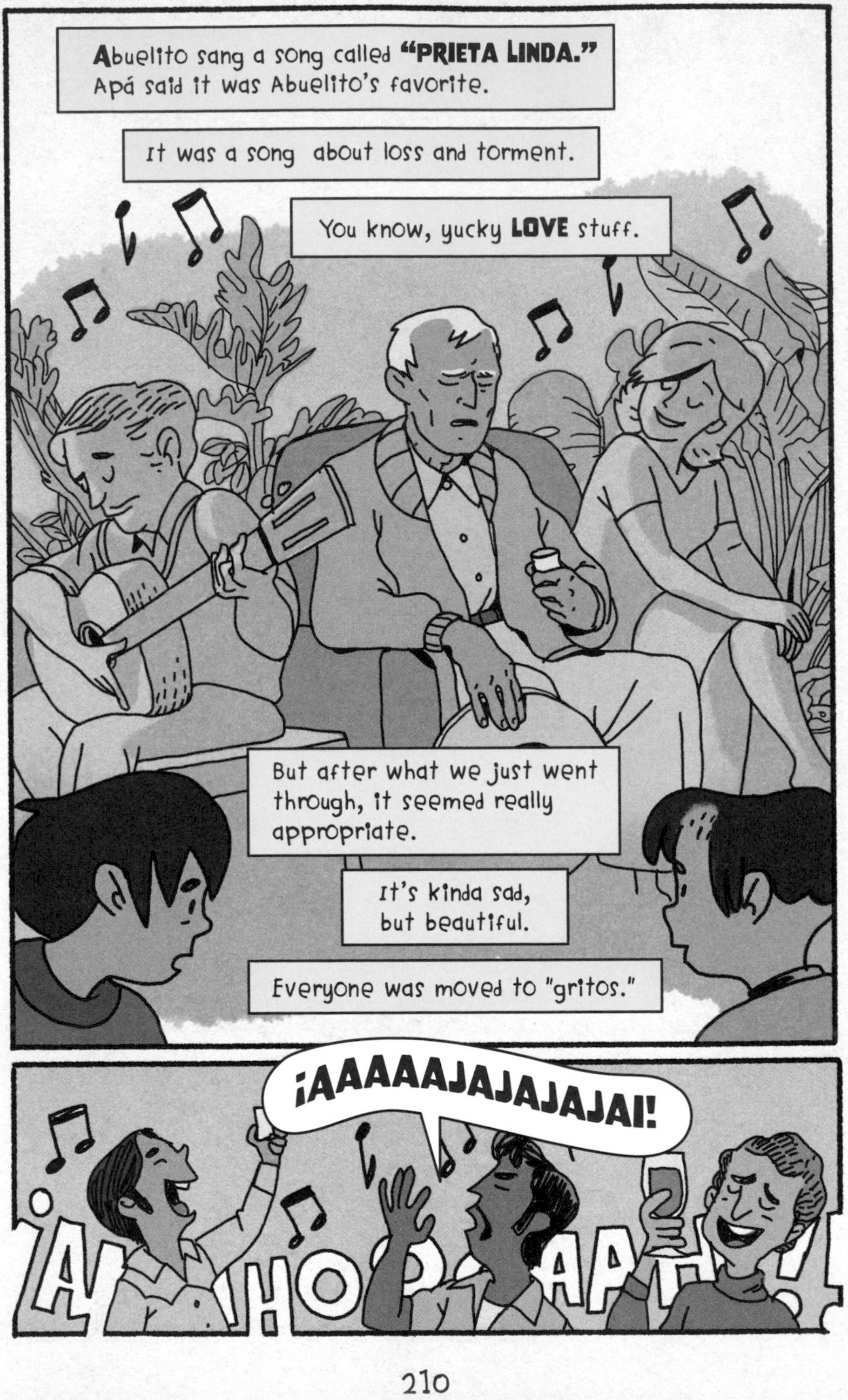
Abuelito sang a song called "PRIETA LINDA." Apá said it was Abuelito's favorite.
It was a song about loss and torment.
You know, yucky LOVE stuff.
But after what we just went through, it seemed really appropriate.
It's kinda sad, but beautiful.
Everyone was moved to "gritos."
¡AAAAAJAJAJAJAI!

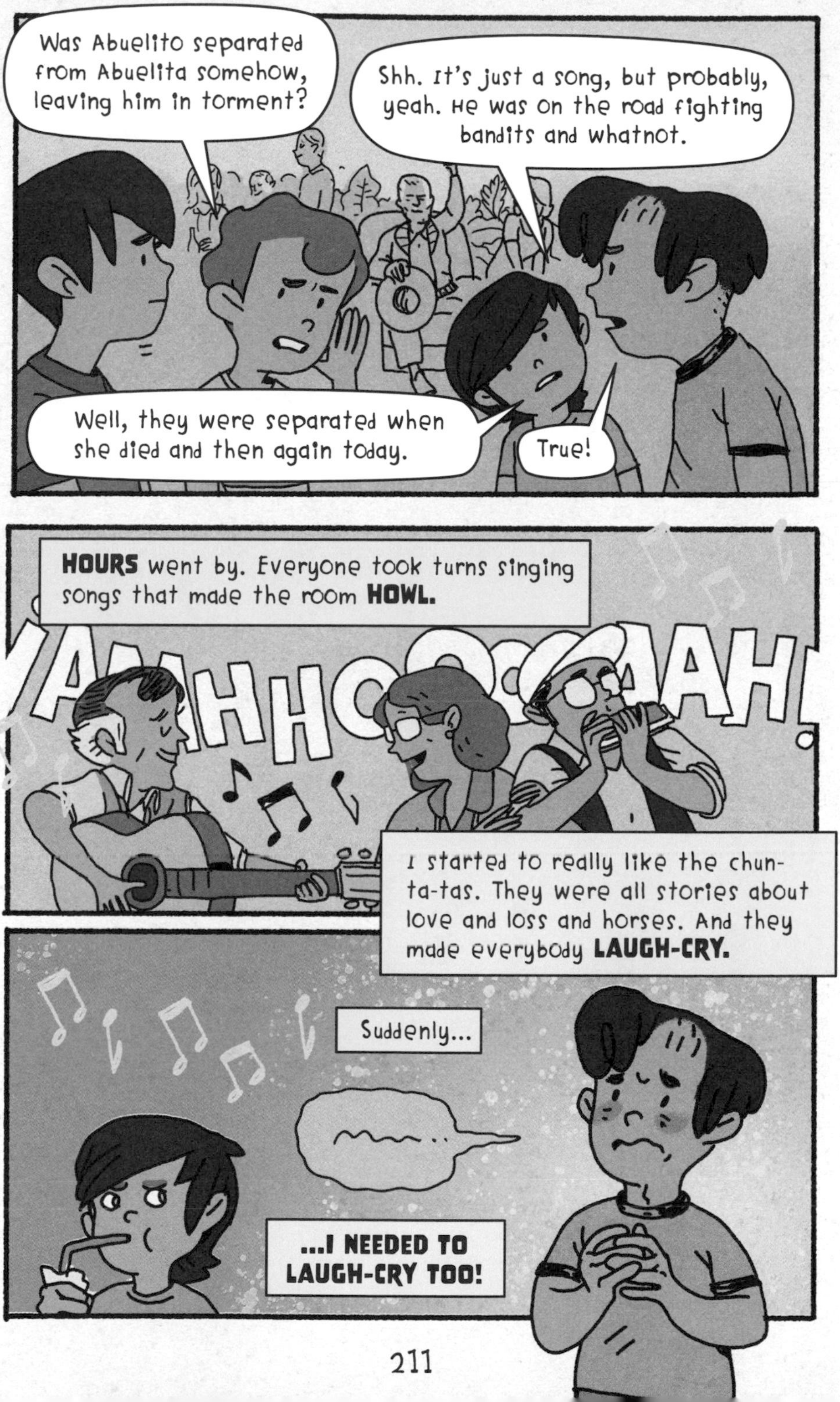
Was Abuelito separated from Abuelita somehow, leaving him in torment?
Shh. It's just a song, but probably, yeah. He was on the road fighting bandits and whatnot.
Well, they were separated when she died and then again today.
True!
HOURS went by. Everyone took turns singing songs that made the room HOWL.
AAAHHOOOOAAH!
I started to really like the chun-ta-tas. They were all stories about love and loss and horses. And they made everybody LAUGH-CRY.
Suddenly...
...I NEEDED TO LAUGH-CRY TOO!

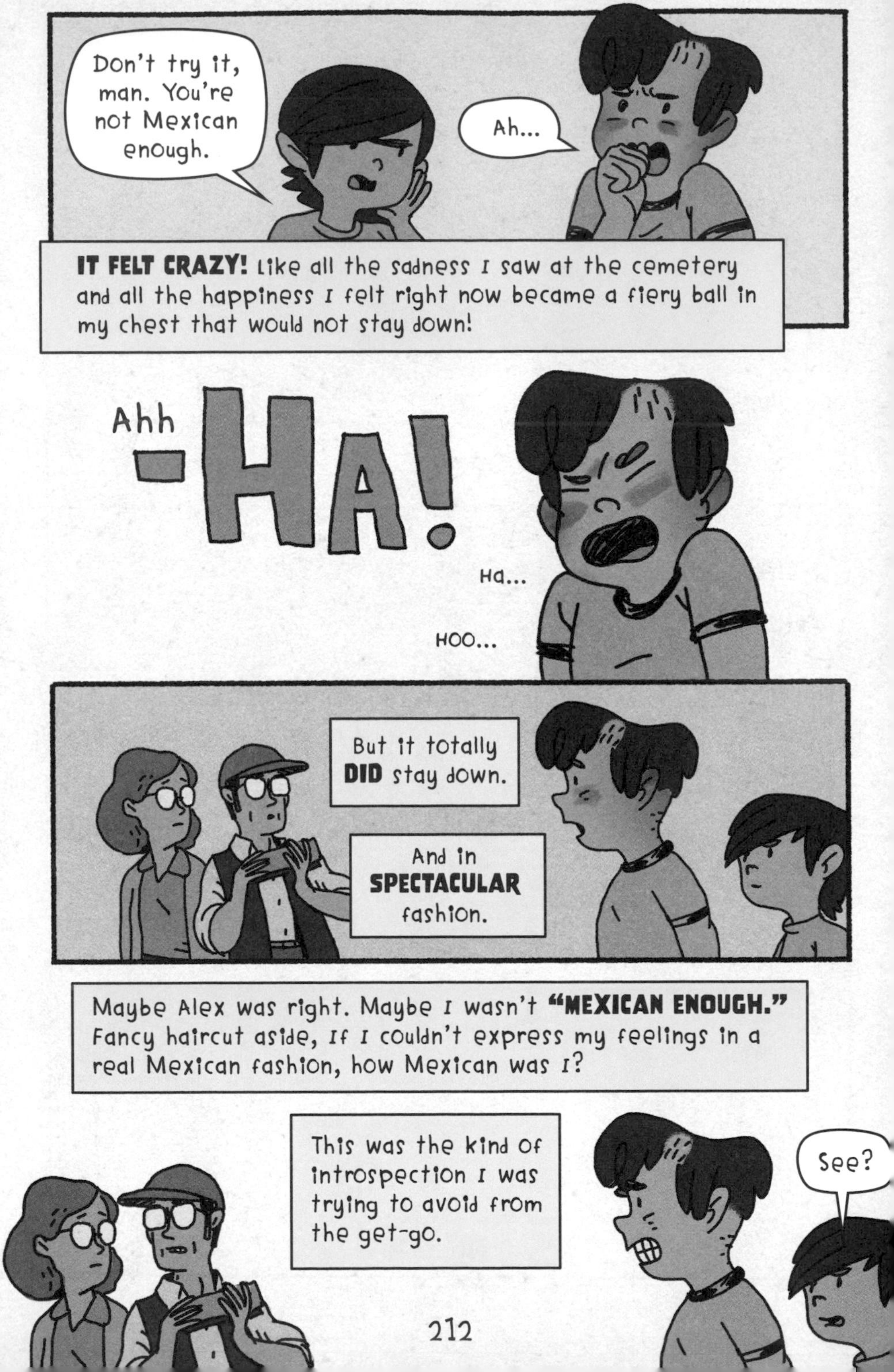

Don't try it, man. You're not Mexican enough.
Ah...
IT FELT CRAZY! Like all the sadness I saw at the cemetery and all the happiness I felt right now became a fiery ball in my chest that would not stay down!
Ahh -HA!
Ha...
HOO...
But it totally DID stay down.
And in SPECTACULAR fashion.
Maybe Alex was right. Maybe I wasn't "MEXICAN ENOUGH." Fancy haircut aside, if I couldn't express my feelings in a real Mexican fashion, how Mexican was I?
This was the kind of introspection I was trying to avoid from the get-go.
See?

It started getting late, so we said our good-nights and shared too many hugs. Everyone kissed Abuelito's hand.

It's what we do.

Promises of our return were made, and plates of food and goodbye gifts were stacked in our arms.

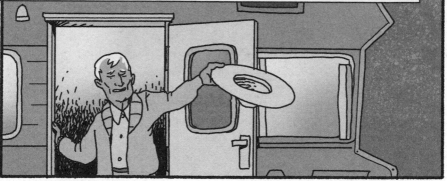

Abuelito stood in the doorway of the motorhome and began his historic farewell speech to the citizens he loved and protected for so many years.

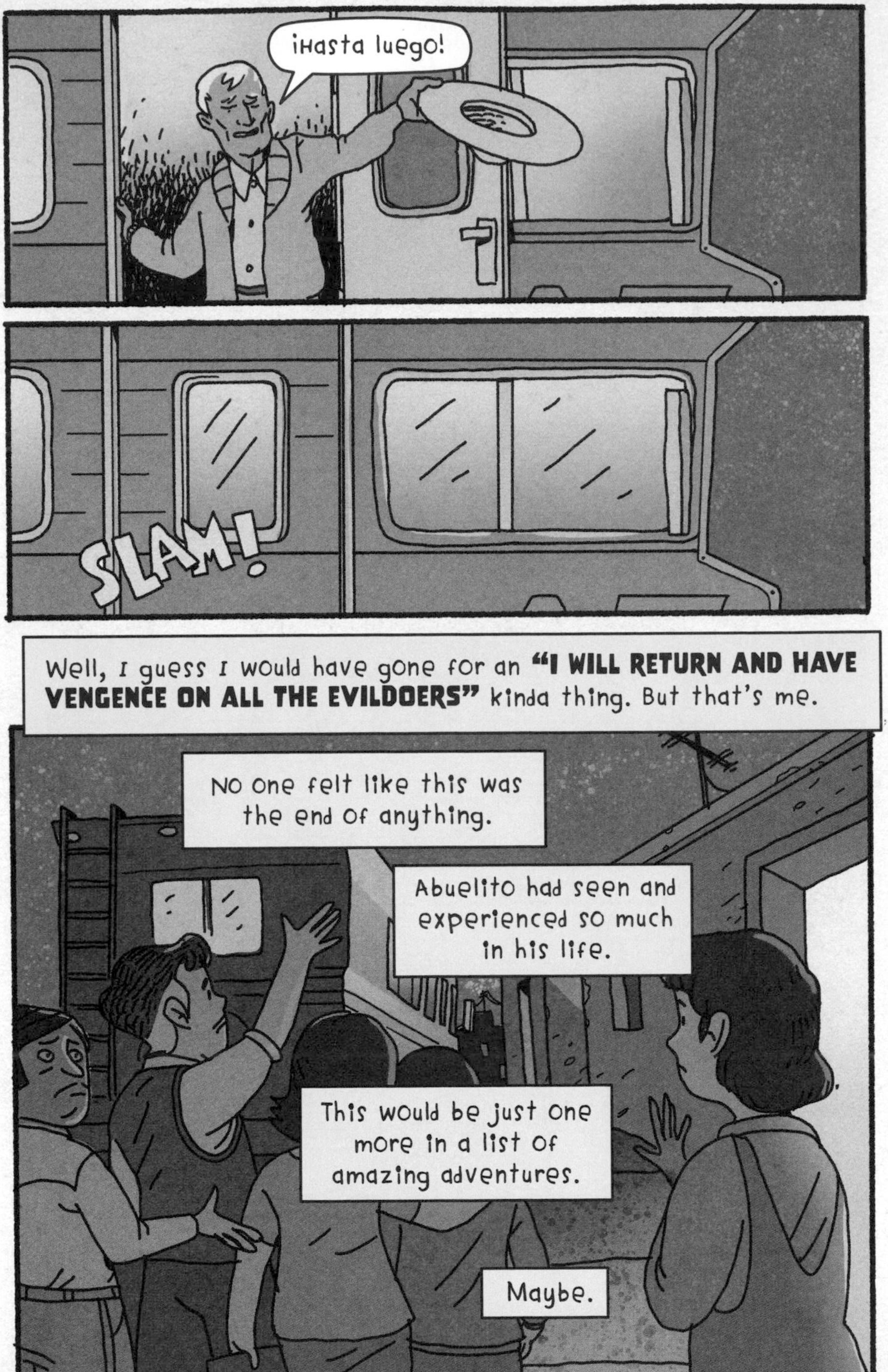
¡Hasta luego!
SLAM!
Well, I guess I would have gone for an **"I WILL RETURN AND HAVE VENGENCE ON ALL THE EVILDOERS"** kinda thing. But that's me.
No one felt like this was the end of anything.
Abuelito had seen and experienced so much in his life.
This would be just one more in a list of amazing adventures.
Maybe.

CHAPTER 16 JUST JUSTICE

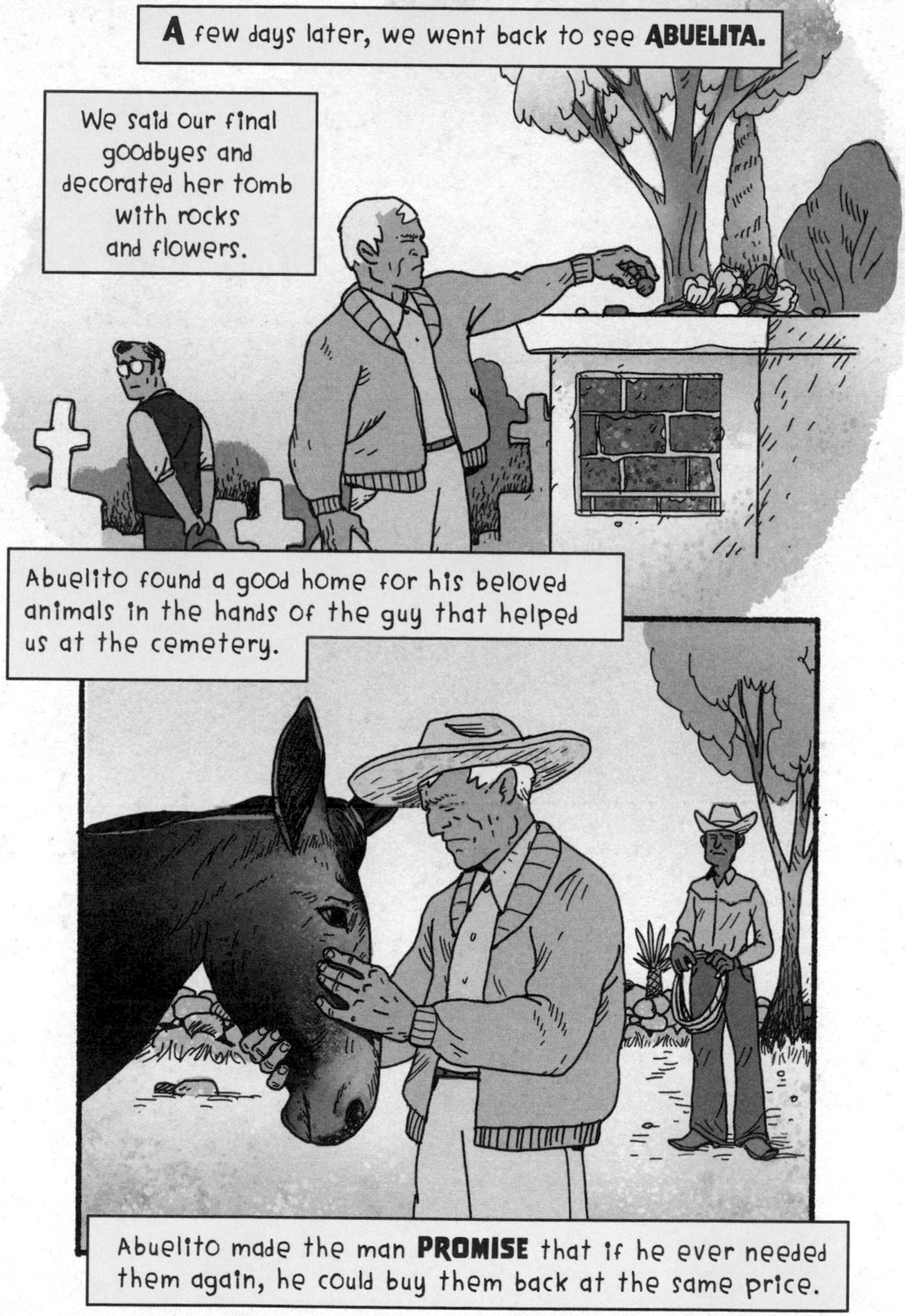
A few days later, we went back to see ABUELITA.
We said our final goodbyes and decorated her tomb with rocks and flowers.
Abuelito found a good home for his beloved animals in the hands of the guy that helped us at the cemetery.
Abuelito made the man PROMISE that if he ever needed them again, he could buy them back at the same price.

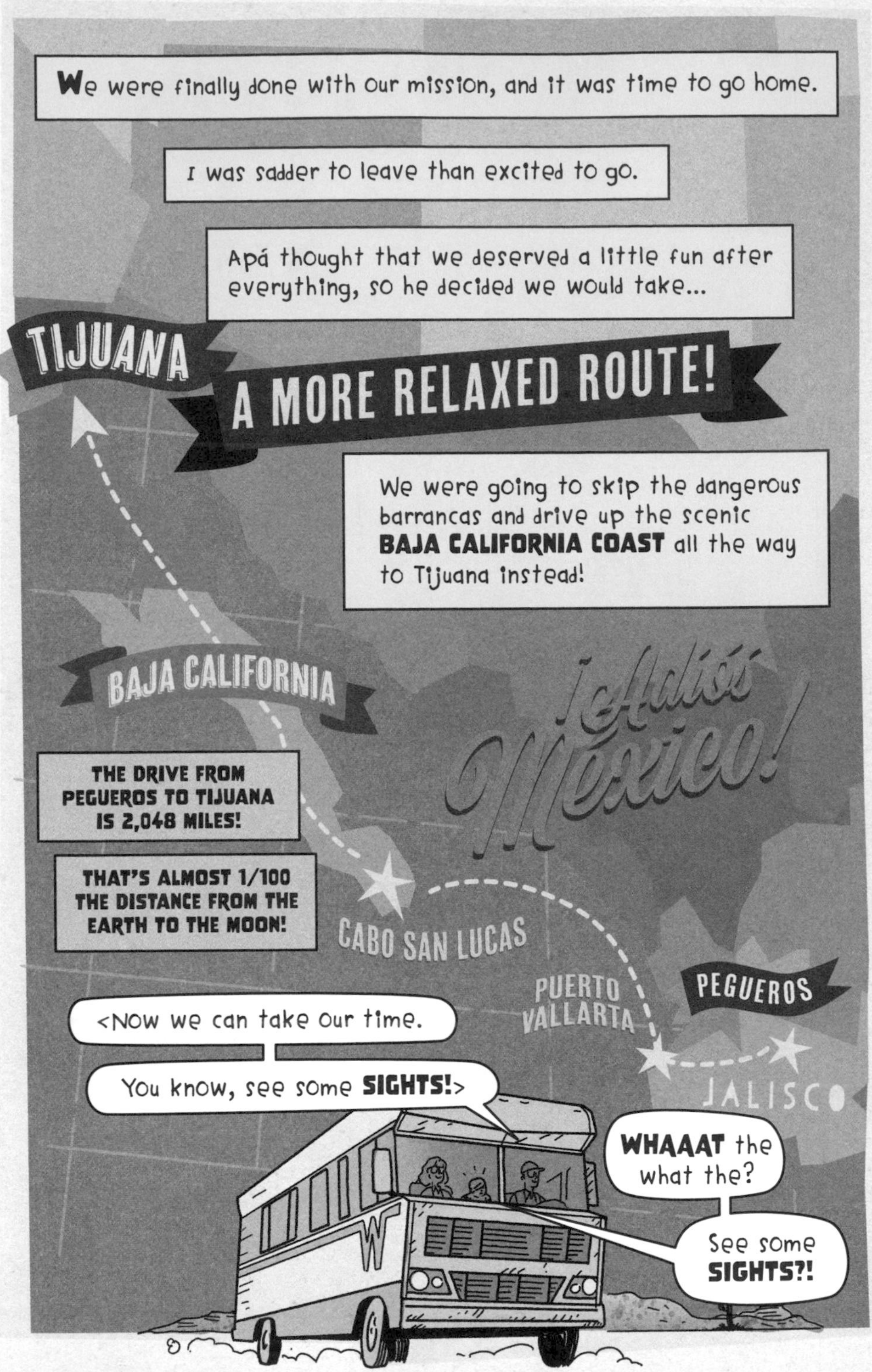
We were finally done with our mission, and it was time to go home.
I was sadder to leave than excited to go.
Apá thought that we deserved a little fun after everything, so he decided we would take...
A MORE RELAXED ROUTE!
TIJUANA
We were going to skip the dangerous barrancas and drive up the scenic **BAJA CALIFORNIA COAST** all the way to Tijuana instead!
BAJA CALIFORNIA
¡Adiós México!
THE DRIVE FROM PEGUEROS TO TIJUANA IS 2,048 MILES!
THAT'S ALMOST 1/100 THE DISTANCE FROM THE EARTH TO THE MOON!
CABO SAN LUCAS
PUERTO VALLARTA
PEGUEROS
JALISCO
<Now we can take our time.
You know, see some **SIGHTS!**>
WHAAAT the what the?
See some **SIGHTS?!**

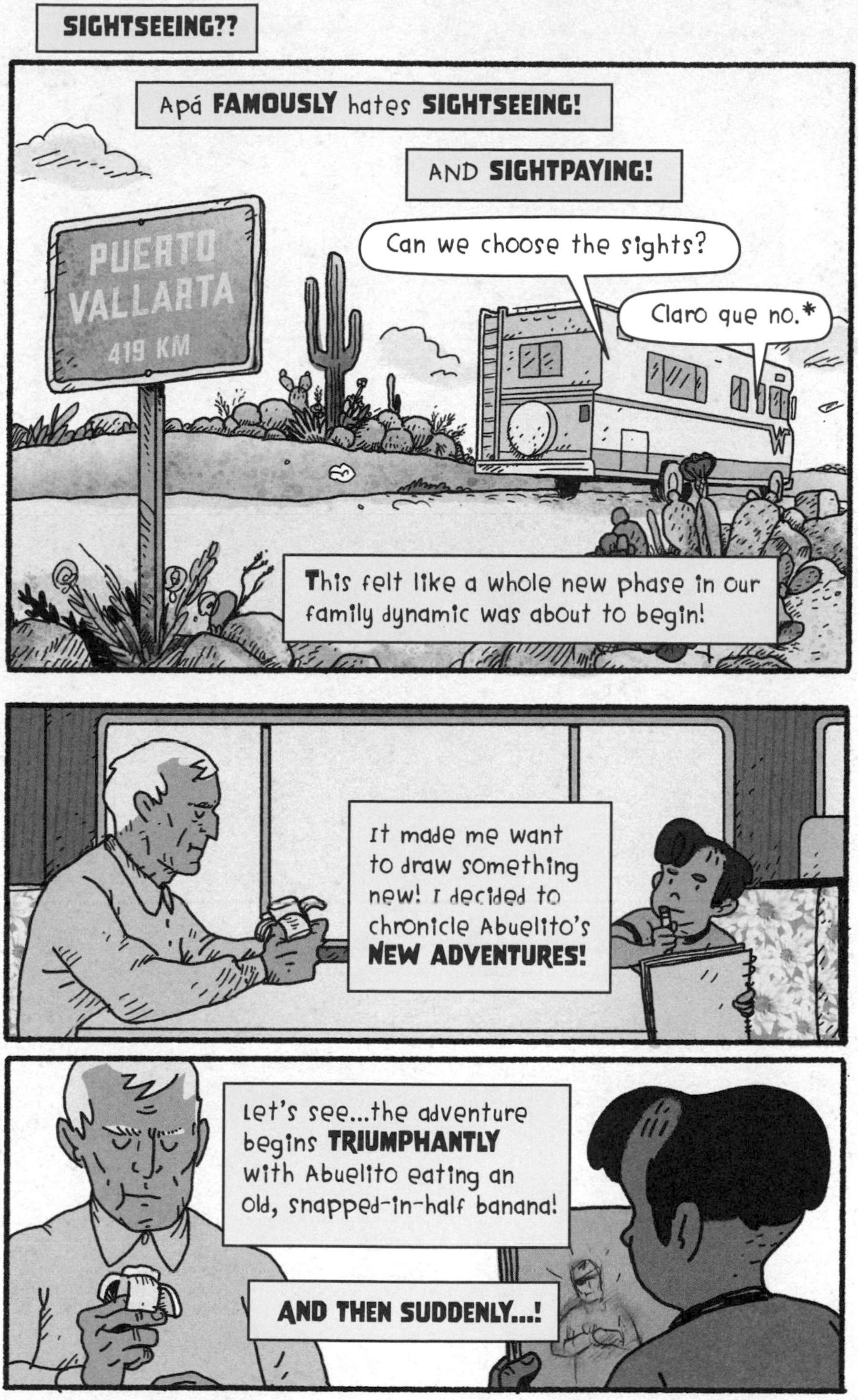
SIGHTSEEING??
Apá FAMOUSLY hates SIGHTSEEING!
AND SIGHTPAYING!
PUERTO VALLARTA 419 KM
Can we choose the sights?
Claro que no.*
This felt like a whole new phase in our family dynamic was about to begin!
It made me want to draw something new! I decided to chronicle Abuelito's NEW ADVENTURES!
Let's see...the adventure begins TRIUMPHANTLY with Abuelito eating an old, snapped-in-half banana!
AND THEN SUDDENLY...!

*Of course not.

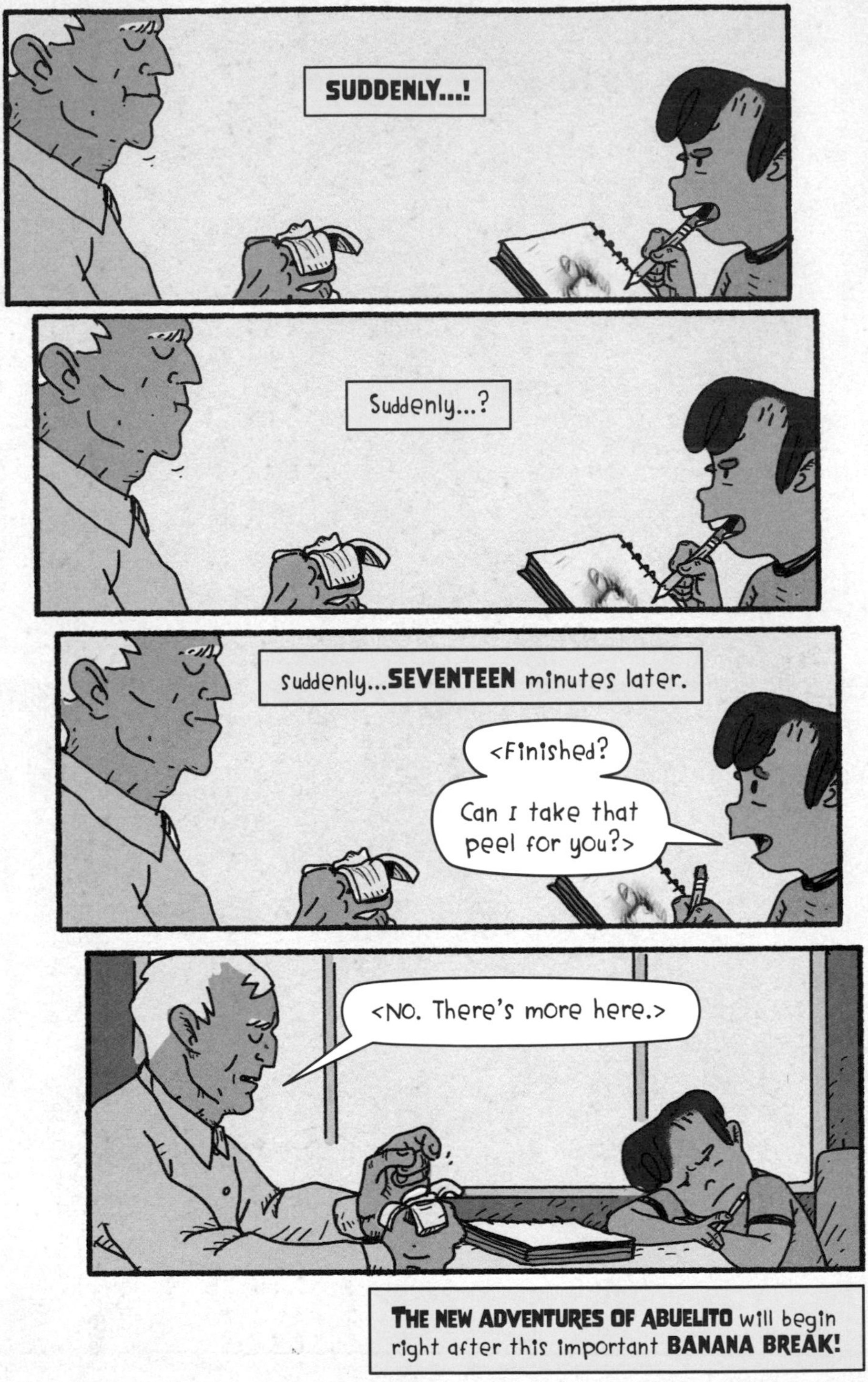
SUDDENLY...!
Suddenly...?
suddenly...SEVENTEEN minutes later.
<Finished?
Can I take that peel for you?>
<NO. There's more here.>
THE NEW ADVENTURES OF ABUELITO will begin right after this important BANANA BREAK!

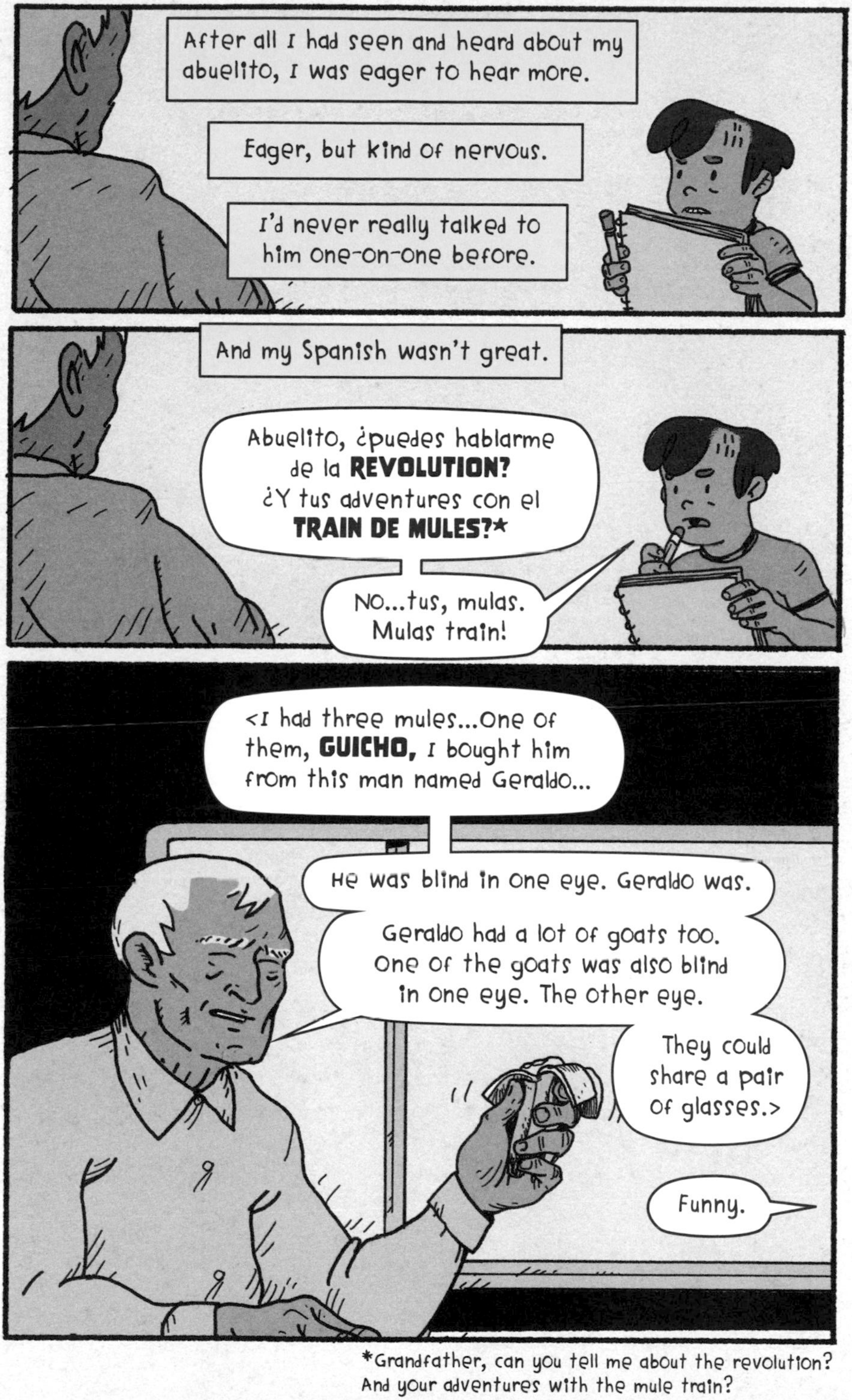
After all I had seen and heard about my abuelito, I was eager to hear more.
Eager, but kind of nervous.
I'd never really talked to him one-on-one before.
And my Spanish wasn't great.
Abuelito, ¿puedes hablarme de la REVOLUTION? ¿Y tus adventures con el TRAIN DE MULES?*
NO...tus, mulas. Mulas train!
<I had three mules...One of them, GUICHO, I bought him from this man named Geraldo...
He was blind in one eye. Geraldo was.
Geraldo had a lot of goats too. One of the goats was also blind in one eye. The other eye.
They could share a pair of glasses.>
Funny.

*Grandfather, can you tell me about the revolution? And your adventures with the mule train?

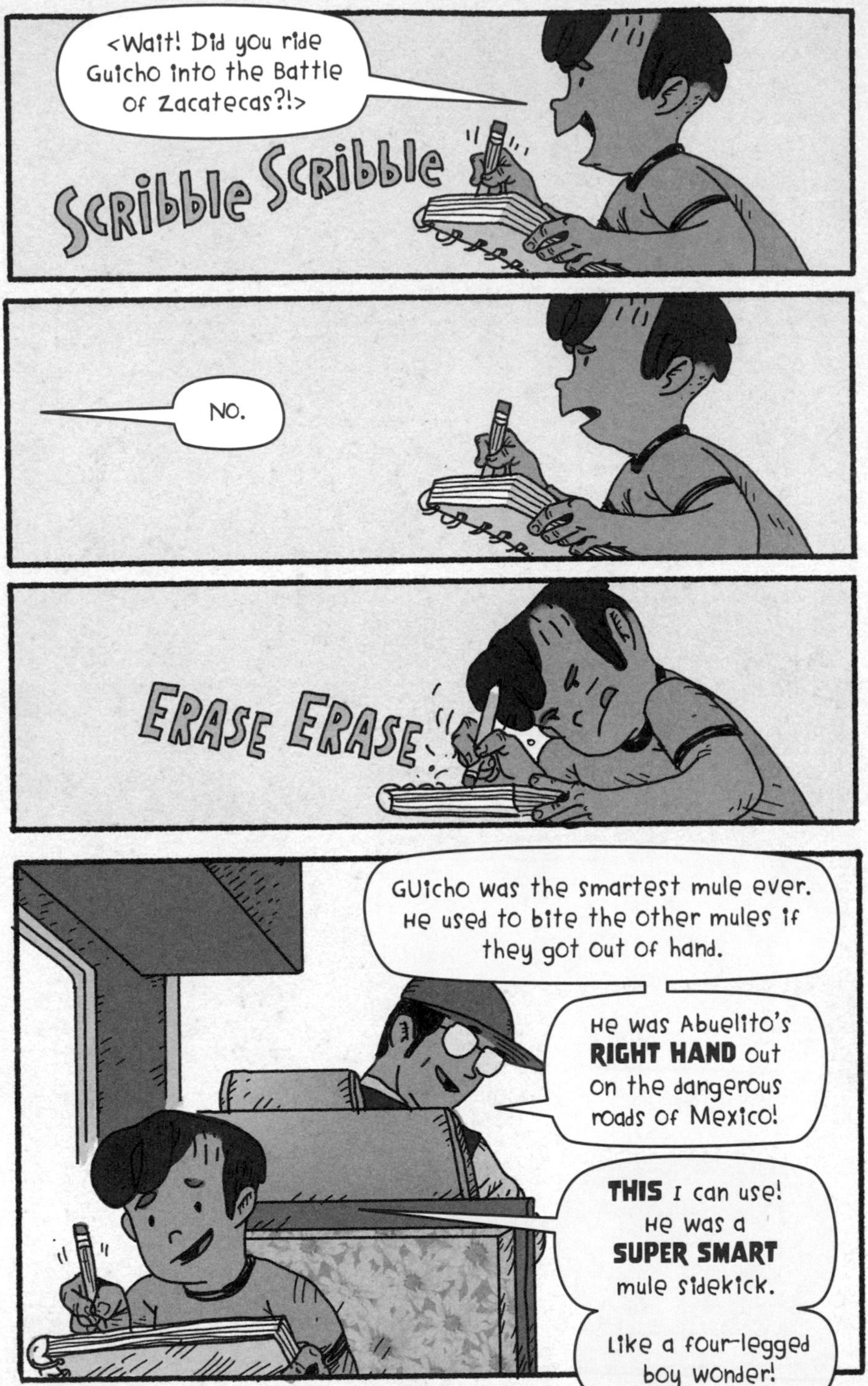
<Wait! Did you ride Guicho into the Battle of Zacatecas?!>
Scribble Scribble
No.
Erase Erase
Guicho was the smartest mule ever. He used to bite the other mules if they got out of hand.
He was Abuelito's **RIGHT HAND** out on the dangerous roads of Mexico!
THIS I can use! He was a **SUPER SMART** mule sidekick.
Like a four-legged boy wonder!

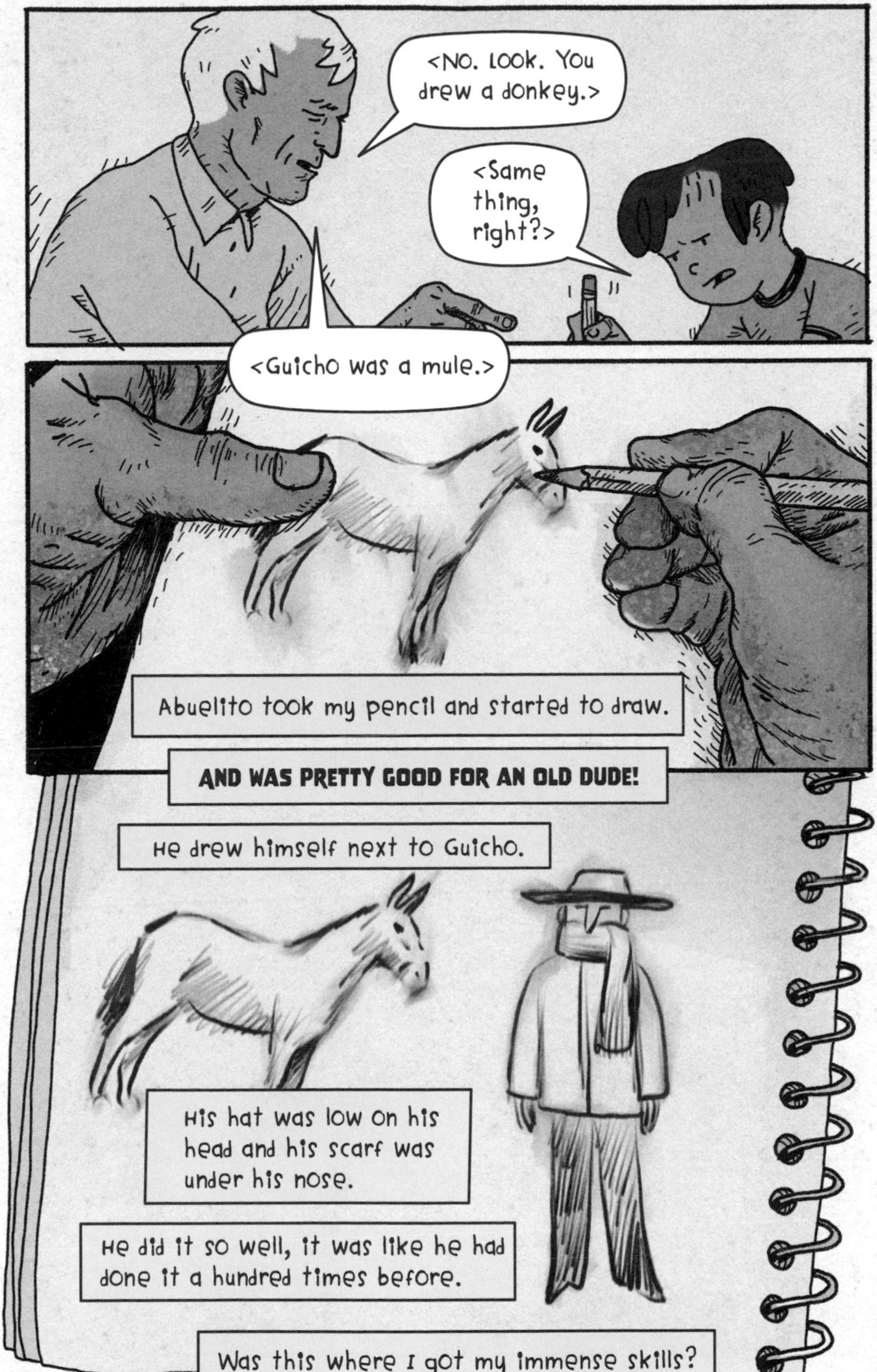
<NO. LOOK. You drew a donkey.>
<Same thing, right?>
<Guicho was a mule.>
Abuelito took my pencil and started to draw.
AND WAS PRETTY GOOD FOR AN OLD DUDE!
He drew himself next to Guicho.
His hat was low on his head and his scarf was under his nose.
He did it so well, it was like he had done it a hundred times before.
Was this where I got my immense skills?

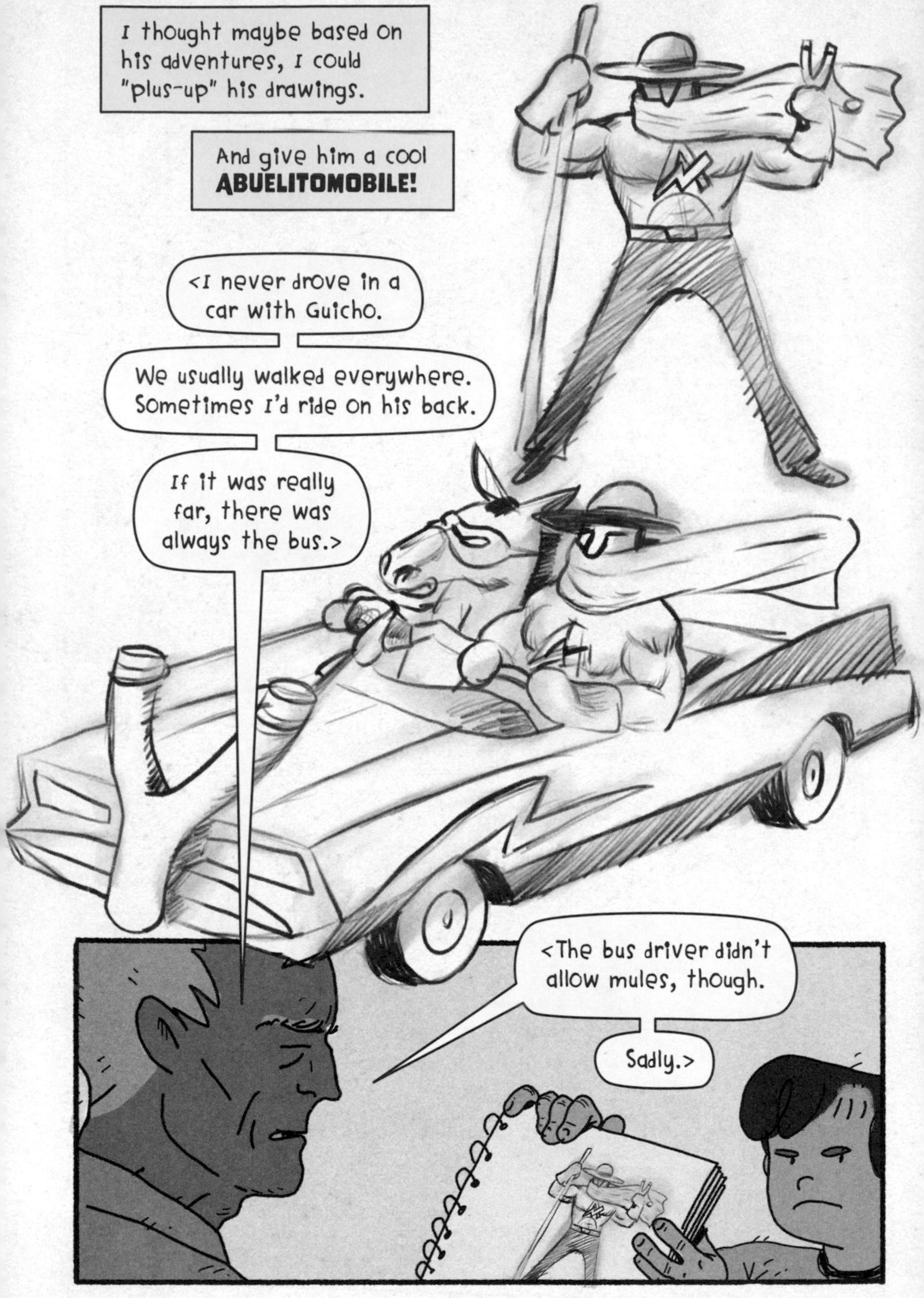
I thought maybe based on his adventures, I could "plus-up" his drawings.
And give him a cool ABUELITOMOBILE!
<I never drove in a car with Guicho.
We usually walked everywhere. Sometimes I'd ride on his back.
If it was really far, there was always the bus.>
<The bus driver didn't allow mules, though.
Sadly.>

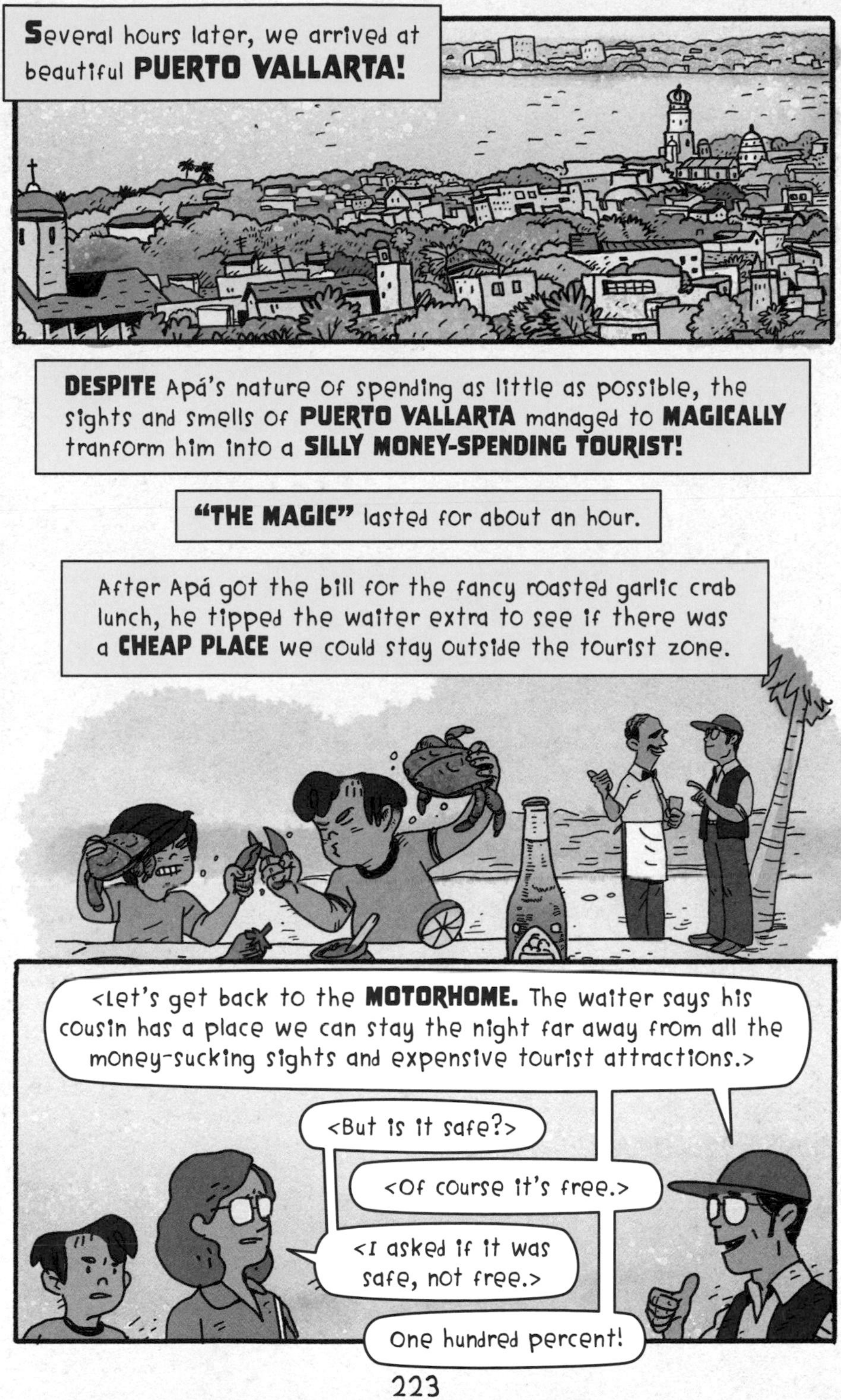
Several hours later, we arrived at beautiful PUERTO VALLARTA!
DESPITE Apá's nature of spending as little as possible, the sights and smells of PUERTO VALLARTA managed to MAGICALLY tranform him into a SILLY MONEY-SPENDING TOURIST!
"THE MAGIC" lasted for about an hour.
After Apá got the bill for the fancy roasted garlic crab lunch, he tipped the waiter extra to see if there was a CHEAP PLACE we could stay outside the tourist zone.
<Let's get back to the MOTORHOME. The waiter says his cousin has a place we can stay the night far away from all the money-sucking sights and expensive tourist attractions.>
<But is it safe?>
<Of course it's free.>
<I asked if it was safe, not free.>
One hundred percent!

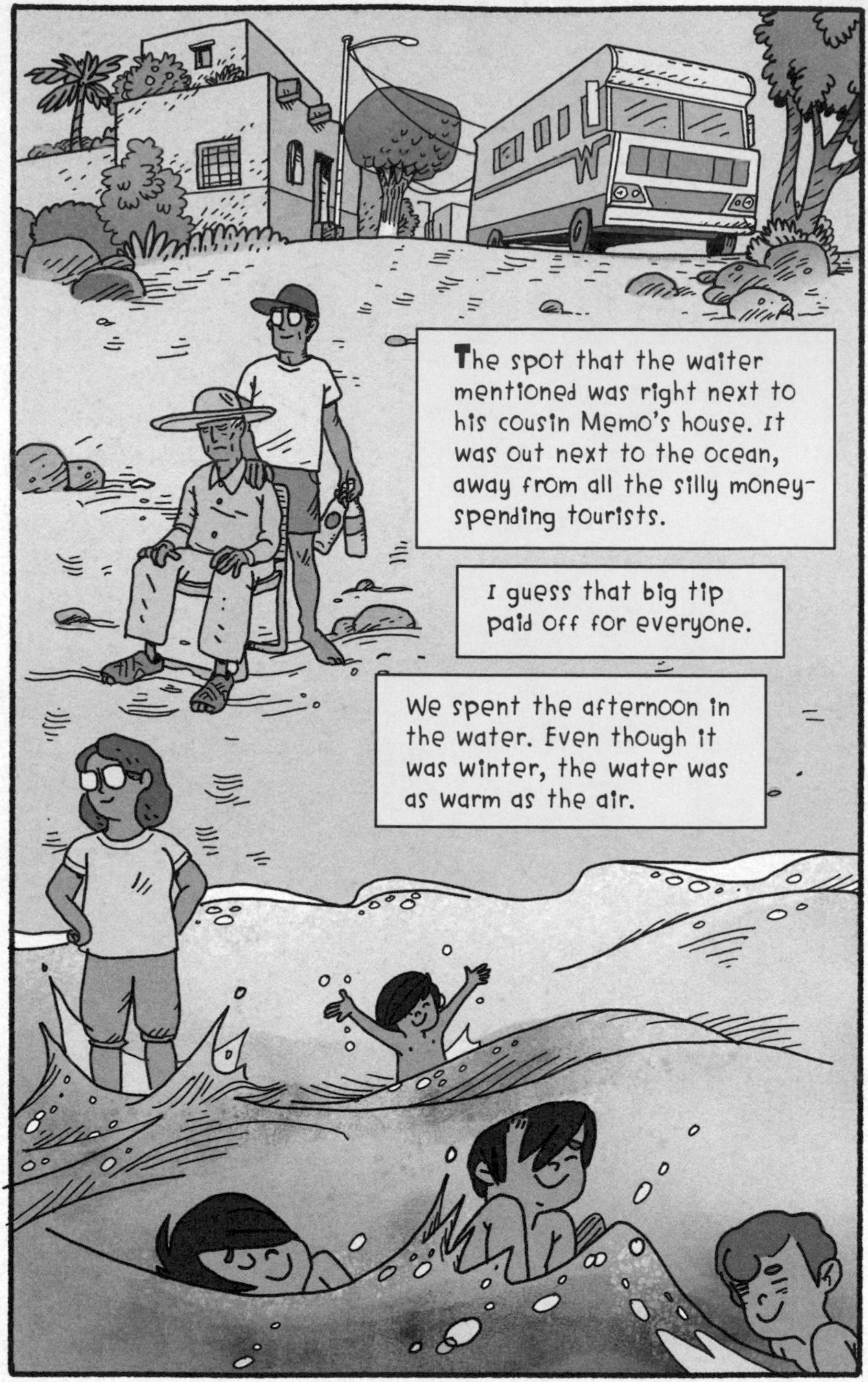
The spot that the waiter mentioned was right next to his cousin Memo's house. It was out next to the ocean, away from all the silly money-spending tourists.
I guess that big tip paid off for everyone.
We spent the afternoon in the water. Even though it was winter, the water was as warm as the air.

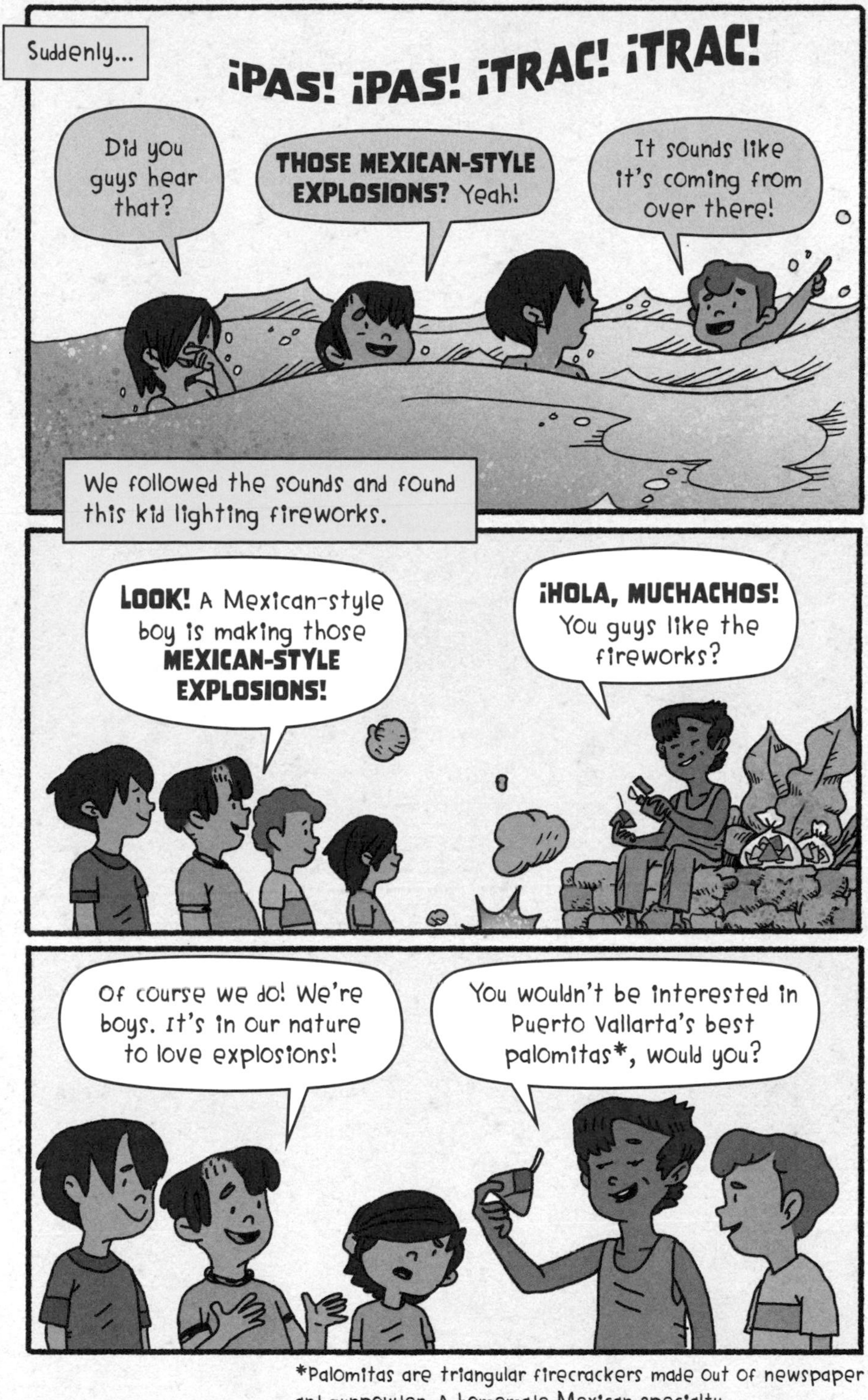
Suddenly...
¡PAS! ¡PAS! ¡TRAC! ¡TRAC!
Did you guys hear that?
THOSE MEXICAN-STYLE EXPLOSIONS? Yeah!
It sounds like it's coming from over there!
We followed the sounds and found this kid lighting fireworks.
LOOK! A Mexican-style boy is making those MEXICAN-STYLE EXPLOSIONS!
¡HOLA, MUCHACHOS! You guys like the fireworks?
Of course we do! We're boys. It's in our nature to love explosions!
You wouldn't be interested in Puerto Vallarta's best palomitas*, would you?

*Palomitas are triangular firecrackers made out of newspaper and gunpowder. A homemade Mexican specialty.

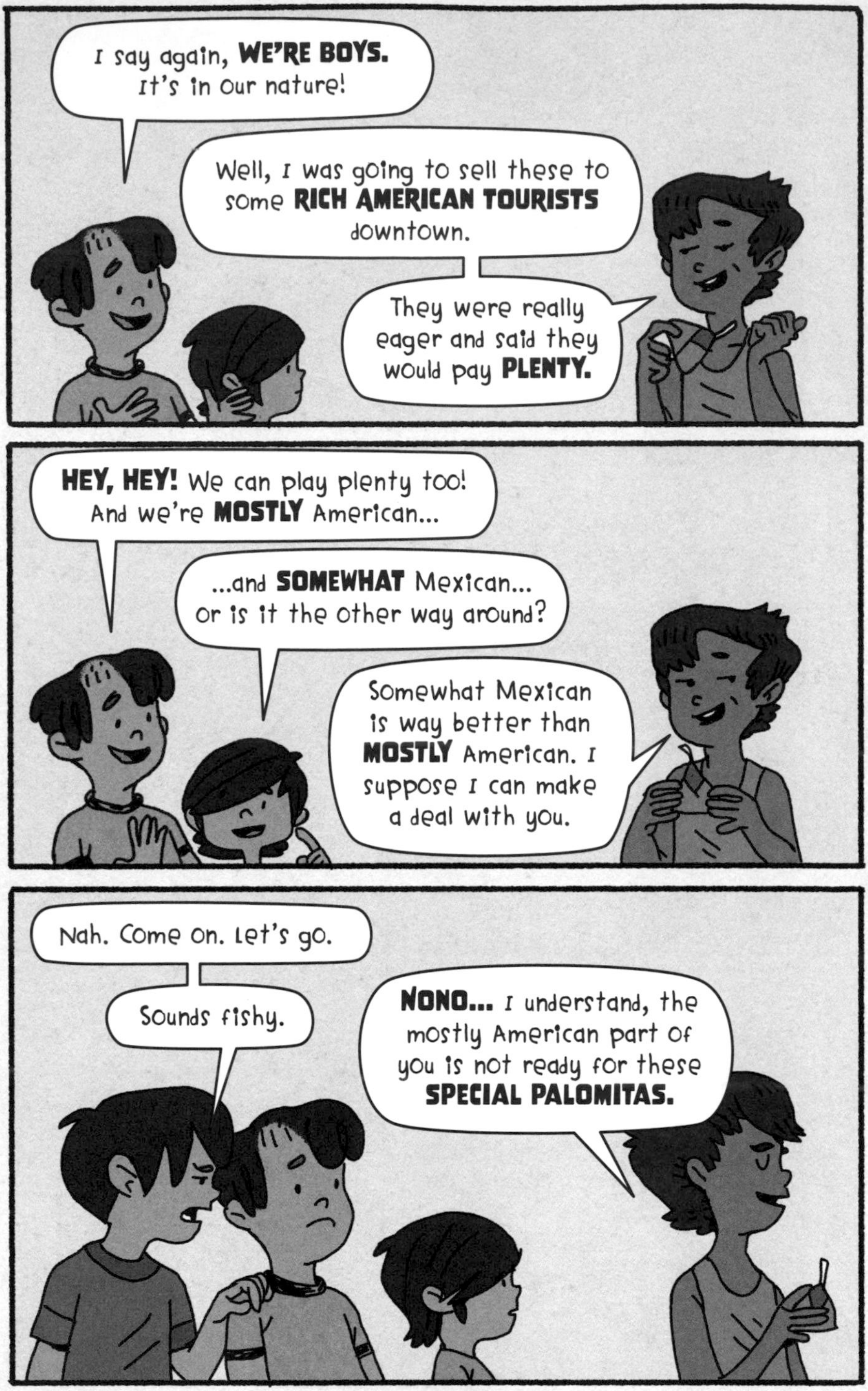
I say again, WE'RE BOYS. It's in our nature!
Well, I was going to sell these to some RICH AMERICAN TOURISTS downtown.
They were really eager and said they would pay PLENTY.
HEY, HEY! We can play plenty too! And we're MOSTLY American...
...and SOMEWHAT Mexican... or is it the other way around?
Somewhat Mexican is way better than MOSTLY American. I suppose I can make a deal with you.
Nah. Come on. Let's go.
Sounds fishy.
NONO... I understand, the mostly American part of you is not ready for these SPECIAL PALOMITAS.

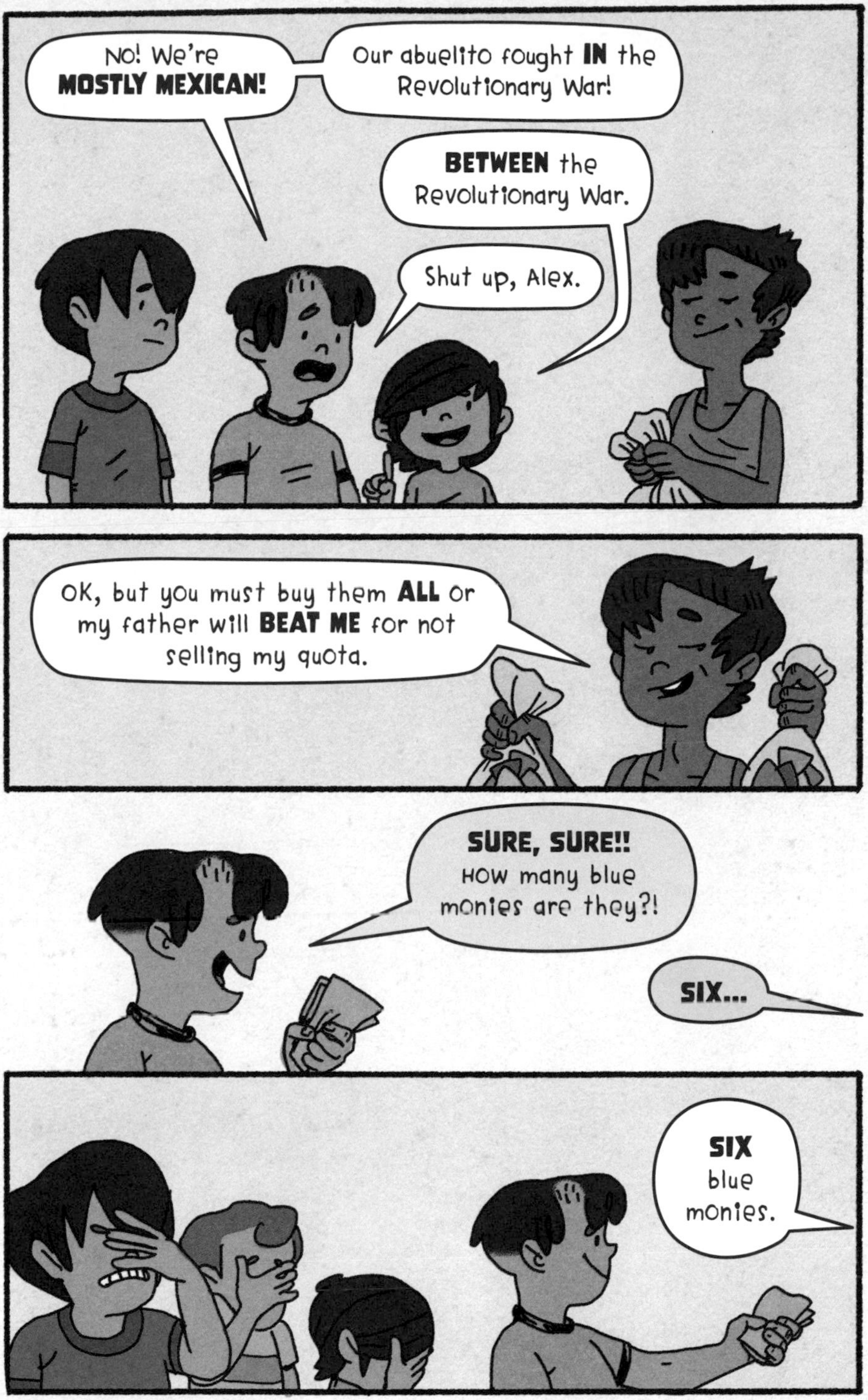
No! We're **MOSTLY MEXICAN!**
Our abuelito fought **IN** the Revolutionary War!
BETWEEN the Revolutionary War.
Shut up, Alex.
OK, but you must buy them **ALL** or my father will **BEAT ME** for not selling my quota.
SURE, SURE!! HOW many blue monies are they?!
SIX...
SIX blue monies.

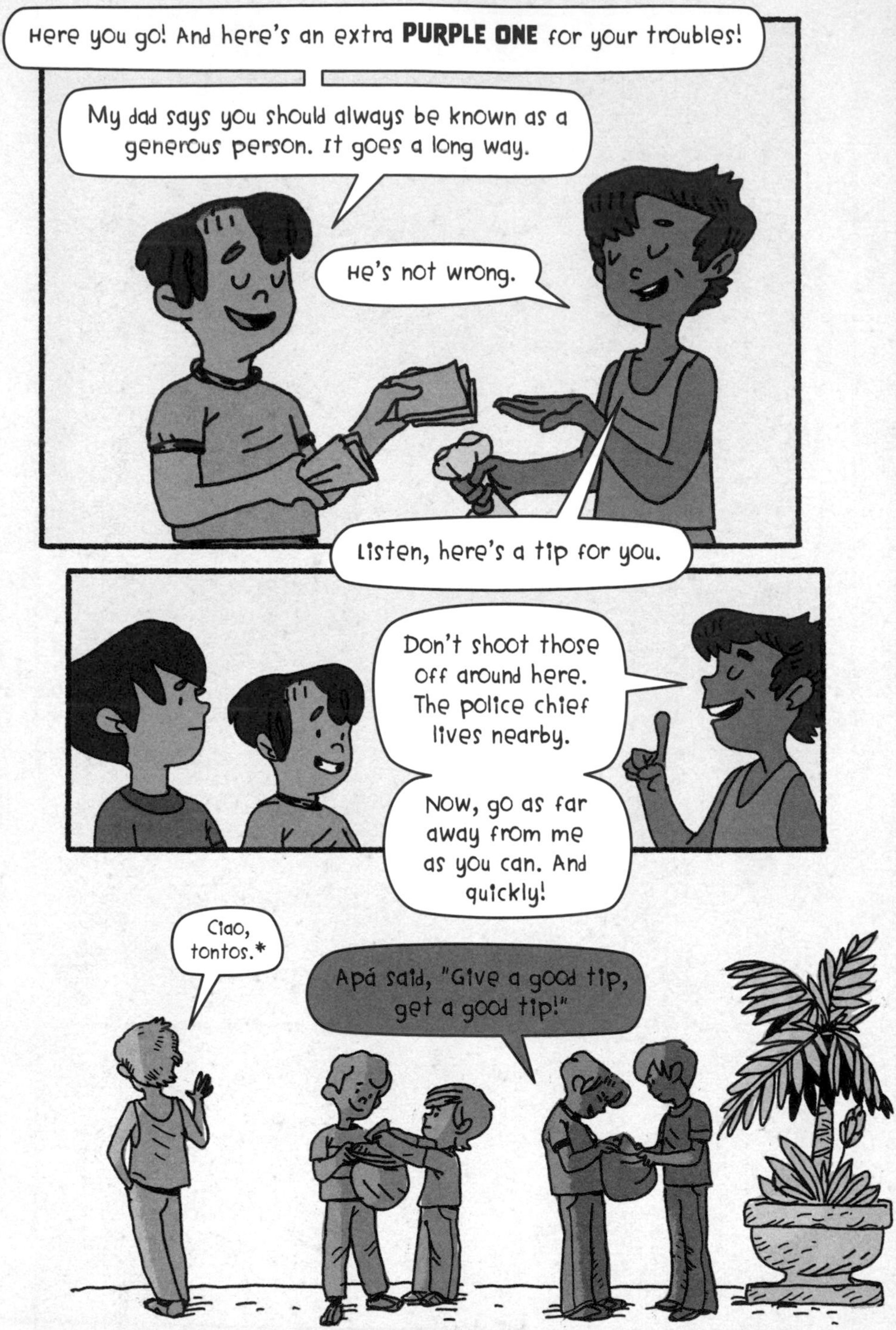

Here you go! And here's an extra **PURPLE ONE** for your troubles!
My dad says you should always be known as a generous person. It goes a long way.
He's not wrong.
Listen, here's a tip for you.
Don't shoot those off around here. The police chief lives nearby.
Now, go as far away from me as you can. And quickly!
Ciao, tontos.*
Apá said, "Give a good tip, get a good tip!"

*See ya, dummies.

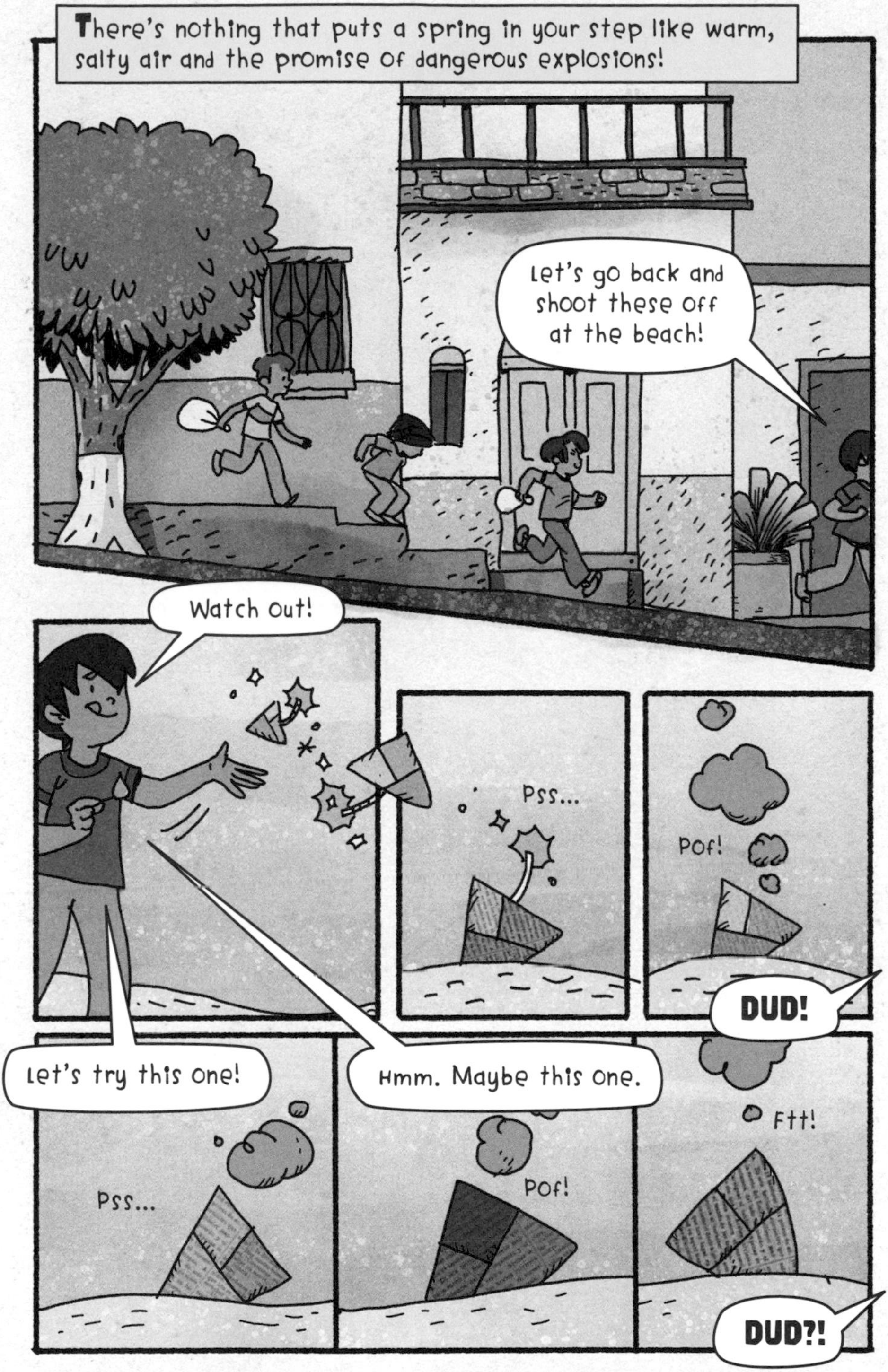
There's nothing that puts a spring in your step like warm, salty air and the promise of dangerous explosions!
Let's go back and shoot these off at the beach!
Watch out!
Pss...
Pof!
DUD!
Let's try this one!
Hmm. Maybe this one.
Pss...
Pof!
Ftt!
DUD?!

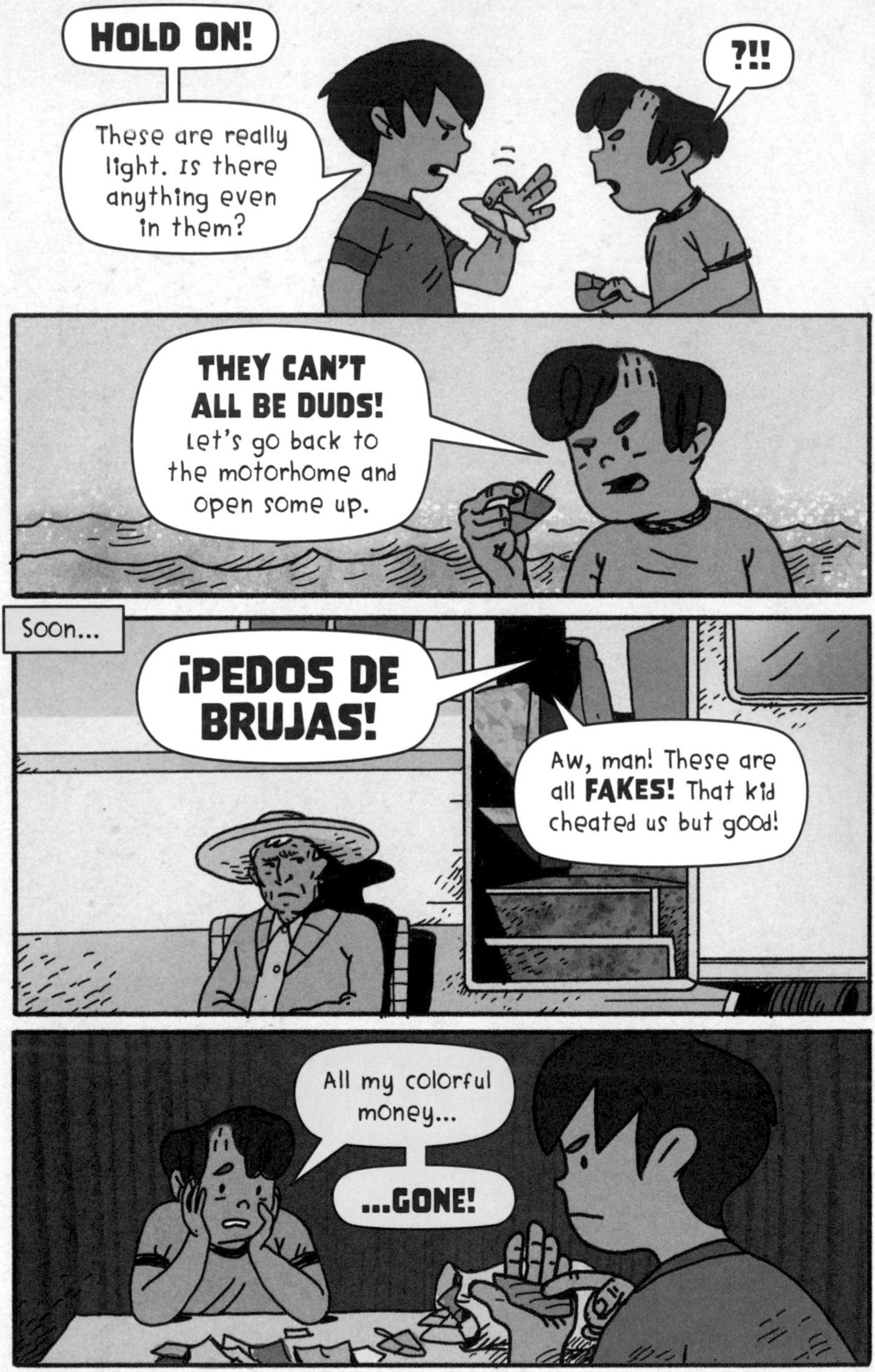
HOLD ON!
These are really light. Is there anything even in them?
?!!
THEY CAN'T ALL BE DUDS! Let's go back to the motorhome and open some up.
Soon...
¡PEDOS DE BRUJAS!
Aw, man! These are all FAKES! That kid cheated us but good!
All my colorful money...
...GONE!

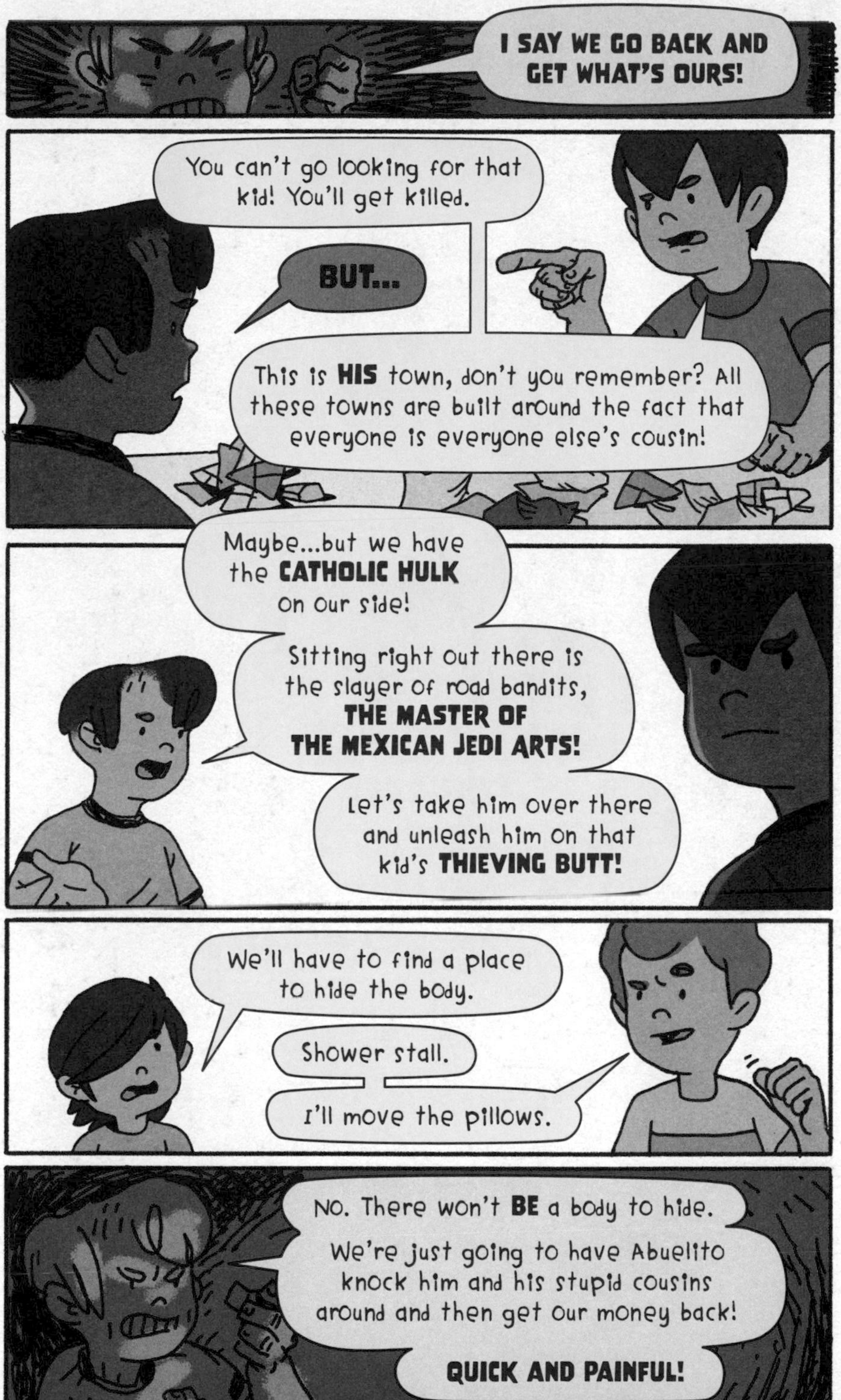

I SAY WE GO BACK AND GET WHAT'S OURS!
You can't go looking for that kid! You'll get killed.
BUT...
This is HIS town, don't you remember? All these towns are built around the fact that everyone is everyone else's cousin!
Maybe...but we have the CATHOLIC HULK on our side!
Sitting right out there is the slayer of road bandits, THE MASTER OF THE MEXICAN JEDI ARTS!
Let's take him over there and unleash him on that kid's THIEVING BUTT!
We'll have to find a place to hide the body.
Shower stall.
I'll move the pillows.
No. There won't BE a body to hide.
We're just going to have Abuelito knock him and his stupid cousins around and then get our money back!
QUICK AND PAINFUL!

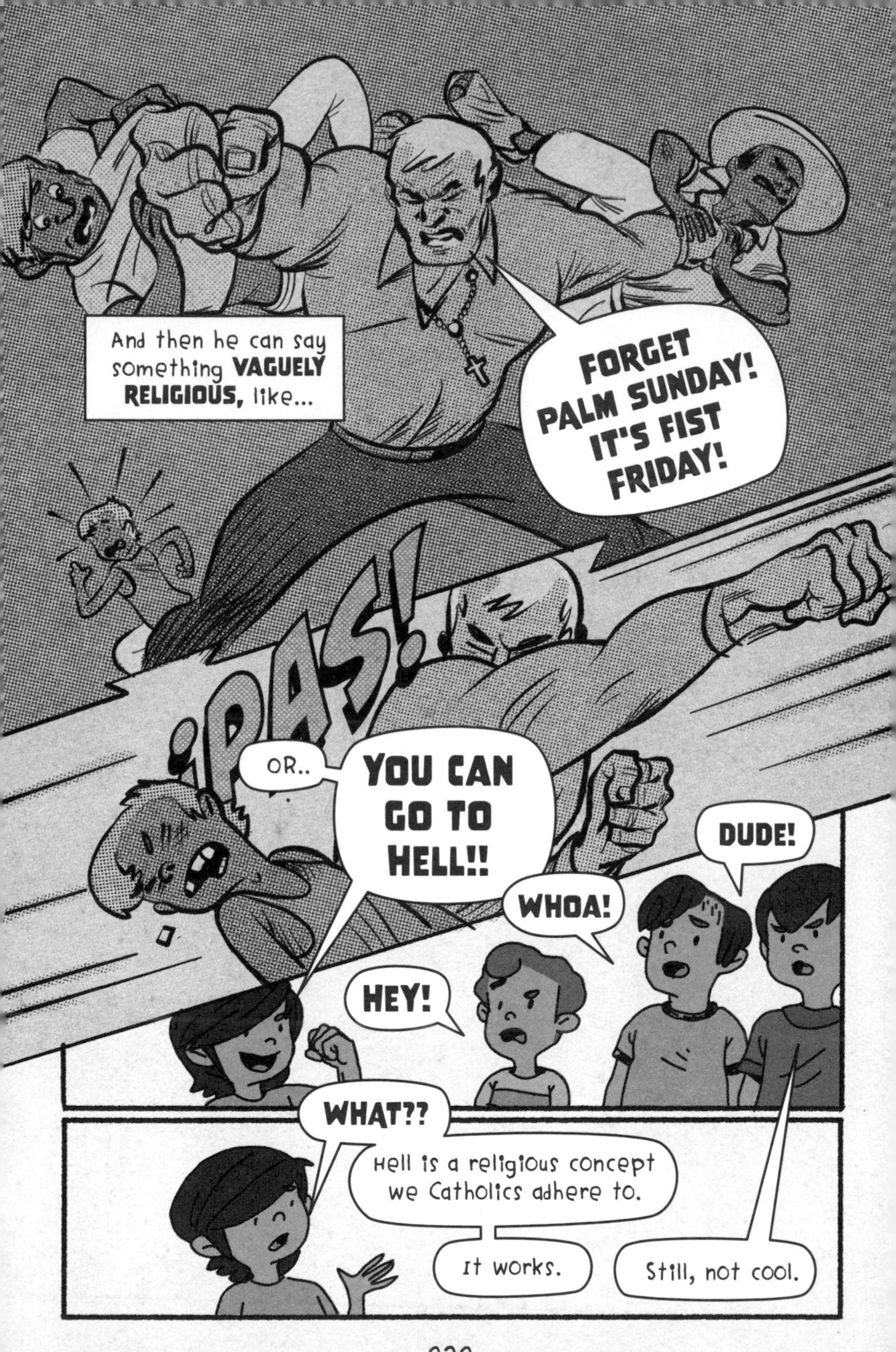
And then he can say something **VAGUELY RELIGIOUS,** like...
FORGET PALM SUNDAY! IT'S FIST FRIDAY!
¡PAS!
OR..
YOU CAN GO TO HELL!!
HEY!
WHOA!
DUDE!
WHAT??
Hell is a religious concept we Catholics adhere to.
It works.
Still, not cool.

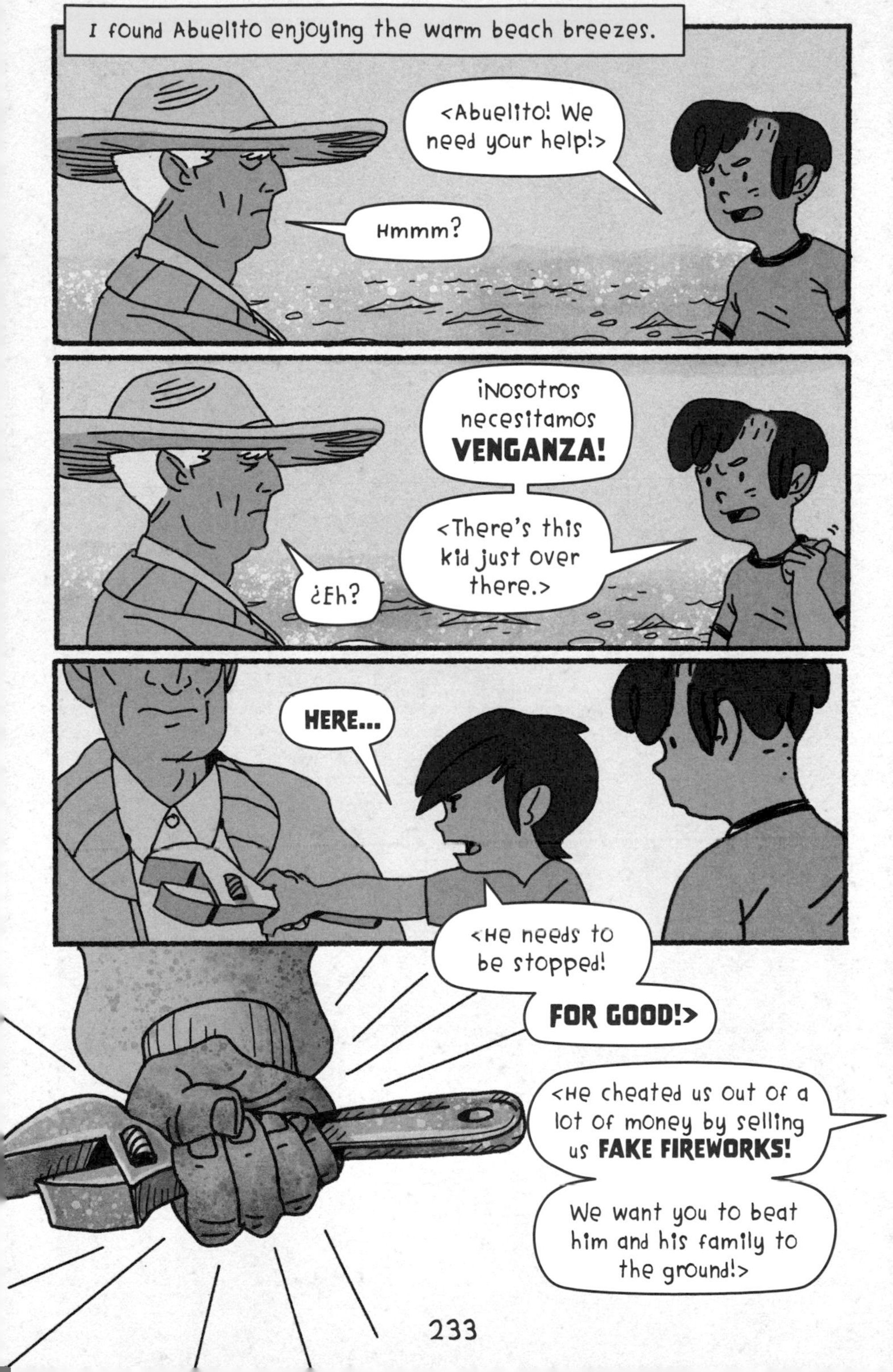
I found Abuelito enjoying the warm beach breezes.
<Abuelito! We need your help!>
Hmmm?
¡Nosotros necesitamos VENGANZA!
<There's this kid just over there.>
¿Eh?
HERE...
<He needs to be stopped!
FOR GOOD!>
<He cheated us out of a lot of money by selling us FAKE FIREWORKS!
We want you to beat him and his family to the ground!>

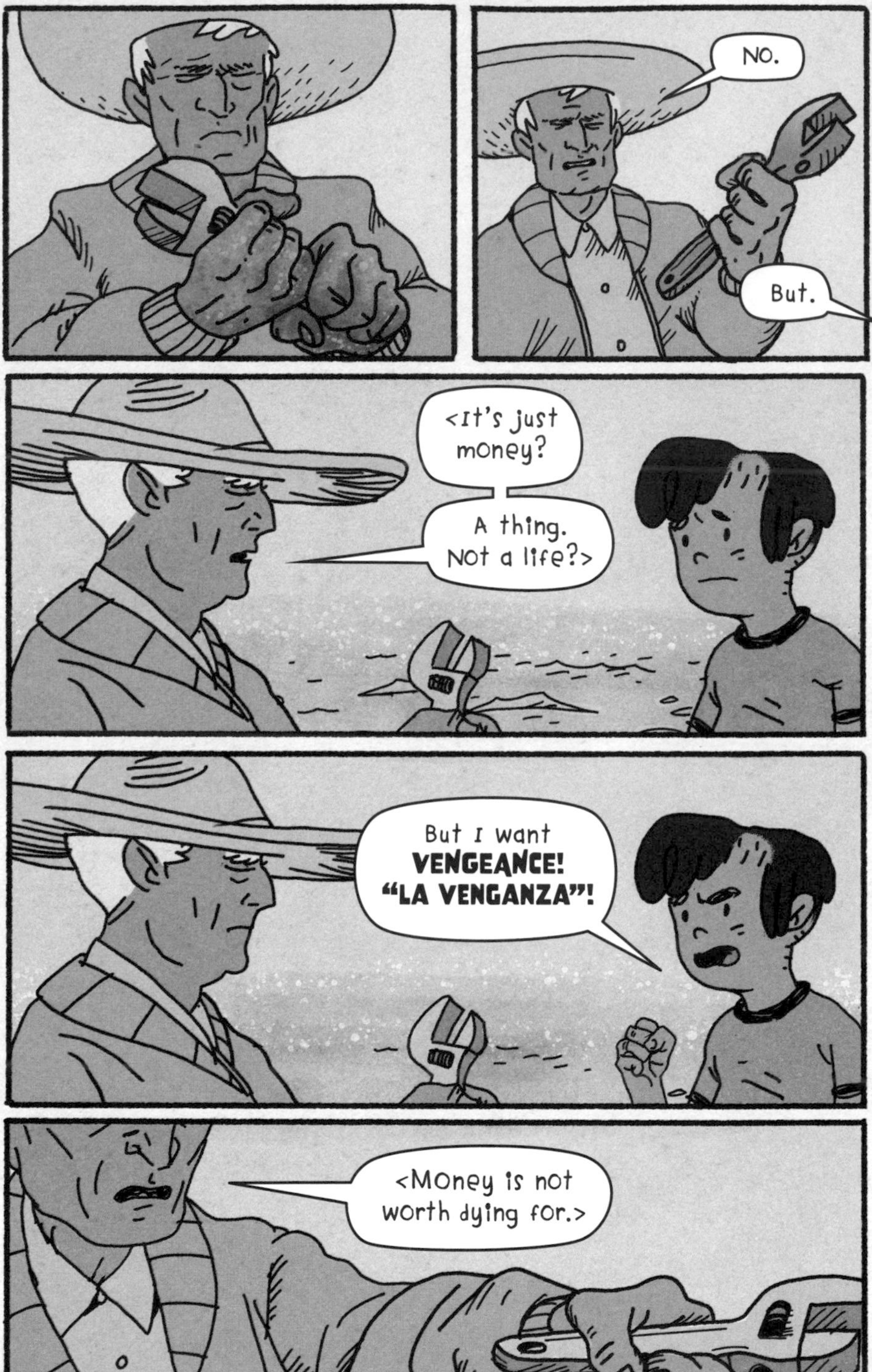
NO.
But.
<It's just money?
A thing. Not a life?>
But I want **VENGEANCE! "LA VENGANZA"!**
<Money is not worth dying for.>

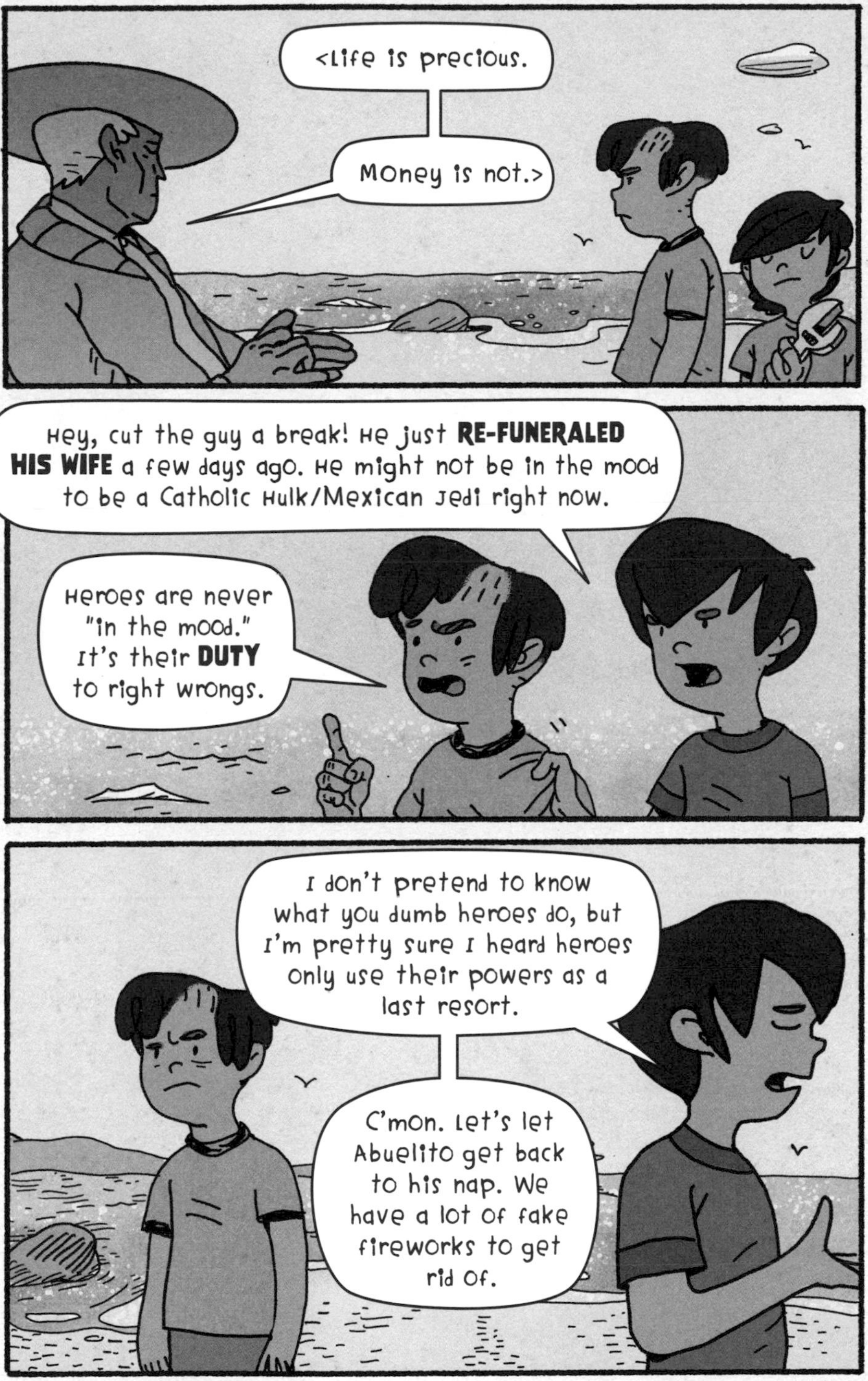
<Life is precious.
Money is not.>
Hey, cut the guy a break! He just **RE-FUNERALED HIS WIFE** a few days ago. He might not be in the mood to be a Catholic Hulk/Mexican Jedi right now.
Heroes are never "in the mood." It's their **DUTY** to right wrongs.
I don't pretend to know what you dumb heroes do, but I'm pretty sure I heard heroes only use their powers as a last resort.
C'mon. Let's let Abuelito get back to his nap. We have a lot of fake fireworks to get rid of.

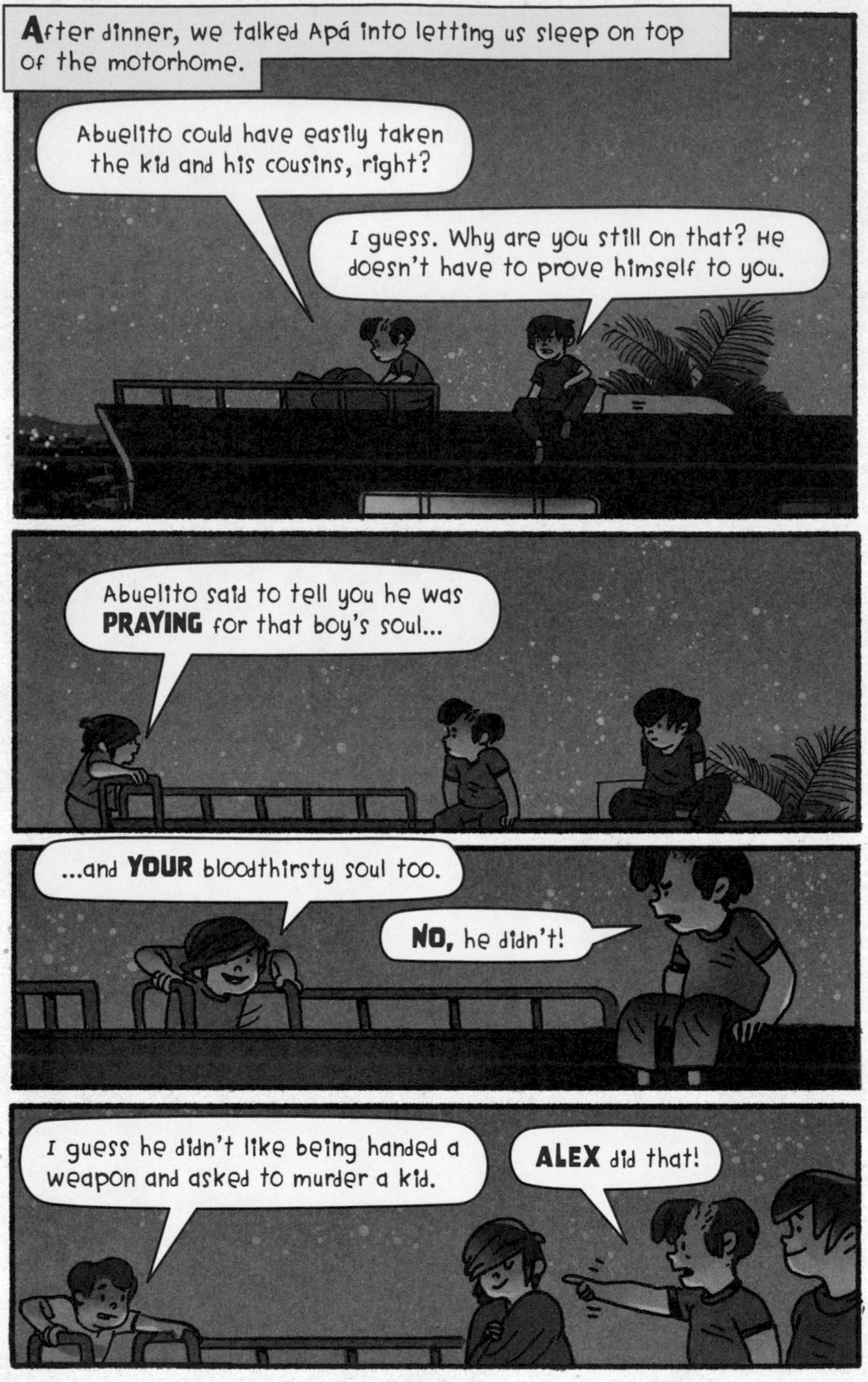
After dinner, we talked Apá into letting us sleep on top of the motorhome.
Abuelito could have easily taken the kid and his cousins, right?
I guess. Why are you still on that? He doesn't have to prove himself to you.
Abuelito said to tell you he was PRAYING for that boy's soul...
...and YOUR bloodthirsty soul too.
NO, he didn't!
I guess he didn't like being handed a weapon and asked to murder a kid.
ALEX did that!

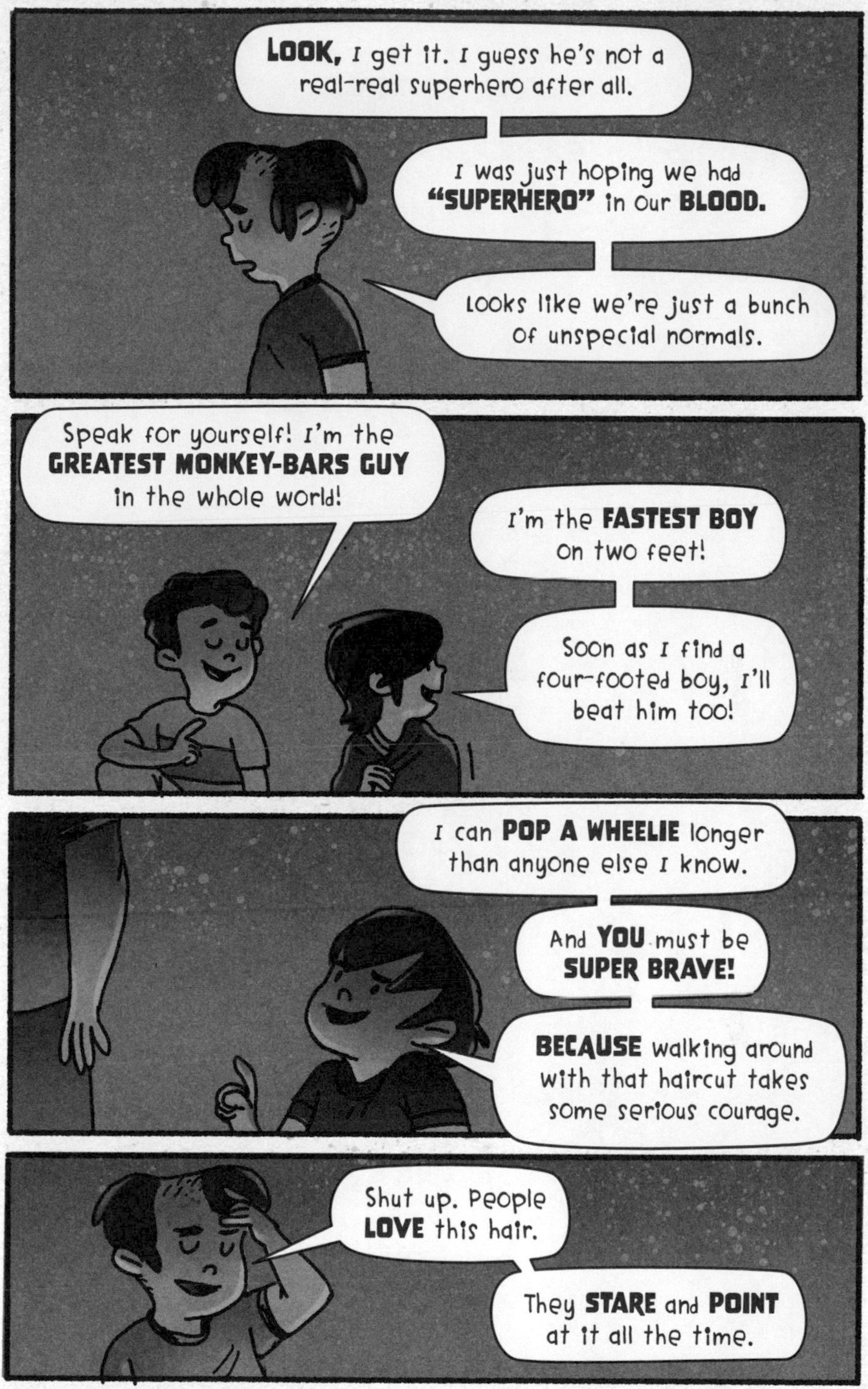
LOOK, I get it. I guess he's not a real-real superhero after all.
I was just hoping we had "SUPERHERO" in our BLOOD.
Looks like we're just a bunch of unspecial normals.
Speak for yourself! I'm the GREATEST MONKEY-BARS GUY in the whole world!
I'm the FASTEST BOY on two feet!
Soon as I find a four-footed boy, I'll beat him too!
I can POP A WHEELIE longer than anyone else I know.
And YOU must be SUPER BRAVE!
BECAUSE walking around with that haircut takes some serious courage.
Shut up. People LOVE this hair.
They STARE and POINT at it all the time.

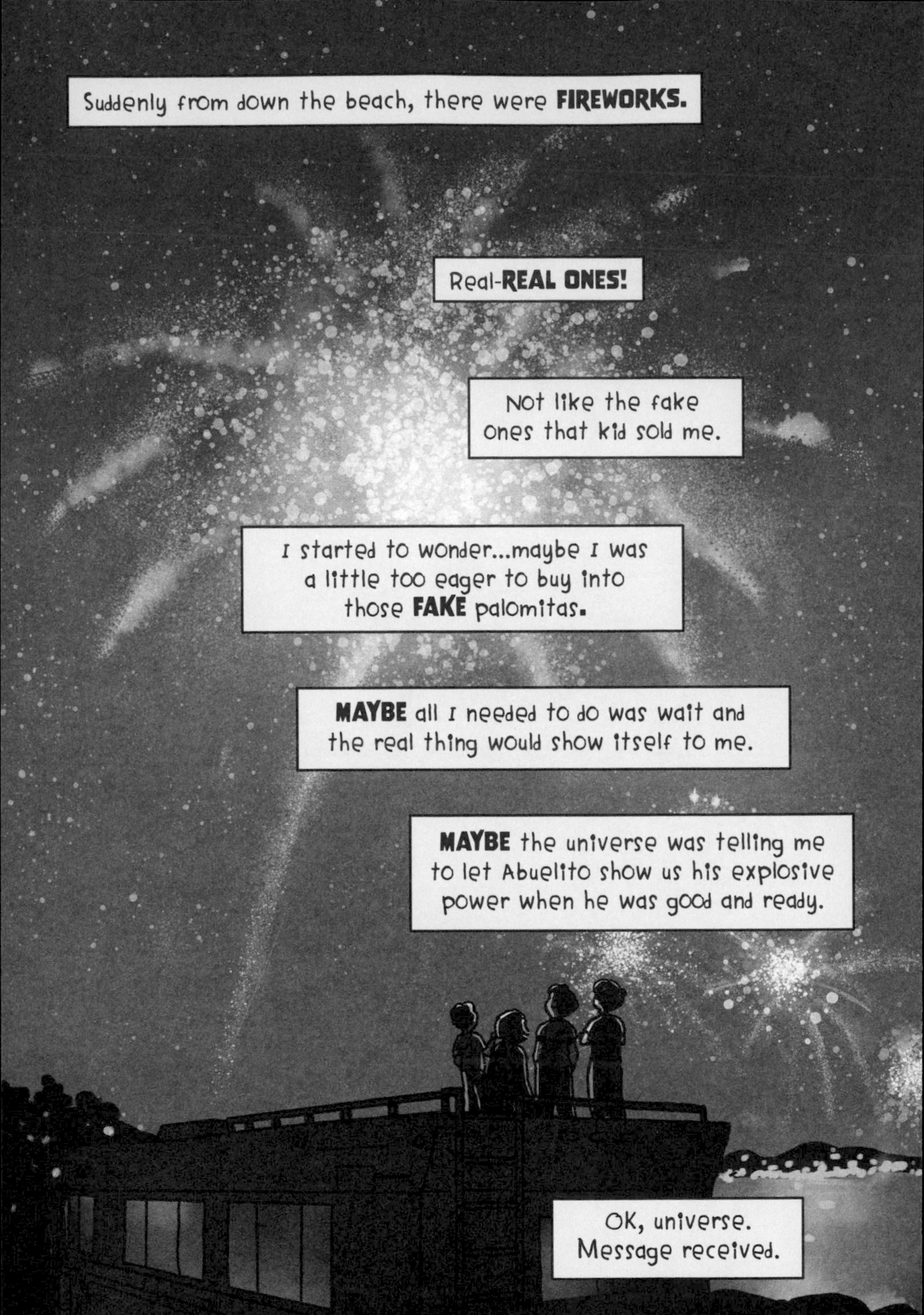
Suddenly from down the beach, there were FIREWORKS.
Real-REAL ONES!
Not like the fake ones that kid sold me.
I started to wonder...maybe I was a little too eager to buy into those FAKE palomitas.
MAYBE all I needed to do was wait and the real thing would show itself to me.
MAYBE the universe was telling me to let Abuelito show us his explosive power when he was good and ready.
OK, universe. Message received.

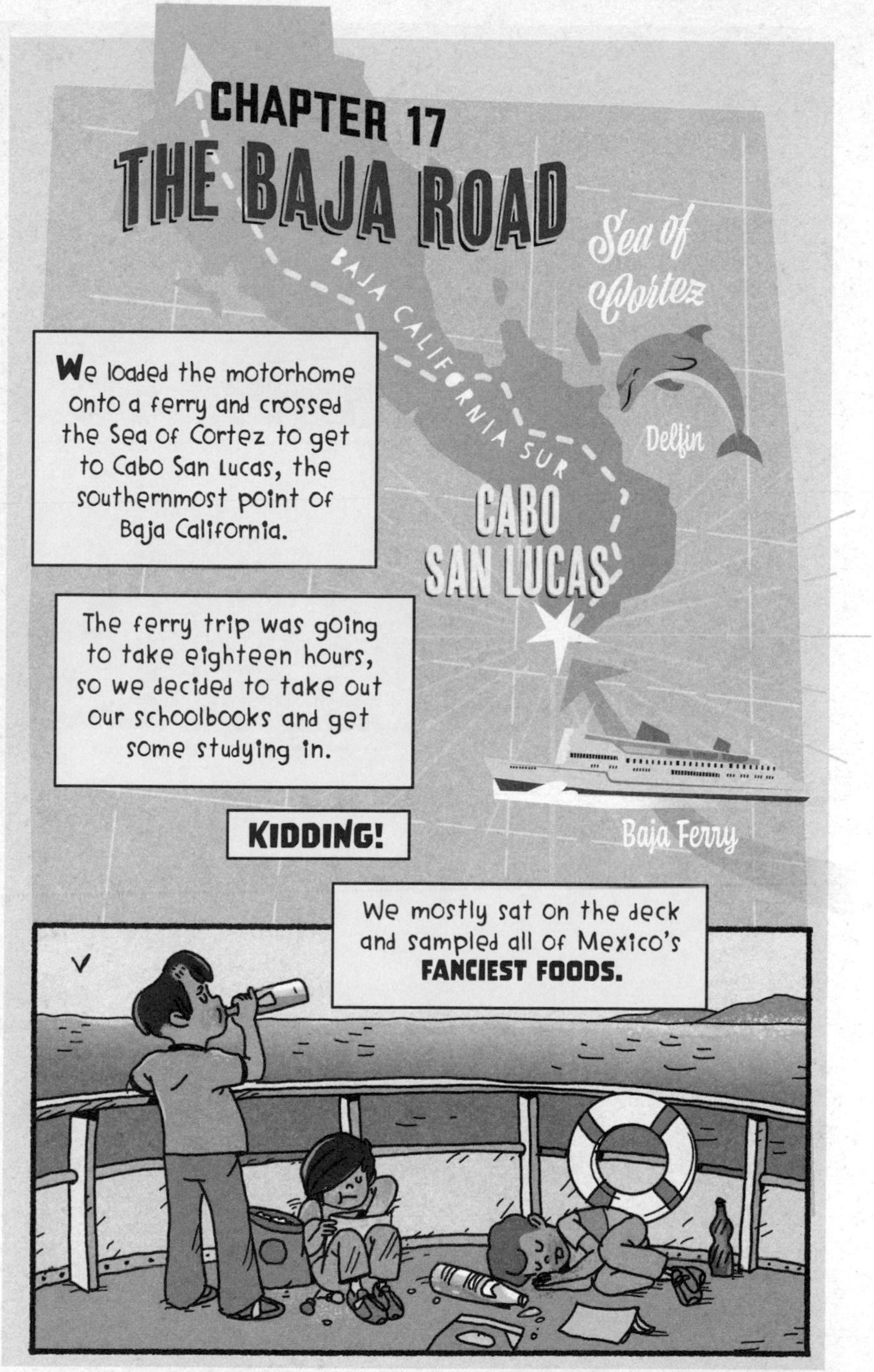
CHAPTER 17
THE BAJA ROAD
Sea of Cortez
BAJA CALIFORNIA SUR
We loaded the motorhome onto a ferry and crossed the Sea of Cortez to get to Cabo San Lucas, the southernmost point of Baja California.
Delfin
CABO SAN LUCAS
The ferry trip was going to take eighteen hours, so we decided to take out our schoolbooks and get some studying in.
KIDDING!
Baja Ferry
We mostly sat on the deck and sampled all of Mexico's **FANCIEST FOODS.**

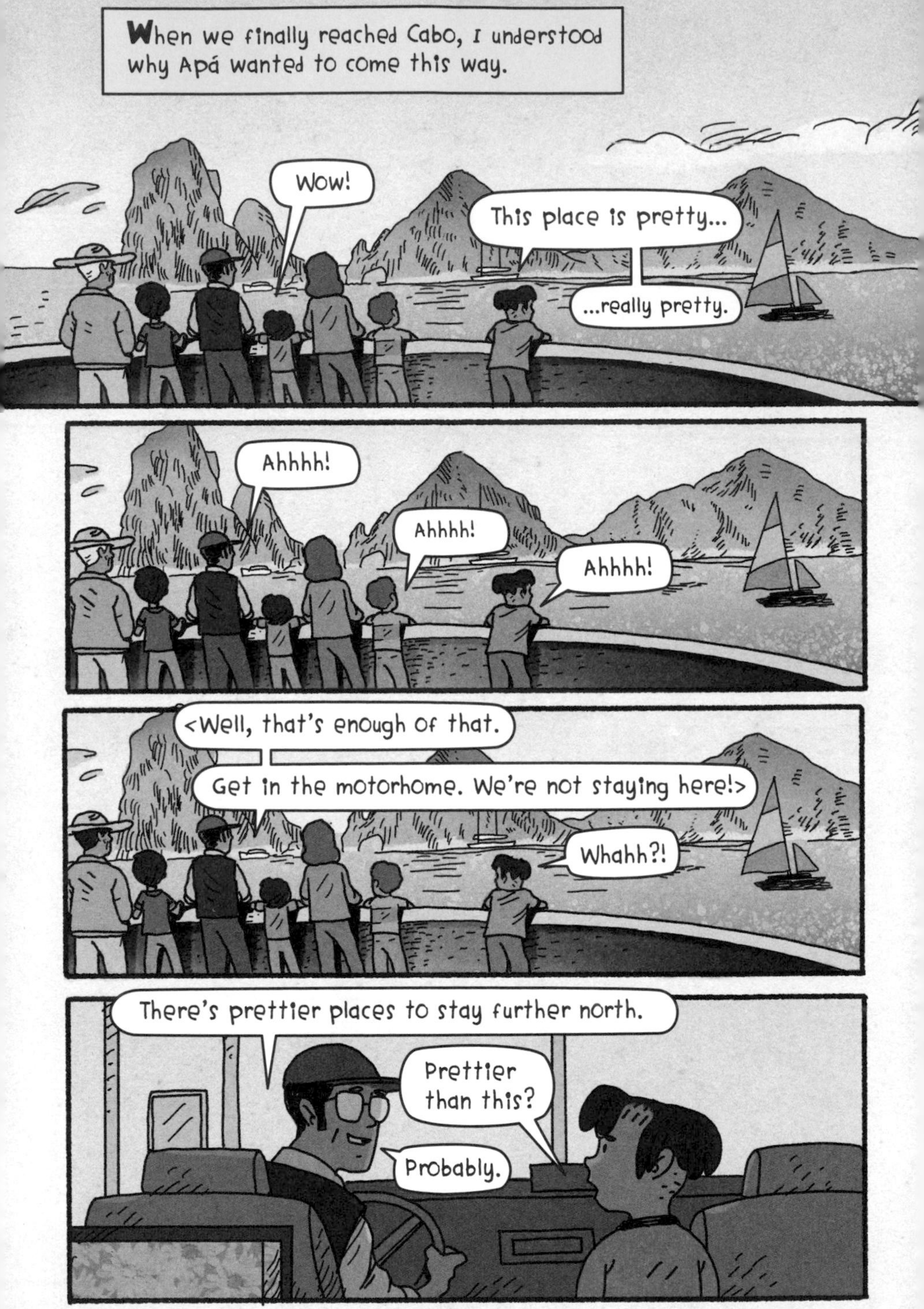
When we finally reached Cabo, I understood why Apá wanted to come this way.
Wow!
This place is pretty...
...really pretty.
Ahhhh!
Ahhhh!
Ahhhh!
<Well, that's enough of that.
Get in the motorhome. We're not staying here!>
Whahh?!
There's prettier places to stay further north.
Prettier than this?
Probably.

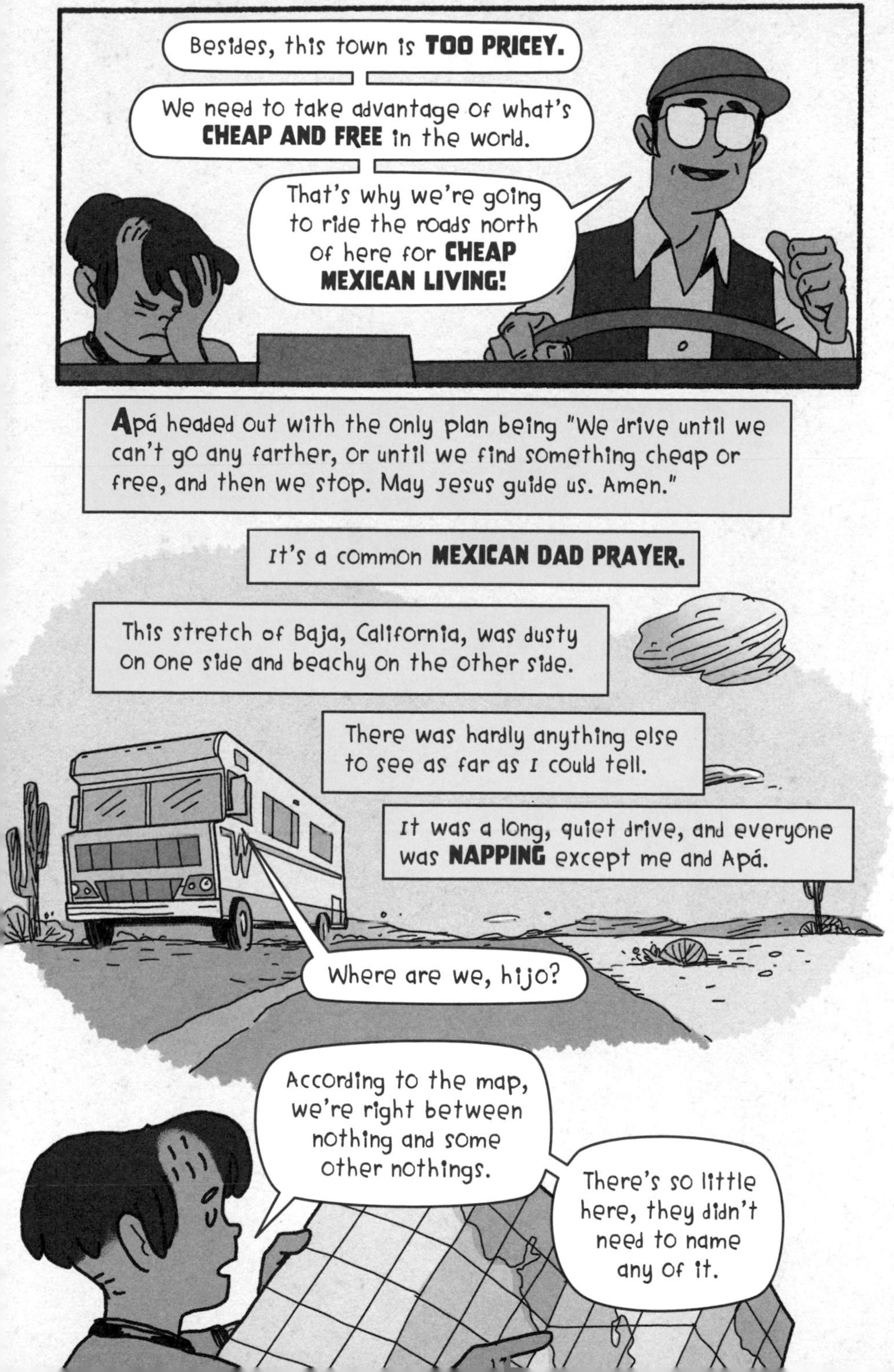

Besides, this town is **TOO PRICEY.**
We need to take advantage of what's **CHEAP AND FREE** in the world.
That's why we're going to ride the roads north of here for **CHEAP MEXICAN LIVING!**
Apá headed out with the only plan being "We drive until we can't go any farther, or until we find something cheap or free, and then we stop. May Jesus guide us. Amen."
It's a common **MEXICAN DAD PRAYER.**
This stretch of Baja, California, was dusty on one side and beachy on the other side.
There was hardly anything else to see as far as I could tell.
It was a long, quiet drive, and everyone was **NAPPING** except me and Apá.
Where are we, hijo?
According to the map, we're right between nothing and some other nothings.
There's so little here, they didn't need to name any of it.

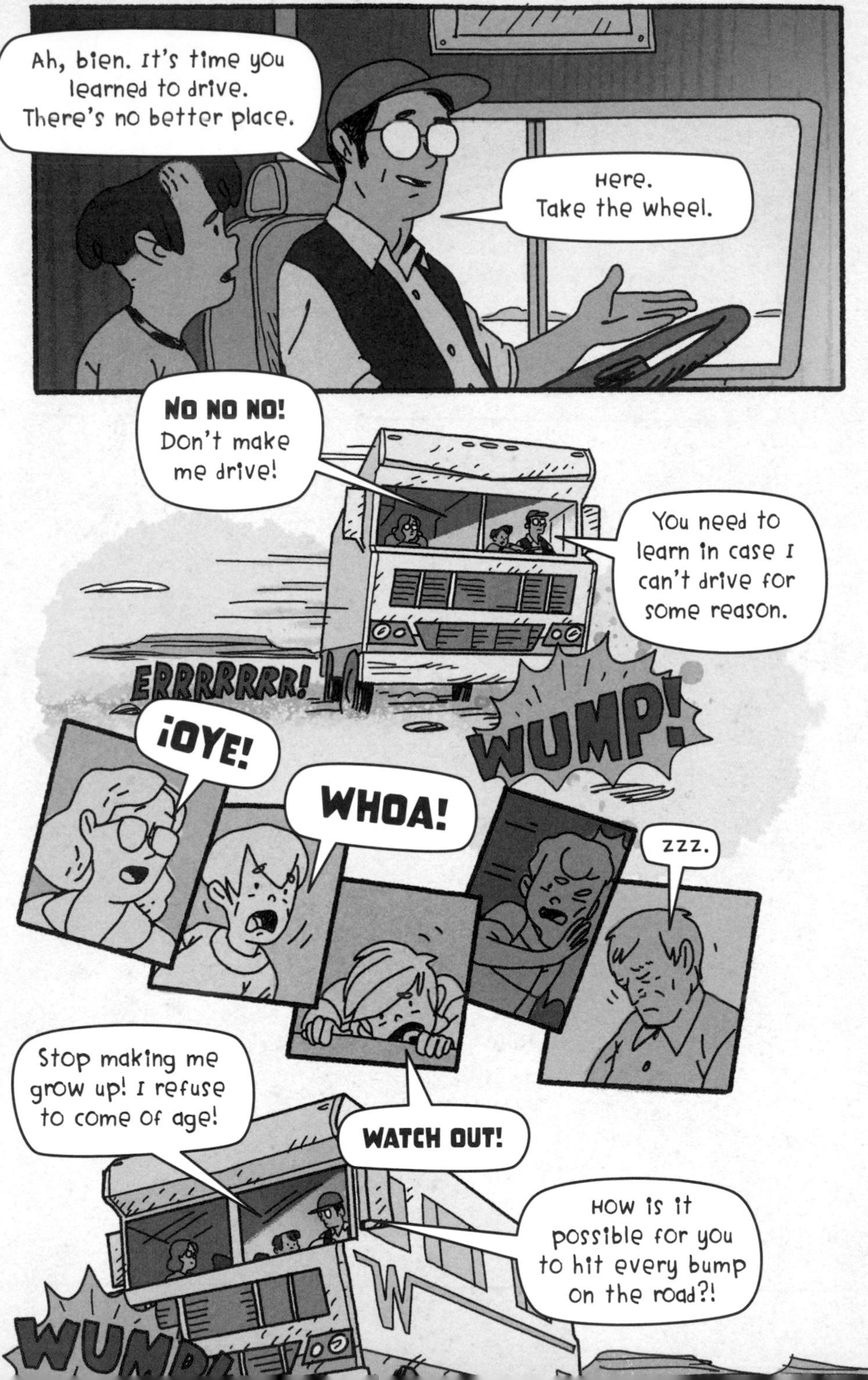
Ah, bien. It's time you learned to drive. There's no better place.
Here. Take the wheel.
NO NO NO! Don't make me drive!
You need to learn in case I can't drive for some reason.
ERRRRRRR!
WUMP!
¡OYE!
WHOA!
zzz.
Stop making me grow up! I refuse to come of age!
WATCH OUT!
How is it possible for you to hit every bump on the road?!
WUMP!

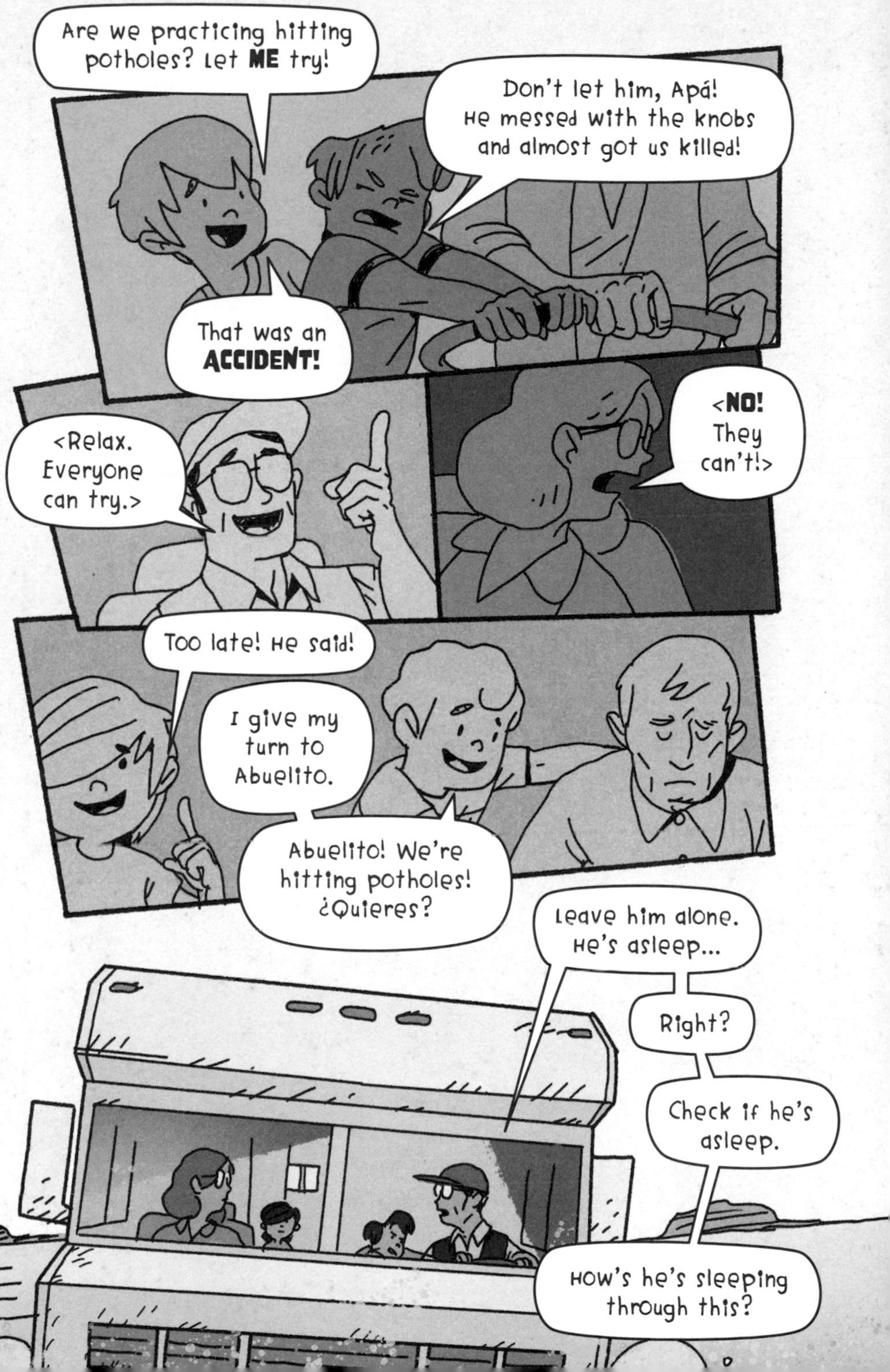
Are we practicing hitting potholes? Let ME try!
Don't let him, Apá! He messed with the knobs and almost got us killed!
That was an ACCIDENT!
<Relax. Everyone can try.>
<NO! They can't!>
Too late! He said!
I give my turn to Abuelito.
Abuelito! We're hitting potholes! ¿Quieres?
Leave him alone. He's asleep...
Right?
Check if he's asleep.
How's he's sleeping through this?

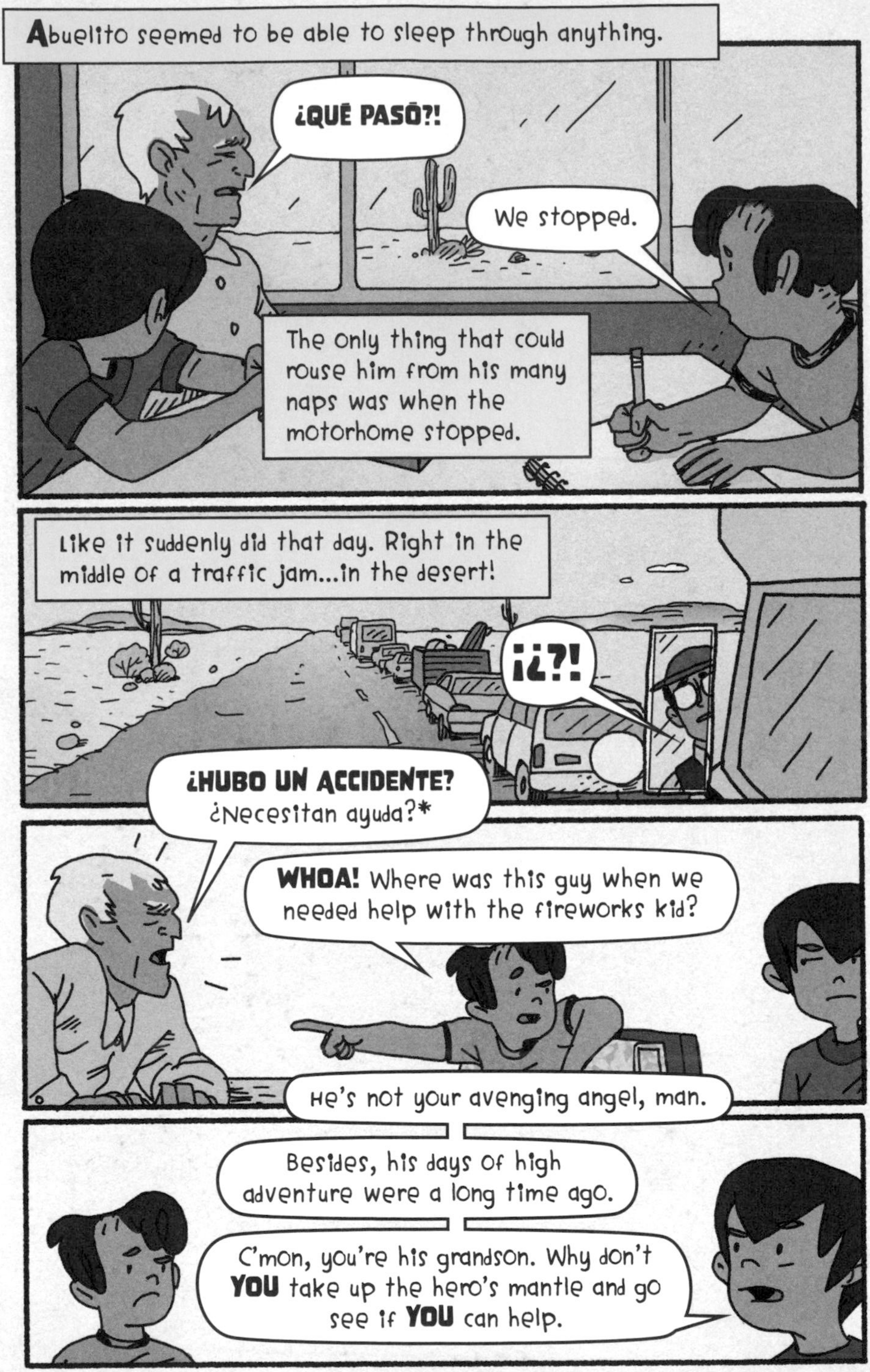
Abuelito seemed to be able to sleep through anything.
¿QUÉ PASÓ?!
We stopped.
The only thing that could rouse him from his many naps was when the motorhome stopped.
Like it suddenly did that day. Right in the middle of a traffic jam...in the desert!
¡¿?!
¿HUBO UN ACCIDENTE? ¿Necesitan ayuda?*
WHOA! Where was this guy when we needed help with the fireworks kid?
He's not your avenging angel, man.
Besides, his days of high adventure were a long time ago.
C'mon, you're his grandson. Why don't YOU take up the hero's mantle and go see if YOU can help.

*Was there an accident? Does someone need help?

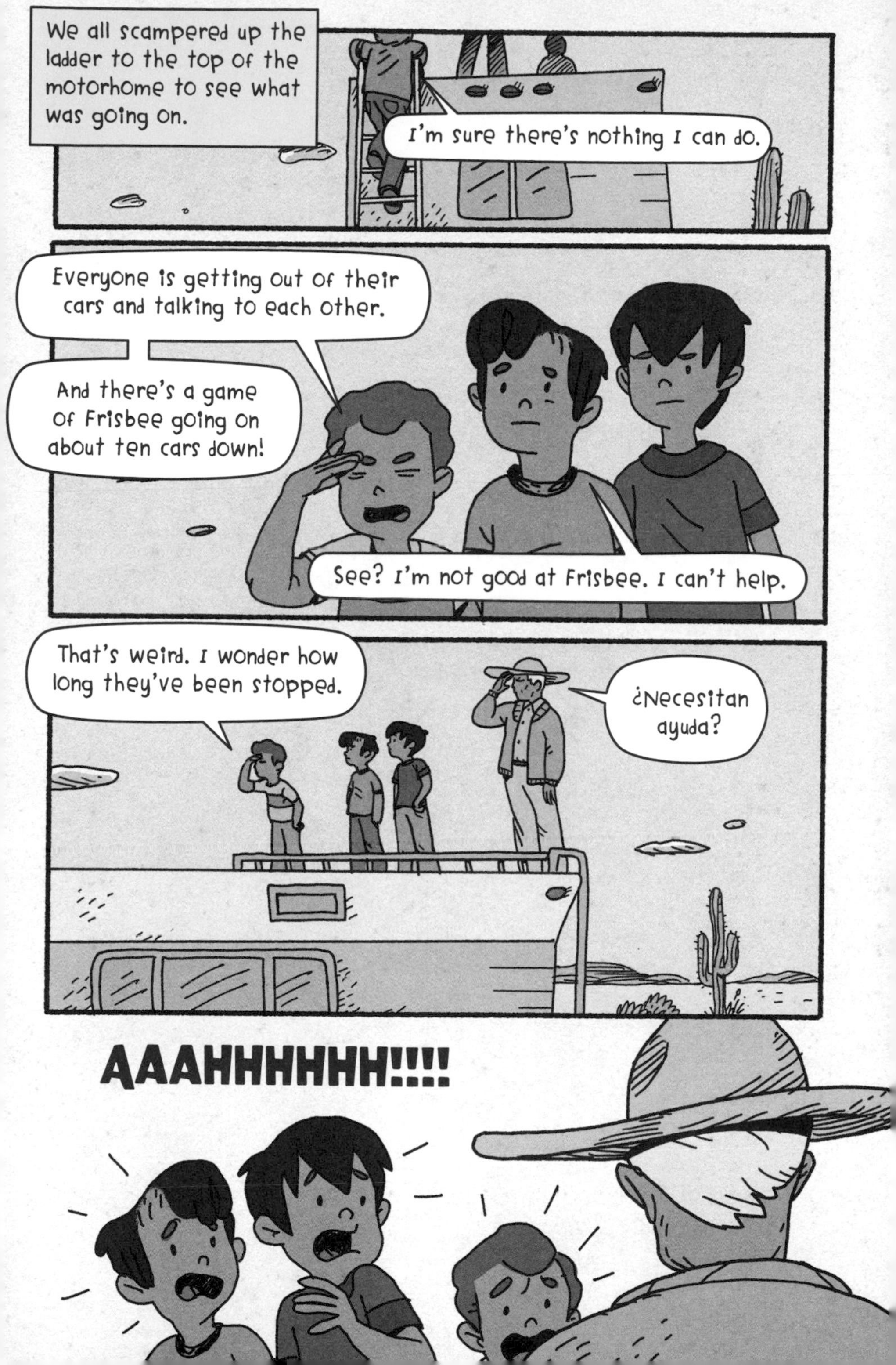
We all scampered up the ladder to the top of the motorhome to see what was going on.
I'm sure there's nothing I can do.
Everyone is getting out of their cars and talking to each other.
And there's a game of Frisbee going on about ten cars down!
See? I'm not good at Frisbee. I can't help.
That's weird. I wonder how long they've been stopped.
¿Necesitan ayuda?
AAAHHHHHH!!!!

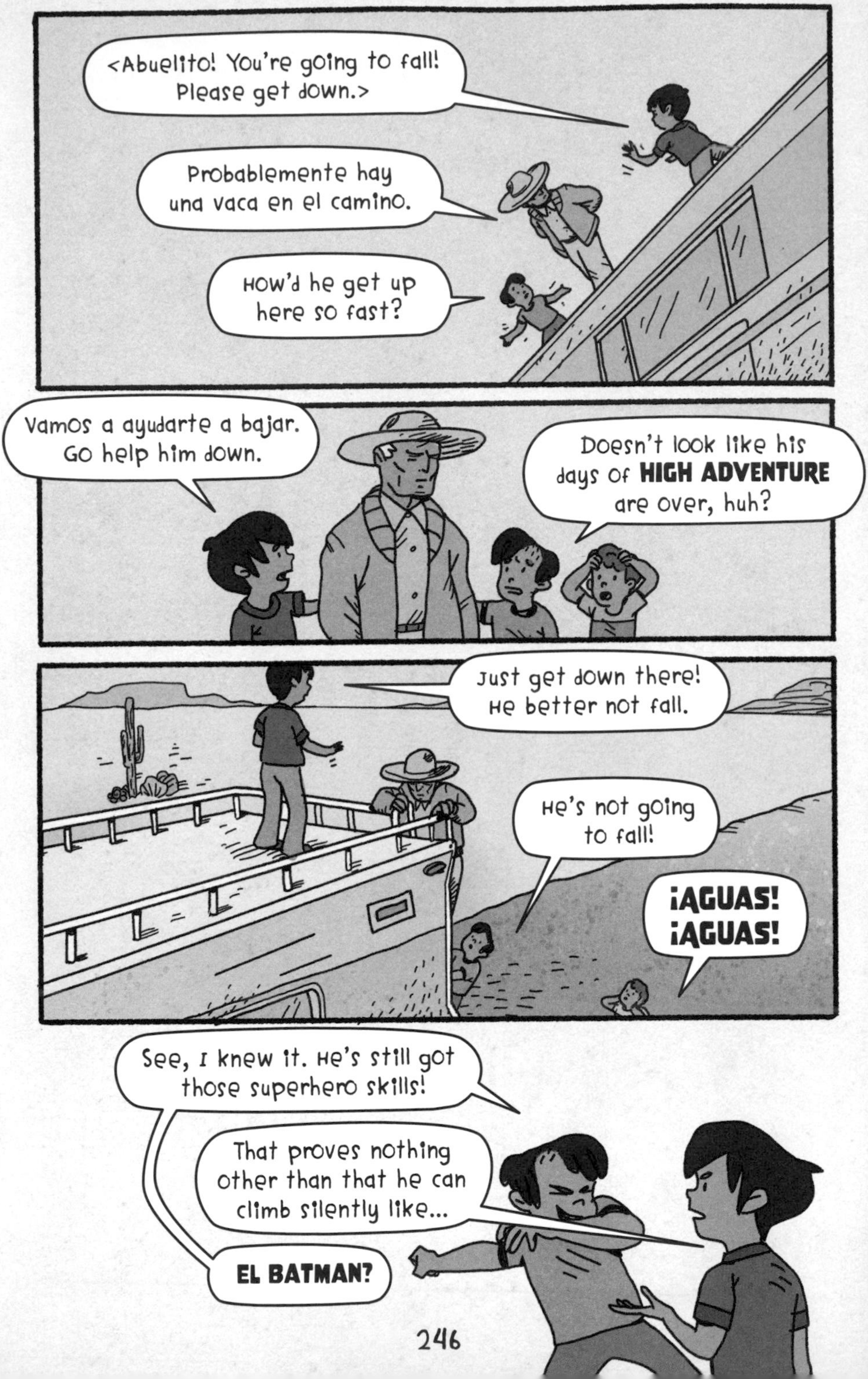
<Abuelito! You're going to fall! Please get down.>
Probablemente hay una vaca en el camino.
How'd he get up here so fast?
Vamos a ayudarte a bajar. Go help him down.
Doesn't look like his days of HIGH ADVENTURE are over, huh?
Just get down there! He better not fall.
He's not going to fall!
¡AGUAS! ¡AGUAS!
See, I knew it. He's still got those superhero skills!
That proves nothing other than that he can climb silently like...
EL BATMAN?

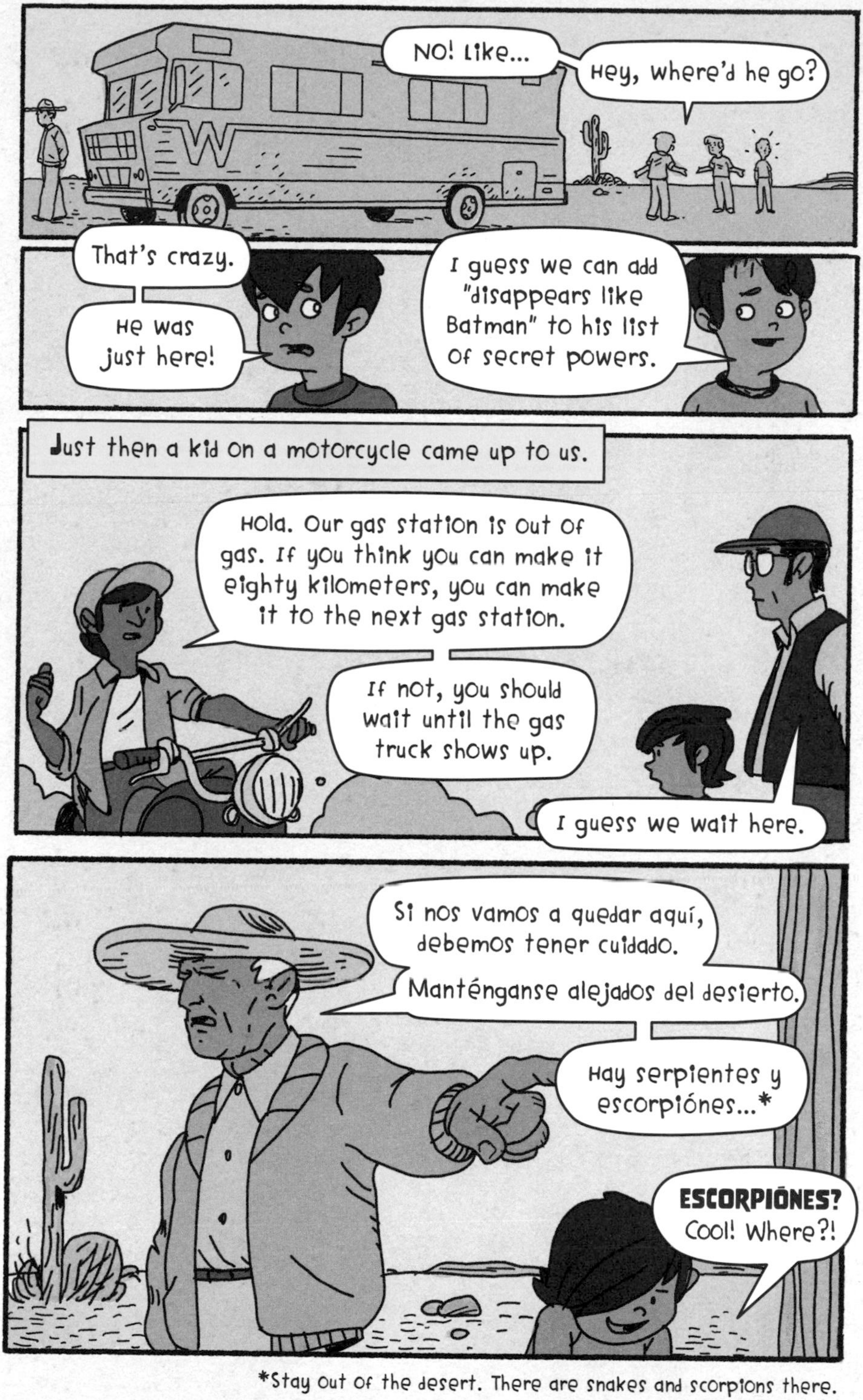
NO! Like...
Hey, where'd he go?
That's crazy.
He was just here!
I guess we can add "disappears like Batman" to his list of secret powers.
Just then a kid on a motorcycle came up to us.
Hola. Our gas station is out of gas. If you think you can make it eighty kilometers, you can make it to the next gas station.
If not, you should wait until the gas truck shows up.
I guess we wait here.
Si nos vamos a quedar aquí, debemos tener cuidado.
Manténganse alejados del desierto.
Hay serpientes y escorpiónes...*
ESCORPIÓNES? Cool! Where?!

*Stay out of the desert. There are snakes and scorpions there.

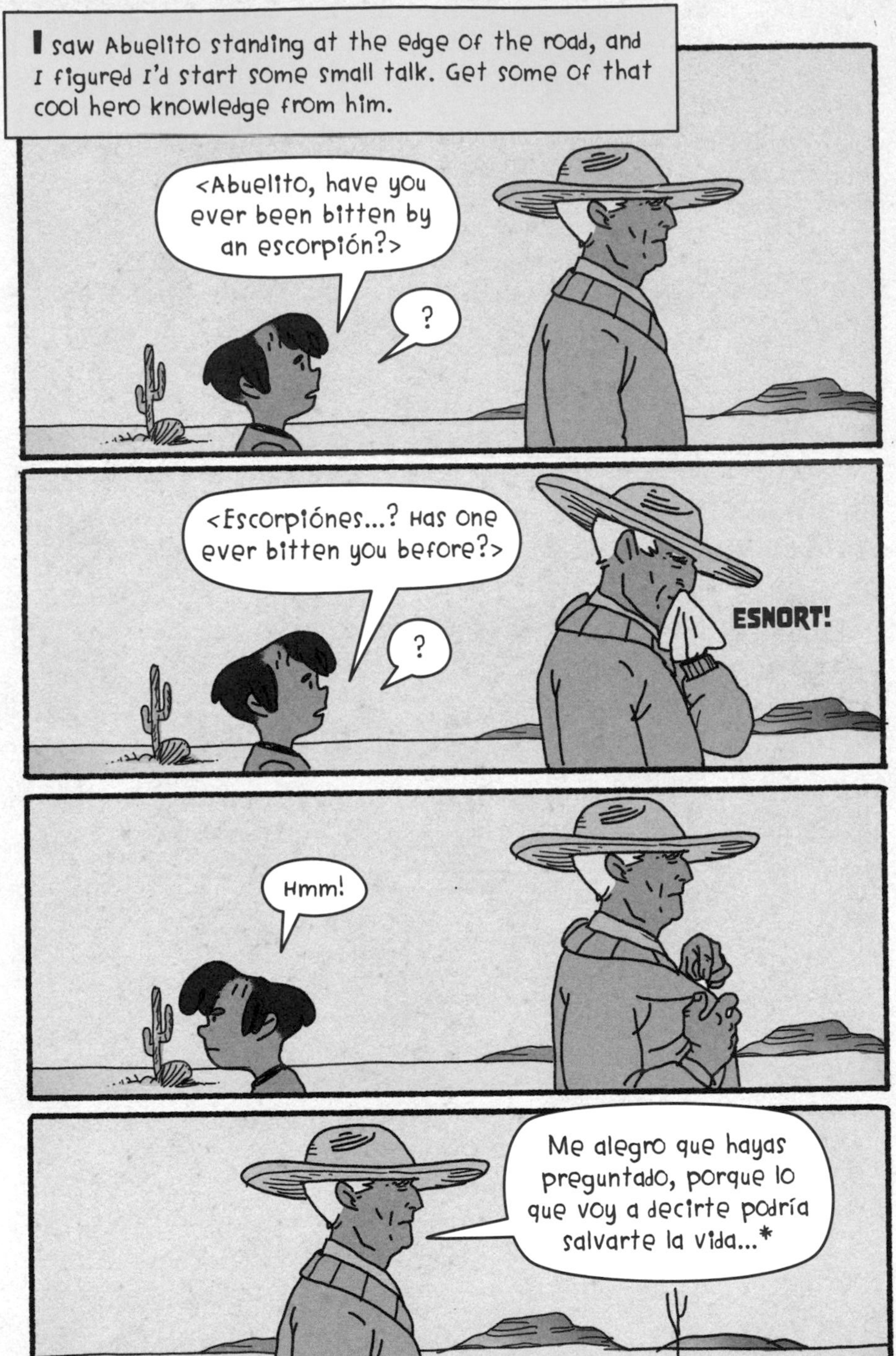
I saw Abuelito standing at the edge of the road, and I figured I'd start some small talk. Get some of that cool hero knowledge from him.
<Abuelito, have you ever been bitten by an escorpión?>
?
<Escorpiónes...? Has one ever bitten you before?>
?
ESNORT!
Hmm!
Me alegro que hayas preguntado, porque lo que voy a decirte podría salvarte la vida...*

*I'm glad you asked because what I'm about to tell you could save your life...

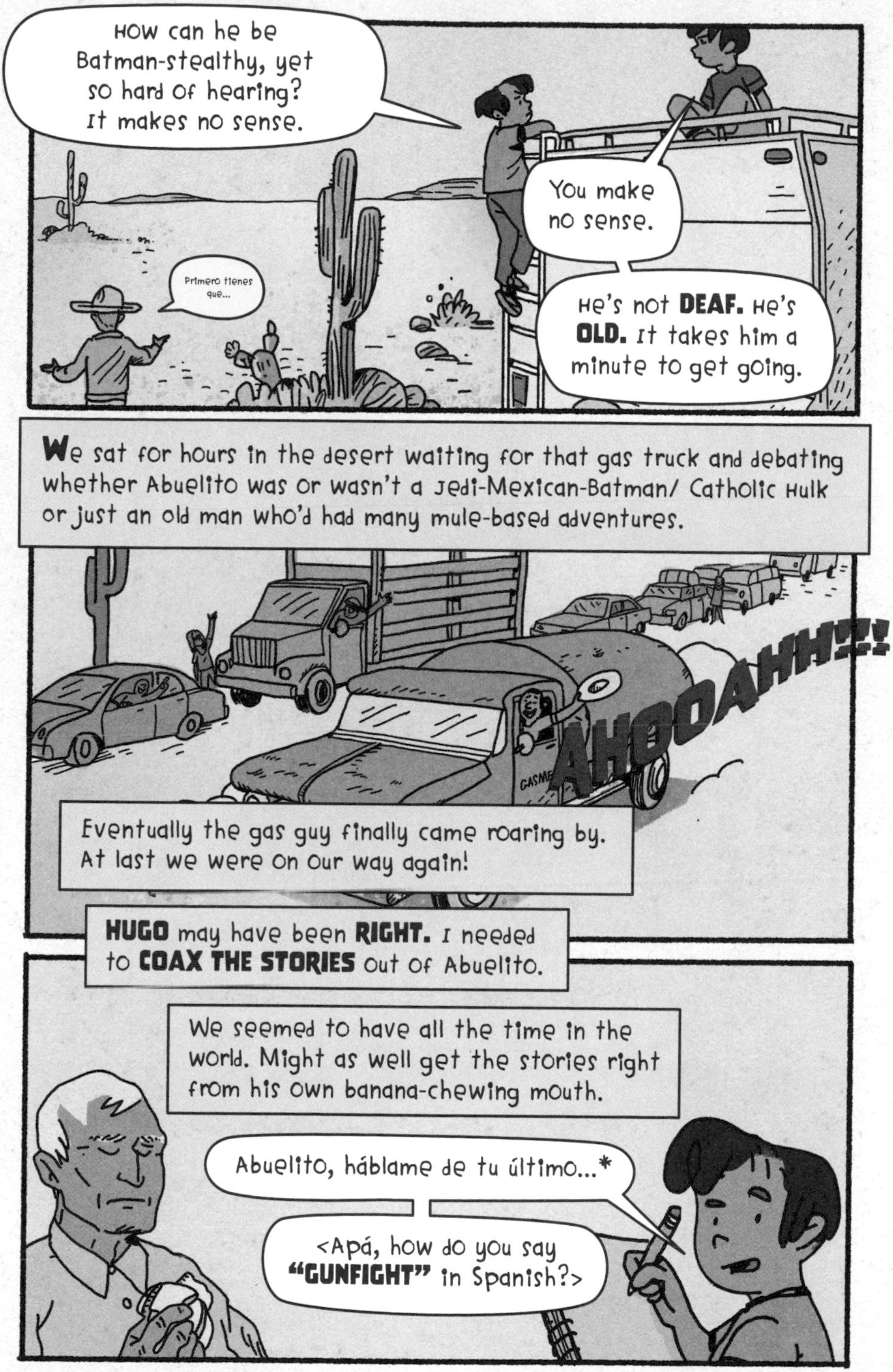

How can he be Batman-stealthy, yet so hard of hearing? It makes no sense.
You make no sense.
He's not **DEAF.** He's **OLD.** It takes him a minute to get going.
Primero tienes que...
We sat for hours in the desert waiting for that gas truck and debating whether Abuelito was or wasn't a Jedi-Mexican-Batman/ Catholic Hulk or just an old man who'd had many mule-based adventures.
AHOOAHH!!!
Eventually the gas guy finally came roaring by. At last we were on our way again!
HUGO may have been **RIGHT.** I needed to **COAX THE STORIES** out of Abuelito.
We seemed to have all the time in the world. Might as well get the stories right from his own banana-chewing mouth.
Abuelito, háblame de tu último...*
<Apá, how do you say **"GUNFIGHT"** in Spanish?>

*Abuelito, tell me about your last...

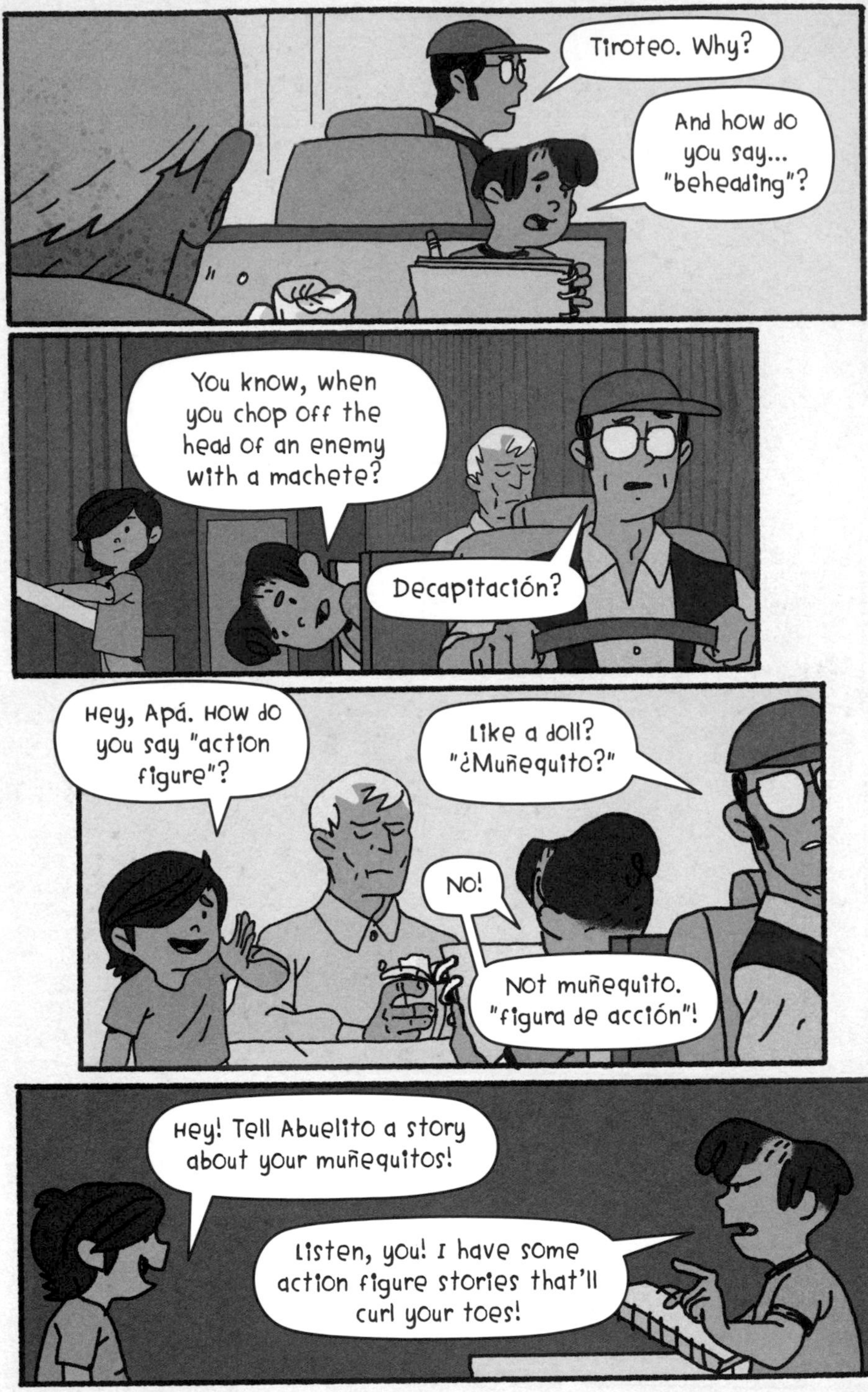
Tiroteo. Why?
And how do you say... "beheading"?
You know, when you chop off the head of an enemy with a machete?
Decapitación?
Hey, Apá. How do you say "action figure"?
Like a doll? "¿Muñequito?"
No!
Not muñequito. "figura de acción"!
Hey! Tell Abuelito a story about your muñequitos!
Listen, you! I have some action figure stories that'll curl your toes!

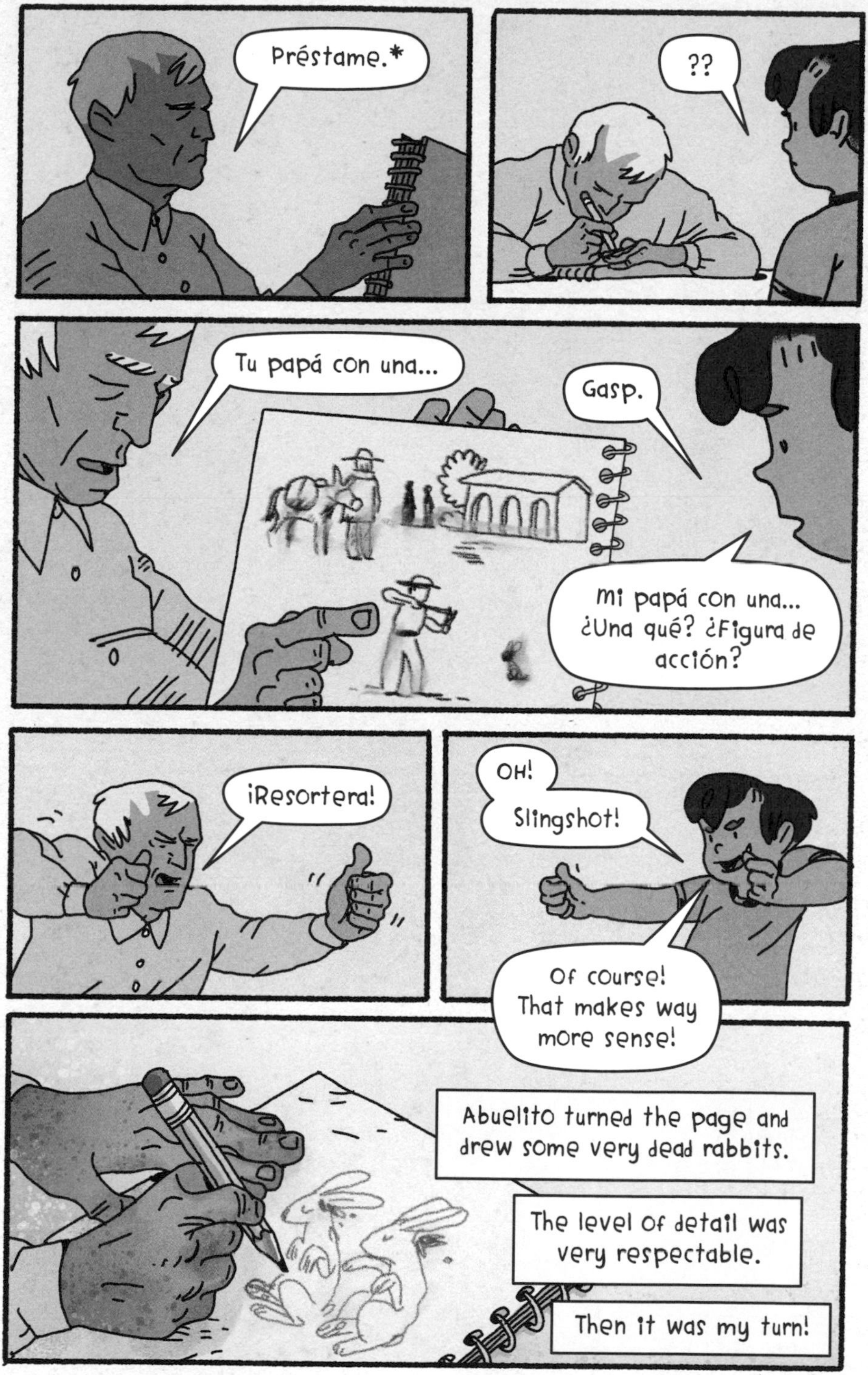
Préstame.*
??
Tu papá con una...
Gasp.
Mi papá con una... ¿Una qué? ¿Figura de acción?
¡Resortera!
OH!
Slingshot!
Of course! That makes way more sense!
Abuelito turned the page and drew some very dead rabbits.
The level of detail was very respectable.
Then it was my turn!

*Lend me.

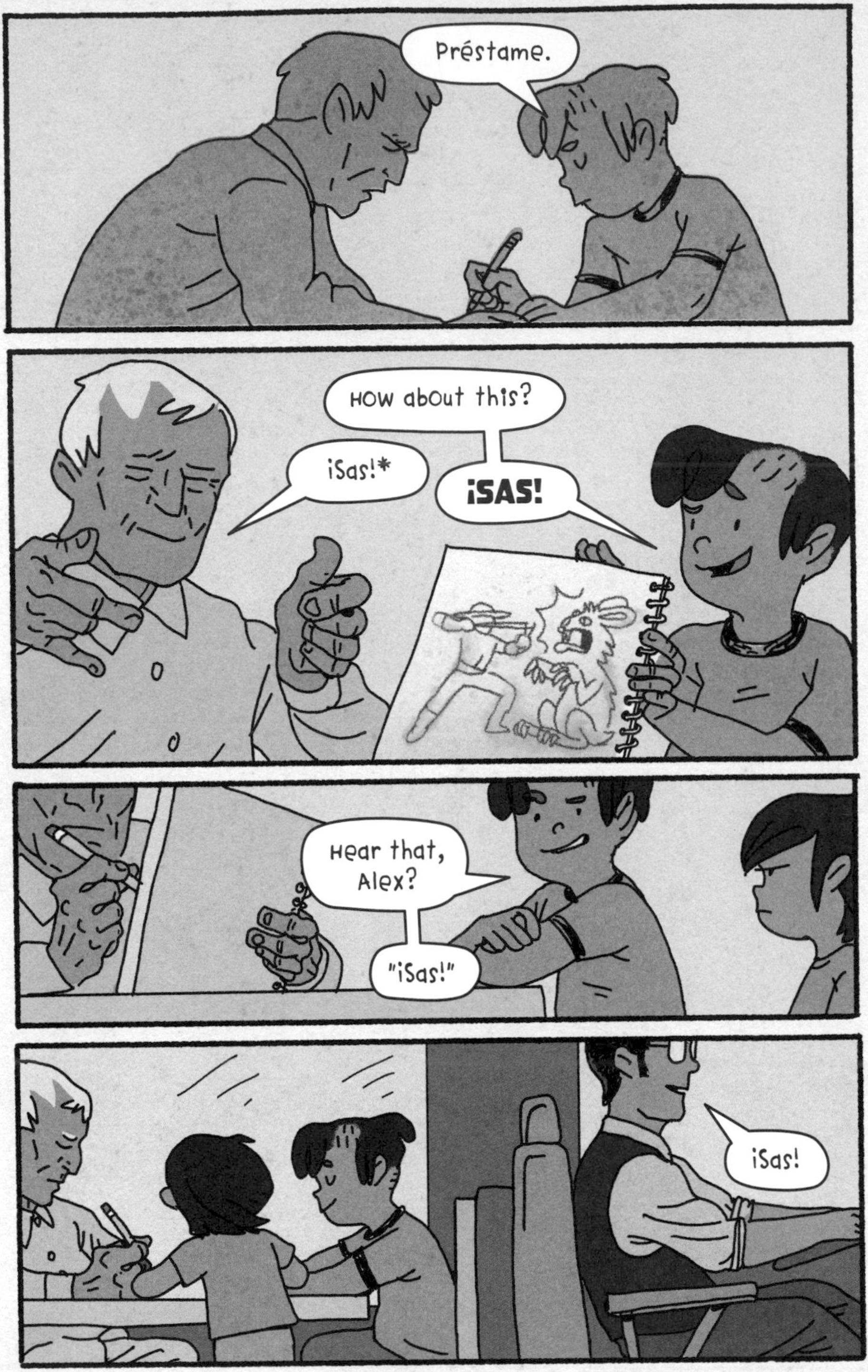
Préstame.
How about this?
¡Sas!*
¡SAS!
Hear that, Alex?
"¡Sas!"
¡Sas!

*POW!

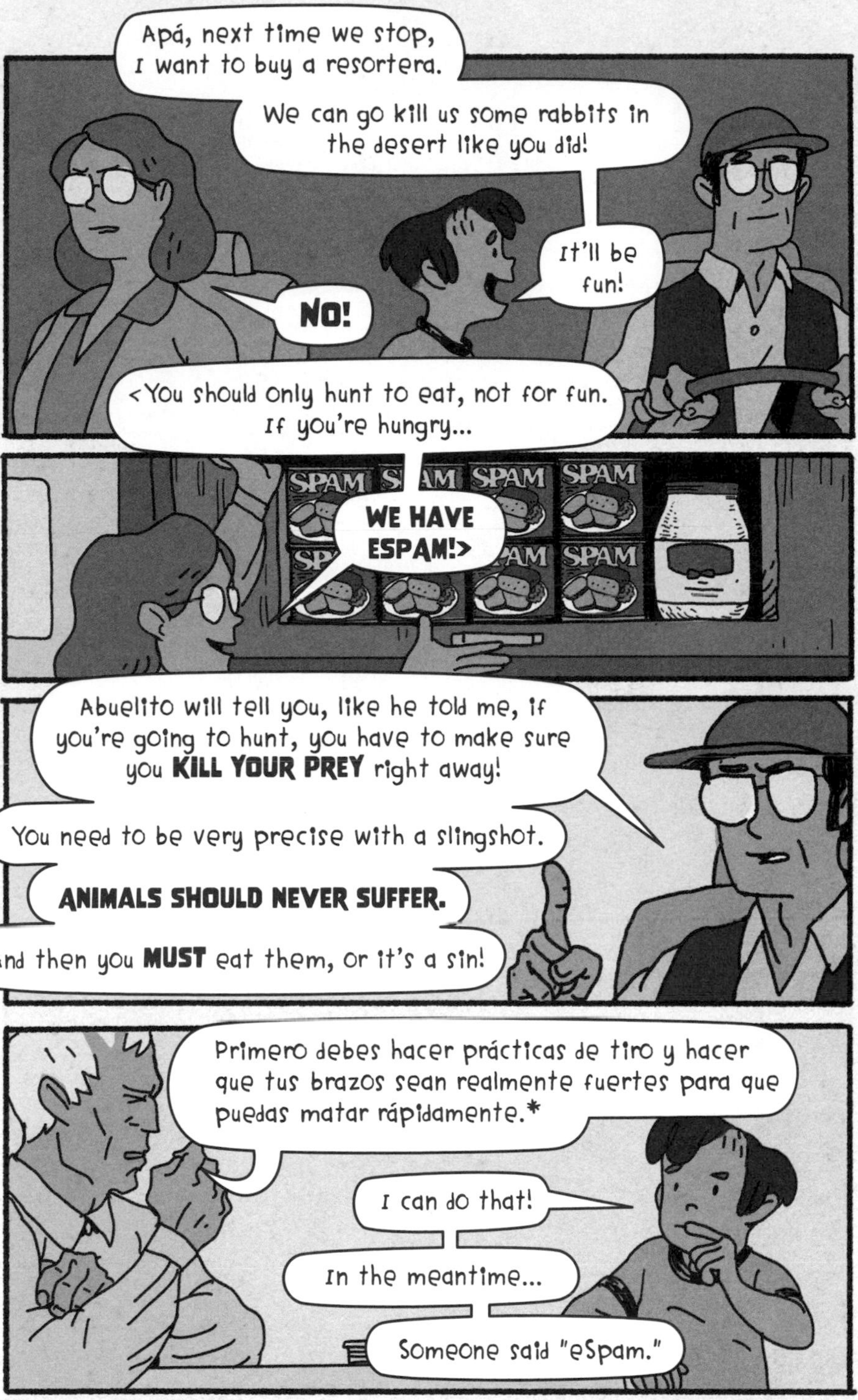
Apá, next time we stop, I want to buy a resortera.
We can go kill us some rabbits in the desert like you did!
It'll be fun!
NO!
<You should only hunt to eat, not for fun. If you're hungry...
WE HAVE ESPAM!>
SPAM
Abuelito will tell you, like he told me, if you're going to hunt, you have to make sure you KILL YOUR PREY right away!
You need to be very precise with a slingshot.
ANIMALS SHOULD NEVER SUFFER.
And then you MUST eat them, or it's a sin!
Primero debes hacer prácticas de tiro y hacer que tus brazos sean realmente fuertes para que puedas matar rápidamente.*
I can do that!
In the meantime...
Someone said "eSpam."

*You need to do target practice first and make your arms really strong so that you can kill quickly.

CHAPTER 18
THE HEROES RETURN

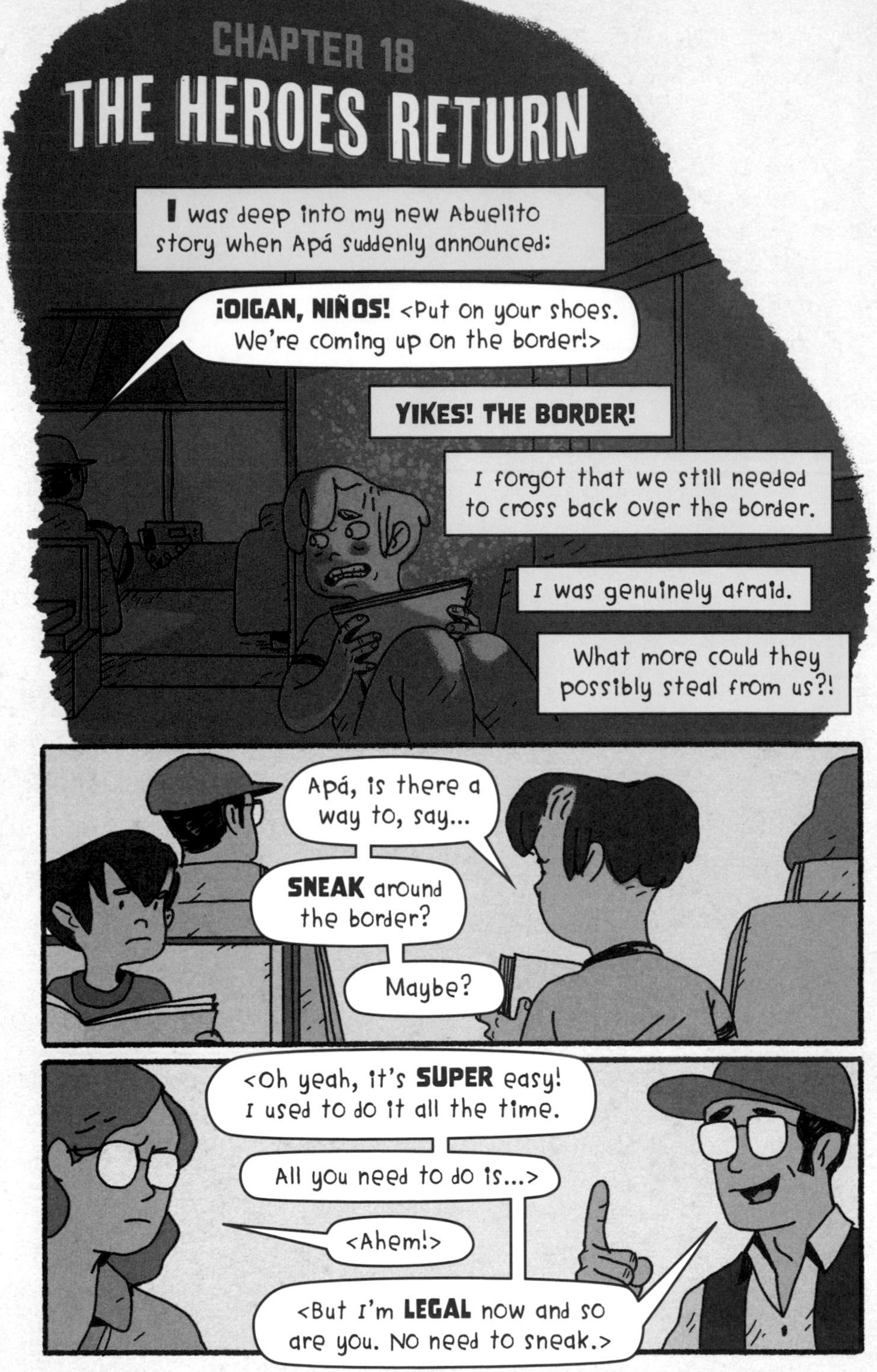
I was deep into my new Abuelito story when Apá suddenly announced:
¡OIGAN, NIÑOS! <Put on your shoes. We're coming up on the border!>
YIKES! THE BORDER!
I forgot that we still needed to cross back over the border.
I was genuinely afraid.
What more could they possibly steal from us?!
Apá, is there a way to, say...
SNEAK around the border?
Maybe?
<Oh yeah, it's SUPER easy! I used to do it all the time.
All you need to do is...>
<Ahem!>
<But I'm LEGAL now and so are you. No need to sneak.>

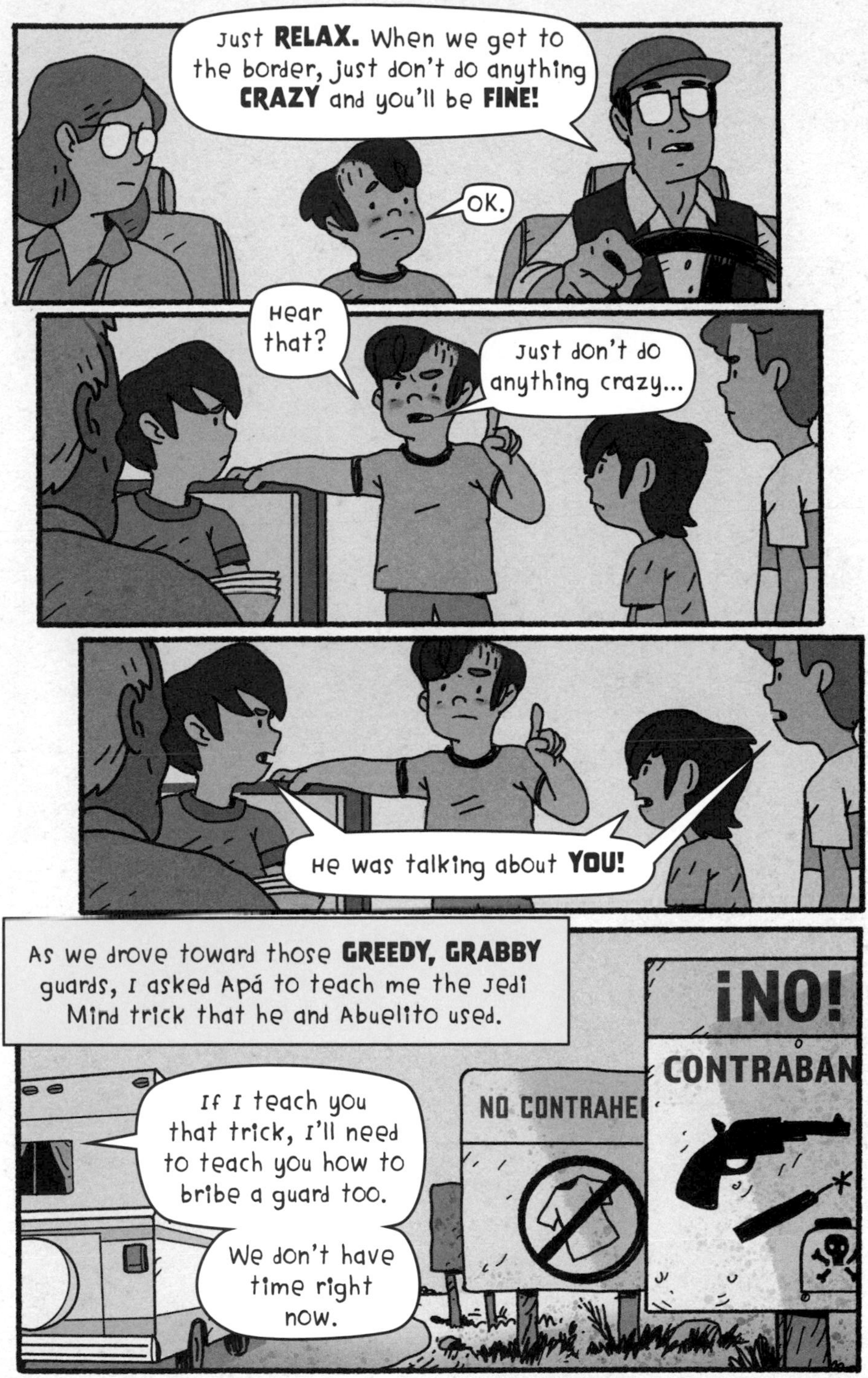

Just RELAX. When we get to the border, just don't do anything CRAZY and you'll be FINE!
OK.
Hear that?
Just don't do anything crazy...
He was talking about YOU!
As we drove toward those GREEDY, GRABBY guards, I asked Apá to teach me the Jedi Mind trick that he and Abuelito used.
¡NO!
CONTRABAN
NO CONTRAHE
If I teach you that trick, I'll need to teach you how to bribe a guard too.
We don't have time right now.

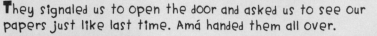

They signaled us to open the door and asked us to see our papers just like last time. Amá handed them all over.

The guard looked at our passports for what seemed like forever. Then he scanned us all like he had **X-RAY VISION.**

YOU!

C'MERE.

Me?

That's what I'd like to know.

Explain.

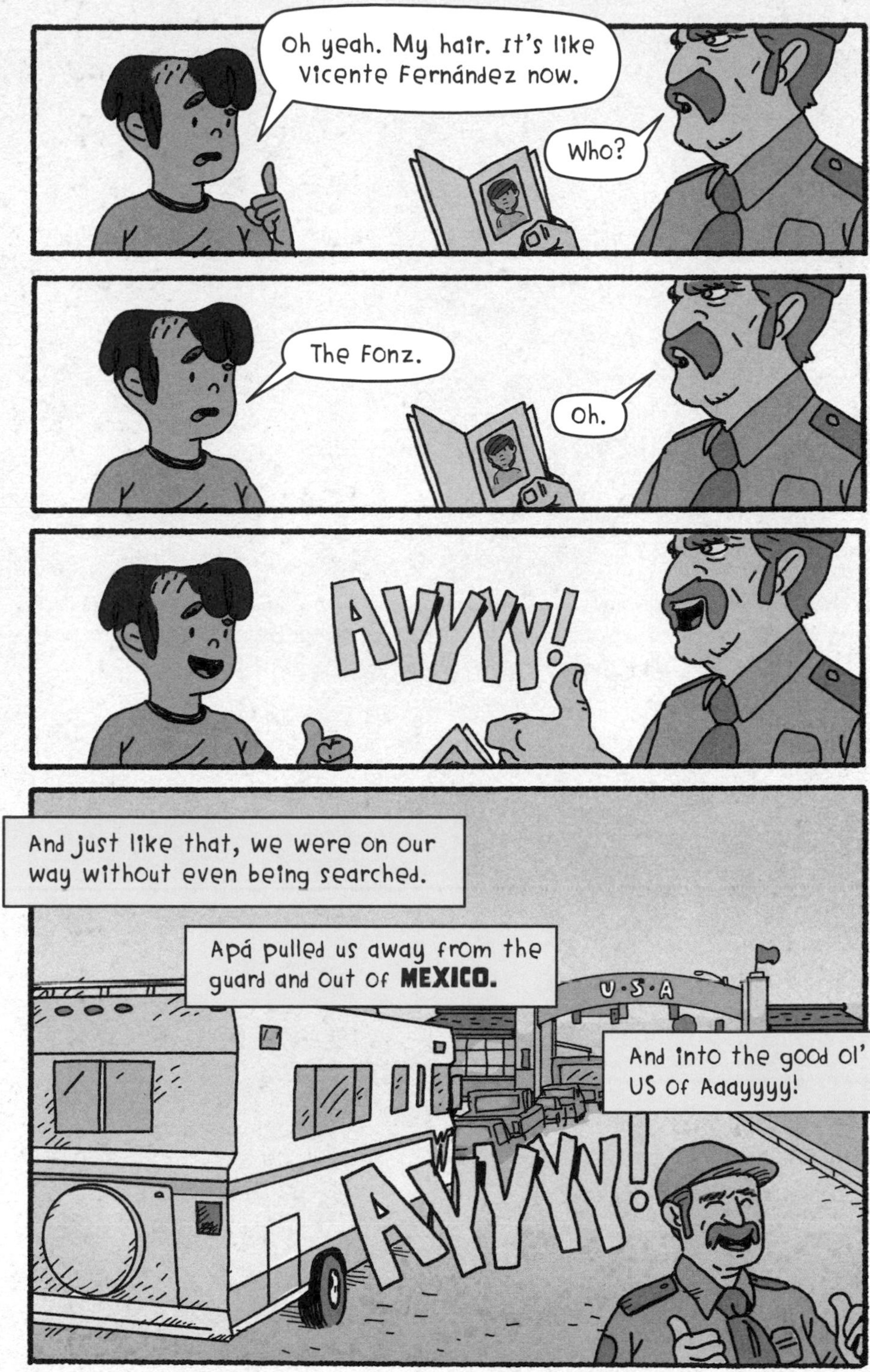
Oh yeah. My hair. It's like Vicente Fernández now.
Who?
The Fonz.
Oh.
AYYYY!
And just like that, we were on our way without even being searched.
Apá pulled us away from the guard and out of MEXICO.
U·S·A
And into the good ol' US of Aaayyyy!
AYYYY!

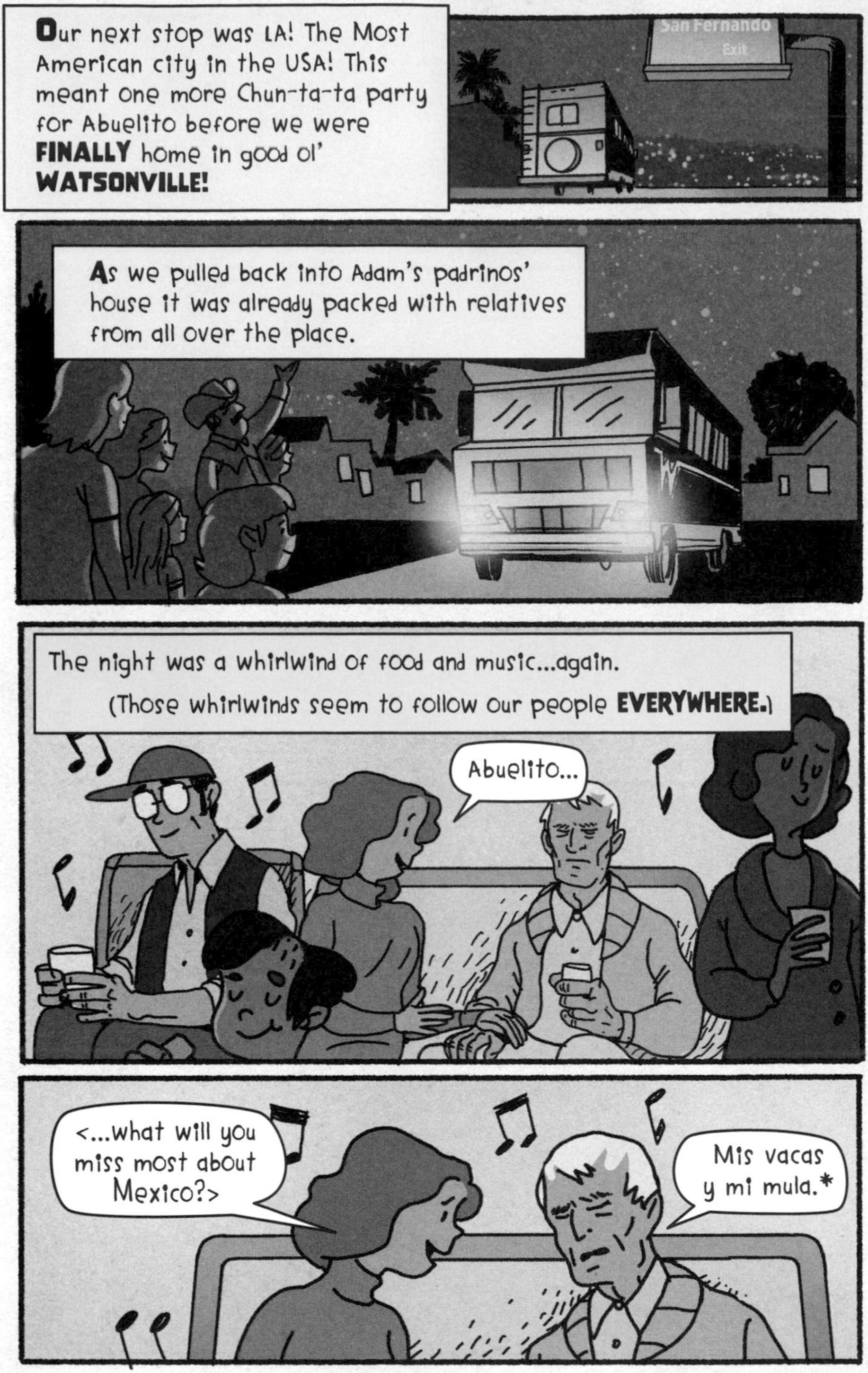
Our next stop was LA! The Most American city in the USA! This meant one more Chun-ta-ta party for Abuelito before we were FINALLY home in good ol' WATSONVILLE!
San Fernando
Exit
As we pulled back into Adam's padrinos' house it was already packed with relatives from all over the place.
The night was a whirlwind of food and music...again.
(Those whirlwinds seem to follow our people EVERYWHERE.)
Abuelito...
<...what will you miss most about Mexico?>
Mis vacas y mi mula.*

*My cows and my mule.

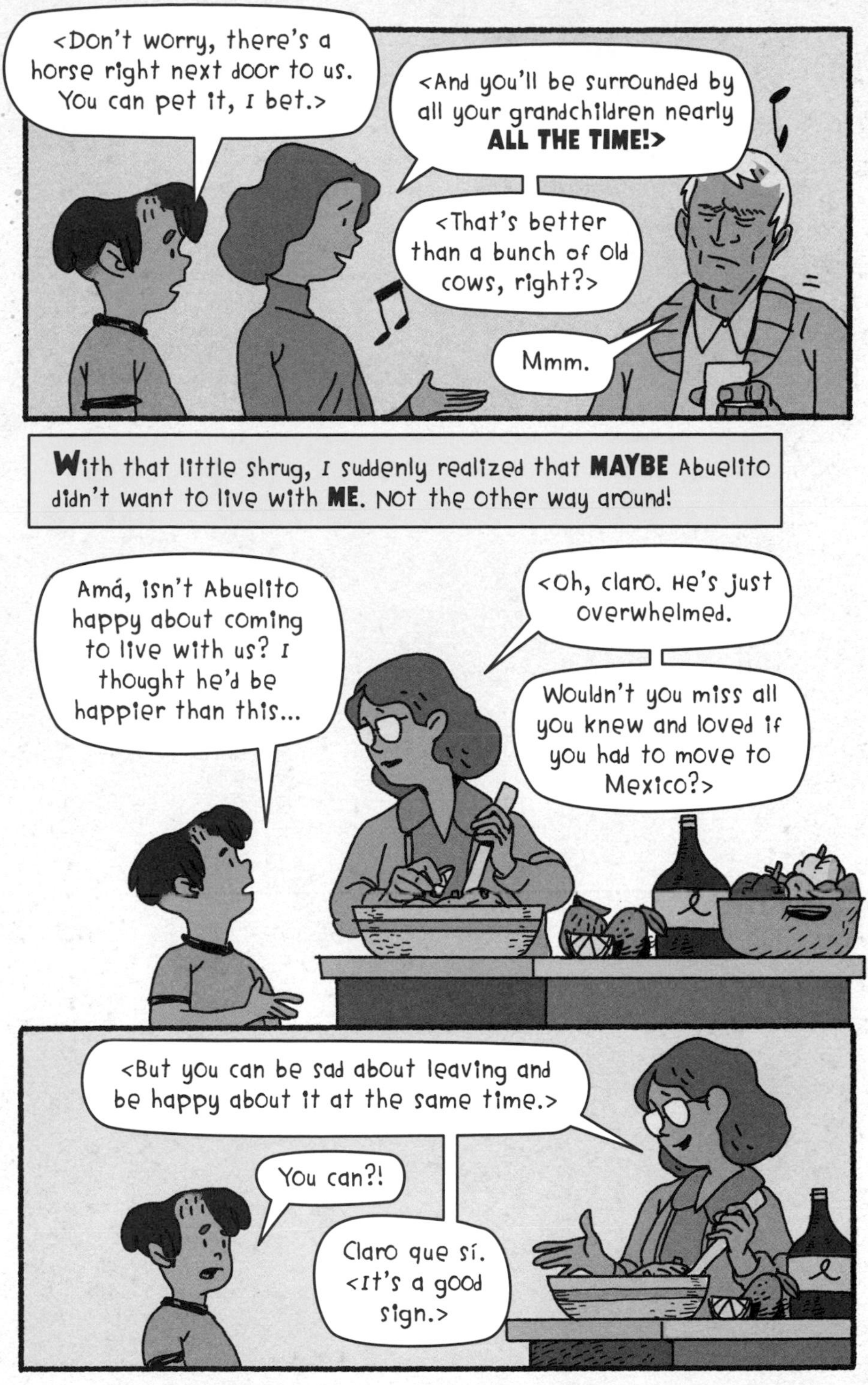
<Don't worry, there's a horse right next door to us. You can pet it, I bet.>
<And you'll be surrounded by all your grandchildren nearly **ALL THE TIME!**>
<That's better than a bunch of old cows, right?>
Mmm.
With that little shrug, I suddenly realized that **MAYBE** Abuelito didn't want to live with **ME**. Not the other way around!
Amá, isn't Abuelito happy about coming to live with us? I thought he'd be happier than this...
<Oh, claro. He's just overwhelmed.
Wouldn't you miss all you knew and loved if you had to move to Mexico?>
<But you can be sad about leaving and be happy about it at the same time.>
You can?!
Claro que sí. <It's a good sign.>

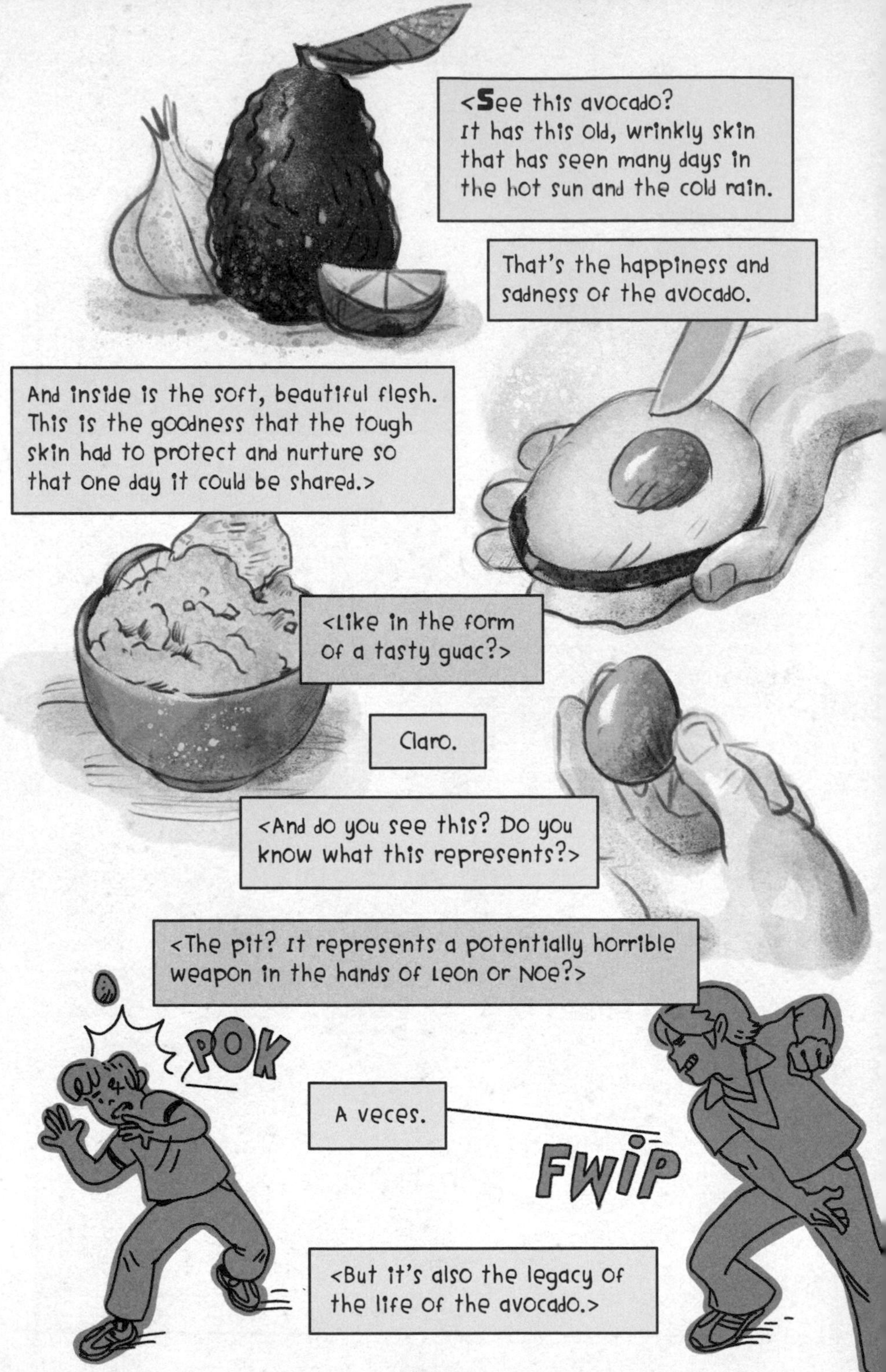
<See this avocado? It has this old, wrinkly skin that has seen many days in the hot sun and the cold rain.
That's the happiness and sadness of the avocado.
And inside is the soft, beautiful flesh. This is the goodness that the tough skin had to protect and nurture so that one day it could be shared.>
<Like in the form of a tasty guac?>
Claro.
<And do you see this? Do you know what this represents?>
<The pit? It represents a potentially horrible weapon in the hands of Leon or Noe?>
POK
A veces.
FWIP
<But it's also the legacy of the life of the avocado.>

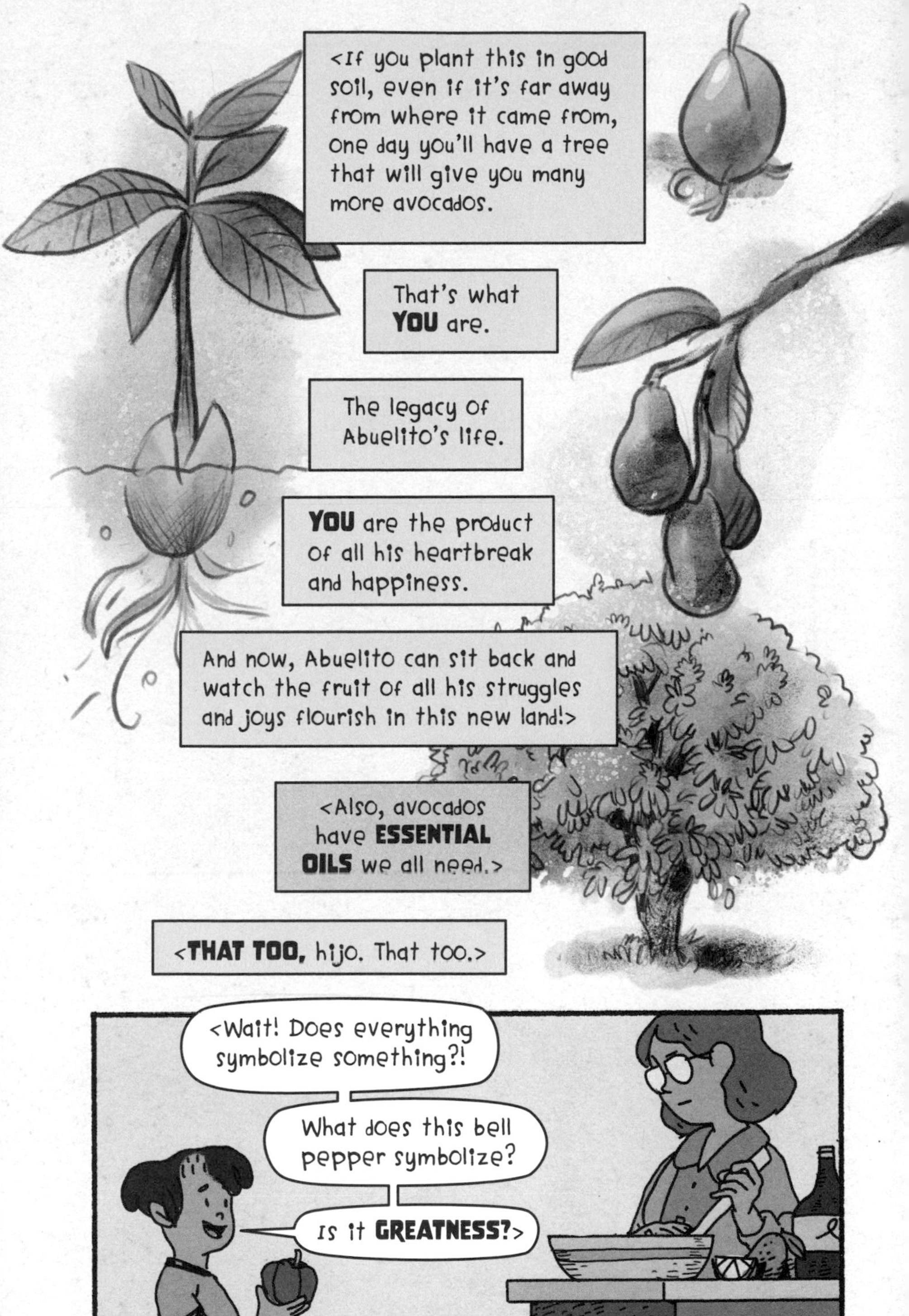
<If you plant this in good soil, even if it's far away from where it came from, one day you'll have a tree that will give you many more avocados.
That's what **YOU** are.
The legacy of Abuelito's life.
YOU are the product of all his heartbreak and happiness.
And now, Abuelito can sit back and watch the fruit of all his struggles and joys flourish in this new land!>
<Also, avocados have **ESSENTIAL OILS** we all need.>
<**THAT TOO,** hijo. That too.>
<Wait! Does everything symbolize something?!
What does this bell pepper symbolize?
Is it **GREATNESS?**>

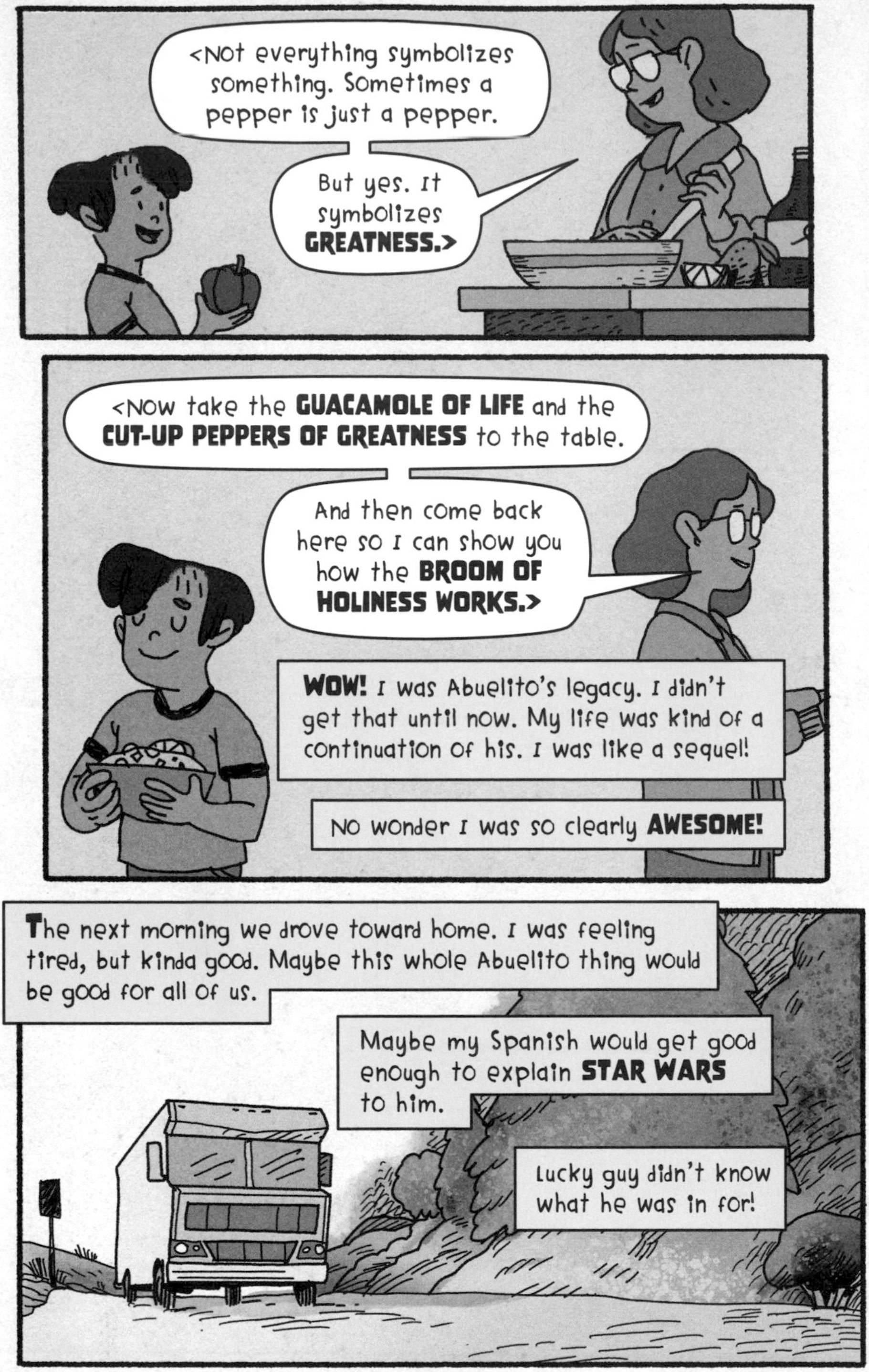

<Not everything symbolizes something. Sometimes a pepper is just a pepper.
But yes. It symbolizes **GREATNESS.>**
<Now take the **GUACAMOLE OF LIFE** and the **CUT-UP PEPPERS OF GREATNESS** to the table.
And then come back here so I can show you how the **BROOM OF HOLINESS WORKS.>**
WOW! I was Abuelito's legacy. I didn't get that until now. My life was kind of a continuation of his. I was like a sequel!
No wonder I was so clearly **AWESOME!**
The next morning we drove toward home. I was feeling tired, but kinda good. Maybe this whole Abuelito thing would be good for all of us.
Maybe my Spanish would get good enough to explain **STAR WARS** to him.
Lucky guy didn't know what he was in for!

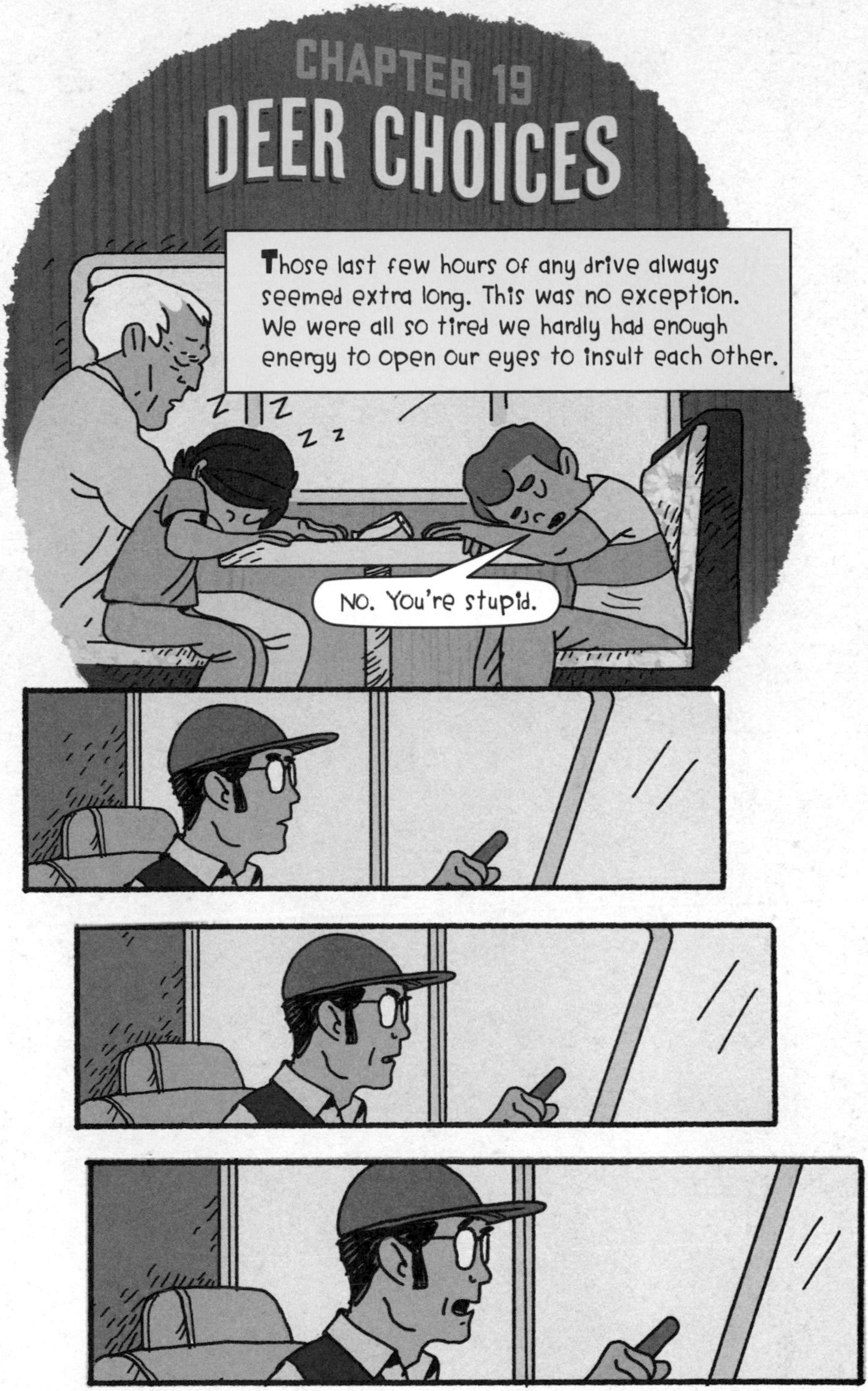
CHAPTER 19
DEER CHOICES
Those last few hours of any drive always seemed extra long. This was no exception. We were all so tired we hardly had enough energy to open our eyes to insult each other.
Z Z
Z Z
NO. You're stupid.

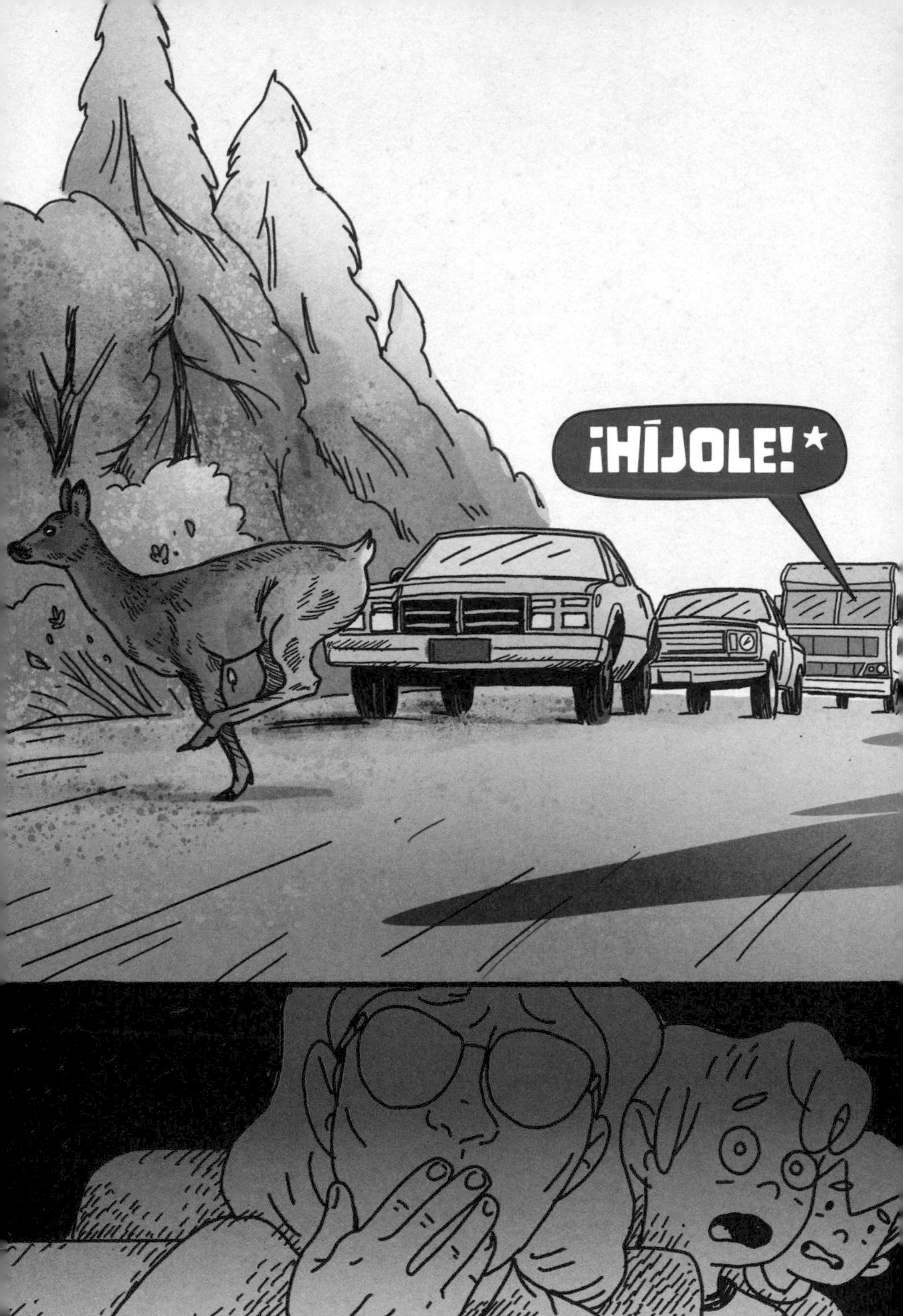
¡HÍJOLE!*

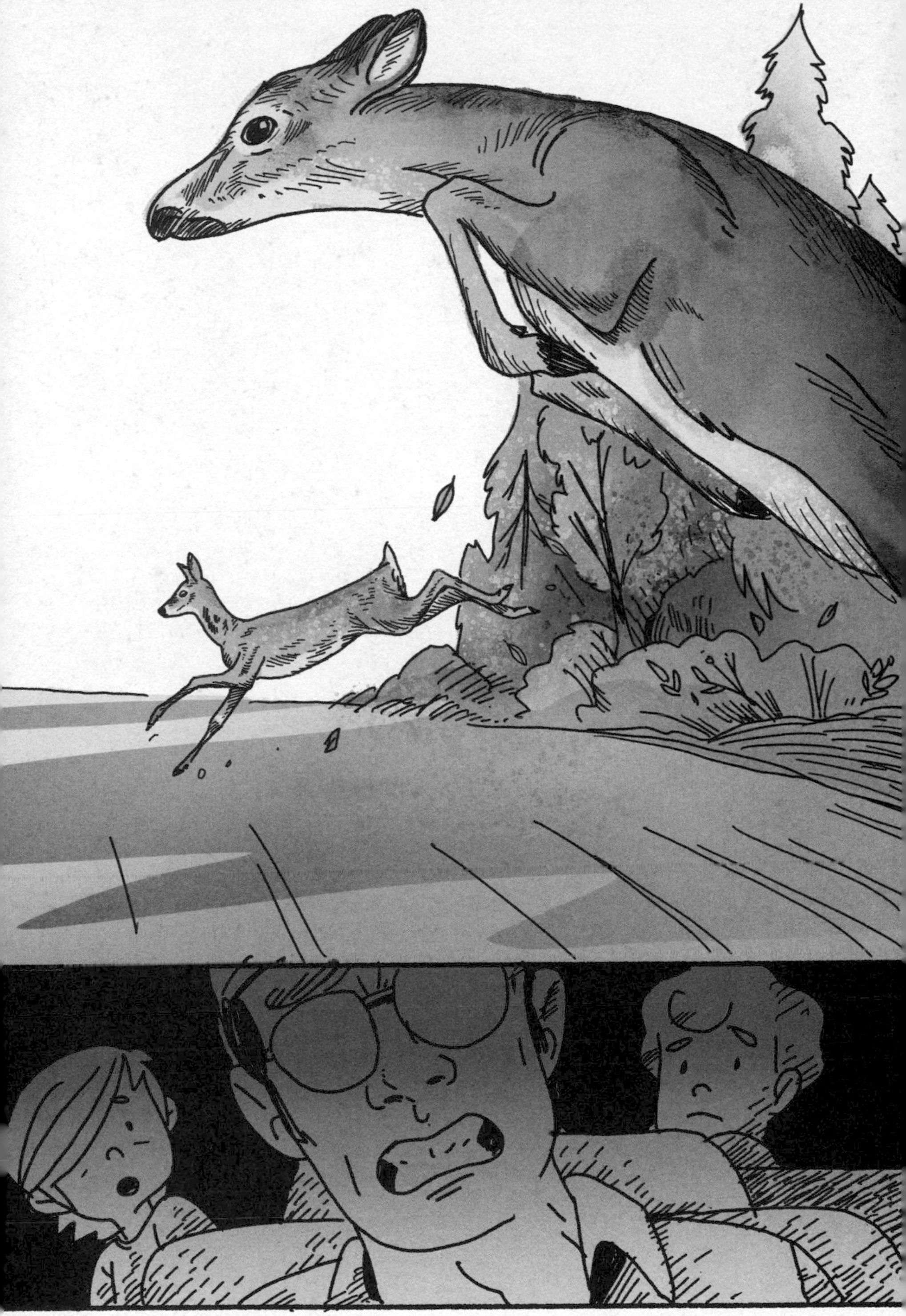

*Holy smokes!

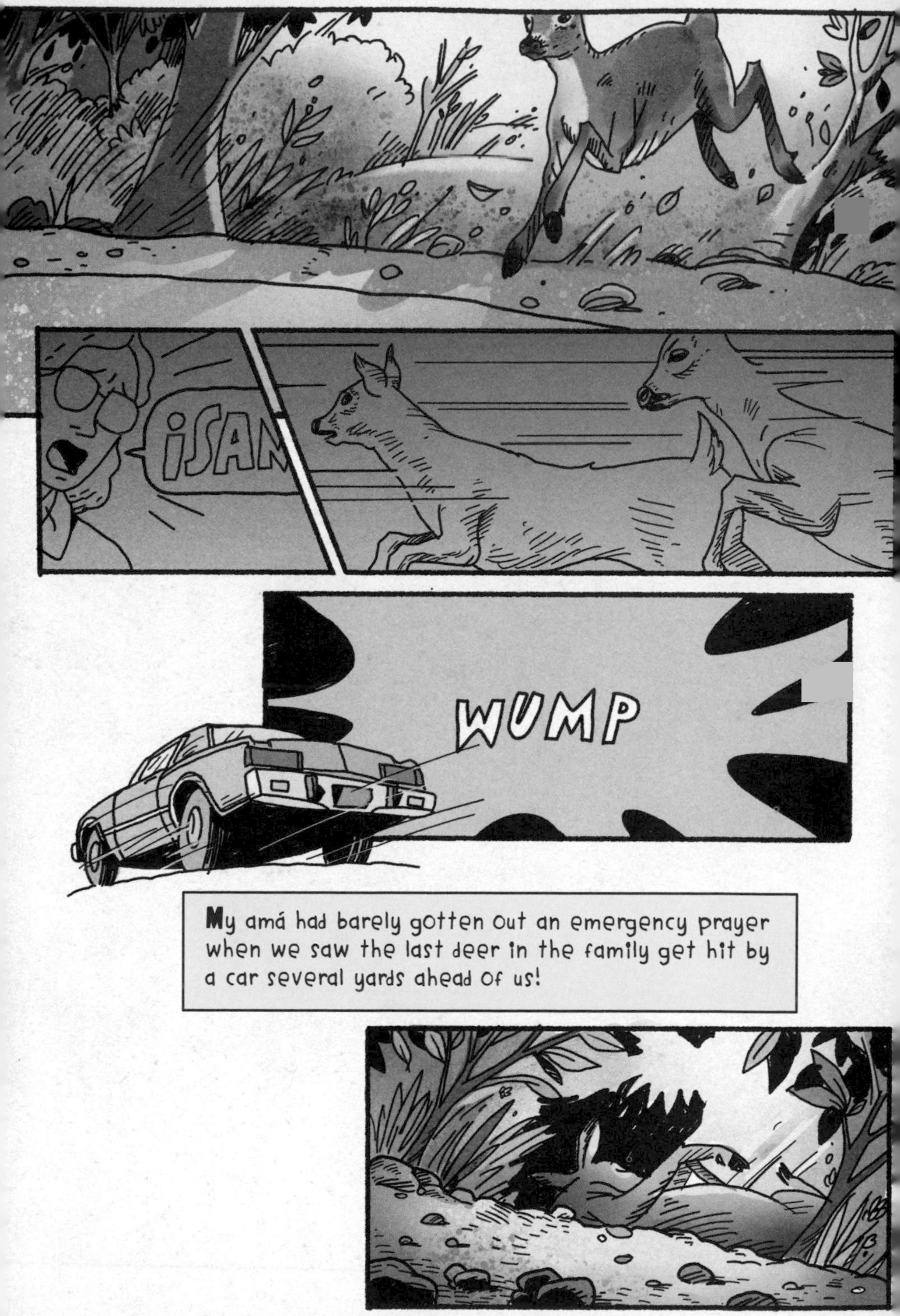
¡SAN
WUMP
My amá had barely gotten out an emergency prayer when we saw the last deer in the family get hit by a car several yards ahead of us!

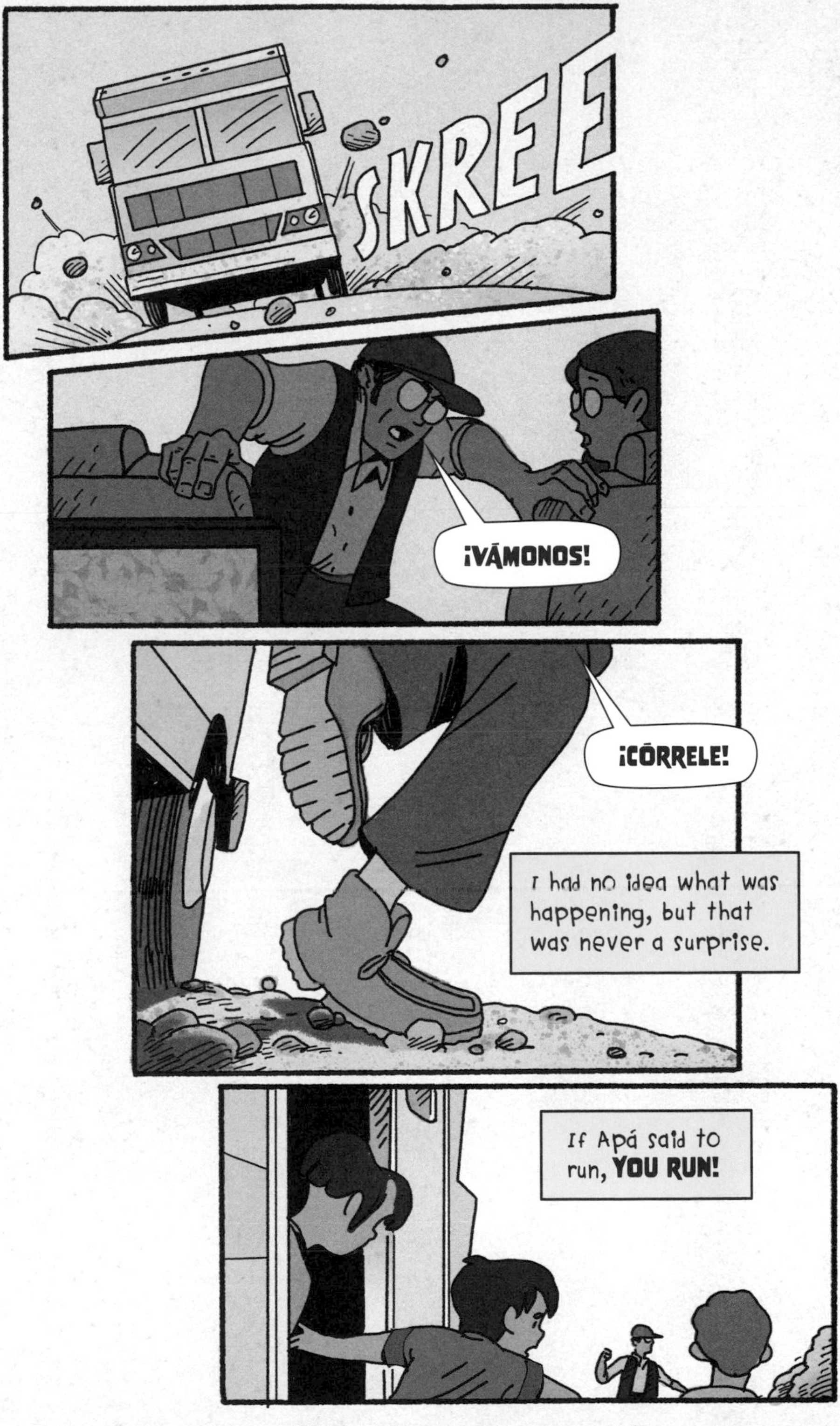
SKREE
¡VÁMONOS!
¡CÓRRELE!
I had no idea what was happening, but that was never a surprise.
If Apá said to run, **YOU RUN!**

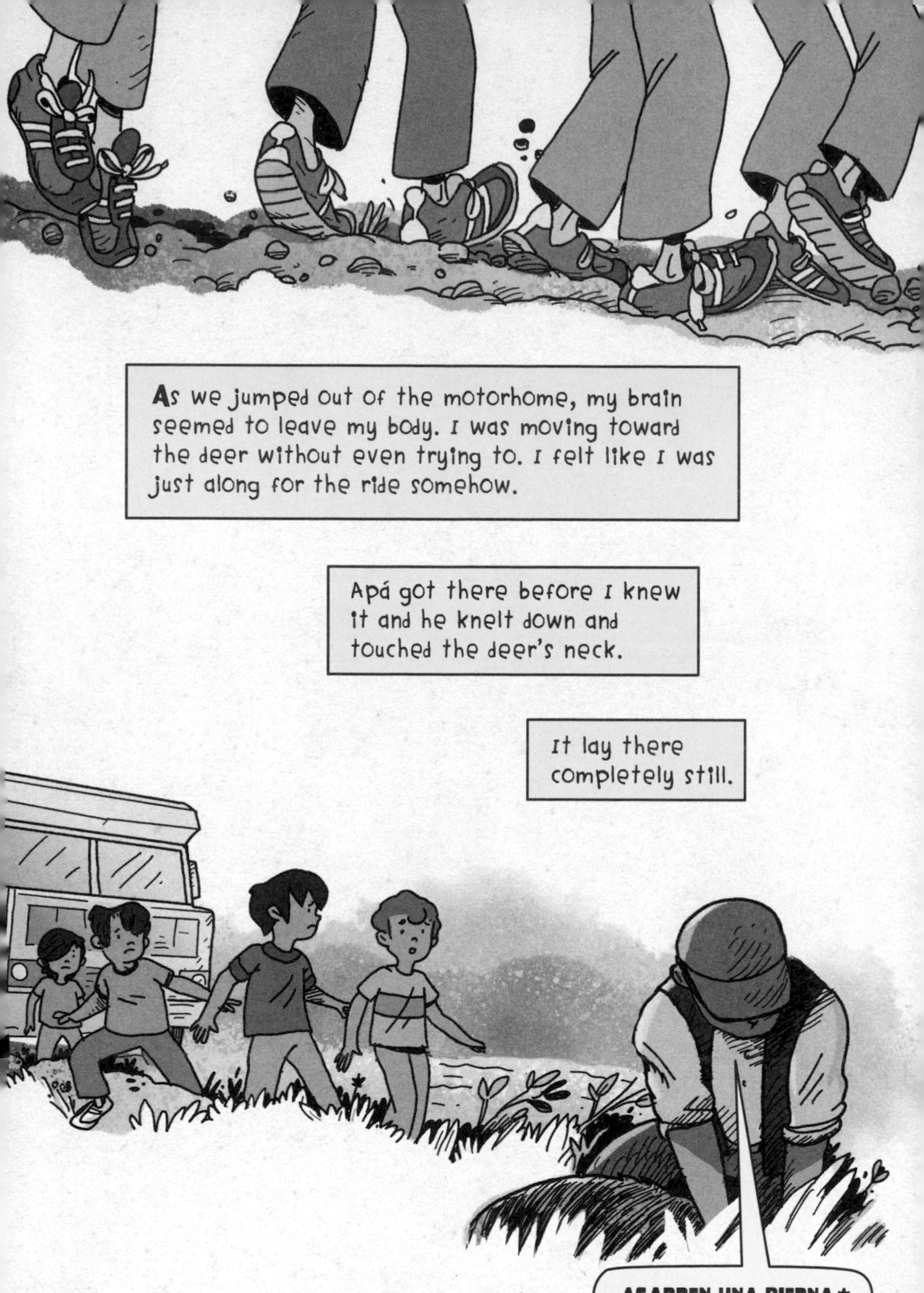

As we jumped out of the motorhome, my brain seemed to leave my body. I was moving toward the deer without even trying to. I felt like I was just along for the ride somehow.
Apá got there before I knew it and he knelt down and touched the deer's neck.
It lay there completely still.
AGARREN UNA PIERNA.*

*Grab a leg.

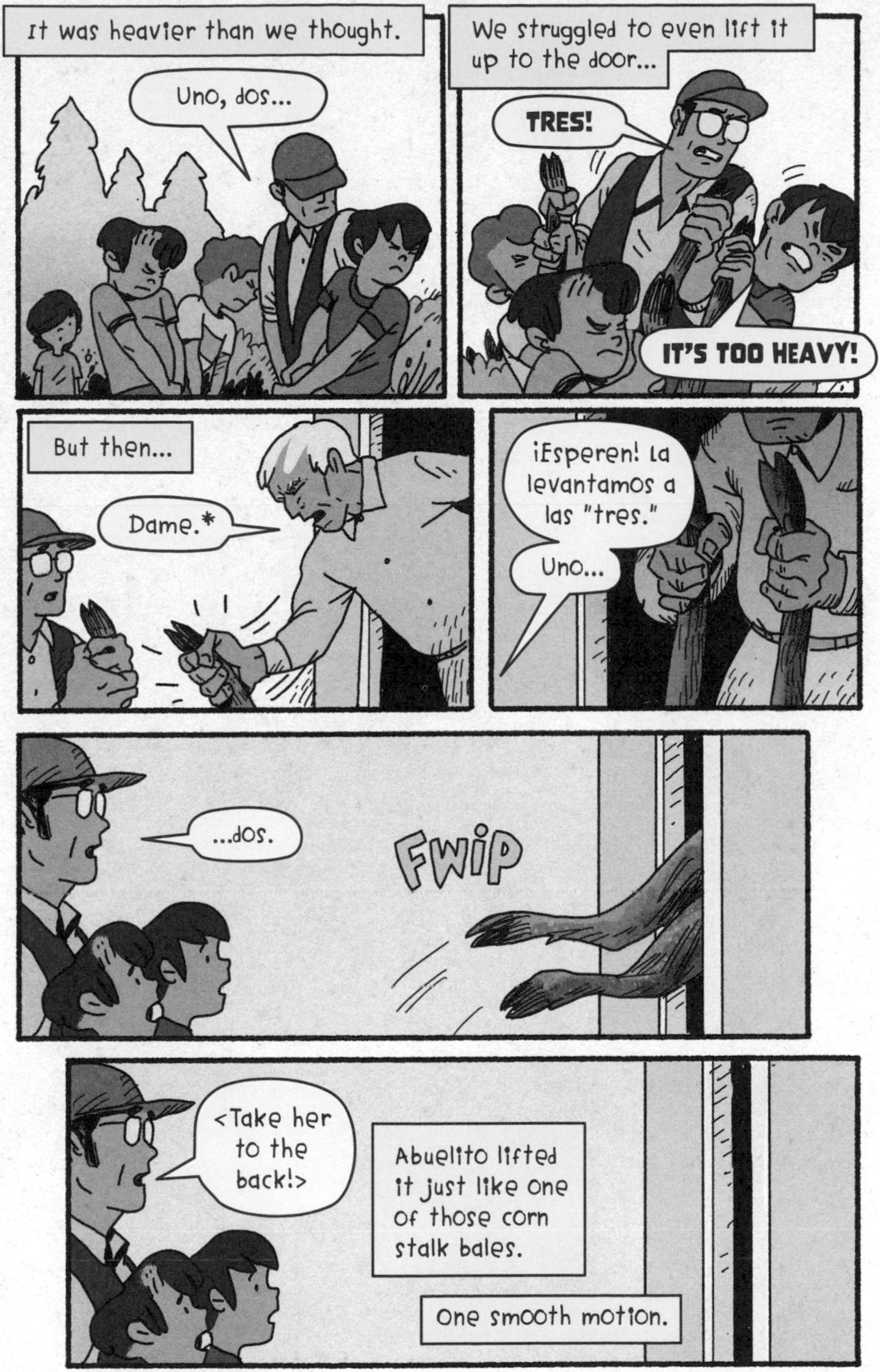

It was heavier than we thought.
Uno, dos...
We struggled to even lift it up to the door...
TRES!
IT'S TOO HEAVY!
But then...
Dame.*
¡Esperen! La levantamos a las "tres."
Uno...
...dos.
FWIP
<Take her to the back!>
Abuelito lifted it just like one of those corn stalk bales.
One smooth motion.

*Give me that.

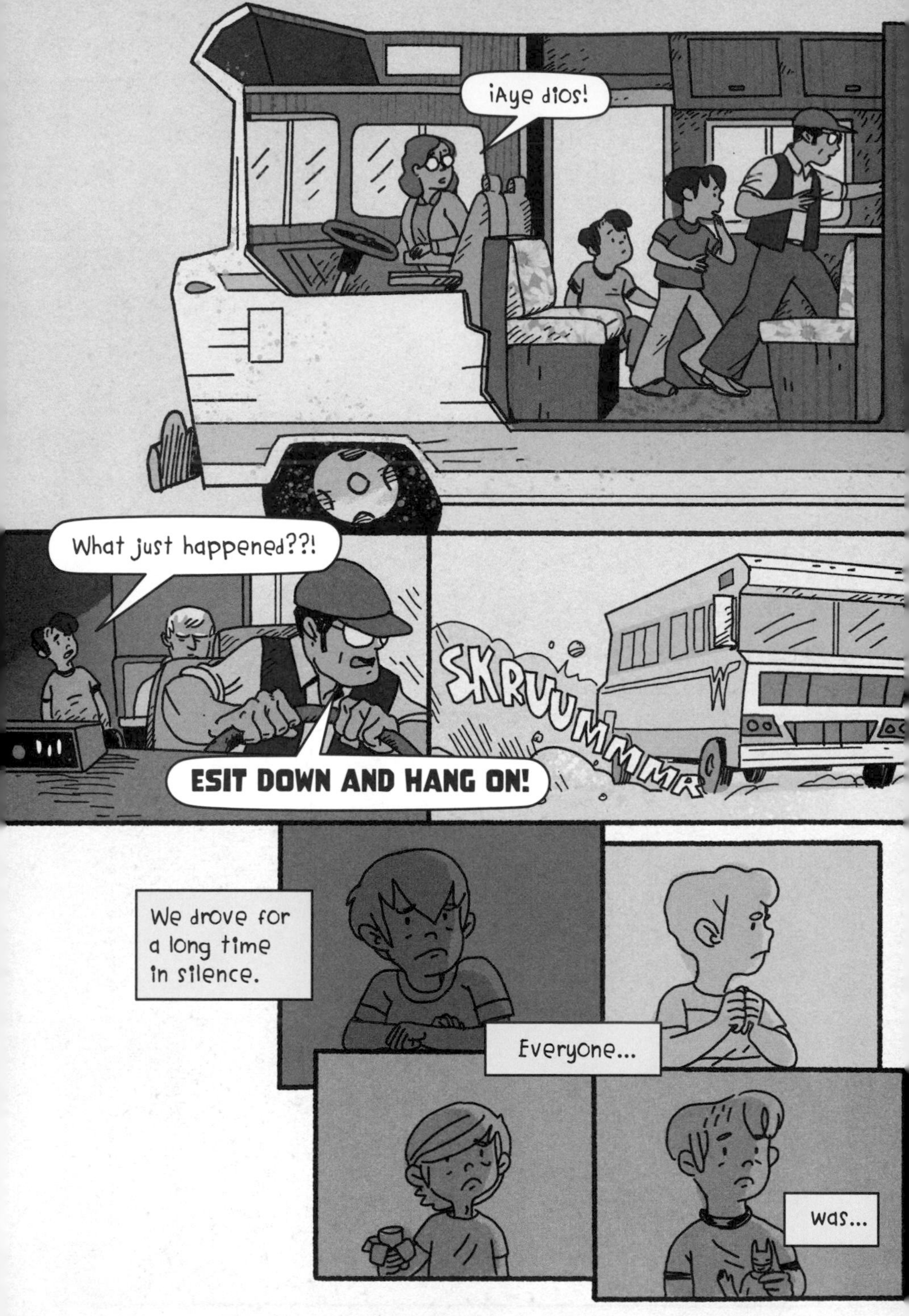
¡Aye dios!
What just happened??!
ESIT DOWN AND HANG ON!
SKRUUUMMMMR
We drove for a long time in silence.
Everyone...
was...

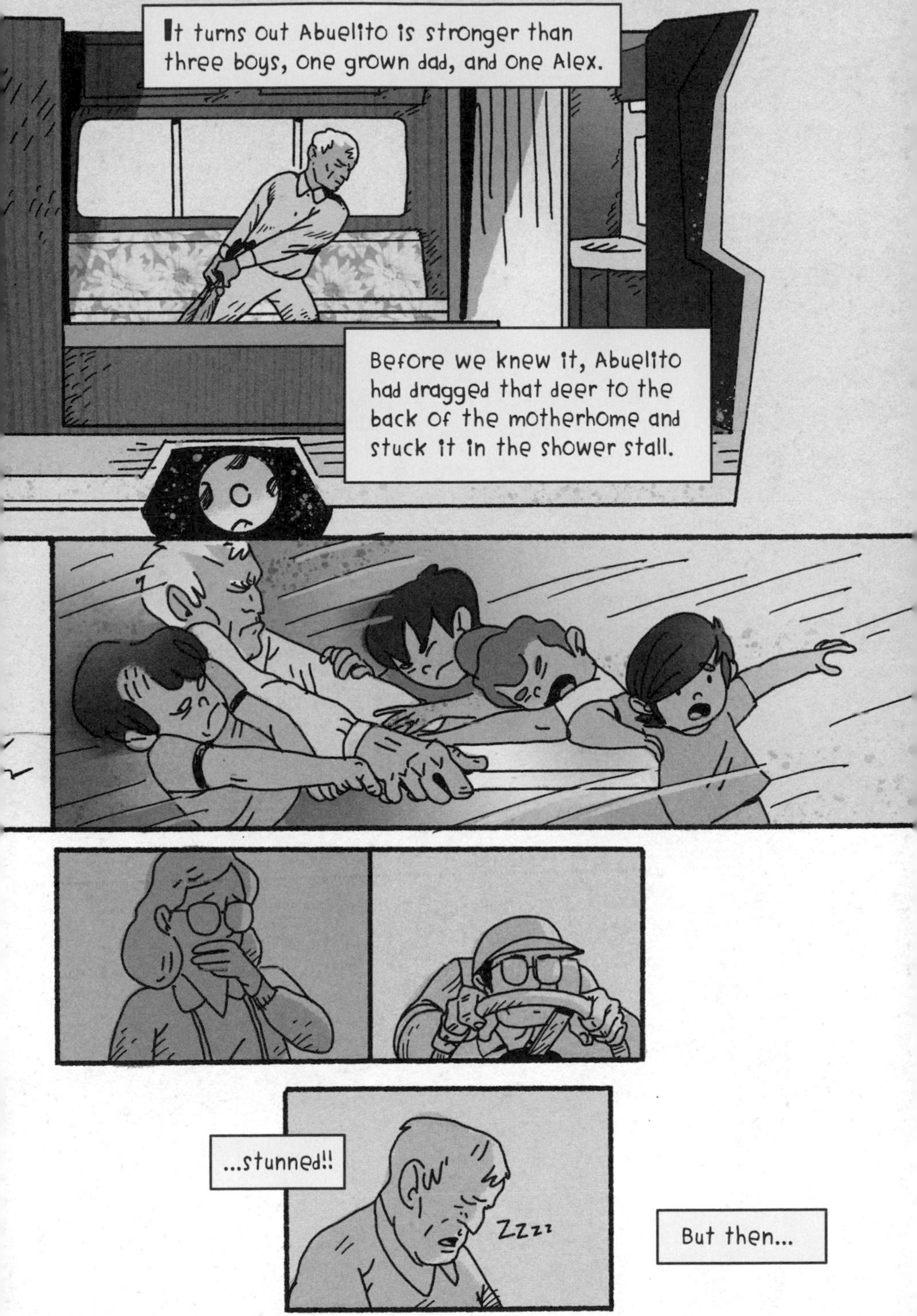
It turns out Abuelito is stronger than three boys, one grown dad, and one Alex.
Before we knew it, Abuelito had dragged that deer to the back of the motherhome and stuck it in the shower stall.
...stunned!!
ZZzz
But then...

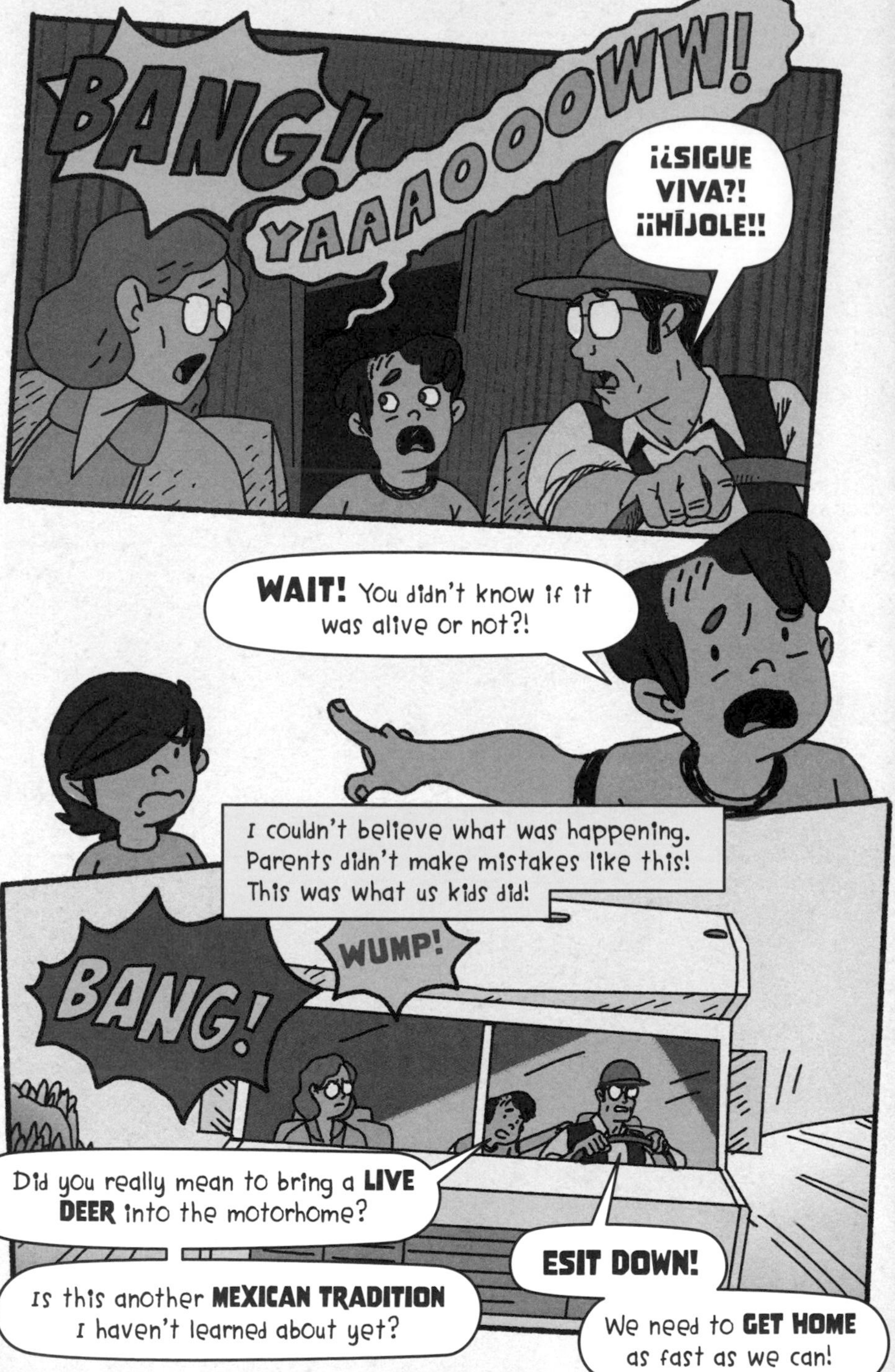
BANG!
YAAAOOOOWW!
¡¿SIGUE VIVA?! ¡¡HÍJOLE!!
WAIT! You didn't know if it was alive or not?!
I couldn't believe what was happening. Parents didn't make mistakes like this! This was what us kids did!
BANG!
WUMP!
Did you really mean to bring a LIVE DEER into the motorhome?
Is this another MEXICAN TRADITION I haven't learned about yet?
¡SIT DOWN!
We need to GET HOME as fast as we can!

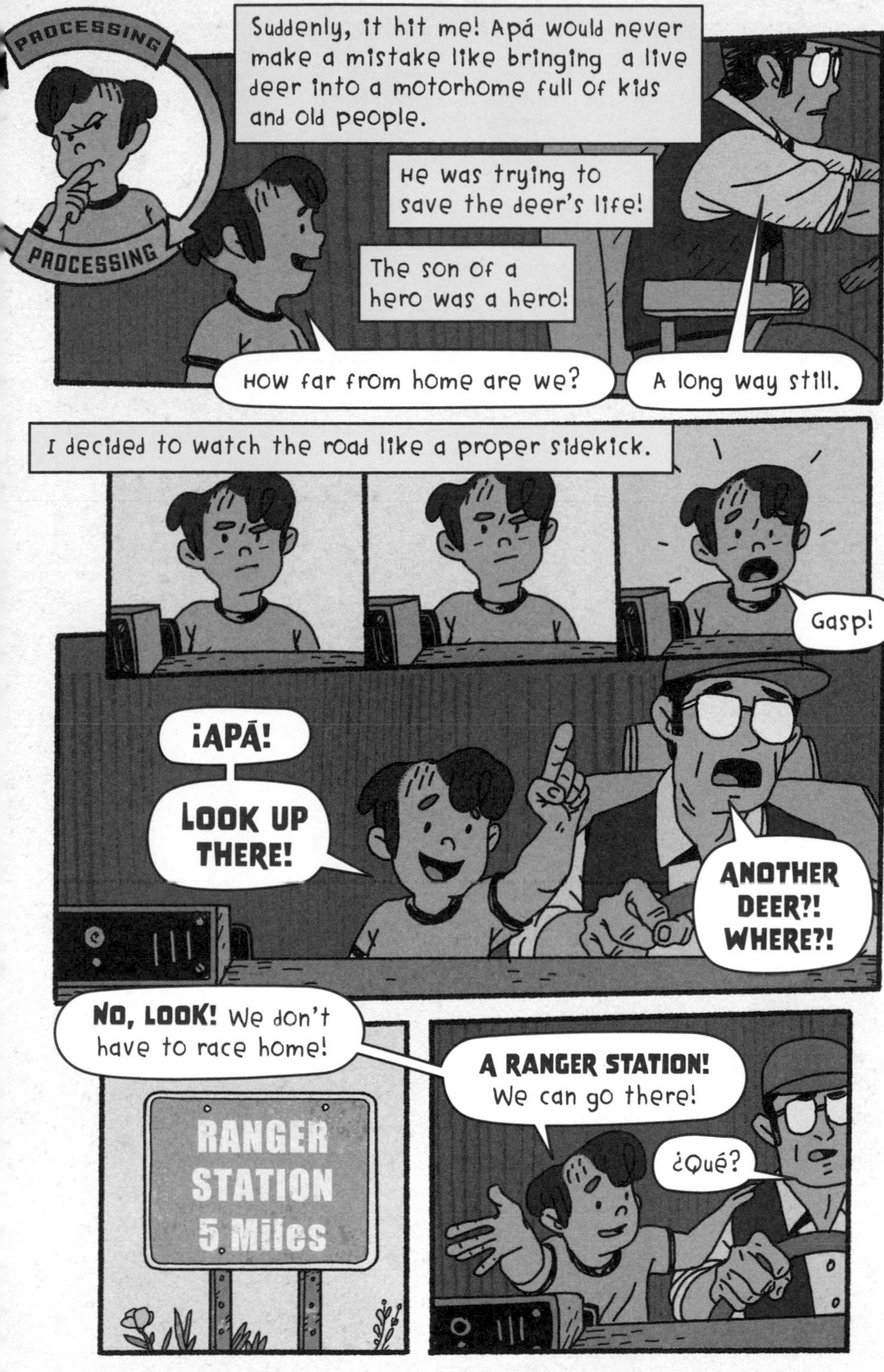
PROCESSING
PROCESSING
Suddenly, it hit me! Apá would never make a mistake like bringing a live deer into a motorhome full of kids and old people.
He was trying to save the deer's life!
The son of a hero was a hero!
How far from home are we?
A long way still.
I decided to watch the road like a proper sidekick.
Gasp!
¡APÁ!
LOOK UP THERE!
ANOTHER DEER?! WHERE?!
NO, LOOK! We don't have to race home!
RANGER STATION 5 Miles
A RANGER STATION! We can go there!
¿Qué?

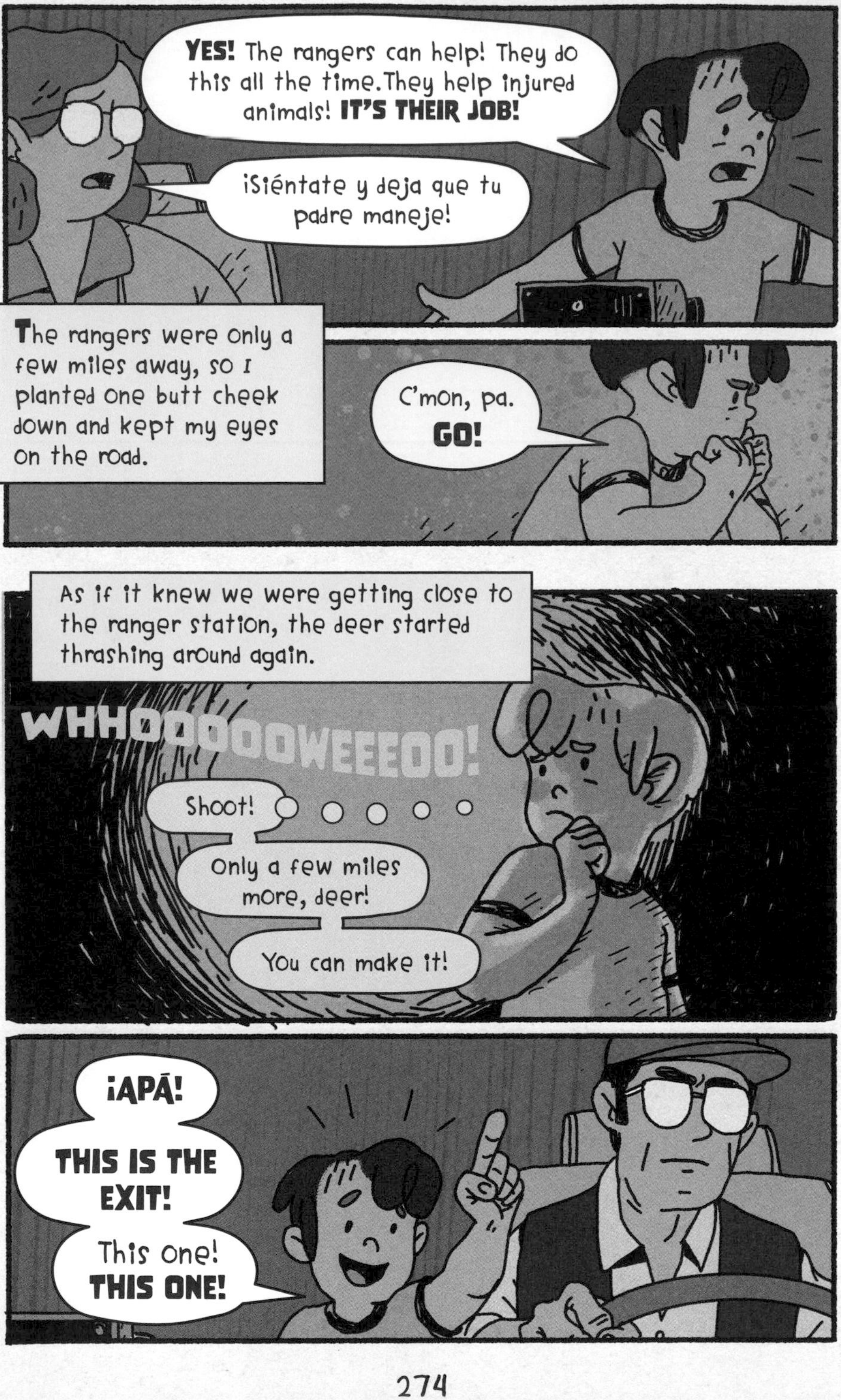
YES! The rangers can help! They do this all the time. They help injured animals! **IT'S THEIR JOB!**
¡Siéntate y deja que tu padre maneje!
The rangers were only a few miles away, so I planted one butt cheek down and kept my eyes on the road.
C'mon, pa. **GO!**
As if it knew we were getting close to the ranger station, the deer started thrashing around again.
WHHOOOOOWEEEOO!
Shoot!
Only a few miles more, deer!
You can make it!
¡APÁ!
THIS IS THE EXIT!
This one! **THIS ONE!**

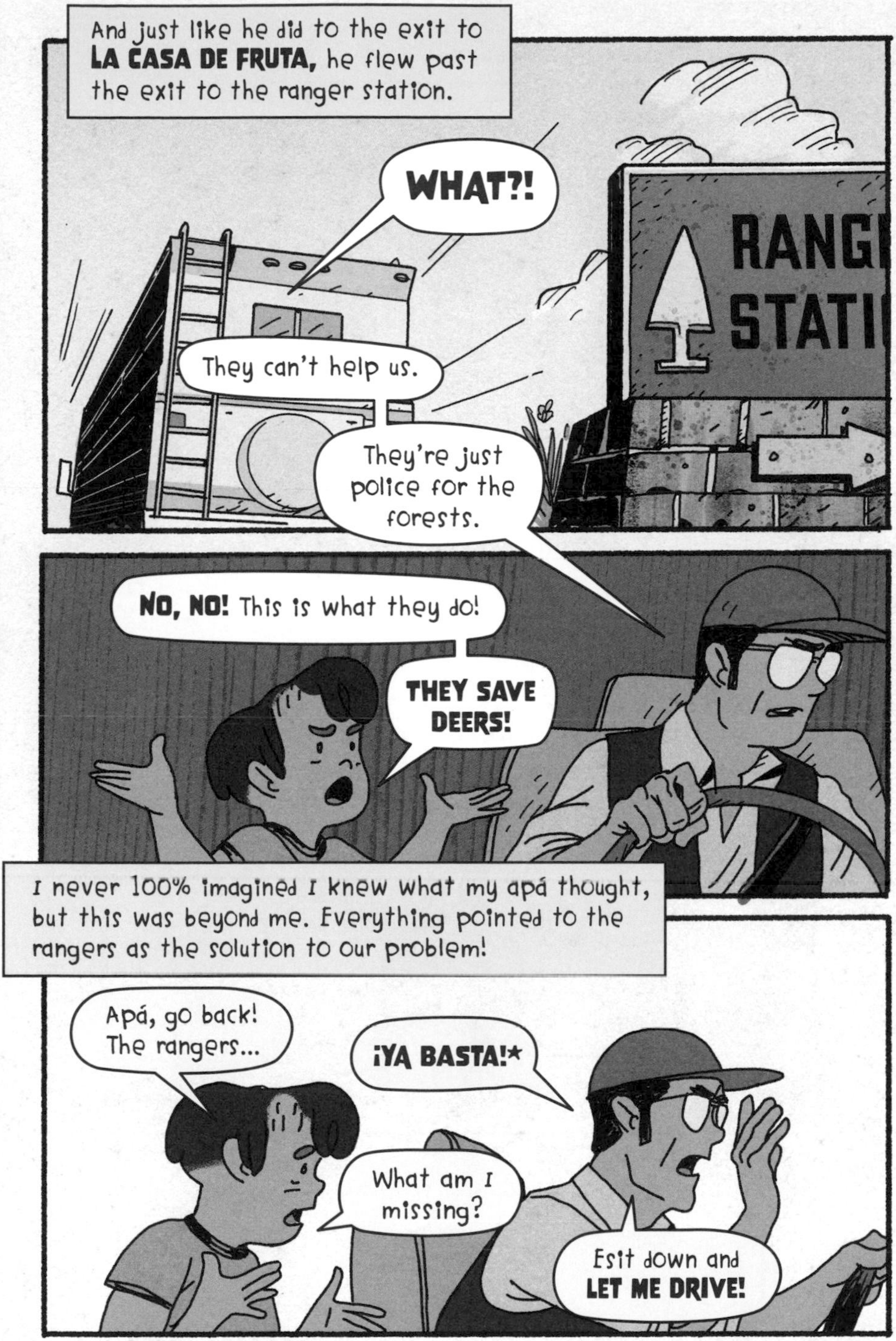

And just like he did to the exit to **LA CASA DE FRUTA,** he flew past the exit to the ranger station.
WHAT?!
RANGE
STATI
They can't help us.
They're just police for the forests.
NO, NO! This is what they do!
THEY SAVE DEERS!
I never 100% imagined I knew what my apá thought, but this was beyond me. Everything pointed to the rangers as the solution to our problem!
Apá, go back! The rangers...
¡YA BASTA!*
What am I missing?
Esit down and **LET ME DRIVE!**

*Enough!

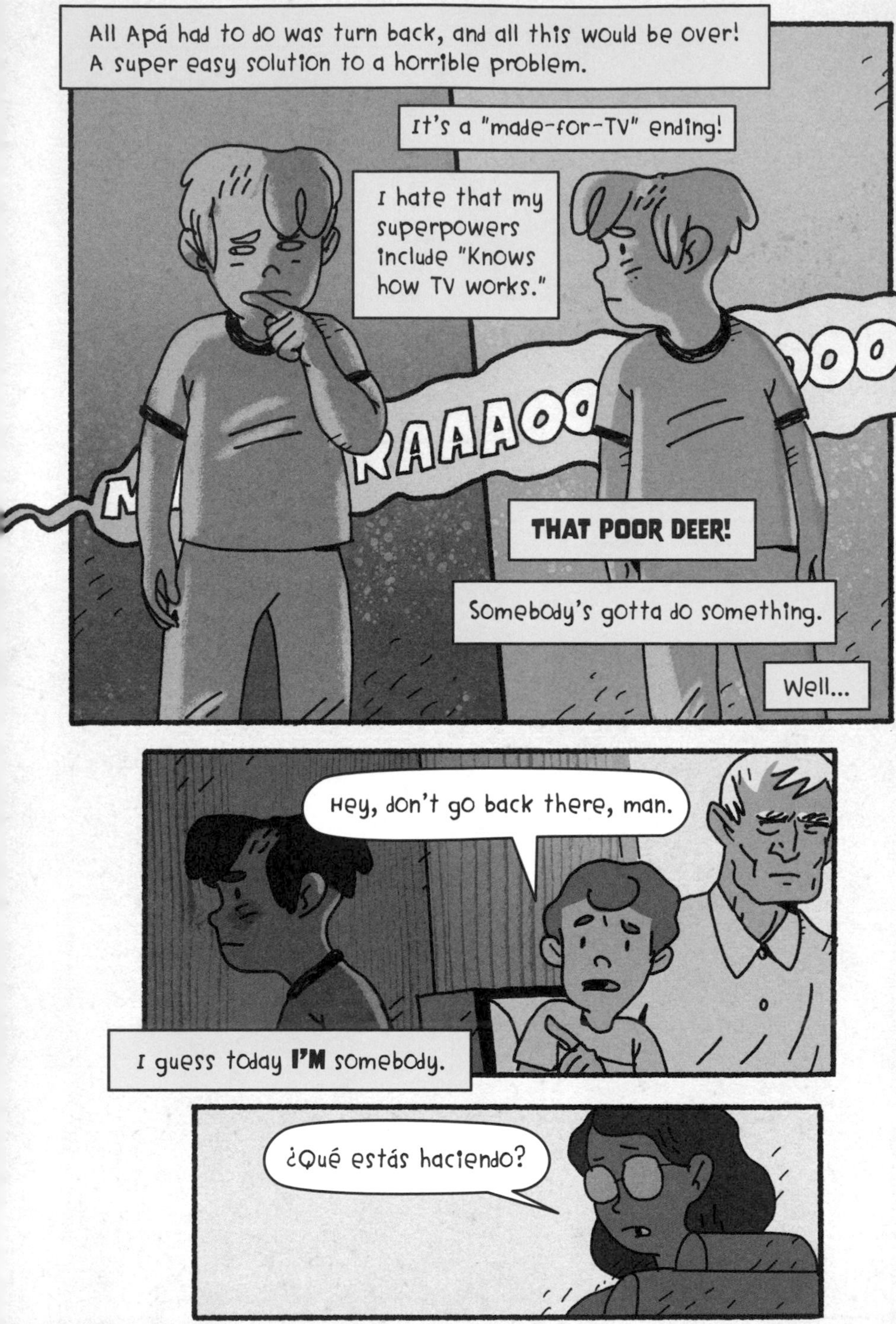
All Apá had to do was turn back, and all this would be over! A super easy solution to a horrible problem.
It's a "made-for-TV" ending!
I hate that my superpowers include "Knows how TV works."
M... RAAAOO... OOO!
THAT POOR DEER!
Somebody's gotta do something.
Well...
Hey, don't go back there, man.
I guess today **I'M** somebody.
¿Qué estás haciendo?

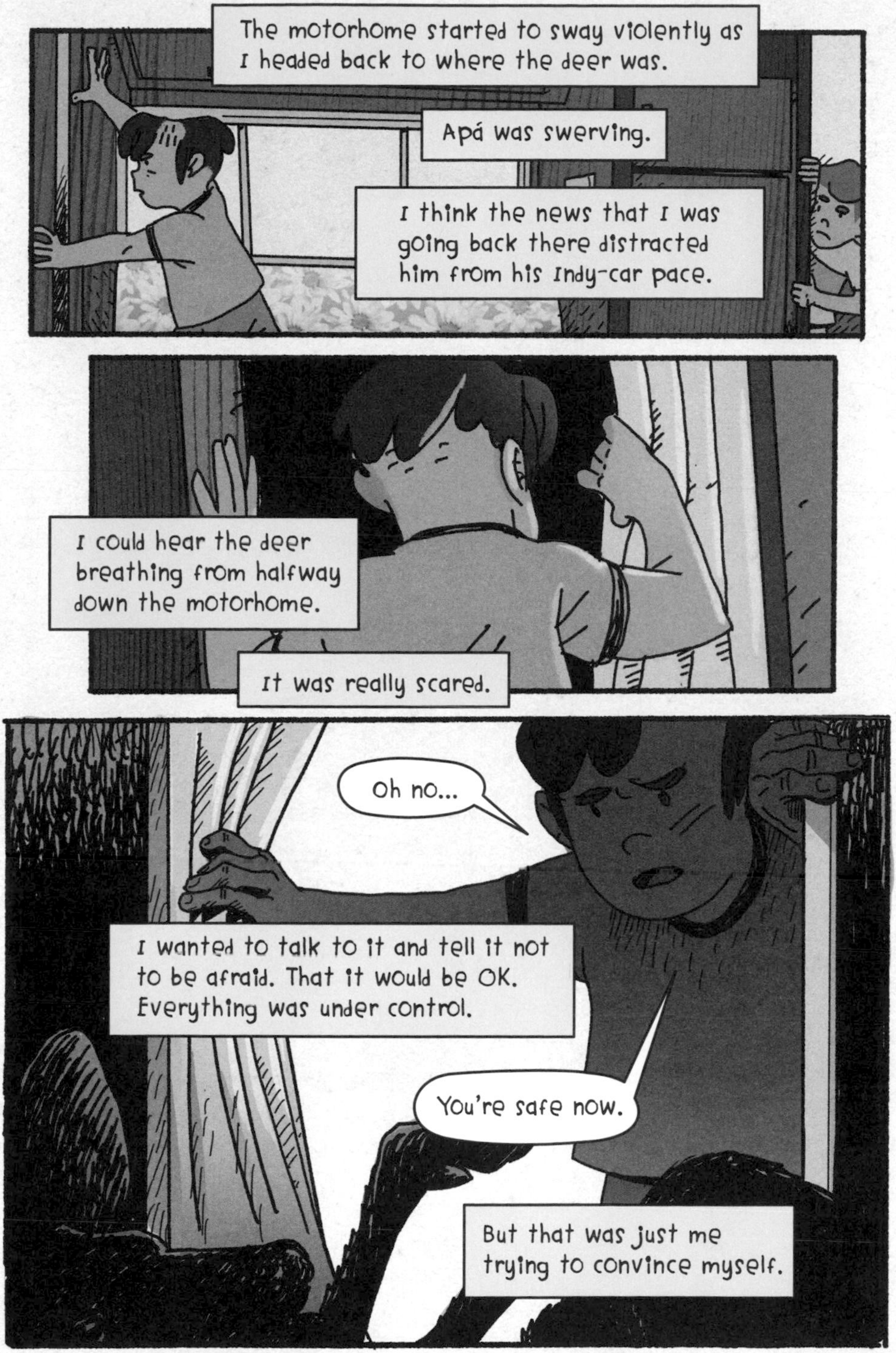
The motorhome started to sway violently as I headed back to where the deer was.
Apá was swerving.
I think the news that I was going back there distracted him from his Indy-car pace.
I could hear the deer breathing from halfway down the motorhome.
It was really scared.
Oh no...
I wanted to talk to it and tell it not to be afraid. That it would be OK. Everything was under control.
You're safe now.
But that was just me trying to convince myself.

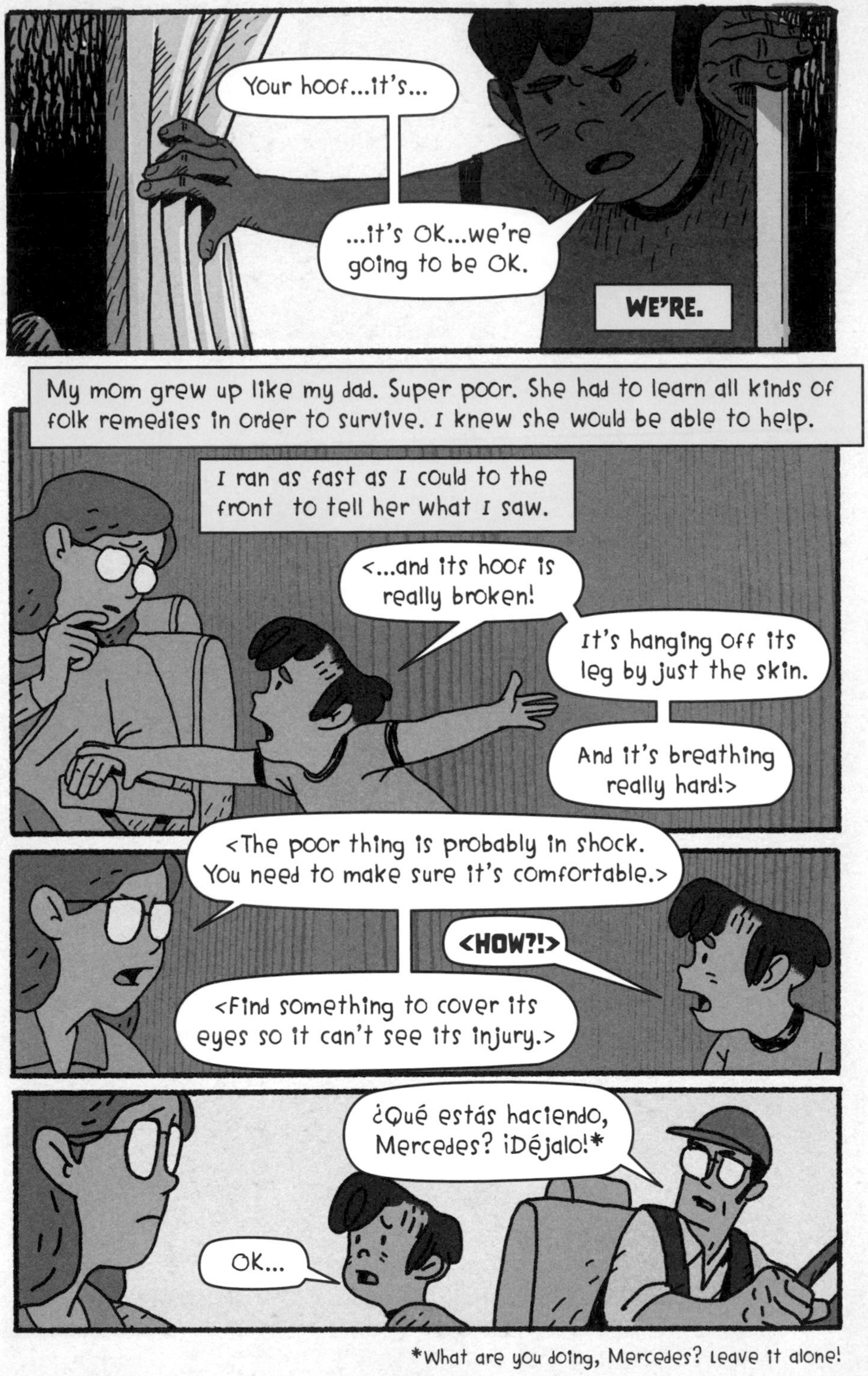
Your hoof...it's...
...it's OK...we're going to be OK.
WE'RE.
My mom grew up like my dad. Super poor. She had to learn all kinds of folk remedies in order to survive. I knew she would be able to help.
I ran as fast as I could to the front to tell her what I saw.
<...and its hoof is really broken!
It's hanging off its leg by just the skin.
And it's breathing really hard!>
<The poor thing is probably in shock. You need to make sure it's comfortable.>
<HOW?!>
<Find something to cover its eyes so it can't see its injury.>
¿Qué estás haciendo, Mercedes? ¡Déjalo!*
OK...

*What are you doing, Mercedes? Leave it alone!

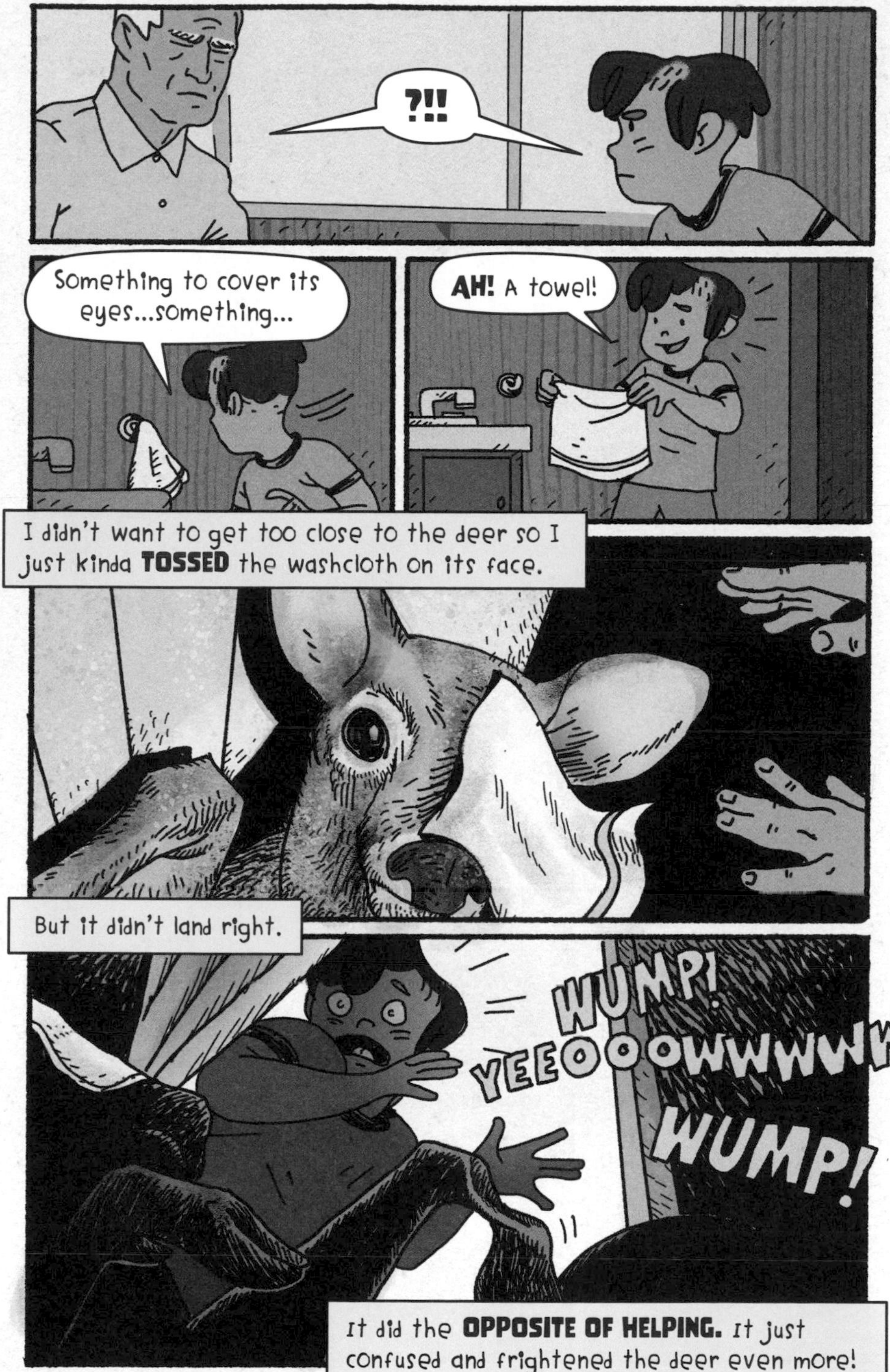
?!!
Something to cover its eyes...something...
AH! A towel!
I didn't want to get too close to the deer so I just kinda TOSSED the washcloth on its face.
But it didn't land right.
WUMP!
YEEOOOOWWWWWN!
WUMP!
It did the OPPOSITE OF HELPING. It just confused and frightened the deer even more!

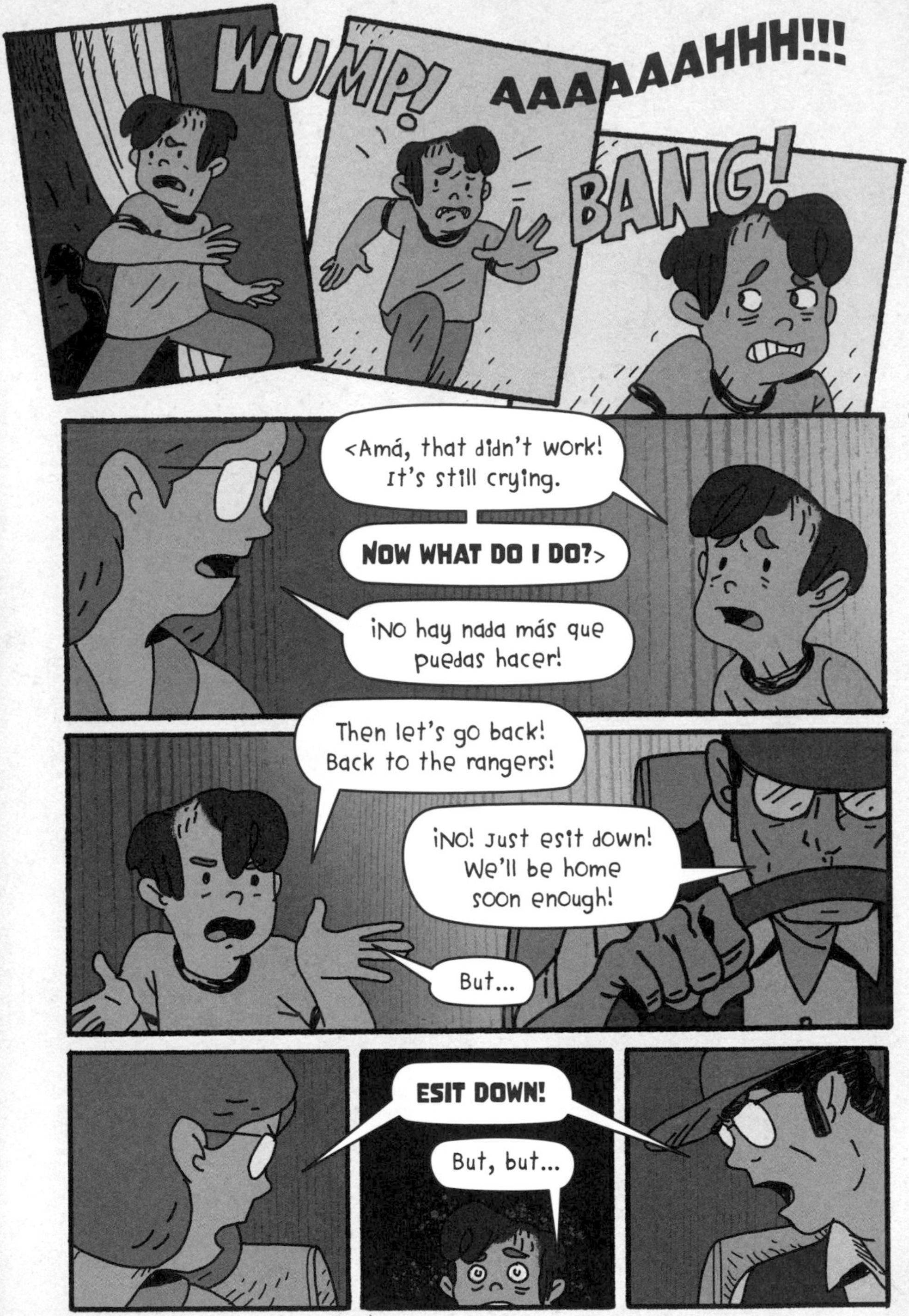
WUMP!
AAAAAAHHH!!!
BANG!
<Amá, that didn't work! It's still crying.
NOW WHAT DO I DO?>
¡No hay nada más que puedas hacer!
Then let's go back! Back to the rangers!
¡No! Just esit down! We'll be home soon enough!
But...
ESIT DOWN!
But, but...

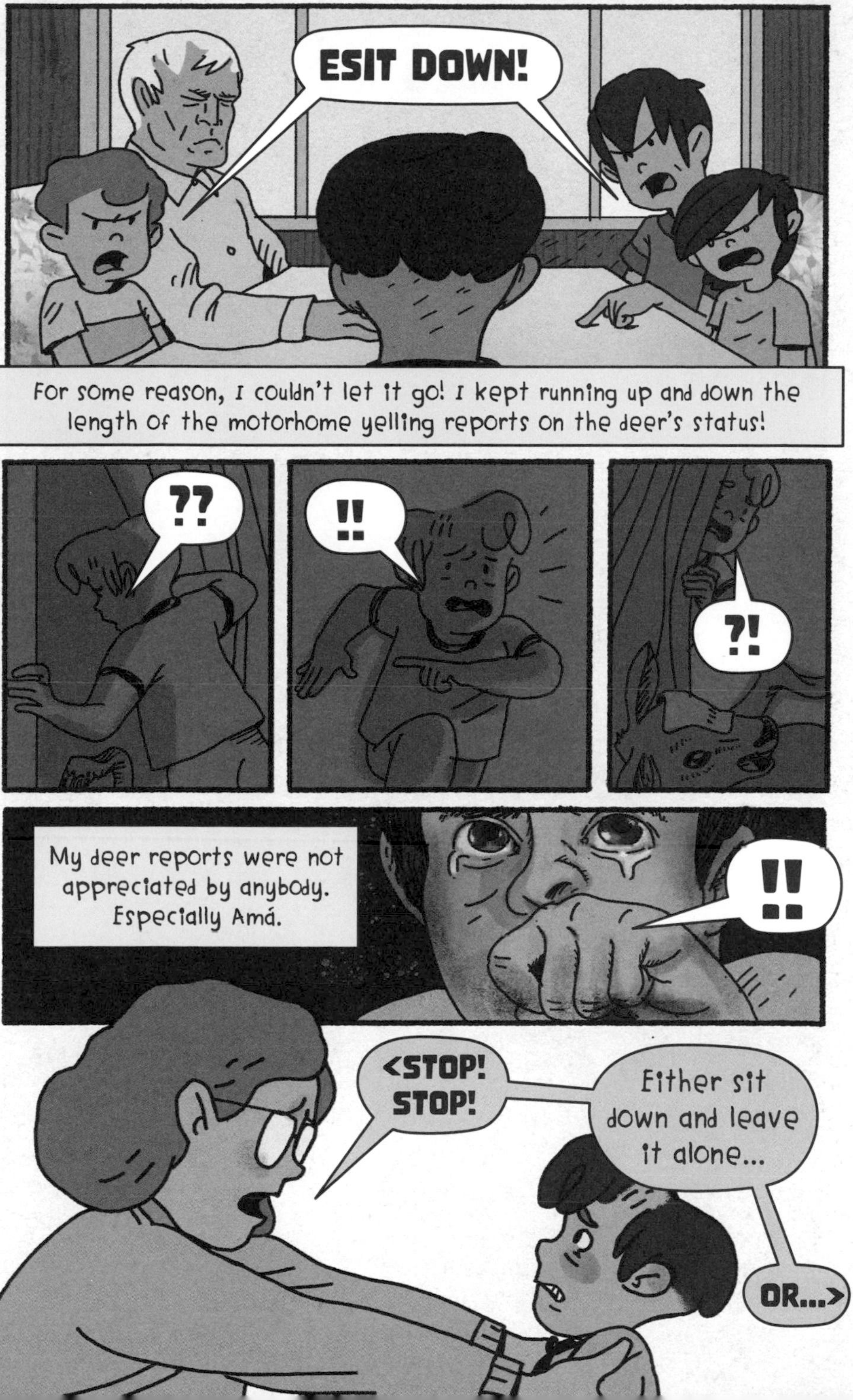
ESIT DOWN!
For some reason, I couldn't let it go! I kept running up and down the length of the motorhome yelling reports on the deer's status!
??
!!
?!
My deer reports were not appreciated by anybody. Especially Amá.
!!
<STOP! STOP!
Either sit down and leave it alone...
OR...>

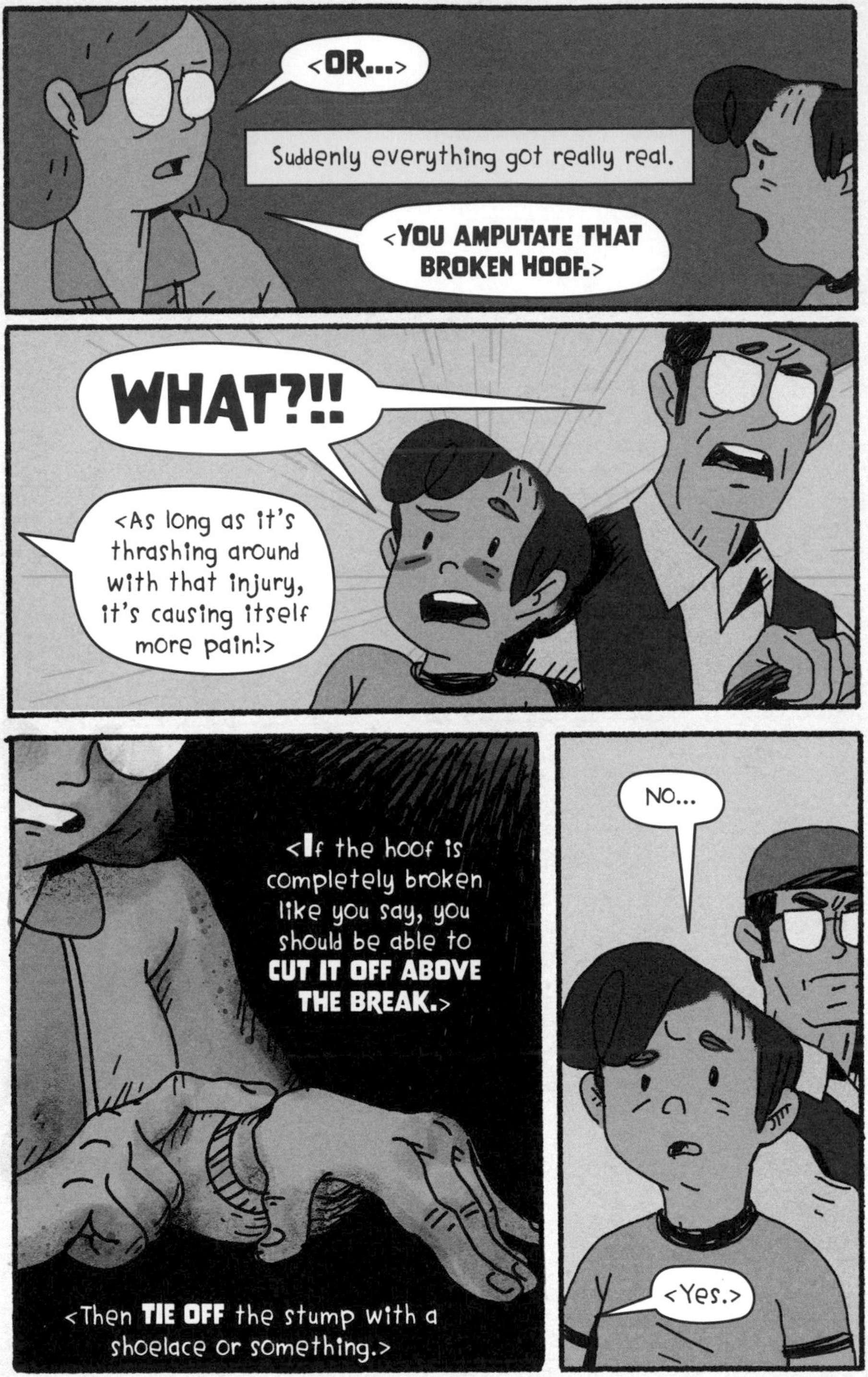

<OR...>
Suddenly everything got really real.
<YOU AMPUTATE THAT BROKEN HOOF.>
WHAT?!!
<As long as it's thrashing around with that injury, it's causing itself more pain!>
<If the hoof is completely broken like you say, you should be able to CUT IT OFF ABOVE THE BREAK.>
<Then TIE OFF the stump with a shoelace or something.>
NO...
<Yes.>

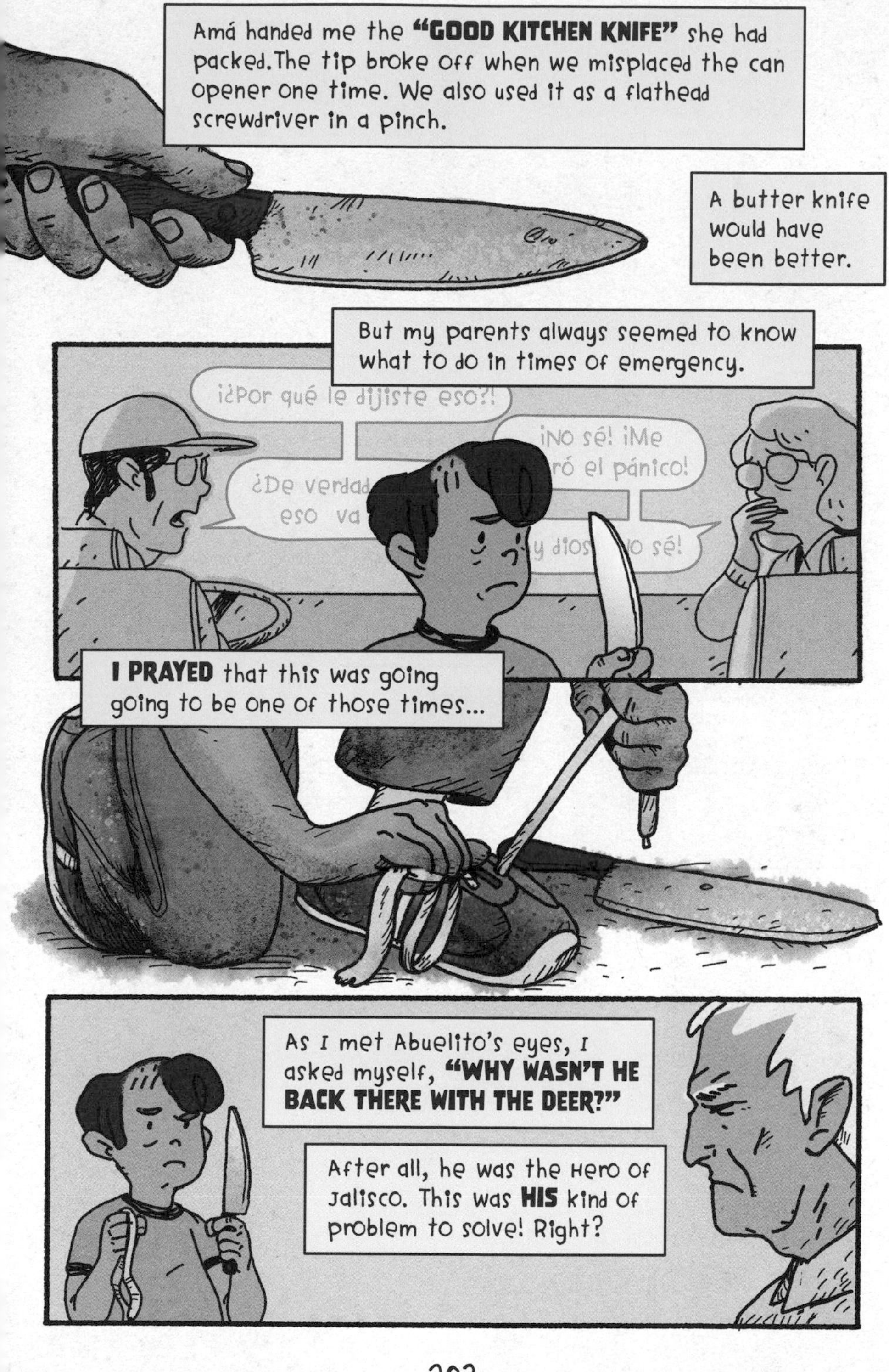
Amá handed me the **"GOOD KITCHEN KNIFE"** she had packed. The tip broke off when we misplaced the can opener one time. We also used it as a flathead screwdriver in a pinch.
A butter knife would have been better.
But my parents always seemed to know what to do in times of emergency.
¡¿Por qué le dijiste eso?!
¿De verdad
eso va
¡No sé! ¡Me
ró el pánico!
y dios
o sé!
I PRAYED that this was going going to be one of those times...
As I met Abuelito's eyes, I asked myself, **"WHY WASN'T HE BACK THERE WITH THE DEER?"**
After all, he was the Hero of Jalisco. This was **HIS** kind of problem to solve! Right?

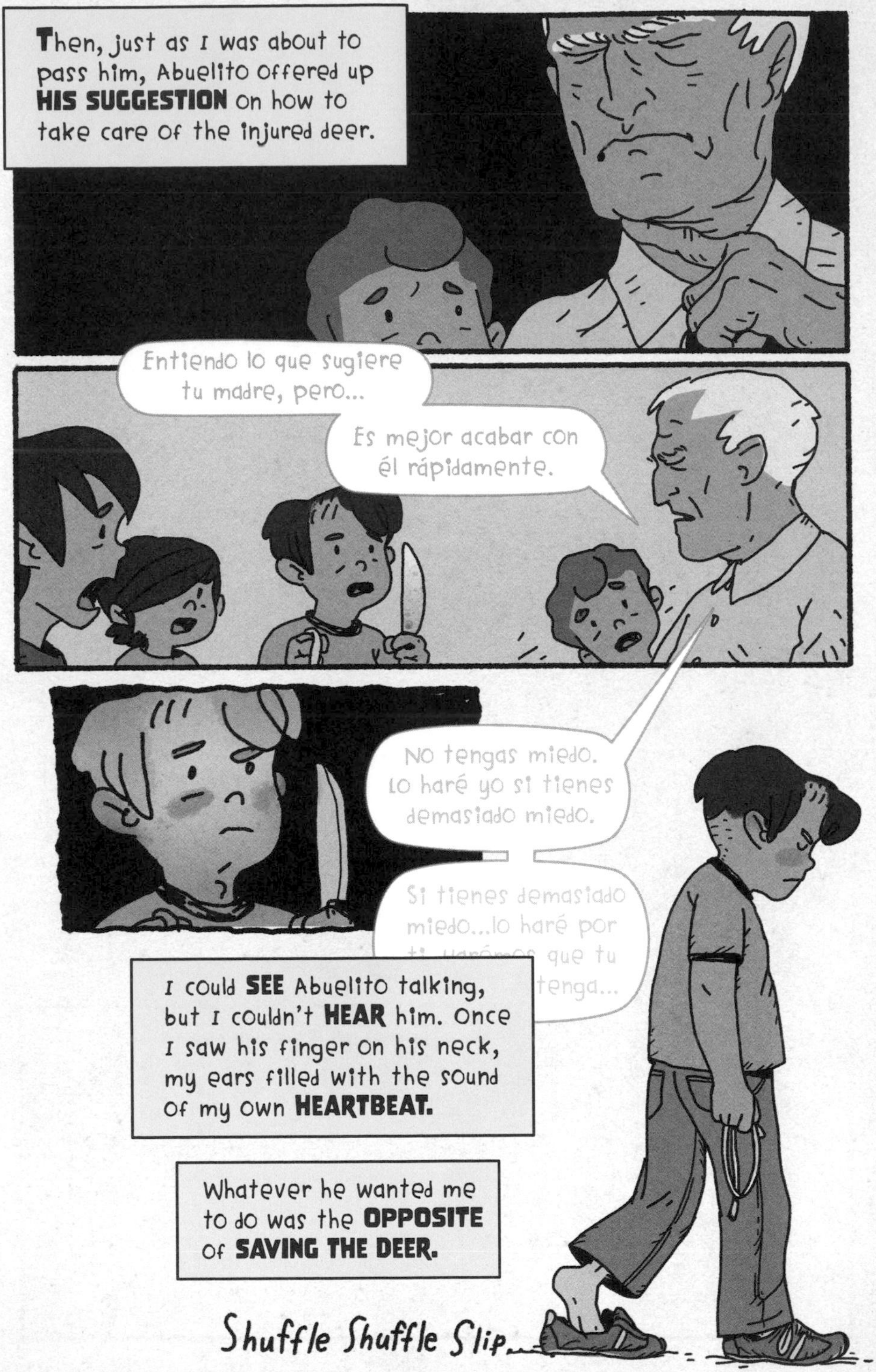

Then, just as I was about to pass him, Abuelito offered up **HIS SUGGESTION** on how to take care of the injured deer.
Entiendo lo que sugiere tu madre, pero...
Es mejor acabar con él rápidamente.
No tengas miedo. Lo haré yo si tienes demasiado miedo.
Si tienes demasiado miedo...lo haré por
que tu
tenga...
I could **SEE** Abuelito talking, but I couldn't **HEAR** him. Once I saw his finger on his neck, my ears filled with the sound of my own **HEARTBEAT.**
Whatever he wanted me to do was the **OPPOSITE** of **SAVING THE DEER.**
Shuffle Shuffle Slip...

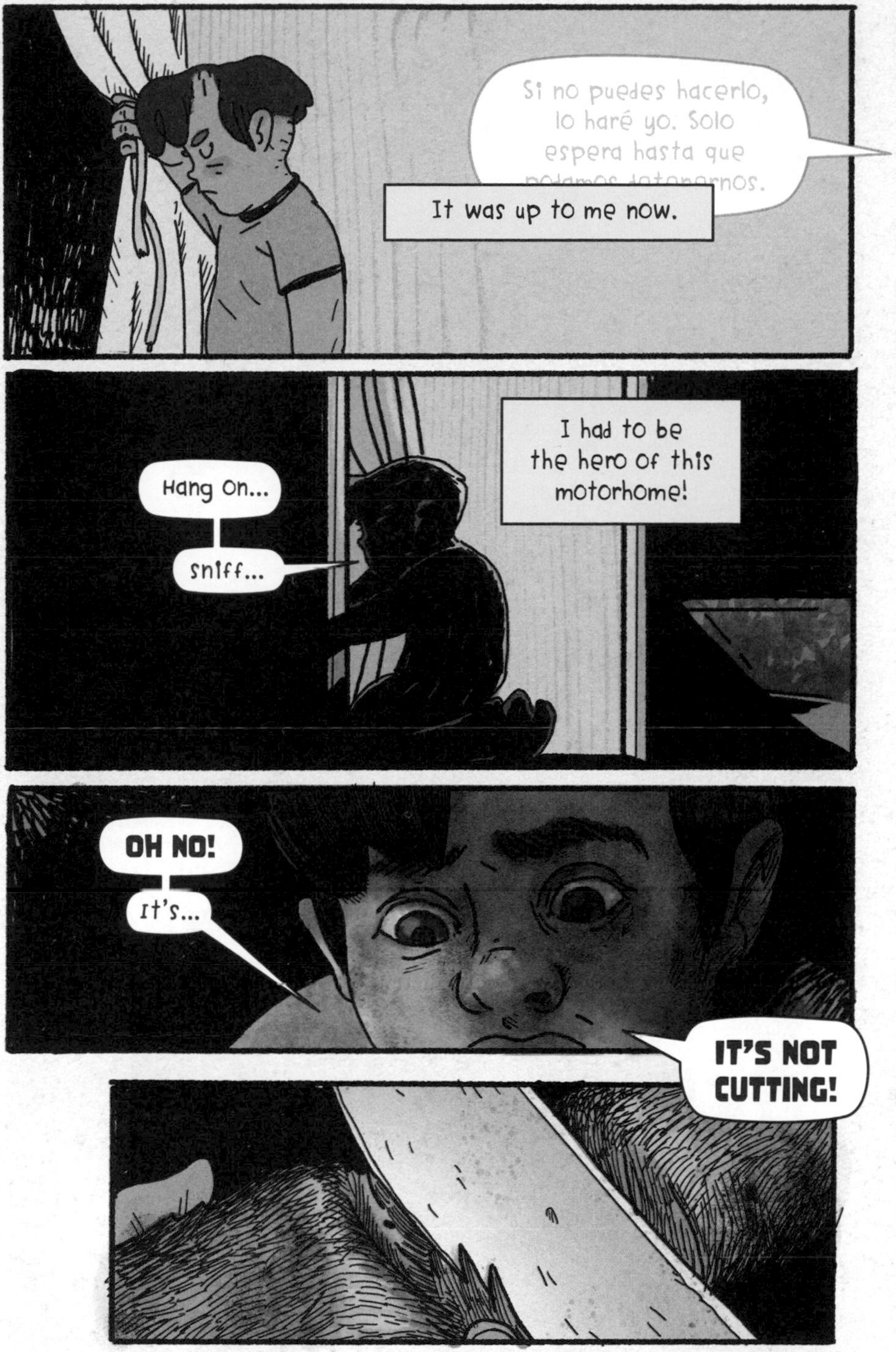

Si no puedes hacerlo, lo haré yo. Solo espera hasta que
It was up to me now.
I had to be the hero of this motorhome!
Hang on...
sniff...
OH NO!
It's...
IT'S NOT CUTTING!

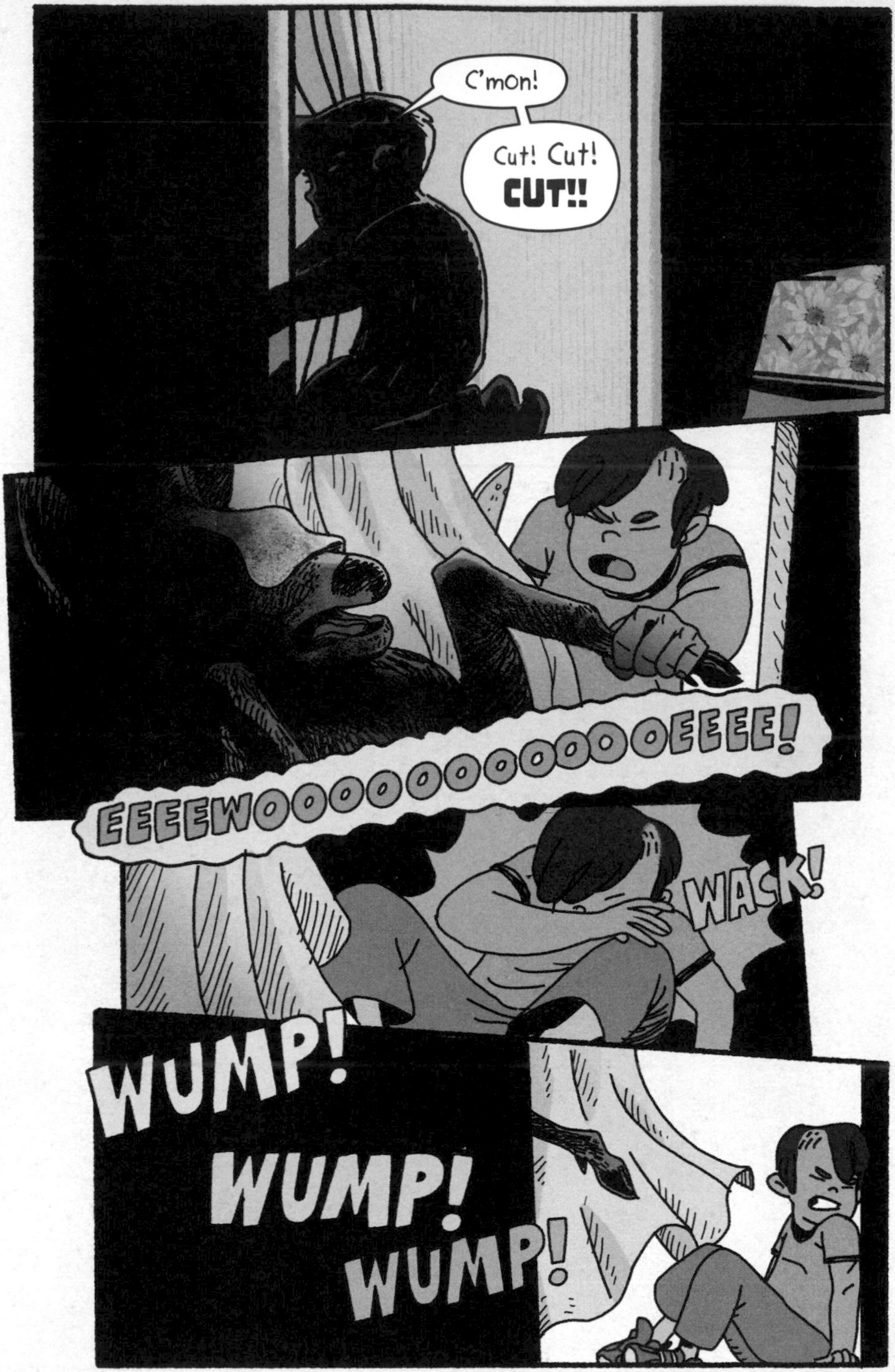
C'mon!
Cut! Cut! CUT!!
EEEEWOOOOOOOOOOOOOEEEE!
WACK!
WUMP!
WUMP!
WUMP!

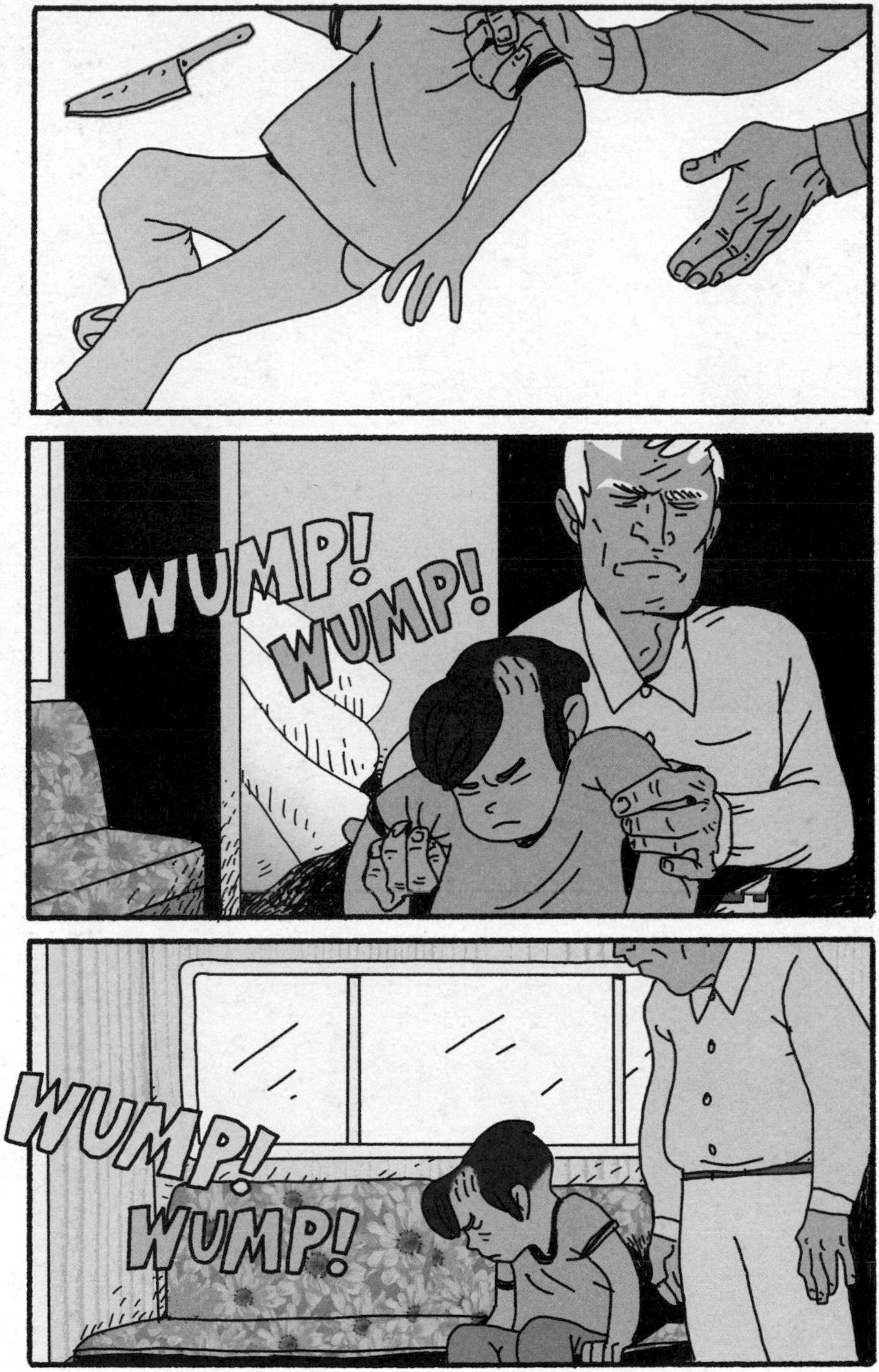
WUMP!
WUMP!
WUMP!
WUMP!

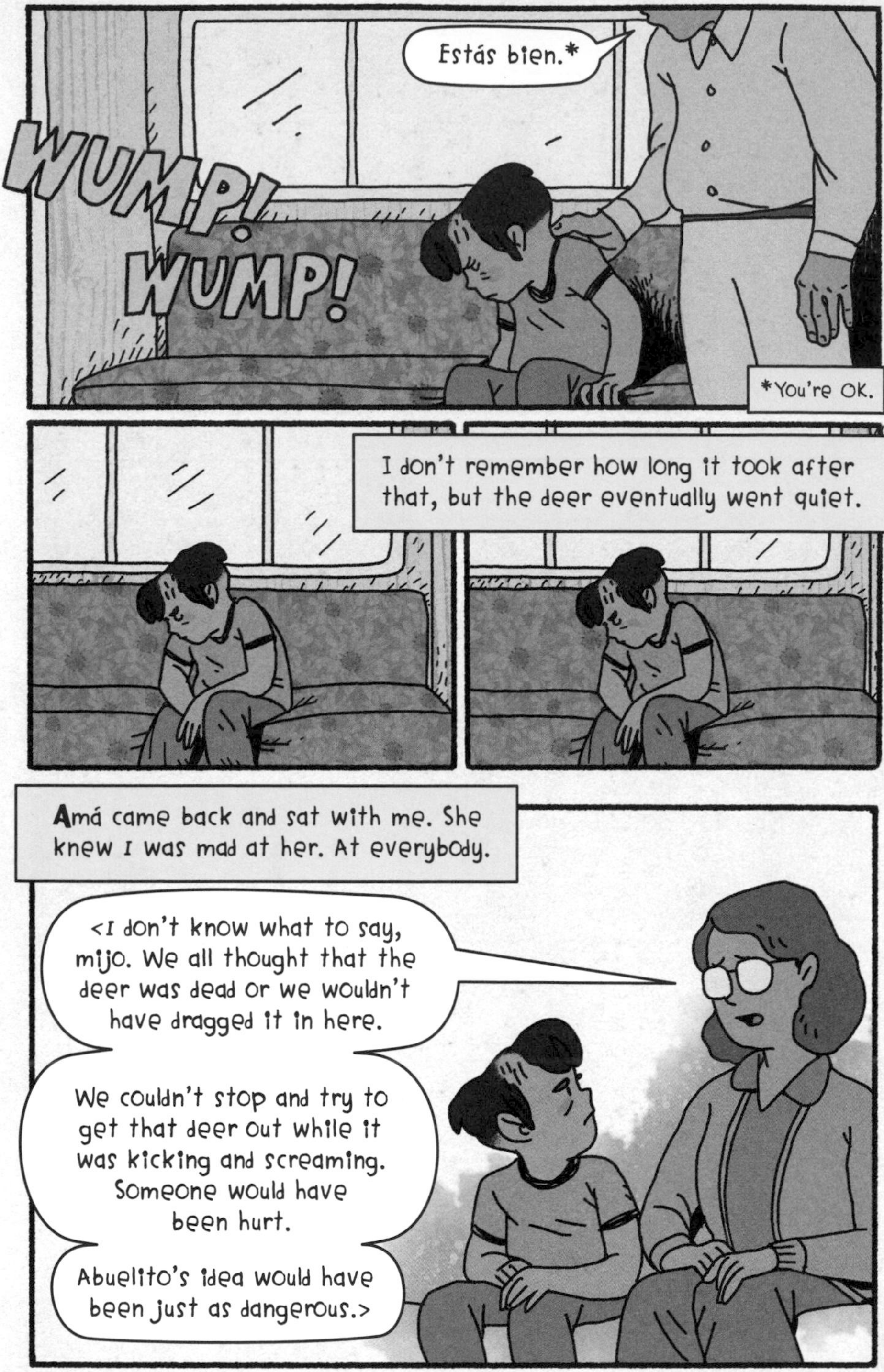
WUMP! WUMP!
Estás bien.*
*You're OK.
I don't remember how long it took after that, but the deer eventually went quiet.
Amá came back and sat with me. She knew I was mad at her. At everybody.
<I don't know what to say, mijo. We all thought that the deer was dead or we wouldn't have dragged it in here.
We couldn't stop and try to get that deer out while it was kicking and screaming. Someone would have been hurt.
Abuelito's idea would have been just as dangerous.>

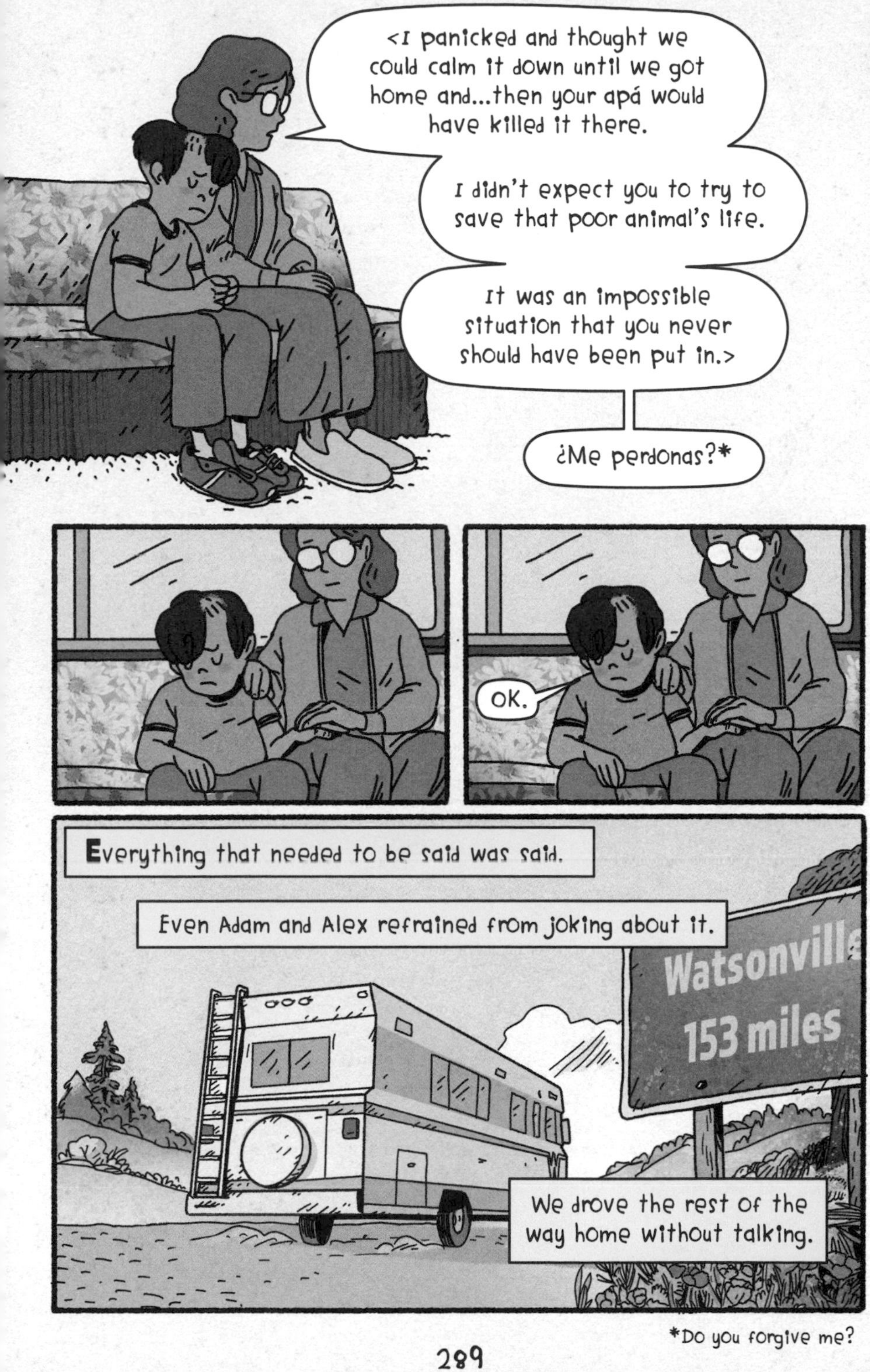
<I panicked and thought we could calm it down until we got home and...then your apá would have killed it there.
I didn't expect you to try to save that poor animal's life.
It was an impossible situation that you never should have been put in.>
¿Me perdonas?*
OK.
Everything that needed to be said was said.
Even Adam and Alex refrained from joking about it.
Watsonville
153 miles
We drove the rest of the way home without talking.

*Do you forgive me?

CHAPTER 20 WELCOME HOME?

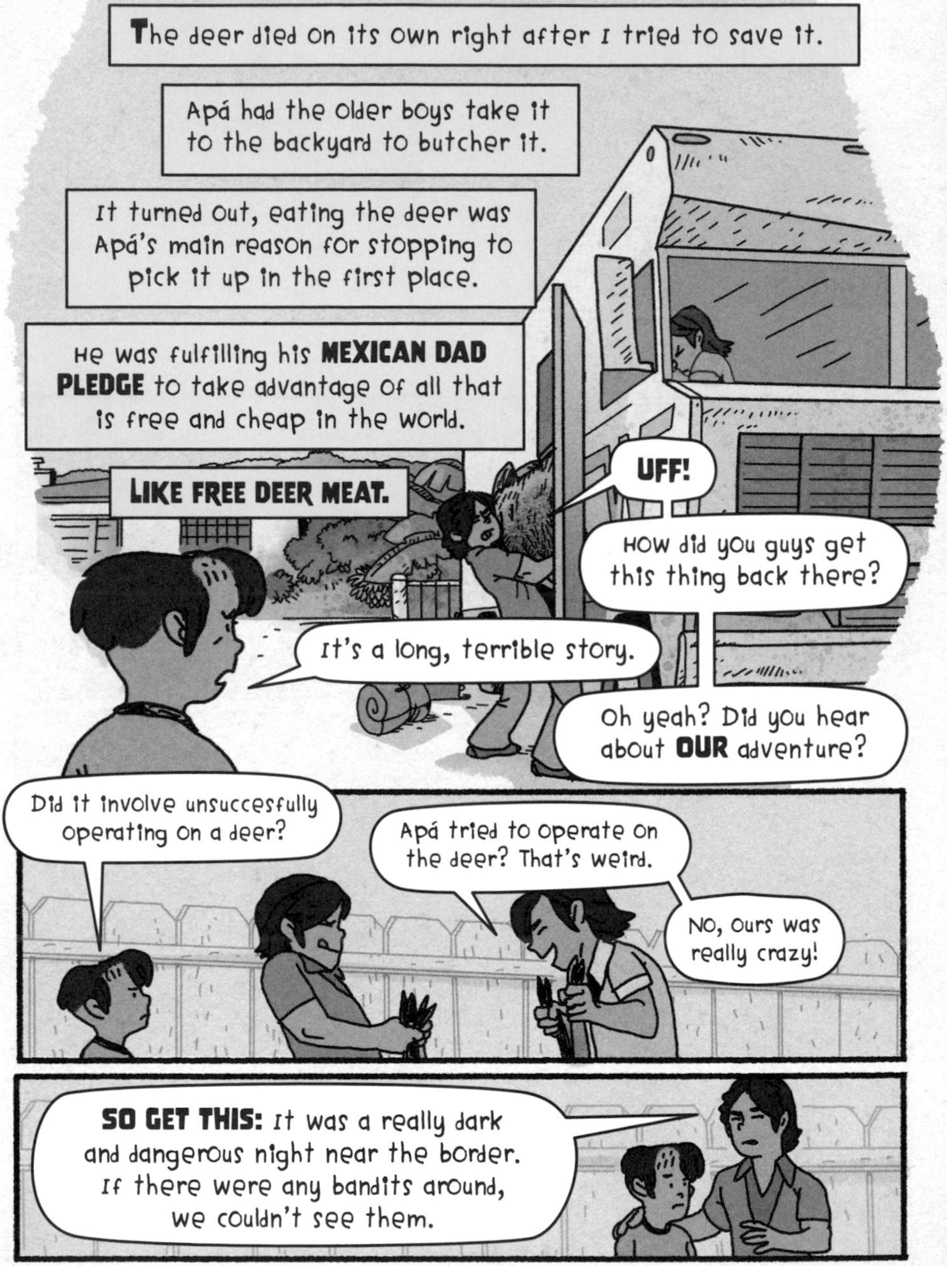
The deer died on its own right after I tried to save it.
Apá had the older boys take it to the backyard to butcher it.
It turned out, eating the deer was Apá's main reason for stopping to pick it up in the first place.
He was fulfilling his **MEXICAN DAD PLEDGE** to take advantage of all that is free and cheap in the world.
LIKE FREE DEER MEAT.
UFF!
How did you guys get this thing back there?
It's a long, terrible story.
Oh yeah? Did you hear about **OUR** adventure?
Did it involve unsuccesfully operating on a deer?
Apá tried to operate on the deer? That's weird.
No, ours was really crazy!
SO GET THIS: It was a really dark and dangerous night near the border. If there were any bandits around, we couldn't see them.

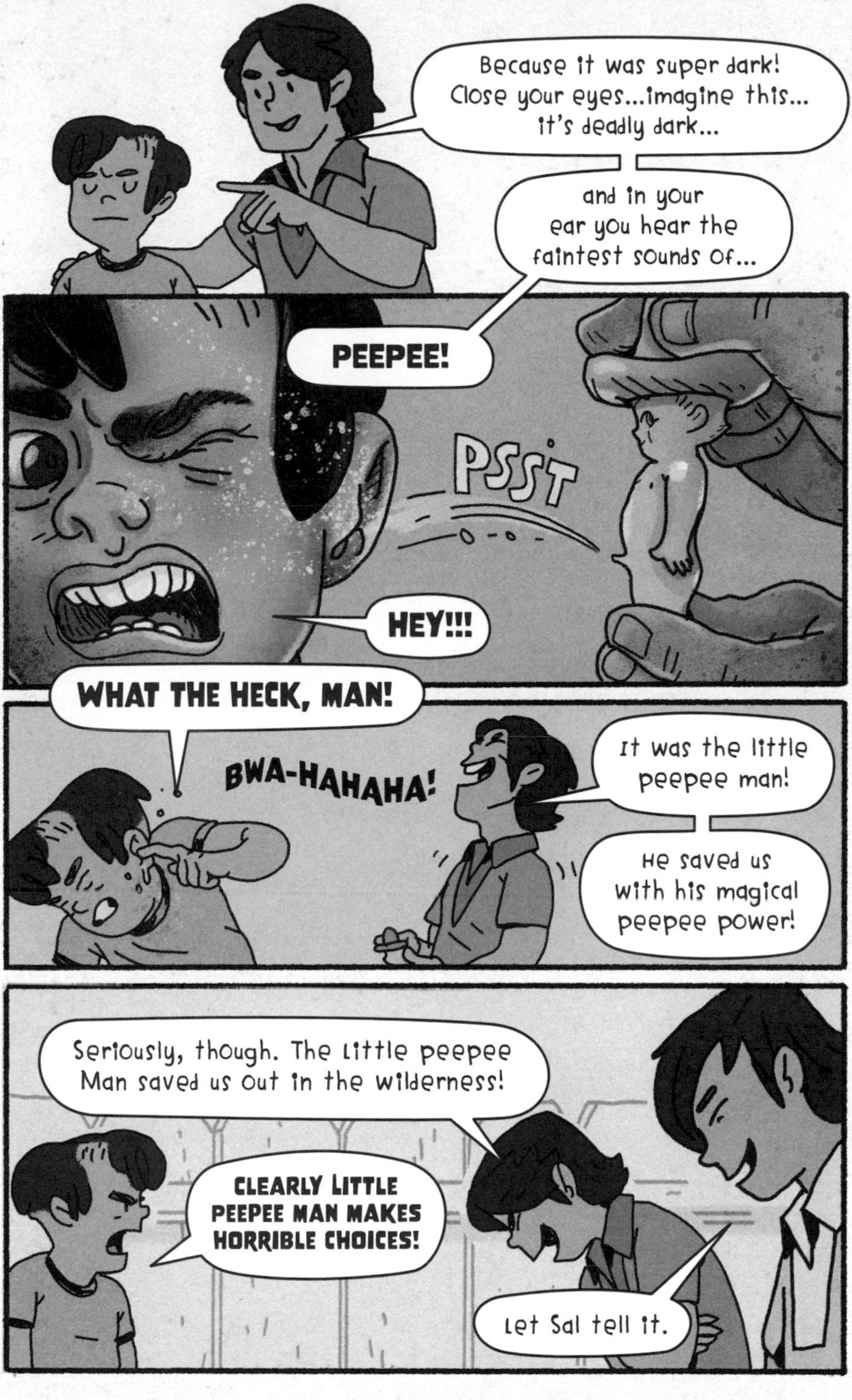
Because it was super dark! Close your eyes...imagine this... it's deadly dark...
and in your ear you hear the faintest sounds of...
PEEPEE!
PSST
HEY!!!
WHAT THE HECK, MAN!
BWA-HAHAHA!
It was the little peepee man!
He saved us with his magical peepee power!
Seriously, though. The little peepee Man saved us out in the wilderness!
CLEARLY LITTLE PEEPEE MAN MAKES HORRIBLE CHOICES!
Let Sal tell it.

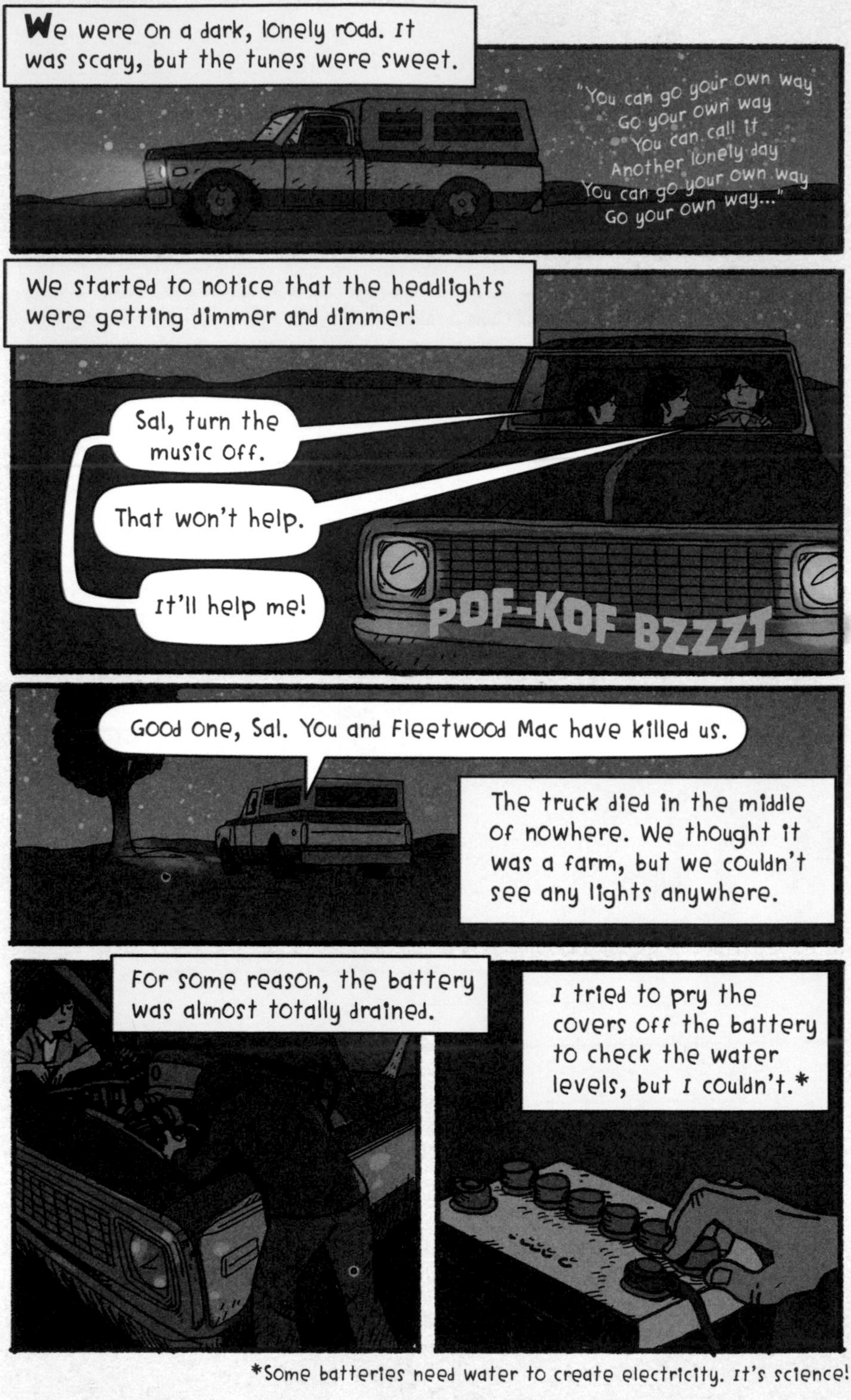
We were on a dark, lonely road. It was scary, but the tunes were sweet.
"You can go your own way
Go your own way
You can call it
Another lonely day
You can go your own way
Go your own way..."
We started to notice that the headlights were getting dimmer and dimmer!
Sal, turn the music off.
That won't help.
It'll help me!
POF-KOF BZZZT
Good one, Sal. You and Fleetwood Mac have killed us.
The truck died in the middle of nowhere. We thought it was a farm, but we couldn't see any lights anywhere.
For some reason, the battery was almost totally drained.
I tried to pry the covers off the battery to check the water levels, but I couldn't.*

*Some batteries need water to create electricity. It's science!

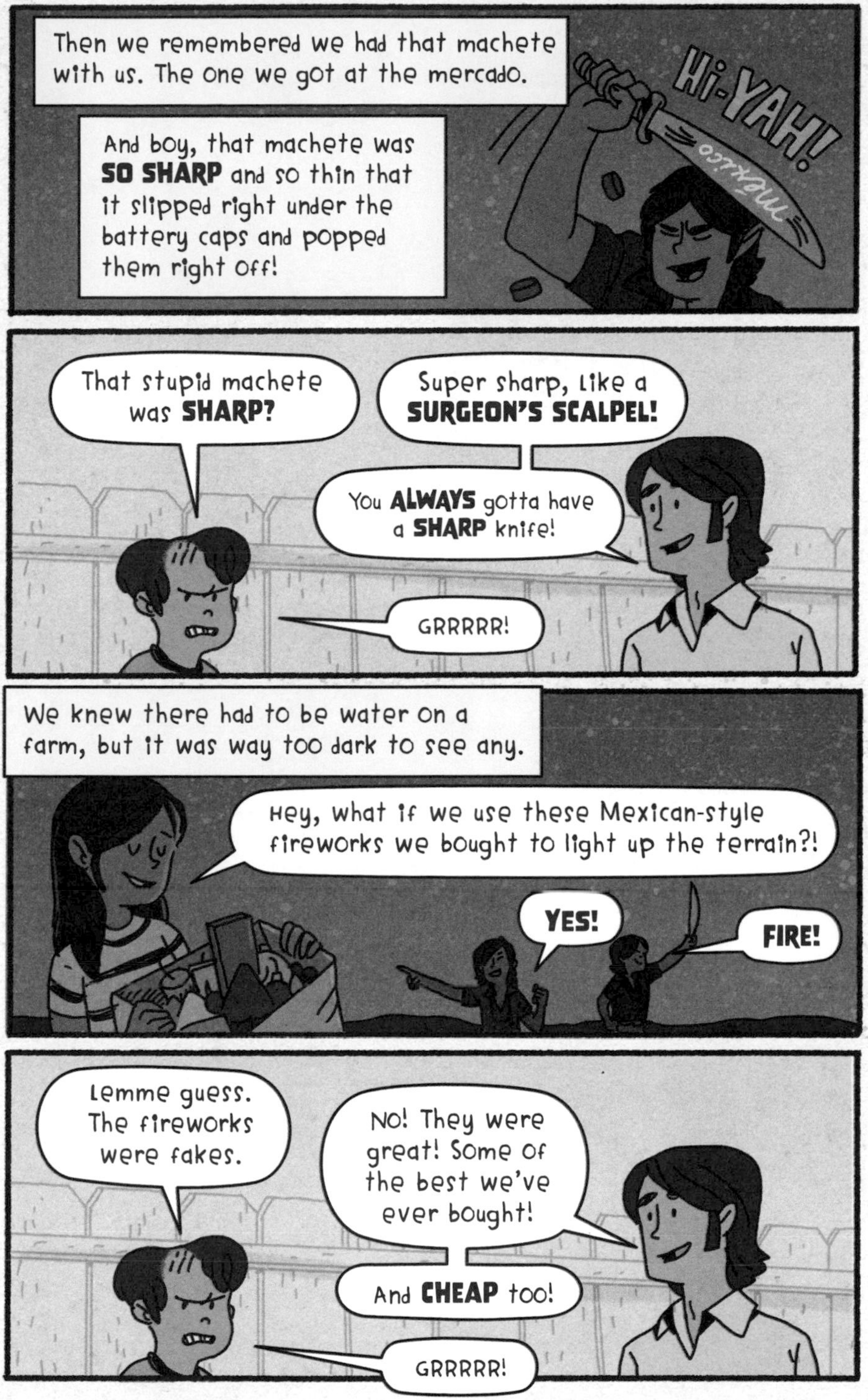
Then we remembered we had that machete with us. The one we got at the mercado.
And boy, that machete was **SO SHARP** and so thin that it slipped right under the battery caps and popped them right off!
HI-YAH!
méxico
That stupid machete was **SHARP?**
Super sharp, like a **SURGEON'S SCALPEL!**
You **ALWAYS** gotta have a **SHARP** knife!
GRRRRR!
We knew there had to be water on a farm, but it was way too dark to see any.
Hey, what if we use these Mexican-style fireworks we bought to light up the terrain?!
YES!
FIRE!
Lemme guess. The fireworks were fakes.
NO! They were great! Some of the best we've ever bought!
And **CHEAP** too!
GRRRRR!

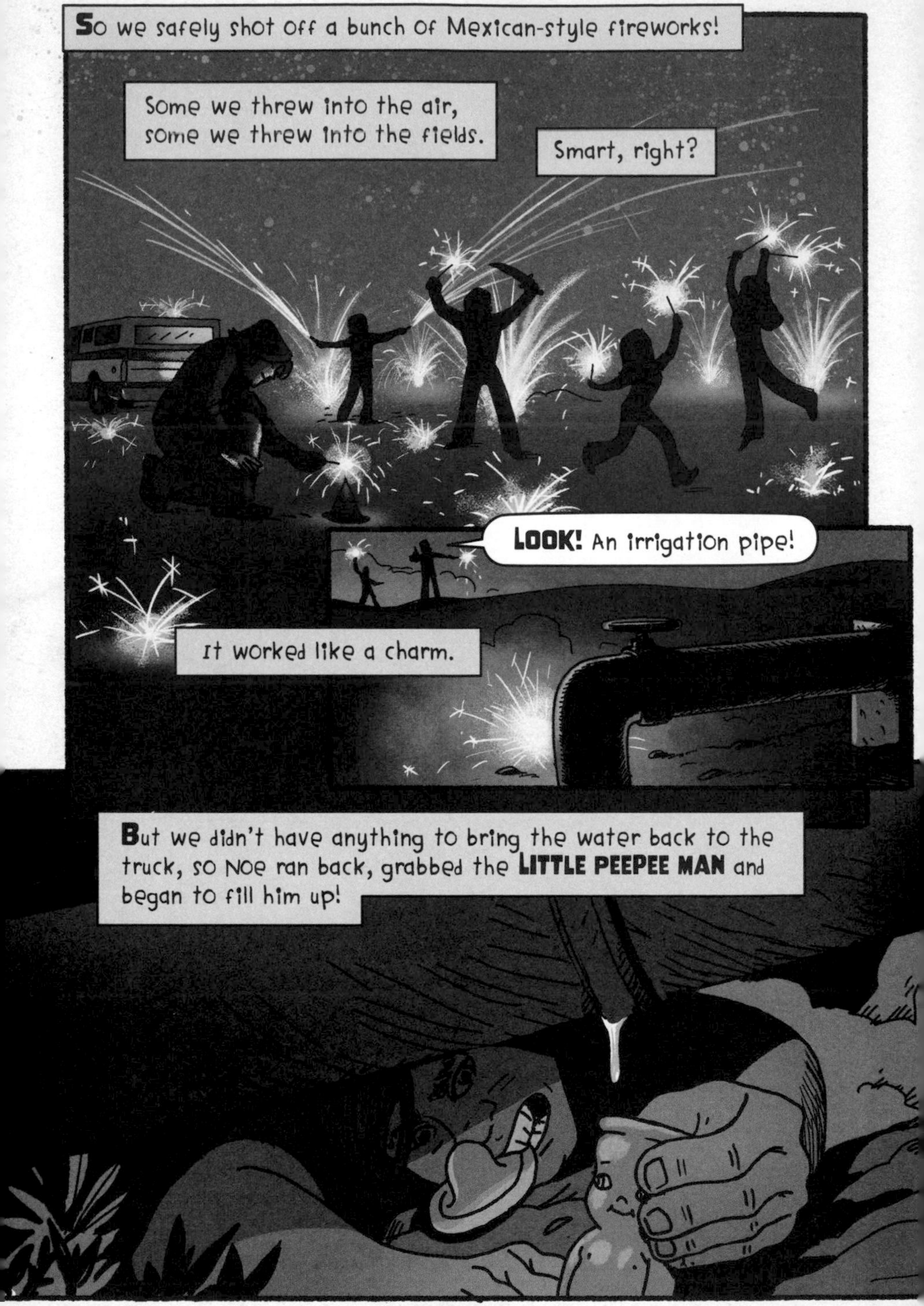
So we safely shot off a bunch of Mexican-style fireworks!
Some we threw into the air, some we threw into the fields.
Smart, right?
LOOK! An irrigation pipe!
It worked like a charm.
But we didn't have anything to bring the water back to the truck, so Noe ran back, grabbed the LITTLE PEEPEE MAN and began to fill him up!

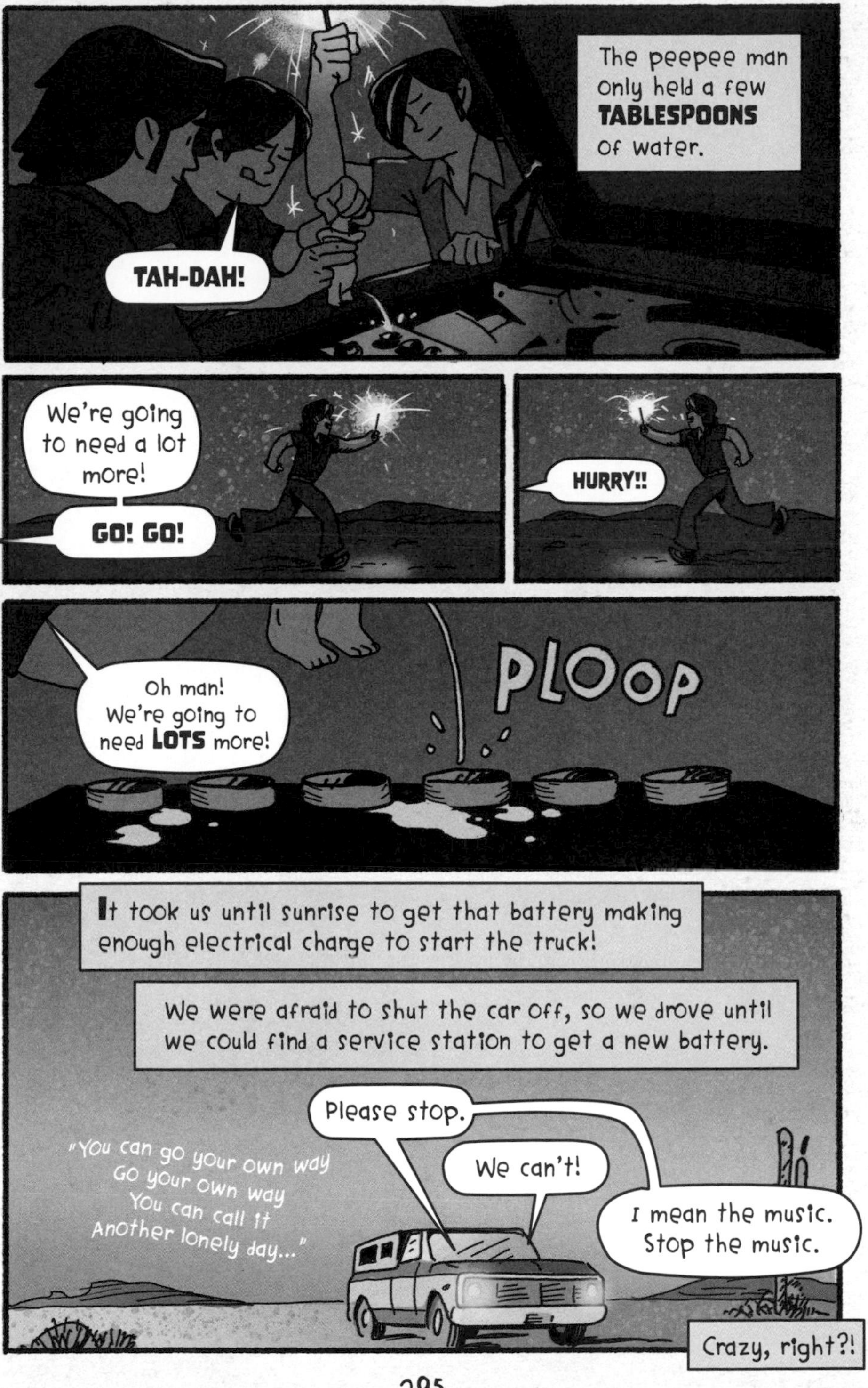
The peepee man only held a few **TABLESPOONS** of water.
TAH-DAH!
We're going to need a lot more!
GO! GO!
HURRY!!
Oh man! We're going to need **LOTS** more!
PLOOP
It took us until sunrise to get that battery making enough electrical charge to start the truck!
We were afraid to shut the car off, so we drove until we could find a service station to get a new battery.
Please stop.
"You can go your own way
Go your own way
You can call it
Another lonely day..."
We can't!
I mean the music. Stop the music.
Crazy, right?!

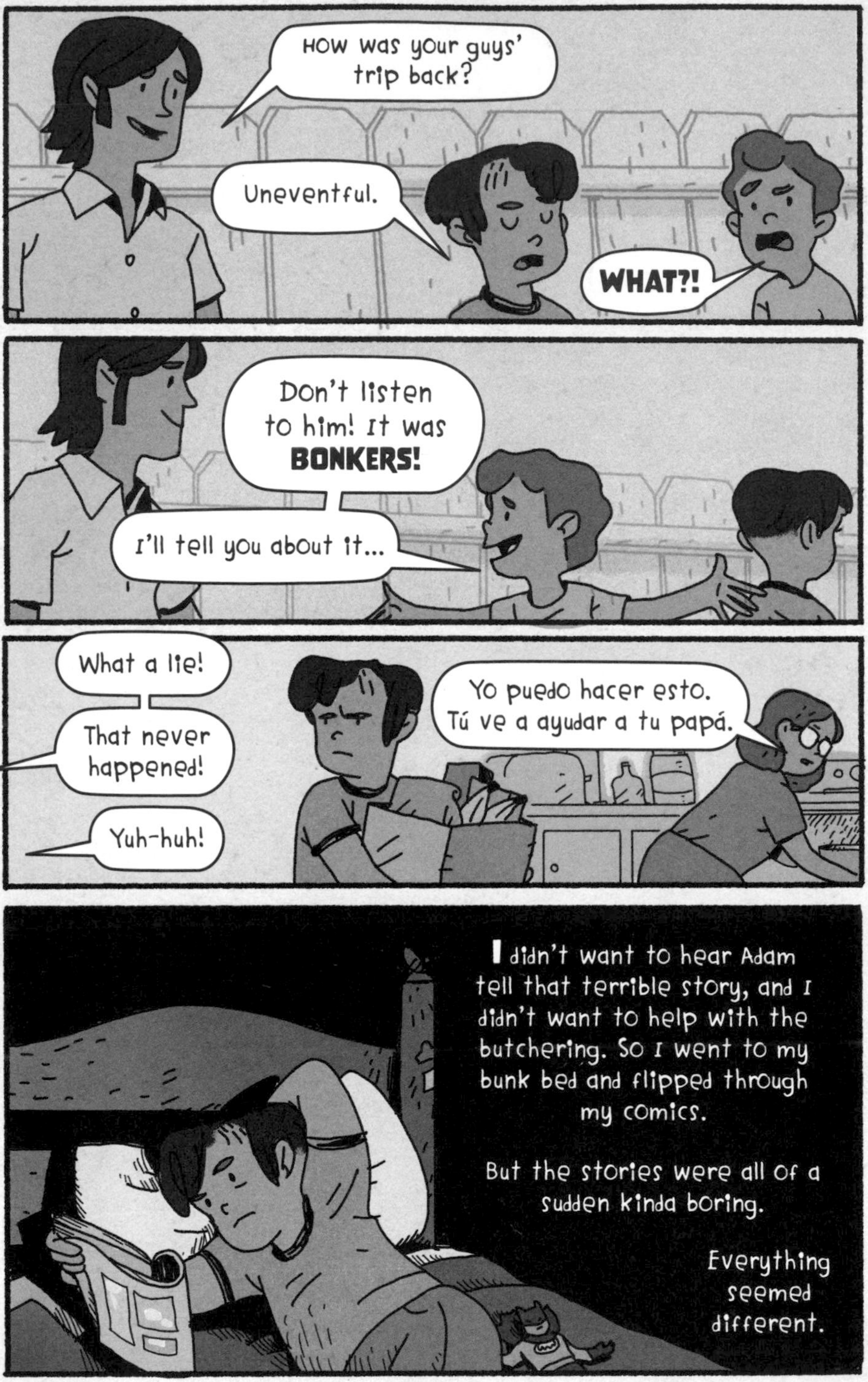
How was your guys' trip back?
Uneventful.
WHAT?!
Don't listen to him! It was BONKERS!
I'll tell you about it...
What a lie!
That never happened!
Yuh-huh!
Yo puedo hacer esto. Tú ve a ayudar a tu papá.
I didn't want to hear Adam tell that terrible story, and I didn't want to help with the butchering. So I went to my bunk bed and flipped through my comics.
But the stories were all of a sudden kinda boring.
Everything seemed different.

The next night, family came from all over town to welcome Abuelito to his new home with a special fiesta!

BONUS! Here's a basic recipe you can use to turn a tragic childhood trauma into a delicious celebration!

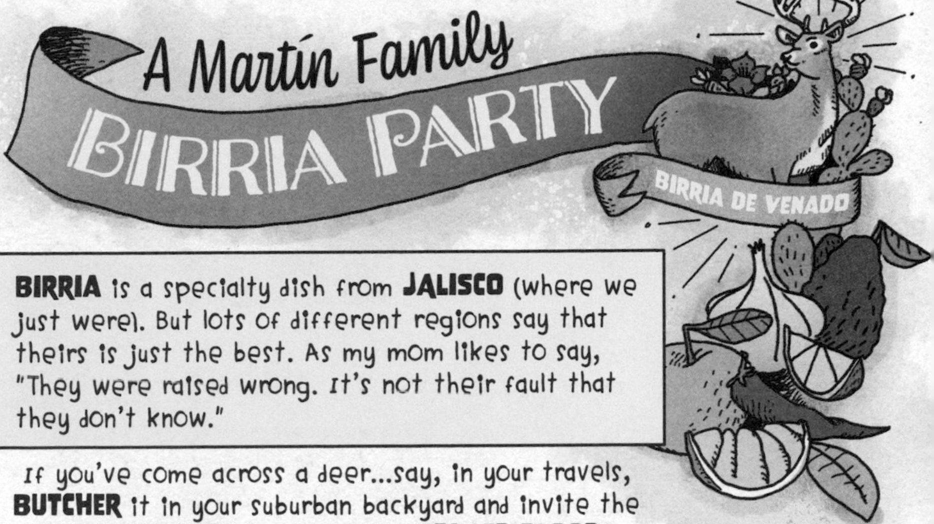
A Martín Family
BIRRIA PARTY
BIRRIA DE VENADO

BIRRIA is a specialty dish from **JALISCO** (where we just were). But lots of different regions say that theirs is just the best. As my mom likes to say, "They were raised wrong. It's not their fault that they don't know."

If you've come across a deer...say, in your travels, **BUTCHER** it in your suburban backyard and invite the **NEIGHBOR CATS** to lap up the **SPILLED BLOOD.**

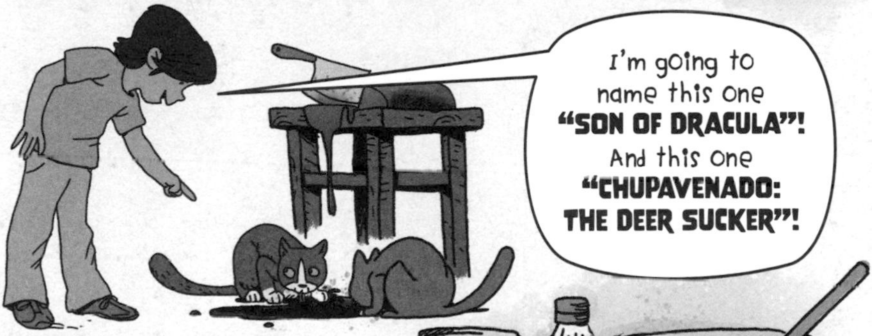
I'm going to name this one **"SON OF DRACULA"!** And this one **"CHUPAVENADO: THE DEER SUCKER"!**

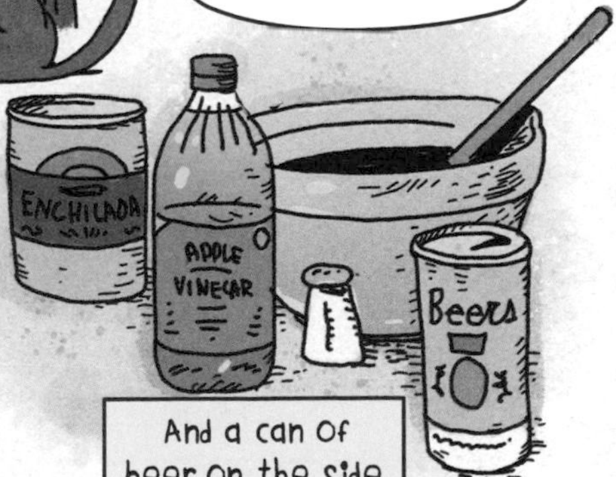
ENCHILADA
APPLE VINEGAR
Beers

MY APÁ likes to soak the meat in a special marinade made of enchilada sauce, tomatoes, bitter oranges, garlic, onions, apple cider vinegar, salt...other things...**AND LOVE!** Lots and lots of **LOVE.**

And a can of beer on the side. (His recipe, not mine.)

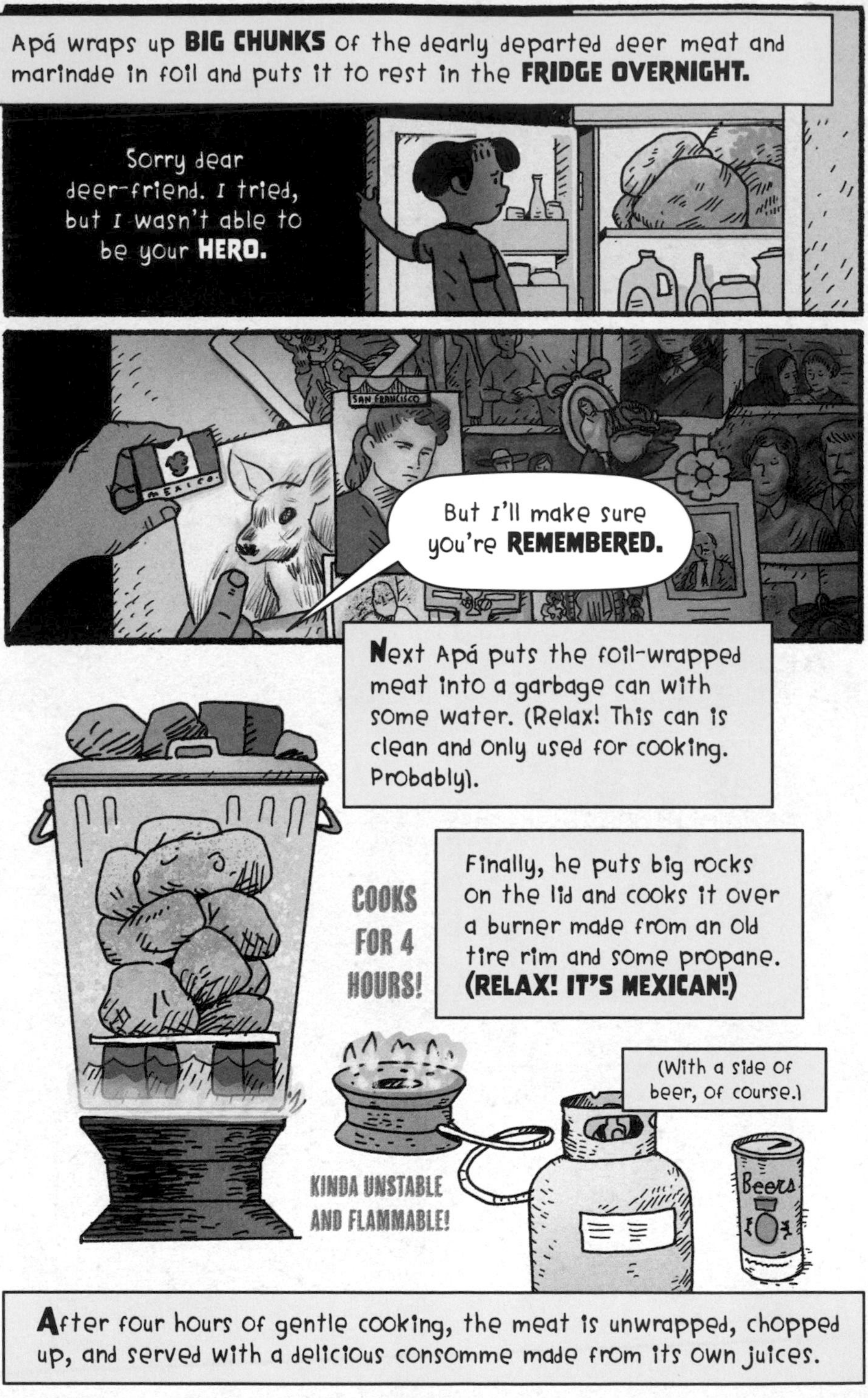
Apá wraps up **BIG CHUNKS** of the dearly departed deer meat and marinade in foil and puts it to rest in the **FRIDGE OVERNIGHT.**
Sorry dear deer-friend. I tried, but I wasn't able to be your **HERO.**
SAN FRANCISCO
But I'll make sure you're **REMEMBERED.**
Next Apá puts the foil-wrapped meat into a garbage can with some water. (Relax! This can is clean and only used for cooking. Probably).
COOKS FOR 4 HOURS!
Finally, he puts big rocks on the lid and cooks it over a burner made from an old tire rim and some propane. **(RELAX! IT'S MEXICAN!)**
(With a side of beer, of course.)
KINDA UNSTABLE AND FLAMMABLE!
Beers
After four hours of gentle cooking, the meat is unwrapped, chopped up, and served with a delicious consomme made from its own juices.

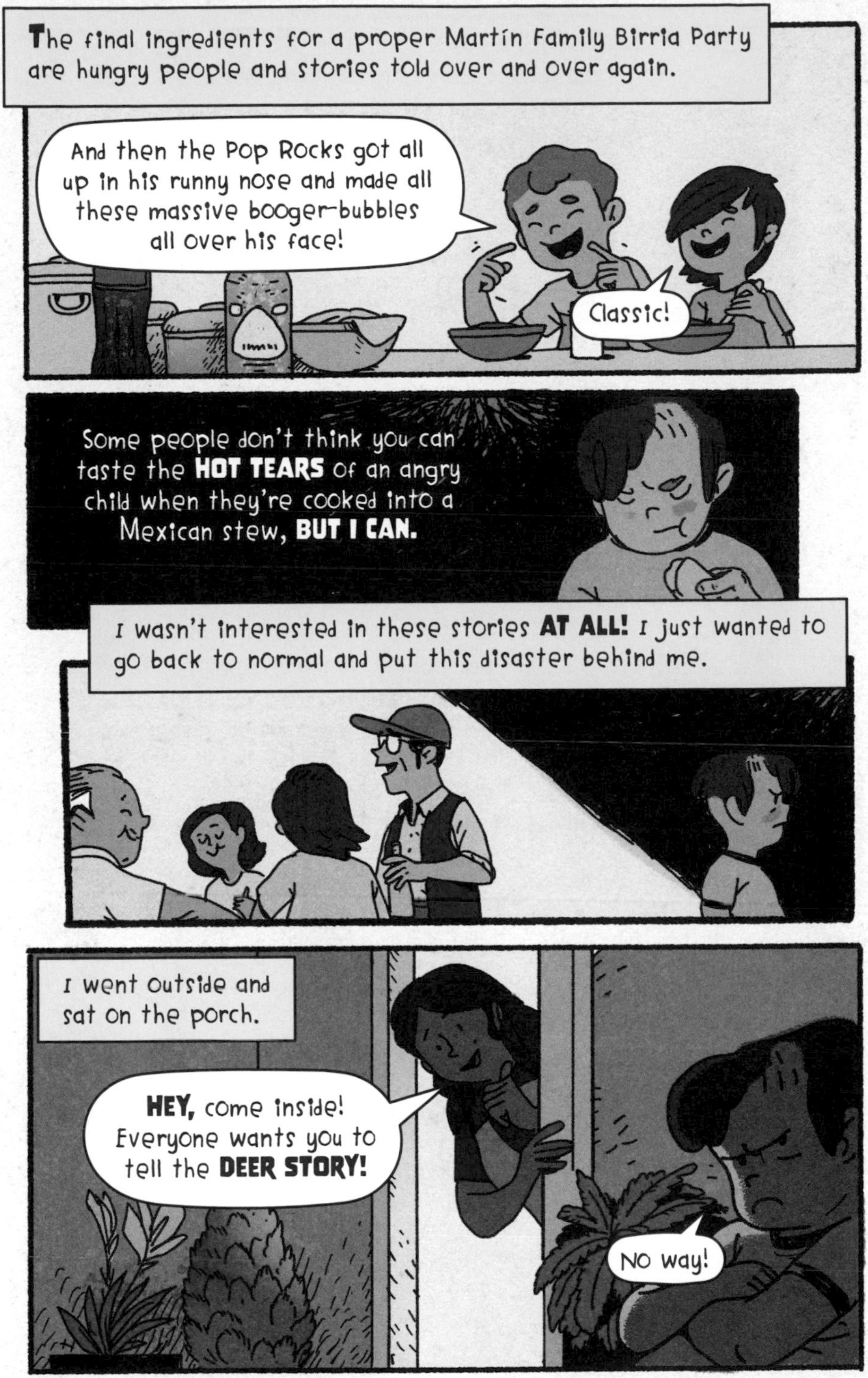
The final ingredients for a proper Martín Family Birria Party are hungry people and stories told over and over again.
And then the Pop Rocks got all up in his runny nose and made all these massive booger-bubbles all over his face!
Classic!
Some people don't think you can taste the HOT TEARS of an angry child when they're cooked into a Mexican stew, BUT I CAN.
I wasn't interested in these stories AT ALL! I just wanted to go back to normal and put this disaster behind me.
I went outside and sat on the porch.
HEY, come inside! Everyone wants you to tell the DEER STORY!
No way!

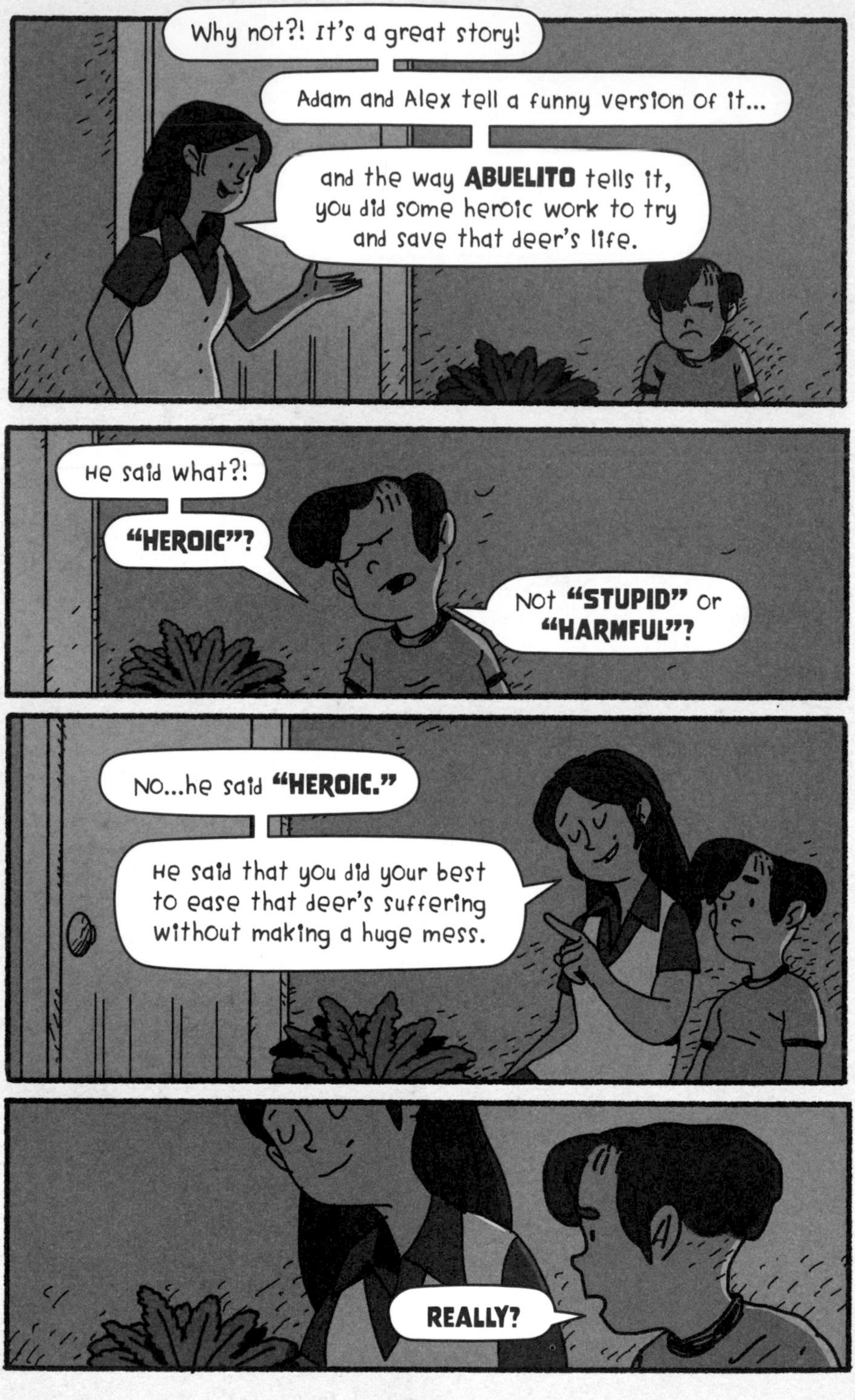
Why not?! It's a great story!
Adam and Alex tell a funny version of it...
and the way ABUELITO tells it, you did some heroic work to try and save that deer's life.
He said what?!
"HEROIC"?
Not "STUPID" or "HARMFUL"?
No...he said "HEROIC."
He said that you did your best to ease that deer's suffering without making a huge mess.
REALLY?

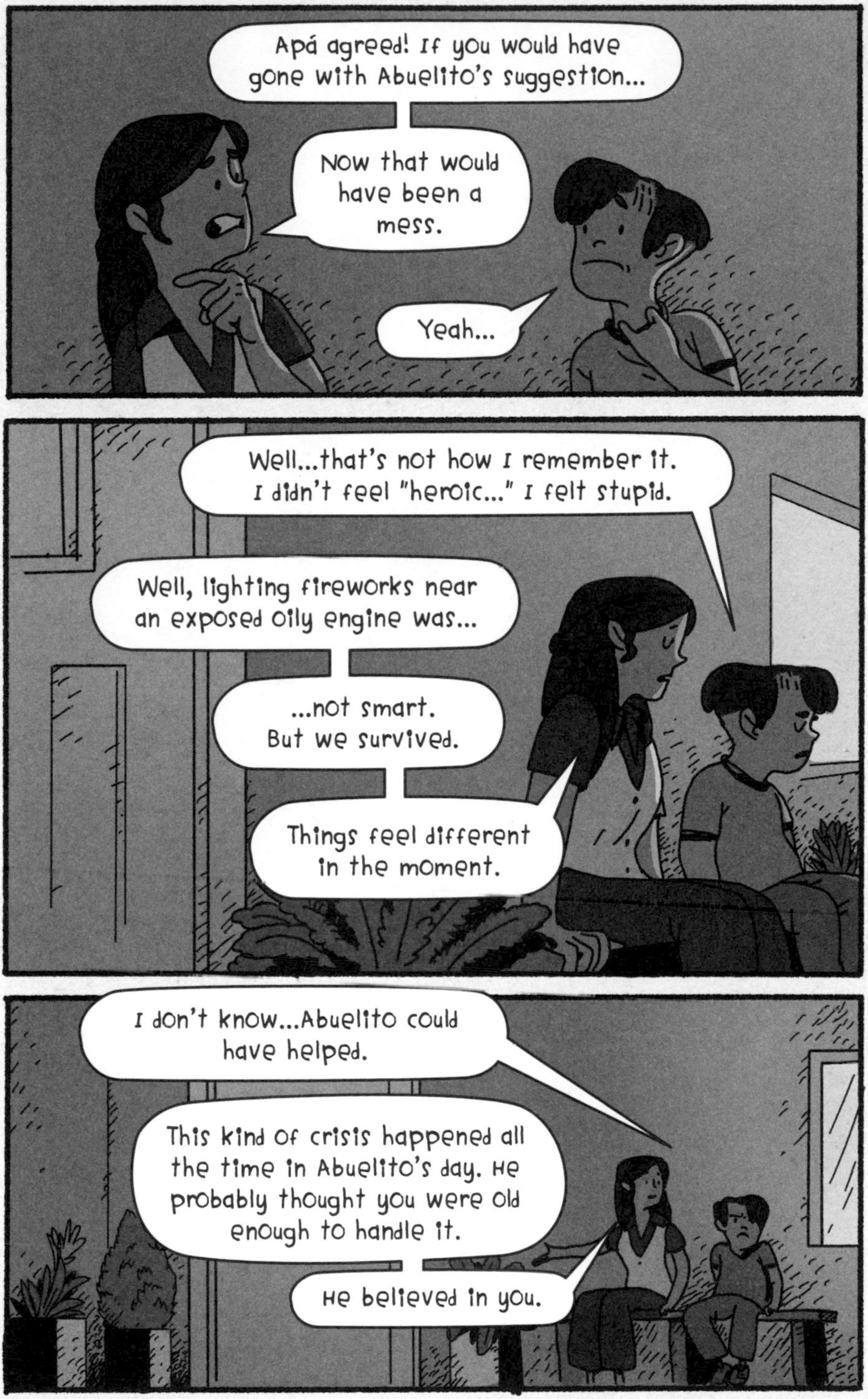
Apá agreed! If you would have gone with Abuelito's suggestion...
Now that would have been a mess.
Yeah...
Well...that's not how I remember it. I didn't feel "heroic..." I felt stupid.
Well, lighting fireworks near an exposed oily engine was...
...not smart. But we survived.
Things feel different in the moment.
I don't know...Abuelito could have helped.
This kind of crisis happened all the time in Abuelito's day. He probably thought you were old enough to handle it.
He believed in you.

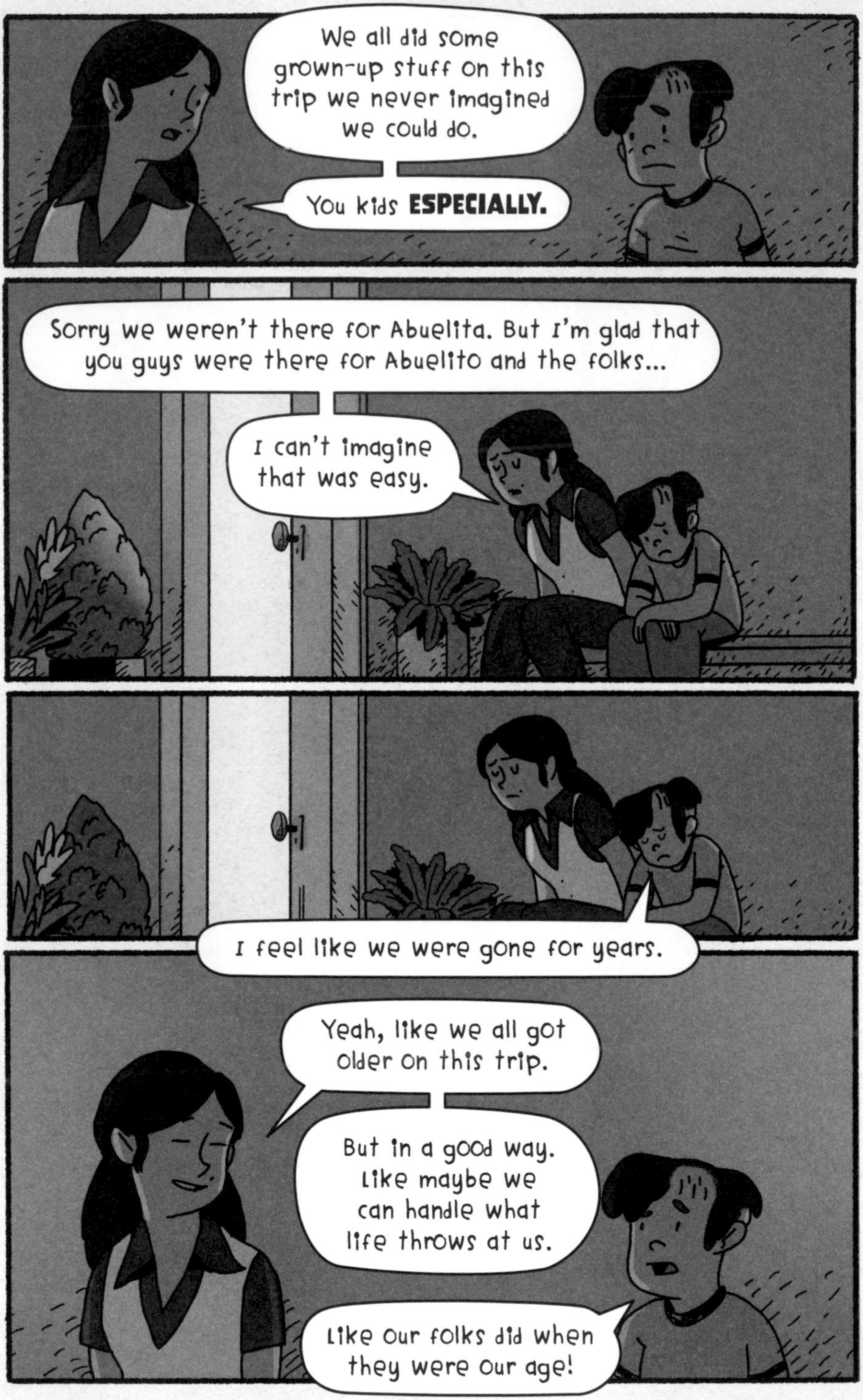
We all did some grown-up stuff on this trip we never imagined we could do.
You kids **ESPECIALLY.**
Sorry we weren't there for Abuelita. But I'm glad that you guys were there for Abuelito and the folks...
I can't imagine that was easy.
I feel like we were gone for years.
Yeah, like we all got older on this trip.
But in a good way. Like maybe we can handle what life throws at us.
Like our folks did when they were our age!

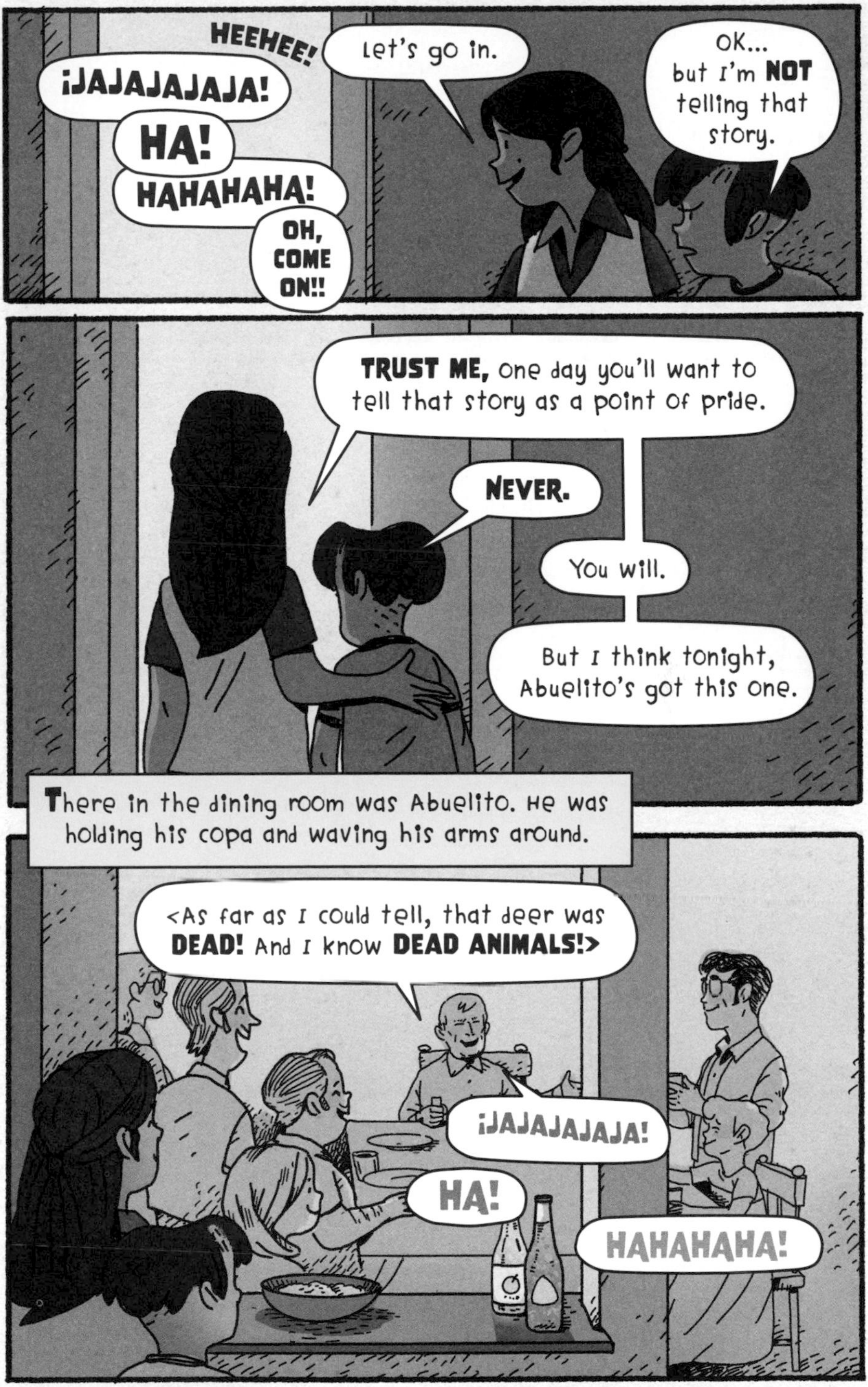
HEEHEE!
¡JAJAJAJAJA!
HA!
HAHAHAHA!
OH, COME ON!!
Let's go in.
OK... but I'm NOT telling that story.
TRUST ME, one day you'll want to tell that story as a point of pride.
NEVER.
You will.
But I think tonight, Abuelito's got this one.
There in the dining room was Abuelito. He was holding his copa and waving his arms around.
<As far as I could tell, that deer was DEAD! And I know DEAD ANIMALS!>
¡JAJAJAJAJA!
HA!
HAHAHAHA!

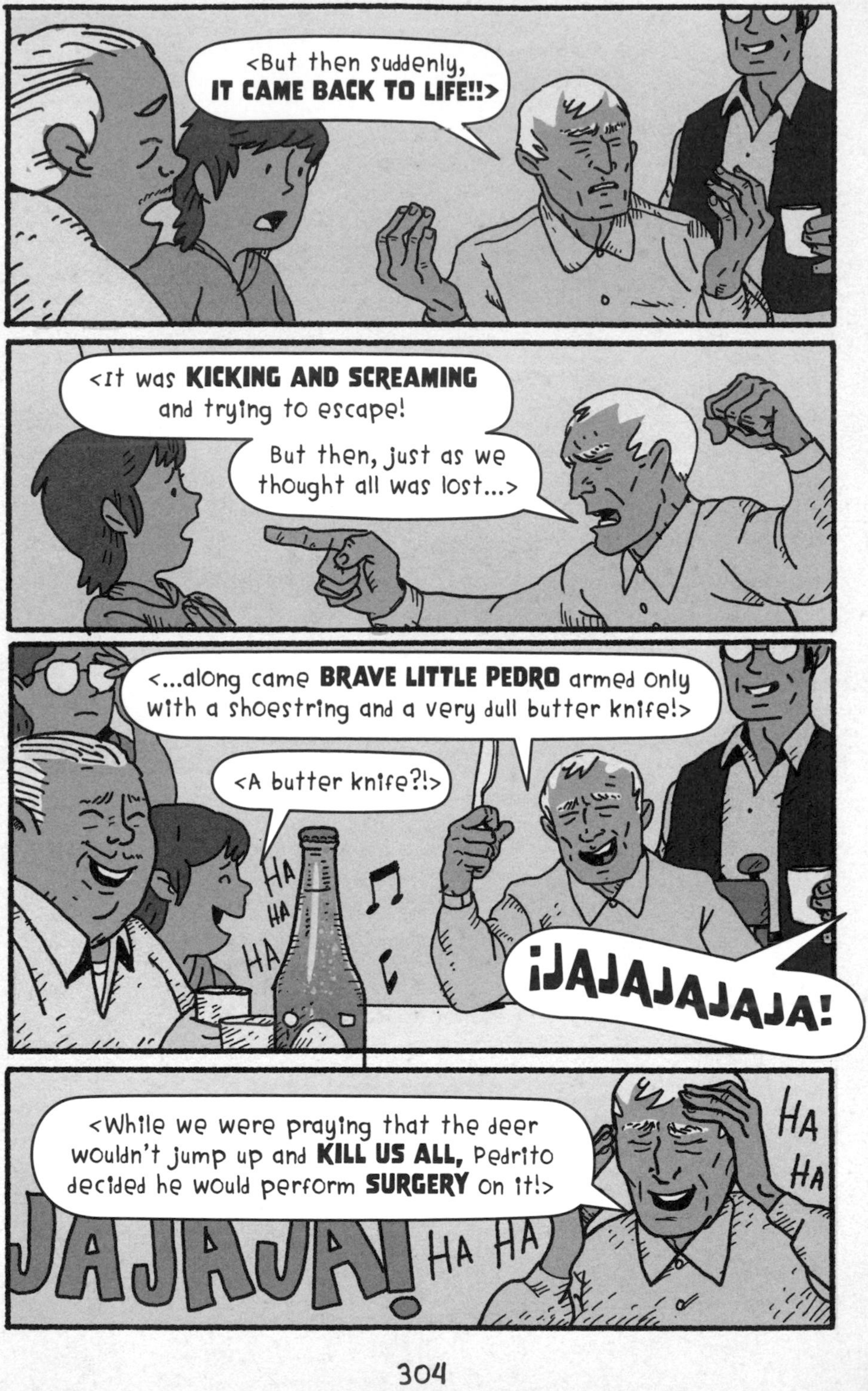
<But then suddenly, **IT CAME BACK TO LIFE!!**>
<It was **KICKING AND SCREAMING** and trying to escape!
But then, just as we thought all was lost...>
<...along came **BRAVE LITTLE PEDRO** armed only with a shoestring and a very dull butter knife!>
<A butter knife?!>
HA HA HA
¡JAJAJAJAJA!
<While we were praying that the deer wouldn't jump up and **KILL US ALL,** Pedrito decided he would perform **SURGERY** on it!>
JAJAJA!
HA HA
HA HA

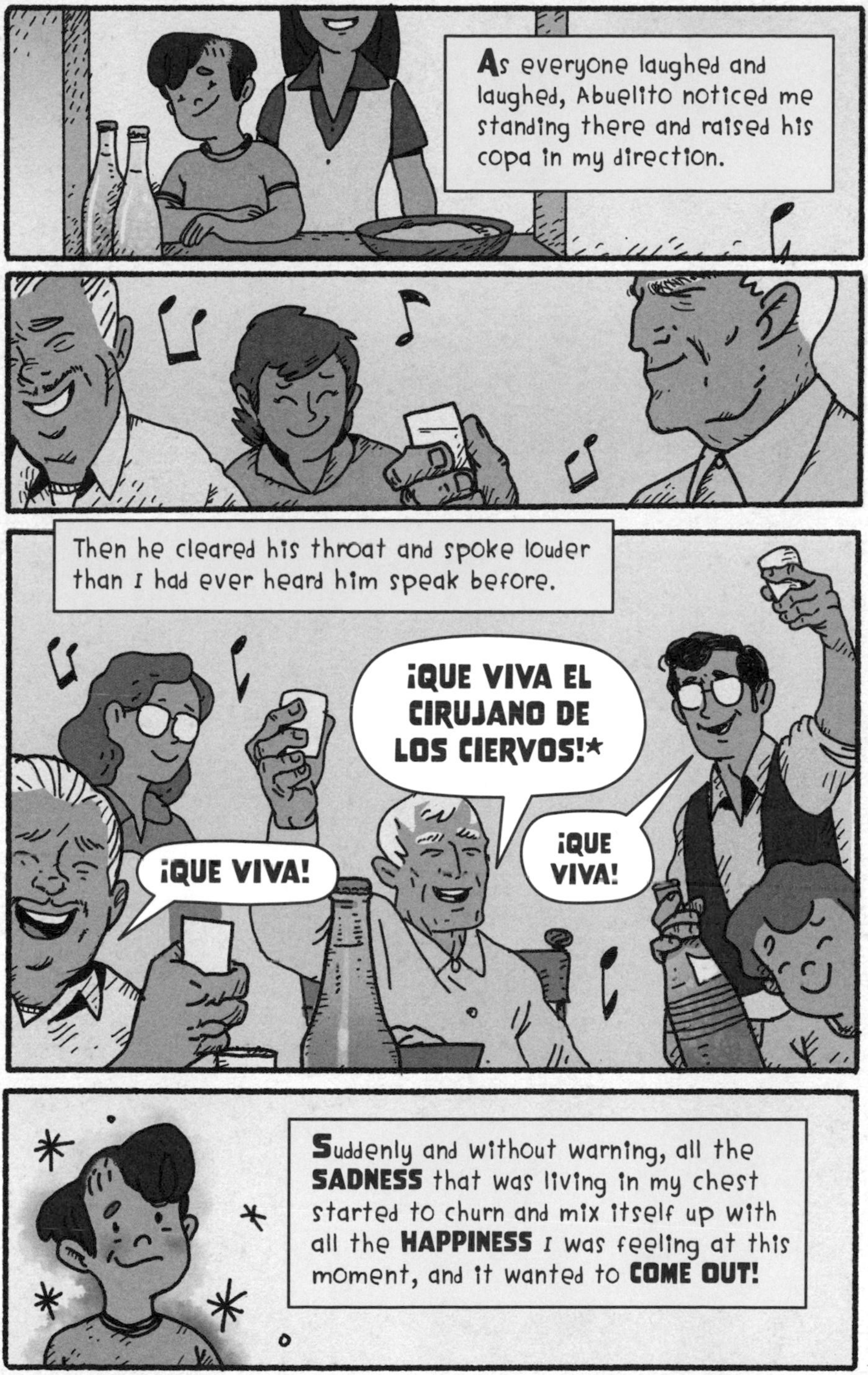
As everyone laughed and laughed, Abuelito noticed me standing there and raised his copa in my direction.
Then he cleared his throat and spoke louder than I had ever heard him speak before.
¡QUE VIVA EL CIRUJANO DE LOS CIERVOS!*
¡QUE VIVA!
¡QUE VIVA!
Suddenly and without warning, all the SADNESS that was living in my chest started to churn and mix itself up with all the HAPPINESS I was feeling at this moment, and it wanted to COME OUT!

*Long live The Deer Surgeon!

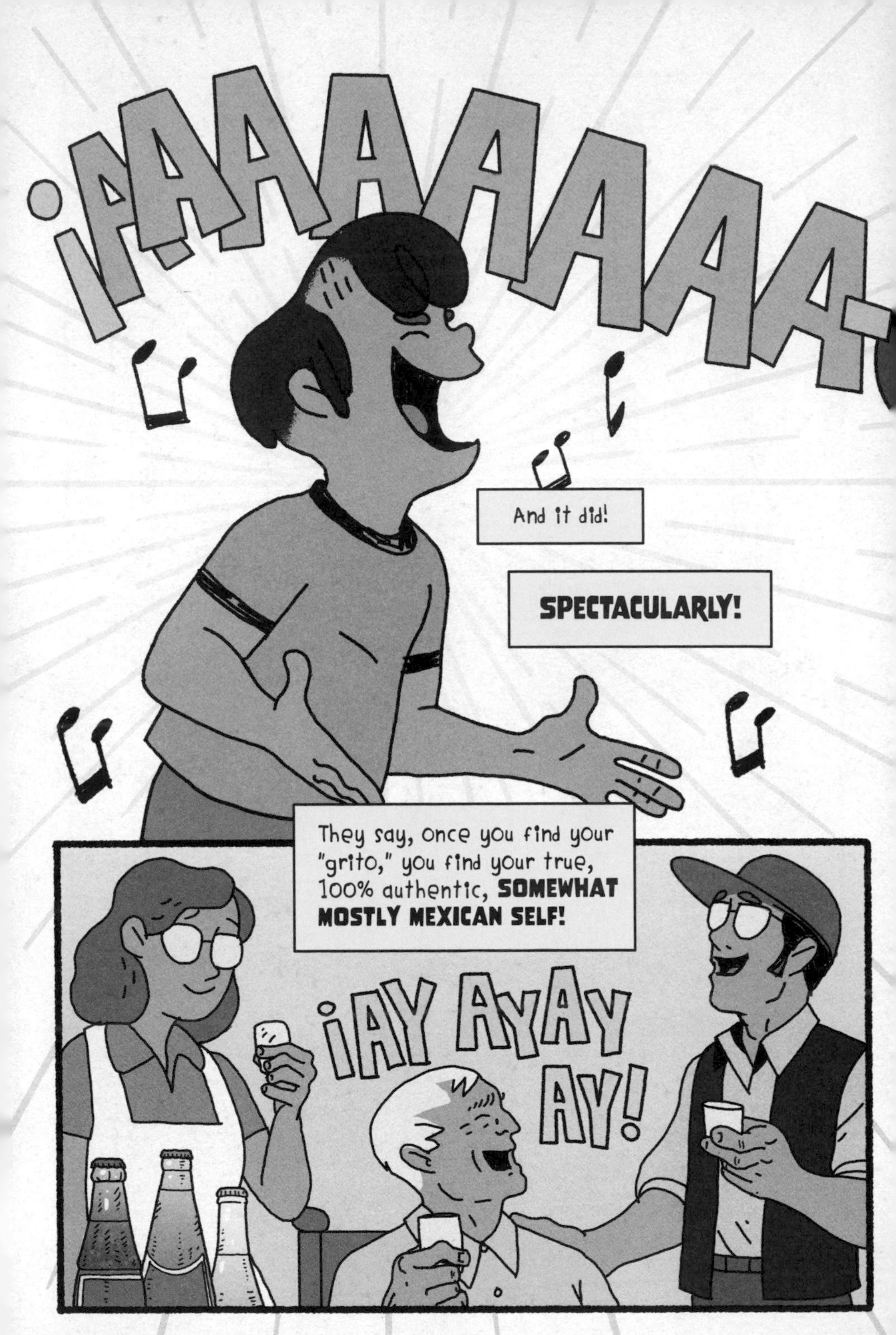
¡AAAAAAAA-
And it did!
SPECTACULARLY!
They say, once you find your "grito," you find your true, 100% authentic, SOMEWHAT MOSTLY MEXICAN SELF!
¡AY AYAY AY!

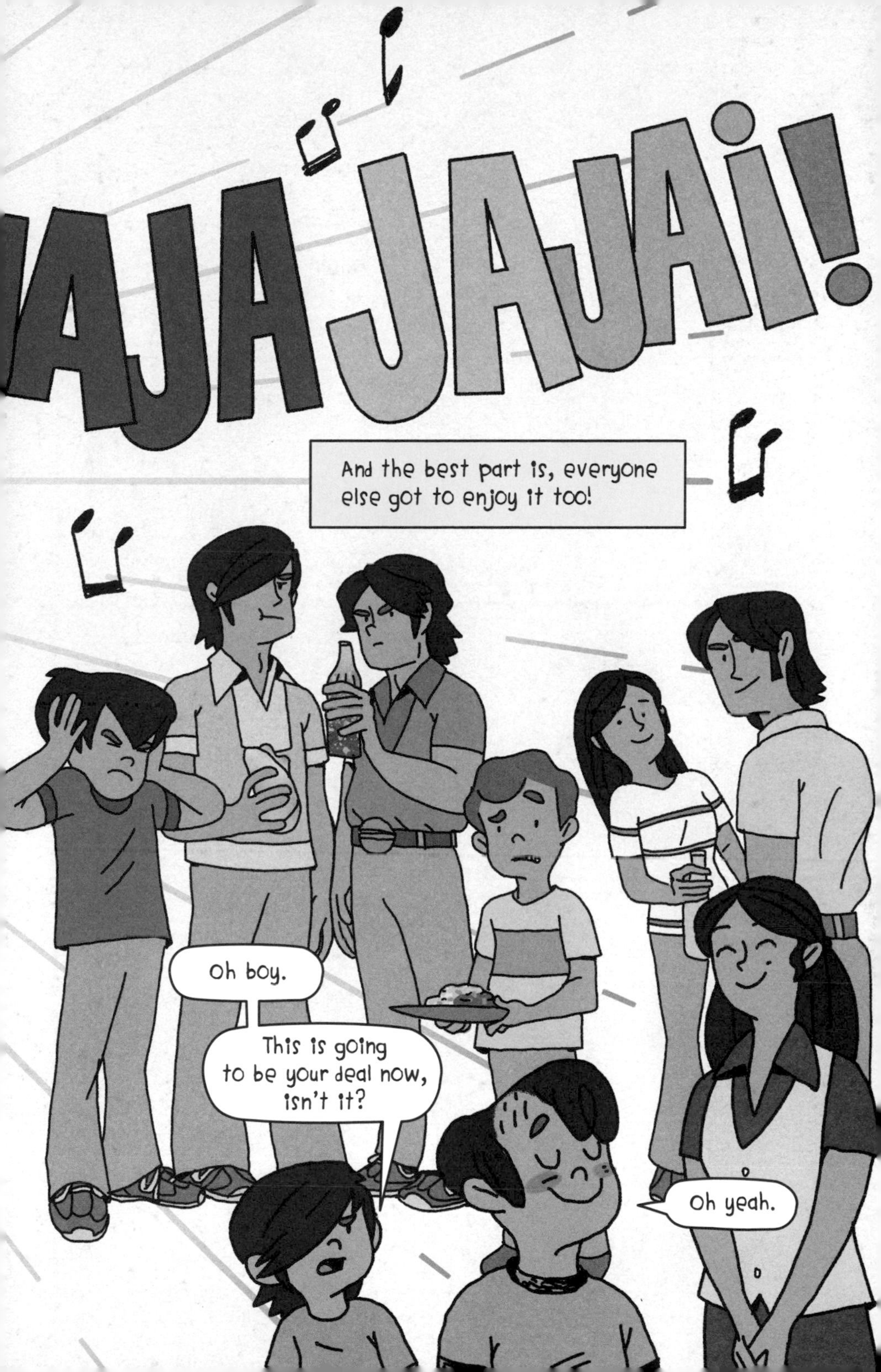

JAJAJAJAJAJA!
And the best part is, everyone else got to enjoy it too!
Oh boy.
This is going to be your deal now, isn't it?
Oh yeah.

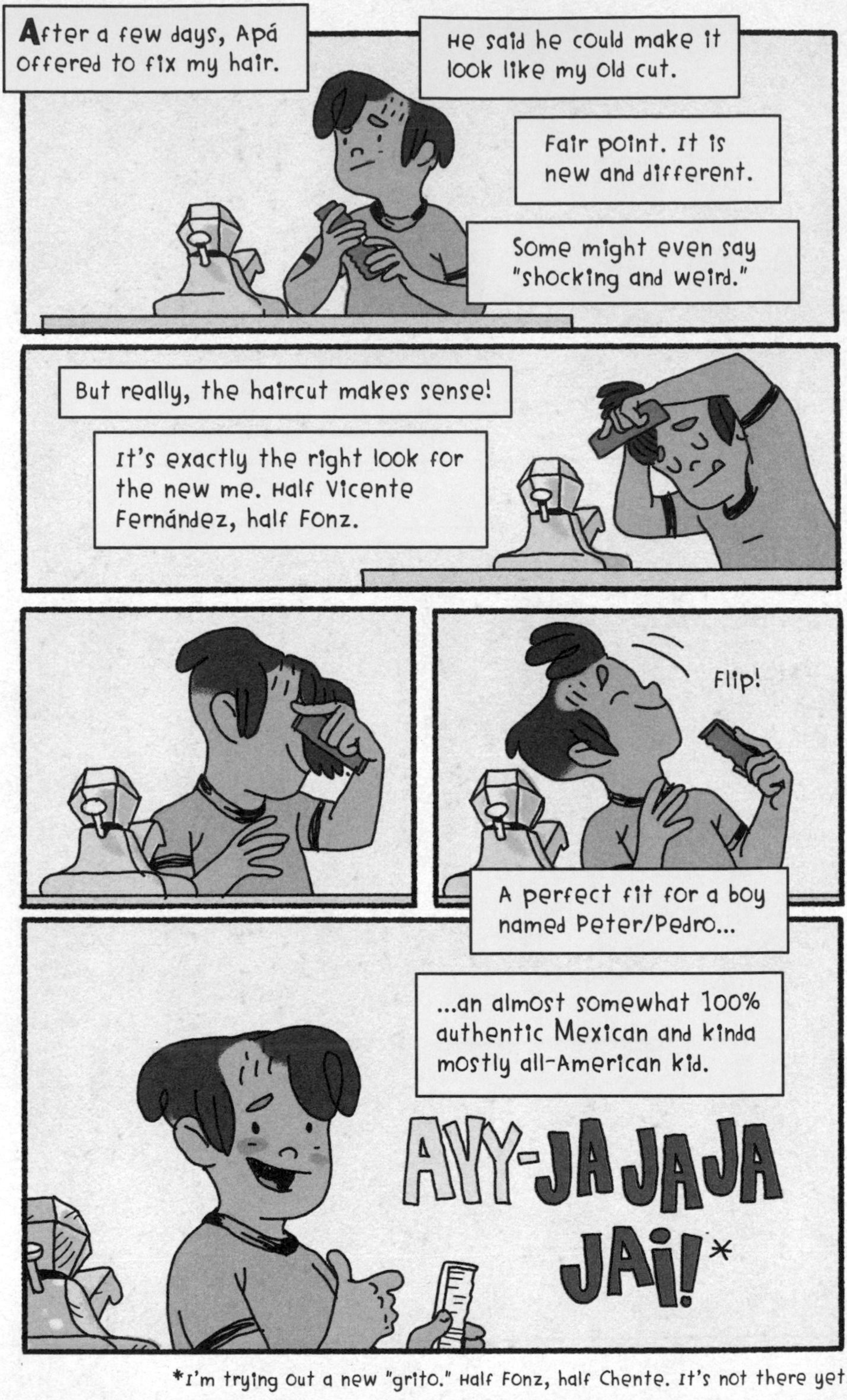
After a few days, Apá offered to fix my hair.
He said he could make it look like my old cut.
Fair point. It is new and different.
Some might even say "shocking and weird."
But really, the haircut makes sense!
It's exactly the right look for the new me. Half Vicente Fernández, half Fonz.
Flip!
A perfect fit for a boy named Peter/Pedro...
...an almost somewhat 100% authentic Mexican and kinda mostly all-American kid.
AYY-JA JAJA JAI!*

*I'm trying out a new "grito." Half Fonz, half Chente. It's not there yet.

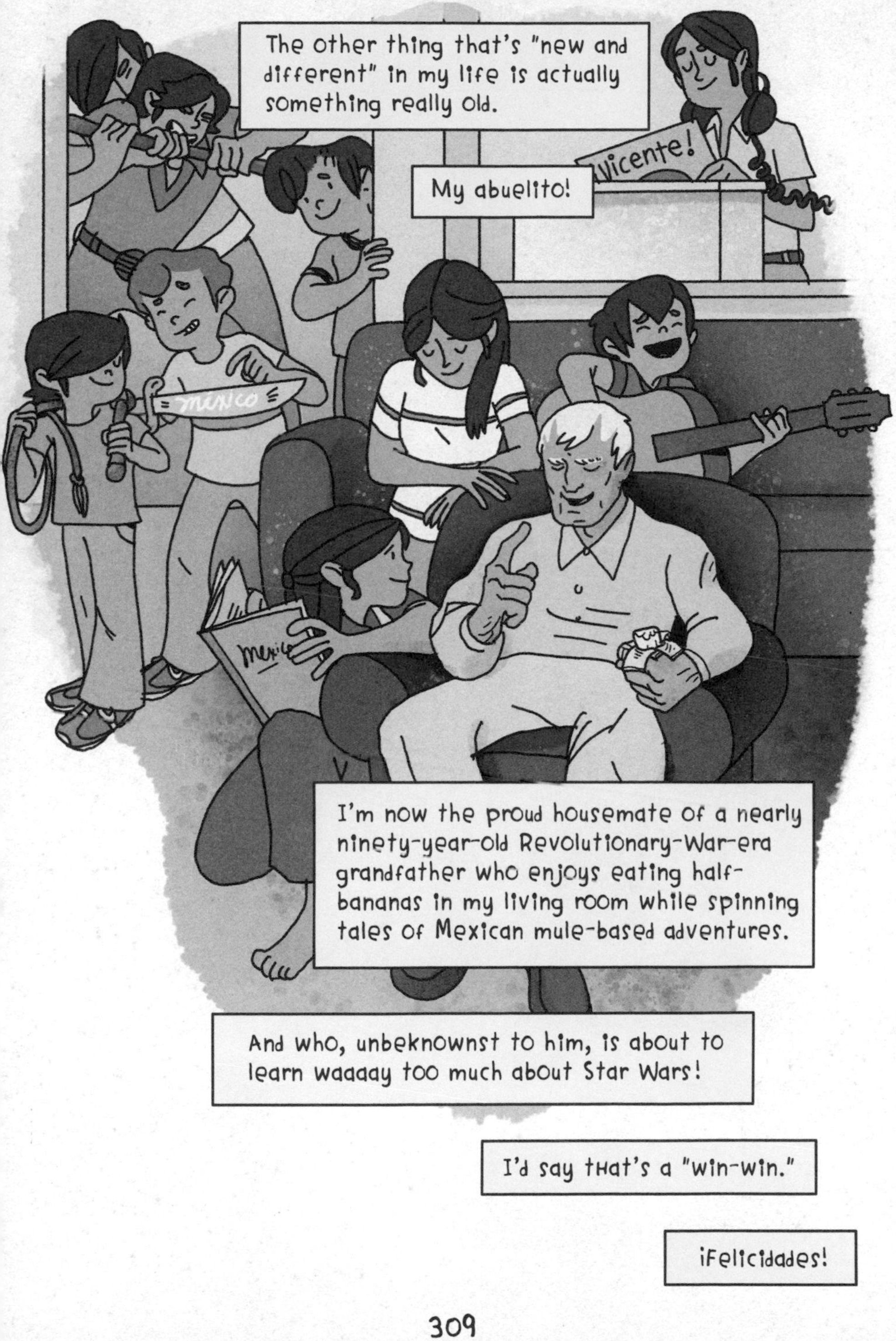
The other thing that's "new and different" in my life is actually something really old.
My abuelito!
Vicente!
México
I'm now the proud housemate of a nearly ninety-year-old Revolutionary-War-era grandfather who enjoys eating half-bananas in my living room while spinning tales of Mexican mule-based adventures.
And who, unbeknownst to him, is about to learn waaaay too much about Star Wars!
I'd say that's a "win-win."
¡Felicidades!

MEET MY REAL-LIFE FAMILIA!

This was my abuelito.
ALEJANDRO MARTÍN

This might be the earliest known picture we had of him.

HE WAS BORN IN 1892!*

*Three years before the invention of the radio!

His favorite food was Menudo, and his favorite drink was Pulque (a beer made from the honey from the heart of the maguey plant).

Immediately after coming to live with us, he began working with my apá out in the fields.

Abuelito admitted he never really liked strawberries, but he loved working in the great outdoors with his son, my apá.

Abuelito lived to be **107** years old.

At the time of his death he had over 53 grandkids, 161 great-grandkids, and 33 great-great-grandkids!

Living

Register-Pajaronian Monday, May 11, 1992 — 3

Centenarian still able to wor

By PAULINE TORRECILLAS
STAFF WRITER

ALEJANDRO MARTIN celebrated his 100th birthday April 26 during an afternoon celebration where he was in the company of several generations of his family. Those attending included his four surviving children: his sons Pedro and Rafael, of Watsonville, his daughter Guadalupe and his son Jose Rosario who both flew from Mexico to be with their father on his centennial.

Mr. Martin was born in Pegueros, Jalisco, Mexico on April 24, 1892.

It was a full afternoon and evening for the honoree. A special mass, celebrated at Valley Catholic Church at 3 p.m. included music by a trio formed by Javier Vargas, Eleazar and Victor Cortes.

Following the service, the Mr. Martin was escorted to the Penny Club gymnasium for a reception in his honor that was attended by more than 350 guests.

The birria was prepared by the honoree's youngest son Pedro. Beans, rice and salad joined the myriad dishes brought by family members and very close friends, turning the serving tables into a huge potluck.

A mariachi played during the

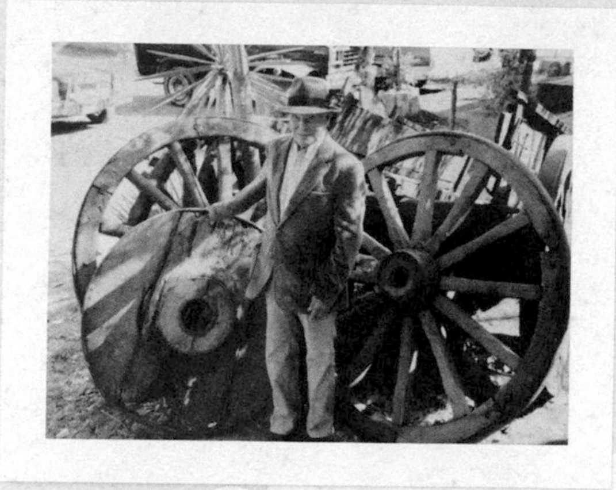

This wagon wheel was the exact one Abuelito made and used during his mule-based adventures back during the Mexican Revolution. I didn't draw the wagon into the story because they are as hard to draw as hands are.

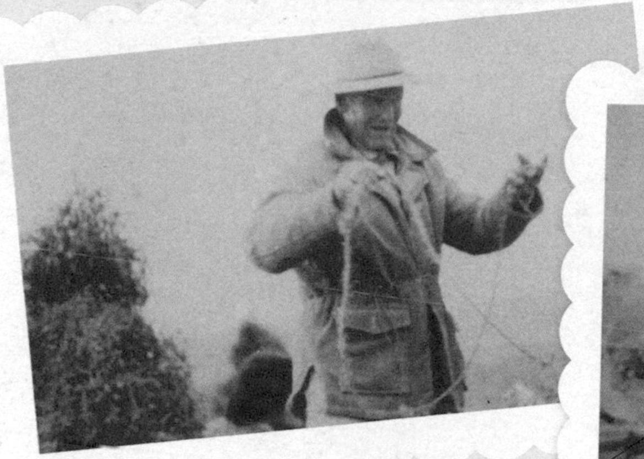

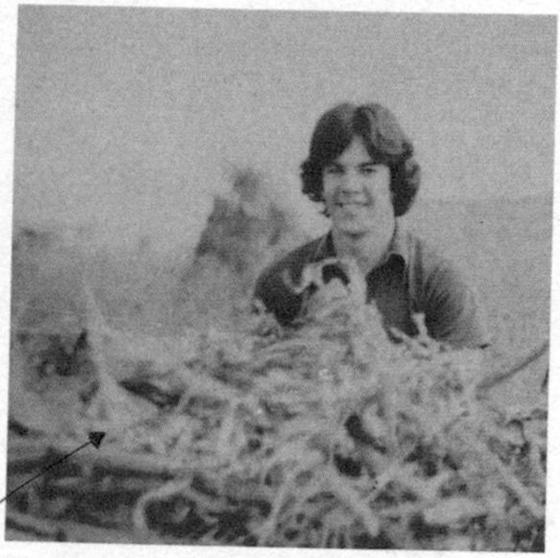

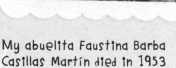

These photos were taken moments before Abuelito out-lifted Noe. Note Noe's misplaced confidence?

My abuelita Faustina Barba Casillas Martín died in 1953 at the age of fifty-six.

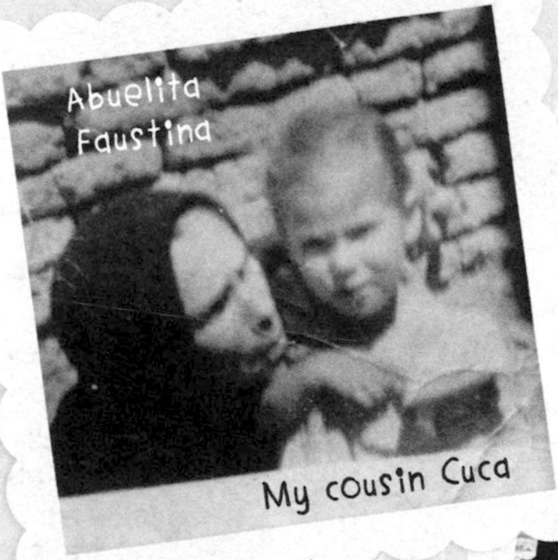
Abuelita Faustina
My cousin Cuca

Abuelita's final, final resting place.

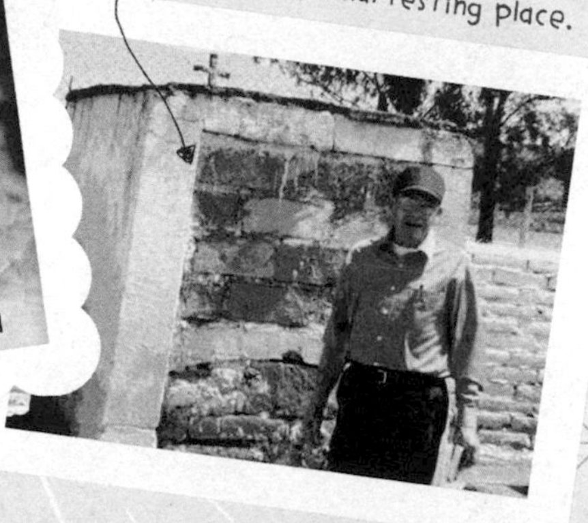

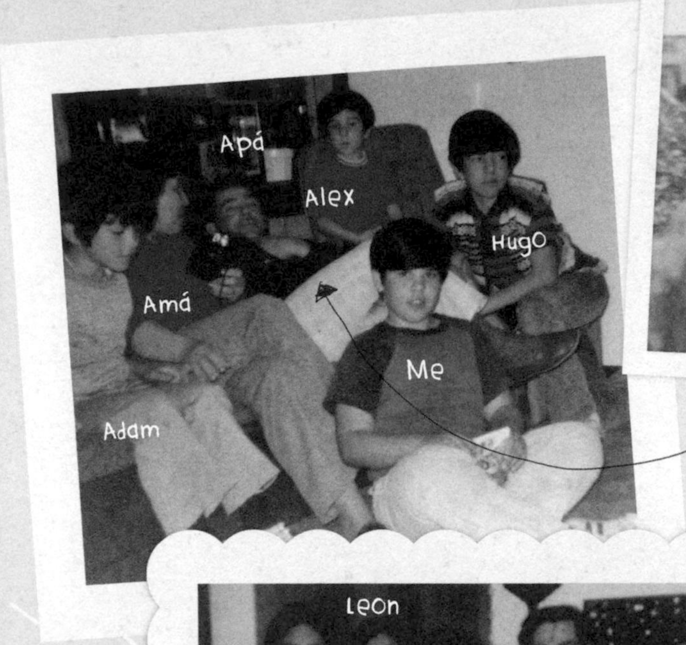
Apá
Alex
Hugo
Amá
Me
Adam

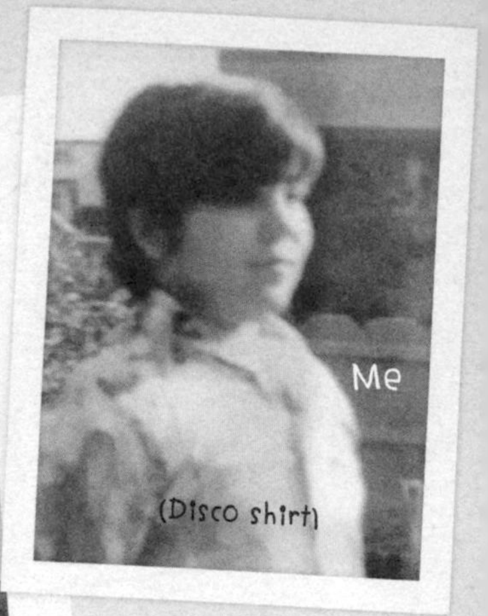
Me
(Disco shirt)

See how tired my apá looks in this picture?

That's nine-kids tired.

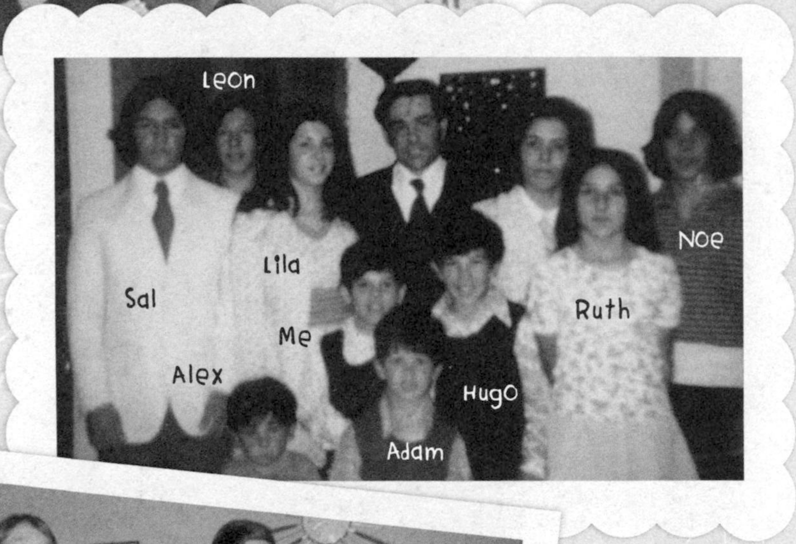
Leon
Lila
Sal
Noe
Ruth
Me
Alex
Hugo
Adam

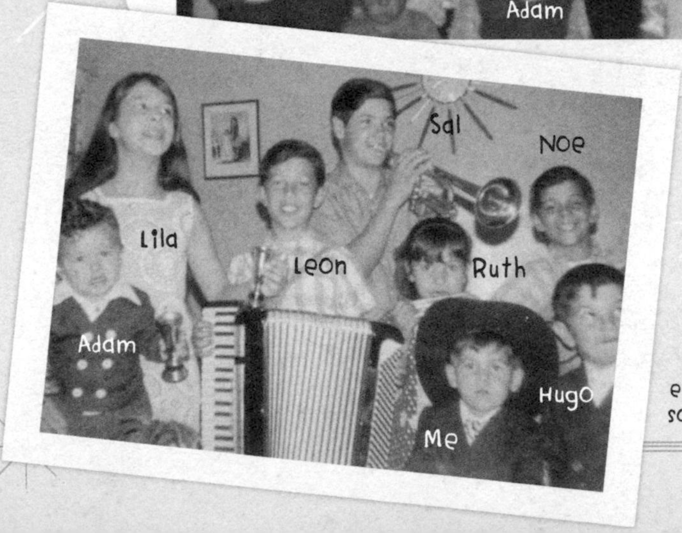
Sal
Noe
Lila
Leon
Ruth
Adam
Hugo
Me

Apá REALLY wanted us to be a family band.

This was as close as he ever got.

We didn't have enough instruments, so I just wore a hat.

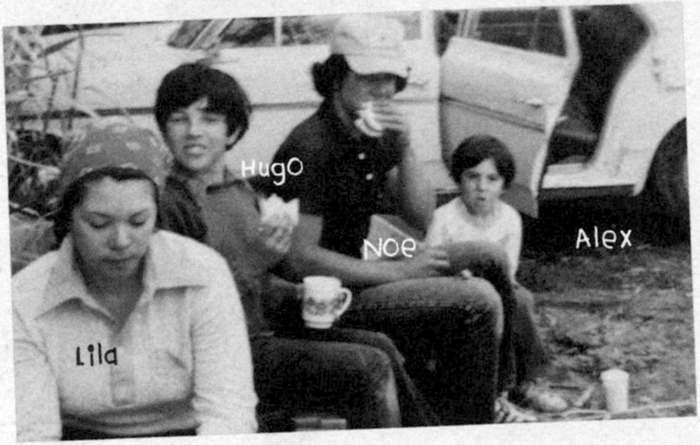
Hugo
Noe
Alex
Lila

Lonche* in the strawberry fields. Amá would always pack a big cooler with "esanweeches" or burritos made from whatever was leftover from the night before. Usually Spam.

*Spanglish for "lunch."

The time Abuelito saw Pope John Paul II!

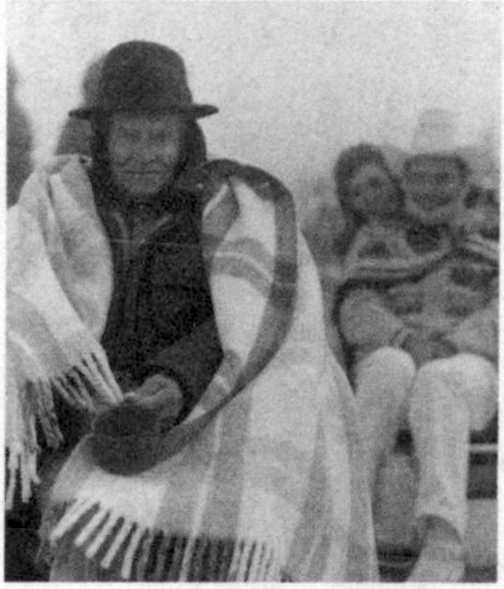

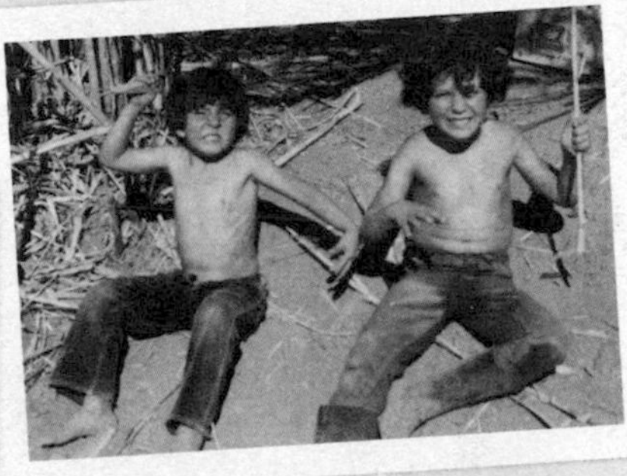

Alex and Adam: Dirt monsters.

Look! El Motorhome!

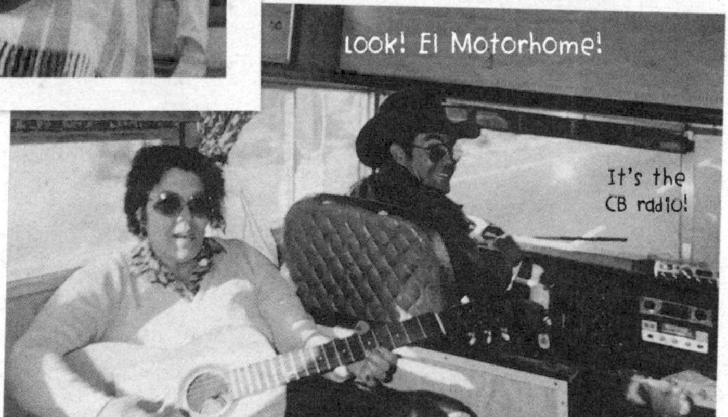
It's the CB radio!

(There are no fewer than nine half-bananas in this picture. Can you spot them all? You can't. That's the magic of the half-bananas. Always there. Never seen.)

SOME OF YOUR QUESTIONS ANSWERED!

WHAT IS A MEXIKID?

It's not what you think. Mexikid is not Meximan's sidekick! (Although...note to self: new comic book idea—The Amazing Meximan!)

Mexikid is what I call a myself. A first generation American-born kid of Mexican parents. Two feet planted on the American side of the border while one heart belonging to both sides.

Being a Mexikid doesn't mean you know everything there is to know about being Mexican. In fact it's the opposite. A Mexikid wants to learn more. A Mexikid is excited to fill in the gaps in his own story with stories of his heritage.

AM I A MEXIKID?

Sure! If you feel like you're more than you are somehow, part of a bigger world...You're your own kind of Mexikid!

WHAT THE HECK IS "SHIPOOPI"?

It's the opening song for act two of Meredith Willson's The Music Man. Some people love it. Most do not. It's silly and doesn't advance the plot one bit. But once you hear it, it will haunt your days. (That, my friends, is a dare. I dare you to listen to it today!)

CAN YOU NAME 10 MORE EUPHEMISMS FOR DIARRHEA?

Pudding Pants. The Choco Cha-cha. Carlito's Spray. An F5 Poop-nado. The Poo-y Decimal System. The big muddy. The chocolate dragster races. The Terracotta Backsplash. A disturbance in the force. We got trouble in River City!

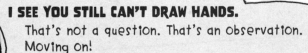

I SEE YOU STILL CAN'T DRAW HANDS.

That's not a question. That's an observation. Moving on!

IS "LITTLE PEEPEE MAN" REAL?
He sure is!! And here's the proof. After years of searching for him, I finally found one in a toy museum in San Miguel de Allende this past fall.

BEHOLD THE 10TH WONDER OF THE MEXICAN WORLD (Many of which are also toys): **LITTLE PEEPEE MAN!**

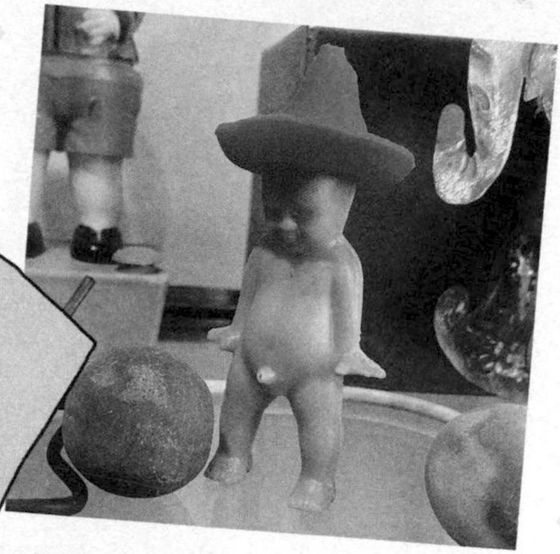

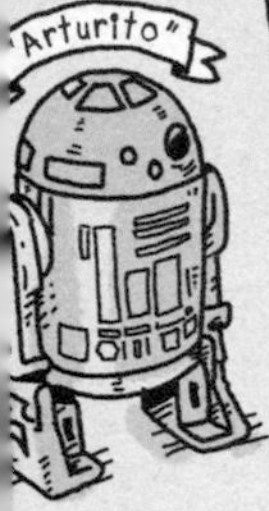
"Arturito"

DID YOU EVER END UP TEACHING YOUR ABUELITO ALL ABOUT STAR WARS?
I think what happened was that he grew to appreciate me enough to know I loved something he could never fully understand. And if it didn't eat into his nap time, he was cool with it.

WAS IT HARD TO WRITE ABOUT YOUR ABUELITA? Writing about someone you've never met is super hard! It's even harder to write about them dying. Abuelita's death was an event that changed the course of many people's lives. I didn't want to hurt anyone by getting it wrong or say so little about it that it didn't mean anything at all. But I had to try.

I relied a lot on my apá and amá to get to know her as much as I could. The things I learned about her were not so much facts, but what she meant to the people she loved. They way they spoke about Abuelita said so much, but who they were because of her, said so much more. She must have been funny, caring, and exceedingly generous, because that's what everyone who knew her was like.

ARE THE THINGS IN THIS STORY 100 PERCENT TRUE?
I like to say that my stories are 100 percent true, 90 percent of the time. My memory and my heart like to play tricks on each other. The results are what makes my stories.

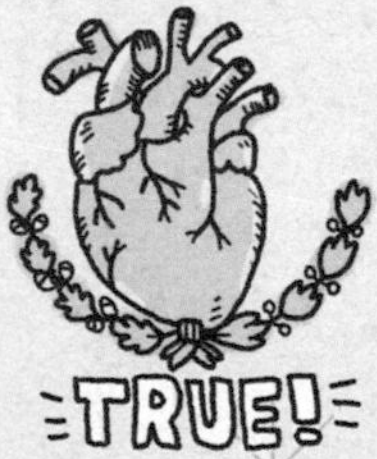
TRUE!

LOVE & ACKNOWLEDGMENTS

I'd like to thank my brothers and sisters. Not only for being part of the story, but for making me who I am today. Suckers!

A special thanks to my brother Leon for sending me family stories and memories almost weekly. Your belief in my quest made this all possible. Sucker!

To my sister Lila. She made me retell "The Deer Story" every time our family would have a get-together. She also made me retell the "Poop Story," which I will spare you for now. Her persistence and joy made me a better story teller.

A big thanks to Aaron Heim, who told me to shoot for the top...and then pointed me in that direction.

To my agent Dan Lazar. When I sent him my original pitch, he threw everything out except for one line. He pointed at that one line and said, "THAT is what this book should be about. Write THAT book." Thank you for helping me grow that one line into a whole book.

To my editor, Kate Harrison, who asked all the hard questions and made me look into myself to find parts of the story I always ignored...you know...the ones that involve human emotions and stuff. Blechh. It's your fault I care!

To my designer, Jennifer Kelly, who gave birth to twins while calmly helping me slash my original 600-page book down to a slim 300 pager. New moms be multitasking!

To Dan Taylor, Bev Carlson, and Emily Monroe for helping me craft those early pitches. Your patience with me was unfathomable. "Unfathomable" is probably the wrong word to use here. What do you suggest?

To the members of The Humor Innovations Group. You know what you did.

To Brian Gordon and Chris Harding, my cartooning godparents. When I first started writing Mexikid Stories, they pulled me aside, slapped my hands, and showed me how it should really be done.

To Warren Ludwig, the creative tornado who believed in my stories.

To anyone who's ever read Mexikid Stories online. Those are some of the longest weekly comics on the internet. Thank you for spending your precious time on my little stories. It really means the world to me.